THE EMBODIED STATE

This edited collection advances a reconceptualisation of state power through emotions. Methodologically, it rethinks the study of the state from the bottom up, by seeking contributions that engage with performances and enactments of state power at the ground level, by frontline staff in direct contact with marginalised populations, and those that reflect on encounters with symbols and practices of state power. Conceptually, it advances a new theory of state power which places values and affects at the heart of its analysis.

In doing so, it seeks to make a crucial intellectual intervention in the study of the people, images and processes involved in the governance of social marginality in various institutional settings – criminal justice, immigration and asylum bureaucracies, the welfare system, the care sector, etc. – to explore how emotions are mobilised, how their expression in contemporary institutional settings of state power connects to broader moral and affective economies, the contradictions, and dilemmas they embody and reproduce, and the implications of these emotionalised forms of governance for state praxis and theory.

The Embodied State will therefore appeal to students and scholars of critical criminology, political sociology, anthropology, migration and border studies, and penology. It will also be of interest to policymakers and professionals involved in these fields.

Ana Aliverti is Professor of Law at University of Warwick's Law School. Her research work looks at the intersections between criminal law and criminal justice, on the one hand, and border regimes, on the other, and explores the impact of such intertwining on criminal justice institutions and on those subject to the resulting set of controls. She has conducted extensive ethnographic work on the police and immigration enforcement, courts and asylum.

Henrique Carvalho is Professor of Law and Co-Director of the Centre for Critical Legal Studies at the University of Warwick. His work investigates issues in criminalisation, punishment, state power and justice through dialogues between legal, social, political and cultural theory. Henrique is the co-author of *Questioning Punishment* (Routledge, 2024).

Anastasia Chamberlen is Professor of Sociology and Co-Director of the Centre for the Study of Women and Gender at the University of Warwick. Her research explores the relations between punishment, embodiment, arts and justice. Anastasia is the co-author of *Questioning Punishment* (Routledge, 2024).

Simon Tawfic is LSE Fellow in Social Policy at the London School of Economics. He holds a PhD in anthropology (2023) from the London School of Economics, having previously completed the joint honours BA in Anthropology and Law there (2017, First Class). Simon was a postdoctoral research fellow on the Vulnerable State project. His research interests include vulnerability, moral labour on the frontline and the everyday politics of care.

Routledge Advances in Criminology

Machine Learning for Criminology and Crime Research
At the Crossroads
Gian Maria Campedelli

Ethical Dilemmas in International Criminological Research
Edited by Michael Adorjan and Rosemary Ricciardelli

Sexuality and Crime
A Neo-Darwinian Perspective
Anthony Walsh

Criminological Connections, Directions, Horizons
Essays in Honour of Nigel South
Edited by Eamonn Carrabine and Anna Di Ronco

An Ontology of Organized Crime
A Meta-Analytical Framework and Enforcement Implications
Stephen Schneider

The Embodied State
Emotions, State Power and Social Marginalisation
Edited by Ana Aliverti, Henrique Carvalho, Anastasia Chamberlen and Simon Tawfic

For more information about this series, please visit: www.routledge.com/Routledge-Advances-in-Criminology/book-series/RAC

THE EMBODIED STATE

Emotions, State Power and Social Marginalisation

Edited by Ana Aliverti, Henrique Carvalho, Anastasia Chamberlen and Simon Tawfic

LONDON AND NEW YORK

Designed cover image: Engelina Zandstra "Composition 7096"

First published 2026
by Routledge
4 Park Square, Milton Park, Abingdon, Oxon OX14 4RN

and by Routledge
605 Third Avenue, New York, NY 10158

Routledge is an imprint of the Taylor & Francis Group, an informa business

© 2026 selection and editorial matter, Ana Aliverti, Henrique Carvalho, Anastasia Chamberlen and Simon Tawfic; individual chapters, the contributors

The right of Ana Aliverti, Henrique Carvalho, Anastasia Chamberlen and Simon Tawfic to be identified as the authors of the editorial material, and of the authors for their individual chapters, has been asserted in accordance with sections 77 and 78 of the Copyright, Designs and Patents Act 1988.

All rights reserved. No part of this book may be reprinted or reproduced or utilised in any form or by any electronic, mechanical, or other means, now known or hereafter invented, including photocopying and recording, or in any information storage or retrieval system, without permission in writing from the publishers.

For Product Safety Concerns and Information please contact our EU representative GPSR@taylorandfrancis.com. Taylor & Francis Verlag GmbH, Kaufingerstraße 24, 80331 München, Germany.

Trademark notice: Product or corporate names may be trademarks or registered trademarks, and are used only for identification and explanation without intent to infringe.

British Library Cataloguing-in-Publication Data
A catalogue record for this book is available from the British Library

ISBN: 978-1-03259-370-8 (hbk)
ISBN: 978-1-03261-705-3 (pbk)
ISBN: 978-1-03261-706-0 (ebk)

DOI: 10.4324/9781032617060

Typeset in Sabon
by Newgen Publishing UK

CONTENTS

List of contributors   *xi*

Introduction   1
Ana Aliverti, Henrique Carvalho and
Anastasia Chamberlen

PART 1
Representing the state, mobilising affect   **19**

1 The Bastille and the French Revolution: Reading an
   icon   21
   Eamonn Carrabine

2 Political affects and embodied states: A psychoanalytic
   framework for theorising the embodiment of state
   power by state representatives   43
   Louise Braddock, Henrique Carvalho and Craig Reeves

3 Postracial sentimentality and the validation of state
   racism   59
   Brett St Louis

PART 2
Producing the state through emotionalised governance   81

4 Manufacturing informants: The emotion work of the Prevent Duty training   83
Sadi Shanaah

5 Disgust and punishment in immigration detention   103
Alethia Fernández de la Reguera

6 State violence and the affective capacity of an inquest   122
Martha McCurdy

7 Staging state embodiment: Performativity, emotional labour, and recalibrating dynamic security in a Philippine City Jail   141
Hannah Nario-Lopez

8 Premature revenge: Feud law among prospective police recruits in Rio de Janeiro, Brazil   157
Eduardo de Oliveira Rodrigues

PART 3
Shifting emotional economies of state power   175

9 The emotional landscape of *prison* managerialism   177
Jamie Bennett

10 Relational aspects of prison work and institutional change: Reflections on Uruguay's prison reform   197
Ana Vigna

11 The affective turn in the criminal process: Stakeholders' emotional labour in child sexual abuse cases in India   215
Shailesh Kumar

PART 4
Unsettling institutionalised emotions   233

12 Disgust at the border: Border work as dirty work   235
    Ana Aliverti

13 Creative emotions: The governance of vulnerability
    and the caring ambivalence of arts therapeutic work
    in prisons   253
    Sally Foreman and Anastasia Chamberlen

14 Institutionalised helper interactions and structurally
    embedded emotions: Welfare assistance as a social form   273
    Åsa Wettergren

15 Beyond the courtroom: Emotions, affects and
    embodied senses of justice in ground-level
    interventions in the judicialisation of an
    environmental disaster   293
    Leticia Barrera

16 In search of institutional affect in Sierra Leone's
    prisons   311
    Andrew M. Jefferson

PART 5
Navigating dilemmas of care and control   331

17 Governing through fear: Affective ambivalences and
    violence in police work   333
    Sara León Spesny

18 Embodying the state in probation practice: Emotional
    labour and self-alienation   349
    *Jake Phillips, Sam Ainslie, Andrew Fowler and
    Chalen Westaby*

19 Circuits of outrage against and within the English
    state of homelessness   369
    Simon Tawfic

20 Plato and the penal reformer's dilemma: Ambivalence, blocked trinity and the failure of integration 387
Amanda Wilson and Alan Norrie

21 Emotional labour and feminisation of work: The case of a 'spontaneous arrival' at a refugee camp in Greece 406
Artemis Christinaki and Erica Burman

Index 426

CONTRIBUTORS

Sam Ainslie is Senior Lecturer at the Sheffield Institute of Law & Justice, Sheffield Hallam University.

Ana Aliverti is Professor at the School of Law, University of Warwick.

Leticia Barrera is a CONICET researcher at Universidad Nacional de San Martin.

Jamie Bennett is Research Associate at the Centre for Criminology, University of Oxford and a senior leader at HMPPS.

Louise Braddock is an independent scholar and former member of the Philosophy Faculty, University of Oxford.

Erica Burman is Professor at the Manchester Institute of Education at the University of Manchester.

Eamonn Carrabine is Professor at the Department of Sociology & Criminology at the University of Essex.

Henrique Carvalho is Professor at the School of Law, University of Warwick.

Anastasia Chamberlen is Professor at the Department of Sociology, University of Warwick.

Artemis Christinaki is Honorary Senior Research Fellow at the University of Manchester.

Alethia Fernández de la Reguera is Associate Professor at UNAM, Mexico and Departmental Lecturer at the Centre for Criminology, University of Oxford.

Sally Foreman is independent researcher, artist, writer and student at the Royal College of Art, London.

Andrew Fowler is Senior Lecturer at the Sheffield Institute of Law & Justice, Sheffield Hallam University.

Andrew M. Jefferson is Senior Researcher at the Danish Institute Against Torture (DIGNITY).

Shailesh Kumar is Lecturer at the Department of Law & Criminology, Royal Holloway, University of London.

Sara León Spesny is Lecturer at the Faculty of Arts & Social Sciences at the University of Sydney.

Martha McCurdy is Postdoctoral Researcher at the University of St. Gallen.

Hannah Nario-Lopez is Assistant Professor at the Department of Sociology, University of the Philippines Diliman.

Alan Norrie is Professor at the School of Law, University of Warwick.

Eduardo de Oliveira Rodrigues is Faculty member at the Colégio Pedro II, Rio de Janeiro.

Jake Phillips is Associate Professor at the Institute of Criminology, University of Cambridge.

Craig Reeves is Senior Lecturer at the School of Law, Birkbeck, University of London.

Sadi Shanaah is Research Fellow at the Department of Politics and International Studies, University of Warwick.

Brett St Louis is Senior Research Fellow at the Centre on the Dynamics of Ethnicity and Department of Sociology, University of Manchester.

Simon Tawfic is LSE Fellow in Social Policy at the London School of Economics.

Ana Vigna is Associate Professor at the Universidad de la República, Uruguay.

Chalen Westaby is Senior Lecturer at the Sheffield Institute of Law & Justice at Sheffield Hallam University.

Åsa Wettergren is Professor at the Department of Sociology & Work Science, University of Gothenburg.

Amanda Wilson is Associate Professor at the School of Law, University of Warwick.

INTRODUCTION

*Ana Aliverti, Henrique Carvalho, and
Anastasia Chamberlen*

This edited collection advances a reconceptualisation of state power through emotions. Methodologically, it rethinks the study of the state from the bottom up, by seeking contributions that engage with performances and enactments of state power at the ground level, by frontline staff in direct contact with marginalised populations, and those that reflect on encounters with symbols and practices of state power. Conceptually, it advances a new theory of state power which places values and affects at the heart of its analysis. In doing so, it seeks to make a crucial intellectual intervention in the study of the people, images and processes involved in the governance of social marginality in various institutional settings – criminal justice, immigration and asylum bureaucracies, the welfare system, the care sector etc. – to explore the place of emotions and values in their everyday work.

Ethnographies of state bureaucracies have long demystified 'the state' as a coherent, rational and monolithic social structure (Hansen and Stepputat 2001, Alexander 2000). Through researching the everyday work of the individuals and institutions that embody 'the state', this scholarship has challenged the binary distinction between state and society implicit in much of the social sciences (Gupta 2012, Auyero 2012, Koch 2018, Laszczkowski and Reeves 2018, Thelen et al. 2017). These interventions highlighted, first, the relational nature of state power which is produced through human interactions, and second, the central place of emotions in the reproduction of the idea of 'the state' and its everyday operation. The state not only sees (Scott 1998) and thinks (Douglas [1986] 2012) through the agents who embody it, but it also feels (Cooper 2019, Fassin 2015, Jupp et al. 2017). Foregrounding the personal, relational and emotional dimensions of statehood, much of this scholarship has prioritised the worlds of frontline staff (welfare relief advisors, asylum caseworkers, immigration judges, police officers, probation and prison staff among others) in their everyday interventions in the lives of the poor (Lipsky 2010, Zacka 2017). They showed how, through their routine practices, social structures are reproduced and occasionally unsettled.

Building on this body of literature, this edited collection seeks to encourage a deeper exploration of the emotional life of the state which advances our understanding of the place of emotions in state power, and the potential of this lens to rethink the state along more innovative and potentially transformative lines. The book invites a novel exploration of the moral and emotional worlds of state workers *qua* relational workers (that is, those at the frontlines in charge of managing socially precarious groups; see Jacobsson and Gubrium 2021).

The growing focus on emotions – largely driven by the 'affective turn' in philosophy and social sciences that has proliferated since the 1990s – is part of a paradigm shift in normative conceptualisations of the self. In criticising liberal theory's conception of subjectivity as autonomous and self-sufficient, feminist philosophers, critical theorists and social interactionists (among others) have argued that we need to understand human beings as interdependent and interconnected. Within this intersubjective dimension, they invite us to recognise the place of vulnerability in constructions of the self and in social relations (Fineman 2008, Butler 2016, Nussbaum 2001, 2013). Emotions such as shame and disgust are responses to the awareness of our vulnerability, and the reassertion of the myth of completeness. Likewise, compassion and empathy arise out of the realisation that one's possibilities and vulnerabilities are similar to those of the sufferer. Emotions are thus, in effect, acknowledgements of one's lack of self-sufficiency. Such a conceptualisation of the self as social, affective, embodied and relational has in turn encouraged enquiries into the place of emotions in state power.

Alongside the interest of moral and political philosophers on the ethical work of emotions, sociologists and anthropologists have identified the social nature of emotions and uncovered new 'emotionalised forms of governance' (Jupp et al. 2017, Laszczkowski and Reeves 2018, Ahmed 2014) which mobilise moral sentiments to 'justify discourses and practices of the government of human beings' (Fassin 2012, 2); they see this as a symptom of contemporary politics. Accordingly, rather than conceptualising emotions as individual dispositions or feelings, we privilege a sociological, anthropological and psychosocial lens (Sclater et al. 2009). In focussing on the moral and affective economies of state power, we seek to place the study of emotions within a wider historical, political and economic context, thus attending to how emotion work forms part of a broader reconfiguration and reconceptualisation of social marginalisation and its governance across various sites and jurisdictions.

This volume is an output of a four-year project on 'The Vulnerable State: Appraising the Ambivalent Economies of State Power', funded by the Leverhulme Trust, and builds on the editors' longstanding research on the moral pains of border controls (Aliverti 2020, 2021, Aliverti et al. 2025), on the moral and emotional economies of the state (Carvalho et al. 2025, Aliverti and Tawfic 2025) and on punishment, justice and emotions (Carvalho and Chamberlen 2016, 2018, Chamberlen and Carvalho 2022, 2019). It contributes to current debates within sociology, anthropology, law, criminology and the social sciences more broadly on the importance of emotions to notions of identity, belonging, order and authority that are central to state power. While heavily informed by developments within criminological scholarship, particularly the efforts to advance a 'criminology of emotions' (Jacobsen and Walklate 2009) and work done on emotional labour (Phillips et al. 2020), on the pains of punishment (Miller 2022, Crewe 2011, Chamberlen 2018) and more recently on 'sensory penalities' (Herrity et al. 2021; see also Martin et al. 2014), this collection aims to foster inter- and multidisciplinary conversations that reach beyond the realm of criminology. At the heart of this project lies the premise that issues of (b)ordering, punitiveness and control are part of a broader matrix of social phenomena which affect the whole constitution and operation of state institutions and processes, whose tensions, ambivalences and dilemmas are most apparent when state power is manifested in the governance of marginalised populations.

In exploring emotions, much of the criminological literature has focussed on revenge, disgust and anger as expressions of the 'punitive turn' in criminal law and criminal justice. However, insufficient attention has been paid to other facets of criminal justice and immigration policies, which privilege compassion and the protection of the vulnerable as a response to moral wrongdoing and human suffering. Furthermore, we have little empirical understanding of the moral and emotional impacts of administering punishment and embodying the punitive facet of the state, and the dilemmas state workers face in doing so, even though these personnel present high levels of work-related stress and trauma (Lumsden and Black 2017, Baillot et al. 2013). As such, the collection seeks to consider these less-explored facets of state work and combines criminological areas of interest with other institutional settings, that are often deemed to belong beyond the realm of criminology.

Situating the State: Embodiment, Social Marginalisation and Contextualisation

As the title indicates, this collection emphasises the embodied character of emotions and, in doing so, seeks to advance an embodied understanding of the state. While metaphors around the body and embodiment have proven useful to ground ideas and understandings around state power and governance (see, e.g., Cooper 2019; Fassin 2015), including the ideological function of 'the body' to justify and naturalise the authority of the state around security and the private spheres of property and individualist self-interest (Epstein 2021), the rhetorical and symbolic power of such images and representations can sometimes mean that the complexity inherent to the embodied dimension of emotions, especially with regard to their experiential aspects, can be neglected or taken for granted. To resist this tendency, in this collection we sought to invite a more grounded and concrete approach to the emotional life of and around the state, by recognising the culturally mediated nature of emotions (Ahmed 2014) while also paying particular attention to phenomenological insights about how emotions are felt by people through their living bodies (Leder 1990; Chamberlen 2018). In other words, we have sought to engage with how the embodied condition of individuals fundamentally shapes not only their subjectivities but also the social world which they inhabit (de Beauvoir 1997, Butler 1990, Young 1990).

This experiential component of embodiment has the potential to significantly ground what are otherwise often innocuous and rather ephemeral understandings of the state and its influence over social and political life. And while there is much that can be gained from acknowledging the influence of the idea of the body to the formation of modern political authority – the state as a 'body politic', a notion that has been relevant at least since the time of Thomas Hobbes – it is important to highlight that an embodied state is ultimately one that is predominantly manifested through the human beings that give it life. An embodied state is also manifested through the concrete products of these beings' agency, which are felt and sensed through their material and symbolic exchanges.

An embodied state is thus inherently relational, as in formed through concrete relations between concrete human beings. Everything else that is also seen to compose the state – symbols, institutions, laws and policies, structures and 'governance' – can be traced back to these human, and therefore intrinsically emotional, relations. Furthermore, such an understanding of the state is also always situated, not only in space and time as in specific geo-historical moments and formations, but also in specific localities and temporalities, positionings that acquire meaning and are felt through the specific ways in which they are experienced by groups and individuals. This approach requires attention to the biographic aspects of state power, how it touches and changes lives, how its symbols can acquire distinct, often contradictory meanings as they meld into the lived experiences of those whom they affect. They also require a sensibility to how these affects and epistemologies are unequally felt and developed, and how they pertain to legacies and sedimentations of oppression, issues that are often effaced by monolithic, colonising and imperialistic ways of imagining and expressing state authority and power; this hegemonic character also serves to conceal the provisionality of 'the state', how states are always 'in-the-making' and require constant reproduction (Hansen and Sepputat 2001). An embodied state is therefore also multifaceted and ambivalent; such a 'state' can at best be understood as a collection of contradictory forces that become manifested – embodied in distinct moments, whose importance is predominantly determined through the marks they leave on the bodies of those subjected to its power. As demonstrated by contributors, when we conceive the state through this embodied and relational lens, matters of race, class and gender take centre stage.

Embodiment and disembodiment have thus been crucial strategies of political domination. While modern state formation rested on its political embodiment – as a strategy of territorial containment, ordering, and differentiation/bonding, the effectivity of its everyday exercise of sovereign power relied on its disembodiment (Epstein 2021). Contrasting the amorphous, elusive, bodiless nature of state power, scholars has long placed attention on the body as a privileged site for the exercise of sovereign power and governance, which work upon and through bodies (Foucault 1977). As feminist and postcolonial scholars have argued, depersonalisation and bodilessness remain a critical feature of the gendered and racialised configurations of the state (Young 1990, Goldberg 1993) and are related to the central function of the state in terms of ordering, differentiation, hierarchisation and exclusion (Scott 1998).

Engrained modern dualisms between nature/culture, reason/emotions, body/mind had a critical role in drawing social boundaries of inclusion and exclusion and shaping the normative subjectivities of the governing and the governed. Relations of domination have been legitimised by the need to protect and control those constructed as 'uncivilised' and irrational – women, the poor, the youth, black and brown people – because of their emotional and corporeal 'excessiveness'. Scholars have interrogated the assumed disembodied and unemotional nature of state power highlighting not only the centrality of emotions for political governance and domination (Stoler 2008, Jupp et al. 2017), but also the epistemological and methodological vantage point that the emotional lens affords. The focus on relationality and emotions allows us to approach the 'state' not as a bounded entity distinct from society, but as field of 'affective entanglements' (Laszczkowski and Reeves 2018) between differently politically situated human beings who collectively enact the 'state'. As such, it leaves analytical space for appraising the uncertainty, messiness and uncontrollable human agency that constitutes 'the everyday state' (Hunter 2015, 16).

This book embraces relationality, embodiment and emotions to deepen our understanding of state power by zooming in to the institutionalised encounters between frontline staff and marginalised populations. As a social category contingent upon socio-cultural, economic and historical factors, 'the marginalised' has been filled with those problematised as 'risky' and 'at risk' and whose lives have been saturated by state intervention and its omnipresence (Sarat 1990, Fernández-Kelly 2015). According to Fassin (2015, 256), this problematisation of precarity and inequality inextricably involves judgement about deservingness and responsibility that in turn engage emotions and values, and the agency of those tasked with the distribution of state pain and protection.

To understand the emotionally charged and complex institutionalised encounters and relationships that make the everyday state, we need to decentre our attention from the Northern criminal justice system and its institutions and actors, a privileged site for criminological research (Carvalho et al. 2020, Aliverti et al. 2023), as necessarily constrained and constraining (Navaro Yashin 2020). With this aim in mind, we sought to engage researchers and practitioners from different disciplines (sociology, anthropology, politics, history, law, philosophy, psychology) researching a range of institutional domains concerned with the social margins (Das and Poole 2004): the prison, the asylum system, the courts, the welfare office, probation, the police or the detention centre, from a variety of jurisdictions to shed light on the multifaceted dimensions of these relationships and their 'state' effects (Mitchell 1990).

Through their grounded explorations of 'statecraft' in a variety of settings and jurisdictions, contributors then interrogate a universalised, decontextualised and unified state form which is assumed in much of the criminological literature. Exploring 'the state' as embodied and relational, they suggest, also means paying attention to its situatedness. They delve into the distinctive emotional economies that are produced in each context. Some of the chapters explore processes of transition and reform as key sites to understand the centrality of state workers' moral agency and emotional mediation in enacting policy change. Others document the strategic use of emotions as a resource to produce order in the context of material and institutional scarcity.

Structure

This book project started as part of a broader intellectual examination of the contradictory and conflicting logics and affects in contemporary practices and policies of governance in what we conceived as a 'punitive-humanitarian complex' (Carvalho et al. 2025). As members of the Vulnerable State Project, based at the University of Warwick, we sought to instigate a wider intellectual dialogue that could not only enrich our understanding of state power but also set an agenda for future research in criminology and beyond that engages the study of state power in more substantive ways with questions of moral agency, embodiment and emotions. Authors were initially invited to participate in the book project in 2023. Draft chapters for this collection were presented and discussed at an online workshop in May 2024. Based on these discussions, editors offered authors written, individual feedback on their work. Revised drafts were subject to subsequent rounds of review by the editors. The different review iterations and collective discussions have been essential for keeping consistency across chapters while also ensuring diversity of methodological approaches and theoretical orientations.

To ensure as much common focus as possible in an endeavour involving an interdisciplinary group of scholars conducting research in various institutional settings and across various jurisdictions, we invited contributors to reflect on the following questions:

1. How are emotions mobilised? What power relationships do they create? And what new solidarities and identifications do (and can) they forge?
2. How does their expression in contemporary institutional settings of state power connect to broader moral and affective economies?
3. What contradictions and dilemmas do they embody and reproduce? How do frontline staff navigate them, and how are these individuals affected by the burden of enacting state power at the ground level?
4. What are the implications of these emotionalised forms of governance for state praxis and theory, and to what extent are they related to broader transformations at the heart of the contemporary state?

The structure of the book is organised around key themes that emerged from the chapters. In the first section, authors explore questions of representation and the central place of affects and emotions in them.

Representing the State, Mobilising Affect

The first section of the book collects contributions that offer insights on the circulation of affects through political icons, narratives and rituals, and on how the state comes to be embodied by those individuals, physical structures and events that come to represent it. In the first chapter, Carrabine offers a meditation on state iconography through a discussion of the many meanings and interpretations given to the French Revolution, and in particular to the fall of the Bastille. After examining how the Revolution itself could be seen as 'a struggle for representation', Carrabine explores the centrality of the storming and fall of the Bastille in the imaginary of the Revolution, the tensions and contradictions involved in the symbolism of the Bastille throughout time, including their reflection in the treatment of the building and its site, and how its persistent symbolic relevance 'tells us something fundamental about the invention of symbols and rituals'.

The second chapter, by Braddock, Carvalho and Reeves, develops a theoretical framework for thinking and investigating the circulation of 'political affects' – affects that have a collective, political dimension – and how these impact the experiences of, and encounters with, state representatives, especially frontline staff in criminal justice. The chapter builds on psychoanalytic theory and semiotics to outline a theory of affect which discusses its place in 'a "self" conceptualised as social, embodied, affective and relational'. A central element of this perspective is the idea that affectivity mediates individuals' conscious apprehension, primarily through what it conceptualises as an iconic mode of presentation through unconscious phantasies that have an affective grip on individuals, shaping their encounters with others and with the world around them by 'turning objects into icons of fear, love, desire, and so on'. The chapter then deploys this framework to reflect on the ways in which the political circulation of affects conditions people's experiences of 'the state', with a particular focus on frontline staff who must actively perform political phantasies as icons of state power.

In the third chapter in the book, and the last in this first section, St Louis draws on James Baldwin's definition of 'sentimentality' as 'the ostentatious parading of excessive and spurious emotion' to examine political rhetorics on immigration control and race equality in the UK, particularly in the aftermath of the Brexit referendum, as a form of postracial sentimentality. The chapter provides a critical exploration of the ambivalent relationship between politics, rationality and emotion, looking at how some senior Conservative politicians from minority ethnic backgrounds have come to prominently advocate policies and laws aimed at severely restricting immigration and weakening race equality. St Louis argues that the key to understanding this phenomenon, which continues to reverberate in contemporary UK politics, is by attending to how it relies on an 'actually-existing postracial society' dialectic which 'presents an emotionally resonant "common sense" that also forestalls criticism of governmental agendas as racist'. This form of postracial sentimentality, St Louis contends, ultimately amounts to 'a dispassionate antipathy toward human flourishing'.

Producing the State through Emotionalised Governance

The second section turns to explore the production of the state through different forms of emotionalised governance. Shanaah's chapter examines the use of emotions to increase the compliance of public sector workers with certain duties under the UK's counter-terrorism programme PREVENT. Under PREVENT, frontline workers – teachers, nurses, doctors, youth workers and other public sector workers – are tasked with detecting individuals showing signs of radicalisation and report them to the police. Through the analysis of the Prevent Duty online training, the chapter explores how possible resistance from public sector workers to the Prevent Duty is managed and their compliance secured via affective governance. In particular, Shanaah reflects on how the online training seeks to attenuate fear of moral and material consequences of reporting radicalisation suspects, activate compassion for radicalisation suspects and increase fear of consequences of not reporting. Shanaah also discusses the contradictions emerging from such emotion work by the government.

In the following chapter, Fernandez de la Reguera conceptualises immigration detention practices and discourses in Mexico as forms of punishment which rely on emotions, most predominantly disgust, to produce punishable subjects. She argues that the agency in charge of these centres routinely creates unhealthy living conditions for detained migrants by limiting access to water, toiletries and medical services. These conditions are not mere accidents but are intended to dehumanise those inside and produce punitive conditions of confinement. The chapter elaborates on the mobilisation of disgust in practices of punishment, arguing that daily punishment in these sites relies on subjugation to filth, making people experience continuously, increasingly abhorrent living conditions. On the other hand, the perception of migrants as disgusting incentivises punishment as well as authorities' non-compliance with regulations, including international protection.

In her examination of inquest proceedings in England, McCurdy documents how emotions are strategically suppressed in the context of the assessment of a border fatality. Drawing on ethnographic observations from the case of Mahammat Abdullah Moussa, who died beneath a vehicle whilst attempting to enter the UK, the chapter explores the various affective registers at an inquest. Inquests are considered fact-finding investigations, sometimes described as therapeutic and cathartic processes. However, McCurdy reflects on how the emphasis on procedural elements during an inquest can lead to an absence of emotion and hinder the preventive potential of the process. As this chapter discusses, an inquest not only produces the legal category of death, but the affective capacity of the process also implicates the adjudication of state violence and, ultimately, the value placed on human life.

Nario-Lopez, in turn, analyses the central role of emotions in prison governance amid conditions of material scarcity, gang violence, overcrowding and understaffing in the Philippines. Based on ethnographic work in one of Manila's most crowded jails, the chapter documents officers' affective strategies in role performances (Goffman 1959) and emotion management (Hochschild 1983) to deliver 'dynamic security' – an approach to prison management that relies on harmonious social relations between staff and residents to ensure prison order. The chapter sheds light on officers' role performance in moderating between highly charged affective forces to deliver 'humane' custody, where calibrating affective dispositions become critical features of state embodiment.

Rodrigues' chapter focusses on the place of revenge for understanding police brutality and discrimination amid rank-and-file police officers. This chapter explores the notion of 'police feud' as articulated by and among young men aspiring to join the military police of Rio de Janeiro. Traditionally seen as a chaotic and personal response, Rodrigues argues that revenge functions as a long-term systemic force mobilised to justify state violence, particularly in response to police victimisation. The chapter posits that state power refines the distribution of emotions and desires already embodied by prospective police recruits, thereby legitimising violence and shaping an emotional economy of policing in Rio de Janeiro.

Shifting Emotional Economies of State Power

The third section brings into focus the emotional dynamics of state power by exploring various processes of institutional reform. In his chapter, Bennett examines the rise of managerialism in prison governance in England and Wales. Building on Bennett's own involvement in prison management, the chapter discusses three aspects of how a sociological understanding of emotions can deepen our understanding of the operation and effects of prison managerialism. First, it looks at how the rhetoric of managerialism drew upon the hopes and fears of prison managers and worked to reshape their subjectivity, including identity and emotions, to increase self-discipline. Second, the chapter explores how managerialism enacted a shift to governing prisoners with diminished emotion. The third area under analysis comprises the intensification of emotional labour, illustrated by ambivalent situations such as managers implementing change they considered harmful, while also acknowledging that the burdens of emotional labour fall unevenly. The chapter sheds light on the affective economy of prison reform, its effects and its relationship with broader structures of power and inequality.

In a similar vein, Vigna situates her chapter within prison reform in Uruguay which sought to change prison work in ways that sought to challenge the dominance of punitive logics. As part of the reform, civil servants gradually entered the workforce, posing a major challenge to the occupational culture of prison officers. Drawing on in-depth interviews with prison staff, the chapter documents the tensions and ambivalences derived from different professional cultures among prison officers in their attitudes towards inmates and prison work. The findings suggest that, despite the deliberate efforts by authorities to modify institutional guidelines, the emotions and values of frontline officers play a fundamental role in the actual conception and implementation of prison policy on a day-to-day basis.

Kumar's chapter focusses on legal and judicial reforms around proceedings involving sexually victimised children in India under the Protection of Children from Sexual Offences Act, 2012 (POCSO). This law focusses on providing a child-friendly and healing criminal justice process with the help of several procedural reforms, such as purposely built customised 'special' courts, and special court personnel like special judges, special prosecutors and support persons. Kumar explores the perceptions and practices of court practitioners in the reform process, discussing the ways in which these actors confront new emotional demands in a stressful work environment without any specific training, and highlighting the relational and cultural features of emotions that are at play in this context.

Unsettling Institutionalised Emotions

The fourth section pays particular attention to emotions' unsettling work in various institutional contexts. First, Aliverti focusses on disgust in immigration policing in the UK. As a moral emotion, disgust pervades certain occupations considered 'dirty' or 'tainted' – physically, socially and morally – and is central for understanding border control work. Immigration officers perform disgust as a professional and moral resource to legitimise a controversial mandate, and in so doing reproduce racialised hierarchies of belonging. Yet, the chapter also shows that disgust is also seized as an affective resource to disrupt these hierarchies and criticise the social, political and economic conditions that make them possible. Ultimately, this chapter reflects on the polyvalent nature of emotions and their potential for exposing the embodied, fragmented and contradictory nature of state power.

Drawing on interviews with arts therapists working in English prisons, Foreman and Chamberlen's chapter examines how these uniquely placed workers perceive their professional status. These therapists straddle competing roles inside and outside the prison, and towards prisoners who they see as patients but whose offending histories they are there to primarily address. The chapter explores these professionals' affectively complex labour. It argues that their work is often compromised by various institutional demands and restrictions, but when enabled, they are able to craft a distinctive space that allows expression (and potentially healing). Importantly, for these therapists, this is also a space that enables a sensorially intersubjective connection, a kind of solidarity between therapist and prisoner, explored here as a paradigmatic case of carceral 'care aesthetics' (Thompson 2022).

Inspired by George Simmels' essay on the poor, Wettergren's chapter explores the emotive-cognitive rationale of welfare assistance, arguing that the state intention behind it is to control recipients rather than to put an end to inequality. The overall purpose is to highlight welfare state assistance as a function of the emotional state. Wettergren argues that the 'institutionalised helper interaction' in welfare assistance practices is a distinct social form oriented by structurally embedded emotions, which shape the emotive-cognitive roles of helpers (social/frontline workers) and receivers (vulnerable citizens and migrants) and constricts the action space of those roles. In connecting this economy of emotions to broader social structures, the chapter suggests that the distribution of these roles and the restrictions that they impose on actors are critical for the reproduction of inequalities.

Building on an ethnography of bureaucratic interventions in the context of environmental social rights litigation in Argentina, Barrera's chapter moves away from the legal process to shed light on the larger phenomenon of judicialisation of social inequalities. She highlights the emotions, affects, senses of belonging and community attachment, agency displays and concrete interactions through which marginalised actors navigate the effects of judicialisation in the everyday while waiting for a solution or remedy to the social injustices experienced. Through this ethnographic account of the dynamics at play in ground-level interventions triggered by the legal process, the chapter shows that the boundaries of the allegedly multiple dimensions (legal moral, emotional, political etc.) of the conflict are blurred and often unsettled in the everyday.

Jefferson's chapter moves us back to the prison to examine the affective force of 'perpetrative institutions'. Drawing on ethnographic work in Sierra Leone, the chapter explores 'the way relations of structure and subjectivity are constituted in and through affect-laden institutional practices', through which personal and institutional identities are forged. Instead of focussing on individual actors, Jefferson broadens the perspective towards 'harm-filled structural intentionality' embedded in carceral settings under punitive conditions; in so doing, the chapter concretises the material dimensions of 'the emotivity of prisons'. The chapter illuminates the way state power is embodied and affectively enforced not only on and through individual actors and intersubjective relations, but also through often effaced and naturalised structures, processes and institutions.

Navigating Dilemmas of Care and Control

The last section of the collection brings together contributions that prioritise shedding light on specific tensions and ambivalences at the centre of the affective and embodied dimensions of state power. In Spesny's chapter, the main focus is on the affective ambivalences displayed and experienced by soldiers of the military police in Rio de Janeiro, Brazil, especially towards favela residents. Based on a year-long ethnography of a military police station located in a favela in Rio, Spesny investigates how, especially through 'explicit and implicit violence, police soldiers are active agents in (re)producing social and racial order'. A central anchor for this ambivalent relation discussed in the chapter is in the similitudes between the biographies of soldiers and of those whom they are tasked with policing. The chapter examines how these relationalities are conditioned by soldiers' embedding in institutional lineages and expectations and contextualised within 'a broader moral economy of police violence'.

In the following chapter, Phillips, Ainslie, Fowler and Westaby explore the affective dimension of probation work in England and Wales through a deployment of Hochschild's concept of emotional labour. The chapter analyses how probation work involves an inherent tension between care and control, and a demand for probation practitioners to be 'efficient' with their emotions, which results in them experiencing 'a disconnect between what they feel and what they think they should feel'. This tension, rooted in the paradoxical character of the emotion rules and expectations around the highly politicised field of probation, has significant consequences, not only to these practitioners' work, but also to their wellbeing, significantly shaping their lives both within and outside of work.

Situating his chapter within the business of ending homelessness in England, Tawfic highlights the mobilisation of outrage at austerity. He charts the circulation of outrage across this industry, paying attention to how it is entangled with compassion in the working lives of NGO workers. Suggesting that the circulation of moral outrage in post-austerity England enables the cultivation of fragile and contested forms of humanitarian authority, it demonstrates that outrage is ultimately a volatile and unstable emotion in this setting: amplifying the moralised division of labour within the industry, it also enrols workers' intimate selves and heightens their experiences of futility.

Wilson and Norrie's chapter, in turn, discusses how the penal system incorporates 'two kinds of psychological embodiment' that are inherently contradictory, one punitive, the other restorative. While the punitive dimension of punishment is dominant, it is nevertheless conjoined with a set of restorative projects which lie, as the chapter argues, at the margins of the penal system. This relation sets the grounds for what Wilson and Norrie call the tragic nature of modern prison life, which the chapter proposes to understand and critically analyse. At the heart of this analysis lies an exploration of the underpinning moral psychology of contemporary penality, which fails to integrate punitive and restorative approaches. The chapter suggests that a deep investigation of this moral psychology reveals the limitations of the modern prison and presses the need to move beyond its punitive dominance, towards what they deem a deep or tendential abolitionist approach to prison reform.

The final chapter in the collection, by Christinaki and Burman, engages with the notion of emotional labour as a pathway to explore the political economies of emotions within humanitarian interventions. Their main focus is on examining what they call the emotional excess of humanitarian labour, which they do through a case study around a family who enters a refugee camp in midland Greece as a 'spontaneous arrival', and who is subsequently asked to leave the camp due to not being officially registered there. The chapter deploys a psychological framework to understand these emotional economies within political discourse and humanitarian work, drawing inspiration from feminist geographers and from discussions on the 'feminisation' of asylum and migration to reflect on the 'feminised' character of work within the humanitarian landscape.

Overall, this collection presents a complex, multifaceted, often kaleidoscopic picture of different perspectives, approaches and empirical findings concerning the embodied, affective and relational character of state power. In so doing, it offers new insights on a burgeoning area of research, to outline and springboard new methodological, theoretical and empirical avenues, and to highlight the importance of continuing to demystify the many issues around hegemonic constructions of the modern state, its authority, values and functions. In pressing for this need, and in exploring ways through which to pursue alternative understandings and, in some cases, alternative visions, this book also hopes to call attention to the importance of exploring possibilities for resistance and contestation.

References

Ahmed, S. 2014. *The Cultural Politics of Emotion*, Edinburgh, Edinburgh University Press.
Alexander, C. 2000. *Personal States: Making Connections between People and Bureaucracy in Turkey*, Oxford: Oxford University Press.
Aliverti, A. 2020. Benevolent Policing? Vulnerability and the Moral Pains of Border Controls. *The British Journal of Criminology*, 60, 1117–1135.
Aliverti, A. 2021. *Policing the Borders Within*, Oxford, Oxford University Press.
Aliverti, A., Carvalho, H., Chamberlen, A. & Sozzo, M. (eds.) 2023. *Decolonizing the Criminal Question; Colonial Legacies, Contemporary Problems*, Oxford, Oxford University Press.
Aliverti, A., Dufraix Tapia, R., Ramos Rodríguez, R., Tapia Ladino, M. & García España, E. 2025. Humanitarianism from Below: Border Police, Professional Identities and Moral Dilemmas. *British Journal of Criminology*. https://doi.org/10.1093/bjc/azaf005
Aliverti, A. & Tawfic, S. 2025. Caring States? Bureaucratic Care, Moral Ideals and Emotional Dilemmas in British Asylum and Policing. *Theoretical Criminology*. https://doi.org/10.1177/13624806241313104
Auyero, J. 2012. *Patients of the State: The Politics of Waiting in Argentina*, Durham and London, Duke University Press.
Baillot, H., Cowan, S. & Munro, V. E. 2013. Second-Hand Emotion? Exploring the Contagion and Impact of Trauma and Distress in the Asylum Law Context. *Journal of Law and Society*, 40, 509–540.

Butler, J. 1990. *Gender Trouble: Feminism and the Subversion of Identity*, London, Routledge.
Butler, J. 2016. *Frames of War: When Is Life Grievable?*, London, Verso.
Carvalho, H. & Chamberlen, A. 2016. Punishment, Justice and Emotions. In: Tonry, M. (ed.) *Oxford Handbooks Online in Criminology & Criminal Justice*. New York: Oxford University Press, 1–16.
Carvalho, H. & Chamberlen, A. 2018. Why Punishment Pleases: Punitive Feelings in a World of Hostile Solidarity. *Punishment & Society*, 20, 217–234.
Carvalho, H., Chamberlen, A. & Lewis, R. 2020. Punitiveness beyond Criminal Justice: Punishable and Punitive Subjects in an Era of Prevention, Anti-Migration and Austerity. *The British Journal of Criminology*, 60, 265–284.
Carvalho, H., Foreman, S., Tawfic, S., Aliverti, A., Chamberlen, A. & Rawson, B. 2025. Modern Slavery and the Punitive-Humanitarian Complex. *The British Journal of Criminology*, 65, 93–109.
Chamberlen, A. 2018. *Embodying Punishment: Emotions, Identities and Lived Experiences in Women's Prisons*, Oxford, Oxford University Press.
Chamberlen, A. & Carvalho, H. 2019. Punitiveness and the Emotions of Punishment: Between Solidarity and Hostility. In: Jacobsen, M. & Walklate, S. (eds.) *Crime and Emotions: Towards a Criminology of Emotions*, London: Routledge, 96–112.
Chamberlen, A. & Carvalho, H. 2022. Feeling the Absence of Justice: Notes on Our Pathological Reliance on Punitive Justice. *The Howard Journal of Crime and Justice*, 61, 87–102.
Cooper, D. 2019. *Feeling Like a State: Desire, Denial, and the Recasting of Authority*, Durham, Duke University Press.
Crewe, B. 2011. Depth, Weight, Tightness: Revisiting the Pains of Imprisonment. *Punishment & Society*, 13, 509–529.
Das, D. & Poole, D. 2004. State and Its Margins. Comparative Ethnographies. In: Das, D. & Poole, D. (eds.) *Anthropology at the Margins of the State*, Santa Fe, School of American Research Press, 3–33.
de Beauvoir, S. 1997. *The Second Sex*, New York, Vintage Classics.
Douglas, M. [1986] 2012. *How Institutions Think*, London, Routledge.
Epstein, C. 2021. *Birth of the State: The Place of the Body in Crafting Modern Politics*, Oxford, Oxford University Press.
Fassin, D. 2012. *Humanitarian Reason: A Moral History of the Present*, Berkeley and Los Angeles, University of California Press.
Fassin, D. (ed.) 2015. *At the Heart of the State: The Moral World of Institutions*, London, Pluto Press.
Fernández-Kelly, P. 2015. *The Hero's Fight: African Americans in West Baltimore and the Shadow of the State*. Princeton: Princeton University Press.
Fineman, M. 2008. The Vulnerable Subject: Anchoring Equality in the Human Condition. *Yale Journal of Law & Feminism*, 20, 1–23.
Foucault, M. 1977. *Discipline and Punish: The Birth of the Prison*. New York: Pantheon Books.
Goffman, E. 1959. *The Presentation of Self in Everyday Life*. New York: Doubleday.
Goldberg, D. T. 1993. Modernity, Race, and Morality. *Cultural Critique*, 24, 193–227.
Gupta, A. 2012. *Red Tape: Bureaucracy, Structural Violence, and Poverty in India*, Durham and London, Duke University Press.

Hansen, T. & Stepputat, F. 2001. Introduction. In: Blom Hansen, T. & Stepputat, F. (eds.) *States of Imagination: Ethnographic Explorations of the Postcolonial State*, Durham and London, Duke University Press, 1–38.

Herrity, K., Schmidt, B. E. & Warr, J. (eds.) 2021. *Sensory Penalities: Exploring the Senses in Spaces of Punishment and Social Control*, Leeds, Emerald.

Hochschild, A. R. 1983. *The Managed Heart: Commercialization of Human Feeling*. Berkeley: University of California Press.

Hunter, S. 2015. *Power, Politics and the Emotions: Impossible Governance?* London: Routledge.

Jacobsen, M. & Walklate, S. (eds.) 2009. *Emotions and Crime: Towards a Criminology of Emotions*, London, Routledge.

Jacobsson, K. & Gubrium, J. F. (eds.) 2021. *Doing Human Service Ethnography*, Bristol, Policy Press.

Jupp, E., Pykett, J. & Smith, F. (eds.) 2017. *Emotional States: Sites and Spaces of Affective Governance*, Oxford, Routledge.

Koch, I. 2018. *Personalizing the State: An Anthropology of Law, Politics, and Welfare in Austerity Britain*, Oxford, Oxford University Press.

Laszczkowski, M. & Reeves, M. 2018. *Affective States: Entanglements, Suspensions, Suspicions*, New York and Oxford, Berghahn.

Leder, D. 1990. *The Absent Body*, Chicago, University of Chicago Press.

Lipsky, M. 2010. *Street-Level Bureaucracy: Dilemmas of the Individual in Public Services*, New York, Russel Sage Foundation.

Lumsden, K. & Black, A. 2017. Austerity Policing, Emotional Labour and the Boundaries of Police Work: An Ethnography of a Police Force Control Room in England. *The British Journal of Criminology*, 58, 606–623.

Martin, T. M., Jefferson, A. M. & Bandyopadhyay, M. 2014. Sensing Prison Climates: Governance, Survival, and Transition. *Focaal—Journal of Global and Historical Anthropology*, 68, 3–17.

Miller, J. 2022. *The Policing Mind*, Bristol: Bristol University Press.

Mitchell, T. 1990. Everyday Metaphors of Power. *Theory and Society*, 19, 545–577.

Navaro-Yashin, Y. 2020. *Faces of the State: Secularism and Public Life in Turkey*. Princeton: Princeton University Press.

Nussbaum, M. 2001. *Upheavals of Thought: The Intelligence of Emotions*, Cambridge: Cambridge University Press.

Nussbaum, M. 2013. *Political Emotions: Why Love Matters for Justice*, Cambridge: Harvard University Press.

Phillips, J., Waters, J., Westaby, C. & Fowler, A. (eds.) 2020. *Emotional Labour in Criminal Justice and Criminology*, Abingdon, Routledge.

Sarat, A. D. 1990. "... The Law Is All Over": Power, Resistance and the Legal Consciousness of the Welfare Poor. *Yale Journal of Law and the Humanities*, 2, 6.

Sclater, S., Jones, D., Price, H. & Yates, C. (eds.) 2009. *Emotion: New Psychosocial Perspectives*, London: Palgrave.

Scott, J. 1998. *Seeing Like a State: How Certain Schemes to Improve the Human Condition Have Failed*, New Haven: Yale University Press.

Stoler, A. L. 2008. *Along the Archival Grain: Epistemic Anxieties and Colonial Common Sense*. Princeton: Princeton University Press.

Thelen, T., Vetters, L. & Von Benda-Beckmann, K. (eds.) 2017. *Stategraphy: Toward a Relational Anthropology of the State*, New York: Verso.

Thompson, J. 2022. *Care Aesthetics: For Artful Care and Careful Art*. London: Routledge.
Young, I. M. 1990. *Throwing Like a Girl and Other Essays in Feminist Philosophy and Social Theory*, Bloomington, Indiana University Press.
Zacka, B. 2017. *When the State Meets the Street: Public Service and Moral Agency*, Cambridge, MA, Harvard University Press.

PART 1
Representing the state, mobilising affect

1

THE BASTILLE AND THE FRENCH REVOLUTION

Reading an Icon

Eamonn Carrabine

Introduction

The storming of the Bastille is often taken to be the defining event of the French Revolution, symbolising the momentous break between the old regime and a new era of freedom. Indeed, it is said to be one of the four great symbols of the Revolution, alongside the Declaration of Rights, the poetic slogan 'Liberté – Egalité – Fraternité' and the national anthem, the *Marseillaise*, composed in 1792 (Lüsebrink and Reichardt, 1997:241). How this notorious fortress-prison came to constitute an iconic cornerstone of the French Revolution is the subject of this chapter, but I am also interested in the forgotten, the buried, and the unfamiliar aspects of this most striking figure of incarceration. For enlightened critics, 'it embodied the secretive, dark, decaying and irrational aspects of the medieval' (Smith, 1999:23). The *lettres de cachet* (loosely, letters of arrest) bearing the King's official seal, which were justified from the principle of divine right, were pivotal here. To modern sensibilities there is nothing more symptomatic of arbitrary, despotic power than these royal decrees that bypassed normal legal proceedings and imprisoned citizens without trial for an indeterminate period. Historians have emphasised how the state fuelled the notoriety of the Bastille by regularly interning its high-profile opponents and well-known personalities there. Among those imprisoned were disgraced ministers, generals accused of treason, courtiers involved in scandal, and writers punished for their subversive, clandestine literature (an odd mix of pornography and politics) who made the Bastille 'the central symbol of radical propaganda before the French Revolution' (Darnton, 1984:155).

Controversial figures like De Sade, Voltaire, and 'the man in the iron mask', who were imprisoned here, established in the collective imagination an understanding of the Bastille as the place where the 'spirit of freedom was imprisoned' (Lüsebrink and Reichardt, 1997:30). Yet for much of the eighteenth century, conditions were by no means as terrible as in other prisons (such as those endured at Bicêtre), and aristocrats were confined in some comfort. I will discuss this growing gap between the reality of prison practice at the Bastille and how its mythology became increasingly significant in defining opposition to state power in what follows, though it is instructive to note that the *lettres* prosecuted not only crimes against the state (espionage, treason, and conspiracies) but in many cases they are pleas by ordinary citizens for social discipline (Farge and Foucault, 1982/2017). The chapter is also attentive to the iconography of the Bastille, where the term iconography is derived from two Greek words: *eikon*, meaning 'image', and *graphe*, meaning 'writing', and is primarily concerned with the meaning, subject matter, or content of works of art. The method addresses the way 'an artist "writes" the image, as well as what the image itself "writes" – that is the story it tells' (Adams, 2010:43).

In other words, the claim is that the use of pictures as historical 'evidence' should not be restricted to a narrow definition; rather, room should be left for the 'imagination', and it may well be better to see such sources as ' "traces" of the past in the present' (Burke, 2001:13). The chapter begins by setting out rival interpretations of the Revolution before discussing how images were active tools of negotiation, parody and defiance – as the struggle over representation was crucial to the unfolding events – and then explores the fate of the Bastille after 14 July 1789. As such, the case study presented here provides a key site for understanding the moral and affective economies of state power and resistance. It is not just that this insurrectionary event, the storming of the Bastille, is celebrated as a national holiday every year, but that this decisive rupture tells us something fundamental about the invention of symbols and rituals. The idea of 'political affects' is explored elsewhere in this collection, especially in Braddock et al.'s contribution, which is developed through fusing insights from psychoanalysis with semiotics to address the 'excess of meaning' generated by state power. This chapter is also concerned with forms of iconic representation, and here the focus is on what has been termed the 'languages of stateness', which refers to the different ways 'the state makes itself real and tangible through symbols, texts, and iconography', that is how it strives to be a state for itself and meet certain expectations, yet such states of imagination also require us to 'move beyond the state's own prose, categories, and perspective and study how the state appears in everyday and localized forms' (Hansen and Stepputat, 2001:5). Struggles over representation help us to better understand the moral and emotional economies of state power and resistance, and as Charlotte Epstein (2021:2) has recently argued, the state's ontology has always been corporeal, and she turns this 'ipseity of the body, its "thereness" into a methodological starting point'. It is this idea of the embodied state that is developed in the chapter.

Approaching the Revolution

It has been said that much of the problem with studying the French Revolution is sifting through what others have said about it. Given that it is one of the most written-about episodes in Western history, this involves a recognition that any attempt to define what happened in 1789, its causes, content, and consequences will be partial and tendentious. It is best understood as a process, perplexing to contemporaries, which stretched over many years, rather than a single event. For some the revolutionary period begins in 1789 with the destruction of the Bastille and continues up to the Consulate of Napoleon in 1799, though for other historians this is problematic as the turbulent era could arguably extend from 1787 to 1815. To write on the French Revolution 'is to throw oneself into a polemical discourse that is itself highly charged with political implications' (Cuno, 1988:13). As an example, Simon Schama's (1989) best-selling chronicle, which turned out to be the success story of the bicentenary, was immediately controversial. His critics accused him of promoting neo-conservative revisionist positions and sounding at times like Margaret Thatcher, if not Edmund Burke, in such passages as:

> the Revolution did indeed invent a new kind of politics…that abolished private space and time, and created a form of patriotic militarism more all-embracing than anything that had yet been seen in Europe. For one year, it invented and practiced representative democracy; for two years, it imposed coercive egalitarianism…But for two decades its enduring product was a new kind of militarized state…The terror was merely 1789 with a higher body count.
> (Schama, 1989:184 and 447, cited in Kates, 1998:11)

Although the connection is not made explicitly, the parallels with modern fascism are inescapable. The main thesis is that violence drove the revolution from the very beginning, insisting that in 'some depressingly unavoidable sense, violence *was* the Revolution itself' (Schama, 1989:xvii, emphasis in original). As early as 1790, Burke was describing the situation in France 'in tones which suggested that massacre and mob rule were already the norm, and total anarchy shortly to arrive' (Andress, 2013:294), predicting that it would take a military dictatorship to end it all – several years before the eventual triumph of a general.

The analysis of the French Revolution has given rise to several competing explanations. These include the conservatism of Burke, but the revolutionary legacy later inspired Marx and Engels, who founded the international communist movement. For much of the twentieth century Marxist interpretations dominated, which maintained that class antagonisms between a feudal old regime and a capitalist bourgeoisie led to the radical rupture in the social order. As it settled into an orthodoxy, the central explanation became one of seeing the French Revolution as the result of a class struggle, where one class was destroyed (the nobility), one awakened (the urban sans-culottes) and another class won control of the state (the bourgeoisie). The position has since been attacked by three distinctive, revisionary approaches. Initially critics argued that the Revolution was not made by the capitalist bourgeoisie; it was instead led by local, petty officials and professionals, and while it was still understood as a social revolution, it was one of 'notables', not capitalists. Their actions not only benefitted landowners in general but also stalled the development of capitalism in France (Cobban, 1964). Throughout much of the nineteenth century France remained an agricultural society, with much of the land now in the hands of the peasantry because of the emancipation in the countryside in the 1790s. Others insisted it was the liberal aristocracy, not a frustrated bourgeoisie, that led the concerted movement against royal despotism (Eisenstein, 1965).

A second influential challenge sees the Revolution in terms of state modernisation. The French state collapsed because of a fiscal crisis generated by Great Power rivalry – fighting three great wars on a worldwide scale had left the monarchy close to bankruptcy in the 1780s. It was not that France lacked the resources to survive as a European force, but that it lacked the system of government to gather fiscal resources from new types of wealth (Goldstone, 1991). The structural weaknesses produced by military needs and international competition resulted in a series of stresses that an agrarian bureaucracy was unable to meet (Skocpol, 1979). In reviving a theme of state failure, this comparative approach recalls Alexis de Tocqueville's (1856/2008) classic argument that the Revolution was a further stage in a centuries-long process of state centralisation, so that no 'one class won the contest' but rather all 'became more equal in their unwitting slavishness to an authoritarian government' (Hunt, 1984:6). Furthermore, de Tocqueville emphasised how by the middle of the eighteenth century 'men of letters' had become leading political figures, and more surprisingly still, it was the court and high nobility who were the main consumers for this work, which did most to undermine their authority. His view was that the old regime brought about its own destruction by 'irresponsibly flirting with ideas it only half understood, but which it found diverting' (Schama, 1989:145) so that when 'the time came at last to act, the nation brought all the habits of literature into politics' (de Tocqueville, 1856/2008:148).

The invitation to place social conflict within an explicitly political framework is one taken up by a third strand of revisionary interpretation. At the vanguard of the anti-Marxist critique is François Furet (1978/1981), who maintained that the Revolution was an autonomous political and ideological movement, not the expression of a social class struggle. By advocating a more considered study of revolutionary rhetoric and ideas, the ambition was to understand why democracy in the French Revolution developed into totalitarianism. Although Furet's understanding is emphatically conservative, it did prompt fresh interest in the cultural history of the era and the institution of a dramatically new political culture. Lynn Hunt's (1984) decisive intervention distilled these revisionist currents in a sophisticated analysis of how the Revolution was essentially driven by ideas, emotions, and symbolic forms. In her reading, democratic republicanism was the most important outcome of the Revolution, seeing it as a potent mix of rhetorical claims, innovative symbols, and collective rituals.

Clearly there are important differences between orthodox and revisionist positions (and they are unlikely to be ever settled), but there are merits in each. Since 1989, the polemics have subsided somewhat, so that no one school dominates the field. Instead, research proceeds along a variety of fronts, where gender relations, religious minorities, slavery, and the colonies have emerged as important new areas. Hunt (2009) has since argued that the study of images may be one of the more productive future directions left to explore, especially since the issue of revolutionary violence is back on the intellectual agenda, and it is that path the rest of the chapter will explore.

Visual Representation

The French Revolution was to a large degree a struggle over representation, and 'violence was one of the most prominent – and unstable – loci of that struggle' (Graybill, 2016:25). The disturbing place of violence in the revolutionary project was a problem well understood by the revolutionaries themselves. How they grappled with their own exceptional present and uncertain efforts to anchor themselves in history is revealed in the images and objects through which revolutionary authority was depicted (Taws, 2013). The struggle for power in the new regime was a struggle over the meaning of violence, which had helped launch the Revolution in 1789, and it was popular violence which also threatened to extinguish the new, fragile social order. Indeed, the explosive energy unleashed by the French Revolution has been attributed to the ongoing struggle between the forces of revolution and those of counter-revolution (Sutherland, 2003). Emancipation in the countryside could only have been accomplished through 'a great deal of insurrectionary violence' against the lords and their seigneurial rights (Markoff, 1998:238).

Defining the new regime involved defining the relationship between violence and legitimacy.

Revolutionary violence itself depended on a 'sharp separation between good People and criminal Other' (Lucas, 1994:74). In this regard a broad range of printed material, intersected with other media, such as songs and images, and assorted ephemera produced by the press, ranging from almanacs, calendars, playing cards, board games, passports, caricatures, and posters to engravings and the newly invented paper currency (*assignats*), all 'carried revolutionary messages into the sphere of everyday life' (Darnton, 1989:xv). Describing this material as 'ephemera' underplays their significance, especially since their fleeting temporality enabled them to respond to fast-moving events in ways that slower and more permanent media such as painting, sculpture, and architecture could not. As these images were sometimes produced in tens of thousands of copies, they also reached large audiences who were unable to read newspapers, pamphlets, or books (Leith, 1989). Indeed, the royal family's ill-fated attempt to flee Paris in 1791, known as the 'flight to Varennes', was ultimately thwarted by a postmaster recognising the King's portrait from an *assignat* he had in his pocket.

Images did more than simply convey information; they actively shaped the way in which events were understood at the time. They were 'historical agents', and this role of 'image as agent' is especially important in the case of revolutions, often helping to make 'ordinary people politically conscious', especially when much of the populace is illiterate (Burke, 2001:145–146). It has been estimated that one-half to two-thirds of the population could not, or could only barely, read and that they lived in a 'traditional world of oral communication'; then the full significance of pictorial representation becomes clear (Reichardt, 1989:224). The downfall of Louis XVI can be read through engravings, which before 1789 had been full of majesty, emphasising the sovereign's divine authority, power, and glory. During the initial, 'liberal' period (1789–91) revolutionaries depicted the monarch in his new, constitutional role, which the dynasty regarded as a humiliating step down. Yet, after the doomed flight to Varennes, the 'caricatures turned hostile; artists depicted the monarch as a drunkard or barnyard animal' (Censer and Hunt, 2001:83). Ridiculing the king and queen through printed images helped prepare the way for their eventual executions in 1793. Though the fact that Marie Antoinette should have been the subject of an extensive pornographic literature both before and during the revolutionary era says much about the 'larger body politic' (Hunt, 1991/1998:279). The sexual sensationalism of the Old Regime, targeted by the obscene *libelles* in this material, has been read as a form of anti-Establishment critique – where the court, church, aristocracy, academies, salons, and the monarchy itself are attacked – communicating 'a sense of total opposition to an élite so corrupt as to deserve annihilation' (Darnton, 1971:111).

Although this 'Grub Street Thesis' continues to be influential, the links between this forbidden literature and the origins of revolutionary ideas remain problematic. The 'low-life', aggressive journalism may have been 'radically destructive', yet it offered up 'no real alternative to the status quo' (Maza, 2013:43). Others suggest that the 'obscene imagery works with a rhetoric that only seems to be radical' as the 'shocking images work with restrictive and even repressive allusions that constantly appeal to popular *mentalités* that are easily mistaken for revolutionary attitudes' (Wagner, 1995:139–140). The shifting meanings are an indication of the dynamic, contradictory processes at the heart of revolutionary visual practice. Indeed, it has been argued that visual 'representation captured the semiotic instability, produced it, and, rather than resolve it, opened the door to a new conceptualization of society itself' (Hunt, 2009:678). At this decisive moment we can see not simply the co-constitution of the state and modern political subject, that is the subject as bearer of rights (to security, liberty, and property), but how these relations 'are neither natural nor eternal'; rather, they 'are less fixed, less firmly in place than we assume and often experience them to be' (Epstein, 2021:2). The origins of the state–subject relation can be traced back to seventeenth-century England, as Epstein (2021) demonstrates, and the figure of the 'citizen' born in the French Revolution, is a crucial development in the evolving and unfolding shaping of the present, where the 'optic of the body' remains crucial. With the collapse of censorship in 1789 images and newspapers were produced in large quantities, and their sheer number points to their crucial significance in addressing a broad social base.

All of which points to a rich and prolific visual culture at work, though one which has not received the attention it should. As the former director of the Museum of the French Revolution put it, there have long been:

> dismissive attitudes toward the visual traces of the Revolutionary period, a corpus of artifacts perceived as rudimentary and an embarrassment for the artisan trades, vulgar caricatures whose meaning had become obscure and irrelevant, and lifeless paintings and sculpture that slavishly imitated classical models.
>
> *(Bordes, 2019:1)*

Of course, the situation has begun to change in the last 30 years or so, with the publication of important scholarship on visual representation and the development of online resources (such as <u>French Revolution Images – Spotlight at Stanford</u>). Rather than try to tackle the entire corpus of images, I will concentrate on a handful of images to provide a sense of their variety and an indication of their role as historical agents. Their selection does not constitute a representative sample in any meaningful sense, and given the space confines of a book chapter, there are further limits placed on the kind of image discussed here. Nevertheless, the overall intention is to demonstrate how a site of punishment became an iconic symbol, the very embodiment of state power. Here it is important to recognise how one of the most important languages of stateness – how the state appears as a myth – operates through a form of 'social fantasy' that is produced through numerous encounters, from mundane practices to those abstracted, fetishised, and manifested in public spectacles (see Hansen and Stepputat, 2001:18–22 for a discussion of the anthropological literature on this point).

The Storming of the Bastille

The storming of the Bastille is the defining event signifying the beginning of the Revolution. Although some maintain that the text of the Declaration of the Rights of Man and Citizen is the most important legacy of 1789, the words of it have never matched the image of the Bastille. Some of the reasons for this symbolic power are conveyed in the following passage:

> The words of the Declaration are rhetorically elevating, but they offer no drama, no story, no violence. All three are embodied and embedded in the image of the Bastille, which signifies a story of liberation, which dramatizes the conflict between the oppressive power of the old regime and the explosive energy of the new republic, and which above all evokes the violent overthrow old order: liberty with a bludgeon in her hand.
> *(Heffernan, 1992:xi)*

To understand how the fall of the Bastille came to represent the bedrock of the French Revolution, it is first necessary to understand the place of the prison in the system of repression practised by the old regime. Built between 1356 and 1382 as an eight-tower fortress to protect Paris, it was gradually refashioned into a state prison and came to embody the obstinate force of eighteenth-century absolutist justice. From 1715 onwards the Bastille was 'increasingly attacked as a concrete embodiment of "ministerial despotism," visible to all, and as a stain on the Enlightenment' (Reichardt, 1989:226). Beginning in the 1720s and 1730s, a group of writers collectively known as *philosophes* produced a series of works critical of the church, the monarchy, and the nobility. They include Voltaire's biting anti-clerical satires, Montesquieu's condemnation of despotism, and the multi-volume *Encyclopédie* that sought to advance knowledge through an irreverent contempt for authority. Yet the idea that 'the Enlightenment' directly caused the French Revolution was rejected by historians several decades ago, for ultimately these writers 'were reformers, not revolutionaries' (Maza, 2013:43). Most were well established in the elite: aristocrats, clerics, lawyers, professionals, and students. They sought to 'enlighten from above', seeking 'the conquest of salons and academies, journals and theatre, Masonic lodges and key cafés, where they could win the rich and powerful to their cause' and in doing so they 'reached a broad public among the middle classes, but they drew the line above the peasantry' (Darnton, 2003:5).

Nevertheless, for Enlightenment thinkers and the population at large, the Bastille epitomised the tyranny of the absolutist state. There were two main reasons for this. First, there was a steady stream of underground literature, much of it produced by former prisoners, which emphasised the dark, oppressive conditions endured at the prison. Comparing their fates 'to the most terrifying form of confinement imaginable: that of being buried alive' (Freedman, 2017:360), these narratives became more horrific, even as conditions greatly improved. Second, the state itself fuelled the notoriety of the Bastille by regularly imprisoning its political opponents there and the Château de Vincennes, both of which were generally reserved for prisoners of social rank and some financial means. Consequently, it has been maintained that 'collective representations of the Bastille over-inflated its objective characteristics', suggesting that 'it was neither as important nor as "bad" as people believed' (Smith, 1999:23). The legends surrounding the Bastille helped sustain a climate of fear, which was the defining principle of despotic government. The 'self-chosen tenet of secrecy, which was supposed to protect state and family interests' (Lüsenbrink and Reichardt, 1997:31), meant that the official silence on the scandals intensified the mythology. Nothing underlines this point more than the fact that when the Bastille was stormed, it contained only seven prisoners. None were political prisoners. Four were forgers, two were mentally disturbed and the other troubled soul was detained at the request of his family.

The immediate cause of the conquest of the prison was the growing urban unrest and popular uprisings in Paris and the provinces. A year of devastating famine had spurred riots across the country, so that all hopes were pinned on the need for major political and economic reforms. The reformers seized their moment because the monarchy was almost bankrupt. When efforts to make the haphazard taxation system more uniform and efficient broke down, the king was pressured to call a meeting of the three estates of the realm – the clergy, nobility, and commoners – to find a solution. The Estates-General, which had not met since 1614, convened in May 1789 and soon fell into acrimony, with the delegates of the Third Estate (mostly filled with ambitious local bureaucrats and professionals) proclaiming they spoke for the entire nation. Reconstituting themselves as the National Assembly and joined by reformers from the other Estates, this effectively meant the end of absolute monarchy and a complete vacuum of power. The collapse was not immediate, and initially a constitutional monarchy, much like England's, was an ambition for many.

In the last week of June 1789, the royal government summoned 20,000 troops to March to Paris, to intimidate the Third Estate deputies and extinguish any further protests. The National Assembly petitioned the king to withdraw the regiments, but instead Louis XVI fired his popular finance minister. The following morning, July 12, Parisians heard the rumour, and it provoked widespread demonstrations and the formation of a citizens' militia to defend against the military attack everyone feared. While the new militia set about finding weapons, the royal authorities were as desperate to hide them. Several thousand invaded the Hôtel des Invalides (the military veterans' hospital), taking 30,000 muskets on July 14, and once news spread that hundreds of barrels of gunpowder had recently been moved to the Bastille from the nearby Arsenal, a crowd of around 1000 (mostly made of small tradesmen, including dozens of locksmiths and some military deserters) arrived at the gates at 10 in the morning. The seemingly impregnable fortress capitulated after a 6-hour siege, and the violence that then followed is said to have been a 'consequence of the indecision of the Bastille's governor, marquis de Launay, the crowd's bitterness at de Launay's apparent violation of the truces, his troops firing into the besiegers, and the crowd's distrust of their own leaders' (Sutherland, 2013:237). Altogether, 6 defenders of the Bastille were killed, and 64 protestors.

The next day the King came to the Assembly to declare that he was ordering the troops encamped around Paris to disperse. His commanders advised him that he could no longer rely on the military, as there were serious morale and desertion problems, which effectively meant the end of royal authority. The storming of the Bastille was significant for several reasons. The first, and most enduring, was the symbolic victory over despotism, and as news spread, similar uprisings took place in towns and cities across the country. Rural revolt was already underway before the July insurrection, so the military and political consequences of the fall of the Bastille were immediately paramount. As a mediaeval fortress, it commanded the entire east of Paris with its guns and was a constant reminder of the might of the old regime, looming over some of the poorest neighbourhoods in the city. The capitulation convinced Parisians that 'they alone had saved the National Assembly from destruction' (Doyle, 2018:111), and the event itself crystallised the principle of the sovereignty of the people, which in turn 'served to legitimize revolutionary violence for the first time' (Lüsenbrink and Reichardt, 1997:45).

Myth Making

However sensational the uprising was, there is no doubt that the Bastille became 'much more important in its "afterlife" than it ever had been as a working institution of the state', not least since it 'gave a shape and an image to all the vices against which the Revolution defined itself' (Schama, 1989:345). The engravings printed in broadsides, newspapers, and pamphlets provide us with telling examples of images in action, where a vibrant mix of picture, sound, and writing circulated in and around these texts. This popular reportage was hawked and performed by street vendors, and the prints circulated widely, while those who could not afford them could see them in the windows of print-shops. An example is provided in Figure 1.1, which sold on 28 July 1789, just two weeks after the fall of the Bastille, depicts the conquest of the Bastille as the governor is seized on the battlements. But what is significant about the picture is how the texts framing it are songs celebrating the conquest, combined with a report of the 'heureuse révolution' distilling key radical messages on the 'necessity to storm the Bastille' beneath the image, while the headline declares the fortress was 'Captured by the Bourgeoisie'.

The print is explicitly addressed to an oral folk culture, and while the image may well be 'naïve and clumsy' in this rendering (by the engraver Jean-Baptiste Gautier of the rue St. Jacques), it served as a model for others to follow (Reichardt, 1989:231–232).

This style of pictorial broadsheet was repeated many times, as in a provincial woodcut (see Figure 1.2) produced by Jean-Baptiste Letourmi of Orléans, which was successfully sold via some hundred outlets across France.

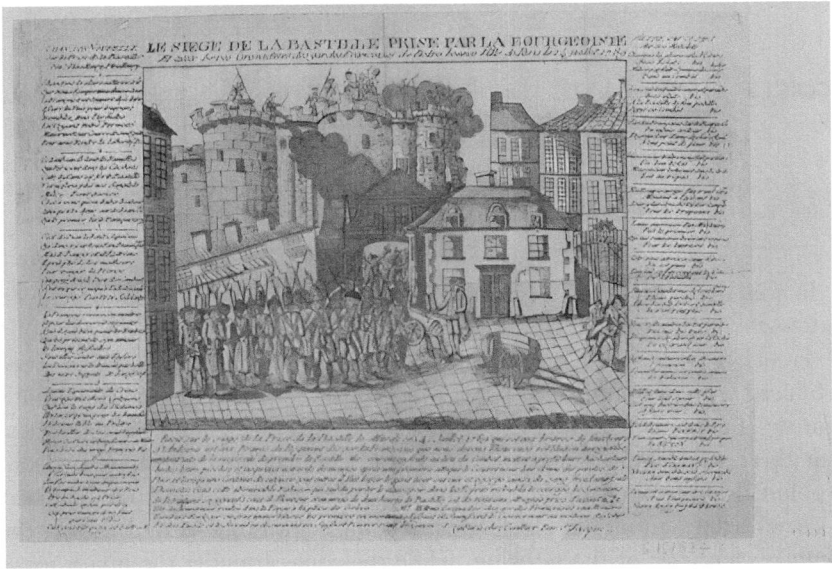

FIGURE 1.1 'The Siege of the Bastille, Captured by the Bourgeoisie' ('Le Siège de la Bastilee prise par la bourgeoisie'). Paris: Gautier, 1789. Colour etching. Bibliothèque Nationale, Cabinet des Estampes, Collection Hennin.

Source: https://purl.stanford.edu/xq102wv2456 (accessed 2024-06-09). Provided by Stanford University Libraries and the Bibliothèque nationale de France.

32 The Embodied State

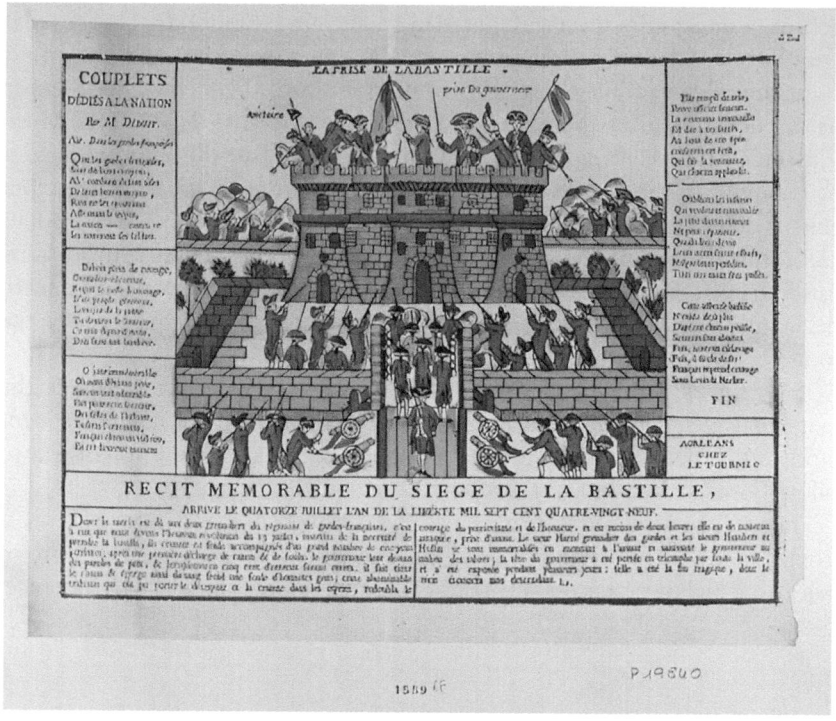

FIGURE 1.2 'The Taking of the Bastille' ('La Prise de la Bastille'). Orléans: Letourni, 1789. Colour woodcut. Bibliothèque Nationale, Cabinet des Estampes, Collection de Vinck.

Source: https://exhibits.stanford.edu/frenchrevolution/catalog/wf081nk0517 (accessed 2024-06-09). Provided by Stanford University Libraries and the Bibliothèque nationale de France.

In this depiction of the storming of the Bastille, the event is portrayed more schematically and less realistically, but it is very much in the style of French woodcuts of saints, known as 'images of Épinal', which were produced in large numbers at this time and even well into the nineteenth century (Burke, 2001:146). Consequently, it is no exaggeration to suggest that this 'emblematic reduction' gives the woodcut the 'effect of an icon, a political devotional image' (Reichardt, 1989:232). The surrounding text borrows from Gautier but places greater emphasis on Liberty and stresses the popular character of the uprising, while the songs framing the image extol the victors as national heroes. Paris was a city 'suffused with songs', and 'the entire kingdom could be described as "an absolute monarchy tempered by songs"', since 'a catchy song could spread like wildfire' (Darnton, 2003:54), especially if it was disrespectful and recited profane verse.

Figure 1.2 depicts the prison and the events surrounding it less exactly than in Figure 1.1, but the image of the Bastille is 'more vivid and doubtless more effective as an illustration of the myth' (Burke, 2001:146). Few understood the myth-making business better than Pierre-François Palloy. He understood immediately that the Revolution had created a demand for a new kind of history – the heroic epic focussing on the common people, rather than princes and nobility. If the idea of a 'bourgeois revolution' is today regarded as problematic, then Palloy is a perfect illustration of how these contradictions might be resolved. Far from being a frustrated failure, he was a dazzling example of old regime capitalism. The son of a small wine merchant, he had become a wealthy architect and was one of the largest building contractors in Paris. He was not the first, nor the last, self-made man to have acquired his fortune by marrying up. In this instance, it was the daughter of his master and taking over the helm of his workshop. On the eve of the Revolution, he employed several hundred workers and owned seven houses, displaying all the lavish trappings of worldly success. By July 1789, at the age of 34, he gave himself the nickname 'the Patriot', identifying with the cause of the *patrie*, and on the 14th of July, he was commandant of his local district militia. Swept along by chance, he claimed to have run to the Bastille and been among the first to enter the inner courtyard of the conquered prison.

While his own account cannot be verified, there is no doubt that he did receive 'a *brevet de vainqueur* to certify that he had been one of the sacred nine hundred' (Schama, 1989:347). Within a day he applied to the Paris Commune for the contract to demolish the Bastille, and once attained, he established a thriving enterprise selling pieces from the ex-prison as souvenirs (see Figure 1.3). These included a set of miniature, replica 'Bastilles' carved from stone blocks reclaimed from the prison rubble and were sent to every

FIGURE 1.3 'Modèle de la Bastille', 1790. Workshop of Pierre-François Palloy.
Source: From Wikimedia Commons.

FIGURE 1.4　Pierre-Etienne and Jacques-Philipp Lesueur, 'Model of the Bastille, Four Men Carrying the Model During Civil Process', gouache mounted on paper, c. 1791. Musée Carnavalet.
Source: From Wikimedia Commons.

French département (there were 83 at the time), which Palloy named 'Relics of Freedom' to be consecrated in festive ceremonies (see Figure 1.4) as '*ex votos* of liberty' (Kohle and Reichardt, 2008:18).

Soon after, the 'aesthetic of fragmentation' that defined this project was replaced by a more opportunistic and no doubt more efficient process, as Palloy 'reduced the prison to its smallest elements before remaking it entirely anew' (Taws, 2013:99). His workshops began to produce miniature models from a Bastille stone dust paste, which were cast from a metal frame and adorned with chiselled detail provided by local artisans.

Throughout the summer of 1789, Palloy and his demolition crew offered paid tours of the basement cells, dungeons, and torture chambers of the disintegrating prison, furnishing their anecdotes with skeletons and bones found under the walls, though these are most likely to have been remnants of fallen construction workers (Lüsenbrink and Reichardt, 1997:120) or the bones of guards buried since the Renaissance. Nevertheless, the opportunity for Gothic sensationalism will have been irresistible, so that they 'were instantly described as the remains of prisoners who had died in captivity, manacled to the walls, forgotten even by their jailors' (Schama, 1989:350). Alongside the tours and replicas, Palloy and his company produced an extensive output of models and medals, furniture and memorabilia, as well as an array of essays, festivals, poems, pamphlets, and plans, which suggest an energetic exploitation of circumstance was to the fore.

Memory Work

Although Palloy was not the only entrepreneur capitalising on the destruction of the Bastille, these objects should not be dismissed as mere commercial flotsam or banal revolutionary kitsch, for their ersatz range speaks to a demand for effective souvenirs among the provincial millions in France for whom the fall of the Bastille was a remote event. Indeed, it has been argued that 'the capital was flooded with the debris of the old regime, helping to stimulate and supply the growing vogue for historical souvenirs' (Stammers, 2008:301). For opportunistic collectors there was ample chance to gather a host of unique, peculiar, and profitable objects. With rich rewards came considerable risks, not least since mementos from the old regime carried the dangerous suggestion of counter-revolution:

> One boy from the provinces stuffed his pockets with records looted from the Bastille in 1789, only to see his mother burn the whole stash four years later. As troops massed nearby for the siege of Lyon, she feared that safeguarding *lettres de cachet* signed by a former King Louis might be political suicide.
>
> *(Stammers, 2008:299)*

Palloy transformed the iron chains from the dungeons into memorial medals of freedom; inkwells were made from fetters; paper found during the demolition was used to make playing cards, as well as fans on which were painted scenes of the 14th of July; smaller stones were carved into little paperweight 'Bastilles', so that the objects repeated, time and again, the form of the prison from its debris. This brisk trade in political devotional objects was one that both inaugurated the Revolution's founding event and, at the same time, dispersed the victorious spoils of the old regime among the patriotic fold. By exploiting 'the unstable boundary between the "authenticity" of the Bastille relics and their palpable artifice', these 'objects were materially as well as politically ambiguous, for they occupied an indeterminate, occasionally parodic territory between sculpture, architecture, and performance' (Taws,

2013:102). Furthermore, they veer from the tiny to the monumental. Before the uprising the Bastille was known for, amongst other things, its immobility and massive size, physical qualities that enabled its strange metamorphosis into every conceivable kind of item.

Indeed, many contemporary images have since been accused of exaggerating the scale of the Bastille, as in Hubert Robert's (see Figure 1.5) Salon oil painting of the early stages of the demolition. It follows Giambattista Piranesi's disturbing images of fantasy prisons set out in his *Carceri d'Invenzione*, published in the middle decades of the eighteenth century, which had an immense influence on artistic sensibility (Carrabine, 2019).

In Robert's composition, the 'masonry of antiquity' falls into 'picturesque decay', presenting a vast elevation of the Bastille, with 'tiny figures scampering jubilantly over its battlements', and the structure itself suggests 'an immense Gothic castle of darkness and secrecy' (Schama, 1989:331). Yet light emanates both from the layer of limestone at the top of the Bastille, where diminutive workers are busy demolishing it, and from every falling stone heaped within the fortress moat. Images displayed in the Salon (the annual exhibit of the Académie des Beaux-Arts in Paris) had a larger and more diverse audience than any print, and those who 'understood the appropriate visual codes' will have 'recognised that the light pointed to the *philosophes*' critiques of established knowledge and

FIGURE 1.5 Hubert Robert, 'La Bastille, dans les premiers jours de sa demolition', 1789, oil on canvas. Musée Carnavalet.

Source: From Wikimedia Commons.

institutions' (Clay, 2012:33). Demolishing the Bastille was not just an act of physical destruction; it generated new signs and category instability.

The act of erasure was also a recipe for ferment. One influential argument is that 'the High Enlightenment recognized the potential agency of things and of the sensuous materials from which things are made', which has 'some altogether peculiar implications for the way the power of objects came to be experienced' (Naginski, 2001:34). The emphasis on the striking mobility of objects during the revolutionary era and how they moved through processes of 'propulsion, dispersion, reassembly' is one that grasps just how radical the transfer of cultural property was after 1789. The material transformation of signs was genuinely disruptive, 'as the patrimony of the clergy, the nobility and the corporations were subjected to confiscation, proscription or re-sale', suggesting the 'discontinuous social life of things' (Stammers, 2019:1–2) and how countless objects were set loose from their traditional settings and swept into 'new circuits of exchange, display and interpretation' (Stammers, 2008:301).

Once destroyed and pulverised into innumerable replicas, the site cried out for an appropriately symbolic resurrection – that even to this day has not yet been achieved. Initially plans were devised to build a new palace for the National Assembly over the haunt of despotism, but these were never realised. By the time of the first anniversary, trees were planted as a stop-gap measure, delineating the old fortress walls. In the following years occasional ritual festivities reinforced the sacred qualities of the area, but it was falling into disrepair. Former moats were now swamps of stagnant water, wild grass grew through scattered stones, and the entire decaying space remained ill-defined and desolate (Smith, 1999:25). When Napoleon sought to halt the semiotic drift, he deliberately reworked revolutionary iconography and directed it toward himself. Initially, an ambitious plan to erect a triumphal arch, supported by elephants and topped by a statue of Hercules, symbolising the might of the people, while commemorating his military victories in the Orient, was proposed. Instead, he retained nothing from this design, except for an elephant, which was placed in the square together with a fountain (Reichardt and Kohle, 2008:113). The Arc de Triomphe was moved to the opposite end of the city, and while many advisors attempted to persuade him that an elephant was a monument in poor taste (if not absurd), the project moved forward. But instead of a bronze statue, it would be a wooden and plaster model standing 24 metres tall that occupied the Place de la Bastille, where it too decayed physically and aesthetically. Few visited the structure, and fewer still could remember what it meant:

> In 1847, the sad history of the elephant came to an appropriate end. It was finally thrown into the canal/sewer on the order of Prefect Rumbuteau. Crowds watched as rats escaped from the sinking monument.
> *(Smith, 1999:28)*

Around 1830 it was moved to a corner on account of its advanced state of decomposition, while at the same time law makers approved a plan to erect a memorial dedicated to the patriots who had made the ultimate sacrifice on 14 July 1789 and to those who perished during 'Three Glorious Days' of urban revolution in July of 1830.

After lengthy discussions it was decided to locate the column on the site of the Bastille. The 50-metre-high Colonne de Juillet was finished on 28 August 1839 and rises from a tomb in which the remains of 504 fallen fighters are buried. Figure 1.6 is one of the few images I could find of the Bastille elephant and the July column, which dates from 1875 and is based on an earlier lithograph from 1841.

It is a somewhat clean and idealised depiction of urban space, anticipating the Hausmannization of Paris in the latter part of the nineteenth century. The architect and planner Baron Haussmann created wide boulevards throughout the city to contain and prevent urban uprisings. Initially, the July memorial served as an expression of the sovereignty of the people and a rallying point for revolutionary activity during the middle decades of the nineteenth century. In 1848, the bodies of 52 protesters shot by the military were arranged around the column to cries of 'Vengence! Aux barricades!' Rituals of revolution were again sparked in 1871 when the Communards erected their own barricades, blocking off every road into the *place* (Welch,

FIGURE 1.6 Fedor Hoffbauer, 'Place de la Bastille (1841)', 1875, colour lithograph.
Source: Brown Digital Repository. Brown University Library.

2022:5). The year 1871 would be the 'last high tide' for the *place de la Bastille* as a site dedicated to 'sacralizing ritualistic activity', as from that date onwards 'it became progressively mundanized and marginalized' as the rise of competing attractions (such as the *Tour Eiffel*) offered 'new packages', more in tune with the changing social and political conditions of post-1871 France (Smith, 1999:30–31). Anthropologists have studied how the myth of the state works as a form of 'social fantasy', where a 'sense of the absurd and surreal suffuses representations of power', and the fetishising of 'things', displays and spectacles, but they only become 'effective as authority' if they are incorporated into the fabric of everyday life (Hansen and Stepputat, 2001:20). The myth of the state is also sustained through more routine and less dramatic practices, and it is significant that many contributions to this edited collection are attuned to how the embodied state is made through these encounters – from traffic lights to taxes (as Braddock et al. perceptively put it) – and raise important questions over when and where affect becomes political.

Conclusion

For many scholars the visual practices introduced during the French Revolution mark a decisive stage in the development of modern visual culture and their relation to political imaginaries and iconographies of state power. During the revolutionary decade, it became compulsory to take political sides and make these allegiances both seen and heard. All manner of objects were mobilised, including:

> the wearing of particular costumes and certain colors, the designing of furniture, letter headings, public spaces to be used for festivals and funerals, songs to be sung on certain occasions, ways of speaking and writing, eating, drinking, and smoking. Shoe buckles and hats, sword hilts and belts, inkwells and fans all carried the revolutionary message and all had to be adapted according to the dictates of the regimes that were in power at any one time.
>
> *(Weston, 2010:18)*

I cite this passage as it conveys the extent to which the politics of visibility permeated everyday life, and it helps to situate the iconoclasm of the Bastille's destruction in these dynamic social changes. In the immediate moment it removed a prison that doubled as an arsenal, as well as a military stronghold that could be used to command a large part of the city, but the symbolic transformation into a revolutionary icon took some effort and a 'successful renegotiation of power relations between people, aristocrats and the king' (Clay, 2012:31).

It is understanding how this physical and symbolic transformation took shape that lies at the heart of this chapter. Of course, the Bastille continues to resonate in the popular imagination as the ultimate reminder of political repression (Welch, 2022). My intention has been to demonstrate how these frames of reference are acquired, at least in part, through the consumption of a diverse, fractured body of material. The concept of 'revolution' implies repetition, as well as rupture, to the extent that 'Revolutions are forced to do stuff with debris, to sort and reframe not only the leftover remnants of the regimes they set out to destroy but the outdated, embarrassing evidence of their earlier selves' (Taws, 2013:1). As such, 'representations of the visible will always show residues and traces of the invisible' (Huyssen, 2003:10). Today the site of the Bastille is a significant transportation node in Paris, while 'the *Colonne de Juillet* stands isolated, unvisited, unapproachable and almost unnoticed in a multi-lane whirlpool of traffic whose roads run over the unmarked locations of the old fortress walls', and thus the 'strange odyssey' continues in the form of 'a giant traffic intersection' (Smith, 1999:33). An appropriate metaphor on which to end.

References

Adams, L. (2010) *The Methodologies of Art*, Boulder, CO: Westview.
Andress, D. (2013) 'The Course of the Terror, 1793–94', in McPhee, P. (ed.) *A Companion to the French Revolution*, Oxford: Blackwell, pp. 293–309.
Bordes, P. (2019) 'The Emotive Artifacts of the French Revolution', *H-France Salon*, 11(18), #2:1–14. www.h-france.net/Salon/SalonVol11no18.2.Bordes.pdf
Burke, P. (2001) *Eyewitnessing: The Uses of Images as Historical Evidence*. London: Reaktion.
Carrabine, E. (2019). 'Reading Pictures: Piranesi and Carceral Landscapes', in Fleetwood, J., L. Presser, S. Sandberg, and T. Ugelvik (eds.) *Emerald Handbook of Narrative Criminology*, Leeds: Emerald, pp. 201–220.
Censer, J. and L. Hunt (2001) *Liberty, Equality, Fraternity: Exploring the French Revolution*. Philadelphia: Pennsylvania State University Press.
Clay, R. (2012) *Iconoclasm in Revolutionary Paris: The Transformation of Signs*, Oxford: Voltaire Foundation.
Cobban, A. (1964) *The Social Interpretation of the French Revolution*, Cambridge: Cambridge University Press, pp. 13–24.
Cuno, J. (1988) 'Introduction', in Cuno, J. (ed.) *French Caricature and the French Revolution, 1789–1799*, California: Grunwald Center for the Graphic Arts.
Darnton, R. (1971, May) 'The High Enlightenment and the Low-Life of Literature in Pre-Revolutionary France', *Past & Present*, 51:81–115.
Darnton, R. (1984) 'A Police Inspector Sorts His Files: The Anatomy of the Republic of Letters', in Darnton, R. (ed.) *The Great Cat Massacre and Other Episodes in French Cultural History*, New York: Basic Books, pp. 145–190.
Darnton, R. (1989) 'Introduction', in Darnton, R. and D. Roche (eds.) *Revolution in Print*, Berkeley: University of California Press, pp. xiii–xv.

Darnton, R. (2003) *George Washington's False Teeth: An Unconventional Guide to the Eighteenth Century*, New York: Norton.
de Tocqueville, A. (1856/2008) *The Ancien Régime and the Revolution*, London: Penguin.
Doyle, W. (2018) *The Oxford History of the French Revolution*, Oxford: Oxford University Press. 3rd edition.
Eisenstein, E. (1965) 'Who Intervened in 1788? A Commentrary on *The Coming of the French Revolution*', *American Historical Review*, 71:77–103.
Epstein, C. (2021) *Birth of the State*, Oxford: Oxford University Press.
Farge, A. and M. Foucault (1982/2017) *Disorderly Families: Infamous Letters from the Bastille Archives*. Minneapolis: University of Minnesota Press.
Freedman, J. (2017) 'The Dangers Within: Fears of Imprisonment in Enlightenment France', *Modern Intellectual History*, 14(2):339–364.
Furet, F. (1978/1981) *Interpreting the French Revolution*, Cambridge: Cambridge University Press.
Goldstone, J. (1991) *Revolution and Rebellion in the Early Modern World*, Berkeley: University of California Press.
Graybill, L. (2016) *The Visual Culture of Violence after the French Revolution*, London: Routledge.
Hansen, T. and F. Stepputat (2001) 'Introduction: States of Imagination', in Hansen, T. and F. Stepputat (eds.) *States of Imagination: Ethnographic Explorations of the Postcolonial State*, Durham: Duke University Press, pp. 1–38.
Heffernan, J. (1992) 'Preface', in Heffernan, J. (ed.) *Representing the French Revolution: Literature, Historiography, and Art*, Hanover, NH: University Press of New England, pp. vii–xv.
Hunt, L. (1984) *Politics, Culture and Class in the French Revolution*, Berkeley: University of California Press.
Hunt, L. (1991/1998) 'The Many Bodies of Marie Antoinette: Political Pornography and the Problem of the Feminine in the French Revolution', in Kates, G. (ed.) *The French Revolution: Recent Debates and New Controversies*, London: Routledge, pp. 279–301.
Hunt, L. (2009) 'The Experience of Revolution', *French Historical Studies*, 32(4):671–678.
Kates, G. (1998) 'Introduction', in Kates, G. (ed.) *The French Revolution: Recent Debates & New Contoversies*, London: Routledge, pp. 1–14.
Kohle, H. and R. Reichardt (2008) *Visualising the Revolution: Politics and Pictorial Arts in Late Eighteenth-Century France*, London: Reaktion.
Leith, J. (1989) 'Ephemera: Civic Education through Images', in Darnton, R. and D. Roche (eds.) *Revolution in Print*, Berkeley: University of California Press, pp. 270–289.
Lucas, C. (1994) 'Revolutionary Violence, the People and the Terror', in Baker, K. (ed.) *The French Revolution and the Creation of Modern Political Culture, Volume 4: The Terror*. Leeds: Emerald, pp. 57–79.
Lüsebrink, H-J. and R. Reichardt (1997) *The Bastille: A History of a Symbol of Despotism and Freedom*, Durham: Duke University Press.
Markoff, J. (1998) 'Violence, Emancipation and Democracy: The Countryside and the French Revolution', in Kates, G. (ed.) *The French Revolution: Recent Debates and New Controversies*, London: Routledge, pp. 279–301.

Maza, S. (2013) 'The Cultural Origins of the French Revolution', in McPhee, P. (ed.) *A Companion to the French Revolution*, Oxford: Blackwell, pp. 42–56.
Naginski, E. (2001) 'The Object of Contempt', *Yale French Studies*, 101:32–53.
Reichardt, R. (1989) 'Prints: Images of the Bastille', in Darnton, R. and D. Roche (eds.) *Revolution in Print*, Berkeley: University of California Press, pp. 223–251.
Schama, S. (1989) *Citizens: A Chronicle of the French Revolution*. London: Penguin
Skocpol, T. (1979) *States and Social Revolutions*, Cambridge: Cambridge University Press.
Smith, P. (1999) 'The Elementary Forms of Place and Their Transformations: A Durkheimian Model', *Qualitative Sociology*, 22(1):13–36.
Stammers, T. (2008) 'The Bric-à-Brac of the Old Regime: Collecting and Cultural History in Post-Revolutionary France', *French History*, 22(3):295–315.
Stammers, T. (2019) 'Transmitting the French Revolution: A Compulsive History', *H-France Salon*, 11(18):1–16.
Sutherland, D. (2003) *The French Revolution and the Empire: The Quest for a Civic Order*, Malden, MA: Blackwell.
Sutherland, D. (2013) 'Urban Crowds, Riot, Utopia, and Massacres, 1789–92', in McPhee, P. (ed.) *A Companion to the French Revolution*, Oxford: Blackwell, pp. 231–246.
Taws, R. (2013) *The Politics of the Provisional: Art and Ephemera in Revolutionary France*, Pennsylvania: Pennsylvania State Press.
Wagner, P. (1995) *Reading Iconotexts: From Swift to the French Revolution*. London: Reaktion.
Welch, M. (2022) *The Bastille Effect: Transforming Sites of Political Imprisonment*, Oakland: University of California Press.
Weston, H. (2010) 'The Politics of Visibility in Revolutionary France: Projecting on the Streets', in Kromm, J. and S. Benforado Bakewell (eds.) *A History of Visual Culture: Western Civilization from the 18th to the 21st Century*, Oxford: Berg, pp. 18–29.

2

POLITICAL AFFECTS AND EMBODIED STATES

A Psychoanalytic Framework for Theorising the Embodiment of State Power by State Representatives

Louise Braddock, Henrique Carvalho and Craig Reeves

Introduction

Although the notion of 'the state' is ubiquitous in contemporary social understandings and the notion that 'state power' exerts a pervasive influence in people's lives has a strong common sense, especially in academic scholarship and debates, the state itself is rather elusive as a concrete idea. This idea is likely at its most intelligible when we think of politics at a macro level, especially in terms of international relations; there, 'the state' appears to be more clearly defined, especially in the guise of its representatives – heads of state, heads of government, diplomatic staff and so on. But on the ground, in people's everyday experiences, the state is much more diffuse and difficult to grasp; as such, understandings of state power tend to be relegated to more obvious episodes, when it is expressed in specific actions and when it is most intrusive, such as in the power to punish criminals and expel illegal migrants. However, there are arguably important reasons why we should pursue a more nuanced understanding of the effect of state power, especially in our affective lives, reasons that a psychoanalytic approach can expose and address.

This chapter will theoretically explore how 'the state' influences and features in individuals' affective lives, especially when it is embodied in the figure of a state official as a central *iconic representation* of state power in social experience – something which, as we will see, has specific connotation and importance for a psychoanalytic understanding of affect. The main issue at the heart of this enquiry is to understand what it means, affectively, to embody the state through one's job as a representative of state power – both to oneself and to others. For this, we aim to advance and clarify the concept of 'political affect'.

DOI: 10.4324/9781032617060-4

We explore how performances of state power are imbricated in the formation and circulation of specific affects, affects that are deemed to be political and discuss how these affects in turn shape the experiences of those individuals involved in these performances of state power. Affect is deemed to be political when it is experienced in the political domain, whether it arises there, is directed towards its institutions or is experienced individually or collectively. Central to this account is an understanding of the individual as a subject who is necessarily situated in relations that are both social and embodied. Affect is experienced by the subject relating to others in social and in bodily engagements. While these experiences often involve some conscious apprehension (for instance, through social construction into specific emotions), affect nevertheless carries an 'excess of meaning' that escapes linguistic articulation. This is usually described in the literature, following a Spinozan approach, as shifts in 'intensity' (on affect and/as intensity, see Massumi, 1995) that are manifested as a positive or negative charge enhancing or inhibiting one's bodily capacities. Hence, affect has a causal influence on actions which eludes rational control in ways that need to be understood if they are to be detected and properly accounted for.

We understand 'political' as meaning 'of' the polity as the domain of regulated social relating. Two key social relations for regulating power in human interaction are collaboration and competition, which are continually in tension as each moderates the other's effects at the level of the social and collective, and at the interpersonal level (see Mouffe, 2005). This tension is intrinsic to human relations since competition and collaboration spring from the same psychological roots. In what has been characterised by the psychoanalyst Jean Laplanche as the fundamental anthropological situation of nurture, there is a tension in the relations that sustain human dependency and make growth and life possible (see Fletcher and Ray, 2014). This situation of basic human vulnerability is one in which psychological relations of attachment and care are needed for meeting vital needs. At the same time, failure to satisfy such needs invites hostility and leads to aggression in the competition for resources.[1]

Vital needs arise throughout life and the drive to satisfy them impels humans to struggle for resources through social relations of collaboration and competition that it is the function of the state to regulate. At the same time, the social individual is also MacIntyre's (2013) 'dependent rational animal', who remains inevitably subject to need, dependency and attachments from which affectivity is inseparable. Affect then is intrinsically relational in being mediated by individual interactions, social situatedness and social needs. The reflections in this chapter employ a psychoanalytically informed framework to elucidate the role that 'the state' as regulator of social power and resources plays in the mediation of individuals' affective life (on affect as inherently mediating and mediated, see Anderson, 2014).

The chapter is divided into three sections. First, it outlines a theory of affect drawn from psychoanalysis to explain affect's place in a 'self' conceptualised as social, relational and embodied. To make sense of how affectivity is simultaneously socially mediating and mediated between bodies, we draw on Richard Wollheim's philosophy of psychoanalysis. Freud proposed that affect arose when the forcefulness of experience was felt in the mind with a negative valence; in his theory, affect was presented as anxiety directed to its origin in experience, or to the frustration of instinctual urges (on Freud's theory of affect, see Rapaport, 1953). Later psychoanalytic theory saw this forcefulness as arising in a dynamic relation with an object that was felt to be its cause, pleasure or pain being attributed to an object as its source, to which the subject was thereby related affectively. This theoretical development, by Melanie Klein and others, is known as psychoanalytic object relations theory. In it, affect is harnessed into the structured content of unconscious imagining through the representation of an affective relation of love (or attachment) or of hate (or aggression) between the subject and the object it is related to. In everyday conscious life we see this imagined relation played out in wish-fulfilling, daydreaming or fantasising. Daydreams, like nocturnal dreams, and like certain sorts of memory (such as flashbacks and *déjà vu* experiences), are states of mind in which immediacy and familiarity conjures up a sense that what is represented is immediately present. In a term owed to Charles Peirce, Wollheim calls this mode of presentation *iconic* (see Wollheim, 1980; 1984; Atkins, 2023). These representations, however, even when conscious, are rarely reflected upon; their immediacy means that their meaning is taken for granted or not consciously examined. Instead, their affective grip shapes the subject's encounters with others and with the world around them by turning objects into icons of fear, love, desire and so on.

The chapter's second section applies this theoretical framework to a reflection on the political circulation of affects, with a specific focus on the construction of socially situated phantasies centred around images of order, security and justice. We discuss how social conditions of insecurity and anxiety feed into the allure of paranoid phantasies where the dominant affect is persecutory, and into the drive for hostile and authoritarian practices of state power. The last section of the chapter relates the idea of political affects back to the experience of embodied selves, by reflecting on the work of frontline staff. In embodying the state through their jobs, these individuals have a direct experience of these political phantasies, having to actively perform them as icons of state power.

Affect and the Embodied Mind

The rise of interest in affect is manifested in the literature of affect theory; this reiterates an idea of a self that is social, embodied, affective and relational (see, e.g., Ambrasat and von Scheve, 2021; von Scheve, 2018; Anderson, 2014). However, if we are to parse the concrete phenomena of a state conceived (as we shall argue) to be predominantly persecutory in a broad range of practices and experiences, there must be a proper conceptualisation of affect which necessarily encompasses these attributes. It is for this reason that we employ the generic, philosophical concept of affect. The more familiar psychological concept of emotion is both too broad, and too socially constructed, for conceptual rigour, while in the prevailing philosophical conception emotion is a species of evaluative propositional attitude. Our Introduction has sketched an account of how we envisage these key factors as intersecting. Our argument here will be that this more holistic, relational account can best be developed in terms of a theory of affect that takes full account of the internal structure of affect-bearing states of mind – with 'mind' being understood as intrinsically embodied.

Psychoanalysis is for several reasons a promising avenue in theorising affect to this end. Not only does psychoanalytic theory offer an account of the individual subject in which affect and relationality together provide a hinge mediating between the external human life of ongoing social relatedness and the internal energetic and affective economy of the minded human body (for a discussion from the perspective of contemporary neuroscience, see Solms and Zellner, 2012). Through these foundational assumptions, psychoanalysis provides a key theoretical source for the embodied mind and the minded body in modern thought; affect is a foundational concept because of its close connection to the vital needs of the body and its mind in the drive for survival. Affect is particularly fundamental to the psychoanalytic theory of object relations in which the subject's basic relation to the other is conceptualised in terms of attachment to the other as an object in the mind, this attachment having either the positive valence of love or the negative valence of hate (Winnicott, 1965; Bion, 1959).[2] In this theoretical approach, anxiety marks the existential threat of disrupting the attachment that is universally necessary for survival.

The mental representation of these relations is a form of imagining that psychoanalysis calls 'phantasy'.[3] Phantasy imaginatively represents the subject's affective experience of its relation to the world of objects. Object relations theory's central tenet is, then, that phantasy's content is object-relational and that the mental regulation of affect is done through the imagination's continual adjustment of the affective relations between the subject and its objects when represented in the inner world of the subject.[4] These relations are imaginatively adjusted to contain, mitigate and re-distribute affective load and quality, in order to maintain a positive (pleasurable) valence of mental experience and thereby defend against anxiety.

Object-relational thought has a prominent status within theoretical psychoanalysis (on this, see, e.g., Greenberg and Mitchell, 1983). In more recent developments, not considered here, object relations theory has had an increasing prominence outside of clinical institutional psychoanalysis, in areas as diverse as critical theory (Honneth, 1992; Allen, 2020), political theory (Gerson, 2004) and 'relational thinking' in cultural and social theory more broadly (Clarke et al., 2008). At the level of social experience, it may be directed to the way social and political affect remains entangled with the substructure of phantasy articulation of affective relations to objects which may subvert linguistic thought and convention. For example, someone may consciously think that a certain person is not a threat – this is the level of conventional meaning – but nevertheless experience that person as a threatening persecutor, a dangerous other, because that other has been recruited into an unconscious phantasy of persecution. The interplay between conscious and unconscious perception and affect can play out in complex ways, perhaps leading to unstable disavowal of the unconscious feeling and guilt or shame associated with it, or perhaps a reworking of conscious thought and feeling under the influence of the phantasy, sustaining the distortions and cognitive dissonance typical to systems of racism and prejudice (see Adorno et al., 2019).

This shift to the social level raises to prominence the question of action causation by phantasy. On the basis of what has so far been set out, we may say that the functional role of phantasy is to re-distribute affective intensity in a relational (an 'object-relational') structure of social and human significance. Phantasy gives that raw, unthought intensity a specific directional structure and thereby makes affect more manageable, though at the same time it provides a pathway to affect's causal effects on action. Wollheim (1993) has argued that phantasy can provoke action through its phenomenology, specifically through its iconicity. As noted, an iconic mental state is one that presents itself, and is experienced, as real.

We can now distinguish the two sides, individual and social, of the way phantasy mediates affective experience via iconicity. Peirce defines the icon as a sign that represents its object by combining resemblance to it with immediacy of presentation, to such a degree that it retains its meaning in the absence of the object itself. When one sees an icon, one immediately relates it with the represented signified object, to the extent that the two become fused – when we see the emoticon '☺', we see 'a smile'. Thus, while a basic affective reaction to an object simply renders a change in intensity, when affect becomes iconic, it becomes a more complex structured feeling associated with specific images and relations, that can become activated whenever an individual encounters an object that they apprehend as bearing this iconic resemblance. In other words, a phantasy 'iconically virtualizes' (Davis, 2010: 276) an affective relation in order to regulate its affective load.

In this way affect becomes psychologically functional: what best mitigates the forcefulness of affect is transforming it into phantasy, repositioning the subject in a structure of and *vis a vis* affective relations with other figures that re-distribute the excess affect.[5] In the individual, phantasy is a psychoanalytical object-relational 'resolution' constructed in the mind; it then reflects back to the subject their imaginative participation in the medium of phantasy, whose iconic immediacy (mis)represents what is imagined as what is real and to be acted on. This then underwrites the continual rearrangement of object-relational configuration in the service of affective regulation; a mediation of affective representation and misrepresentation that evades rational conscious scrutiny in the space of reasons but is nevertheless accessible to psychoanalytic interpretation.[6]

By the same token the individual's social experience is mediated by their phantasies, so that the affective charge of every encounter with others is both refracted through the structure of the individual's internal world and impacts upon it to change it, not always towards the realistic. One does not experience phantasies as phantasmagorical superimpositions hovering above 'real' objects; every encounter with an object in the world is simultaneously also a psychic encounter. In this way, phantasy-formation is causally effective in interaction with others and with the world itself, by imaginatively turning objects there into iconic bearers of meaning.

When Affect Becomes Political

The theoretical discussion in the previous section supplies the foundation for a framework for understanding the political circulation and manipulation of affects, when the construction of socially situated phantasies centres around affectively charged iconic representations of, for instance, order, security and justice. To further develop this framework, however, it is necessary to highlight that this iconic presentation of affect in phantasy-formation, besides mediating an individual's practical and political consciousness, is also itself mediated by their embodied and situated relationality. As mentioned, affect is both cause and effect of the subject's relations with others.

Every encounter carries an affective charge, and one's situatedness in relation to others is a primary, if not the primary, source of anxiety. Phantasy-formation works to regulate this anxiety, re-distributing it among different objects and circumstances. This phantasy-formation is both historical and continuous: its building blocks are linked to the individual's history, and psychoanalysis places particular emphasis on the formation of complexes during the early years; but phantasies are continuously reshaped by experience, the inner world constantly transformed by additions, removals and superimpositions as the individual is exposed to new environments, experiences, relations and traumas. The inner and outer world are thus in constant interchange, and while the subject's consciousness is filtered through the phantastic tapestry in its imagination, these phantasies are themselves weaved from and through the subject's interaction with and apprehension of objects in the outside world. Furthermore, and of particular interest to this theoretical formulation, these constant interactions often result in the production of socially situated phantasies – iconic affective articulations that circulate socially and that can attach to certain socially and politically constructed objects. For instance, the 'gang' has become a widely circulated icon of urban criminality and violence, emulating – fearsome and loathsome, but also alluring – images of danger and deviance, pervasively produced by allusion to racialising, marginalising and stigmatising tropes, which underpin a dominant pattern of blaming in Anglo-American societies (on this, see Carvalho, 2023).

There is a long tradition of critical thought that examines how politics and the political are intimately related to the articulation of affectively charged images and allegories, often through an engagement with discussions of ideology and aesthetics, particularly in cultural and critical theory (see Adorno et al., 2020; Jameson, 1981; Eagleton, 1990; Hall et al., 1978; Ahmed, 2004; see also Carrabine, this volume). In a way, the whole dimension of 'the political' can be understood as a socially constructed and circulated phantasy-formation – a socially and historically situated set of iconic virtualisations which regulates the distribution of capacities – of drives and anxieties – in accordance with economies and hierarchies of cooperation and competition. From this perspective, a political affect can be conceptualised as an affect that arises in this interchange between individual and political phantasy-formations.

This idea of mutual interchange must be emphasised to resist the conclusion that political affects are 'external' forces/images that are imposed on and passively internalised by the individual. First, even when these socialised images 'enter' into the psychic world of individuals, they are transformed as they interact with individual phantasies shaped by their unique histories and experiences, so that each individual has and develops their own version of political allegories. Second, these political phantasies are themselves influenced – indeed, constituted – by shared individual drives and anxieties, so that the two dimensions are inextricably imbricated. Political affects are as much products as they are producers of socially and historically structured images of order, community and belonging. And third, every encounter between individual and political phantasy worlds will have its own aspects of uniqueness that can shape its associated affective experience. As such, political affects are simultaneously mediated by these iconic affective structures on the one hand and possessed of an intrinsic openness that escapes determination on the other.

However, while political affects can escape full determination, they are not immune to conditions of what Althusser (2006), following Marx, called over-determination – 'the effects of the contradictions in each practice' linked to 'the pattern of dominance and subordination, antagonism or non-antagonism of the contradictions in the structure in dominance' (Brewster in Althusser, 2006: 252–53; see also Althusser, 1969) that can be established by socio-political circumstances. Individuals' affective lives are significantly mediated by power relations linked to the structure in dominance in any historical moment. The culturally dominant character of this structure means that it exerts substantial pressure in the shaping of political phantasy-formations, and therefore conditions their influence in the regulation of affect. Of particular interest to this chapter is how within the contemporary 'structure in dominance' (Althusser, 2006), there are elements – structural inequalities and violence grounded on colonial and patriarchal legacies etc. – that feed into the allure of political phantasies which are predominantly persecutory, paranoid in character (Reeves, 2019; Reeves et al., 2019), and that thus encourage hostile affective relations and dynamics.

Many of these patterns appear in the allegoric framework of dominant phantasy-formations as conditions or structures which underpin more specific aspects of social imagination. A broader example of this is the idea of 'ontological insecurity' as a general condition of late modernity (Giddens, 1991), but more nuanced elaborations point to how contemporary social and political experiences are pervaded by a chronic sense of anxiety, or how contemporary socio-economic conditions feed into experiences of precarity (see Anderson, 2014, especially Chapter 4). In political terms, such insecurities can get patterned around relations of cooperation and competition, of solidarity and hostility (Chamberlen and Carvalho, 2019; Carvalho and Chamberlen, 2024), which can then be crystallised around images of security and dangerousness. For instance, 'danger formations' can shape around figures such as the illegal migrant or the urban gang, channelling broader social anxieties into specific personifications (Carvalho et al. 2020; Carvalho, 2023).

Moreover, political phantasies also significantly rely on the institutionalisation of these patterns and relations around symbols of order and authority, which play a central role in the allegoric framework of the political imagination. In particular, a structure cannot be dominant unless it has seeped into the complex iconic formation of the state. For instance, socio-economic anxiety can be seen as a dominant feature of our contemporary political phantasy-formation not only because it is manifested in images around precarity, homelessness and dispossession, but because these are inextricably linked to the imbrication of state power in these conditions through the neuropolitics (Isin, 2004) of austerity, Brexit, crisis, inflation and so on. Likewise, danger formations are inseparable from state-related apparatuses such as punitive populism, hostile environment etc. (Carvalho et al., 2020).

As such, 'the state' appears as an iconic nexus for these political phantasy-formations, in at least three senses. First, the state comes to represent these conditions as the protagonist in the political allegory: a political imagination pervaded by insecurity cannot be decoupled from the sense that the state is somehow primarily involved in or responsible for this insecurity. Second, the state is likewise tasked with the responsibility for addressing any adverse effects of such conditions; political problems immediately orient us to the state for solutions. And third, the configuration of the state within these formations defines the orders and boundaries of belonging, shaping dynamics of identification and estrangement (Sparks, 2018). Together, these dimensions illustrate how the state has a predominant function in the over-determination of political affective life. This way, the performance and deployment of state power can also be seen as a primary affective *apparatus*, which targets and conditions individuals' affective experiences and indeed, the political dimension of their sense of self.

Before we move on to consider the implications of this understanding of the place of state power in the framework of political affect, a couple of points need to be stressed. First, as mentioned, 'overdetermination' does not mean simple, full determination. There are patterns that exert pressures and tend to channel political imagination – and political affect – in specific directions; but these are still heavily mediated by individuals' own histories and their situatedness. Affective life is, as the name indicates, *alive*, and thus always in motion, and each encounter can give rise to a new interpretation. A hostile political imagination does not mean that an individual's affective reaction to an Othered other will always be hostile, but merely that there will be a strong tendency in this direction. Second, and relatedly, in a strong sense, no one encounters 'the state'. In many ways, the state is itself a product of political imagination, a thing of phantasy. At the same time, as discussed in the previous section, an individual's experience cannot easily distinguish between phantasy and reality, and the iconic character of phantasy-formations means that psychic objects are imbued with a sense of immediacy through resemblance. So, when someone encounters an icon of state power, one can have the experience of a real encounter with the state. What happens in these encounters, especially when the state icon in question is being personified by another individual, is the focus of the next section.

Embodying the State

While symbols of state power and law, broadly conceived, are ubiquitous in contemporary everyday life – from traffic lights, to taxes, to warnings in train and underground stations – these subtle signs are often not apprehended as manifestations of the state by our practical consciousness, at least not until something reminds us of their solemn status – for instance, when we believe we may have been caught crossing a red light. And even then, the connection between the coercive threat of a penalty or fine and the 'state' as an entity or complex might not be straightforward in every circumstance; the question of what turns an object or encounter into an icon of state power in the psychoanalytic sense is complex and demands further analysis. This is because, as this chapter suggests, this identification depends on the interaction between individual and social phantasy-formations, so that especially with regard to more subtle symbols like the ones mentioned above, the answer to what gives rise to a political affect in the sense we have been discussing can be significantly contingent.

However, some representations of the state are more iconic, and thus can more safely be assumed to grab a hold on imaginaries of state power. In particular, criminal justice officers are traditionally some of the more iconic representations of the state, performing a prominent cultural role in 'mediat[ing] the state-society relationship' (Jefferson, 2009: 126). Thus, whereas it is important to acknowledge the difficulty of defining what comprises 'the state' in broader anthropological terms (Taussig, 1997), it is relatively uncontroversial to suggest that, when someone sees or meets a police officer, a Crown prosecutor or a prison officer exercising their function, one has a keen sense of being before someone who is personifying the state – a state *representative* (Jefferson, 2009).

This imbrication between a particular individual and the official role they perform as a manifestation and an agent of state power raises important questions regarding the role of the state in political affectivity. There is an interesting 'practical interface between personhood and institutional arrangements' (Jefferson, 2009: 128) that needs to be acknowledged and scrutinised. For instance, when someone encounters a police officer in uniform, one is both encountering an icon of state power and a specific person. In terms of the psychoanalytic account proposed in this chapter, there is a strong sense in which the iconic representation affectively over-determines the encounter. The immediacy and familiarity inherent in icons provides a fast link into a virtualised affective relation that is superimposed over the actual encounter, so that 'all' one sees is the icon. This subsumption is likely to be even more powerful when the icon in question is linked to a persecutory phantasy (Reeves, 2019) which tends to essentialise complex encounters into 'good' or 'bad' objects. The punitive impulse in criminal justice can be seen as a manifestation of a political persecutory phantasy-formation that tends to channel anxiety into a defensive and hostile position against those seen as dangerous others (Reeves et al., 2019; Carvalho et al., 2020). As such, a criminal justice state officer is often embodying such a phantasy as much as they are embodying 'the state' more generally.

Therefore, when someone meets or interacts with a police officer or a prison officer, in their eyes they may not only be encountering the state but a persecutory state, someone who they will immediately identify as a protector against dangerous forces and individuals or – especially if the person in question is a member of a minoritised, marginalised or oppressed population – as a hostile, threatening figure. This identification can potentially affect not only the impression of the officer but also the situation more broadly, as the affective hold of the encounter spills into its surroundings. For instance, seeing many police officers at a train station can instantly give rise to the impression that there might be something wrong happening – or, if someone was feeling insecure, it might give rise to a sensation of security and reassurance. Of course, this dominant valence with regard to the affective relation may be frustrated and lead to ambivalence or amplify anxiety if such expectations are frustrated or distorted by the actual situation. But the point is that one way or another, the encounter is primarily conditioned by the affective hold of the phantasy-formation and its iconic representation.

There is an additional level of complexity when the individual in question is not simply encountering the state in the person of a criminal justice officer but is embodying the state themself by exercising that function. Anthropological studies on criminal justice officers talk about how such individuals let aspects of their jobs seep into their personal lives, often incorporating disciplinary techniques, routines and values in a way that makes it difficult to determine where the icon ends and the individual begins, espousing 'a life more or less possessed by the state' (Jefferson, 2009: 132; see also, more generally, Karpiak and Garriott, 2018). Of course, this 'possession' is not always seamless, and experiences of it may vary significantly, depending on many factors. For instance, there can be several degrees of resonance and dissonance between values and expectations held by the individual and imposed by or expected of the function, which may be magnified by symbols or impressions attached to the individual's personal characteristics. For instance, a Black police officer may feel uncomfortable wearing the uniform, given the constant emergence and resurgence of issues surrounding institutional racism in the police (Holdaway and O'Neill, 2006). At the same time, specific encounters and relations may further influence these dynamics; for instance, depending on the situation, a Black police officer interacting with their local community may feel less or perhaps even more uncomfortable with their iconic embodiment. Furthermore, the individual may not be aware of the impact of these dissonances on the way they feel, or they may be conscious of it; if the latter, this can potentially lead to opportunities for resistance or subversion, or even a sense of political responsibility (on this, see Young, 2011).

It is thus important to bear in mind that the over-determination imposed by a political phantasy-formation is underpinned by a dialectic between structure and agency, both with regard to those who embody the state and those who encounter such embodiments, which 'is constantly being produced and reproduced' (Jefferson, 2009: 128). In this regard, it is useful to think of these state officials, following Barker, Harms and Lindquist, as 'figures' – as 'real people who also operate as symbols that embody the structures of feeling associated with larger, seemingly impersonal conditions of a particular time' (Barker et al., 2014: 3, cited in Cabot, 2018: 211). These figures can express and even reinforce the political phantasy they are iconically representing, but they can also challenge it or at least disturb or distort its affective valence and meaning. When someone encounters a police officer, the iconic character of the office may over-determine the interaction, but so can that individual's agency end up over-determining the phantasy they are embodying. Thus, a particular police officer's actions can become, for someone who experiences their particular kindness or brutality, for instance, the model for every police officer subsequently encountered, and possibly even for 'the police' or 'the state'.

Moreover, from this perspective, criminal justice officials not only embody the state as an institutional or even political entity, but also as an apparatus and as a manifestation of collective affects. Their iconic representation is not only linked to the idea of the state as government, as power or as enforcement, but also to the state as a configuration of circumstances, historical contingencies and power relations. For instance, the police officer as icon of British state power in the 2011 riots, which predominantly expressed the anger and dissatisfaction of racialised and marginalised populations, is distinct from the same icon in relation to the 2024 riots, which were directed *against* racialised and marginalised migrants; there are several continuities but also important differences, which can significantly change the affective framework around each figure. One way or another, however, the affective grip of embodying an iconic representation of such a dominant political phantasy substantially conditions the social experience and political consciousness of those who encounter it, especially those who are tasked with bringing it to life.

Conclusion

This chapter has deployed a psychoanalytic philosophical account of affect to examine the performance and experience of state power in interpersonal relations, particularly with regard to those individuals who embody the state through their functions as criminal justice officials. At the heart of this account is an understanding of affect as iconic, and as linked to the production and reproduction of individual and social phantasy-formations that are geared at the management of affect – especially of affect's manifestation as anxiety. Phantasy-formations populate our psychic and cultural worlds, prefiguring attitudes, assumptions, sensibilities and emotions, and over-determining social relations as a result. Through the interaction between individual and social phantasy-formations, political phantasies and their iconic representations filter into the lifeworld of individuals, conditioning their social experience. The iconic character of phantasies means that these familiarities have a sense of immediacy that pre-empts conscious apprehension and reflection – they influence practical consciousness but usually escape conscious scrutiny. To us, these phantasies appear just as 'the world as we see it', making it difficult to distinguish or examine them without considerable effort.

As a result, then, our perception of and engagement with the world, especially of the social world, is shaped by our affective experience as mediated by our phantasies – including those political phantasies which we internalise. When someone encounters a criminal justice officer, therefore, they encounter an individual as well as an affectively charged iconic representation of a political phantasy-formation, one that tends to have strong persecutory connotations. For those who embody such icons, this becomes an even more immersive and potentially overwhelming incursion into the phantastic affective life of the state.

If this account is sound – and it seems to chime with many insights coming from anthropological accounts of state officials, especially in criminal justice – then we ought to pay more attention to the ways in which state power relates to, and to a significant extent depends on, the prevalence and social distribution of anxiety in contemporary social settings, as well as how such circumstances tend to privilege defensive, persecutory discourses and practices. From this perspective, state power, rather than being conceived as largely detached from and merely impacting on people's social and political experiences, becomes something intrinsically embedded in their affective life worlds – a thing of phantasy.

Notes

1 Need is essentially social since among vital needs is the need for recognition by the other. For more on vital needs, see Wiggins (1998).
2 The different psychoanalytic schools posit different baseline relations in terms of constructed 'emotions': love, gratitude, attachment; hate, anger, 'primary' aggression.
3 Although derided by some writers as a psychoanalytic affectation, the English term is derived as translation from the German *phantasieren* (presumably with a nod at Aristotle).
4 The object-relational nature of phantasy is posited by Klein as constitutive of the mind; it derives from German (Hegel-inspired) idealist theories of subjective consciousness as necessitating consciousness of objects.
5 Wollheim's use of the idea of psychic function owes something to the teleological terms of the original Freudian theory of organismic mind, where uptake of affective (psychic) force serves to maintain psychic equilibrium (i.e. under the pleasure principle) and so becomes established as functional.

6 In Peirce's theory what specifies the sign as index, icon or symbol is not the object itself (though its presence or absence is germane) but the nature of the relation of sign to object (causal/contiguous, resemblance, convention) and the interpretant or 'significate effect'; the Peircean icon is a sign connected to its object through a relation of resemblance, such that it continues to designate in the object's absence. Peirce's theoretical distinction between index and icon as signs has been criticised on the ground that there can be no icons anyway. Nevertheless, as an analytic distinction it remains useful for describing a sign that retains its meaning in the absence of its object (is iconic) and one that signals or indexes the presence of its object. It is the conceptual possibility of affect's (*affectus*'s) mobility between them that we exploit/explore here (and in more depth elsewhere (Braddock, forthcoming).

References

Adorno, T., Benjamin, W., Bloch, E., Brecht, B., Lukacs, G. (2020) *Aesthetics and Politics*. London: Verso.
Adorno, T., Frenkel-Brunswik, E., Levinson, D. J., Nevitt Sanford, R. (2019) *The Authoritarian Personality*. London: Verso.
Ahmed, S. (2004) *The Cultural Politics of Emotion*. Edinburgh: Edinburgh University Press.
Allen, A. (2020) *Critique on the Couch: Why Critical Theory Needs Psychoanalysis*. New York: University of Columbia Press.
Althusser, L. (1969). Contradiction and Overdetermination. *For Marx*, 114: 15–35.
Althusser, L. (2006) *For Marx*. London: Verso.
Ambrasat, J., von Scheve, C. (2021) Affective Meanings and Social Relations: Identities and Positions in the Social Space. *Emotions and Society* 4(2): 161–180.
Anderson, B. (2014) *Encountering Affect: Capacities, Apparatuses, Conditions*. London: Routledge.
Atkins, A. (2023) Peirce's Theory of Signs. In E. Zalta, U. Nodelman (eds), *The Stanford Encyclopedia of Philosophy* (Spring 2023 Edition). Available Online at https://plato.stanford.edu/archives/spr2023/entries/peirce-semiotics/ (Accessed 14 August 2024).
Barker, J., Harms, E., Lindquist, J. (2014) *Figures of Southeast Asian Modernity*. Honolulu: University of Hawai'i Press.
Bion, W. R. (1959) Attacks on Linking. *The International Journal of Psychoanalysis* 40: 308–315.
Cabot, H. (2018) The Good Police Officer: Ambivalent Intimacies with the State in the Greek Asylum Procedure. In K. Karpiak, W. Garriott (eds), *The Anthropology of Police* (pp. 209–229). London: Routledge.
Carvalho, H. (2023) Dangerous Patterns: Joint Enterprise and the Culture of Criminal Law. *Social and Legal Studies* 32(3): 335–355.
Carvalho, H., Chamberlen, A. (2024) *Questioning Punishment*. London: Routledge.
Carvalho, H., Chamberlen, A., Lewis, R. (2020) Punitiveness beyond Criminal Justice: Punishable and Punitive Subjects in an Era of Prevention, Anti-Migration and Austerity. *British Journal of Criminology* 60(2): 265–284.
Chamberlen, A., Carvalho, H. (2019) The Thrill of the Chase: Punishment, Hostility, and the Prison Crisis. *Social and Legal Studies* 28(1): 100–117.

Clarke, S., Hahn, H., Hoggett, P. (2008) *Object Relations and Social Relations: The Implications of the Relational Turn in Psychoanalysis*. London: Routledge.

Davis, W. (2010) *Queer Beauty: Sexuality and Aesthetics from Winckelmann to Freud and Beyond*. New York: Columbia University Press.

Eagleton, T. (199) *The Ideology of the Aesthetic*. Cambridge: Blackwell.

Fletcher, J., Ray, N. (eds) (2014) *Seductions and Enigmas: Cultural Readings with Laplanche*. London: Lawrence & Wishart.

Gerson, G. (2004) Object Relations Psychoanalysis as Political Theory. *Political Psychology* 25(5): 769–794.

Giddens, A. (1991) *Modernity and Self-Identity: Self and Society in the Late Modern Age*. Redwood City: Stanford University Press.

Greenberg, J. R., Mitchell, S. A. (1983) *Object Relations in Psychoanalytic Theory*. Cambridge: Harvard University Press.

Hall, S., Roberts, B., Clarke, J., Jefferson, T., Critcher, C. (1978) *Policing the Crisis: Mugging, the State, and Law and Order*. London: Macmillan.

Holdaway, S., O'Neill, M. (2006) Institutional Racism after Macpherson: An Analysis of Police Views. *Policing and Society* 16(4): 349–369.

Honneth, A. (1992) *The Struggle for Recognition: The Moral Grammar of Social Conflicts*. Cambridge: MIT Press.

Isin, E. (2004) The Neurotic Citizen. *Citizenship Studies* 8(3): 217–235.

Jameson, F. (1981) *The Political Unconscious: Narrative as a Socially Symbolic Act*. London: Routledge.

Jefferson, A. M. (2009) On Hangings and the Dubious Embodiment of Statehood in Nigerian Prisons. In S. Jensen, A. Jefferson (eds), *State Violence and Human Rights: State Officials in the South* (pp. 122–138). London: Routledge.

Karpiak, K., Garriott, W. (eds) (2018) *The Anthropology of Police*. London: Routledge.

MacIntyre, A. (2013) *Dependent Rational Animals: Why Human Beings Need the Virtues*. London: Bloomsbury Academic.

Massumi, B. (1995) The Autonomy of Affect. *Cultural Critique* 31: 83–109.

Mouffe, C. (2005) *On the Political*. London: Routledge.

Rapaport, D. (1953) On the Psycho-Analytic Theory of Affects. *The International Journal of Psycho-Analysis* 34(3): 177–198.

Reeves, C. (2019) What Punishment Expresses. *Social and Legal Studies* 28(1): 31–57.

Reeves, C., Norrie, A., Carvalho, H. (2019) Between Persecution and Reconciliation: Criminal Justice, Legal Form and Human Emancipation. In E. Christodoulidis, R. Dukes, M. Goldoni (eds), *Research Handbook on Critical Legal Theory* (pp. 379–406). Cheltenham: Edward Elgar.

Solms, M., Zellner, M. (2012) Freudian Affect Theory Today. In A. Fotopoulou, D. Pfaff, M. A. Conway (eds), *From the Couch to the Lab: Trends in Psychodynamic Neuroscience* (pp. 132–144). Oxford: Oxford University Press.

Sparks, R. (2018). Degrees of Estrangement: The Cultural Theory of Risk and Comparative Penology. In P. Six (ed), *The Institutional Dynamics of Culture, Volumes I and II* (pp. 1096–1113). London: Routledge.

Taussig, M. (1997) *The Magic of the State*. New York: Routledge.

von Scheve, C. (2018) A Social Relational Account of Affect. *European Journal of Social Theory* 21(1): 39–59.

Wiggins, D. (1998) *Needs, Values, Truth*. Oxford: Oxford University Press.

Winnicott, D. (1965) *The Family and Individual Development*. London: Tavistock.
Wollheim, R. (1980) *Art and Its Objects* (2nd ed). Cambridge: Cambridge University Press.
Wollheim, R. (1984) *The Thread of Life*. London: Cambridge University Press.
Wollheim, R. (1993) *The Mind and Its Depths*. Cambridge: Harvard University Press.
Young, I. M. (2011) *Responsibility for Justice*. New York: Oxford University Press.

3
POSTRACIAL SENTIMENTALITY AND THE VALIDATION OF STATE RACISM

Brett St Louis

Drawing on James Baldwin's definition of 'sentimentality' as 'the ostentatious parading of excessive and spurious emotion… the mark of dishonesty, the inability to feel,' this chapter examines the empirical example of UK Conservative governmental rhetoric on immigration control and race equality as postracial sentimentality. Given that the Conservative governments of the late 2010s and early 2020s were the most ethnically diverse ever, two key questions are addressed: Why did some senior Conservative politicians from minority ethnic backgrounds advocate policies and laws to severely limit immigration and weaken race equality? And why was their support for such a harsh agenda often so enthusiastic? To start, the chapter explicates the ambivalent relationship between politics, rationality and emotion, followed by an account of their interplay within British post-war race relations. Moving forward, senior minority ethnic Conservative politicians' anti-race equality and strong border control positions are explained as indicative of an 'actually-existing postracial society' dialectic. When spoken through postracial tribunes, this dialectic is intended as an emotionally resonant 'common sense' protecting the government from criticism as racist. Overall, these politicians' powerful affective appeal against race equality and immigration exemplifies a sentimentality that, in Baldwin's estimation, amounts to a dispassionate antipathy towards human flourishing.

Introduction

Politically, post-Brexit Britain has faced momentous questions and seen numerous dramatic changes. The challenge of enacting an exit from the EU led to significant conflicts within government, between the 'soft' exit

DOI: 10.4324/9781032617060-5

retaining freedom of movement in order to access the European single market, advocated by Theresa May's administration, and the harder line including relinquishing full access to the EU single market and customs union espoused by her successor Boris Johnson. Consequently, the composition of Cabinet changed appreciably. 'Remainers' and pragmatists were removed from influential positions with a hardline, pro-Brexit phalanx installed in their stead. Alongside this shift in ideological inclination, the composition of Cabinet also transitioned towards greater ethnic diversity as some senior black, Asian and minority ethnic Conservative MPs were prepared to support this hardline, nationalist position. As minority ethnic politicians, their support for this position helped forestall charges of xenophobia levelled at the government. At the moment of its formation, the 2019 Cabinet was the most ethnically diverse in British history, with six ministers of black, Asian and minority ethnic backgrounds accounting for 18% of members (Diversity UK 2019). Moreover, upon becoming prime minister in September 2022, Liz Truss' appointment of Suella Braverman, James Cleverly and Kwasi Kwarteng as Home Secretary, Foreign Secretary and Chancellor of the Exchequer, respectively, saw the first time that none of the four major offices of state within the British government was held by white men. Rishi Sunak's initial Cabinet formed in October 2022 contained 5 people of minority ethnic backgrounds including himself (Uberoi and Carthew 2023), down from 7 in Truss' first Cabinet, both from a total of 31 (Jones 2022).

This era of greater diversity of MPs happened alongside a forceful wider political agenda including on civil liberties, immigration and asylum that has been characterised as an 'authoritarian turn' adversely impacting minority ethnic groups (Webber 2021). A key issue, then, is whether this radical political agenda was enacted in spite of or aided by an increasingly diverse Cabinet. This question contains an allied conundrum of the correspondence between ethnic identity and political persuasion, namely the assumption that the minority ethnic population empathise—or should empathise—with migrant welfare and race equality. However, this assumption simply does not hold for black, Asian and minority ethnic people, whether politicians or not. Conservative social attitudes have increased among black Britons (Warmington 2015) and among affluent, socially mobile British South Asians who have been characterised as committed to high levels of educational attainment, securing entry into the professions and middle-class status as 'model minorities' (Saini 2022, 2023). Furthermore, on the specific issue of immigration, black, Asian and minority ethnic voters concur with the general view of UK voters that immigration should be reduced (Migration Watch UK, 2015), and there are instances where some migrants themselves propagate the distinction between 'deserving' and 'undeserving' migrants (Dhaliwal and Forkert 2015). Therefore, it is perhaps unsurprising that an ethnically diverse Cabinet has not supported race equality and pro-immigration policies.

This chapter addresses two key issues emerging from this problematic. First, why did some senior Conservative politicians from minority ethnic backgrounds advocate laws and policies on strong immigration control and weakening of race equality? And second, why was their support for such a punishing and vitiating agenda often so vociferous and enthusiastic? These questions engage the understanding of state power developed in *The Embodied State*. This chapter compliments the focus on 'street-level' practices explored throughout the collection—for example the delivery of social services and practices of social control—with an analysis of how the ideas enacted at the local level also reflect top-down governmental directives. Addressing affecting themes such as the 'threat' supposedly posed by migrants countered by punitive government policy, this chapter also examines the role of emotions in state power and related moral economies. Additionally, the postracial postures of senior minority ethnic Conservative politicians evaluated below embody the contradictions and dilemmas manifest in the formation and wielding of state power detailed throughout the collection. Ultimately, the objective of understanding the emotional and moral registers of state power and its wider implications within *The Embodied State* is realised in the critique of senior minority ethnic Conservative politicians' ambivalent positioning as British others that propagate discriminatory policies while denying the government's racist motivations and impacts.

The chapter begins by setting the context with an overview of the ambivalent relationship between politics, rationality and emotion, followed by exposition of the interplay of these themes within hierarchical historical processes of racialisation and British post-war race relations. Using Enoch Powell's 'Rivers of Blood' speech as an indicative example, the latter section establishes the interaction and tension between emotive and rational responses to immigration control and race equality. I then move to examine the two main issues. First, I explain senior minority ethnic Conservative politicians' support for strong immigration control and weakening of race equality as indicative of an 'actually-existing postracial society' dialectic: race and racism are said to have diminished, yet the politicians' racial-ethnic backgrounds and lived experiences serve to underscore their impassioned promotion of a British colour-blind meritocracy. That diversity is not a panacea for racism is evident in these politicians' ethnic identity tacitly serving to indemnify the government from charges of discrimination, just as the hope that a more diverse criminal justice workforce will increase black, Asian and minority ethnic people's confidence in and outcomes from that same system they are overrepresented within (Ministry of Justice 2020). Second, these politicians' visceral objections to 'mass immigration' are understood as the emotive performativity of Britishness used to gain inclusion and acceptance. James Baldwin's understanding of sentimentality as an insensitive, mawkish depiction of a social idyll that pointedly ignores human experience and feeling is applied across both of these sections. Sentimentality in Baldwin's formulation provides a means to understand how immigration and race equality are forged as 'the migrant crisis' and 'woke' threat and used to foment discord. This perspective is then applied to an understanding of senior minority ethnic Conservative politicians' function as postracial tribunes.

Methodologically, this chapter develops an interpretive analysis of senior Conservative MPs' approach to immigration control and race equality using their political speeches and critical literature from relevant interdisciplinary debates. The following speeches were selected using purposive sampling: Kemi Badenoch's (2021) Minister for Equalities' speech on the Commission on Race and Ethnic Disparities' report; Priti Patel's (2021) Home Secretary's opening speech for the second reading of the Nationality and Borders Bill in the House of Commons; Suella Braverman's (2023) speech to the Conservative Party Conference; and Rishi Sunak's (2024) Prime Ministerial address on extremism. These speeches were deemed relevant as important policy and position statements by Cabinet ministers from minority ethnic backgrounds speaking on issues relating to immigration control and race equality. These public speeches were also identified as indicative of the different politicians' positions as they were intended to be informative and persuasive and widely reported. In analysing these speeches and related critical literature, the chapter uses a processural racial eliminativist approach as a theoretical framework.

This perspective focuses primarily on race as a constituting category and concept instead of an empirical group descriptor—the focus, therefore, is on what reference to race does instead of what race purportedly is. The prevalent postracial concept referred to in this chapter is the figurative notion of an 'actually-existing' postracial society suggesting the declining significance of race and waning racism. Because a processural form of racial eliminativism is used, reference to race is not debarred. Therefore, the term race is used in this chapter to reflect its common meaning and usage within literature, debates and discourse, while the term racialisation is used to denote the production of racial groups.

Politics, rationality and the ambivalence of emotion

When James Carville coined the now well-known phrase 'It's the economy, stupid' while an advisor to Bill Clinton's 1992 presidential election campaign, he crystallised a key principle within political analysis. Carville's maxim encapsulated the ideal of voters as rational actors pursuing their interest which in that case could be reduced to the economic. Such idealisation of political action as the exercise of reason, especially regarding major parties and the state within democratic societies, is typified within the post-war Keynesian consensus. In Joseph Schumpeter's (1950) classic articulation of this viewpoint, the electorate review competing party programmes and a government is formed once a majority selects the one that best reflects their wishes.

This dominant perspective on political action, as stimulated by rational self-interest, in turn considered emotions as an aberration or unwelcome intrusion into politics. As such, emotion is a deficient trait ascribed to individuals and extra-legislative pressure groups acting according to narrow partisan interest; emotion within politics is outside the norm of equanimity and lucid calculation. Emotionally driven political action is, then, cast as exceptional, evident within major touchstone issues such as capital punishment and abortion (Ost 2004). Conversely, the executive, legislative and judicial branches of state power are commonly understood to remain above the fray, issuing dispassionate pronouncements according to constitutional precedent.

Recent examples of this perspective are evident in commentaries on the rise of populist nationalism exemplified within the 2016 seismic shocks of Brexit and the US presidential electoral success of Donald Trump. The Brexit/Trump axis was read as a rebellion of the 'left behind,' stoked by anti-immigration sentiment (Bailey 2017; Edwards, Haugerud and Parikh 2017) as well as nostalgia for and desired return to revered 'tradition' (Gusterson 2017). Characterisations of these malcontents as 'low information' emotional voters (Fording and Schram 2017) further highlight their affective motivation as deviant political behaviour. Notably, however, this emotional predilection is not confined to the populist political right. Rather, following the 2008 financial crisis, the emergence of leftist, right-wing and non-partisan parties, movements and leaders such as Podemos in Spain, Syriza in Greece, Momentum and Jeremy Corbyn's Labour Party leadership in the UK in addition to the earlier Tea Party movement in the US, all point to an 'intensification of affective animus vis-à-vis their partisan opponents' (Page and Dittmer 2016: 76). Taken together, these examples from across the political spectrum point to the recent derogation of sober-minded politics, thus reiterating the normativity of informed, rational voting.

And so, emotion holds an ambivalent position within politics. On one hand, reason is regarded as the norm, an ideal to be maintained amidst rising unruly, passionate sentiments that are seditiously threatening. An ideologue conjures an image of a fervent adherent of an extreme politics, problematic in their zealotry. Conversely, the 'statesman'-like politician provides a comforting image of patrician stability, primed to act benevolently in the public good. On the other hand, however, the inherent emotionality of politics is assiduously obscured through a deliberate, discursive sleight of hand. Feminist political theorists, for example, have long pointed out the gendered, patriarchal separation of reason and emotion, arguing instead for a humanist feminism that can combine empathetic understanding with ethical rationality (Green 1995). The ambivalence of emotion is clear with the 'deliberately ambiguous' core Brexit Vote Leave slogan, 'Take back control,' as operating simultaneously in substantive and affective registers with reference to concrete National Health Service funding proposals alongside nebulous notions of sovereignty (Gietel-Basten 2016). I suggest that the key issue when evaluating this ambivalent position on emotion is not whether an emotional aspect of politics is desirable or not, but rather what objectives are harboured within each idealisation.

Moreover, I question the supposedly recent emergence of political emotionality with the rise of populist nationalism within debates on Brexit/ Trump. The Leave campaign was premised on long-standing notions of an exceptionalist and isolationist English nationalism (Virdee and McGeever 2018), while Trump's electoral success was 'not an aberration but perhaps a more transparent revival of nationalist tendencies and white supremacy that is an integral part of US history through the erasure of native people, slavery, and the Jim Crow era' (Gökariksel and Smith 2016: 80). The affective political dimension evident within Brexit/Trump is not a new phenomenon but, as we now turn to see, a timeworn strategic aspect of the politics of race-making.

Racialisation, racism and the politics of sentiment

'In the middle of the nineteenth century,' wrote Hannah Arendt, 'race opinions were still judged by the yardstick of political reason,' citing Tocqueville's admonishment of Gobineau's views on Europeans' physical, intellectual and moral superiority over all other racial groups (2004: 210). For Arendt, prior to the apogee of imperialism and its birthing of methodical racial ideologies, race-thinking was but one—highly impressionistic—perspective amongst others and contestable once subject to reasoned scrutiny. However, another way of approaching Arendt's proposition is to reflect on the extent to which speculative racial thinking was underwritten by reason. An exemplary critique of this fault line is Charles W. Mills' (1997) theory of the 'racial contract' whereby the classic value-free formation of universal liberal ideals such as freedom, equality and democracy were conceived of and enacted in racially restrictive ways. Legitimised violence such as settler colonialism and land theft were rationalised and simultaneously emotionally rendered. Therefore, racial theorists' profoundly visceral prose disdaining abject racialised others was not extraneous to reason. Rather, it served to create and distinguish those mature and worthy Kantian 'persons' from the inveterate contrast class of immature and unworthy racialised 'subpersons' (Mills 1997). As Jean-Paul Sartre held in relation to anti-Semitism, the judicious defence of indefensibly specious political programmes motivated by feelings of disgust and repulsion requires mobilising a 'logic of passion' (1995: 10). For Sartre, deep animosity towards others was not derived from actual experiences but resulted from an idea of that other developed for expedient purposes—passionate racist hatred, therefore, emanated from a decision to hate. In a more measured formulation, an aspect of Enlightenment rationalism attributed observable behavioural differences between populations to intrinsic racial traits. Even though supposedly dispassionate, this racial reasoning contained moral judgements of groups' inherent being that informed the establishment of racial hierarchy and exclusions to liberal universality (Goldberg 1993).

The not-so-strange fusion of reason and emotion in the politics of racial thinking is readily discernible in post-war Britain. As the advent of mass migration from the 'new Commonwealth' brought colonial subjects to the metropole, concerns about race relations began to build through the 1950s, with the 1958 'race riots' in Nottingham and Notting Hill marking a pivotal moment with discordant 'coloured' immigration deemed their cause in both policy debates and media coverage (Solomos 2003). Concerns over immigration causing grave social harms became a major electoral political issue during the 1964 general election (Banton 1967). These concerns were perhaps rehearsed most notably in Enoch Powell's (1968) infamous 'Rivers of Blood' speech (hereafter 'Rivers'). In that address, Powell—a Conservative MP—inveighed against the Race Relations Bill that would be enacted into law in a few short months after for exacerbating the crisis brought about by new Commonwealth immigration and the resulting threat posed to Britain. Much has been written about the practical impact of Powell's speech for normalising extreme positions such as the repatriation of migrants (Solomos 2003). In addition, some interesting evaluation of Powell's political oratory using 'rhetorical political analysis' demonstrates how 'Rivers' marks a conscious and purposeful departure from his customarily unexciting, analytical speeches: 'Rhetorically the use of anecdotes underpinned his pathos, and with the assistance of his emphasis on numbers and the anecdotes presented as facts, these constructed his logos' (Crines, Hepple and Hill 2016: 82). Moreover, this affective-logical composition demonstrates the circular fusing of reason and emotion in racial thinking whereby the authentic experiential testimonies of 'ordinary people' are taken to provide a substantive evidential basis for the claims made. Sociologically, this mutually reinforcing relation between reason and emotion is understood more generally where emotional experience is rationally interpreted as positive or negative in relation to power and prestige, with gaining and losing power leading to positive and negative emotions such as and anxiety and fear, comfort and satisfaction (Kemper and Collins 1990). This applied rational calculation of emotions is evident within classical race relations literature gesturing towards the psychic impact of host populations' perceived loss of status resulting from their social and economic competition with incoming migrants (Banton 1967).

'Rivers' is significant for the discussion at hand here in two senses. First, as Nasar Meer puts it, an unresolved tension 'between the policy objectives of race equality and migration control... remains a characteristic of "race talk" in Britain since Powell' (2022: 59). This tension is evident in 1968, for example, in the contrast between the Race Relations Act with its provisions to address migrant welfare, social adjustment and discrimination, and the Commonwealth Immigration Act featuring ethnic restrictions on British citizenship eligibility and entitlement to enter Britain. More recently, this tension is evident in the contrast between the protections from discrimination, harassment and victimisation contained in the Equality Act (2010) and the Conservative government's 'hostile environment' for immigrants and floating of a British Bill of Rights to supplant the European Convention on Human Rights.

Second, the rhetorical and emotional tenor of the pronouncements are notably familiar. 'Rivers' was pitched in a highly emotional register in order to exploit empathy for the suffering of the vulnerable (specifically the elderly, women and children), inflame passions at the injustice of Britons now 'made strangers in their own country' and stoke resentment and anger towards unassimilable immigrants. All of these points resonate eerily within contemporary Britain as undeserving economic migrants are said to benefit at the taxpayers' expense, thus marginalising decent, hardworking Britons (Braverman 2023; Patel 2021). Powell's (1968) portrait of 'ordinary, decent, sensible people' expressing 'rational' concerns over the 'privileges' granted to migrants yet fearful of 'penalties or reprisals' as indicative of a growing sense of 'being a persecuted minority' dovetails neatly with contemporary discourse bemoaning the disenchanted 'left behind' silenced by 'metropolitan elites' and a pervasive, omnipotent 'woke' agenda. Taken together, this rational-emotional amalgam running from the past to the present sets a politics of grievance in train whereby the privileging of migrants is said to be both empirically verifiable in demographic terms and keenly felt by the now disadvantaged local white population (Dench, Gavron and Young 2006). Practical, policy-driven directives are presented as rational responses to practical social problems of 'uncontrolled migration,' complimented by an affective appeal to the Powellian sense of 'alarm and resentment' felt by the host British population as well as impending 'national danger.'

Postracial sentimentality and British identity politics

Mobilising the emotional political register in defence of 'decent people' against mass immigration and its 'woke' advocates is a demanding feat, requiring shrewd messaging and compelling messengers. In a characteristically insightful analysis of *Uncle Tom's Cabin*, James Baldwin refers to sentimentality as a major motif in American cultural politics. 'Sentimentality, the ostentatious parading of excessive and spurious emotion,' Baldwin wrote, 'is the mark of dishonesty, the inability to feel' (1985a: 28). Baldwin is concerned with how Harriet Beecher Stowe's famous work, lauded as an anti-slavery novel, is replete with normalised violence detailing infanticide, rape, murder, beatings and sadistic cruelty yet neither details the feelings of those people experiencing this legalised terror nor explains why it takes place. Instead, the melodramatic plot drives a naïve moralistic narrative designed to provoke an overwrought emotional response that easily and inevitably denounces slavery as evil. Crude and pre-determined, this response is ultimately insincere and circumvents the magnitude of slavery in human and social terms. Moreover, it obviates responsibility and a reckoning for slavery. Sentimentality, then, is a disingenuous performativity of emotion calculated to confect moral outrage and trite axioms that deliberately obscure nuanced understanding and obstruct appropriate ameliorative action.

Baldwin's formulation of sentimentality provides a useful conceptual tool to help understand the current tension between progressive cosmopolitan approaches to open borders and equalitarian and punitive approaches to migration control and race equality within governmental policy. Just as the sentimentality within *Uncle Tom's Cabin* provides a gestural denunciation of slavery without a full accounting, senior Conservative Cabinet ministers from a minority ethnic background repeated this sophistry regarding race equality and immigration policy. Kemi Badenoch (2021), for example, asserted that 'racism is still a real force which has the power to deny opportunity and painfully disrupt lives' then adding the caveat that 'many factors other than racism are often the root cause [of racial disparities]. Among these are geography, deprivation, and family structure.' The Commission on Race and Ethnic Disparities (CRED) report on race and ethnic disparities in education, employment, crime, policing and health that Badenoch is referring to in her speech mirrors this diminishing of racism at greater length: racism is said to exist but active claims to and experience of its existence are largely dismissed as often overblown, misguided and divisive (CRED 2021). The melodramatic facet of sentimentality identified by Baldwin and its emotional aspect is manifest within the confected scourge of the 'migrant crisis' and 'woke' critical race theory that misrepresent social conditions and is orchestrated to stir up a febrile atmosphere. While the existence of racism is rehearsed in an obligatory manner but its actuality is disavowed, the tangible, extant inequities and injustices are those experienced by 'the British people' who, while 'generous and compassionate,' nonetheless 'have had enough of open borders and uncontrolled migration' (Patel 2021). This paean to British decency set against the machinations of devious migrants typifies Baldwin's view of sentimentality as a form of performative outrage. The emotive expression is not only devoid of an adequate material justification but does not need to be as it is an end in itself. Creating figures of hate that evoke a visceral response is a guileful attempt to conjure a retaliation without a provocation (Sartre 1995).

This sentimental messaging is effectively expressed through the artful use of effectual messengers. As much as this conjured catastrophe of Britain's 'open borders' echoes the feverish tone and anxieties of 'Rivers,' there is an immense difference. While Powell struck an especially defiant note as a white man refusing to be silenced from criticising racial integration as a 'dangerous delusion,' Conservative Cabinet diversity means that many governmental figures do not share his ethnic encumbrance. And so, senior minority ethnic Conservative politicians serve as 'post-racial gatekeepers,' bringing diversity to the government and Cabinet as a means to 'soften' the Conservative Party image from that of 'the nasty party' and broaden its electoral appeal (Saini, Bankole and Begum 2023). Governmental foregrounding of neo-liberal themes, including equality of opportunity, meritocracy and the centrality of normative cultural values, while downplaying ethnic inequality and racism (Goldberg 2015; Wise 2010), underscore the practical relevance and critical cogence of the postracial as a critical term.

Joining the governmental chorus promulgating the notion of a meritocratic Britain, the sentimental pronouncements of these senior Conservative government politicians carry an additional emotional charge as minority ethnic tribunes speaking from personal experience. During the Conservative Party leadership election in the summer of 2022, candidates Kemi Badenoch, Sajid Javid, Rishi Sunak and Nadhim Zahawi all provided narratives of their personal trajectories towards integration into Britishness and/or availing themselves of opportunities within Britain that facilitated their personal advancement and professional achievement (Saini, Bankole and Begum 2023). In Badenoch's estimation, for example, Britain is 'one of the fairest countries in the world' (HM Government 2022: 7). Rishi Sunak's (2024) speech on terrorism further demonstrates the ideal of British openness and beneficence:

> I stand here as our country's first non-white Prime Minister, leading the most diverse government in our country's history to tell people of all races, all faiths and all backgrounds it is not the colour of your skin, the God you believe in or where you were born, that will determine your success but just your own hard work and endeavour.

Notably, however, Sunak's multi-faith and cross-cultural largesse is undercut by the primacy of Britishness, its institutions, conventions and ideals. At first, combining ethnic religious identity with civic pride and committed British citizenship is 'underpinned by the tolerance of our established, Christian church' (Sunak 2024). And then,

> our Britain must not be a country in which we descend into polarised camps with some communities living parallel lives. It is not enough to live side-by-side, we must live together united by shared values and a shared commitment to this country.
>
> *(Sunak 2024)*

This form of postracial sentimentality establishes the primacy of Britishness—'this country'—with markers of racialised difference such as skin colour and religion subsumed within the nation. While Powell in 'Rivers' found migrants to be a threateningly different presence and thus unassimilable, Sunak suggests an amenable form of difference, mutable to the extent that it lacks menace. A simplistic, sentimental contrast is drawn between varied forms of difference building a Manichean contrast between acceptable respectability and Powellian interlopers who 'hold the whip hand.' Biddable others, personified within Sunak's non-threatening self-representation, are compatible with and can be incorporated into a normative national self-image. The ominous 'forces here at home trying to tear us apart' (Sunak 2024), on the other hand, constitute an enemy within.

Embodying the postracial de-toxification of racism

The compelling critique of postracial gatekeeping as a form of nationalist incorporation on the part of senior minority ethnic Conservative politicians bears further development in terms of its dynamic existential and affective dimensions. Firstly, however, it is notable that the applicability of the term itself is flatly disavowed with the definitive claim that Britain is not 'a postracial society' (Badenoch 2021; CRED 2021: 9). Moreover, race is explicitly referred to in many senior minority ethnic Conservative politicians' speeches. Sunak (2024) spoke as the 'first non-white Prime Minister,' while Badenoch—who would succeed Sunak as Conservative Party leader after the 2024 general election—positioned herself as a 'black woman.' Ironically, these interventions deployed the storytelling mode central to much-derided critical race theory—Badenoch, for example, underscored her 'passionate' belief in the meritocratic ideal as reflecting her 'lived experience' (HM Government 2022: 7). Nevertheless, as stated above, claims that race is of diminishing significance and racism is in decline while meritocratic idealism is ascendant suggest a postracial society in figurative terms.

This in/significance of race is indicative of a constitutive dialectical tension within what I have referred to as a disingenuous notion of the 'already-existing postracial society' where race is transcended (St Louis 2016). But within this perspective, race is not transcended in absolute terms and racism has not been eradicated. To 'transcend' race is to exist, somehow, separate from race—whatever that means—but not to eradicate it. Similarly, colour-blindness means to disregard colour. In other words, to ignore race which, again, is not to eradicate it altogether. Therefore, the 'post' in this version of the postracial is not an absolute break. Rather, within this already-existing postracial formulation, race is characterised as of diminishing significance which, in turn, has a proportionate impact on racism which is said to be in decline. Nevertheless, race remains as a trace that has to be mentioned, implied or alluded to in its supposedly weakened form and minimised effects.

Regarding the CRED (2021) report, Kemi Badenoch (2021) expresses 'abhorrence at the appalling abuse meted out to the Commissioners' for publishing positive findings and being falsely accused of disingenuousness such as minimising the 'atrocities of slavery.' Badenoch then asserts that it is 'irresponsible—dangerously so—to call ethnic minority people racial slurs like "Uncle Toms", "Coconuts", "House slaves or House Negroes" for daring to think differently.' The issue raised here is not simply intemperate personal criticism of commissioners, but the use of epithets designed to signal a dissonant internal whiteness or treacherous subservience that questions a person of colour's racial authenticity (Ford 2005). As nine of the ten commissioners 'were from ethnic minority backgrounds' (HM Government 2022: 7), this specific concern with 'racial slurs' foregrounds not only racial ontology but also criticises a discriminatory unilateral racial excommunication. By attempting to revoke the Commissioners' racial authenticity and falsely accuse them of racial disloyalty, those critics' actions are deemed dangerously irresponsible. However, the slurs are not simply offensive because they misinterpret the commissioners' views. Rather, they are offensive in part because they are hurtful; they disregard a deep interior sense of self-identity that Linda Martín Alcoff (2006) refers to in 'contextualist' terms as attuned to the 'lived experience of racialization' and 'how race is constitutive of bodily experience, subjectivity, judgment' (2006: 183). Consequently, the slurs are not simply utterances and words heard or read by the recipient but they can also be experienced as an attack and felt as a form of injury. Badenoch's objection, therefore, attempts to garner public sympathy and support by pointing to the emotional ills of bullying behaviour, coercive tactics and personal insult.

Nonetheless, accepting racialised experience at face value runs the risk of naturalising felt racial experience as 'fully self-presenting' (Alcoff 2006: 184). This is an important caveat because some senior Conservative politicians pointedly rehearse familiar, deeply sentimental tropes of British decency and fairness from specific experiential positionalities—for example Badenoch 'a black woman, a first-generation immigrant,' and Sunak as 'a practising Hindu and a proud Briton.' Framed in this way, Badenoch and Sunak's experiences and feelings—such as the latter's professed 'love' for Britain—are deeply internalised and indisputable; they act as a rhetorical form of closure. A heartfelt bond such as Sunak's love cannot be rationalised but instead conveys a deep emotional connection precisely because it is felt and lived. But while Badenoch and Sunak's speeches reflect politically salient, emotionally charged lived experiences, as Joan Scott (1991) points out in a classic intervention, the meaning of experience is not self-evident but requires interpretation with reference to its formative context. 'To think about experience in this way,' writes Scott, 'is to historicize it as well as to historicize the identities it produces' (1991: 780). When applied to Badenoch and Sunak's speeches, their personal testimonies are not literal reflections of their authentic selves. Rather, their speeches function as political discourse heavily mediated through the narration of lived experience designed to elicit specific feelings. Their varied ethnic, religious and cultural differences aside, Badenoch, Braverman, Patel and Sunak's speeches are intended to instigate and confirm heartfelt popular sentiments. 'The British people have repeatedly voted to take back control of our borders,' Patel (2021) intones, 'They finally have a government that is listening to them. Our priorities are the people's priorities.' Senior black, Asian and minority ethnic Conservative MPs, therefore, share the public's feelings over mass immigration and its adverse impact.

Crucially, reference to the personal experience of senior minority ethnic politicians who have experienced professional advancement and social mobility serves to mitigate and undermine wider issues of racism in the society at large and demonstrate British openness. Badenoch (2021) expressed concern with attacks on commissioners' racial authenticity as 'deplorable tactics... designed to intimidate ethnic minority people from their right to express legitimate views.' These 'legitimate views' are the controversial findings of the report, perhaps crystallised in the following quote contrasting the continued existence of racism, albeit lessening, with

> an increasingly strident form of anti-racism thinking that seeks to explain all minority disadvantage through the prism of White discrimination. This diverts attention from the other reasons for minority success and failure, including those embedded in the cultures and attitudes of those minority communities themselves.
>
> *(CRED 2021: 11)*

And so, minority ethnic communities bear some responsibility for their social marginalisation, as a result of their own cultural characteristics and level of industriousness. As evidenced by their elevated social status, those politicians and/or their families are implicitly 'good' migrants. They came in the right way under acceptable circumstances such as being expelled from their homelands; they are deserving of characteristic British generosity and are profoundly grateful for it. Conversely, the supposedly duplicitous, criminal and indolent are undeserving, 'bad' migrants. And the recognition of the latter by the former is striking.

Quite simply, the implication is that government policies emanate from an ethnically diverse Cabinet and, as a result, cannot be discriminatory. Minority ethnic politicians' experience-based negative comments on migrants and race equality initiatives have an important impact, obviating the arduous work commonly required when racism is denied from a white perspective (Van Dijk 1992). As Home Secretaries, Priti Patel (2021) and Suella Braverman's (2023) speeches on immigration and border control are crafted as forthright tell-it-as-it-is statements of fact. Conveyed colloquially, the crafting of such 'stories' in relation to everyday situations normalise racism within commonsense narratives that feel correct and are thus compelling to their audience (Van Dijk 1993). Furthermore, the denial of racism is also understood as a form of violence against the very experiences of those racialised people subject to racism (Lentin 2018). Consequently, the experience-based views of minority ethnic Conservative politicians utilise the racial trace to denude the charge of racism. Mirroring Badenoch and others, Braverman (2023) acknowledges her background as the child of migrants in her call for greater border control. If this declaration should appear contradictory given her familial circumstance, Braverman's positionality is intended to bolster her policy position. The emotional appeal to family contextualises and justifies the need for managed migration and tighter border control as an irreproachable, rational calculation insofar as even the child of migrants can support the policy.

The effectiveness of attacks on immigration and race equality depends significantly, and often tacitly, on the racialised subject position of the speaker. That Home Secretaries of Asian descent such as Patel and Braverman could speak so vociferously for strong controls on migration enabled their pronouncements to be framed as demonstrably reasonable and obviously non-discriminatory. Furthermore, Braverman (2023) attacks the Labour Party opposition and their voluntary sector 'allies' on migration control: 'Some of whom openly declare that they oppose national borders merely on principle. And all of them bleating the same incessant accusation: Racist. Racist. Racist.' Whereas postracial racism denial usually requires de-legitimising claims to the existence of 'public racism' (Lentin 2016) through a series of evasions, this variety of postracial racism denial is able to mount a direct, scathing attack. Echoing the CRED report findings, Braverman notes the charge of racism as a weaponised moral taboo wielded by the left and the 'woke.' Insidious diversity, equity and inclusion policies, Braverman continues, have pedalled 'pernicious nonsense' such as 'White privilege' and 'Anti-British history' with dangerous consequences whereby 'those who fail to conform are persecuted.'

Speaking from a tacit insider position enabled by the racial trace and a familial migrant experience provides an existential basis for minimising the impact of racism. The sentimentally overwrought narrative of an alien invasion demands a robust response that is truculent in tone and punitive in practice. Like Baldwin's critique of *Uncle Tom's Cabin*, any complex understanding of the social forces driving migrants as well as the ethical and legal responsibilities of the British state towards them is dissembled by a calculated dishonest and unfeeling incitement of 'excess and spurious emotion.'

Expulsion dreams: Postracial sentimentality and the relativity of privilege

In a now infamous speech at a fringe event at the 2022 Conservative Party Conference, Braverman remarked, 'I would love to have a front page of the Telegraph with a plane taking off to Rwanda, that's my dream, it's my obsession' (Dearden 2022). Braverman's political commitment to deporting asylum seekers to file their applications in Rwanda instead of the UK is unequivocal. But when stated as a 'dream' and an 'obsession,' Braverman's fervour to fulfil the policy objective is remarkable. In a separate ardent declaration, Braverman's predecessor as Home Secretary, Priti Patel, offered the following:

> The British people have had enough of open borders and uncontrolled migration. Enough of: costly failed asylum system, illegal migrants, economic migrants posing as refugees, adults pretending to be children to claim asylum, foreign criminals—including murderers and rapists—who abuse our laws and then game the system so we can't remove them.

Patel then continues, referring to gangs profiting from people smuggling as 'truly evil,' with the British government having 'a moral duty to prevent them.' Then, Patel graphically denounces the indefensible action of these facilitators using 'violence and the threat of violence—including rape—to control people. We are talking about *unimaginable wickedness*' (emphasis added).

Set against what Simon Clarke (2003) terms a 'double fear' of wider social disorder as well as a threat to individuals' private existence within emotive racist discourse, this visceral rhetoric displays a virulent aversion to and rejection of asylum seekers. Reacting against the 'double fear,' Braverman's message is notably positive as her 'obsession' and 'dream' are volitional. Therefore, the enervating sense of passivity engendered by the 'double fear' amidst a migrant 'invasion' is aggressively countered by a sense of agency. Braverman presents herself as striking back, as it were, fuelling a combative emotional response from her sympathetic audience. Patel's speech, on the other hand, presents a more dispiriting image that stokes the double fear. The reference to 'true evil' underscores the extreme malevolent threat facing Britain. This Manichean opposition between the Good—British decency—and Evil and unimaginable wickedness conjures the spectre of an irredeemable outsider central to the fomenting of racist hatred (Sartre 1995). Patel's portent of doom exacerbates fear and instils anger. As it was the case with the figure of the migrant in 'Rivers', such inveterate deviance cannot be incorporated into the polity and must be expelled.

'Postracial gatekeeping' offers an instrumental explanation of the unsympathetic attitude towards migrants exhibited by some senior minority ethnic Conservative politicians. This incendiary rhetoric garners a passionate emotional response from its intended audience and, in doing so, clears a path into the British establishment. But understanding the practical means/ends reasons for such attitudes, whether access to positions of power or incorporation into Britishness, does not account for the *tenor* of the pronouncements. Much of the governmental anti-migration discourse articulated by black, Asian and minority ethnic politicians was enthusiastically vitriolic, inviting a simple question: Why was that the case? Why were politicians like Patel and Braverman so passionately vehement in their denunciation of migrants and protection of Britain?

An answer lies in the emotional landscape of power relations experienced by an intermediate social grouping examined in Albert Memmi's classic text, *The Colonizer and the Colonized*. In that work, Memmi explores the situation of the minor European in the colony—the 'small coloniser'— situated above the colonised mass and below the colonial masters. Indeed, this figure is often exploited by the colonial master and yet is, 'in most cases, a supporter of colonialists and an obstinate defender of colonial privileges' (Memmi 1990: 76–77). For Memmi, the small coloniser adopts this posture because they enjoy a relative privilege in comparison to the native colonised population. And by receiving tangible benefits, for example in access to education and employment, and enjoying social status above that of the colonised, the small coloniser is positioned precariously between integration into the colony and loyalty to their own native land. As a European, the small coloniser has a sense of cultural commonalty with their superiors that brings them 'sentimentally closer' and yet never fully integrated or accepted, they 'live in painful and constant ambiguity' (Memmi 1990: 80, 81).

Alongside the figure of the small coloniser is the migrant, a new arrival neither a member of the colonising power nor native population subject to colonial occupation. Upon entering the colony, the migrant is a social competitor to the small coloniser, positioned below the colonial elite but locating themselves above the colonised. The migrant's mentality and social positionality is crystallised in Memmi's analytic portrait, which bears repeating at length:

> The recently assimilated place themselves in a considerably superior position to the average colonizer. They push a colonial mentality to excess, display proud disdain for the colonized and continually show off their borrowed rank, which often belies a vulgar brutality and avidity. Still too impressed by their privileges, they savor them and defend them with fear and harshness; and when colonization is imperilled, they provide it with its most dynamic defenders, its shock troops, and sometimes its instigators.
>
> *(1990: 82)*

This portrait of attitudes and behaviours mirrors that of the politicians articulated in their speeches discussed above. The marginality of those 'recently assimilated' is redolent of South Asians' generally precarious inclusion within Britishness as they are positioned within 'a liminal space of privilege and prejudice' (Saini 2022: 110). The excessive promulgation of a superior British disposition is continually rehearsed in the eulogising of British fairness, decency, meritocracy and so on, both in itself and as a world-leading trait. Taking joy in disregarding the vulnerable is manifest in the demonisation of migrants played out performatively for maximum emotional impact. Revelling in the power of their office is shown in devising objectives aimed at delivering sanctioned discrimination, such as ensuring that Prevent is 'focused on the main security threat to the British public, Islamist extremism' (Braverman 2023). They do so with 'vulgar brutality and avidity' which is arguably the intention of Braverman's 'dream' and 'obsession' contrasting with the reductive caricatures of 'woke' permissiveness and 'luxury beliefs.' And the extravagant cruelty in dreaming of deportation flights leaving Britain provides a sign of pleasure derived from and defending their privilege 'with fear and harshness.'

These attitudes and behaviours aggressively reduce people to categories and dehumanise them as at best unwanted and at worst venal. In turn, these archetypes embody a simplistic problem—'the migrant crisis'—that poses a dual threat to person and polity. The disciplinary circuit is then completed by the zealous defence of the nation required to quell this alien threat. To borrow from James Baldwin (1985b), there is a sense that minority ethnic Conservative politicians' support for hardline anti-immigration policies and opposition to race equality is the 'price of the ticket' for both their political careers and certified Britishness. But this political acquiescence cannot work if perceived as instrumental naked ambition. Rather, their exceptionalist and exclusionary Britishness must be demonstrably inhabited and earnestly performed with devotion so as to be convincing. Hence the spectacular cruelty of Braverman's 'dream' and 'obsession' confirm her Britishness and belonging to the nation.

Conclusion: Postracial sentimentality and 'the price of the ticket'

'The price the white American paid for his ticket,' wrote James Baldwin, 'was to become white' (1985b: xx). This whiteness amounts to social status, a marker of entitlement to rights and regard. Whiteness, in this formulation, signifies power which constrains all in different ways. 'Part of the price of the black ticket' Baldwin held was 'the dream of becoming white' (1985b: xiv), that is, simply the gift of life and freedom. But the object of this reverie is itself a delusion as 'white people are not white: part of the price of the white ticket is to delude themselves into believing that they are' (1985b: xiv). And so, in Baldwin's estimation, the pursuit of whiteness 'choked many a human being to death' (1985b: xx), both the non-white people denied the right to live and the whites who, by systematically brutalising, enslaving and murdering others, dehumanised themselves.

The in/significance of race for Baldwin as well as what it signifies and obscures is replicated within the political positionality of senior Conservative minority ethnic politicians discussed in this chapter. They occupy a precarious postracial position as worthy recipients of non-racial meritocratic professional opportunity and social advancement while their ethno-racial and religious identities mark them as different, thus requiring incorporation into Britishness. This subjective oscillation between being racially marked and unmarked enables a strategic positioning deployed to minimise and deny racism. Postracial positioning and sentimental rhetoric, therefore, work hand-in-hand. Given the fervid tenor of the debate, these politicians' emotive and impassioned pronouncements, often undergirded by their own personal experience, are intended to both justify restrictive policy positions on migration, border control and race equality and indemnify them from criticism as racist.

In the example discussed above, sentimentality functions as a means to emotionally cohere the state and the people and enable both to attempt to deny their self-debasement. Speaking to the Conservative Party Conference in 2023, Suella Braverman recognised that 'Every human, every single person, has the right to aspire to a better life. As Conservatives, that is one of the cornerstones of our philosophy. And, indeed, without that dream, I wouldn't be standing before you today.' In stark contrast with that of her parents, Braverman's own infamous 'dream' as well as her 'obsession' belies the cruel sentimentality Baldwin draws attention to. 'Mass immigration' although understandable from the viewpoint of those economic migrants, let alone those seeking asylum, is now 'uncontrolled and unmanageable' and thus callously rejected as impractical and unrealistic. For Braverman (2023), humane petitioning against the vilification of migrants and legal objections to the unlawful treatment of refugees are 'luxury beliefs... promoting seductive but irresponsible ideas.' Even when enshrined in international treaties, fairness and justice are not universally applicable but reserved for particular local beneficiaries. Using Baldwin as a critical lens, the wilful misnaming of 'the migrant crisis' spawned by a sentimental impulse is replete with an unfeeling detailing of terror and violence, confected anger and championing of a facile and emotionally satiating response.

References

Alcoff, L.M. (2006) *Visible Identities: Race, Gender, and the Self*, Oxford: Oxford University Press.

Arendt, H. (2004) *The Origins of Totalitarianism*, New York: Schocken Books.
Badenoch, K. (2021) 'Minister for Equalities' speech on the Commission on Race and Ethnic Disparities' report', 20 April. Available at www.gov.uk/government/speeches/minister-for-equalities-speech-on-the-commission-on-race-and-ethnic-disparities-report
Bailey, D. (2017) 'Class struggle after Brexit', *Capital and Class*, 41(2): 333–372.
Baldwin, J. (1985a) 'Everybody's Protest Novel', in *The Price of the Ticket: Collected Nonfiction, 1948–1985*, New York: St. Martin's Marek.
Baldwin, J. (1985b) 'Introduction: The Price of the Ticket', in *The Price of the Ticket: Collected Nonfiction, 1948–1985*, New York: St. Martin's Marek.
Banton, M. (1967) *Race Relations*, London: Tavistock.
Braverman, S. (2023) 'Speech to Conservative Party Conference', 3 October. Available at www.ukpol.co.uk/suella-braverman-2023-speech-to-conservative-party-conference/
Clarke, S. (2003) *Social Theory, Psychoanalysis and Racism*, Basingstoke: Palgrave Macmillan.
Commission on Race and Ethnic Disparities (2021) *Commission on Race and Ethnic Disparities: The Report*, London: HMSO.
Crines, A., Heppell, T., and Hill, M. (2016) 'Enoch Powell's "Rivers of Blood" Speech: A rhetorical political analysis', *British Politics*, 11(1): 72–94.
Dearden, L. (2022) 'Suella Braverman says it is her 'dream' and 'obsession' to see a flight take asylum seekers to Rwanda', *Independent*, 5 October. Available at www.independent.co.uk/news/uk/politics/suella-braverman-rwanda-dream-obsession-b2195296.html
Dench, G., Gavron, K., and Young, M. (2006) *The New East End: Kinship, Race and Conflict*, London: Profile Books.
Dhaliwal, S. and Forkert, K. (2015) 'Deserving and undeserving migrants', *Soundings*, 61: 49–61.
Diversity UK (2019) 'Britain's most ethnically diverse Cabinet ever', 25 July. Available at https://diversityuk.org/britains-most-ethnically-diverse-cabinet-ever/
Edwards, J., Haugerud, A., and Parikh, S. (2017) 'Introduction: The 2016 Brexit referendum and Trump election', *American Ethnologist*, 44(2): 195–200.
Ford, R.T. (2005) *Racial Culture: A Critique*, Princeton: Princeton University Press.
Fording, R.C. and Schram, S.F. (2017) 'The cognitive and emotional sources of Trump support: The case of low-information voters', *New Political Science*, 39(4): 670–686.
Gietel-Basten, S. (2016) 'Why Brexit? The toxic mix of immigration and austerity', *Population and Development Review*, 42(4): 673–680.
Gökariksel, B. and Smith, S. (2016) '"Making America great again"?: The fascist body politics of Donald Trump', *Political Geography*, 54: 79–81.
Goldberg, D.T. (1993) *Racist Culture: Philosophy and the Politics of Meaning*, Oxford: Blackwell.
Goldberg, D.T. (2015) *Are We All Postracial Yet?* Cambridge: Polity.
Green, K. (1995) *The Woman of Reason: Feminism, Humanism and Political Thought*, Cambridge: Polity Press.
Gusterson, H. (2017) 'From Brexit to Trump: Anthropology and the rise of nationalist populism', *American Ethnologist*, 44(2): 209–214.
HM Government (2022) *Inclusive Britain: The Government's Response to the Commission on Race and Ethnic Disparities*. London: HMSO.

Jones, I. (2022) 'Less diverse, fewer women: Key statistics about Rishi Sunak's new Cabinet', 26 October, Evening Standard. Available at www.standard.co.uk/news/politics/rishi-sunak-cabinet-diversity-women-suella-braverman-michael-gove-gillian-keegan-dominic-raab-b1035222.html

Kemper, T.D. and Collins, R. (1990) 'Dimensions of microinteraction', *American Journal of Sociology*, 96: 32–68.

Lentin, A. (2016) 'Racism in public or public racism: doing anti-racism in 'post-racial' times', *Ethnic and Racial Studies*, 39(1): 33–48.

Lentin, A. (2018) 'Beyond denial: "not racism" as racist violence', *Continuum*, 32(4): 400–414.

Meer, N. (2022) *The Cruel Optimism of Racial Justice*, Bristol: Policy Press.

Memmi, A. (1990) *The Colonizer and the Colonized*, London: Earthscan.

Migration Watch UK (2015) 'Immigration policy and black and minority ethnic voters', Briefing paper 11.37, 25 March. Available at www.migrationwatchuk.org/pdfs/BP11_37.pdf

Mills, C.W. (1997) *The Racial Contract*, Ithaca: Cornell University Press.

Ministry of Justice (2020) *Tackling Racial Disparity in the Criminal Justice System: 2020 Update*, February. Crown Copyright.

Ost, D. (2004) 'Politics as the mobilization of anger: Emotions in movements and in power', *European Journal of Social Theory*, 7(2): 229–244.

Page, S. and Dittmer, J. (2016) 'Donald Trump and the white-male dissonance machine', *Political Geography*, 54: 76–78.

Patel, P. (2021) 'Home Secretary opening speech for Nationality and Borders Bill', 19 July. Available at www.gov.uk/government/speeches/home-secretary-opening-speech-for-nationality-borders-bill

Powell, E. (1968) 'Speech at Birmingham', 20 April. Available at www.enochpowell.net/fr-79.html

Saini, R. (2022) 'The racialisation of class and the racialisation of the nation: ethnic minority identity formation across the British Asian middle classes', *South Asian Diaspora*, 14(2): 109–125.

Saini, R. (2023) 'The racialised "Second Existence" of class: Class identification and (de-/re-)construction across the British South Asian middle classes', *Cultural Sociology*, 17(2): 277–296.

Saini, R., Bankole, M., & Begum, N. (2023) 'The 2022 Conservative leadership campaign and post-racial gatekeeping', *Race & Class*, 65(2): 55-74.

Sartre, J.-P. (1995) *Anti-Semite and Jew: An Exploration of the Etiology of Hate*, New York: Schocken Books.

Schumpeter, J.A. (1950) *Capitalism, Socialism, and Democracy*, New York: Harper & Brothers.

Scott, J.W. (1991) 'The evidence of experience', *Critical Inquiry*, 17(4): 773–797.

Solomos, J. (2003) *Race and Racism in Britain*, Third edition, Basingstoke: Palgrave Macmillan.

St Louis, B. (2016) 'Can Race Be Eradicated? The Post-Racial Problematic', in K. Murji and J. Solomos (eds.) *Theories of Race and Ethnicity: Contemporary Debates and Perspectives*, Cambridge: Cambridge University Press.

Sunak, R. (2024) 'PM address on extremism', 1 March. Available at www.gov.uk/government/speeches/pm-address-on-extremism-1-march-2024

Uberoi, E. and Carthew, H. (2023) 'Ethnic diversity in politics and public life', 2 October, House of Commons Library. Available at https://researchbriefings.files.parliament.uk/documents/SN01156/SN01156.pdf

Van Dijk, T.A. (1993) 'Stories and racism', *Narrative and Social Control: Critical Perspectives*, 21: 121–142.

Van Dijk, T.A. (1992) 'Discourse and the denial of racism', *Discourse & Society*, 3(1): 87–118.

Virdee, S. and McGeever, B. (2018) 'Racism, crisis, Brexit', *Ethnic and Racial Studies*, 41(10): 1802–1819.

Warmington, P. (2015) 'The emergence of black British social conservatism', *Ethnic and Racial Studies*, 38(7): 1152–1168.

Webber, F. (2021) 'Britain's authoritarian turn', *Race and Class*, 62(4): 106–120.

Wise, T. (2010) *Colorblind: The Rise of Post-Racial Politics and the Retreat from Racial Equity*, San Francisco: City Lights Books.

PART 2
Producing the state through emotionalised governance

PART 2

4
MANUFACTURING INFORMANTS
The Emotion Work of the Prevent Duty Training

Sadi Shanaah

In this chapter, I will analyse how the UK government attempts to increase the compliance of public sector workers with the Prevent Duty by working on, and through, their emotions. The Prevent Duty was created by the Counter-Terrorism and Security Act 2015, which mandates all workers in local governments, education and childcare, health and social care, criminal justice, and police to "have due regard to the need to prevent people from being drawn into terrorism" (Counter-Terrorism and Security Act, 2015). In effect, the Prevent Duty, as it is evident from its name, makes it a duty for millions of people in the country to actively participate in Prevent, which is the UK's counter-radicalisation strategy. Such responsibilisation of a large part of the society to co-produce national security is symptomatic of the general trend to enlist the public to police a whole range of public safety issues, from immigration and welfare fraud to sexual offences (Aliverti, 2015).

The goal of Prevent is to stop individuals from becoming terrorists or supporting terrorism by early recognition of signs of their radicalisation (HM Government, 2011). Spotting these signs and reporting them to the police have thus become a legal requirement for teachers, nurses, doctors, youth workers, and other public sector workers. This has been characterised as constituting "a total net of surveillance" (Boukalas, 2019, p. 468), where public sector workers act as "informants" (Faure-Walker, 2019). Somewhat surprisingly, various studies showed that the vast majority of public sector workers accepted this new role with little resistance (Busher et al., 2019; Heath-Kelly & Strausz, 2019).

It has been argued that the broad acceptance of the Prevent Duty is the result of the government framing it as part of traditional and uncontroversial safeguarding of vulnerable people and situating Prevent referrals (i.e.,

DOI: 10.4324/9781032617060-7

reporting signs of radicalisation) in the logic of care rather than security (Dresser, 2019; Edwards, 2021; Heath-Kelly & Strausz, 2019). While this is true, I will extend these accounts in two ways. First, I will provide a detailed empirical analysis of the key government communication of the Prevent Duty to public sector workers. Empirically rich accounts of government discursive strategy that aims at making the Prevent Duty acceptable to front-line workers are rare. Second, I will focus on the affective dimension of this strategy to draw out the "emotionalities of rule" – the affective component of governmentality (Campbell, 2010). Although Prevent has been described as "a structure of governance" (Boukalas, 2019, p. 473), the affective part of governing through Prevent has been mostly only implied.

My argument is that we cannot explain the apparent buy-in of public sector workers into the Prevent Duty merely by pointing to the fact that the government sold it to them as safeguarding. We already know that changes in attitudes and behaviour usually result from the interaction of both cognitive and emotional processes (e.g., Clore, 2011; Lerner et al., 2015) and that, for this reason, persuasive communication usually includes both emotional and rational appeals (Petty & Briñol, 2015). Therefore, to be able to fully understand the government discursive strategy aimed at making public sector workers comply with the Prevent Duty and explain its success, we need to analyse whether and how the government discourse attempts to work on the emotional level. To do so, I examine government online courses that have been primarily designed for the purpose of training public sector workers covered by the Prevent Duty.

Using this data, I argue that the government in its communication to public sector workers does not only convey factual instructions on how to fulfil the duty or its rational justification, but it also, and perhaps mainly, tries to pre-empt possible resistance and boost compliance by amplifying and abating emotions of the target audience related to (1) the act of referring radicalisation suspects, (2) the radicalisation suspects themselves, (3) consequences of inaction. As with any technique of governance, this attempt to shape the attitudes and behaviour of public sector workers includes some contradictions that I will describe in more detail in further sections of this chapter. They are not just contradictions of logics but also of emotions, which are brought into conflict by, among others, the appropriation of vulnerability language for counter-radicalisation – a poor fit made even more visible by recent efforts of the government to replace "vulnerability" by "susceptibility" while still containing it under the rubric of safeguarding.

(Counter)Terrorism and Emotions

The "affective turn" in the humanities and social sciences has been slow to substantially affect both mainstream and critical terrorism studies (Clément,

2021). The reluctance to engage emotions was in part caused by the legacy of a long academic struggle in this field against the earlier popular notion of the irrationality of terrorism. Mainstream terrorism scholars have re-engaged emotions as drivers of political violence following 9/11 and the invention of the radicalisation process, something made easier by widely circulated Western racialised and gendered prejudice about Muslim men and their alleged proclivity for emotionally driven action (Wright-Neville & Smith, 2009).

Of course, the word terrorism itself already evokes emotions – terror, fear, anxiety, anger, and desperation, to name some of them. But these relate to the alleged intended effect of acts described as terrorism. Unsurprisingly then, much work across the mainstream and critical terrorism studies investigates the socio-political effects of emotions resulting from political violence. In the critical stream, this includes studies on the production of terrorism knowledge (e.g., Heath-Kelly & Jarvis, 2017), use of emotions to justify and increase support for government militarised responses to terrorism (e.g., Clément et al., 2017), collective identity shaping through post-attack emotion work (e.g., Hutchison, 2010), emotional impact of counter-terrorism policies and the War on Terror on suspect populations (e.g., Ahmed, 2015; Anderson, 2010), the emotional dimension of securitisation (Eroukhmanoff, 2019), affective atmospheres of counter-terrorism (e.g., Fregonese & Laketa, 2022), and political construction and maintenance of terrorism fear (Jackson, 2013).

These and other valuable accounts of the important role that affect and emotions play in the emergence and impact of political violence usefully reveal the "multiplicity of forces that mark the relationship between the political and the corporeal, highlighting their unpredictable linkages and their mobile, volatile nature" (Laketa, 2021, p. 20). However, the extant literature has not yet addressed the way government engages in emotional governance of front-line workers to exercise power over its population through surveillance. Emotional manipulation of public sector workers to elicit compliance with counter-terrorism policy that remakes them into security agents is qualitatively different from manipulating public emotions such as fear and anger to buttress support for foreign military interventions and limiting civil liberties at home. And while framing counter-terrorism as safeguarding (with attendant affective potentialities) has become more common in government communication towards the public in recent years, public sector workers occupy a very different contextual space from a regular citizen and one can expect that the emotionalities of rule (Campbell, 2010) surrounding the Prevent Duty would, therefore, differ from methods used to responsibilise ordinary citizens to co-produce counter-terrorism (for an analysis of the responsibilisation and training of the general public for counter-terrorism, see Rodrigo Jusué, 2022).

The Prevent Duty and Its Affective Potential

Despite the lack of explicit empirical investigation of the affective dimension of the Prevent Duty, there is no shortage of studies that touch on its emotional side. Firstly, a number of scholars point out how modern counter-terrorism policies colonised the care sector and deployed its language – safeguarding, vulnerability, care – to make pre-crime interventions in individual lives "palatable" but also possible (e.g., Boukalas, 2019; Brown & Mohamed, 2022; De Goede & Simon, 2013; Heath-Kelly & Gruber, 2023). Millions of public sector workers are tasked with counter-terrorism duties which are deliberately normalised as banal safeguarding (Finch & McKendrick, 2019). At the heart of safeguarding is the vulnerable subject who needs protection and nurturing. Vulnerability can be defined as "a living at the mercy of someone else's agency" (Schoonheim et al., 2022, p. 80). Protection from potential malign agency of others exercised over vulnerable individuals is part of care, which could be also understood as the management of vulnerability (Costello, 2020). But care is not only a logic; care is underpinned by emotions. A key emotion of care is compassion (Pulcini, 2017), which in the context of vulnerability can be thought of as a sympathetic concern for the well-being of somebody who is at the mercy of the potentially malign agency of other people. And so, when we think about public sector workers, emotions such as compassion are at stake when counter-terrorism becomes framed as safeguarding.

Critical terrorism scholars also call attention to the way the traditional understanding of vulnerability, as a reduced physical or mental capacity necessitating special support and protection, mutated in the context of counter-terrorism into a label that carries at its core the notion of dangerousness and public security threat (Heath-Kelly, 2023a; Heath-Kelly & Strausz, 2019). This is because in the counter-terrorism discourse a vulnerable person came to denote an individual thought to display signs of sympathy to ideas regarded as extreme (Heath-Kelly & Strausz, 2019), which in turn is regarded as potentially leading to the engagement in or support for terrorism (i.e., radicalisation). It was pointed out how this new quality of vulnerability inadvertently combines with biases, stereotypes, and prejudices of those who are tasked with spotting signs of radicalisation, resulting in discrimination, especially of Muslims (Fernandez, 2024; Pettinger, 2020). Dangerousness and risk imply the emotions of fear and anxiety that could be aroused by vulnerable suspects in the bodies of those who are mandated to guard the public order. However, fear compromises compassion and, hence, the discharge of good care (Pulcini, 2017).

The affective potential of the Prevent Duty is also revealed in studies on the practical implementation of the duty by front-line workers, especially teachers. While some seem to endorse it as an appropriate remedy to what they perceive as a significant and widespread social problem, thus possibly feeling relieved, content, and confident, others express fear and anxiety about either the possibility of stereotyping students or the consequences of missing genuine radicalisation cases (for the radicalised child(ren), themselves and their colleagues, or the school) (Busher et al., 2019). An extra layer of emotional burden is felt by public sector workers who might be racialised by others as "Muslims" and, thus, feel as potential targets of the Prevent Duty, in addition to being responsibilised for its implementation (Fernandez, 2024). The emotional unease about the Prevent Duty is amplified by the substantial public criticism of UK counter-terrorism and counter-radicalisation policies in general and Prevent in particular (Lister, 2023). Some of the alleged Prevent Duty incidents have been highly publicised for example when a 10-year-old boy was reportedly questioned without the consent of his parents by the police for writing at school about living in a "terrorist" (rather than "terraced") house (Lundie, 2019).

It is thus apparent that the Prevent Duty is not affect-less. On the contrary, it can give rise to a multitude of emotions. It is often pointed out that "emotions do things" (Ahmed, 2004), that they affect our cognition as well as behaviour. This is not lost, at least on the intuitive level, by policy-makers. It would be, therefore, only rational to expect policy-makers to try to "render practicable" to public sector workers "how to feel" about the Prevent Duty (Campbell, 2010). The most straightforward technology that the government can use to achieve this is creating a training programme for public state workers, which I analyse in the following section.

The Emotion Work of the Prevent Duty Online Training

The usual understanding of "emotion work" follows the original coinage of the term by Hochschild who described it as synonymous to the emotion-management of the self – "the act of trying to change in degree or quality an emotion or feeling" (1979, p. 561). Hochschild does mention the possibility of emotion work being done "by the self upon others, and by others upon oneself" (1979, p. 562), but she seems to refer to situations where one sets up an "emotion-work system" to use others (e.g., friends) to reinforce one's efforts at managing one's own emotions. Hochschild also acknowledges that emotion work can include efforts to regulate the emotions of other people (2012). This has been taken up by Oliker (1989) in her description of how friends help to change emotions of individuals going through marriage crisis. When I write about emotion work of the Prevent Duty online training, I extend this approach to the government's efforts to regulate emotions of public sector workers. Following Hochschild (1979), such regulation could be achieved through providing guidance on how to interpret a certain situation – *framing rules* – and how to feel in that situation – *feeling rules*.

To uncover emotion work done by policy-makers on public sector workers covered by the Prevent Duty, I analyse below the content of three courses that make up the Prevent Duty online training: Awareness Course, Referral Course, and Channel Course.[1] The courses consist of texts interspersed with occasional exercises and short videos of 3 minutes on average (whose transcriptions accompany the clips on the training website). According to the website, the first two courses take between 30 and 40 minutes, while the third takes between 50 and 60 minutes to complete. There is also Refresher Awareness Course (20–30 minutes), which is excluded from the analysis as it is duplicitous.

Authorities covered by the Prevent Duty are required to provide training to their staff and the Prevent Duty guidance material published by the government directs the authorities in England and Wales towards the online training analysed here (HM Government, 2023). That said, the guidance does not rule out other types of training, including face-to-face trainings, which are either provided by the authorities in-house or by external parties vetted by the government. In fact, before the government published the online training in 2022, and even before Prevent became a matter of statutory obligation, public sector workers had been trained to spot and report signs of radicalisation in face-to-face Workshops to Raise Awareness of Prevent (WRAP). WRAP trainings still take place, but the trainers rely heavily on government-provided scripts and DVDs. Strausz and Heath-Kelly described how WRAP facilitators steer the audience towards using their "gut feeling" to detect vulnerability to radicalisation in their clients' emotions and feelings such as isolation, belonging, and frustration (Strausz & Heath-Kelly, 2019). These emotions are depicted as a cause of concern that gives rise to the need for protecting clients (now suspects) against potential radicalisation. What remains to be analysed, though, is the affective dimension of the training in the form of emotional work done on the audience. The emotional messages conveyed by the government through the training are at their clearest form found in the online training, which was designed, scripted, rehearsed, and edited to achieve the maximum intended effect, which is often diluted by forms of adaptation by WRAP trainers, who often find it impossible to "stick to the script" (Heath-Kelly & Strausz, 2019, p. 99).

In the following analysis, I approach the study of affect and emotions in line with those scholars who argue that the two are mutually constitutive rather than distinct categories (Stenner, 2018; Wetherell, 2013) and that discourse is "productive not only of linguistically constructed identities and meanings, but also various kinds of affective structures, conditions, and orientations" (Koschut et al., 2017, p. 499). In other words, I understand discourse as a framework that shapes what emotions can be felt, expressed, and understood as socially acceptable. In this sense, discourse is key to constructing *framing rules*, which in turn define *feeling rules*. Hence, critical discourse analysis – a method I use in the following analysis – can be usefully deployed to reveal how government discourse nested in the Prevent Duty online training strategically constructs framing rules through language (including its affective/emotional dimension) to reframe the Duty and promote certain emotional orientations over others. I group this emotion work into three interrelated and overlapping themes outlined in the introduction: (1) attenuating fear of moral and material consequences of reporting radicalisation suspects, (2) activating compassion for radicalisation suspects, and (3) increasing fear of consequences of not reporting radicalisation suspects.

Don't Worry, Refer Them!

The Prevent Duty came to force in 2015 in the context of already existing widespread criticism of and unease about the government's counter-radicalisation Prevent Strategy. Prevent appeared already in 2003 as a part of CONTEST, the government's counter-terrorism strategy, but it was fully rolled out following the 2005 London bombings. Since then, Prevent has been heavily contested in the UK public sphere, especially by academics and human rights activists who have portrayed it as unfairly targeting racialised Muslim minorities and being built on deeply illiberal logics of pre-crime interventions. Prevent was even characterised as a "cradle-to-grave police state" (Mohammed & Siddiqui, 2013). Following the introduction of the Duty, some public sector workers organised to express their opposition, especially teachers (Adams, 2016). One of the slogans of resisting academics at the time was "Educators, not informants!" (Greer, 2016).

It is this fear of becoming an informant, a security agent for the police state, that the online training heavily engages. The very first sentence of the first video of the first course is, in fact, this: "I think for me, the first thing that I would always say to a teacher is that there is nothing to be scared of. This is about safeguarding". The sentence is articulated in a friendly, empathetic voice of a female employee of the Department of Education. In this 2-minute video, there are two more female speakers. In every subsequent video of the three courses, there are either female speakers only or the ratio of female to male speakers is heavily skewed in favour of the former (e.g., 6 to 1). In general, women tend to speak when the topic is about emotions and care/safeguarding, while men are brought in when the language turns into more "serious" matters of radicalisation and terrorism expertise and policing, which follows the traditional gender stereotypes and norms around caring femininity versus masculine authority. Women provide the reassuring, caring framing to dispel fears, while men supply the legitimacy and expertise on the threat of radicalisation. These paralinguistic cues in the form of speakers' gender seem to be strategically deployed to shape the affective dimension and emotional orientations promoted towards the Prevent Duty.

Emotionalised pronouncements along the line of the opening sentence quoted above abound in the training. Public sector workers are repeatedly reminded that they "cannot get in trouble for sharing information" and "will not be judged or held responsible" for referring people to the police. They are repeatedly assured that referring people "is not about punishment" and "isn't about criminalising people". The act of referring is framed as "safeguarding", "protection", and "support" in the same way people are safeguarded, protected, and supported in case of "drug usage or exploitation". The training material implores the trainees: "Just treat it as normal safeguarding". The frequency of the deployment of the word "safeguarding" (around 80 times throughout the three courses, most of it concentrated in the first two courses) can be seen as a type of overcompensation denial that, ironically, validates the pre-existing concerns about the Prevent Duty not being just another form of safeguarding.

The training tries to assuage potential anxiety and fear of referring people also by creating the illusion that instead of public workers being responsibilised for counter-terrorism, the responsibility resides outside of them. They are told that they "do not need to be an expert" and that if they have a concern, they "don't have to hold that risk yourself, you can share that risk, share it with people. There are professionals there who know and can look into things *for you*" (emphasis added). Furthermore, the trainees are told, when deciding to make a referral, "not [to] worry at that point about things that are happening wider afield". Their action of referral is described as "signposting" individuals "to the people that can help them". The act of a referral, thus, becomes an act of a deferral. Deferral of responsibility to other people into the future, which should alleviate potential negative emotions of a referral.

One aspect of emotion work involved in the Prevent Duty was well illustrated in a video segment in the third course on Channel. Channel is a multi-agency programme putting together representatives of various public sector agencies to discuss Prevent referrals and manage interventions on those deemed at risk of radicalisation. In the video, a chair of one of the Channel Panels described her role as "making the participants relaxed enough to be able to feel able to share the information". By participants, she meant the representatives of other public agencies, especially those operating under the logic of care as opposed to the security logic of the police, which is present at the meetings too. In the video, the Channel chair assured such potentially reluctant co-producer of counter-terrorism policy that

> [t]hey can feel perfectly safe being around that table and giving their opinions. There's no reason to be nervous. I know it's Home Office Channel and that seems scary, but it's not. It's just like being requested to attend any meeting.

As in the case of the initial referral act, the participation in the more advanced stage of the counter-radicalisation process is made banal, like "any meeting". The goal is to eliminate negative emotions that might prevent the circulation of information vital to the security apparatus.

Sharing of information, including the very act of referral, is the ultimate goal of the training, since Prevent is dependent on the "willingness of the lay public and professional practitioners to escalate information to authorities". Appeals to public sector workers to report radicalisation suspects and share information are omnipresent in the training and they are parallel and complementary to the efforts to make practitioners feel better about them. Trainees are instructed to "[c]ollect as much contextual information as possible to be shared with the police" and be suspicious because "[t]here may be scenarios that look normal on the outside" but, in fact, carry security risk. The training text insists that "[a]nyone could be radicalised" regardless of "how old the individuals is". Sharing of radicalisation concerns and information about suspected individuals is described as "an intrinsic part of any frontline practitioner's job". The training repeatedly underlines that sharing concerns is a duty and a responsibility and that it should be done as early as possible.

Finally, fear and anxiety over reporting suspects are to be replaced by a positive feeling of confidence and trust in oneself and those who will handle the cases afterwards. On many occasions, the training instructs public sector workers about the "need to feel confident" and "trust their own instincts". In this way, new feeling rules are being established for the situation of detecting and reporting signs of radicalisation so that these activities are undergirded and propelled by positive emotions instead of hindered by negative ones.

Be Compassionate, Refer Them!

As mentioned earlier, UK governments have tried to frame Prevent as a form of safeguarding since the updated Prevent Strategy was released in 2011. In doing so, they have relied on the concept of vulnerability, copying thus a broader trend of deploying this concept beyond the care sector, for example, in criminal justice policies (Aliverti, 2020). However, while the incorporation of vulnerability into the work of the police was a novel thing with a potential of humanising its practices, efforts to sell counter-terrorism to care workers as protection of vulnerable people have been criticised for having the opposite effect of securitising care practices (Heath-Kelly, 2023b; Heath-Kelly & Strausz, 2019).

Public sector workers engaged in caring services had already worked with the concept of vulnerability, but one that had the traditional meaning of denoting individuals with "care and support needs" who needed to be protected against abuse and harm (Heath-Kelly & Strausz, 2019).

Practitioners were bound to these individuals through the ethics and ethos of care, which are intertwined with emotions such as compassion or even love, motivating protective, supporting, and helping behaviour. Linked to counter-terrorism, vulnerability foregrounds its risk dimension and changes its direction from the vulnerable individual to the rest of society, which is now at risk. The vulnerable individual is then necessarily contaminated with the suspicion of being a source of threat and danger, a source of terror.

And yet, the Prevent Duty online training tries to mobilise positive emotions about individuals vulnerable to radicalisation by framing referrals as helping, protecting, and supporting. These three words are used extremely frequently throughout the training with "support" in the first place, reaching almost 200 counts (it is also present in the web address of the training itself). For example, trainees can read that "Prevent is not about getting people into trouble. It's about supporting people" or that "Prevent is about helping people make better choices and staying safe".

Emotional appeals to refer people are sometimes quite direct as in a video segment depicting potentially strange behaviour of radicalising children as follows: "It may be a cry for help, they may actually want some support to get away from whatever it is that they're going down". In fact, children are brought up many times in the training (by female speakers) to evoke compassion and motivate referrals as acts of care. For example, the Vulnerability Assessment Framework, a much-criticised tool for assessing vulnerability to radicalisation, is described in the following terms: "It's the same as looking at a child that's potentially going to be involved in child sexual exploitation".

At places, the course material tackles head on the core of the criticism of the Prevent Duty – that it is an intrusive securitisation of public sectors, which operate under a completely different logic (of care) and differ fundamentally from the traditional understanding of safeguarding. The counter in the training is, "Rather than reporting a terrorist, it's reporting a vulnerable person and actually it's not so different from what we all do every day anyway". The everyday activity here refers to safeguarding, which is forcefully equated to the Prevent Duty in the following video segment:

> If I don't share [the radicalisation concern], why would I not be sharing it? Rather than thinking I shouldn't be sharing it. So, challenging yourself as a professional around that. But if you look at this through a lens of "this is a safeguarding issue" this is about supporting somebody who is at risk, I think that generally starts peeling away layers of why you shouldn't be doing something.
>
> [...]
>
> If you thought someone was at risk of domestic violence, you wouldn't go: Do I need to tell them? Do I need to tell them where they live? Should

I tell anyone? You go, "I need to protect that person". And it's exactly the same.

Apart from framing radicalisation referrals as safeguarding in order to activate positive emotions connected to the already existing professional ethics of care, the training sometimes suggests to public sector workers to use the safeguarding approach in order to collect private information related to non-criminal attitudes and behaviour for the purpose of pre-crime[2] risk assessment, which, ironically, validates the accusations levied on Prevent for being a tool of nation-wide surveillance policing people's mind:

> I think what's key to actually emphasise when you do make the approach to those individuals that are being referred in, is that you give the emphasis around safeguarding, protection and support. [...] We're here to help you [...] There's no point going in and being like "we don't like what you're doing on the internet" or "we don't like who you're associating with" because people are just going to clam up. Because I would. If someone came up to me and said, "I don't like what you're doing", I'd be like who the hell are you to tell me? [...] so it's got to be couched in exactly the right language.

Prevent a Catastrophe, Refer Them!

The third and final theme through which the Prevent Duty online training works on emotions of public sector workers concerns the evocation of fearful consequences should they not refer radicalisation suspects. This theme is inherently lodged in the name of the counter-radicalisation strategy itself and the corresponding duty – Prevent. To prevent means to stop something from materialising; in the case of the Prevent Duty, it means preventing people from becoming terrorists or supporting terrorism. The term terrorism is loaded with negative emotions and visions of tragedy, suffering, and destruction. Evoking such dark emotions and visions makes any acts designed to prevent them good and noble.

However, too much fear can lead to paralysis and too much talk about security can lead to public sector workers feeling securitised. This is likely why the training material uses such catastrophic security language economically and constantly assures trainees that security matters will be taken care of by experts further up the chain.

In the training, the evocation of negative consequences is achieved by the mere deployment of the words *terrorism*, *extremism*, and *radicalisation* and reminders of what they stand for – "a threat to people". The risk of terrorism needs to be reduced "so people can go about their daily lives freely". Trainees are also reminded that the threat of terrorism today does not lie with old-fashioned terrorist organisations but "is dominated by individuals and small groups acting outside" of them. Anyone could be radicalised, anyone could be a terrorist. A metaphor of an iceberg is employed in the training, where the tip of the iceberg above surface is the visible terrorist attack, but the vast body below in "dark waters" consists of "hidden activity that builds and builds". The importance of Prevent, according to the training, is that it "sits down at the bottom of the iceberg, away from terrorist-related criminal activity".

Hence, if public sector workers tasked with the Prevent Duty do not comply, physical violence might erupt: "Sadly, there are instances where concerns haven't been shared […] and as the risk progresses up the iceberg, the results of such inactivity can be unthinkable". Again, the emotional figure of a child is used to evoke fear of noncompliance: "[In the cases of] children that have come to harm, the biggest single issue that is repeated again and again, is the failure of agencies to share information".

There are clear overlaps with the other two themes. In almost hydraulic fashion, raising fear of consequences of not referring diminishes fear of referring:

> Perhaps you'd worry that you're overreacting. That you don't have the level of understanding or knowledge needed to raise a concern. Or that you'd be threatened, wasting people's time, or be accused of racism. Or that you'd start a criminal investigation against the very person you're concerned about. Time to remember the iceberg that represents terrorism.

The powerful iceberg metaphor is frequently used in Prevent trainings, because it "recontextualises everyday experiences of vulnerability by positioning them in a causal chain that necessarily leads to violence" (Strausz & Heath-Kelly, 2019, p. 167). Therefore, it has the potential to change how public sector workers see vulnerabilities in other people, inserting negative feeling of dread associated with violence represented by the tip of the iceberg alongside pre-existing feeling of compassion. But how to square these two seemingly contradictory feelings?

The tension created by raising fear of consequences of not referring, done through the insertion of negative feelings linked to violence at the top of the iceberg, is resolved by reframing the referral as an act of compassion, which enhances the well-being of the vulnerable person. "[I]t's about supporting people, stopping something happening before they can get into difficulties". Referring people means giving them the chance to receive support that would turn them "in a different direction to the way that it might have progressed if you hadn't intervened". In the embodiment of the dual nature of the new meaning of vulnerable subjects – those that are simultaneously at risk and risky – direct appeals to public sector workers to comply with the Prevent

Duty combine the spectre of terrorism risk with the notion of protecting and helping the individual at risk of radicalisation: "You can make a huge difference in safeguarding those who may be radicalised, turning them away from terrorism, so they can't be exploited by others, and helping them to achieve a positive outcome".

Ironically, while working on emotions of trainees, the training material explicitly addresses the topic of emotions, but only insofar as the assertion that "the process of radicalisation feeds on emotions". According to the material, these emotions include anger, frustration, and confusion, which is important to recognise, because care practitioners can work on them in order to prevent catastrophic consequences: "You can stop them from feeling such a huge sense of frustration or injustice that they entertain the idea of causing harm to themselves or others".

Another recognition of the role of emotions comes in the form of a warning about the success of nebulous radicalisers unless emotional labour by public sector workers is exerted in the battle for hearts:

> The radicalisers are normally very successful because they provide that emotional support that a person sometimes misses in life. So anybody like teachers, parents, friends can also have a counteracting pull by having the same kind of regard for the person's emotional needs.

This quote reveals the degree of power the Prevent Duty training credits emotions with when it comes to driving catastrophic scenarios and preventing them from happening. Simultaneously, deflecting the blame for a potential future violence to "radicalisers" serves to strengthen the second theme of referring out of compassion for vulnerable individuals. Yet, this shift of blame cannot fully erase the dangerousness of public sector workers' clients created by the training's "pedagogy of suspicion" (Strausz & Heath-Kelly, 2019), leading to tensions and contradictions described in the next section.

Contradictions

As other governmentality projects, the Prevent Duty is afflicted by contradictions. At the heart of these contradictions are two issues. First, vague definitions of radicalisation and extremism situating them in the pre-crime space. Second, the dual at risk/risky nature of the newly invented vulnerable subjects. The resulting tensions seep into the emotion work that the Prevent Duty does on public sector workers.

Vague, pre-crime definitions of radicalisation and extremism make it difficult for the Prevent Duty training to dispel fear of referring people. On one hand, as demonstrated in the analysis, the training tries to assuage public sector workers by suggesting that the Prevent Duty is like any other safeguarding, that it does not require specialist knowledge (which is transferred to "professionals" up the chain), and that it is completely sufficient to follow one's instinct:

> You do not need to be an expert [...] the important thing is that you feel comfortable to speak up any time you feel concerned.
> It's not about an assessment. We are not expecting our housing officers, our youth workers, our social workers to assess this. What we are asking them to do, is if you see something where you have an instinct that it's not quite right. It's like any other safeguarding agenda.
> The behaviours we might expect from a person being radicalised are not as unpredictable or unrecognisable as we might have imagined.
> There are professionals there who know and can look into things for you.

On the other hand, the training material tacitly admits, by implication, that radicalisation and extremism are not as straightforward safeguarding issues as, for example, drug use or sexual abuse:

> [...] a blurring of ideologies with personal narratives makes it harder to assess the risk that people may pose.
> It's important to take social, cultural, regional and historical considerations into account to discover alternative justifications [of signs that could mean radicalisation].
> It's important that you feel confident in your knowledge and understanding of radicalisation so you can spot the signs and know what to do.

In turn, the dual nature of radicalisation vulnerability makes it difficult to motivate referrals based on compassion for the radicalisation "victim". The traditional understanding of vulnerability, which evokes compassion and produces safeguarding needs, is one of a defenceless person open to exploitation by others. The main if not the only danger is that which threatens the vulnerable person. But in the context of counter-radicalisation, a vulnerable person is "already conceptualised as dangerous" (Boukalas, 2019, p. 477) to others and becomes vulnerable merely by the fact that they sympathise with whatever is thought to be a political extreme (Heath-Kelly & Strausz, 2019). It is a person potentially capable of supporting or causing deliberate mayhem and destruction, thus possessing strong agency unlike a vulnerable person in the classic sense. Therefore, trying to motivate public sector workers to refer radicalisation suspects out of compassion and desire to help would only be effective if radicalisation worked in the same way as exploitation, dragging defenceless, agency-lacking individuals into danger to themselves. This, however, does not reflect the reality.

The Prevent Duty training recognises this tension, but it is unable to solve it without resigning on the notion that Prevent Duty is just another safeguarding. According to the training website, the material was first published online on September 1, 2022, but the "wording" was updated on July 25, 2023, following the *Independent Review of Prevent*. This means that the training videos are original, while the textual material around them was updated. As a result, the language in the videos is one of "vulnerability to radicalisation", while the textual information uses the language of "susceptibility to radicalisation". There is also a short dedicated (textual) section of the training that discusses the difference between vulnerability and susceptibility, making it clear that:

> Not all people susceptible to radicalisation will be a vulnerable person. A person can be vulnerable if they need special care, support or protection because of age, disability, risk of abuse or neglect. There are other circumstances, needs, or other underlying factors that may make a person susceptible to radicalisation that do not constitute a vulnerability.

Such a distinction means a substantial change in how vulnerability used to be understood in Prevent and a return to more traditional definition of the concept. It reflects the criticism of the use of the term by William Shawcross, the author of the *Independent Review of Prevent* (2023, pp. 41–42):

> [...] the term "vulnerable" should be reserved for those who, because of circumstances beyond their control, are at particular risk of falling prey to exploitation or abuse. That is not the case for most of those likely to be radicalised.
> [...] the characterisation of Prevent work as wholly focused on supporting vulnerable individuals fails to adequately identify the majority of individuals who become terrorists or support terrorist activity.
> Presenting Prevent as a largely safeguarding initiative may cause confusion, for practitioners and frontline professionals alike, about what it is that the scheme is seeking to do.

The update of the Prevent Duty training apparently addressed this criticism by replacing the word vulnerability by susceptibility in the textual material and adding the short clarification described above. However, not only were the videos left as they were, but the newly added section that clarifies the difference between vulnerability and susceptibility ends with the following statement: "Every person who is susceptible to radicalisation will receive the same level of support regardless of whether there are vulnerabilities present". What it says, in effect, is that regardless of the new vocabulary, the Prevent Duty should still be perceived as safeguarding and provision of support. Moreover, both terms still imply passivity, lack of agency, and individual mental weakness, and, hence, work towards depoliticisation of Prevent, which could be seen "as part of a wider system aimed at manufacturing consent" (Skoczylis & Andrews, 2020, p. 362). Susceptibility is the new vulnerability.

Conclusion

In this chapter, I analysed how the UK government attempts to work on emotions of public sector workers in order to increase their compliance with the Prevent Duty, which tasks them with detecting and reporting radicalisation suspects. I argued that the government tries to establish new *feeling rules* that would guide emotions of public sector workers in situations when they come across radicalisation concerns, so that these emotions motivate and facilitate referrals to the police.

The Prevent Duty online training could then be considered as a technique of the state's *emotionalities of rule*, defined as "discursive and material forms which propose and suppose particular ways of feeling about the world" (Campbell, 2010, p. 39). In such perspective, emotions are harnessed and managed as part of the state's exercise of power under the understanding that citizens are not just rational but also, and, perhaps, mainly, "neurotic" subjects (Isin, 2004). Through the Prevent online training, the state simultaneously incites (in)security-related neurosis among public sector workers and regulates this neurosis to govern public security.

The degree of instrumentality on the side of the state as well as the embodied effects the training has on its target audience lie outside the scope of the chapter and would be a fruitful focus of further studies. What is important, though, is that this effort carries deep emotional contradictions, which stem from the attempt to merge two fundamentally incompatible logics governing the care and security sectors. The former is underpinned by the emotion of compassion with the target subject while the latter by fear of the target subject. By positioning Prevent, a security policy, within the safeguarding/care paradigm, in order to increase public sector workers' compliance with the policy, the state inevitably introduces negative emotions that stick to public sector workers' clients such as students and patients. Moreover, by simultaneously insisting on the everyday simplicity of "radicalisation" and "extremism" knowledge and their complex "social, cultural, regional and historical" context, the state adds another level of conflicting emotions of self-confidence in and fear of making a good/wrong referral.

The importance of the affective/emotional dimension in the governance of public security exemplified in this chapter also makes a case for exploring the emotionalities of rule in other policy domains of contemporary societies because the trend of responsibilisation that ideologically facilitates the Prevent Duty extends beyond (and precedes) the prevention of extremism into many other public policies (O'Malley, 2012; Rose, 1999).

Acknowledgement

The work on this chapter was made possible thanks to my role in the project "Neoliberal Terror: The Radicalisation of Social Policy in Europe" funded by the ERC Starting Grant 851022 (2020–2025). I would like to thank Professor Ana Aliverti and Professor Henrique Carvalho (both from the University of Warwick) for their inspiring comments on an earlier draft of the chapter.

Notes

1 The training is publicly accessible through the following website, which also states that members of public may take it if they want to learn how to identify "behaviours that cause concern": www.support-people-susceptible-to-radicalisation.service.gov.uk/
2 For a discussion of the concept of "pre-crime", see Zedner (2017).

References

Adams, R. (2016, March 28). Teachers back motion calling for Prevent strategy to be scrapped. *The Guardian.* www.theguardian.com/politics/2016/mar/28/teachers-nut-back-motion-calling-prevent-strategy-radicalisation-scrapped

Ahmed, S. (2004). Affective economies. *Social Text, 22*(2), 117–139. https://doi.org/10.1215/01642472-22-2_79-117

Ahmed, S. (2015). The 'emotionalization of the "war on terror"': Counter-terrorism, fear, risk, insecurity and helplessness. *Criminology & Criminal Justice, 15*(5), 545–560. https://doi.org/10.1177/1748895815572161

Aliverti, A. (2015). Enlisting the public in the policing of immigration. *British Journal of Criminology, 55*(2), 215–230. https://doi.org/10.1093/bjc/azu102

Aliverti, A. (2020). Benevolent policing? Vulnerability and the moral pains of border controls. *The British Journal of Criminology, 60*(5), 1117–1135. https://doi.org/10.1093/bjc/azaa026

Anderson, B. (2010). Morale and the affective geographies of the 'war on terror.' *Cultural Geographies, 17*(2), 219–236. https://doi.org/10.1177/1474474010363849

Boukalas, C. (2019). The Prevent paradox: Destroying liberalism in order to protect it. *Crime, Law and Social Change, 72*(4), 467–482. https://doi.org/10.1007/s10611-019-09827-8

Brown, K. E., & Mohamed, F. N. (2022). Logics of care and control: Governing European "returnees" from Iraq and Syria. *Critical Studies on Terrorism, 15*(3), 632–658. https://doi.org/10.1080/17539153.2021.2016092

Busher, J., Choudhury, T., & Thomas, P. (2019). The enactment of the counter-terrorism "Prevent duty" in British schools and colleges: Beyond reluctant accommodation or straightforward policy acceptance. *Critical Studies on Terrorism*, 12(3), 440–462. https://doi.org/10.1080/17539153.2019.1568853

Campbell, E. (2010). The emotional life of governmental power. *Foucault Studies*, 35–53. https://doi.org/10.22439/fs.v0i9.3057

Clément, M. (2021). Emotions and affect in terrorism research: Epistemological shift and ways ahead. *Critical Studies on Terrorism*, 14(2), 247–270. https://doi.org/10.1080/17539153.2021.1902611

Clément, M., Lindemann, T., & Sangar, E. (2017). The "Hero-Protector Narrative": Manufacturing emotional consent for the use of force. *Political Psychology*, 38(6), 991–1008. https://doi.org/10.1111/pops.12385

Clore, G. L. (2011). Psychology and the rationality of emotion. *Modern Theology*, 27(2), 325–338. https://doi.org/10.1111/j.1468-0025.2010.01679.x

Costello, G. (2020). On care and vulnerability. *Solitude Journal*, 1. www.akademie-solitude.de/wp-content/uploads/costello_solitude.pdf

Counter-Terrorism and Security Act. (2015). § c. 6, part 5. www.legislation.gov.uk/ukpga/2015/6/part/5

De Goede, M., & Simon, S. (2013). Governing future radicals in Europe. *Antipode*, 45(2), 315–335. https://doi.org/10.1111/j.1467-8330.2012.01039.x

Dresser, P. (2019). "Trust your instincts – act!" PREVENT police officers' perspectives of counter-radicalisation reporting thresholds. *Critical Studies on Terrorism*, 12(4), 605–628. https://doi.org/10.1080/17539153.2019.1595344

Edwards, P. (2021). Surveillance, safeguarding and beyond: The prevent duty and resilient citizenship. *Critical Studies on Terrorism*, 14(1), 47–66. https://doi.org/10.1080/17539153.2020.1855018

Eroukhmanoff, C. (2019). *The securitisation of Islam: Covert racism and affect in the United States post-9/11*. Manchester University Press. https://doi.org/10.7765/9781526128959

Faure-Walker, R. (2019). Teachers as informants: Countering extremism and promoting violence. *Journal of Beliefs & Values*, 40(3), 368–380. https://doi.org/10.1080/13617672.2019.1600321

Fernandez, S. (2024). When counter-extremism 'sticks': The circulation of the Prevent Duty in the school space. *Identities*, 1–19. https://doi.org/10.1080/1070289X.2024.2318092

Finch, J., & McKendrick, D. (2019). Securitising social work: Counter terrorism, extremism, and radicalisation. In S. A. Webb (Ed.), *The Routledge handbook of critical social work* (pp. 244–255). Routledge Taylor & Francis Group.

Fregonese, S., & Laketa, S. (2022). Urban atmospheres of terror. *Political Geography*, 96, 102569. https://doi.org/10.1016/j.polgeo.2021.102569

Greer, S. (2016, May 23). *Universities and counter-terrorism in the UK: 'Educators Not Informants!', 'Boycott Prevent!'?* https://legalresearch.blogs.bris.ac.uk/2016/05/universities-and-counter-terrorism-in-the-uk-educators-not-informants-boycott-prevent/

Heath-Kelly, C. (2023a). An introduction to vulnerability: Merging social policy with the national security state. In C. Heath-Kelly & B. Gruber (Eds.), *Vulnerability: Governing the social through security politics* (pp. 1–18). Manchester University Press.

Heath-Kelly, C. (2023b). Counterterrorism and psychiatry: Re-bordering vulnerability and securitisation in UK public protection. In C. Heath-Kelly & B. Gruber (Eds.), *Vulnerability: Governing the social through security politics* (pp. 98–118). Manchester University Press.

Heath-Kelly, C., & Gruber, B. (Eds.). (2023). *Vulnerability: Governing the social through security politics*. Manchester University Press.

Heath-Kelly, C., & Jarvis, L. (2017). Affecting terrorism: Laughter, lamentation, and detestation as drives to terrorism knowledge. *International Political Sociology*, 11(3), 239–256. https://doi.org/10.1093/ips/olx007

Heath-Kelly, C., & Strausz, E. (2019). The banality of counterterrorism "after, after 9/11"? Perspectives on the Prevent duty from the UK health care sector. *Critical Studies on Terrorism*, 12(1), 89–109. https://doi.org/10.1080/17539153.2018.1494123

HM Government. (2011). *Prevent strategy*.

HM Government. (2023). *Prevent duty guidance: Guidance for specified authorities in England and Wales*. https://assets.publishing.service.gov.uk/media/65e5a5bd3f69457ff1035fe2/14.258_HO_Prevent+Duty+Guidance_v5d_Final_Web_1_.pdf

Hochschild, A. R. (1979). Emotion work, feeling rules, and social structure. *American Journal of Sociology*, 85(3), 551–575.

Hochschild, A. R. (2012). *The managed heart: Commercialization of human feeling* (Updated ed.). University of California Press.

Hutchison, E. (2010). Trauma and the politics of emotions: Constituting identity, security and community after the Bali bombing. *International Relations*, 24(1), 65–86. https://doi.org/10.1177/0047117809348712

Isin, E. F. (2004). The neurotic citizen. *Citizenship Studies*, 8(3), 217–235. https://doi.org/10.1080/1362102042000256970

Jackson, R. (2013). The politics of terrorism fears. In S. J. Sinclair & D. Antonius (Eds.), *The political psychology of terrorism fears* (pp. 267–282). Oxford University Press. https://doi.org/10.1093/acprof:oso/9780199925926.003.0015

Koschut, S., Hall, T. H., Wolf, R., Solomon, T., Hutchison, E., & Bleiker, R. (2017). Discourse and emotions in international relations. *International Studies Review*, 19(3), 481–508. https://doi.org/10.1093/isr/vix033

Laketa, S. (2021). (Counter)terrorism and the intimate: Bodies, affect, power. *Conflict and Society*, 7(1), 9–25. https://doi.org/10.3167/arcs.2021.070102

Lerner, J. S., Li, Y., Valdesolo, P., & Kassam, K. S. (2015). Emotion and decision making. *Annual Review of Psychology*, 66(1), 799–823. https://doi.org/10.1146/annurev-psych-010213-115043

Lister, M. (2023). *Public opinion and counter-terrorism: Security and politics in the UK* (1st ed.). Routledge. https://doi.org/10.4324/9781003244585

Lundie, D. C. (2019). Building a terrorist house on sand: A critical incident analysis of interprofessionality and the Prevent duty in schools in England. *Journal of Beliefs & Values*, 40(3), 321–337. https://doi.org/10.1080/13617672.2019.1600283

Mohammed, J., & Siddiqui, A. (2013). *The Prevent Strategy: A cradle to grave police-state*. Cage. https://assets-global.website-files.com/6364ebb4927fbc4330221d8f/65ca2996adae60898fc49386_ZCb3Wk8XWj0xwS6Yd41JdFpE36sQUxvscvUGosv3o4E.pdf

Oliker, S. J. (1989). *Best friends and marriage: Exchange among women*. University of California Press.

O'Malley, P. (2012). *Risk, uncertainty and government*. Routledge-Cavendish.

Pettinger, T. (2020). CTS and normativity: The essentials of preemptive counter-terrorism interventions. *Critical Studies on Terrorism, 13*(1), 118–141. https://doi.org/10.1080/17539153.2019.1658412

Petty, R. E., & Briñol, P. (2015). Emotion and persuasion: Cognitive and meta-cognitive processes impact attitudes. *Cognition and Emotion, 29*(1), 1–26. https://doi.org/10.1080/02699931.2014.967183

Pulcini, E. (2017). What emotions motivate care? *Emotion Review, 9*(1), 64–71. https://doi.org/10.1177/1754073915615429

Rodrigo Jusué, I. (2022). Counter-terrorism training "at your kitchen table": The promotion of "CT citizens" and the securitisation of everyday life in the UK. *Critical Studies on Terrorism, 15*(2), 290–310. https://doi.org/10.1080/17539153.2021.2013014

Rose, N. S. (1999). *Powers of freedom: Reframing political thought*. Cambridge University Press.

Schoonheim, L., Vervoort, T., & Ferrarese, E. (2022). The politics of vulnerability and care: An interview with Estelle Ferrarese. *Krisis|Journal for Contemporary Philosophy, 42*(1), 77–92. https://doi.org/10.21827/krisis.42.1.38697

Shawcross, W. (2023). *Independent Review of Prevent*. Dandy Booksellers Ltd.

Skoczylis, J., & Andrews, S. (2020). A conceptual critique of Prevent: Can prevent be saved? No, but .... *Critical Social Policy, 40*(3), 350–369. https://doi.org/10.1177/0261018319840145

Stenner, P. (2018). Bridging the affect/emotion divide: A critical overview of the affective turn. In L. Zhang & C. Clark (Eds.), *Affect, emotion, and rhetorical persuasion in mass communication* (1st ed., pp. 34–56). Routledge. https://doi.org/10.4324/9781351242370

Strausz, E., & Heath-Kelly, C. (2019). Seeing radicalisation? The pedagogy of the Prevent strategy. In J. Edkins (Ed.), *Routledge handbook of critical international relations* (pp. 161–176). Routledge.

Wetherell, M. (2013). Affect and discourse – What's the problem? From affect as excess to affective/discursive practice. *Subjectivity, 6*(4), 349–368. https://doi.org/10.1057/sub.2013.13

Wright-Neville, D., & Smith, D. (2009). Political rage: Terrorism and the politics of emotion. *Global Change, Peace & Security, 21*(1), 85–98. https://doi.org/10.1080/14781150802659390

Zedner, L. (2007). Pre-crime and post-criminology? *Theoretical Criminology, 11*(2), 261–281. https://doi.org/10.1177/1362480607075851

5
DISGUST AND PUNISHMENT IN IMMIGRATION DETENTION

Alethia Fernández de la Reguera

Terrence DesPres, a Holocaust scholar, recounts that in Nazi camps, dirt and excrement were permanent conditions of existence and that subjection to filth was a daily element of a survivor's ordeal (DesPres, 1976, p. 53). In May 2022, I visited Auschwitz-Birkenau. I walked through the camp twice, the first time accompanied by the guide and a group who joined the tour in Spanish and the second time in silence, accompanied only by my thoughts and memories from earlier fieldwork with detained migrants in Mexico. After conducting an institutional ethnography for three years in *Estacion Migratoria Siglo XXI* (EMSXXI) [XXIst Century Migration Station], I found some elements of resemblance between these two historically and geographically faraway places. How my memory related one space to another was a painful and terrifying experience. After this experience, it was even clearer to me that punishment through filth, cruelty and dehumanisation is at the heart of Mexican immigration policy.

In 2023, I interviewed a colleague from an NGO in Chiapas (on the southern border of Mexico) that provides psycho-legal support and assistance to detained people on the move in EMSXXI. He told me the following:

> In 2022, we were contacted by the Honduran Consulate to ask for help. They reported that a young man from Honduras needed assistance as he was detained at *Estación Migratoria Siglo XXI* and had "a problem". Apparently, he was being sexually harassed by a private security guard. We immediately went inside the detention centre to look for this person. Before the agents from the *Instituto Nacional de Migración* (INM) [National Institute of Migration] gave us access, they somehow knew why we were going, so they shared with us their perspective of what was going on with this young man. Later that day, we had the opportunity to speak

DOI: 10.4324/9781032617060-8

to him, and he confirmed that he was experiencing sexual harassment from a private security guard and that the authorities were doing nothing about it. He also asked us to provide him access to a doctor, psychologist, or psychiatrist. We notified the INM agent about this situation; we told him how we saw the young man and the need for urgent attention to his physical and mental health. They told us they would help him, but they did not. Two days later, when we returned, they informed us that we could not see him because he was experiencing an extreme mental health crisis, and that earlier that day, whilst in the kitchen and dining area, he had defecated and eaten his faeces in front of his peers and INM officials. How could that happen? We had previously notified the authorities from the INM of the seriousness of the case. Unfortunately, we could no longer talk to him. We contacted the *Comisión Nacional de Derechos Humanos* (CNDH) [National Commission of Human Rights] to ask to assist him urgently. We also spoke to the director of the immigration detention centre to ask for immediate support through a health institution. He told us they had no contacts and could not refer him to any public health institution. So, we told the authorities to allow us to take care of him; we asked for a humanitarian visitor's card to get him outside the detention centre and take him to a hospital. We told them we would ask for support from an organisation that could provide care. Whilst waiting for INM to provide him with the humanitarian visitor's card, the CNDH advised that they had released him. We tried to find him, but we never saw him again.

This case is one of the most dehumanising I have identified in this place. It is not an exceptional case, as NGOs have reported instances of cruel treatment that even end with the loss of the lives of migrants (Del Río & Kerwin, 2024). However, in addition to outrage, it seems very relevant to analyse what happened as it demonstrates how a person's life and safety are put at risk by being detained by the state. It also shows how the authorities do not comply with the protocols established in the Migration Law to guarantee access to health services and dignified and safe conditions in immigration detention centres.[1] Moreover, it suggests the risks of privatising security services in these places,[2] as responsibilities for guaranteeing detainees' human rights are diluted and fragmented. Furthermore, in the case above, the authorities knew about the seriousness of the situation, and the solution was to leave this person free in the city of Tapachula, exposed to many risks due to his vulnerability and mental health condition. How can we analyse this case? Why did the authorities fail to prevent and protect him against sexual abuse? Was negligence and abandonment a punishment for having spoken to the NGO colleagues? Was it also a preventive punishment for the other people in the dining room?

Through my ethnographic research of immigration officers' subjectivities in immigration detention centres, I have acknowledged the relationship between emotions and punishing practices (Fernández de la Reguera, 2024). I have studied punishment as a key institutionalised practice in immigration detention centres that in one hand channels emotions of immigration agents derived from anxieties and frustrations, and on the other hand promotes a sense of institutional belonging and the illusion of order and control. My research runs in parallel with other studies demonstrating that emotions are fundamental to analysing punishment in these places and settings (Aliverti, 2021; Bosworth, 2014; Griffiths, 2023; Hall, 2012).

In this chapter I reflect on the relationship between disgust and punishment. What is the institutional function of disgust? How does disgust relate to the implicit and explicit forms of punishment of immigration detention? Is disgust a factor affecting decisions on immigration regularisation procedures and access to international protection? Over the past eight years, I have learned to observe and reflect on disgust as an emotion that is ever-present in our daily interactions and even more so in punitive and prison settings. Disgust is an emotion anticipated by an anti-migrant discourse[3] and institutionally generated through the material conditions of detention centres. The institution creates unsanitary conditions to dehumanise migrants but also goes to extreme cases of human rights violations, punishment, torture and crimes associated with unsanitary conditions.

Between 2017 and 2020, I conducted 14 semi-structured interviews with immigration agents of the *Instituto Nacional de Migración* (INM) and more than 30 interviews with people in immigration detention, mainly in Tapachula, Chiapas. The focus of the research was to understand the impact of the subjectivities of immigration agents on the implementation of immigration policy and the power relations within an immigration detention centre. Moreover, between July and September 2023, as part of my research on the effects of the militarisation of borders, I conducted ten in-depth interviews (in person and virtually) with civil society organisations that provide psycho-legal services to detained people on the move in southern, central and northern Mexico. Together with the organisation *Fundacion para la Justicia y el Estado Democratico de Derecho A.C.* [Foundation for Justice and the Democratic Rule of Law], I contacted organisations that have documented and supported or legally represented cases of human rights violations of migrants involving the Armed Forces, especially the *Guardia Nacional* [National Guard]. In this chapter, I analyse some of the testimonies of detained migrants, former INM agents, cleaning staff at EMSXXI, and NGO staff who constantly access immigration detention centres nationwide.

In my previous research, I identified the centrality of disgust in generating social boundaries between INM staff working in immigration detention centres and people on the move and also as part of an institutional dehumanising practice (Fernández de la Reguera, 2020, 2022). In this chapter, I delve deeper into the relationship between disgust and punishment. On the one hand, through the narratives of criminalised and detained migrants, I identify the experience of unsanitary conditions as a form of institutional punishment. On the other hand, I analyse disgust as a punitive emotion (Dubreuil, 2010) promoted within institutional practices, which inhibits immigration officers' empathy and generates distancing, facilitating prolonged punishment and impacting decision-making (Hofmann et al., 2018). I argue that daily punishment relies on subjugation to filth, making people experience continuously increasing abhorrent living conditions. Moreover, the perception of migrants as disgusting inspires authorities' non-compliance with regulations, including international protection, for example by slowing down or denying access to a humanitarian visa such as the case I described in the introduction.

The chapter has five sections. In the first section, I present some theoretical and conceptual elements for understanding disgust as a physical, political and moral emotion; in other words, as part of an institutional culture in immigration detention centres, and some key ideas to understand punishment through an emotional perspective. The second section discusses how we can learn to categorise the objects and subjects of disgust. Later, I present an ethnographic account of how I began to observe unhealthy practices in EMSXXI, followed by the narratives showing how disgust facilitates punishment and is experienced as a punishment. Finally, I present some cases that demonstrate that disgust can become a criterion and justification for authorities to not comply with regulations and legal obligations, exposing people to unjustified deportations and denying them international protection.

The culture of punishment and disgust in immigration detention

The sociology of emotions has become a vibrant field to analyse immigration policies, particularly institutionally based interactions between State actors and people on the move (Ariza, 2024). Emotions are part of daily interactions and decisions taken within socially, culturally and institutionally implicit and explicit rules. According to Sara Ahmed's theory of affective economies, "[...] emotions are not 'in' either the individual or the social, but produce the very surfaces and boundaries that allow the individual and the social to be delineated as if they are objects"(Ahmed, 2014, p. 10). Through social interactions, we continually and fluidly create and exchange our emotions.

As emotions create tensions, connections and attachments in institutional settings, they allow us to understand power relations between different actors. Approaching subjectivities to understand power relations in a detention centre led me to analyse emotions not only as expressions of subjectivities but as a result of the institutional contexts where interactions occur (Aliverti, 2021).

Therefore, even though emotions are subjectively embodied, their circulation often results from both tacit and codified institutional rules, such as providing a bucket instead of a toilet. In immigration detention centres, emotions have an institutional function related to the centrality of punishment as a daily practice, which provides a sense of belonging and allows distancing from incarcerated migrants (Fernández de la Reguera, 2024).

Even though disgust has only been a proper subject of research for the past three decades (Chapman & Anderson, 2012), there is a vast literature mainly from psychology, but lately from other fields such as philosophy, sociology, anthropology and law. It is a fascinating emotion since it is considered a primary, moral and very bodily (physical) emotion which acts as "a psychic need to avoid reminders of our animal origins" (Miller, 1997, p. 6). It is an emotion of proximity and survival but also a political emotion that acts as a bodily and moral boundary (Miller, 2018).

Ahmed explores the relationship between disgust and offensiveness and explains that the latter is an affective response to being disgusted by an object or the proximity of the object. "Disgust is about an object, such that one's feelings of sickness become attributed to the object" (Ahmed, 2014, 85). Therefore, a person feels disgusted by the presence or the idea of closeness to something or someone she rejects. Through disgust we establish boundaries and reject objects and persons that we believe might pollute us, cause harm or remind us of our vulnerability to animality and mortality (Nussbaum, 2004).

As a visceral emotion, disgust is usually considered a survival instinct; however, it is closely linked to socialisation. Interestingly, it is an emotion of dual nature. Disgust is ambivalent as we feel repulsion or rejection as we are attracted to the object (Ahmed, 2014; Joensuu, 2020). We reject what is unknown and strange to us, but usually there is a simultaneous desire for the abject.

The philosopher Julia Kristeva (2024) explains the dual relationship with the abject:

> Loathing an item of food, a piece of filth, waste or dung. The spasms and vomiting that protect me. The repugnance, the retching that thrusts me to the side and turns me away from defilement, sewage and muck. The shame of compromise, of being in the middle of treachery. The fascinated start that leads me toward and separates me from them.
>
> *(p. 2)*

One of the critical aspects of this definition is the incorporation of a contaminant. As Martha Nussbaum (2004) explains, the danger of pollution – by incorporation into the self – with its anticipated consequences is one crucial element to analyse disgust, not only as rejection but as offensiveness of a real or imaginary disgusting object. My analysis of disgust as punishment in immigration detention is mainly based on hygiene disgust experimented by both migrants and officers and the moral disgust implicit in daily treatment from authorities towards migrants (Chapman & Anderson, 2012). Both types of disgust are reinforced by a public discourse that frames migrants as a threat to national security and health. The very precarious material conditions I have documented in immigration detention centres include limited access to drinking water, broken and a lack of toilets, rotten food, dirty mats and pests. Within these contexts, daily interactions between INM agents and people on the move are mediated by ideas of particular kinds of danger, pollution or contamination through proximity.

Punishment fulfils an essential function in societies, as it orders and establishes social hierarchies. The social and cultural understanding of punishment must integrate an emotional and transdisciplinary perspective (Carvalho & Chamberlen, 2024). At the subjective and social level, it functions in a complex manner. While punishment is a consequence of a condemnatory response to specific behaviours (Canton, 2022), it also generates some satisfaction in the person who punishes. "This complex interplay between hostility and satisfaction suggests that the emotionality of punishment influences our self-perceptions and, though focusing on punishing others, it also seeks to make us feel better about ourselves" (Carvalho & Chamberlen, 2024, p. 35).

Taking as a basis one of the classic definitions of punishment established by Antony Flew (1954), Rob Canton critically analyses current forms of punishment in societies (2022). According to Flew's definition, punishment implies that the authority imposes pain on an offender for an act considered offensive. However, it is necessary to critique how an offence is defined, the type of punishment applied and the actor who punishes it. Irregular migrants in Mexico are punished with detention, which has become one of the most essential deterrence policies in the last decade. The degradation and cruelty experienced by migrants in detention expose a retributive punishment inconsistent with a legal framework that protects the rights of migrants and considers irregular entry into Mexico as an administrative offence. Moreover, shaming punishment incentivised by disgust makes it easier to prolong the punishment in detention (Canton, 2022).

My research explores disgust as a complex institutional practice related to punishment with effects on both immigration agents and migrants. On the one hand, staff feel disgusted by migrants. Unhealthy conditions of the areas occupied by detained migrants and the provision of rotten food create social boundaries, and migrants are often seen as morally and physically disgusting. On the other hand, through these common practices, imprisoned migrants report feeling disgust and discomfort, as well as getting sick in this place.

Learning to feel disgust

Eleonora Joensuu asks: What do we learn and teach through disgust? She analyses the relationship between disgust and epistemology, as she explains that disgust is a way of giving meaning to the rejected otherness and causing harm (2020, p. 6). Moreover, what is often considered disgusting and threatening results from previous experiences before the actual proximity to the object (Miller, 1997). Since early childhood, we learn to classify objects as disgusting, so we can feel disgusted by having direct contact or potential contact with that object or person, but also with an object or person which has been in contact with an object previously identified as disgusting (Miller, 2018). For example, people who have been in contact with faeces, blood or vomit. In the case of incarcerated migrants, as they are forced to live in unhealthy and filthy conditions while detained, they quickly become objects of disgust for having slept on pest-ridden mats and having to use dirty toilets.

Disgust as a pedagogy has been studied in public health communications, particularly in obesity education campaigns. These studies conclude that disgust is embodied through bodily responses and affects learned to assist governmental imperatives (Leahy2009). As previously mentioned, disgust against particular objects and groups is promoted by public discourse, as they become disgusting through speech acts by naming the object and the subject as disgusting (Ahmed, 2014). These everyday pedagogies function through the reproduction of dichotomous representations (at both the symbolic and discursive levels) that construct aesthetics and morals out of opposites: white people and black people, beautiful people and ugly people, clean people and dirty people. Along with discourses of hygiene, they produce "[...] common places and senses, linked to moral concerns; they underpin, deepen and reproduce the hatred of democracy, the racist and classist rejection of subaltern, excluded and impoverished groups, cornered between exploitation, marginalisation and political clientelism" (Asselborn, 2012, p. 23).

Despite the cultural variants that may exist, pedagogies of disgust focus on a differentiation that, from a Western perspective, prioritises what is considered aesthetically beautiful, clean and desirable over what is considered aesthetically ugly, dirty and disgusting. Societies teach to reject certain social groups considered repugnant or potential contaminants (Nussbaum, 2004). Moreover, the state is a central transmitter of messages about polluting subjects. These are the social groups on the margins, the categories of the excluded, the lower social classes, the sick, prisoners and migrants.

Sara Ahmed explains that this kind of speech act not only designates an object or a subject as disgusting but "[...] generates a community of those who are bound together through the shared condemnation of a disgusting object or event" (2014, p. 94). In other words, disgust not only allows dominant groups to establish boundaries against disadvantaged ones but also creates social cohesion through hostility towards disadvantaged or "disgusting" groups.

Martha Nussbaum (2004) shows that:

> So powerful is the desire to cordon ourselves off from our animality that we often don't stop at faeces, cockroaches, and slimy animals. We need a group of humans to bound ourselves against, who will come to exemplify the boundary line between the truly human and the basely animal. If those quasianimals stand between us and our own animality, then we are one step further away from being animal and mortal ourselves,
>
> *(p. 107)*

These authors suggest that social cohesion through disgust might be crucial as part of an institutional process that designates migrants, especially certain groups, as disgusting. The establishment of boundaries and hierarchies also binds together INM agents who, in their "superiority", feel disgusted. I have previously analysed other emotions that together with disgust promote a group identity among immigration officers in detention centres (Fernández de la Reguera, 2024). For example, the constant fear among staff of losing their jobs, as well as other institutional consequences of disobeying orders, together with the fear caused by external working conditions such as operating in places controlled by organised crime, facilitates the existence of a community of punishers.

It seems that through the learning and practising of disgust, moral communities are created as "[...] co-sharers of the same sentiments, as guardians of property and purity" (Miller, 1997, p. 195). Constant access to the immigration detention centre allowed me to compare the unhealthy and very precarious material conditions in the areas where migrants are detained with the areas where INM staff work, which tend to be clean and ventilated. Implicitly and explicitly, moral and hygienic disgust differentiate officers from migrants and facilitate punishment.

The stigmatised and often punished groups may feel guilt for their own stigma and eventually develop feelings of shame, self-disgust and self-contempt (Miller, 1997). I have interviewed the same people inside and outside detention. When detained, it is very common that at the time of the interview, as well as asking for support with paperwork, they ask us to help them get a deodorant or a sanitary pad. I have clearly noticed how they act and talk differently once they are no longer deprived of their freedom. The reasons might be that they are no longer detained, surveilled or even threatened. However, significantly, they can wear clean clothes, have access to toiletries, can shave again, wear makeup etc. In other words, they can practice daily cleaning, hygiene, and beauty routines. People regain confidence and dignity after being forced to withstand harsh conditions, including feeling disgusted and self-disgusted while detained.

The bucket

In February 2017, I arrived for the first time at the EMSXXI on the outskirts of the city of Tapachula, Chiapas. Inaugurated by the INM in March 2006, this facility possesses the capacity to detain 960 people and was named *Siglo XXI* (21st Century) because of its outstanding "technology" imported from the United States, along with the privatisation of prison services, including the outsourcing of food preparation, cleaning services and security to private companies. For more than a decade, multiple NGOs, including the *Comisión Nacional de Derechos Humanos* (CNDH) [National Commission of Human Rights], have documented the inadequate quality of the food under these contracted companies as well as serious human rights violations with the participation of private security staff (Avila et. al, 2017; Comisión Nacional de los Derechos Humanos, 2019).

That day, I entered without really understanding how the place worked. My task was to support my colleagues from the human rights organisation *Centro de Derechos Humanos Fray Matías de Córdova A.C.* [Fray Matías de Córdova Human Rights Centre] by taking care of the children while they interviewed their parents. I observed the space, intending to capture and preserve in my mind its design – the corridors and the white bars covering all the windows, avoiding any possible interaction-. I first entered the office where the so-called middle management immigration agents were. My colleagues and I had a list of around 30 people, including women, men and families whose cases had been referred to this organisation, either through United Nations High Commissioner for Refugees (UNHCR), other people in detention or relatives of detainees, requesting legal and psychological assistance.

Once we had handed over the lists with the names of the people we would see that day, we moved to the male entrance hall. About 30 men sat on concrete benches waiting to register their biometric data, remove their shoelaces, and have their personal belongings checked and secured. I observed the bars, the shoes, the faces, the crusts of blood, the mud, the suitcases, the looks and the bars again. Following the entrance hall, first, there was the biometrics area and a room where the suitcases of the new arrivals were kept; then, there was a corridor with two tiny offices where we would see the detainees that day. As this was my first day, my job was to help my colleagues organise the people on the list whom the INM agents had previously called to come with us; I was also in charge of offering sheets of paper and colour pencils to the children who were present while their mothers were being interviewed.

As I sat there, I detected an unpleasant smell: a mixture of detergent, chlorine and urine. Guided by the foul smell, I looked towards the end of the corridor, and there was a white plastic bucket full of urine. How can a place called *Siglo XXI* not have enough toilets? That was my first thought. From that day on, I started to investigate why that bucket was there, why migrants had to urinate in front of everyone, and why nobody did anything about it. It was as if the bucket was invisible to the bureaucrats and other people who passed by daily, except for the male migrants, the cleaning lady and me, the "newest" in the place.

The only person with whom I could talk about the bucket was "naturally" the cleaner, who, in mid-2019, had been working there for 13 years. On a visit later that year, I found out she had been fired as the INM had terminated the further contract with the cleaning company. In my last conversation with her months before, the woman was frankly annoyed by the arrival of Central American caravans,[4] and at having to empty and wash the bucket twice and even three times a day. She told me the following:

> I had to take out a bucket without handles [a repurposed litter bin], so I had to get an old bucket and throw away the pee. I have been working here for 13 years and have never seen this. They are pigs. I am not going to be left behind by some foreign asshole. They should arrive to our country with their tails between their legs instead of going around demanding.

After three years of regularly visiting the EMSXXI, I have inquired about the presence of the bucket at every possible opportunity. I learned by asking staff members from *Centro de Derechos Humanos Fray Matías de Córdova A.C.*, detained migrants and immigration agents that it had been the solution that people on the move themselves had initially devised as a response to not being allowed to go to a toilet until the entire group with which they entered was registered correctly. Apparently, once the bucket began to be used for urinating, INM agents decided to leave it in that place and for that use. A Salvadorean who had been detained for four months explained to me that "they [the INM agents] put it there to urinate; when someone comes, as there are no toilets, they put it there, and that is where most of them urinate". Located at one of the most critical border crossing points on Mexico's southern border, this immigration detention centre receives hundreds of people detained throughout the country every day. People arriving on buses often travel for long periods, sometimes more than 12 hours, without access to a toilet. On arrival, instead of access to toilets, they are greeted by an improvised bucket.

Experiencing disgust as a punishment

Disgust as a daily practice of border control is central to power relations as it keeps boundaries between bodies and hierarchies (Aliverti, this volume). Who has the right to feel disgusted, and who does not? What are the institutional consequences of hierarchising subjects according to their disgust threshold? Disgust makes it possible to humiliate, punish and take institutional cruelty to the extreme, as people forced to live in unhealthy and outrageous conditions might end up facing mental health problems, sexual abuse and torture, as I will show in the following testimonies.

In my interviews, I have documented how INM agents constantly hear pleas from migrants to access drinking water, a toilet, a sanitary pad or a soap. Detained people perceive that access denial is a way to punish them. Still, at the same time, these daily practices suggest that the institution considers that people can tolerate the degrading conditions of the place because their threshold of disgust is higher than theirs. For example, when I asked a former INM agent to describe how the food was served at immigration detention centres, she characterised it in the following terms:

Former INM agent: No, the food is deplorable.
Alethia: Okay. So?
Former INM agent: It's very, very [...]
Alethia: Wouldn't you eat it?
Former INM agent: Of course not!
Alethia: Okay.
Former INM agent: No, never, no, no, no, no. I tried it two or three times, and it was disgusting food.
Alethia: Okay, why was it disgusting?
Former INM agent: I don´t know.
Alethia: People always tell me: "It is not tasty", "It doesn't have salt", but I don't know if it's because it's not fresh or if the taste is [...], or if it's too greasy. Could you describe it to me?
Former INM agent: I can only think of a rotten roast.
Alethia: Okay, you mean as something spoiled?
Former INM agent: Yes, it's like an awful rice. It's food that you're literally giving to the dog because you have leftovers. And because it's been in the fridge for three days with that sour taste.

Why would they (INM agents) think that a migrant person can eat rotten food? Why would you give that food even to a dog? In this testimony, the person describes the food but does not question why migrants would not be disgusted by something as she is. As my research demonstrates, immigration detention centres in Mexico are places where unhealthy conditions are the result of implicit rules and discretionary practices in order to institutionally establish social differences and hierarchies for disciplining and punishment.

Regulations on the operation of immigration detention centres in Mexico guarantee the wellbeing and safety of detained migrants; however, in many cases, these allow for discretion in the day-to-day administration of the different areas of the immigration detention centre. For example, the law establishes that all persons entering immigration detention centres must have access to medical services and receive a toiletry kit. However, on many occasions, I have documented that depending on the guard in charge, migrants may or may not have access to medical services and receive toiletries. Moreover, budget allocation can aggravate material conditions. For example, in May 2019, during an interview with the director of EMSXXI, she told us that the Federal Government had reduced the budget for fumigation, and they could not fumigate in three months. During that visit, many outbreaks of skin infections were reported.

The following is a testimony from a person I interviewed in 2023 who works for an NGO that has access to immigration detention centres in various parts of Mexico. She is explaining the conditions of a temporary detention centre in Chiapas.

> The conditions are inhuman. We talk about torturing spaces. There is a lot of overcrowding. In a place originally intended to keep four people, we found up to 90 people lying on mattresses, windows without glass, a broken roof, and a wall with holes. It was not only cold, but sometimes it was wet and full of cockroaches and mosquitoes.

The misuse, deterioration and abandonment of the INM facilities have been publicly denounced for more than a decade by the National Human Rights Commission and various civil society organisations (Comisión Nacional de los Derechos Humanos, 2019; Consejo Ciudadano del Instituto Nacional de Migración, 2017; Macías Delgadillo et al., 2013). There has been no political will or budget to guarantee dignified spaces. On the contrary, political and budgetary efforts have been focused on the securitisation and militarisation of immigration detention centres (Fundacion para la Justicia y el Estado Democratico de Derecho A.C. et al., 2021; García Alanís, 2024).

In Mexico, irregular and racialised migrants, especially dark-skinned people from Honduras, Cuba, Haiti and African countries such as Angola, Congo and Senegal, are usually stigmatised as potential carriers of diseases. I have seen this not only in the treatment they receive while detained or as they wait for their transit permits outside INM offices but also in the racist news spread by local newspapers in Tapachula (Recamier, 2019). Because of the imagined places they are coming from or the type of work they do, they are considered potential pollutants or carriers of diseases (Round & Kuznetsova, 2016). Moreover, a punitive immigration policy that prioritises detention as the central deterrence policy reinforced the stigma against people on the move as deviants or transgressors of the law. In such an institutional context, migrants easily become targets of disgust and discrimination. The following narrative is from a Salvadorean man who was detained for three months in EMSXXI. He explained to me about the way officers were treating migrants from India, Nepal and Bangladesh.

> These kids are brown; they are from India and Nepal. They are humbler, like those from Bangladesh. I have observed officers with arrogance; they speak to them loudly, they call them rude names, they call them "bastard" to offend them because they do not understand Spanish and on many occasions, I have seen how they are beaten.
> *(interview with a Salvadorean man detained at EMSXXI, 2018)*

A Honduran woman told me that when she was detained with her two children, there was a family of Garifuna (black people from Honduras) in the next cell. She recalled that the guards said that no one could get close to this family because they had tuberculosis, and that initially, INM guards refused to give them food, but eventually, *the officer approached them wearing gloves and a mask, opened the cell and disgustedly brought them food*. Both testimonies show the racism and stigma towards black and non-Spanish-speaking people. There is openly differential treatment, use of force and stigmatisation. The Garifuna family did not have tuberculosis, and they were locked in a cell with no medical diagnosis and limited access to food. Racism was reinforced by disgust derived from a stigma of disease.

Disgust and the exceptionality of immigration law

Martha Nussbaum (2004) has theorised the role disgust plays in the law. She is critical of the way it has justified the making of some acts illegal, significantly affecting stigmatised groups such as homosexuals or sex workers. She emphasises how, in the Western tradition, legal barriers based on disgust have been considered part of the civilising process as society transmits disgust to its members by enacting laws. Mexican immigration law can be an example of this: even though it lies within the domain of administrative law, it is closer to criminal law as it frames its targets as potentially punishable. Moreover, it is not only punitive but also racialised, as people on the move are stigmatised as threats to national security and as "potential pollutants". She is very critical of why disgust in any way should not provide information relevant to legal regulation and opposes any possibility in which disgust can be a criterion to classify and regulate actions (Kahan, 2000). In my research, I have not identified cases where disgust is openly used as a criterion to regulate immigration laws. However, I have found implicit practices that suggest that disgust might be a decisive factor for deportation, just as in the following case narrated by a former INM agent in 2017.

> I remember that I started talking to them [a group of Indians who rejected the INM agents], and I asked them: "Do you need vegetarian food?" They said yes. I also asked: "Why don't you take a bath?" One of them answered that in their culture they bathe every second or third day, but they were also on strike. I told him: "Look, they are not going to take you out [released from detention] even if you go on strike for fifteen days without bathing". I explained him his rights. Then he asked me: "What is an *amparo*[5]?" I told him: "Look, the *amparo* is..." and explained what he could do. He said: "Ah, okay! I have a friend out there who can help me". I told him: "Tell your friend to send a lawyer here; they have to let him in so he can give you legal advice". The only INM agent who had talked to them was me. My boss asked me, "Why did you tell them about the *amparo*?" I told him that it was their right. Then he told me: "They will be there [in the detention centre] for six months!" I said, "Oh, sorry!" My colleagues told me: "How could you? They do not bath, and we have to give them special food". Then the control and verification officer wanted to deport them, and I said: "But you cannot deport them," and he said: "Why not?" I explained that they belong to a tribe and that if they return to their country, they will be killed. So, eventually they got legal protection. It was obvious that they were going to win the trial because if they went back to their country, they would be killed; the *amparo* lasted six months[6]. The truth was that I got emotionally tired of explaining to my bosses why human rights should be respected. Many times, they told me: "It seems like you are a representative of the National Commission of Human Rights".

This testimony highlights how disgust, in a context of ignorance, racism and neglect of other cultural practices, is a factor that can determine a person's eligibility to apply for an *amparo* to avoid deportation. The National Institute of Migration itself, through a wide range of discretion, makes decisions on the right or not of a person to apply for asylum. Moreover, within an environment of racism and disgust, it might be preferable to deport a group of people even if that implies the risk of death, before allowing them to initiate an asylum application. In this case the right to present an *amparo* meant having them longer in detention, causing "discomfort" to the INM agents because of their smell and the provision of a vegetarian diet.

The following is a testimony documented in 2023 from a NGO staff member who has access to different immigration detention centres in the country.

> There is legal uncertainty because migrants never have information about their procedure, or they make them sign deceitful documents. I know many cases where INM officers tell them: "I am going to give you toothpaste", "I am going to give you soap", and "I am going to give you this". In return, they will have to sign documents for voluntary returns. So, I think it is very evident that this is happening. Also, we have seen that they condition them with access to water. It is like, "They are making a lot of noise, so we are going to take the water out of the migratory station", and at least here in Villahermosa [because of the high temperatures], if they leave you without water, it is equivalent to torture.

This narrative shows the discretion on the part of the authority to provide essential goods within a detention centre, such as water, soap and toothpaste. In addition, it shows that one way to punish people for making too much noise or other misbehaviour is the deprivation of water, which can have serious consequences, even for guaranteeing the right to life. It is an example of how the institution, through these practices, punishes by generating unhealthy conditions, increasing risks of diseases, as well as the disgust that people feel at having to be crammed into spaces without access to water. Finally, it also shows that people are easily deceived and that the fundamental principle of ensuring non-refoulement and the right to seek asylum is violated in international refugee law. While asking for basic toiletries, people are deceived and voluntarily sign their request to return to their countries of origin. In this case, it seems that the authorities do not consider that migrants deserve to be treated with dignity; they are criminalised, and their punishment is to be dehumanised and deported.

When disgust is a criterion or a factor associated with classifying acts as illegal, there is a risk of increased punishment. "Underscoring disgust thus could increase the severity of criminal punishment in ways related not to the gravity of the offence but simply to the size and disgust coherence of the group" (Massaro, 2000, p. 99). In the case of migrants, not only are punitive policies and the criminalisation of migration strengthened, but human rights and basic principles of international protection are undermined. In the cases presented in this chapter, the authorities should have at least granted a visitor's card for humanitarian reasons and facilitated access to the asylum procedure. However, they ended up being deported. Very unfortunately, in the first case of the young Honduran, he was released in the middle of the night whilst in a mental health crisis, so it is not possible to know what happened to him.

Conclusion

The case of Ashley Smith, who died on October 19, 2007, at the age of 19 while imprisoned in Ontario, Canada, shows how disgust is an essential characteristic of punishment in prison settings (Joensuu, 2020). She strangled herself whilst correctional officers watched her from outside her cell.

> By stripping individuals of liberty – a venerated symbol of individual worth in our culture – and by inflicting countless other indignities – from exposure to the view of others when urinating and defecating to rape at the hand of other inmates – prison unambiguously marks the lowness of those we consign to it.
> *(Kahan, 2000, p. 1642)*

As in other prisons globally, the reports on Ashley's case show the existence of incidents with "disgusting objects" such as urine, faeces or spit in her cell, which was interpreted by the guards as a threat from her (Joensuu, 2020). Eleonora Joensuu (2020) analyses how in this case the institution acts as the "disgusted subject" and Ashley as the "disgusting object". She was living in filth, dehumanised and then left to die.

On March 27, 2023, at around 9:30 p.m., the Ciudad Juarez, Chihuahua immigration detention centre caught on fire; 40 migrants died, and 27 were seriously injured. The fire originated in the cell where men were being held, protesting that they had no access to drinking water or food and that the place was overcrowded. They were detained even though many of them were asylum seekers. A 32-second surveillance footage circulated on social media shows the moment when the fire starts and how the guards walk unhurriedly in front of the cell where the migrants were locked up, the smoke rises rapidly, and the guards do not reappear.

Countless cases of extreme punishment and violence are documented every year by NGOs monitoring immigration detention centres in Mexico. Extreme cases such as the Juarez fire are still in the process of being brought to justice. Overcrowded, filthy and unsanitary conditions are forms of daily punishment disguised as indifference and based on disgust that we practice daily towards people who are different from us. It is necessary not only to critically analyse disgust as a central element of punishment, but also to understand that it is a physical and intimate emotion with profound moral and political weight. Access to justice begins by radically eradicating stigma and practices of dehumanisation through disgust and contempt, with which, while extreme in detention settings, we are all complicit.

Notes

1   Articles 106 and 107 of the Migration Law establish the following obligations for the National Migration Institute and the provision of services within immigration

detention centres which according to the law are called migration stations: (1) to provide medical, psychological and legal assistance services; (2) to offer three meals a day; (3) Keeping men and women in separate and secure locations; (4) Ensuring respect for human rights; (4) Maintaining adequate facilities to prevent overcrowding; (5) Having spaces for sports and cultural recreation; (6) Allowing access to legal representatives, or a person of trust, and consular assistance (Diputados, 2011).
2 In some immigration detention centres, private security guards are hired to provide surveillance services 24/7 inside detention areas.
3 The anti-migrant discourse has been gaining strength in Mexico in the last decade. It has become institutionalised in national security and public security forces, with migrants being one of the groups identified since 2012 as a threat to national security in the National Security Plan (Presidencia de la República, 2014).
4 Migrant caravans are mass migrations (between 3,000 and 13,000 people have been documented) that visibly move in groups. They generally come from Central America and are in transit to the United States through Mexico. They usually use traditional and highly visible routes of passage and access to the territory. These are strategies to avoid migrating clandestinely and reduce risks and costs (Gandini et al., 2020).
5 In Mexico, an *amparo* is a judicial action to protect an individual from the acts or omissions of the authorities that violate human rights and guarantees.
6 The process of filing an *amparo* against deportation took six months. This allowed them to avoid deportation and begin their asylum application.

References

Ahmed, S. (2014). *The Cultural Politics of Emotion* (Second edition). Edinburgh University Press.
Aliverti, A. (2021). *Policing the Borders Within*. Oxford University Press.
Aliverti, A. (2024). Bordered orders and affective states: Unravelling, rethinking, abolishing. In M. Bosworth, K. Katja Franko, M. Lee, & M. Rimple (Eds.), *Handbook on Border Criminology* (pp. 25–40). Edward Elgar Publishing,
Ariza, M. (2024). Migration, institutions and emotions. In H. Flam (Ed.), *Research Handbook on the Sociology of Emotions* (pp. 313–329). Edward Elgar Publishing.
Asselborn, C. J. (2012). Asco y Política. Reflexiones intempestivas sobre sensibilidades sedimentadas y democracia. *Revista Intersticios de La Política y La Cultura*, 1(1), 21–30.
Avila Morales, A., Díaz de León, L., & Andrade, J. (2017). *Informe En el umbral del dolor: acceso a los servicios de salud en estaciones migratorias*.
Bosworth, M. (2014). *Inside Immigration Detention*. Oxford University Press.
Cámara de Diputados. (2011). *Ley de Migración*. Congreso de la Unión.
Canton, R. (2022). *Punishment*. Routledge.
Carvalho, H., & Chamberlen, A. (2024). *Questioning Punishment*. Routledge.
Chapman, H., & Anderson, A. (2012). Understanding disgust. *Annals of the New York Academy of Sciences*, Special Issue *The Year in Cognitive Neuroscience*, 1251 (1), 62–76.
Comisión Nacional de los Derechos Humanos. (2019). *Informe Especial. Situación de las Estaciones Migratorias en México, hacia un Nuevo Modelo Alternativo a la Detención*.

Consejo Ciudadano del Instituto Nacional de Migración. (2017). *Personas en detención migratoria en México. Misión de Monitoreo de Estaciones Migratorias y Estancias Provisionales del Instituto Nacional de Migración.*

Del Río, J., & Kerwin, H. (2024). *Informe Incendio en la Estancia Migratoria de Ciudad Juárez "No nos dejen morir aquí."*

DesPres, T. (1976). *The Survivor an Anatomy of Life in the Death Camps.* Oxford University Press.

Dubreuil, B. (2010). Punitive emotions and norm violations. *Philosophical Explorations, 13*(1), 35–50. https://doi.org/10.1080/13869790903486776

Fernández de la Reguera, A. (2020). *Detención migratoria. Prácticas de humillación, asco y desprecio.* UNAM.

Fernández de la Reguera, A. (2022). Immigration detention, the patriarchal state and the politics of disgust in the hands of street-level bureaucrats. *Feminist Encounters: A Journal of Critical Studies in Culture and Politics, 6*(2), 30. https://doi.org/https://doi.org/10.20897/femenc/12353

Fernández de la Reguera, A. (2024). Punitive subjectivities and emotions in immigration detention. *Migration Politics, 3*(4), 1–21. https://doi:10.21468/MigPol.3.1.004

Fundación para la Justicia y el Estado Democrático de Derecho A.C., Sin Fronteras I.A.P, Derechos Humanos Integrales en Acción, Derechoscopio, Uno de Siete Migrando e Instituto para las Mujeres en la Migración A.C. . (2021). *Bajo la Bota. Militarización de la política migratoria en México.*

Flew, A. (1954). The justification of punishment. *Philosophy, 29*(111), 291–307.

Gandini, L., Fernández de la Reguera, A., & Narváez, J. C. (2020). *Caravanas.* Universidad Nacional Autónoma de México, Secretaría de Desarrollo Institucional.

García Alanís, P. (2024). *La militarización del Instituto Nacional de Migración y sus implicaciones en las violaciones a derechos humanos de las personas migrantes.* Universidad Iberoamericana.

Griffiths, M. (2023). The emotional governance of immigration controls. *Identities*, 1–22. https://doi.org/10.1080/1070289X.2023.2257957

Hall, A. (2012). *Boder Watch Cultures of Immigration, Detention and Control.* Pluto Press.

Hofmann, W., Brandt, M. J., Wisneski, D. C., Rockenbach, B., & Skitka, L. J. (2018). Moral punishment in everyday life. *Personality and Social Psychology Bulletin, 44*(12), 1697–1711. https://doi.org/10.1177/0146167218775075

Joensuu, E. (2020). *A Politics of Disgust Selfhood, World-Making, and Ethics.* Routledge.

Kahan, D. (2000). The progressive appropriation of disgust. In S. Bandes (Ed.), *The Passions of Law* (pp. 63–79). NYU Press.

Kristeva, J. (2024). *Powers of Horror: An Essay on Abjection.* Columbia University Press.

Leahy, D. (2009). Disgusting pedagogies. In J. Wright & V. Harwood (Eds.), *Biopolitics and the Obesity Epidemic Governing Bodies* (pp. 180–190). Routledge.

Macías Delgadillo, A., Hernández Méndez, A., Carreño Nigenda, C., Martínez Medrano, D., Castro Lobato, M., Oehler Toca, M., & Cano Padilla, S. (2013). *La Ruta del Encierro. Situación de las personas en detención en estaciones migratorias y estancias provisionales.* Sin Fronteras.

Massaro, T. (2000). Show (some) emotions. In S. Bandes (Ed.), *The Passions of Law* (pp. 80–120). NYU Press.

Miller, S. B. (2018). *Emotions of Menace and Enchantment Disgust, Horror, Awe, and Fascination*. Routledge.
Miller, W. I. (1997). *The Anatomy of Disgust*. Harvard University Press.
Nussbaum, M. (2004). *Hiding from Humanity Disgust, Shame and the Law*. Princeton University Press.
Presidencia de la República. (2014). *Programa para la Seguridad Nacional 2014 – 2018. Una política multidimensional para México en el siglo XXI*.
Recamier, M. (2019, October 8). África, un continente perdido en Chiapas. *Reporte Indigo*. www.reporteindigo.com/opinion/Africa-un-continente-perdido-en-Chiapas-20191008-0024.html
Round, J., & Kuznetsova, I. (2016). Necropolitics and the migrat as a political subject of disgust: The precarious everyday of Russia's labour migrants. *Critical Sociology*, *42*(7–8), 1017–1034.

6
STATE VIOLENCE AND THE AFFECTIVE CAPACITY OF AN INQUEST

Martha McCurdy

Introduction

The coroner's court in England and Wales has evolved over 800 years towards its role in investigating unnatural, suspicious and violent deaths, including those at the hands of the state (Courts and Tribunals Judiciary, 2023). These investigations are called inquests, and the importance of these processes lies in their ability to establish the truth surrounding a person's death and provide closure for bereaved families (Jacobson et al., 2024). A coroner can identify harmful practices or policies and produce recommendations to prevent future harm (Coroners and Justice Act, 2009). When 'put right', an inquest's 'potential preventive value' and role in providing 'public scrutiny' is not only in the interests of the bereaved but also the wider public (Justice Committee, 2020). In recent years, inquests have spotlighted the cruelty of state detention (Medical Justice, 2016)[1] and exposed systemic failings made by individuals and organisations responsible for such institutions (Taylor, 2019a).[2] However, evidence suggests that the process can be perfunctory and limited in scope (Aitken, 2022; Baker, 2016; Green, 1992). As a result, inquests can reproduce patterns of state violence and disregard for human life (Arthur, 2022; Nijjar, 2019). Bereaved families often deal with a rigid and technical system and have expressed aggrievement with the process (INQUEST, 2023; Jacobson et al., 2024; Taylor, 2019b). In the face of limited legal remedy, families and non-governmental organisations have been compelled to pursue alternative forms of justice. Through grassroots activism that memorialises loved ones and challenges institutional failings, they seek to prevent future harm and bring about accountability (Oppenheim, 2024).[3]

State violence and the affective capacity of an inquest   123

This chapter discusses how an inquest not only produces the legal category of death but the affective capacity of the process also implicates the adjudication of state violence and, ultimately, the value placed on human life (Butler, 2004). This chapter draws upon data collected between 2018 and 2019, including interviews with NGOs and legal professionals and analysis of inquest reports and observations. It first outlines the legal framework of the UK's coroner's court and, subsequently, an inquest's affective capacity to address state violence. The focus of this chapter is ethnographic material collected from the inquest into Mahammat Abdullah Moussa, who died whilst trying to enter the UK beneath a vehicle. Despite some concern for the circumstances relating to his death, the inquest's focus on administrative detail and remoteness towards Moussa and his family came at the expense of addressing more complex questions relating to state violence and prevention (Aitken, 2022). This chapter subsequently refers to the historical inquest into Blair Peach's death as a contextual point to examine the limitations of the inquest process to provide closure. Blair Peach was killed by the police in London during an anti-fascist demonstration in 1979. The inquest was described as a 'shadow of an inquiry' and blamed for allowing a police cover-up (Searle, 2014). Failures in legal processes beyond just the Peach case continue to motivate non-governmental and activist groups to advocate for victims of state-related deaths and demand improvements to the inquest system (Bourne, 2009).[4] By exploring the tensions between different affective registers at an inquest (Griffiths, 2024), this chapter supports calls for an inquest's (often unrealised) potential as a site for pursuing justice and mobilising challenge against state violence.

The UK Coroner's Court

A coroner is an independent judicial officer who, unlike the rest of the judiciary, is appointed by the local authority. A coroner holds an inquest to investigate 'a violent or unnatural death', where the 'cause of death is unknown', or if the 'deceased died while in custody or otherwise in state detention' (Coroners and Justice Act, 2009, part 1, chapter 1, s.1 , ss. 2 a–c). The first coroner's office in the UK dates back to 1194. At this time, there is 'little sense that the bereaved were at the heart of the process' (Courts and Tribunals Judiciary, 2023, point no.15). Instead, an inquest's original purpose was to secure revenue for the Crown following an unnatural death (Courts and Tribunals Judiciary, 2023).[5] Over time, this institution has evolved to investigate unnatural deaths 'for the benefit of the community as a whole' (The Coroner's Society of England and Wales, n.d.). The shift in the role of inquests over several centuries, along with the measures established in the Coroners and Justice Act (2009), has placed much greater emphasis on the needs and interests of bereaved families (Courts and Tribunals

Judiciary, 2023). This includes granting families access to relevant material, allowing them to question witnesses during the inquest and providing families with the right to appeal a coroner's decision (Courts and Tribunals Judiciary, 2023).

Depending on the death, inquests take on varying forms, with more complex cases involving multiple parties and jury members (Coroners and Justice Act, 2009; INQUEST, 2023). Article 2 of the European Convention on Human Rights, introduced in 2004, mandates that states prevent unlawful killings and investigate suspicious deaths, including those involving the state. Inquests in such cases often involve a jury and a more expansive scope to investigate the circumstances surrounding a person's death (Coroners and Justice Act, 2009). Other inquests, such as Moussa's, involve relatively fewer parties and are much shorter in duration. As part of the inquest process, a coroner is legally required to establish who, where, when and how a person died. The final determination of a person's death must be recorded on the Record of Inquest, generally read in an open court. A coroner must also prepare a Prevention of Future Death (PFD) or Regulation 28 report if they are concerned about the risk of future deaths. Regulation 28 or PFD reports are integral to an inquest's preventive function. By outlining malpractice or failings and submitting their findings to relevant parties, these reports aim to prevent future harm (Chief Coroner, 2013) Recipients are required to respond to these reports, which are 'intended to improve public health, welfare and safety' and 'wherever possible, designed to have practical effect' (Chief Coroner, 2013, p.1).

At the discretion of the judiciary, coroner's reports may be published on the judiciary website or available on request. Some reports may be redacted or summarised to protect individuals' privacy or the public from potentially harmful information (Chief Coroner, 2013) However, as this chapter illustrates, there is a discrepancy in how inquests are recorded. Finally, a coroner's final report cannot 'determine any question of criminal' or 'civil liability' (Coroners and Justice Act, 2009, part 1, chapter 1, section 10, subsection 2 a,b). As such, an inquest serves an inquisitorial rather than accusatorial function, meaning that it can establish facts about the circumstances surrounding a person's death, but it cannot pursue a conviction (Aitken, 2022). The promise of an inquest to provide closure and impact on society can also be examined by analysing the emotional registers that circulate during the process.

Affective Registers and State Violence

The role of emotions in court settings is a topic of ongoing academic concern (Blix & Wettergren, 2018; Roach Anleu & Mack, 2019). Restorative justice scholars argue for further integration of emotions within the law (Karstedt,

2016; Rossner, 2017). A relevant discussion for this chapter is whether inquests can serve a 'therapeutic' function (Freckleton, 2007), acting as a 'cathartic' moment for the bereaved to achieve closure and resolve (Aitken, 2022, p.486). Whilst some believe that coroners must maintain emotional distance and impartiality, others argue that sympathy and compassion play a clear role in death investigations (Tait et al., 2016). The call for a more therapeutic approach highlights the affective potential of an inquest to provide closure (Tait et al., 2016). However, in practice, this function can be undermined. The needs of the bereaved may be sidelined as families are outnumbered by representatives and the interests of government departments or organisations (Aitken, 2022; INQUEST, 2023). Cases following border fatalities involving some of the most marginalised and racialised individuals raise further issues in addressing structural forms of violence.

This chapter draws inspiration from Griffiths' (2024) research on the 'affective governance' of the UK's immigration system. Griffiths (2024, p.84) discusses the 'charged affective register' that exists at every level of the asylum process, expressed through anger, coldness, distrust, suspicion and indifference. The splenetic affective registers, such as suspicion or aggression exhibited by an immigration officer, contrast with displays of disinterest or coldness in asylum court proceedings. These differing emotions work simultaneously to produce hierarchies of inclusion and exclusion (Griffiths, 2024). Griffiths (2023, n.p.) writes that the 'mobilisation and suspension of emotions sustains social stratification and subjugation to produce deportable and disposable persons'. The emotional framing of deaths at state borders[6] also operates on multiple levels. On the one hand, there is a striking political indifference, with these deaths often reduced by governments and the media to mere unfortunate accidents.[7] On the other hand, this detachment is coupled with a highly charged rhetoric of criminality (De León, 2015; Eschbach et al., 1999; Jones, 2016; Michalowski, 2007). By manipulating affective responses, states can effectively frame border deaths as unfortunate accidents or the result of individual choices rather than the direct outcome of their policies (Institute of Race Relations, 2020, p.5). The response to border fatalities also relates to hierarchies of exclusion and the 'differential allocation of grievability' (Butler, 2004, p.xiv). People who die at state borders often 'remain unacknowledged, unprotected, unremembered, and ungrieved' (Perl, 2016, p.199).

An inquest not only determines the legal cause of death, but as this chapter examines, the affective capacity of the inquest process is also relevant to how wider questions of state violence and marginalisation are addressed. Legal systems, such as the inquest process, may perpetuate as well as conceal forms of structural violence (Galtung, 1990; Farmer, 2004; Scheper-Hughes & Bourgois, 2004).[8] Throughout the British legal system, government policies and entangled histories of institutionalised racism are minimised as inconsequential or peripheral (Arthur, 2022; El-Enany, 2019; Shilliam, 2018). The contemporary British legal system is premised on enforcing public order at the expense of safeguarding and protection (Aliverti, 2020). In depriving 'certain individuals of legal capacity' (Tuitt, 2019, p.127), the legal system produces abject classes of 'failed' and 'stateless' citizens who fall outside of the legal protections of citizenship whilst being subject to the full force of state power (Tyler, 2013). In her ethnography of a deindustrialised town in England, Willis (2023, p.211) highlights how structural violence, which manifests in reduced health and life expectancy, is 'pushed out of sight' and 'deemed irrelevant'.

By examining the circumstances that lead to an 'unnatural' or 'violent' death, an inquest has the potential to examine broader systemic issues. However, as Aitken (2022, p.493) argues, inquests following self-inflicted deaths in prisons often opt for a narrower focus, circumventing more exploratory questions. By favouring 'factual details and administrative minutiae', these investigations choose to overlook debates about structural violence in prisons, wider questions relating to punishment and whether the suffering experienced in incarceration is justifiable (Aitken, 2022, p.481). As Aitken (2022, p.487) finds, inquests are not 'entirely inquisitorial proceedings concerned with fact-finding and consensus-building'. As revealed by Aitken's (2022) interviews with coroners and lawyers, an imbalance in legal representation nurtures a 'partially adversarial' and unequal setting (Aitken, 2022). The interests of the bereaved in learning the truth about the death of their loved one can become overlooked. In the context of state-related violence, the promises of an inquest to provide closure can therefore be undermined.

Case Studies

Mahammat Abdullah Moussa Inquest

The following ethnographic material collected from the inquest into Moussa's death illustrates the limitations of this process to serve a remedial or therapeutic function. The affective registers included both technical and emotionless discussion of the case as well as some vague concern for the circumstances relating to Moussa's death. The inquest foreclosed any wider debate, such as the structural violence associated with border policies or the political responsibility for such fatalities. Ultimately, the procedural elements took precedence in this case, which failed to provide any tangible steps to prevent future harm.

The inquest into the death of Mahammat Abdullah Moussa was held on 18 April 2019 at the Archbishop's Palace in Maidstone. Moussa, a 25-year-old Chad national, died on 18 November 2018 whilst entangled underneath a coach travelling from Brussels to the UK. His body was discovered underneath the coach by French border police at the Eurotunnel terminal in Folkestone (Williams, 2019). There was little information before the inquest, which the court had initially listed as 'Unknown Male' found at the Channel Tunnel. I learnt about this case via the 'Deaths at the Calais border' database. In 2009, the Calais Migrant Solidarity (CMS) project was born out of the collective action in the refugee camp in Calais, France. This group offers solidarity, support and advice to 'people with and without papers facing daily harassment and abuse from the border regime' (Calais Migrant Solidarity, n.d.). The Deaths at the Calais border database continues to record fatalities in Northern France and in attempts to reach the UK.

At the time of the inquest, two short lines on the CMS website read that a 'man [was] found dead under a bus at the Eurotunnel terminal in Folkestone in UK'. This was later updated to 'an exiled man is found dead under a bus at the Eurotunnel terminal in Folkestone in the UK. He will be later identified as Mahammat Abdullah Moussa, 25, from Chad' (Calais Migrant Solidarity, n.d.). Their database seeks to challenge this silence and confront the violence of the border regime (Calais Migrant Solidarity, n.d.) Between 2014 and 2024, 321 migrants have been recorded as missing or deceased in attempts to reach the UK via the English Channel (International Organisation for Migration, n.d.). This largely includes vehicle-related deaths or drownings, as well as deaths caused by violence or destitution (International Organisation for Migration, n.d.). As the collective writes, many of these deaths are 'ignored, the facts covered up or altogether unreported', with many 'unnamed' and 'without families or friends to advocate on their behalf'(Calais Migrant Solidarity, n.d.). Interviews I held with personnel of NGOs working in Northern France and existing literature (Institute of Race Relations, 2020) challenge this indifference and failure to confront the structural violence associated with borders.

The original reporting of this death was also impersonal. The BBC (2018) reported the 'body of suspected migrant found under bus in Folkestone'. As existing literature argues, following a border fatality the individual who died is often overlooked in news reports and political debate. Instead, the deceased are typically represented by the media in blanket or anonymous terms (Institute of Race Relations, 2020; Webber, 2004). Media reports in the immediate aftermath of such deaths (e.g. Hopkins et al., 2000; Tran, 2000) often focus 'on the distress of those who had found the bodies and on the criminality of those who had brought them, rather than attempting to understand the issues thrown up by the deaths' (Webber, 2004, p.134). This stands in contrast to the hysteria often associated with 'small boats', where febrile language is used to affect fear and panic (Griffiths, 2023; Institute of Race Relations, 2020).

The inquest was held in an old-fashioned registry office at the Archbishop's Palace in Maidstone. The Palace is a grand historic building situated by the riverside, and as a coroner's court, it is also used for wedding receptions. The joy of the wedding party outside of the lawn in bright colours contrasted with the cold and estranged atmosphere of the inquest. The only parties in attendance were the coroner, the court usher, a local journalist, a police detective and myself. The inquest was scheduled for 11.30 am, and when I arrived, I enquired with the receptionist, who knew nothing about it. She asked me to wait upstairs and after about half an hour, I returned to the reception. The receptionist apologised, explaining that she had forgotten about me. The remiss of the receptionist, as well as the inquest being delayed for several hours, contributed to a sense of insignificance. As Mulcahy and Rowden (2020) argue, court architecture, design and spatial hierarchies are not neutral. A court's architectural and spatial configurations direct the kinds of cues and behaviours that take place. These spatial dynamics enable and restrict who can (and cannot) access or participate in the court proceedings. For example, in the context of criminal trials, Mulcahy (2011) finds that the spatial isolation of a defendant leads to their marginalisation and inability to participate. Following Mulcahy and Rowden (2020), I suggest that the architectural space and involvement only of strangers were highly emblematic of the remoteness at this inquest.

Encapsulating the narrow and procedural scope of the inquest, the coroner started the inquest by stating, 'I will be touching upon the death' and 'I am calling upon pathological [and police] evidence, and that is all the evidence I am going to call in this case'. Bereaved families have described the inquest process as 'alienating' and 'disempowering' (Jacobson et al., 2024, p.1), despite promises by the court and Chief Coroners that they should be at the 'heart' of the process (Jacobson et al., 2024, p.5). In some cases, families have emphasised the importance of sharing 'pen portraits' of the deceased, which humanised 'what was otherwise experienced as a cold, impersonal process' (Jacobson et al., 2024, p.6). The information about Moussa was scant and limited to the technical details surrounding his death. The pathologist's report was briefly summarised by the coroner. This report determined Moussa's death as 'unnatural', citing several grievous injuries that Moussa had sustained whilst below the axle of the bus. Reading from the pathologist report, the coroner stated that this comprised a large defect to the left of Moussa's back, missing organs and an amputated left leg, as well as injuries to his head and chest. The focus on medical and technical language gave no sense of who Moussa was, further illustrating how emotion (or lack of it) lends to humanising or dehumanising the life that has been lost.

The emotionless and technical ways the pathologist's report and evidence were dealt with were complicated by comments made at the close of the inquest. After the inquest had concluded, I left the Archbishop's Palace with the journalist and the police detective. They commented on the grimness of the case. This backstage interaction is more informal and unscripted (Goffman,

1959) and sheds light on the different emotions that circulate an inquest. While the pathologist's report and the evidence presented by the police officer described in some detail the events surrounding Moussa's death, they were scripted, pre-prepared and procedural. The comments made after the inquest are a reminder of the different modes of interpreting and engaging with a case, which are not limited to the courtroom. Professionals working with death find coping strategies and must maintain decorum and professionalism with the outside world (Timmermans, 2006). However, some cases may also personally or emotionally affect medical examiners (Timmermans, 2006). Comments made outside the courtroom elicit a more unstructured kind of emotion, that may be more compassionate or sympathetic. The remark regarding the grimness of the inquest hints at the cruelness of Moussa's death. This complicates the kinds of emotion that exist around an inquest. However, reserving these sentiments to outside the courtroom suggests a preference for more procedural affective registers.

During the inquest, the coroner did offer some sensitivity towards the circumstances of Moussa's death, specifically by vaguely acknowledging the severity of the risk of hiding beneath a bus. However, her focus was largely on assessing the responsibility of another party. She asked the police detective, 'as far as you can tell, no third party was involved?'. In his response, the police detective stated, 'no, this is a fairly frequent occurrence of people trying to secure passage underneath vehicles'. He further stated that Brussels 'is a place where a large proportion of people are trying to enter the UK'. The coroner responded that Moussa had 'sadly misjudged' something that 'was completely risky' and the police detective highlighted the regularity of such risk-taking, which is widely known. Despite grasping these risks, neither addressed the structural conditions underlying such fatalities. The coroner hinted at the need for a deeper understanding of the risks involved, stating that the risks are 'maybe something that people need to clearly understand. They take some very severe risks'. And yet, the inquest fell short of fully addressing more open-ended and complicated questions (Aitken, 2022) relating to border regimes and structural vulnerabilities that illegalised individuals face. This was underlined by a mutual understanding between the detective and the coroner that the broader context would not impact the outcome of the inquest.

The exclusion of the bereaved further pronounced the superficiality of the inquest process and the emotionless dealing with facts. The family were neither present nor represented. The police officer stated that Moussa 'had no family here' and only briefly suggested that the Chad Embassy had been contacted during their investigation. No more details were provided. Referring to the mobile phone found on Moussa's body, the coroner asked the detective, 'I understand one of the numbers was mon papa?'. He replied, 'the phone was in French, and we had difficulties reviewing it in my limited French.

I understood that to be his father'. The absence of Moussa's family from the inquest contradicts the principle that the bereaved should be at the centre of the process. This exclusion significantly limits the scope of an inquest and its affective potential. In an ideal arrangement, bereaved relatives or those who represent them should have the opportunity to question witnesses and be involved in setting the terms of an inquest. However, in this case, the fact that the family were neither present nor extensively involved may account for the limited scope. Griffiths (2024) describes the neglect and disinterest exhibited by the Home Office towards people trying to navigate the UK's asylum system. In a similar vein, the limited concern towards the bereaved family or neglect to translate Moussa's phone are further displays of suspended emotions. Like Griffiths' (2024) analysis, these kinds of emotional registers, in reducing important details or treating them as irrelevant, contribute to a devaluation of a person's life. In the context of migrant deaths at the US–Mexico border, Timmermans et al. (2024) discuss the additional violence involved in repatriating bodies. As a result of different state policies, some families are unable to return their loved ones home or bury them according to cultural and religious customs (Timmermans et al., 2024). This is another important example of how the administration of death can prevent closure by not allowing some bodies to be 'claimable' (Timmermans et al., 2024) or 'grievable' (Butler, 2004).

An interesting tension between the different affective registers at the Moussa inquest relates to the coroner's deliberation and conclusion. In assessing intent and signalling towards deterrence, the coroner's final statement suggests a conceivable wider scope. She stated, 'I think I have two options to consider this an 'accident' or 'misadventure'. As she continued:

> [Moussa] clearly intended to put himself in a position without understanding the risk or danger; it was his intention, no third party was involved, and he was not locked in. I am wondering, he clearly did not mean for this to happen. 'Misadventure' is an unintended consequence of the intended action [...] I am concerned that 'accident' could be misinterpreted; this was clearly no fault of the driver. So, I turn to the balance of probabilities – I think it is more accurate to say 'misadventure' and maybe something people need to clearly understand that they take some very severe risks.

As Green (1992) and Baker (2016) highlight, the legal definition of death is ambiguous. Such decisions 'are produced through a moral analysis of the facts surrounding a death and through the resulting process of demarcating them from other, more culpable, deaths' (Green, 1992, p.373). The coroner in Moussa's case was concerned that 'accidental' death could be 'misinterpreted' and implicate the driver. As Green (1992, p.385) states, '[d]espite being in itself a morally neutral term [...] the label of "accidental" points to the possibilities of responsibility for a death'. The coroner in Maidstone decided that 'misadventure' carried less ambiguity and did not risk implicating the driver. This seems to be a more legally acceptable understanding of the cause of death. The detective described these circumstances as a 'fairly frequent occurrence'. By suggesting that people need to understand the severe risks, the coroner also alluded to deterrence or prevention strategies. However, in the face of an almost complete lack of publicity or visibility of such procedures, this further illustrates the differing affective registers at inquests, where the procedural approach often undermines the preventive potential.

Blair Peach Inquest

In considering the affective capacity of an inquest, specifically in the context of state-related deaths, this chapter references the following historical inquest. It is illustrative of more overt forms of obstructing and denying state violence. It offers further insight into how different emotional registers contribute to the ongoing devaluation of certain lives and adjudication of state violence.

Blair Peach, a teacher from New Zealand, was killed on 23 April 1979 by the police during a demonstration against an election meeting held by the National Front in Southall Town Hall. Many protestors were first- and second-generation British Asians concerned about racist attacks carried out by the Front, such as the stabbing of 16-year-old Gurdip Singh Chaggar on Southall High Street in 1976. Blair Peach and a group of his friends joined over 2,000 other demonstrators. Over 2,700 police attended the demonstration, with the Special Patrol Group (SPG), a mobile unit within the Metropolitan Police Service, behaving particularly violently during the anti-racist protest. The police used 'heavier than normal' truncheons against the demo, and one man remained in a coma for five months after being struck on the head by a police baton (Renton, 2020). Peach and his friends decided to leave the demonstration at around 7.45 pm. It was just as he was leaving that he received a fatal blow to his head from a police officer. He died later that evening in hospital. As well as the killing of Peach, 64 people sustained injuries at the hands of the police. It was subsequently found that the SPG had taken unauthorised weapons to the demo, including large truncheons, crowbars and metal coshes (Renton, 2020).

The inquest into Peach's death lasted four weeks and was held at West London Coroner's Court (Pallister, 2012). The coroner initially refused a jury; however, following an appeal by the family, the case was overturned by the High Court (Renton, 2014). The inquest heard evidence from ten witnesses and from a raid that had found unauthorised weapons in the possession of the SPG officers. The coroner maintained that the police force had acted lawfully and proportionately (Scraton & Chadwick, 1986). Contrary to statements made by friends and family regarding Peach's character, the coroner painted him as a 'militant, violent extremist' whose participation in the protest was partly to blame for his death (Scraton & Chadwick, 1986, p.106). This was contrary to the Cass Report, which the coroner did not make available to the jury, the family or their representatives. The Cass Report, organised by Commander John Cass, chief of the Metropolitan Complaints Investigation Bureau, presented an in-depth enquiry and found that one of the police officers killed Peach. The report did not establish self-defence or reasonable force in favour of the police officer responsible for his death because it found that Peach had been trying to get away from the protest at the time of his killing. The report also indicated discrepancies in the police accounts. The police officers who gave evidence denied their involvement or remembering any details about the death (Renton, 2014). This obstruction of facts was supported by the coroner, who is described as 'sowing confusion' and 'divert[ing] attention' from the police involvement in his killing (Renton, 2014, n.p.). Peach's partner, Celia Stubbs, described how the coroner sympathised with the officers but 'harangued Asian witnesses' for translation errors (Stubbs, 2010). On 27 May 1980, the verdict 'death by misadventure' was reached. As a result, no criminal prosecutions were mandated. This killing of Blair Peach and the failure of the inquest process was one of the catalysts for the setting up of the charity INQUEST, which is the only UK organisation that provides expertise on state-related deaths to support bereaved families and advocate for reforms to the inquest process (INQUEST, 2023).

The inquest into Peach's death is remembered by lawyers for its 'manifest injustice' and in particular the coroner's refusal to allow the jury or family access to the report that revealed the truth and identified the likely perpetrator (Renton, 2020, n.p.). Stubbs had hoped to achieve an 'unlawful killing' verdict, which would have resulted in accountability from the police. However, the coroner's refusal to publish the Cass Report, which identified the responsibility of the police, sustained this injustice over several decades. The report was only made publicly available in 2010 following the murder of Ian Tomlinson. Tomlinson died after being pushed to the ground by the police during a G20 summit protest (Renton, 2014). After three decades of campaigning, this death renewed the demands of Peach's family for the Cass Report to be published (Lewis, 2010; Renton, 2014). Stubbs described the relief and vindication that the publication of the report brought. Although the names of the police officers were redacted, it brought some closure by stating that the police struck the fatal blow that killed Peach (Stubbs, 2010). However, the release of this information has not led to any further investigation or prosecution (Renton, 2020). The affective capacity of this inquest supports the blame, denial and cover-up by the authorities for several decades in contrast to the exhaustion and demoralising sentiment that his partner has described in suffering such a bereavement and facing 'such determined intransigence' from the authorities (Undercover Policing Inquiry, 2020, p.29).

The final verdict from both Moussa and Peach's inquest was death by 'misadventure'. Blair Peach was framed as having attended the demonstration at his own risk (UK Parliament, 1980). The coroner in the Peach inquest made excessive attempts to exonerate the police of their guilt by denying the family and their lawyer access to the Cass Report and painting Peach as partly responsible (Renton, 2014; Scraton & Chadwick, 1986). In the Moussa inquest, the coroner believed that Moussa understood his risk in hiding beneath a bus and suggested that individuals should understand these dangers. As Griffiths (2024, p.100) argues elsewhere, overt forms of denial and suspicion (such as in the Peach case), alongside disinterest and indifference (such as in the Moussa case), frame individuals as 'responsible for their own suffering'. Both cases highlight the different yet comparable ways in which the inquest process can exonerate systemic forms of violence through its affective registers.

Outside of its legal and procedural role in establishing the cause of death, an inquest is capable of identifying areas to prevent future deaths. In their report 'No More Deaths', INQUEST (n.d.b) document how delays and fragmentation within the system are further hindrances to the promise of the investigatory process (INQUEST, n.d.b, p.5). One of their major concerns, which reflects that of many bereaved families, is the effectiveness of inquest conclusions and PFD reports. INQUEST highlights inconsistencies in recipients responding to PFD reports and the recommendations. Furthermore, the lack of an oversight body which could monitor recommendations further disrupts the affective capacity to provide closure. As Deborah Coles, Director of INQUEST, stated before the Justice Committee:

> There needs to be a national oversight mechanism to provide a clear framework for following up on what happens to these reports. Families repeatedly tell us that they go through these processes in the hope of meaningful change and, yet they subsequently find out about deaths in similar circumstances, which, you can imagine, really does add to the trauma and can be very re-traumatising.
>
> *(Justice Committee, 2020)*

A legal professional shared a similar sentiment to me during an interview: 'at certain inquests it feels like they are trying to limit the blame, rather than acknowledging what has happened'. Often, similar concerns appear 'time and time again', especially 'concerns around the monitoring of mental health or around monitoring safety'. This quote reveals how inquests are themselves contested processes, where deliberations by the coroner may focus on the minutia (Aitken, 2022). The neglect of addressing issues relating to public safety or safeguarding appears to contradict the preventive function of an inquest process. Finally, the frustration that the legal professionals and families exhibit further illustrates the varying emotions that different parties feel when an inquest repeatedly fails in its preventive function.

In the case of Peach, the truth about his death was deliberately obstructed for several decades. The reporting of Moussa's case was minimal. INQUEST has criticised the inaccessibility of coronial records online (Justice Committee, 2020). Whilst a report of an inquest can be found online, and it is possible to request a copy of the verdict, 'only a minority of inquests' receive media coverage (Citizens Information, 2021). Juliet Cohen (Head of Doctors, Freedom from Torture) found that there is no centralised or official record of suicides among asylum seekers. The ONS (Office for National Statistics) collects data on births and deaths. As Cohen (2021) states, she was surprised to find the lack of data on asylum seekers. Every incident of a possible suicide must be considered by a coroner, who is required to submit a form following an inquest. Cohen (2021, n.p) demonstrates the implications of failing to collect this information, stating, 'what is the point of an investigation into such a tragedy if not to try to reduce the risk of it happening to others?' As Cohen (2021, n.p) argues, this kind of 'data is vital to us because it tells a story about the lives of people who live among us but are marginalised and voiceless. This absence of information tells us they are not counted even in death'.

In my correspondence with legal professionals, I also found a similar omission of data as coroner's are not required to document the migration status of the deceased. Despite evidence that Black and racialised people in the UK experience 'some of the most violent, neglectful and contentious deaths at the hands of the state', issues of race and racism do not feature in post-death investigations (INQUEST, 2024a, p.7).[9] This omission severely hinders the opportunity for an inquest 'to establish the truth about the death and offer a measure of catharsis for bereaved families, who were often acutely aware of the role racism played in the death of their loved one' (INQUEST, 2024a, p.8). A stark reminder of the failings in prevention is the fact that deaths at the hands of the police continue apace. In 2024, INQUEST (2024b) found that 'every year, more people are dying in and following police custody', with 1,910 deaths recorded since 1990 (INQUEST, n.d.a). The exclusion of important facts regarding a person's identity, especially in cases of marginalisation or racialisation, further discounts the possibility of addressing forms of structural violence and preventing further harm.

Conclusion

This chapter focuses on ethnographic material collected from the inquest into the death of Mahammat Abdullah Moussa. This case illustrates how a number of emotions circulated during the inquest process, including indifference, remoteness and some vague sensitivity towards the circumstances surrounding his death. To situate this case within a broader discussion on how inquests deal with state violence, this chapter also referred to the historical case of Blair Peach. This case revealed intense struggles over the inquest process, which ultimately legitimised 'the wrongdoing of the authorities' and exonerated the police involved (Bourne, 2009, n.p.). The affective registers at an inquest can influence how society chooses to address state-related violence, including the violent realities of the UK's immigration system and policing. Emotional registers that individualise violence, favour cold scientific facts and fail to put the bereaved at the heart of the process may continue the ongoing devaluation of racialised and marginalised bodies. Whilst the inquest process has the potential to provide a sense of closure, the proceedings and systems of reporting often fail to address issues relating to structural violence and racism. Instead, the inquest process may focus on technical or administrative details (Aitken, 2022). Demands made by bereaved families and non-governmental organisations are important interventions in struggles for justice. These interventions and their inclusion in legal frameworks can and should provide a crucial challenge to the law where it silences and, by extension, perpetuates state violence.

Notes

1 Without the inquest into the death of Jimmy Mubenga, a detainee originally from Angola, who was killed aged 46 on 12 October 2010 whilst being forcedly restrained by three private security guards during a deportation flight (Taylor & Booth, 2014), 'the truth about his death would never have emerged' (Medical Justice, 2016). The inquest into his death 'exposed [the] racism and unlawful practices used in deportations' (INQUEST, 2013).
2 In 2019, I observed the inquest following the death of Tarek Chowdhury, from Bangladesh, who was fatally assaulted by another detainee at an immigration removal centre. The inquest found 'failures to properly assess and share information' regarding the perpetrator's mental health and violent tendencies. Due to 'inappropriate staffing and handover arrangements' in Colnbrook and despite the perpetrator displaying 'aggressive' and 'odd' behaviour, safeguarding measures were not escalated (Taylor, 2019a).
3 The United Families and Friends (UFFC) is a network that began in the 1990s as a group of Black people whose relatives were killed whilst in police custody. They campaign against institutionalised racist killings and meet on the last Saturday in October every year in Trafalgar Square to remember those killed by the state and to demand changes in the justice system. Available at: www.inquest.org.uk/blog/25-years-on-the-origins-of-uffc-from-the-archive
4 The charity INQUEST was partly formed as a result of the failings of this inquest. It is the only charity which supports bereaved families and investigations in cases involving state-related deaths. They advocate for changes to the system (Bourne, 2009; INQUEST, 2023).

5   This included securing treasures from shipwrecks, as well as forfeiture of estates or objects following self-inflicted deaths or murders.
6   The term border death has become synonymous with the deaths of migrants and refugees at the European-Mediterranean and US–Mexico state borders, who without the legal right to cross state borders are forced into clandestine and potentially deadly options to traverse sea, desert and land borders.
7   Existing academic research on migrant deaths challenges notions upheld by states that these deaths are 'natural' or 'tragic' (De León, 2015; Eschbach et al., 1999; Jones, 2016; Michalowski, 2007).
8   Structural violence, presented by these authors, is where suffering and violence are inflicted through social, political and economic conditions of poverty, political exclusion and unequal access to life support.
9   There is currently no existing case law in the coronial system to investigate racism or racial discrimination; however, principles from case law in employment tribunals and civil claims offer routes for advocating for racial justice and including questions of race and racism in the inquest process (INQUEST, 2024a, p.54).

References

Aitken, D. (2022). 'Investigating prison suicides: the politics of independent oversight', *Punishment and Society*, 24(3), 477–497.
Aliverti, A. (2020, September). 'Benevolent policing? Vulnerability and the moral pains of border controls', *The British Journal of Criminology* 60(5), 1117–1135.
Arthur, C. C. (2022). 'Make believe: police accountability, lying and anti-blackness in the inquest of Sean Riff', *Crime, Media, Culture*, 19(3), 362–379.
Baker, D. V. (2016). *Deaths after police contact: constructing accountability in the 21st century*. London: Palgrave Macmillan.
BBC. (2018, November 18). 'Body of suspected migrant found under bus in Folkestone', *BBC News*. Available at: www.bbc.co.uk/news/uk-england-kent-46255088?fbclid=IwAR1jRTgNxnlhtxfc2b7A-s1ncx5RfnTtPXexuSGYcsWrsNVLNQm6bqi-BNs (Accessed: 18 February 2022).
Blix, S. B. and Wettergren, A. (2018). *Professional emotions in court: a sociological perspective*. Abingdon; Oxford: Routledge.
Bourne, J. (2009). 'The political legacy of Blair Peach', *Institute of Race Relations*. Available at: https://irr.org.uk/article/the-political-legacy-of-blair-peach/ (Accessed: 18 December 2024).
Butler, J. (2004). *Precarious life: the powers of mourning and violence*. London: Verso.
Calais Migrant Solidarity. (n.d.). Deaths at the Calais Border. Available at: https://calaismigrantsolidarity.wordpress.com/deaths-at-the-calais-border/ (Accessed: 3 February 2022).
Chief Coroner. (2013). 'Guidance No.5: reports to prevent future deaths', *Courts and Tribunals Judiciary*. Available at: www.judiciary.uk/wp-content/uploads/2013/09/guidance-no-5-reports-to-prevent-future-deaths.pdf (Accessed: 18 December 2024).
Citizens Information. (2021). Inquests and Inquest Reports. Available at: www.citizensinformation.ie/en/death/sudden_or_unexplained_death/inquests.html (Accessed: 8 February 2022).

Cohen, J. (2021, March 29). 'Asylum seeker suicides aren't officially recorded – but they deserve to be', *Metro*. Available at: https://metro.co.uk/2021/03/29/asylum-seeker-suicides-deserve-to-be-officially-recorded-14159210/ (Accessed: 14 February 2022).

Coroners and Justice Act. (2009). Available at: www.legislation.gov.uk/ukpga/2009/25/contents (Accessed: 18 December 2024).

The Coroner's Society of England and Wales. (n.d.). History. Available at: www.coronersociety.org.uk/the-coroners-society/history/(Accessed: 18 December 2024).

Courts and Tribunal Judiciary. (2023). Speech by the Chief Coroner: Death and Taxes – The Past, Present, and Future of the Coronial Service. Available at: www.judiciary.uk/speech-by-the-chief-coroner-death-and-taxes-the-past-present-and-future-of-the-coronial-service/ (Accessed: 23 December 2024).

Courts and Tribunals Judiciary. (n.d.) Coroner Publications. Available at: www.judiciary.uk/publication-jurisdiction/coroner/ (Accessed: 18 February 2022).

De León, J. (2015). *The land of open graves: living and dying on the migrant trail*. Oakland, CA: University of California Press.

El-Enany, N. (2019). 'Before Grenfell: British immigration law and the production of colonial spaces', in Bulley, D., Edkins, J. and El-Enany, N. (eds.) *After Grenfell: violence, resistance and response*. London: Pluto Press, pp. 50–61.

Eschbach, K., Hagan, J., Rodriguez, N., Hernandez-Leon, R. and Bailey, S. (1999). 'Death at the border', *The International Migration Review*, 33(2), 430–454.

Farmer, P. (2004). 'An anthropology of structural violence', *Current Anthropology*, 45(3), 305–325.

Freckelton, I. (2007). 'Death investigation, the coroner and therapeutic jurisprudence', *Journal of Law and Medicine*, 15(2), 242–253.

Galtung, J. (1990). 'Cultural violence', *Journal of Peace Research*, 27(3), 291–305.

Goffman, E. (1959). *The presentation of self in everyday life*. New York: Anchor Books.

Green, J. (1992). 'The medico-legal production of fatal accidents', *Sociology of Health and Illness*, 14(3), 373–389.

Griffiths, M. (2023). Mixed Emotions Make Migrants Threatening, Polluting and Irrelevant. Available at: www.birmingham.ac.uk/news/2023/mixed-emotions-make-migrants-threatening-polluting-and-irrelevant (Accessed: 1 April 2024).

Griffiths, M. (2024). 'The emotional governance of immigration controls', *Identities*, 31(1), 82–103.

Hopkins, N., Vasagar, J., Kelso, P. and Osborn, A. (2000, June 20). 'Grim find of 58 bodies in lorry exposes smugglers' evil trade', *The Guardian*. Available at: www.theguardian.com/uk/2000/jun/20/immigration.immigrationandpublicservices3 (Accessed: 23 March 2022).

INQUEST. (n.d.a). Deaths in Police Custody. Available at: www.inquest.org.uk/deaths-in-police-custody (Accessed 18 December 2024).

INQUEST. (n.d.b). No More Deaths. Available at: www.inquest.org.uk/Handlers/Download.ashx?IDMF=b480f898-7fbd-4c9c-a948-50dd3fad3a04 (Accessed: 18 December 2024).

INQUEST. (2013, August 5). 'Coroner for the inquest into the death of Jimmy Mubenga publishes critical rule 43 report', *INQUEST Media Releases*. Available at: www.inquest.org.uk/jimmy-mubenga-coroner-rule-43-report-published (Accessed: 14 February 2022).

INQUEST. (2023). Unlawful Killing [Audio Podcast]. Spotify. Available at: https://open.spotify.com/show/0t6KTt9azEhp8sLQHIcj6L

INQUEST. (2024a). Achieving Racial Justice at Inquests. Available at: https://files.justice.org.uk/wp-content/uploads/2024/02/22174259/Feb-2024-Achieving-Racial-Justice-at-Inquests-1.pdf (Accessed: 4 July 2024).

INQUEST. (2024b). IOPC Statistics for England and Wales 2022/23. [online] Available at: www.inquest.org.uk/iopc-stats-2023-4 (Accessed: 18 December 2024).

Institute of Race Relations. (2020). Deadly Crossings and the Militarisation of Britain's Borders. Available at: https://irr.org.uk/wp-content/uploads/2020/11/Deadly-Crossings-Final.pdf (Accessed: 20 December 2024).

International Organisation for Migration. (n.d.). Europe, Missing Migrants Project. Available at: https://missingmigrants.iom.int/region/europe?region_incident=4061&route=3896&incident_date%5Bmin%5D=&incident_date%5Bmax%5D= (Accessed: 16 July 2024).

Jacobson, J., Templeton, L. and Murray, A. (2024). 'I feel like I've been swept along on a tsunami': Bereaved People's Experiences of Coroners' Investigations and Inquests Research Findings Summary. Voicing Loss. Available at: https://voicing-loss.icpr.org.uk/sites/default/files/2024-06/VL%20Research%20Findings%20Summary.pdf (Accessed: 18 December 2024).

Jones, R. (2016). *Violent borders: refugees and the right to move*. London; New York: Verso.

Justice Committee. (2020). Oral evidence: The Coroner Service, HC 282. Available at: https://committees.parliament.uk/oralevidence/1092/pdf/ (Accessed: 22 March 2022).

Karstedt, S. (2016). 'The emotion dynamics of transitional justice: an emotion sharing perspective', *Emotion Review*, 8(1), 50–55.

Lewis, P. (2010). 'Blair Peach killed by police, Met report finds', *The Guardian*. Available at: www.theguardian.com/uk/2010/apr/27/blair-peach-killed-police-met-report (Accessed: 18 December 2024).

Medical Justice. (2016). Death in Immigration Detention 2000 – 2015: Medical Justice. Available at: https://medicaljustice.org.uk/wp-content/uploads/2022/02/2015_Death-In-Immigration-Detention_Final.pdf (Accessed: 14 February 2022).

Michalowski, R. (2007). 'Border militarization and migrant suffering: a case of transnational social injury', *Social Justice*, 34(2), 62–76.

Mulcahy, L. (2011). *Legal architecture: justice, due process and the place of law*. Abingdon, Oxon; New York: Routledge.

Mulcahy, L. and Rowden, E. (2020). *The democratic courthouse: a modern history of design, due process and dignity*. Abingdon, Oxon: Routledge, Taylor & Francis Group.

Nijjar, J. S. (2019). 'Southall: symbol of resistance', *Race and Class*, 60(4), 65–69.

Oppenheim, N. (2024). 25 Years On: The Origins of UFFC from the Archive. Available at: www.inquest.org.uk/blog/25-years-on-the-origins-of-uffc-from-the-archive (Accessed: 18 December 2024).

Pallister, D. (2012). 'Police use unauthorised weapons, Blair Peach jury told', *The Guardian*. Available at: www.theguardian.com/theguardian/2012/may/28/archive-1980-blair-peach-inquest (Accessed: 18 December 2024).

Perl, G. (2016). 'Uncertain belongings: absent mourning, burial, and postmortem repatriations at the external borders of the EU in Spain', *Journal of Intercultural Studies*, 37(2), 195–209.

Renton, D. (2014). 'The killing of Blair Peach', *London Review of Books*, 36(10). Available at: www.lrb.co.uk/the-paper/v36/n10/david-renton/the-killing-of-blair-peach (Accessed: 3 July 2024).
Renton, D. (2020). 'On deadly policing and the 1979 Southall protests', *Lit Hub*. Available at: https://lithub.com/on-deadly-policing-and-the-1979-southall-protests/ (Accessed: 3 July 2024).
Roach Anleu, S. and Mack, K. (2019). 'A sociological perspective on emotion work and judging', *Oñati Socio-Legal Series*, 9(5), 831–851.
Rossner, M. (2017). 'Restorative justice in the 21st century: making emotions mainstream', in Liebling, A., Maruna, S. and McAra, L. (eds.) *The Oxford handbook of criminology*. Oxford: Oxford University Press, pp. 967–989.
Scheper-Hughes, N. and Bourgois, P.. (2004). 'Introduction: making sense of violence', in Scheper-Hughes, N. and Bourgois (eds.) *Violence in war and peace: an anthology*. Oxford: Blackwell Publishing, pp. 1–27.
Scraton, P. and Chadwick, K. (1986). 'Speaking Ill of the Dead: institutionalised responses to deaths in custody', *Journal of Law and Society*, 13(1), 93–115.
Searle, C. (2014). 'The truth behind the murder of Blair Peach?', *Institute of Race Relations*. Available at: https://irr.org.uk/article/the-truth-behind-the-murder-of-blair-peach/ (Accessed: 20 December 2024).
Shilliam, R. (2018). *Race and the undeserving poor*. Newcastle: Agenda Publishing.
Stubbs, C. (2010, April 30). 'The Cass report brings justice for Blair Peach closer', *The Guardian*. Available at: www.theguardian.com/commentisfree/2010/apr/30/cass-report-blair-peach-justice (Accessed: 18 December 2024).
Tait, G., Carpenter, B., Quadrelli, C. and Barnes, M. (2016). 'Decision-making in a Death Investigation: emotion, families, and the coroner', *Journal of Law and Medicine*, 23(3), 571–581.
Taylor, D. (2019a, March 25). 'Catalogue of failings led to death of 'gentle' man at detention centre', *The Guardian*. Available at: www.theguardian.com/uk-news/2019/mar/25/catalogue-of-failings-led-to-death-of-gentle-man-at-detention-centre (Accessed: 16 February 2022).
Taylor, D. (2019b, October 7). 'Hostile environment ruled not a factor in death of Windrush man', *The Guardian*. Available at: www.theguardian.com/uk-news/2019/oct/07/hostile-environment-ruled-not-a-factor-in-death-of-windrush-man (Accessed: 21 February 2024).
Taylor, M. and Booth, R. (2014, December 16). 'G4S guards found not guilty of manslaughter of Jimmy Mubenga', *The Guardian*. Available at: www.theguardian.com/uk-news/2014/dec/16/g4s-guards-found-not-guilty-manslaughter-jimmy-mubenga (Accessed: 15 February 2022).
Timmermans, S. (2006). *Postmortem: how medical examiners explain suspicious deaths*. Chicago: University of Chicago Press.
Timmermans, S., Prickett, P. and Martinez-Aranda, M. (2024). 'Unclaimed and Unclaimable Deaths: weaponizing migrant mourning', *Mortality*, 1–17. https://doi.org/10.1080/13576275.2024.2418971
Tran, M. (2000, July 5). 'Dover victims' relatives too afraid to come forward, says lawyer', *The Guardian*. Available at: www.theguardian.com/uk/2000/jul/05/immigration.immigrationandpublicservices (Accessed: 23 March 2022).
Tuitt, P. (2019). 'Law, justice and the public inquiry into the Grenfell Tower fire', in Bulley, D., Edkins, J. and El-Enany, N. (eds.) *After Grenfell: violence, resistance and response*. London: Pluto Press, pp. 119–129.

Tyler, I. (2013). *Revolting subjects: social abjection and resistance in neoliberal Britain*. London: Zed Books.

UK Parliament. (1980). Blair Peach, Hansard, 11 June. Available at: https://hansard.parliament.uk/Commons/1980-06-11/debates/be37c238-a2fe-40da-92f2-390272771fd4/BlairPeach (Accessed: 18 December 2024).

Undercover Policing Inquiry. (2020). Opening Statement on Behalf of Core Participants Represented Set Out in an Annex Represented by Hodge Jones & Allen, Bhatt Murphy and Bindmans Solicitors. Available at: www.ucpi.org.uk/wp-content/uploads/2020/11/20201026-Opening_Statement_CPs_represented-by_HJA_BM_Bindmans-MRQC.pdf (Accessed: 18 December 2024).

Webber, F. (2004) 'The war on migration', in Hillyard, P., Pantazis, C., Tombs, S. and Gordon, D. (eds.) *Beyond criminology: taking harm seriously*. London: Pluto Press, pp. 133–155.

Williams, S. (2019, April 23). 'Migrant died after clothes tangled under coach at Folkestone's Eurotunnel terminal', *KentOnline*. Available at: www.kentonline.co.uk/folkestone/news/migrant-found-dead-under-coach-203192 (Accessed: 16 February 2022).

Willis, R. (2023). *A precarious life: community and conflict in a deindustrialised town*. Oxford: Oxford University Press.

7

STAGING STATE EMBODIMENT

Performativity, Emotional Labour, and Recalibrating Dynamic Security in a Philippine City Jail

Hannah Nario-Lopez

Introduction

In *Asylums* (1968:18), Goffman observed that

> [e]ach grouping tends to conceive of the other in terms of narrow hostile stereotypes, staff often seeing inmates as bitter, secretive, and untrustworthy, while inmates often see staff as condescending, high-handed, and mean. Staff tends to feel superior and righteous; inmates tend to feel inferior, weak, blameworthy, and guilty.

I argue, however, that such oversimplification flattens the complexity of social relations within penal facilities. Instead, I view prisons as unique social environments where compound affective strategies occur.

I use the case of the Philippines, a country whose jails and prisons have been perpetually operating below international and national minimum standards (Nario-Lopez, 2017, 2020a, 2021a). Administration offices are deteriorated and powered by unsafe electrical wiring; toilets are lacking and do not have clean water. Detainees take turns sleeping, are malnourished, and often fall ill from respiratory illnesses, digestive diseases, and skin infections.[1] In the context where prison minimum standards remain an aspiration and material deprivation (food, space, beds, programmes) is widespread, human resources (correctional staff, psychological services, and rehabilitation expertise) become overstretched (Nario-Lopez, 2017, 2020b, 2021b). Officers in this study justify inattention to the "philosophical" concerns around punishment as superfluous to daily jail operations. In their words, what they need is to simply "get through the day" despite their best efforts to respond to their role as "justice frontliners" (Nario-Lopez, 2017:181).

Data from this chapter come from a total of three years of ethnographic research, from 2015 to 2018, in a jail located in the Philippines' capital city Metro Manila. This site was selected as case of focus of this research for its qualities that represent features that are universal in the country's detention and correctional facilities. The qualities include the following: (a) facility structure that is not intended for penal purposes; (b) poor and deteriorated buildings; (c) resident overcrowding; (d) understaffing; and (e) general lack of basic provisions such as food, medication, sanitation units, beds, and rehabilitation programmes. The ethnographic research is composed of frequent whole-day visits to the field site, ranging from three to four days a week. This allowed me, as an outsider of the penal profession, to achieve and sustain rapport with the actors in the field. In these visits, I spent time shadowing jail officers and "hanging out" in their offices and common areas where I was able to observe them as they work and interact with co-officers, residents, visitors, and higher-ups of the Bureau of Jail Management and Penology (BJMP). I had informal conversations, shared meals, and developed a deep sense of understanding about officers' personal perspectives about their profession. Towards the end of the ethnographic research, I conducted several focus group discussions with officers who were grouped according to rank to compare personal insights to shared group sentiments.

Throughout the research process, I remained attentive on how my presence might affect their conduct. I did my best to be present in the field regularly and in sustained periods of time to secure the officers' trust on my intentions. Among the primary things I reflected on is my positionality as a female researcher and highly masculinized setting. My reflections on my positionality were recorded in a journal and later published as a methodological piece (Nario-Lopez, 2018) wherein I highlighted how I responded to interactions and how I managed my own affective states during my observations. In the piece, I also explained that I resolved these concerns by approaching "sexist attitudes" from a perspective of understanding the officers' occupational culture, which at the end of my ethnographic research I addressed by conducting as gender-sensitivity training workshops among officers.

I refer to "institutional embodiment" in this chapter to investigate how institutions become tangible through their physical manifestations. While institutional embodiment can be achieved through physical manifestations like buildings, symbols, rituals, and bureaucratic process (Celermajer, Churcher, and Gatens, 2021), I focus on the agents of the state (workers or employees) as embodiments through administrative frameworks, institutional values, and power relations manifested in the setting. Specifically, in this piece, jail officers acting on behalf of the state perceive and try to achieve institutional embodiments by resorting to performativity and emotional labour. By highlighting the importance of emotion management in the institutional structure and the relational structure of the penal organization under study, I emphasize that due to lack of infrastructural support, officers' emotional labour and performativity techniques are used as a means for officers to achieve embodiment the institution they represent. Through this framing, the chapter advances our understandings of prison institutions as embodied structures that include both the institutional and relational structure of an organization (Elder-Vass, 2008). This chapter enriches the contribution of this volume by expanding the discussion on state embodiments in criminal justice settings, engaged in the chapters by Jefferson who focussed on how state power is embodied and affectively enforced through frontline state officials in Sierra Leone, Philips et al who scrutinized how probation workers embody the state by negotiating the emotional labour demands placed on them, and McCurdy who analysed how inquest proceedings implicate the adjudication of state violence, and the value placed on human life.

I start the discussion by detailing this prison context. Then, I move to scrutinize how emotions are managed for prison security, which I argue is a dynamic form of security. Dynamic security is a contemporary form of prison management, coined by Ian Dunbar in 1985 (Leggett and Hirons, 2006). Dynamic security maximizes the pragmatic functions of positive relationships within prison settings—between higher authorities, staff, and residents—banking on trust and reasonable accommodation of each other's stakes to maintain order. I analyse how officers use emotion management techniques to secure order despite the absence of basic provisions in the penal setting such as standardized housing units, supply of food and medication, and technological tools to ensure security and safety of residents. In this piece, I argue therefore that officers are subjected to intense emotion management to overcompensate for the state. Overcompensating means to try too hard to correct a problem, which can lead to creating a new problem, new difficulty, or lack of balance. In the case of the officers in the city jail under study, jail officers through emotional labour and performativity make up for the lack of and absence of specific state provisions to its penal institutions.

My work contemplates the invisible aspect of correctional work: performativity and emotion management. Using Goffman's theory of performativity and Hochschild's concept of emotional labour to examine how jail officers embody state institutions, the chapter analyses how officers manage their emotions and perform their roles to maintain order in challenging prison environments. The chapter examines the dynamics of officers' front and backstage behaviour, and the strategies they use to maintain control and standardize interactions through alternative interpretations of dynamic security. Hochschild's concept of emotional labour (1983) is incorporated in the analysis of how officers' emotional routines are part of their job performance. I consider how officers' emotional expressions adhere to cultural scripts based on institutional norms. Both Goffman's dramaturgy and Hochschild's concept of emotional labour focus on individuals following cultural scripts that dictate appropriate emotions for interactions; following them signifies role mastery and enhances performance credibility. Hochschild further introduces "display rules," which are societal norms that dictate which emotional expressions are acceptable in specific contexts. In this milieu, effective management by prison guards becomes indispensable. To survive each shift, staff turn to emotions and value feeling management as the most useful tool kit in delivering their duties (Nario-Lopez, 2017, 2020a, 2021a). The analysis connects performative acts with the maintenance of dynamic security to emphasize that social institutions are not abstract but are embedded and shaped by social practices, with workers serving as embodiments of these institutions. I conclude this chapter by forwarding questions for critical reflection on how such carceral conditions implicates staff members to surrender their emotions and what this means for the state's end in delivering justice.

Walking on a Tightrope: The Theatrics of Prison Security in the Philippines

In this section, I discuss the context of the study by describing the prison space and how the strains it presents affect the ways in which officers deliver their duties. Likening the jail as a site of officer role performance, I focus on how its features affect their view of and interactions with senior officers of the institution and residents, showing how officers maintain the design and structural integrity of the Goffmanian stage despite subhuman conditions.

Since the 1990s, the BJMP has operated at 300% occupancy (Nario-Lopez, 2017). Using an old police building with a quadrangle the size of a basketball court, the jail facility is not designed for detention. As a result, the interior spaces are crammed together, and the rooms are furrowed using light materials such as plywood and discarded furniture. The space complicates security measures because the presence of numerous crevices in makeshift bunk beds and small rooms which can be likened to cubicles become spaces where contrabands are crafted. Budget constraints limit the number of officers manning the facility. These conditions have serious consequences for jail security in two prominent ways. First, many tasks such as heading the scheduled counts, serving as errand boys and messengers for officers, and managing the schedule of cleaning chores are delegated to detainees. Such delegation creates competition for dominance that has natural risks including violence, circulation of contraband, and gang formation. Due to a lack of manpower, officers are unable to swiftly address these violations. Second, this also inverts the flow of power between staff and detainees, heightening the professional liabilities of officers for any ensuing jail disorder. When sour social contacts, passive–aggressive exchanges, verbal fights, and riots erupt, the officers on duty are responsible for these interactions; their careers are jeopardized (Figure 7.1).

Problems with jail conditions always point to officers' discontent with the BJMP. The officers believe that their role in the bureau is as simple as "just follow[ing] orders" ("*kasi sa bureau, basta sundin mo nalang*"). According to Officer V, they must do what needs to be done and say what needs to be said and all will be well. Early in their career as cadets, officers are ordered to "humbly accept" ("*tanggapin nalang*") how the structure of authority operates in a bureaucratized institution (Nario-Lopez, 2017). Through acquiescence that such is life in their profession, they can do what is commanded of them. Officers reveal their common sentiment that they must internalize that when they wear their uniform, they become a "different person" ("*ibang tao*")—not their private selves—and are representatives of the institution, the government, and the nation. On the one hand, these statements speak to the officers' awareness that they are actors merely playing out a role dictated to them and that they must embody an institution, a goal, and an entity larger than themselves. On the other hand, the bureau is seen by the officers as directors who impose the storyline through mandates from the BJMP Operations Manual, active protocols, and rolling memos. Routines, however, are not easy to glean if one is unfamiliar with the bureaucratic inner workings of carceral facilities.

From the focus group discussions and informal interviews I conducted with staff, officers referred to the administrators in the bureau as people who are "*nasa taas*" (above the ranks, bureaucracy). Focus groups were composed of personnel who man the facilities from the ranks of Jail Officer 1 to Senior Jail Officer 4 and see themselves as "*nasa baba*" (below the ranks, bureaucracy) or working on the ground. They are at the bottom of the chain of command and are made to be aware since the intake training that they need to set aside criticisms and place their complete trust in the state institution they serve. The officers recognize that the vertical structure in the bureaucracy is a natural characteristic of the bureau—it is a given—and they alluded to the bureau's paramilitary structure where orders flow downward. The officers see themselves as enactors of orders from above, portraying scenes and enunciating scripts aligned with broader institutional goals. From this perspective, officers view the bureau as their stage director. This is further manifested in several ways.

First, officers believe that they are always left out of the planning, not consulted, and are simply expected to take and execute orders. There are times that officers wish that the higher ranks from the national headquarters would take the time to understand how jails struggle to operate. One officer shared that a visit per quarter to do "performance checks" is not enough to see the real volatility of their positions. Second, most officers believe that

146 The Embodied State

FIGURE 7.1 Panoramic view of the jail from the courtyard. To the left of the photo are the offices. And to the centre and right are the living quarters for residents.

the BJMP Operations Manual (2015) is severely outdated and that the top ranks perceive that they can run a show robotically. The manual is essential because it details routines on how to run the jail, enforce rules, and deal with residents. According to the officers, the manual is removed from how jails are feasibly managed on the ground. It is "too ideal," without consideration of social dynamics. Perspectives that do not align, they claim, produce unsubstantiated instructions that are often detrimental to the social order and relational harmony in the facility. Officer B further emphasizes that the manual was written by people who have police training and thus do not have a background in custodial management. For example, a directive was placed to eradicate makeshift bunks (*kubols*) immediately. *Kubols* are important to detainees because they serve as private spaces to rest and receive residents' families. These small spaces were destroyed in a very cinematic display before the media to exhibit how stern BJMP is enacting rules. After the operation, staff are left behind to appease detainees. The officers explained that while they understood the order follows the manual, the National Headquarters did not give them any alternatives. The officers believe that their blind following is futile and can even be hazardous to securing the footing of their authority and their relationships with residents.

Assembling Emotions and Recalibrating Dynamic Security

Due to substandard jail conditions and conflicting orders from the jail management, the relationship between officers and the resident population are constantly in flux. In this section I outline the ways in which officers attempt to mend incongruences between jail mandates and practices, discussing repertoires by which officers manage their emotions as "performances" of "being paramilitary" to arrive at an alternative form of dynamic security. Moreover, I delve deeper into how officers negotiate their roles by reconfiguring security measures and how they use emotions as a resource to overcompensate for material deficiencies and gang ascendancy to embody their state-mandated roles.

To achieve dynamic security, detainees are taught how to communicate respectfully to each other and deal with conflict by conferring to the process of mediation facilitated by officers. Language is recast to more constructive vocabularies and pleasant tones. According to the warden, this is a big shift because now they are sensitive to the fact that they are manning "persons"— who have humanity—and therefore deserve respect. This change helps direct each staff interaction, big and small, to rehabilitating detainees through needs-based approaches to care. In the city jail, however, administering dynamic security is a challenge due to the difficulty experienced by officers in discerning gangs' genuine intentions. Butler, Slade, and Dias (2018) warned that prisons struggle to standardize operations due to gangs' organizational sophistication. Gangs have strong leverage in prison order (Jones, 2014) because of their capacity to recruit, maintain the loyalty of members, and strengthen clout (Lyman, 1989). In the context of the Philippines, officers accommodate gangs because they provide indispensable resources such as food, medication, and human resources from members that have become essential in completing tasks that officers can no longer take on (e.g. cleaning, cooking, and routine counts) (Narag, 2005; Gutierrez, 2012).

Though prison scholarship has long emphasized the need for staff control (Dilulio, 1987), contemporary scholars have expanded the understanding of how hierarchy is negotiated by staff and residents to achieve prison order. Prison systems can be decentralized, with prisoner self-governance, or centralized, with co-governance between staff and residents (Skarbek, 2020). Self-governance is more common in the Global North, while co-governance is observed in the Global South, where resident-delegates act as a link between formal rules and informal norms. This expansion of how residents groups are valued by officers is also apparent in the case of this study. In the Philippines, residents groups, known as *"mga pangkat,"* are viewed as an alternative to formal prison structures, contributing to social cohesion and harmonious relationships among residents. These groups are seen as essential to jail order. Jail officers acknowledge they cannot eliminate gangs, and that jail order depends on pangkat magna carta, which holds gang leaders accountable for their members' actions. Officers rely on residents' networks to provide necessities; however, some officers view the guidance within gangs as favouritism. Officers are aware that detainees study their behaviour and can use this information to manipulate them, creating emotional tension.

Officers have resigned to the fact that gangs will endure until structural improvements are made (Nario-Lopez, 2021a, 2021b). In my interview with the warden, he clarified that this is the main reason why, for the time being, a shift in perspective is needed. The warden even argued that close ties and loyalty within resident groups can be foundations to build a "compassionate community." While all officers who support the warden's perspective see this alternative form of governance as a positive development in prison culture, they are aware of how this too can inhibit the bureau's administration. To circumvent this predicament, jail officers calibrated how they enforce security. Through their specific form of dynamic security, officers reconstruct prison management that complies with prison standards and institutional mandates, while deliberating with and appeasing detainees. To them, the management of social relations is imperative because it directly relates to security and safety within the facility.

Staff try their best to manoeuvre threat and fear out of social dynamics, so accountability of parties is achieved. Through consistent open communication, via regular meetings with gang *mayores* (leaders), agents of the bureau hear out residents' concerns while residents cooperate, volunteer "intelligence information," and forward suggestions. It is in this deliberative process that the jail can run despite the chaos. The way they practise dynamic security may not be the most ideal form of prison order, but in their peculiar prison setting, it helps dissipate outbursts of violence. As such, relational assets proceeding from close observance and calculation of role performance charged with the appropriate emotions become the most reliable feature of the interactive process to secure the continuity of peaceful social relations. The challenge of practising dynamic security is in the term "dynamic." It is ongoing and proactive, where a balance of seemingly disparate qualities of prison management is hard to poise. Finding the midpoint between effective communication and staff vigilance; immediate intervention and mindful action; surveillance and care; and restraint and rehabilitation involve emotional gauging and calibration.

In prison work, as revealed by the officers in this study, dynamic security is composed of assemblages of affective routines and emotional labour. In synergistic spaces, routines are critical in administering normative order. Goffman (1971a, 1971b) explains that the durability of interaction is necessary to sustain relationships. And it is in these relations that social order is intuitively achieved. In my observations of routines in the jail facility, interaction stability is facilitated not by the design of space—like other affluent prison settings with panoptic structures, or more progressive Scandinavian-style prisons (Fowler, 2015)—but through expressive controls. Officers vividly portray and emphasize certain emotions to command attention and beckon behaviours. They employ two strategic lines of expressive control: (a) behavioural strategies usually comprised altering gestures, actions, and conduct to appear that one is feeling the suitable emotion; and (b) cognitive processes, which include the methodical manipulation of raw grasp and judgement of the affective focus to authentically replicate feelings in agreement to the appropriate emotion.

Workers are required to exhibit specific emotions as part of their job responsibilities. The successful adherence to these display rules signifies the fulfilment of their professional roles as a "good officer." Display rules and the emotional labour that come with them (Nario-Lopez, 2021a, 2021b) demands officers to keep a "face" or put on different "masks" when they perform before superiors and before detainees. At the front stage, officers portray the idealized jail officer as it was taught in training and constantly imposed by bureau protocols, guidelines, and reminder memos. When curtains open, officers need to keep a face as somebody competent and credible enough to carry four core competencies to uphold the bureau's mission and vision. Acting as deeper goals and values shared by officers and the bureau are (a) "continuous skills enhancement of personnel; (b) ability to establish linkages and partnerships; (c) responsive planning; (d) timely decision-making; and (e) expedient implementation" (Bureau of Jail Management and

Penology (BJMP), 2010). All personnel are also expected to commit to and respect human rights, have efficiency and competence, and cooperate with teamwork as their core values (Bureau of Jail Management and Penology (BJMP), 2015). This idealization of the perfect officer assumes flawless delivery of personal fronts (Goffman, 1959). However, when I asked officers what being an "ideal officer" means to them, they shared different qualities that involved emotional training and management: (a) respectable; (b) calm and collected; and (d) disciplined. All these are essential in the perfection of performances or until it is portrayed with "unthinking ease" (Goffman, 1959:75).

To encapsulate these ideals, officers use a common term: "paramilitary." Maintaining control of how one reacts is crucial to uphold idealized impressions and preserve credibility before other actors. "Being paramilitary," before detainees, connotes the masculine comportment of being stoic, tough, and must not be carried away by emotions (*"huwag magpadala sa emosyon"*) before detainees. This adjustment is particularly crucial in the presence of detainees who are adept at detecting emotions and may interpret them as vulnerabilities. The officer explained that displaying ambiguity in the confined space of the city jail makes them susceptible to manipulation and potential attacks. Becoming emotional, according to her, creates an impression of vulnerability and weakness, which can be exploited by others. This concern raised by a female officer and the same concern is also raised by other officers who have different gender identities. Similarly, even though officers empathize with detainees' struggles, they need to display stern dispositions to personify supervision and control (Bureau of Jail Management and Penology (BJMP), 2015). This is especially true in circumstances where officers need to follow instructions from courts and other authorities. Situations where officers need to separate residents from their children, even when sick or dying, break officers' hearts the most. One officer said that they simply needed to do it due to court orders, even though they may endure outrage from the public and the media.

In contrast, before bosses, to be "paramilitary" means operating within the tradition of rank. Such commitment goes so far as changing personalities. Officers display feminized traits, such as subservience, docility, patience, and servitude. The officers parallel their bureau (BJMP) with other uniformed services such as the Philippine National Police (PNP) and Armed Forces of the Philippines (AFP) that follow the culture and customs (*"Ang paramilitary sumusunod sa culture (..) customs and tradition ng uniformed service mapa-BJMP, PNP, AFP"*) especially in terms of alluding to rank when receiving orders or assignments. When I asked if these different traits conflict with their role performance before the residents, one officer said it is how it is, it is a part of it (*"ganun talaga iyon, parte talaga iyon"*). One interviewee appraised subservience as a cogent and respectable choice when they comport themselves towards their superiors, going so far as to change their personalities. For example, a female senior officer explains how patience is just one of the many facets in being a part of the bureau. To her, you must love your job and from this, you will learn how to be "careful" and have "self-control."

> Ako, ang pinaka-natandaan ko lang talaga, mag-ingat sa duty. Ingatan ang duty, mahalin... Kailangan mabago ang personalidad. Noong nagtraining kami nabago iyong pagkatao ko. Dahil dati may "civilian mentality" nga kami eh. Unipormado ako, may baril ako, di porket may baril ako mamamaril ka na ng tao. Dapat may kontrol ka rin sa sarili mo.

> (For me, what I have learned in my years of service is that you need to be careful. You need to be careful while you are on duty. You need to love the job... you need to change your personality. When we were training, our personality has changed. Because before, we have "civilian mentality." Now, we are uniformed. We have guns but just because we carry guns, it does not mean we can shoot people. We should have control of ourselves).

At the backstage, officers engage in the rehearsal of scripts and discuss various strategies to enhance the maintenance of "expressive control" (Goffman, 1959), which they practise with co-officers. In meetings and individual consultations with the warden, officers are often advised to concede to "the plan," the performance of the collective. Taken together, individual emotion management processes carried out by each officer result in a more cohesive implementation of bureau rules, fortifying the bureau's institutional identity. According to officers, managing their personal emotions is part of the job. They value emotional management as a fundamental skill because it implicates the ability to differentiate between "emotions" and "principles." According to one officer, principles are grounded in logic and practicality ("*dapat nasa tamang rason at praktikal*") needed in the job, while emotions are ("*makasarili*") selfish. This denotes that being "emotional" is perceived as being egotistic (i.e. taking things personally), whereas principles are based on ideals that benefit everyone (i.e. taking one for the team). Officer G emphasized that officers should not display any indications of being emotional while on duty, especially emotions that suggest they feel victimized or confronted with individual moral dilemmas. They must proceed, according to a younger officer, even though they are deeply hurt: "*Tuloy ang trabaho kahit masakit*" (keep on going even though it is a pain).

From the Goffmanian perspective, "internalization" is a sign of affective idealization. In the case of the officers, they self-regulate emotions and manage outward displays of feelings and moods to keep themselves in check and aligned with institutional requisites. Careful deployment, to the officers, is critical for their unit to achieve dynamic security.

Institutional Embodiments through Expressive Controls

In this section, I extend the earlier analysis of officers' role performances and emotion management strategies to analyse efforts employed by officers at the institutional level to embody the state. In the jail setting under study, officers systematically rehearse and practise state embodiments at the institutional level in six salient ways: (a) by creating "adaptive mechanisms" to secure peaceful relations within the facility; (b) by formalizing communication channels for collaboration and resolving grievances; (c) by trusting the wisdom of senior officers and following procedures stipulated in the operations manual; (d) by rehearsing with co-officers discrepancies in past role performances; (e) by maintaining confidentiality of their emotional management practices; and (f) by carefully calculating the emotional climate of the resident population before arriving at decisions.

First, symmetry of interaction is achieved through the review of incidents and the perception of outcomes in interactions with detainees. Illustrations of ways by which they perform "adaptive mechanisms" include roleplaying during professionalization workshops, training on the therapeutic community modality programme, and the *Katatatagan Kontra Droga* (drug rehabilitation) modules, where officers look back at previous interactions and try to address issues that had hindered proper communication and negotiation between conflicting parties. During consultative meetings and team building sessions, officers also calibrate past performances, so they achieve intended outcomes (usually aligned with security and to keep the "peace in the facility") in interacting with detainees. For instance, I was invited to observe "special concerns" meetings between specific detainees and officers from the welfare unit. I observed that officers express empathy for detainees' requests but draw limits to how much consideration they will provide. In particular "special cases," the *mayores* are involved to ensure sanctions are imposed on detainees who break prison rules.

Second, the warden and pertinent unit heads conduct routine meetings with resident leaders (*mayores*) to establish formal avenues of collaboration and standardize grievance mechanisms. In these meetings, resident leaders communicate to officers' ongoing troubles experienced by their members. Officers act as mediators of grievances, file official paperwork, and impose necessary sanctions. In these meetings officers and residents both decide on priority projects, plan activities, and disseminate various updates on rehabilitation programmes. I have observed that in these meetings, while remaining advocates for their groups, detainees enthusiastically volunteered participation of their members. Officers, in my observations, treated detainees professionally as if they were colleagues and yet instilled rules (*patakaran*) as their contribution for the well-being of all (*pakikisama*, being one with others). These meetings foster positive social relations between officers and residents and make it easier for officers to communicate with higher-ranking officers because decisions arise from actively consulting stakeholders who are involved. Adapting formalistic routines make it easier to communicate decisions to the higher-ups.

Third, officers seek guidance from trusted personnel for wisdom on how to talk over faulty interactions that have transpired. If things get worse, they turn to the operations manual, document incidences, and course concerns through official lines of bureaucracy. In seeking help through channels, officers are guaranteed that they are resolving problems within their institutional safety nets. Officers have faith in the bureau's "due process" because as stated above, they are most careful in their interactions with gang members, especially leaders. For example, if they need to speak with gang leaders, they never do it in dorms because these spaces are considered gang territories. An officer explained, "*I-consider mo 'yung no-no sa trabaho mo ang komprontahin sila sa loob ng kanilang bahay sa teritoryo, wala ka pong kalaban-laban. Kahit opisyal ka, kahit si warden, hindi pwede kumonpronta sa loob.*" (Always consider the no-no's of the job, like confronting *mayores* in dorms, their homes, their territory, where you do not have clout and protection. Even if you are an official, even the warden, he cannot confront detainees inside [dorms].)

Fourth, individual officers seek the cooperation of other team members to patch up discrepancies in performance. Senior officers also proactively approach junior members of the team to correct mistakes. As a group, unit heads meet with members every Monday to evaluate performances and incidents, if any, that occurred over the past days. Often, it is the newly hired jail officers who need the most help in effectively communicating detainees' soft diplomacy in the "correct way" ("*tamang paraan*")—depending on the type of relationship, mood, and personality of the detainee, and the emotional climate of the whole prison population. Like an orchestra, custodial officers act or play upon the command of the warden who acts as their conductor—making sure that everyone executes their work at the proper time and tempo; all facets of jail work are delivered in harmony. This delicate task is done backstage, discreetly, to achieve mystification (Goffman, 1959:67).

Fifth, officers methodically practise state embodiments by maintaining the confidentiality of their emotion management strategies. Mystification of "being paramilitary" is important because officers need to withhold information from detainees to manage perceptions and maintain professional distance. In routines and rehearsals, such cautiousness can also be observed because officers have varying ways of interpreting "definitions of the situation." They consider, for example, the position of the detainee whom they are interacting with in the *pangkat* by maintaining a balance between distance and mutual trust as a standard for interaction. As observed during the ethnographic work, officers maintain distance by keeping conversations in a professional tone while also communicating that they understand the concerns of the detainees, even personal ones. An officer warned, "*Hindi mo hawak ang isip nila eh, may isa lang na aburrido diyan saksakin ka sa loob, wala ka na.*" (You cannot have a handle of their minds. Even if there is just one of them who is aggravated, you might be stabbed, and then you are gone!). Such emotion management informal rules enable officers to move about while also balancing bureau goals and soliciting cooperation from detainees.

Last, officers evaluate interactions in terms of the emotional climate of the prison population and consider the gravity of consequences if the situation escalates. Anticipating emotional outbursts is perhaps the hardest to learn, according to the officers, because detainee moods are hard to interpret and come in flux and surges. Amid this uncertainty, officers remain watchful in every social contact—in speech and even non-verbal communication—as detainees' impending engagements are unpredictable. One officer highlighted how detainees have all their waking hours to watch jail staff, studying their movements, routines, and personalities. The officer feared that this gives detainees enough information to manipulate or even threaten them. So, if for example, detainees' requests do not compromise jail operations, officers often grant them to maintain understanding and cooperation. One officer shared, "*Oo, trained to care. Para kaming caregiver eh. Kasi tao yan eh na nakakaramdam din ng sakit. Dapat di sila sinasaktan. Challenge satin 'yun.*" (Yes, we are trained to care. We are like caregivers. We know that the residents are humans and feel pain. We should not hurt them.). Despite being undervalued, officers continue to tread through because, in their minds, they are public servants who are under oath. An officer proudly shared, "*[b]ilang public servant, nagnanais din tayo na somehow, makatulong din.*" (As a public servant, I also wish that I can help somehow.). Seeing themselves as public servants is central to the professional identity among officers (Nario-Lopez, Piers, and Entienza, 2020). For them, their badges represent not only their ranks but their duty to embody the state.

The nexus between the individual emotional labour and institutional embodiments is bonded because officers maximize the sway and effect of their collective performances and interpersonal processes. Officers optimize all resources and means available, even though this means that often the demand for emotional labour begs more than mere control of emotional expressions. Officers admit that they often feel burnout and regret losing time with their families to be able to attend to long hours on the job. They, however, express strong pride in the opportunity to serve and the invisible efforts they make to run a judicious detention facility despite many challenges.

Conclusion

In this chapter, I analyse how officers strive for ideal role performances and institutional goals despite material constraints and challenges to their authority through concepts of frontstage role performances and backstage processes. Using Goffman's work on social life as theatre and Hochschild's concepts of display rules and emotional labour, I explore how constraints in a prison setting in the Global South foist officers to create an assemblage of emotional displays to overcompensate for the material constraints within the institution they represent. In their narratives and reflections, officers deploy dynamic security through the reconstruction of emotional expressions as individuals and as teams. Officers align these affective strategies with paramilitary stances in their work culture. In officers' championing of their institutionalized embodiments, the meticulous reorganization of emotions is warranted. And, while I agree that officers' resilience and determination must be lauded, I also maintain how surrendering emotions to embody the institutions misuses deep socialization to excuse state negligence. I hope to see further examinations of how embodiments of state institutions continue to reify human suffering not only to its subjects but also to its agents.

To end, I encourage researchers to confront how normative, regularized, and seemingly innocent aspects of our everyday life, while beneficial in perceiving resilience, particularly in public service, are also used to justify abandonment by structures of authority. I continue to believe in the task of sociology in unravelling indiscernible yet salient driving forces that shape human conduct and the ways by which we define the limits of how we relate with each other and make use of resources according to social roles and artificial entitlements. Lastly, I wish to express my profound gratitude to scholars who continue to communicate sociological knowledge in accessible language at the policy front, with non-government organizations and open spaces to publicly discuss germane features of our social life—in all its amusing charm and absurdity.

Note

1 The daily food budget is PHP 60 (Philippine pesos, or US$1.25) and daily medicine budget is PHP 8 (US$0.15).

References

Bureau of Jail Management and Penology (BJMP). (2010). About BJMP. Retrieved from www.bjmp.gov.ph/about.html
Bureau of Jail Management and Penology (BJMP). (2015). *Jail Operations Manual*.
Butler, M., Slade, G., & Nunes Dias, C. (2018). Self-Governing Prisons: Prison Gangs in an International Perspective. *Trends in Organized Crime*.
Celermajer, D., Churcher, M., & Gatens, M. (Eds.). (2021). *Institutional Transformations: Imagination, Embodiment, and Affect*. New York: Routledge.
Dilulio, J. J. (1987). *Governing Prisons: A Comparative Study of Correctional Management*. New York: London Free Press.
Elder-Vass, D. (2008). Integrating Institutional, Relational and Embodied Structure: An Emergentist Perspective 1. *The British Journal of Sociology*, 59(2), 281–299.

Fowler, M. (2015). The Human Factor in Prison Design: Contrasting Prison Architecture in the United States and Scandinavia. *103rd ACSA Annual Proceedings: The Expanding Periphery and the Migrating Center.*

Goffman, E. (1959). *The Presentation of Self in Everyday Life.* Garden City: Anchor Books Doubleday and Company Inc.

Goffman, E. (1968). *Asylums: Essays on the Social Situations of Mental Patients and Other Inmates.* Garden City: Anchor Books Doubleday and Company Inc.

Goffman, E. (1971a). *Relations in Public: Microstudies of the Public Order.* New York: Basic Books.

Goffman, E. (1971b). *Encounters: Two Studies in the Study of Interaction.* Middlesex: Penguin Books Ltd.

Gutierrez, F. (2012). Pangkat: Inmate Gangs at the New Bilibid Prison Maximum Security Compound. *Philippine Sociological Review*, 60(1), 193–237.

Hochschild, A. R. (1983). *The Managed Heart.* Berkeley and Los Angeles: University of California Press.

Jefferson, A. M., & Gaborit, L. S. (2015). *Human Rights in Prisons: Comparing Institutional Encounters in Kosovo, Sierra Leone and the Philippines.* London: Palgrave Macmillan UK.

Jones, C. (2014). Prison Gangs and Prison Governance in the Philippines. *Griffith Asia Quarterly*, 2(1), 57–74.

Leggett, K., & Hirons, B. (2006). Security and Dynamic Security. In M. Parker (Ed.), *Dynamic Security: The Democratic Therapeutic Community in Prison* (pp. 232–241). London: Jessica Kingsley Publishers.

Lyman, M. (1989). *Gangland.* Illinois: Springfield.

Narag, R. (2005). *Freedom and Death Inside the Jail: A Look into the Condition of the Quezon City Jail.* Manila: Supreme Court of the Philippines.

Nario-Lopez, H. G. (2017). Emotional Labor among Officers in a Philippine City Jail. Quezon City: University of the Philippines Diliman MA Sociology Thesis.

Nario-Lopez, H. G. (2018). Doing Qualitative Research on Emotional Labor in a Philippine City Jail. *Philippine Social Science Review*, 70(1), 73–97.

Nario-Lopez, H. G. (2020a). The Potential and Plausibility of Rehabilitative Prison Culture: A Philippine Example. *Social Science Diliman: A Philippine Journal of Society and Change*, 16(2), 29–65. https://journals.upd.edu.ph/index.php/socialscienceddiliman/article/view/8501

Nario-Lopez, H. G. (2020b). Managing a Congested Jail Population: An Interview with a City Jail Warden. In F. C. Gutierrez (Ed.), *Crime and Punishment in the Philippines: Beyond Politics and Spectacle* (pp. 255–266). Quezon City: Philippine Social Science Council.

Nario-Lopez, H. G. (2021a). Diskarte Lang: Dealing with Operational Challenges in a Philippine City Jail. *Social Transformations: Journal of the Global South*, 9(1), 159–194. https://ajolbeta.ateneo.edu/stjgs/articles/228/2551

Nario-Lopez, H. G. (2021b). Emotional Labor Dynamics as Precursors to Mundane Violence in a Philippine City Jail. *MovimentAção*, 8(14), 65–93. https://doi.org/10.30612/mvt.v8i14.15019

Nario-Lopez, H. G., Piers, S., & Entienza J. (2020). Embodying the Promises of the People Power Revolution: Public Service as Civic Engagement among Millennial Officers in a Philippine City Jail. *Philippine Social Science Review*, 72(2), 43–89.

Skarbek, D. (2020). *The Puzzle of Prison Order.* New York: Oxford University Press.

8
PREMATURE REVENGE

Feud Law among Prospective Police Recruits in Rio de Janeiro, Brazil

Eduardo de Oliveira Rodrigues

Introduction

Feud law has garnered significant attention in scholarly literature, with many scholars engaging in lively debates about its role in both past and present contexts, as well as in Western and non-Western societies (Christensen, 2016; Gluckman, 1955; Marques, 2002; Pitt-Rivers, 1977; Povolo, 2015). Viewed as antithetical to the modern rule of law, Willian Miller (1998, pp. 162–163) argues that feuds are often conceptualised as a "crazed, uncontrolled, subjective, [and] individual" way of managing conflicts, "admitting no reason, no rule of limitation." For others, feuds can also function as a parallel system of "power balance" between warring groups (Robert, 2007, pp. 28–29), framing criminal and political violence in environments often associated with so-called "failed", "collapsed," or "weak" states in the Global South (Geiβ, 2009; Howard, 2016; Rotberg, 2010).

Yet feud law has evolved into a persistent informal system that coexists and entangles with formal criminal justice institutions in Brazil. In cities like Rio de Janeiro, the police mobilise feud law as a legitimising mechanism for lethal state violence, often justified as an immediate response to police victimisation. According to Terine Coelho (2017, pp. 151–152), deaths caused by on-duty officers in Rio tend to rise following the murder of an agent. In percentage terms, within the seven days following an officer's murder, the likelihood of a civilian being killed increases by 125%. This figure rises to 350% the following day and dramatically escalates to 1150% on the same day. More recent statistics from the data lab "Fogo Cruzado" reveal that, of the 305 "slaughters"[1] that occurred between August 2016 and December 2021, 223 were carried out during "police raids,"[2] while 82 were attributed to "criminal and unofficial actions" by illegal groups (Hirata et al., 2022a, p. 4). Of the total 1,184 deaths recorded, 878 were the result of direct state action, while 306 were attributed to criminal groups (Hirata et al., 2022a, p. 5). In summary, police interventions resulted in nearly three times as many "slaughters" as armed criminal groups and caused the deaths of almost three times as many people over the past eight years in the RMRJ.

Considering the scenario above, this chapter responds to one of the prompts in this edited collection by asking: *How does the desire for revenge create an emotional moral economy of policing in Rio's impoverished neighbourhoods?* Following Didier Fassin (2009, p. 14), I understand a "moral economy of policing" here as the analysis of the "production, distribution, circulation, and use of moral sentiments, emotions and values, norms, and obligations in the social space" by the police. To address this problem, I propose a dual shift in focus compared to more traditional scholarship: (a) from the violent acts of revenge to the emotions they evoke; (b) from current to potential avengers— that is, from police officers to prospective recruits who may become involved in future feuds.

As will be demonstrated, the emotions driven by revenge are linked to a process that begins even before individuals formally join the Military Police of Rio de Janeiro (PMERJ).[3] The aspiration to "become the police," I argue, is part of a *state effect* (Abrams, 1988; Trouillot, 2001) that emerges from the very "ground of the city" my research interlocutors inhabit. By examining how the state may also be embodied through revenge by these civilian prospective police recruits, I aim to contribute, from a bottom-up perspective, to scholarship that challenges the binary distinctions often found in the social sciences—such as state/society, reason/emotion, and civilian/ military (Brigagão, 1985; Fassin et al., 2015; Gupta, 2012; Laszczkowski & Reeves, 2018; Lima & Dias, 2022).

My analysis is structured in three interconnected parts. First, I unpack a paradox shared by one of my main research interlocutors. While Ricardo[4]—a professional driver and aspiring police recruit—wants to patrol the streets of poor, violent zones in the suburbs of Rio, he prefers to drive his Uber in the city's wealthy, safer neighbourhoods. I explore this paradox by ethnographically examining his desire to pursue a police career in Rio's northern suburbs and the reasons behind his "seeking revenge against criminals" following a violent incident he experienced while attending an Uber ride. In the next section, I analyse how his experience with criminal violence sets the stage for understanding not only the emotions driven by revenge, but also how Ricardo and some of his peers prematurely embody these emotions in their journey of "becoming the police." Finally, I conclude that state power, by "educating the proper distribution of sentiments and desires" (Stoler, 2007, p. 9), shapes an emotional economy of policing central to understanding the high levels of police lethality in Rio de Janeiro.

Safe Driving, Dangerous Policing

When I first met Ricardo, he was working as an Uber driver for 12 hours a day. His busy schedule made it challenging for us to find time to talk, as his only day off was Monday. He could never join me and other prospective recruits for drinks after evening classes, nor could he watch football on TV during the weekends. The best way for me to learn more about his life and his interest in a career in policing was to ride with him whenever possible. Whenever I needed an Uber, I would request Ricardo's services, especially for longer rides.[5] Informally texting and booking him via WhatsApp was also beneficial, as it allowed for engaging conversations and helped him avoid the 25% commission charged by the app.

Besides being his most loyal client, I also met him twice a week in the evenings at a preparatory course for the PMERJ academic tests, where I had begun my fieldwork. My doctoral research involved 15 months of in-depth interactions with hundreds of police career aspirants from June 2019 to September 2020. As candidates needed to pass multiple tests to join the force,[6] I often found myself tutoring them in humanities studies during class breaks. As our relations deepened, some candidates came to trust me beyond the classroom, inviting me into their workplaces, homes, and leisure activities across impoverished areas of the city. Following their daily lives allowed me to observe how Military Police Officers (PMs) share vital aspects of their routines with prospective colleagues, as they also maintain civilian connections as family members, friends, neighbours, employers, and acquaintances. Ricardo, for example, had a young cousin who was a constable and an uncle who was a long-term sergeant already serving in the Military Police. As will be shown, having police relatives was crucial for Ricardo to pursue a career in policing.

My interlocutor was, at the time, a 25-year-old Black man, married to his wife Paula for four years, and currently living in a modest studio in his mother's backyard. After losing his job at a unionised motor carrier, Ricardo had to start driving for Uber and move back to his mother's property to save money (much to his wife's dismay). The young couple had previously lived in a small two-room apartment in the northern suburbs of Rio, where most of my research interlocutors also reside. In fact, living in Rio's "suburbs" carries more of a social than a geographical meaning. It does not align with the classic North American or British definition of suburbia as "peripheral in location vis-à-vis a centre, residential, low-density, with a distinctive way of life and municipal political autonomy" (Harris & Larkham, 1999, p. 8). Instead, as explained by Roberta Guimarães and Frank Davies (2018), the term "suburb" in the Marvelous City refers to a social category encompassing representations of "poverty," "subaltern," and "popular classes," in contrast to wealthier urban areas.

Not every location far from Rio's CBD is considered a suburb, but rather only the northern and western disadvantaged neighbourhoods served by train lines. Nélson Fernandes (2011, p. 53) explains that there was no suburban stigma until the end of the 19th century, as white middle-class segments inhabited several outlying neighbourhoods surrounding the city. Yet the urban remodelling proposed by Mayor Pereira Passos (1902–1906) drastically altered Rio's downtown area. While hundreds of poor homes and tenement buildings were demolished, thousands were forced to seek shelter in the emerging favelas or move to available land in more distant northern neighbourhoods (Abreu, 1987). In the following decades, unequal public policies and institutional practices contributed to the establishment and reinforcement of both material and symbolic segregation between the city's northern (poor) and southern (wealthy) zones.

While conducting my fieldwork, I observed that Ricardo and many other police career candidates aspired to patrol the streets and favelas of Rio's impoverished areas once they joined PMERJ. They believe working as a PM in the suburbs carries a higher social status and officers are generally more respected there than in the city's wealthier neighbourhoods. As Ricardo puts it:

> Being a cop in the Southern City? No way! Many judges, deputies, preppies and other "VIP wannabe" live there. If you find dope in some playboy's car, you can't even slap him in the face. It's too risky, you can easily get into trouble. But here [in the suburbs] it's different, you know? Cause people look at the police... they look at the uniform, the rifle, and show some respect. They know the police can harm them. You may also work more relaxed... no sergeant or captain will piss you off for nothing. Not to say the girls! They look at the PMs up and down and always smile when they drive down the street. You know how cars turn girls on, right? That's why I wanna be a PM in the suburbs... it's where you can get respected being the police.

Living in the low-police-accountability environments found in favelas and suburbs, most candidates argue that the notion of "respect" among military cops in Rio is driven by fear, often fuelled by the potential use of violence (Ramos, 2017, p. 20). Ricardo clearly understands that, in addition to "respect," police violence can also be capitalised on for profit by leveraging his family connections to learn more about PMERJ. His cousin, Ezequiel, was assigned to one of the deadliest police units in the city. His division would frequently raid favelas, allegedly to fight local drug gangs, including in the northern suburbs. Ricardo wants to join Ezequiel's unit because he has always said his primary goal in the police force was "to make money quickly" to "improve his life." Ezequiel frequently advised him that "police raids" are the most lucrative "scheme" for a street cop to get involved in. For Ricardo and many other candidates, a "scheme" is a native term that describes the set of relations and skills needed to operate in a particular market, sometimes linked to illegal practices. Because of this boundary between the legal and illicit, "schemes" are always based on personal trust and secrecy (Rodrigues, 2022).[7]

Despite being a rank-and-file officer, Ezequiel lived a lavish lifestyle, complete with a luxury vehicle, a comfortable apartment, and a summer house. Ricardo admired his cousin's life, believing he was respected for his accomplishments. My interlocutor experienced Ezequiel's wealth first-hand when they rode in his gleaming white Toyota pickup truck, went to bars and parties, interacted with his police friends, and saw his photos with different women on Instagram. Ricardo did not care that Ezequiel's income came from illegal arms and drug seizures. He had amassed his wealth and reputation as a "feared cop" mainly through these illegal "schemes," which PMs informally referred to as "war spoils." No wonder Ricardo aspired to emulate Ezequiel's path by becoming a cop in the northern suburbs of Rio, where most of the police raids allegedly take place to fight armed drug gangs.[8]

On the other hand, Ricardo avoids driving in the same northern suburbs to stay safe while working as an Uber driver. He has developed defensive strategies to protect himself, such as never entering unfamiliar favelas and staying in the city's southern areas or close to downtown Rio whenever possible. These strategies have become "survival tactics" for him after experiencing two incidents of criminal violence. The first occurred when he drove to pick up a supposed passenger after completing a nearby stop on the outskirts of Rio. Unfamiliar with the area, he followed the GPS directions through narrow streets that led him into a different municipality, where two armed men were waiting for him. They stole all his cash, cell phone, and watch, amounting to nearly half of his monthly salary, which was around 600 dollars at the time in 2018.

The second incident occurred early on a Sunday, just the week after Ricardo had told me what had happened. He decided to accept one last ride on the app, almost on his way home. Two well-dressed men and a woman boarded the vehicle near a nightclub, supposedly leaving the party together. They asked Ricardo to take the woman to a nearby favela and then continue to a final stop where the men would get off. As previously mentioned, the prospective police recruit had a professional policy of not entering unfamiliar favelas to pick up or drop off passengers: "I'd rather miss the ride than be embarrassed when some fucker puts a rifle in my face," he used to say. When the passengers told him their intended destination, Ricardo warned them he would not go there, agreeing instead to drop the woman off at a nearby location. An argument broke out during the drive, with the passengers complaining about Ricardo's refusal to take them to their desired destination.

My interlocutor mentioned that "things got really tough" when the man in the front seat suggested that Ricardo didn't want to enter the favela because he was allegedly a cop. He knew there was some truth to the statement, as he had often heard people remark on his "police look." His athletic build, shaved beard, military-style haircut, large golden watch, and aviator sunglasses were all part of the "police outfit" commonly worn by off-duty officers and "police wannabes" in the northern suburbs (Rodrigues, 2024). Judging by Ricardo's appearance, the man in the front seat warned him that "many cops have been killed" in that neighbourhood recently. The passengers in the back seat agreed, stating that if Ricardo wasn't "really a cop," he was, at the very least, someone "who wanted to become a cop very bad."

The tension escalated when he suddenly felt the muzzle of a revolver pressed against the back of his head, and the passengers announced a robbery. They began searching the entire vehicle, threatening to execute him if anything identifying Ricardo as a police officer was found. He was most concerned about his cell phone, which contained his conversations with Ezequiel. Along with text messages and audio files about the police entrance exams, the chat history included photos, videos, and other digital content related to the police world. Amid the threats and verbal abuse, the robbers searched not only his wallet but also the glove compartment and the front carpets of the car for valuables and any possible police ID or weapon. Ricardo told me, "If they start snooping through my cell phone, I swear to you, I'd speed up and hit the first lamppost. Fuck them all! I would die, but I certainly wouldn't die alone."

Fortunately, the phone did not attract much attention. The robbers took it, along with Ricardo's watch and cash. The woman collected all his belongings while he was instructed to stop on a quiet street a few blocks from their destination. Before letting him go, one of the criminals struck Ricardo hard in the chest with a pistol, warning him to "respect robbers" next time. Confused and still breathless, he drove alone in silence, speeding home. Back in the modest studio in his mother's backyard, he told Paula what had happened, swearing that no criminal would ever humiliate him like that again.

Anthropophagic Revenge

Ricardo was not the only one with hard feelings. Throughout my fieldwork, many other candidates shared stories with me about violent incidents involving themselves, relatives, friends, neighbours, and acquaintances. These first- and second-hand experiences of violence included common crimes such as muggings, robberies, extortion, and threats by criminals, which occurred in everyday places like trains, buses, streets, and beaches, as well as at their homes in poor neighbourhoods and favelas. Hearing those stories made it clear that the candidate's resentment was not only about the loss of their belongings, but also about the symbolic violence shown by criminals towards their victims. As Luís Roberto Cardoso de Oliveira (2008) argues, although physical violence has an indisputable objective dimension, the moral dimension of aggression is essentially symbolic and immaterial, implying devaluation or denial of the victim's rights or identity.

In addition to Ricardo, another important interlocutor named Cássio also shared his experiences of violence. One summer afternoon, two armed motorcyclists robbed him as he arrived home. They took his wallet and phone and forced him to lie on the hot asphalt in front of his house, with his head down, staring at the pavement. This left him with no chance to react and caused burns all over his legs and arms. Similar to Ricardo's experience, the incident caused severe emotional damage to the candidate due to the nature of the crimes, fuelling his hatred towards the attackers. When the Uber story was shared, Cássio and other prospective recruits emotionally supported Ricardo by recounting their own experiences of victimisation. I witnessed the spontaneous "emotional support session" during a lunch break at the preparatory course, where their individual experiences, through a collective entanglement, were transformed into shared narratives of moral insults (Cardoso de Oliveira, 2008, pp. 136–137) against their honour.

Such moments of emotional catharsis indicate that honour can also be collectively understood as social solidarity among peers (Pitt-Rivers, 1965, p. 35). Just as individual dishonourable conduct can tarnish the honour of the whole community, an insult directed at one of its members can trigger solidarity within the group. When Ricardo mentioned that he had promised himself and his wife that he would never be humiliated again, his classmates immediately identified with the story. As male prospective police recruits, being dishonoured by criminals seemed an even greater insult, considering their current male identity and future roles as law enforcers. Following Raewyn Connell and James Messerschmidt (2005, pp. 829–830), immediate responses to any aggression encompass a set of behaviours related to the "hegemonic masculinities" within the police in Rio. Eliminating criminals whenever possible, though sometimes illegal, is considered a legitimate form of preventive *réplica* [retaliation] (Zucal, 2010, p. 91), as it represents a more honourable and widely recognised way of being both "a man" and "a cop."

A couple of weeks after the "emotional support session," I found myself back in Ricardo's Uber. I was sitting in the same seat where one of his attackers had been, and I asked him if he remembered the faces of any of them. He said he could not remember but added that it did not matter because "criminals were all the same." Surprised by his answer, I pressed him on what that statement meant. Ricardo paused briefly, reflecting, and explained that they were all the same because "they were all cowards." He continued, "I almost died because of my phone! If they had found Ezequiel's messages, they'd have killed me... they'd showed no mercy at all." Had other candidates heard his confession, they would have strongly agreed, as Ricardo was not a lonely voice among his peers. During class breaks or on other occasions outside the course, I heard stories from candidates about off-duty officers being tortured and killed simply because they were identified. The fear of brutalisation was the main reason they said they would always carry a gun once in the force. Beyond "punishing offenders" in the face of a "failed" formal criminal justice system, fear is also a key element for them in justifying preventive *réplica* to avoid future and unnecessary confrontations.

Most of these stories reflect an important principle of revenge connecting police officers to criminals in Rio de Janeiro. This principle is discursively justified by the "defense of honor" (Pitt-Rivers, 1965, p. 30), particularly in response to the ongoing material and moral aggression against the police. Criminals are not the only ones responsible for killing and humiliating agents in the streets and favelas; society, on one hand, also plays a role by often overlooking the lives of officers, while the state is complicit by supporting an ineffective and lenient criminal justice system. Police *réplica* typically takes two different but complementary forms (Fassin, 2013, p. 199). The first is as an "arbitrary punishment," where someone is killed to "take the rap" for others. The second is as a "punitive expedition," involving violent retaliatory operations targeting social spaces associated with criminal territoriality, such as favelas or impoverished neighbourhoods.[9]

Furthermore, Rohden (2006, p. 114) argues that this same principle can challenge any universal concept of honour, presenting it instead as a process of individualisation within the context of a given feud system. But curiously, when asked about their attackers, Ricardo and Cássio could not recall their names or recognise their faces. None of the other candidates with whom I spoke were able to provide details about police officers who had been murdered and featured in the media, such as their names, physical descriptions, or information about their grieving families. Unlike past Mediterranean vendettas (Pitt-Rivers, 1965, 1977), deadly encounters in Rio follow a logic distinct from personal victims and perpetrators. Instead, I propose that the local feud system operates in a more fragmented and impersonal manner, influenced by an "anthropophagic rationale" (da Cunha & de Castro, 1986). Anthropophagy plays a crucial role in perpetuating a form of revenge where cannibalism becomes the essential condition for the "continuation of hatred" (da Cunha & de Castro, 1986, p. 66). Among the different Tupinambá groups living in pre-Columbian Brazil, all participants in anthropophagic rituals were considered potential victims in subsequent battles. Winning warriors, after partaking in the feast, became enemies to the rival tribe, by consuming the flesh of the defeated.

This feud law architecture frames the police–criminal blood quarrels primarily through a second stage of the conflicts, focussing on the symbolic devouring of bodies. Police officers, drug dealers, and militia groups actively create their own narratives of the battles, sometimes in the form of photos, videos, music, and audio files circulating within their WhatsApp and Telegram groups. Yet not only participants in the feuds engage with these symbolic artefacts. For example, during my fieldwork, I received dozens of digital contents depicting brutal episodes of violence, such as executions, torture, rape, decapitations, and other severe violations involving rival criminal groups and the police. Most of this content was shared by civilian candidates who, like Ricardo, had prior contact with legitimate law enforcement or lived in areas under the territorial control of drug or militia groups throughout the RMRJ.

Among all the stories I heard directly from candidates or indirectly through shared digital content, the notion of "anthropophagic rationale" was particularly evident in narratives where elements of social performance were re-fused (Alexander, 2006, pp. 33–34). Candidates often engage with police storytelling in two ways. First, narratives of officers being wounded or killed by ruthless criminals highlighted the dangers of police work in Rio. Second, interactions between agents and criminals were described through scenarios involving the subjugation of bandits and their ongoing demoralisation during events such as arrests, assaults, and murders. It was common for some interlocutors to emphasise the necessity (or even the desire) to humiliate outlaws. Beatings, torture, and even massacres were seen as "pedagogical bloodbaths" (Costa, 2024) by these candidates, as they were considered the only way to communicate with bandits. In police storytelling, violence serves as a cultural idiom that re-fuses meaning in police performances, especially before specific audiences, such as prospective recruits.

Violent acts may take on symbolic significance when linked to a shared cultural background between perpetrators and victims (Botelho & Magnoni, 2017, p. 111). Criminals, police officers, and the civilian audience who consume these war narratives perceive violence as a socially constructed category shaped by the actors involved in feuds. At times, violence is seen as relevant, justifiable, or even necessary, with its moral implications and meanings subject to ongoing negotiation and dispute. Even before joining the PMERJ, candidates share with legitimate police officers a similar view of the ongoing conflicts. Like Ricardo and many of his peers, they develop an early understanding of revenge based on their personal experiences with criminal violence and prior interactions with police officers. This is why the violent acts performed by agents strongly resonated with those I spoke to. Violence functions as a common language for candidates in the many places they circulate—places where both criminals and PMs are present.

In these communities of violence, revenge is atomised among opposing groups through conflicts where identifying specific victims and perpetrators is not essential. Feuds are viewed as part of a broader conflict between general categories such as "o polícia" [police] and "o bandido" [bandit], which encompass the individual identities of the adversaries. This allows unknown faces and names to become integral to the everyday narratives of war emerging from favelas and impoverished neighbourhoods, alongside the circulation of violent videos, photos, and audio files on social media. Similar to the Tupinambás, the defeated who are consumed lose their individual identities and become part of the collective memory of the wars. Revenge is more about the past and future of opposing groups—those who have perished and those who will perish at the hands of the enemy. In this sense, revenge ensures the preservation of social memory, linking "the dead of the past to the dead of the future through the living" (da Cunha & de Castro, 1986, p. 69).

Final Remarks

In this chapter, I have presented feud law not merely as an "irrational" method of conflict management or a system for balancing power between enemy groups. Instead, police feuds were defined as persistent legitimising mechanisms for state violence in urban Brazil. Focussing specifically on Rio de Janeiro, I have demonstrated how feuds foster a highly emotional economy of policing in favelas and poor suburbs, intertwining with formal criminal justice institutions through the police. Echoing Walter Benjamin's remarks (1978, p. 286), agents may become "ignoble" due to the force of their discretionary authority, particularly in low-police-accountability environments. This allows the police institution to effectively "create the law" in those areas rather than merely "enforce" or "preserve" it. Most prospective police recruits are aware of how violence can be instrumentalised into both material and symbolic gains. They recognise the police as a social actor that operates differently within the social and spatial hierarchies of the city, navigating between poor and wealthy neighbourhoods.

By shifting the analytical focus to the emotions that revenge evokes in potential future avengers, this chapter has also explored the narratives of vendettas in two complementary ways. On the one hand, it considered violence a "symbolic action" (Botelho & Magnoni, 2017, p. 111) that unites police officers and criminals within the same moral community of values, beliefs, and emotions. On the other, it suggested that once immersed in these communities, lethal violence adheres to an "anthropophagic rationale" (da Cunha & de Castro, 1986, p. 66). Victims and perpetrators lose their individual identities and become part of the collective memories of warring groups. Rather than targeting specific individuals, revenge is widely dispersed among adversaries through narratives of the past and expectations of future massacres. Nevertheless, police revenge represents a corrupt form of anthropophagy, detached from the Tupinambás' cosmology and alterity.

Instead of respect for their enemies, it sets the stage for the depersonalisation and bestialisation of the defeated, transforming them into "artefacts of consumption" (Feldman, 2002, p. 247).

Police prospective recruits, as argued, prematurely experience these emotions by playing a dual role in conflicts: as either crime victims or "spectators" of feuds. They view police feuds as something relevant, justifiable, or even a "necessary evil" in a world where criminals only understand the language of violence. This tension between a principle of justice and a logic of resentment – one of the main features animating what Didier Fassin (2013, pp. 200–203) refers to as the "moral economies of law enforcement" – leads both agents and police recruits to perceive their illegal (future) actions not as deviant, but as legitimate. The apparent paradox between their motivations and the fact that they often become entangled in the very illegal economies they claim to fight against can be understood through the disentangling between the "moral" and "legal" spheres in policing (Civico, 2012; Fassin, 2013; Kant de Lima, 1995; Zucal, 2010). This is particularly evident in Rio de Janeiro, where informal and illegal rules and knowledge have historically influenced police work and ethics among both civil and military officers (Caruso, Patrício & Pinto, 2010; Kant de Lima, 1995; Muniz, 1999; Pires & Albernaz, 2022; Poncioni, 2004).

Furthermore, the early participation of prospective police recruits in the described moral economy of policing draws our attention to the unstable nature of the state's boundaries. One might slightly complicate the argument presented in this edited collection by asking: Since the state not only "sees" and "thinks" but also "feels" through its agents, when exactly do individuals start to embody the state? What, after all, does the embodiment of the state entail? If affections are also "one of the constitutive conditions of state formation" (Gupta, 2012, p. 113), revenge in many parts of Rio de Janeiro becomes one of the most relevant "zones of contact" between embodied subjects and the political state apparatus (Linke, 2006, p. 208). Revenge sometimes produces "victims"; other times, however, it may contribute to the desire to become the "future avengers." Emotions such as hate and resentment towards criminals are tied to the everyday lived experiences of many of my interlocutors, as seen in the stories of Cássio and, particularly, Ricardo.

As highlighted by Ann Stoler (2007, p. 9), state power consent is made possible "by shaping appropriate and reasoned affect, by directing affective judgments, by severing some affective bonds and establishing others, by adjudicating what constitutes moral sentiments." The state not only controls or creates but also refines the distribution of emotions already embodied by individuals to strengthen its own power. (Future) Agents also "feel" through the state, as they are not monads but social beings holding intentional states, such as belief and desire, related to their agency and subjectivity.

Acknowledgements

Previous versions of this text were presented in 2024 at the 34th Brazilian Anthropology Association (ABA) Meeting in Belo Horizonte, Brazil, and at the Writing Workshop "Crime and Punishment in Latin America" in Santa Fé, Argentina. I want to thank Dr. Natália do Lago and Dr. Roberto Efrem for organising the panel on "Violence, Criminalisation, and Imprisonment" at the 34th ABA meeting, and Dr. Ana Aliverti, Dr. Vanessa Barker, and Dr. Máximo Sozzo for organising the Writing Workshop. I also wish to thank all the valuable feedback received on both occasions from other panellists, especially Dr. Ana Aliverti and Dr. Déborah Goldin, for their careful reading, and literature recommendations. I would also like to thank Dr. Henrique Carvalho for his insightful comments on the second version of the text.

Notes

1 The "Fogo Cruzado" data lab considers "slaughter" the death of three or more people in episodes of violence involving state agents or criminal groups.
2 As Elizabete Albernaz and Eduardo Rodrigues (2022, p. 617) point out, the category of "police raids" is often used interchangeably to describe any police intervention in areas of ongoing urban violence. This term encompasses a wide range of operational and militarised actions aimed at combating mostly drug trafficking in the favelas and impoverished outskirts of Rio de Janeiro city and its Metropolitan Region (RMRJ). There is considerable ambiguity and uncertainty surrounding this category, as there are also no official public data or transparency regarding the protocols for police actions.
3 Brazil has several police agencies operating at different government levels, each with its own personnel, ordinances, institutional structures, and functions. At the federal level, the country has two national full-cycle police organisations: the Federal Police and the Highway Federal Police. The former is responsible for investigating and preventing nationwide federal and international crimes, while the latter handles traffic offences on interstate highways. At the state level, every Brazilian state and the Federal District have two distinct forces operating within their territorial borders. The Military Police is the principal ostensive police agency, responsible for preventing crimes, while the Civil Police focusses on crime investigations. In addition, Municipal Guards enforce local bylaws concerning public order and the security of municipal property. For more literature on the organisation of Brazilian police forces, see Leandro Carneiro (2021) and Wesley Skogan and Vicente Riccio (2018).
4 All names in the chapter are changed to protect my interlocutors' identities.
5 I often took long rides with Ricardo to attend weekly seminars, classes, and research meetings at UFF (Fluminense Federal University), where I pursued my PhD studies. The travel time from home to UFF ranged from 45 to 90 minutes, depending on traffic conditions.
6 At the time of fieldwork, PMERJ required candidates to have theoretical knowledge in the following subjects: Brazilian Portuguese (writing and grammar), Brazilian History, Geography, Sociology, Traffic Legislation, Human Rights, and IT.

7 Hearing stories of illicit police activities from agents, and particularly from prospective recruits, was an important element of my fieldwork. Although deeply controversial, such stories are not exceptional in scholarship on policing in Rio and elsewhere (Albernaz, 2018; Fassin, 2013; Hornberger, 2017; Jauregui, 2013; Zucal, 2010). In fact, ethnographic writing on policing and criminal groups requires strong situational ethical practices (Barbosa et al., 2021; Calvey, 2023; Dekeyser & Garrett, 2021), given the relative nature of the moralities involved. I developed dialogical and situated ethical practices with my interlocutors, ensuring their right to anonymity and confidentiality while guaranteeing that my data would not cause them harm. However, by asking them to explain their (past and potential future) illicit practices, and by negotiating their perspectives into my own understanding of these actions, I transgressed moral and legal boundaries with them to some extent. In line with Beatrice Jauregui (2014, p. 147), it is not possible for the ethnographer to be "pure" when "observing, analysing, writing, and representing," even if one aims to be so in intention. Although uncomfortable, being critically aware of my *complicity* with them allowed me to use it strategically to understand the multivocality of my interlocutors and how their *situated moralities* (Eilbaum, 2012, p. 379) pave the way for some of their illicit and sometimes violent future actions.
8 Rio's policing landscape comprises a variety of groups that challenge the state's monopoly on the legitimate use of violence (Civico, 2012; Diphoorn, 2015; Feltrán, 2020; Hills, 2014). In different contexts, (il-)legitimate police forces, private security, paramilitary groups, and other criminal gangs control settlements for markets involving drugs, protection rackets, property sales, or utilities (Pires et al., 2020). For further exploration of Rio's hybrid forms of policing, see Daniel Hirata et al. (2022b), José Alves (2020), and Michel Misse (2019).
9 Scholarly literature indicates that police feuds in Rio de Janeiro have led to lethal retaliatory violence against innocent civilians or even criminals who were not directly involved in the murder of any state agent (Coelho, 2017; Farias, 2015; Hirata et al., 2022a; Montes & Lins, 2017). However, most of the victims are identified by social markers such as gender (male), class (poor), race (Black), and location (favela), which contribute to what Michel Misse (2010, p. 22) refers to as "criminal subjection." The most recent data show that police lethality in Rio mirrors national trends. In 2023, 6,393 civilians were killed by state agents in Brazil. Of these, 82.3% were Black, 71.7% were aged between 12 and 29, and 99.3% were male. For more information, see the annual report published by the Fórum Brasileiro de Segurança Pública (2024).

References

Abrams, P. (1988). Notes on the difficulty of studying the state. *Journal of Historical Sociology, 1*(1), 58–89.

Abreu, M. de A. (1987). *Evolução urbana no Rio de Janeiro*. Prefeitura do Rio de Janeiro: Pereira Passos.

Albernaz, E. (2018). 'Palácios sem reis, democracias sem cidadãos: Política, cotidiano e a formação de mercados da exclusão em dois contextos do "sul-global"'. PhD thesis, Universidade Federal Fluminense.

Albernaz, E., & Rodrigues, E. de O. (2022). Operações policiais: Um exercício multi-situado e multiescalar de regionalização dos impactos da violência armada em favelas durante a pandemia no Rio de Janeiro. *Farol: Revista de Estudos Organizacionais e Sociedade, 25*, 1–18.

Alexander, J. C. (2006). Cultural pragmatics: Social performance between ritual and strategy. In J. C. Alexander, B. Giesen, & J. Mast (Eds.), *Social performance: Symbolic action, cultural pragmatics and ritual* (pp. 29–90). Cambridge University Press.

Alves, J. (2020). *Dos barões ao extermínio: Uma história da violência na Baixada Fluminense*. 2. ed. Consequência.

Barbosa, A., Biondi, K., & Renoldi, B. (2021). 'Os crimes da etnografia: Considerações sobre método e experienciação nas práticas de pesquisa antropológica sobre violência e criminalidade'. *Cuestiones Criminales, 4*(7/8), 410–459. https://ri.conicet.gov.ar/bitstream/handle/11336/183366/CONICET_Digital_Nro.ea6c44bb-1fff-4144-af65-d57b96ba6535_B.pdf?sequence=2&isAllowed=y

Benjamin, W. (1978). Critique of violence. In H. Arendt (Ed.), *Reflections: Essays, aphorisms, autobiographical writings* (pp. 277–300). Harcourt Brace Jovanovich.

Botelho, N. A., & Magnoni, J. A. (2017). *Sociologias de la violencia – Estructuras, sujetos, interacciones y acción simbólica*. FLACSO.

Brigagão, C. (1985). *A militarização da sociedade*. Zahar.

Calvey, D. (2023). Deception, situated ethics, and police ethnography. In J. Fleming & S. Charman (Eds.), *Routledge International handbook of police ethnography*. Routledge. https://doi.org/10.4324/9781003083795

Cardoso de Oliveira, L. R. (2008). Existe violência sem agressão moral? *Revista Brasileira de Ciências Sociais, 23*(67), 135–146.

Carneiro, L. P. (2021). The organization and functioning of police forces in Brazil. In J. M. Mbuba (Ed.), *Global perspectives in policing and law enforcement* (pp. 329–341). Rowman & Littlefield.

Caruso, H., Patrício, L., & Pinto, N. M. (2010). Da escola de formação à prática profissional: um estudo comparativo sobre a formação de praças e oficiais da PMERJ. *Segurança, justiça e cidadania: pesquisas aplicadas em segurança pública, 2*(4), 101–118.

Christensen, K. R. (2016). *Revenge and Social Conflict*. Cambridge University Press.

Civico, A. (2012). "We Are Illegal, But Not Illegitimate": Modes of policing in Medellín, Colombia. *PoLAR, 35*(1), 77–93. http://dx.doi.org/10.1111/j.1555-2934.2012.01180.x

Coelho, T. H. (2017). *Medindo forças: A vitimização policial no Rio de Janeiro* (Master's thesis). Rio de Janeiro State University, Rio de Janeiro.

Connell, R. W., & Messerschmidt, J. W. (2005). Hegemonic masculinity: Rethinking the concept. *Gender & Society, 19*(6), 829–859.

Costa, A. S. (2024). A espetacularização das operações militares como banhos de sangue pedagógicos. In L. Pires, E. Albernaz, & E. de O. Rodrigues (Eds.), *Margens em disputa: Ilegalismos, territórios armados e práticas militarizadas* (pp. 50–72). Autografia.

Da Cunha, M. L. C., & de Castro, E. B. V. (1986). Vingança e temporalidade: Os Tupinambás. *Anuário Antropológico, 10*(1), 57–78.

Dekeyser, T., & Garrett, B. (2021). Illegal ethnographies: Research ethics beyond the law. In S. Henn, J. Miggelbrink and K. Hörschelmann (Eds.), *Research ethics in human geography* (pp. 153–167). Routledge.

Diphoorn, T. (2015). Twilight policing: Private security practices in South Africa. *British Journal of Criminology*, 56(2), 1–19. http://dx.doi.org/10.1093/bjc/azv057

Eilbaum, L. (2012). "O bairro fala": conflitos, moralidades e justiça no conurbano bonaerense. Hucitec.

Farias, J. (2015). Fuzil, caneta e carimbo: Notas sobre burocracia e tecnologias de governo. *Confluências – Revista Interdisciplinar de Sociologia e Direito*, 17(3), 75–91.

Fassin, D. (2009). Moral economies revisited. *Annales. Histoire, Sciences Sociales*, 64(6), 1237–1266. Editions de l'EHESS.

Fassin, D. (2013). *Enforcing Order: An Ethnography of Urban Policing*. Polity.

Fassin, D., Bouagga, Y., Coutant, I., Eideliman, J.-S., Fernandez, F., Fischer, N., Kobelinsky, C., Makaremi, C., Mazouz, S., Roux, S., & Brown, P. (2015). *At the heart of the state: The moral world of institutions*. Pluto Press.

Feldman, A. (2002). Strange fruit: The South African Truth Commission and the demonic economies of violence. *Social Analysis*, 46(3), 234–265.

Feltrán, G. (2020). *The entangled city: Crime as urban fabric in São Paulo*. Manchester: Manchester University Press.

Fernandes, N. Da N. (2011). *O rapto ideológico da categoria subúrbio: Rio de Janeiro 1858/1945*. Apicuri.

Fórum Brasileiro de Segurança Pública. (2024). *Anuário brasileiro de segurança pública 2024 (Ano 18)*. Fórum Brasileiro de Segurança Pública. ISSN 1983-7364.

Geiß, R. (2009). Armed violence in fragile states: Low-intensity conflicts, spillover conflicts, and sporadic law enforcement operations by third parties. *International Review of the Red Cross*, 91(873), 127–142.

Gluckman, M. (1955). The peace in the feud. *Past & Present*, 8(1), 1–14.

Guimarães, R. S., & Davies, F. A. (2018). Alegorias e deslocamentos do "subúrbio carioca" nos estudos das Ciências Sociais (1970–2010). *Sociologia e Antropologia*, 8(2), 457–482.

Gupta, A. (2012). *Red tape: Bureaucracy, structural violence, and poverty in India*. Duke University Press.

Harris, R., & Larkham, P. J. (1999). *Changing suburbs*. E & FN Spon.

Hills, A. (2014). What is policeness? On being police in Somalia'. *The British Journal of Criminology*, 54, 765–783. https://doi.org/10.1093/bjc/azu049

Hirata, D., Grillo, C., Dirk, R., & Lyra, D. (2022a). Chacinas policiais – relatório de pesquisa. Heinrich Böll Stiftung. Available at: https://geni.uff.br/wp-content/uploads/sites/357/2021/02/document_open_icon_181096.png

Hirata, D. V., Cardoso, A., Grillo, C. C., dos Santos Junior, O. A., Lyra, D. A., & Dirk, R. C. (2022b). The expansion of milícias in Rio de Janeiro. Political and economic advantages. *Journal of Illicit Economies and Development*, 4(3), 257–271.

Hornberger, J. (2017). The belly of the Police. In J. Beek (Eds.), *Police in Africa: The street level view* (pp. 199–212). Oxford Academic.

Howard, T. (2016). *Failed states and the origins of violence: A comparative analysis of state failure as a root cause of terrorism and political violence*. Routledge.

Jauregui, B. (2013). Beatings, beacons, and big men: Police disempowerment and delegitimation in India. *Law & Social Inquiry*, 38(3), 643–669.

Jauregui, B. (2014). Dirty anthropology: Epistemologies of violence and ethical entanglements in police ethnography. In A. M. S. Leclerc & T. G. Z. Barnes (Eds.), *Ethnography at the edge: Crime and Ethnography in the Violence of Policing* (pp. 125–145). Routledge.

Kant de Lima, R. K. (1995). *A polícia da cidade do Rio de Janeiro: seus dilemas e paradoxos*. Forense.

Laszczkowski, M., & Reeves, M. (2018). Affective states: Entanglements, suspensions, suspicions. Berghahn.

Lima, A. C. de S., & Dias, C. G. (2022). *Maquinaria da unidade; bordas da dispersão: Estudos de antropologia do Estado*. 7Letras.

Linke, U. (2006). Contact zones: Rethinking the sensual life of the state. *Anthropological Theory, 6*(2), 205–225.

Marques, A. C. (2002). *Intrigas e questões: Vinganças de família e tramas sociais no sertão de Pernambuco*. Relumé Dumará.

Miller, W. I. (1998). Clint Eastwood and equity: Popular culture's theory of revenge. In A. Sarat & T. R. Kearns (Eds.), *Law in the domains of culture* (pp. 161–202). University of Michigan Press.

Misse, M. (2010). Crime, sujeito e sujeição criminal: Aspectos de uma contribuição analítica sobre a categoria 'bandido'. *Lua Nova, 79*, 15–38.

Misse, M. (2019). The puzzle of social accumulation of violence in Brazil: Some remarks. *Journal of Illicit Economies and Development, 1*(2), 177–182. https://doi.org/10.15406/sij.2017.01.00012

Montes, G. C., & de O. A. Lins, G. (2017). Evidências para os efeitos de deterrence, desenvolvimento socioeconômico e revanche policial sobre a violência nos municípios do Estado do Rio de Janeiro. *45º Encontro Nacional de Economia da Associação Nacional dos Centros de Pós-Graduação em Economia*. Natal/RN.

Muniz, J. de O. (1999). *Ser policial é, sobretudo, uma razão de ser: Cultura e cotidiano da Polícia Militar do Estado do Rio de Janeiro* (Doctoral thesis). Insituto Uiversitário de Pesquisas do Rio de Janeiro (IUPERJ), Rio de Janeiro.

Pires, L., & Albernaz, E. R. (2022). "Na teoria, a prática é outra coisa!": socialização "escolar", estrutura bipartida e conflitos na Polícia Militar do Estado do Rio de Janeiro (PMERJ). *Revista Brasileira de Segurança Pública, 16*(1), 232–251.

Pires, L., Hirata, D., & Maldonado, S. (2020). 'Apresentação: mercados populares, ilegalismos e suas regulações pela violência'. *Antropolítica—Revista Contemporânea De Antropologia, 50*, 7–31. https://doi.org/10.22409/antropolitica2020.i50.a47749

Pitt-Rivers, J. (1965). Honour and social status. In J. Peristiany (Ed.), *Honour and shame: The values of Mediterranean society* (pp. 19–77). Weidenfeld & Nicolson.

Pitt-Rivers, J. (1977). *The fate of Shechem, or the politics of sex: Essays in the anthropology of the Mediterranean*. Cambridge University Press.

Poncioni, P. (2004). *Tornar-se policial: A construção da identidade profissional do policial no Estado do Rio de Janeiro* (Doctoral thesis). Faculdade de Filosofia, Letras e Ciências Humanas, Universidade de São Paulo (FFLCH-USP), São Paulo.

Povolo, C. (2015). Feud and vendetta: Customs and trial rites in medieval and modern Europe: A legal-anthropological approach. *Acta Histriae, 23*, 195–244.

Ramos, L. dos S. (2017). *Entre a "judaria interna", a "pista salgada" e o "medo de se entregar": Uma etnografia das representações de medo entre policiais militares do Estado do Rio de Janeiro* (Undergraduate thesis on Public Safety). Fluminense Federal University, Niterói.

Robert, P. (2007). *Sociologia do crime [La Sociologie du Crime]*. Vozes.

Rodrigues, E. de O. (2022). *Sociedade dos esquemas: Uma etnografia sobre candidatos à carreira policial no subúrbio carioca* (Doctoral thesis). Fluminense Federal University, Niterói.

Rodrigues, E. de O. (2024). Fake officers/real police: What are Pi-lícias doing in the streets of Rio de Janeiro? *The Cambridge Journal of Anthropology, 42*(2), 97–113.

Rohden, F. (2006). Para que serve o conceito de honra, ainda hoje? *Campos, 7*(2), 101–120.

Rotberg, R. I. (Ed.). (2010). *When states fail: Causes and consequences*. Princeton University Press.

Skogan, W. G., & Riccio, V. (2018). *Police and society in Brazil*. Routledge.

Stoler, A. L. (2007). Affective states. In *A companion to the anthropology of politics* (pp. 4–20). Blackwell.

Trouillot, M. (2001). The anthropology of the state in the age of globalization: Close encounters of the deceptive kind. *Current Anthropology, 42*(1), 125–138.

Zucal, J. G. (2010). "Se lo merecen": Definiciones morales del uso de la fuerza física entre los miembros de la policía bonaerense. *Cuadernos de antropología social, 32*, 75–94.

PART 3
Shifting emotional economies of state power

PART 3

9
THE EMOTIONAL LANDSCAPE OF *PRISON* MANAGERIALISM

Jamie Bennett
University of Oxford

Introduction

As the millennium turned, the rise of managerialism marked a sea change in the culture and practices of management in English prisons. The coming of managerialism can be situated in the emergence of neo-liberalism in the Western world, particularly during the 1980s. Neo-liberalism describes a return to laissez-faire economics, including facilitating the mechanisms of production and exchange, enabling mass consumption, expanding the reach and control of commercial organisations, and legitimising inequalities in wealth. This is not solely an issue of economics but has complex social, political, legal and cultural dimensions that have permeated the life of the contemporary Western world (Bell, 2011). In management, it has been observed that a dominant approach has evolved (Parker, 2002), which includes a movement towards larger organisations with hierarchical structures that attempt to monitor and control the behaviour of employees through target setting and the use of information technology. This dominant approach involves not only technical practices and structures but also an attempt at "governing the soul" (Rose, 1999) of employees by deploying psychological technologies including human resource management techniques such as recruitment, reward, appraisal, development, communication and consultation to align the ways that employees think about their work with the needs of the organisation and the broader political economy. Together, these trends, combining tighter, centralised structures and re-engineering professional identity, have sometimes been termed "managerialism".

These developments refashioned prison management in England and elsewhere (see Vigna in this volume). There has been the proliferation of technologies of monitoring, including the introduction of performance targets and indicators, audits and ratings systems. It is important to recognise that such changes are not merely technical but also have a significant cultural impact, altering professional orientations and outlooks (Cheliotis, 2006). The prison management that has emerged has been described critically as one that over-uses targets, audits and other measures so leaving little space for individuality, creativity and autonomy; over-emphasises compliance with measures for their own sake without meaningful connection with the social context, and; nurtures compliant behaviour and uniformity amongst prison managers with the aim of producing identikit corporate citizens (Bennett, 2020).

While global changes, such as the expansion of managerialism, are influential, often eroding local cultures, they do not entirely sweep them away (Kennedy, 2010). This is the case in English prisons, where there are deeply rooted local cultures. The primary elements of the traditional prison occupational culture are: insularity, that is prison staff have an internal focus, strong bonds of solidarity and feel cut off professionally and socially from those outside of prisons; hierarchical staff–prisoner relationships; and masculinity, due to prisons being predominantly male-dominated settings. In prison management there has been a dialectical relationship between global changes brought about by managerialism and the existing local culture. For example, targets and audits reinforced insularity by creating a set of internal measures rather than drawing upon external human rights or legal standards; the hierarchical structure was reinforced by the layers of surveillance and control; and the competitive individualism of the managerial environment aligned with masculine ideals. The inter-relationship between the global forces of managerialism and embedded local cultures was an important mediating factor in shaping the working lives of managers. Given this inter-relationship, it is appropriate to refer to "*prison* managerialism", reflecting the way in which this took distinct form within the local context (Bennett, 2015a, 2024). The terms "managerialism" and "*prison* managerialism" will be used interchangeably in this chapter, but both are intended to refer to the distinctive developments in English prisons.

This chapter draws upon ethnographic research conducted between 2007 and 2022, which traces the evolution of *prison* managerialism. The data will be revisited to consider the role of emotions and affect in prison governance and the working lives of prison managers, an issue that has not previously received sustained scholarly attention. This chapter will attempt to explore emotions and affect at the macro level, in the rhetoric and discourse on prison management; at the meso level, in the institutional practices and culture; and at the micro level of individual experiences. There will be an attempt to discuss how these manifestations of emotion and affect are interconnected in an "affective economy" (Ahmed, 2014: 8) where emotions are not only individual experiences but are embedded in social contexts, shaping and being shaped by social structures and power relations.

Emotions and prison governance

In common use and in psychology, emotions are often understood to be individual experiences and feelings:

> Emotions are conscious mental reactions (such as anger or fear) subjectively experienced as strong feelings usually directed toward a specific object and typically accompanied by physiological and behavioral changes in the body.
> *(American Psychological Society, 2024)*

In contrast, the sociological approach seeks to understand emotions, not as solely individual experiences, but as being interconnected with the wider social context (Turner & Stets, 2005; Ahmed, 2014). Emotions are created through interactions with the social world and may be patterned so that they are shared across groups. Scholars have started to pay attention to, for example, how states consciously seek to manage emotions through rhetoric or as an aspect of national resources, such as by incorporating quantifications of "happiness" into measures of gross national product and surveys of quality of life (Pykett et al., 2017). There has been particular attention directed towards the management, deployment and commodification of emotions in the workplace. Notably, the seminal work of Arlie Hochschild (1983) describes "emotional labour", that is the way that workers manage their feelings to display appropriate social presentation. The management and deployment of emotional labour has increasingly become the subject of human resource practice as contemporary organisations seek more profound control over workers, regulating not only their actions and behaviour, but also their emotions and identities (Rose, 1999).

Although the place of emotions in prison governance has not received focused attention, emotion has not been entirely absent from research on prison managers. By sifting through the literature, it is possible to find indications of the areas in which further attention might be directed.

Emotions have long been part of the discourse about criminal justice, encompassing negative emotions that sustain punitiveness, including anger and shame, but also more positive emotions that support rehabilitation, reintegration and normalisation, including empathy and compassion. The shift from the bloody spectacle of public punishments to the institution of imprisonment in the industrial age marked a shift from expressive attachments to punishment to a modern version of punishment that has been presented as more rational and civilised (Foucault, 1977). The post-War Welfare state held a degree of optimism in the capacity of prisons to be a vehicle for reform and rehabilitation. The rise of neo-liberalism since the 1980s, it has been argued, has seen a further turn from: "the instrumental reasoning of crime control analysis towards the visceral emotions of identification and righteous indignation" (Garland, 2001: 144). This historical evolution suggests that underlying ideologies of punishment are both constituted by and expressed through emotions (Carvalho & Chamberlen, 2016).

At an institutional level, there have been studies of prison managers that have sought to excavate their guiding values and ideologies. Andrew Rutherford (1993)'s study of criminal justice leaders, identified three broad credos that shape practice: punitive (a strongly held dislike of prisoners and desire to see them punished); liberal humanitarian (empathy for offenders and victims, desire to respect their rights and offer opportunities for rehabilitation); and expedient managerialism (concerned with disposing of the task at hand as efficiently as possible). Although these credos were largely discussed in terms of political beliefs, Rutherford also illuminated how they are steeped in emotion – including hatred, anger and empathy – and their formation is rooted in both personal backgrounds and professional turning-points that are often emotionally powerful. Similarly, Ben Crewe and Alison Liebling (2015) describe that prison managers often had emotionally charged motivations, such as a desire to challenge abuses of power or valuing public service. These studies point towards emotions being an element of penal ideologies in society broadly, and in the more specific professional community of prison managers.

There have been several studies on the work of prison managers (e.g. Bryans & Wilson, 2000; Bryans, 2007; Coyle, 2008; Brookes et al., 2008; Bennett, 2015a, 2024). While none have explicitly focused on emotions, they have all placed emphasis on how prison managers influence staff, prisoners and the relationships between them, giving attention to the cultural and relational aspects of leadership. One of the studies described managing "the 'softer' elements of a prison (such as culture, emotions, tensions, expectations)" (Bryans, 2007: 178). Crewe and Liebling (2015) described how prison managers would ameliorate the potential harshness of managerialism by giving attention to the feelings of staff and providing space to express themselves and influence change. Together these works suggest that emotions and their management are integral aspects of people management in prisons.

While there has been work exploring the emotional labour of prison officers (e.g. Nylander and Bruhn, 2020), there is no equivalent on prison managers. There has, nevertheless, been a significant contribution focussing on the well-being of prison managers, recognising the emotionally demanding nature of the work and the harmful consequences of a masculine working culture that encourages managers to present an image of (managed) coping, even if they are experiencing unhealthy stress (Harrison et al., 2024). Within this dominant masculine culture, women report having to engage in gendered emotional labour, presenting a front, in Goffman's sense, and containing their authentic selves in a culture where behaviour perceived as "female" is discouraged (Bennett, 2015a; Crewe & Liebling, 2015; Smith, 2021). Prison managers from minority ethnic groups have also reported having to undertake emotional labour, constructing psychosocial defences to insulate themselves in an environment in which race can evoke hostility and suspicion (Morgan, 2018). These studies start to reveal the nature of emotional labour undertaken by prison managers, how that labour is distributed and its relationship to power and inequality.

This brief survey suggests that the current literature points to three potentially fruitful areas of inquiry – the role of emotion in discourses and ideologies of prison management; the role of emotion in prison governance, including the implications for staff and prisoners; and the nature of the emotional labour undertaken by prison managers.

Research context

The chapter draws upon a series of insider ethnographies conducted with prison managers over a 15-year period. The first study took place in 2007–8, involving 62 days of observation and 60 semi-structured interviews in two medium security prisons in England (Bennett, 2015a) and focused on the embedding of managerialism. Deploying Bourdieu's concept of the habitus (Bourdieu, 1977), it was argued that the changing structure of prison management through the rise of managerialism had led to transformations in the dispositions, attitudes, values and actions of managers. These alterations in the culture and professional identity of prison managers intensified and deepened managerialism.

A follow-up study in one of the original research sites during 2014 and 2015 included ten days of observations and interviews with 20 managers. It explored how prison managers had been affected by the austerity policies being implemented in the UK, and other countries, following the financial crisis of 2007–8 and subsequent recession (Bennett, 2015b). These policies aimed to control and reduce national debts, in part through increased taxation, but more significantly through reductions in public spending (Blyth, 2013). As part of the plans to reduce public expenditure, the National Offender Management Service was required to deliver savings of £900 million, equivalent to 24% of the overall budget, between 2011 and 2015 (National Offender Management Service, 2014). Budget cuts were achieved through a range of measures, including the "benchmarking programme" (Mulholland, 2014), which created a framework against which the resources and service delivery expected of similar security category prisons would be standardised. This standardisation largely entailed a reduction in resources and staffing levels. Facilities management services, including maintenance and cleaning, were privatised, and the prison estate underwent "restructuring" in order "to open new efficient places at lower cost" (National Offender Management Service, 2014: 24) by closing smaller prisons, replacing them with new, larger prisons and building additional accommodation in other prisons. Finally, staff pay and conditions were reformed to reflect market rates, with the intention to: "Enable public sector prisons to remain a competitive force in an increasingly diverse market place" (National Offender Management Service, 2012: 8). As with other public sector organisations, the Prison Service was subject to pay restraint, and civil service pensions were reformed including increased employee contributions, a change from final to average salary calculation and a raised retirement age (Prison Service Pay Review Body, 2014).

A third study examined the operation of a "reform prison" in 2017 and comprised ten days of observations and interviews with 16 managers (Bennett, 2019). Four "reform prisons" were established by then Justice Secretary Michael Gove, empowered to have "operational autonomy and genuine independence" as well as "greater freedom" (Gove, 2015), an approach drawing upon the experience of academy schools. The attempt at structural reform ultimately foundered. The process of "managerial clawback" revealed the resilience of managerialism as an idea and set of practices (Bennett, 2019).

The fourth study was carried out in one of the original sites while prisons were continuing to respond to the coronavirus pandemic in 2021 and included ten days of observations and interviews with 20 managers (Bennett, 2023). The study considered how the exceptional circumstances of the pandemic led to managerial structures being disrupted for a protracted period, with measurement and monitoring suspended. Over time, as the pandemic receded, the managerial infrastructure was reintroduced as part of a return to "normality".

In all, the research has included 92 days of observations and interviews with 116 managers. The studies were primarily concerned with the emergence, entrenchment and subsequent evolution of *prison* managerialism. Although emotions were not the primary focus of the research, the ubiquity and commonplace nature of emotions meant that they were ever-present. This chapter revisits those studies to explore the salience of emotions in the working lives of prison managers and the governance of prisons, focussing on the themes suggested in the extant literature – discourse and rhetoric, governance and emotional labour.

The rhetoric of *prison* managerialism

In the years leading up to the millennium, neoliberal reforms included the introduction of private prisons and the curtailment of prison workers' right to strike. Following the election of the Labour government in 1997, there was a focus across the public sector on improvement through target-setting, performance monitoring and intervening to address poor services (Prime Minister & Minister for the Cabinet Office, 1999). As the century turned, the introduction of a managerial infrastructure accelerated in prisons with a rapid growth in key performance targets, audits and the development of a league table of prison performance. There was resistance from prison managers, some of whom saw this as eroding their autonomy and diminishing the relational aspects of prison governance (e.g. Wilson, 1995). Senior managers advanced various justifications for adopting a managerial approach, including that it could improve order in prisons following a decade that had seen major disorder and security breaches (Spurr & Bennett, 2008). Increased management control, they suggested, would ensure that the good intentions of liberal managers could be translated into reality by addressing overcrowding, poor conditions, abuse and lack of safety (Wheatley 2005). The then Director General of Prisons argued that there was a direct connection between meeting managerial targets and moral conduct:

> show me a prison achieving all its [Key Performance Indicators] and I will show you a prison which is also treating prisoners with dignity.
> *(Liebling assisted by Arnold, 2004: 68)*

These arguments deliberately conflated managerialism and the progressive ambitions of many prison managers, suggesting an indelible connection. The rhetoric was a conscious attempt to draw upon the emotions and moral aspirations of prison managers, offering hope. This period has been characterised as one of "managerialism-plus" (Liebling & Crewe, 2013: 292), where the techniques of monitoring and control were "overtly welded to better standards for prisoners and to greater control and encouragement of staff" (p. 293).

Over the next decade, as will be described below, not only did resistance dissipate, but managerialism became embedded within the professional culture and identity of prison managers. The period of austerity saw significant reductions in prison resources and changes to how they operated. Within the UK generally, there was public and institutional acquiescence with austerity policies in the face of concerns that the economy was at a breaking point (Clarke & Newman, 2012). It was only over time that the approach was contested as the social costs became apparent and the economic validity was questioned (Blyth, 2013). In this context, the changes implemented in prisons were largely accepted as inevitable and a necessary part of the wider national economic programme. Alongside the economic argument, the potential of privatisation also loomed. In 2010, the government announced that eight public sector prisons would be opened for commercial competition; a significant change in strategy as previously competitions had predominantly been limited to newly constructed prisons (Institute for Government, 2012). In 2012, the competitions were abandoned following agreement to implement the austerity reforms described previously, including the "benchmarking" programme and changes to pay and conditions. Rather than the hope and aspiration that shaped the rhetoric when managerialism emerged, the approach during austerity was instead grounded in fear of privatisation and insecurity in the economic context.

The hegemony of managerialism was challenged by the development of autonomous "reform" prisons during 2016–17 and then due to the disruptions of the coronavirus pandemic in 2020–22. In the reform prisons, the changes were introduced in the context of a significant decline in safety as the reductions in resources due to austerity began to have an impact on prison conditions (HM Chief Inspector of Prisons, 2013, 2014, 2015). At the same time, psychoactive substances became more widely available, reinvigorating the drug market and organised crime (Gooch & Treadwell, 2020). In such uncertain times, even if illusory, managerialism, with its familiar focus on targets, audits and hierarchical controls, offered a sense of order and certainty. In contrast, the disruption of managerialism during the initial stages of the pandemic was broadly welcomed. In this context, the lockdown regime with prisoners confined in their cells for longer periods and only unlocked in small groups for limited activity, and the concentration of prison staff on public health, offered a simplification of prison life in which managers had a clarity of purpose. As the pandemic eased, the reassembly of the managerial infrastructure was broadly accepted by managers as part of a return to "normality". In these two contexts, there were processes of "managerial clawback" in which managerialism was re-established following reform or disruption. Rather than being justified and promoted through emotional rhetoric appealing to the hopes and fears of managers, managerialism was instead accepted as offering some comfort or reassurance as part of the status quo.

The rhetoric of *prison* managerialism has altered over time as conditions changed. At the inception, the language of hope and aspiration was used to appeal to the positive emotions of managers, legitimising change and motivating engagement. By the time of austerity, managerialism had been embedded and its continuity was sustained through fear and insecurity as managers were concerned about the national economic context and the more specific threat of prison privatisation. The hegemony of *prison* managerialism later became such that attempting reform induced anxiety and insecurity. This long view illustrates how emotions are deployed and entangled in processes of change from initiation, to embedding and conservation.

Governance and emotions

Governance is concerned with the systems through which organisations are managed and organised. Previous literature on prison managers has recognised not only the technical aspects, but also the relational, cultural and emotional elements of their work (e.g. Bryans, 2007; Crewe & Liebling, 2015). This literature focuses on prison managers as subjects or agents who are consciously engaging in the governance of the emotional life of prisons. Yet, in the age of managerialism, prison managers are also the object of institutional governance through affective means, as will be described.

As *prison* managerialism emerged, there was initially some resistance from managers, used to operating with greater autonomy. However, this culture gradually shifted, aided by the recruitment of new managers, greater competition through published performance league tables and line management becoming more assertive, enabled by surveillance through performance data (Cheliotis, 2006). By 2007-8, managers largely acknowledged that managerial measures had a dominant role in their working lives, as captured in descriptions such as: "The whole day is affected by key performance indicators"; "they dominate my life"; "they're my bread and butter". For many prison managers, performance measures became: "our core business". While not uncritical, managers generally accepted, indeed embraced managerialism. Many considered that it offered a process through which priorities could be established and management rationalised; they felt empowered by having a tool to direct, motivate and hold to account those they managed; and they experienced a sense of achievement from meeting targets. There were, however, also many who were driven by a fear of failure. It was widely perceived that monitoring was underpinned by a disciplinary process in which those who failed would "get a kicking", "get absolutely hammered", "get our arses kicked" or oppressive managers would "throw a few fucks into them". Such aggressive management responses were not an objective reality, and instead, accountability was generally exercised reasonably. Managers were, nevertheless, conscious that they would be professionally judged on their achievement of targets and their future career prospects and reputation were at stake. This felt to them like monitoring was being "used as a stick" and could have personal consequences.

The fear and insecurity generated by managerialism have been more broadly observed, including in education (Clarke, 2016). Prison managers' drive to achieve was shaped by positive emotions – satisfaction, happiness – and negative – fear. This drive often coalesced into an intensive internalised desire to attain targets, which sometimes manifested in unhealthy behaviours. Many had an unswerving commitment, using phrases such as: "you don't miss a [target], you just don't do it"; "I don't like to fail things"; and "I guard them with my life". One manager described how they found it "devastating" that they had failed to meet a target, even though this was caused by a large increase in the prisoner population. Another manager appeared drained and visibly shaken when asked about what they would do if they could not meet a target, describing that it "makes me feel ill thinking about it". These intense emotional and physiological responses were elicited by the drive that these individuals had regarding targets. It was clear that performance monitoring played a powerful and dominating role in how managers viewed themselves, their self-worth, and it potentially affected their well-being.

Emotions were bound up with the rise of *prison* managerialism and are critical to understanding the operation and effects of power in prisons. There was a gradual movement from resistance by prison managers to acceptance and later to the embodiment of managerial logics. Prison managers not only operated systems of managerialism, but these structures were given depth and weight as managers internalised the new expectations, altering their professional identity and habitus (Bourdieu, 1977). While habitus was conceived by Bourdieu as being comprised the dispositions, attitudes, values and actions of a particular social group, in prisons it was not only that managers started to see and understand their world differently, but they also started to feel differently, experiencing emotions including the satisfaction of attaining targets, the security of perceiving they had greater control, as well as the fear of failure and insecurity of being more intensively scrutinised. Emotions, both positive and negative, were entangled in the constitution of a managerial habitus.

The growth of managerialism had implications for how prison managers, as subjects, approached the relational and emotional dimensions of their work. As described previously, the early 2000s have been characterised as "managerialism-plus" (Liebling & Crewe, 2013: 292), where techniques of monitoring and control were deployed to improve standards for prisoners and engagement of staff. Gradually, however, this started to alter as managers increasingly viewed their work through the managerial lens of targets, audit outcomes and financial cost (Bennett, 2015a), adopting a perspective of "economic rationality" (Liebling, 2011: 3). With the era of austerity, this coalesced into a period characterised as "managerialism-minus", a "no-frills" form of imprisonment in which "economy and efficiency are prioritized above any moral mission" (Liebling & Crewe, 2013: 294). The reconstitution of prisons from a social organisation to a business operation risked minimising the human impacts and effects. Zygmunt Bauman has argued that the conditions in the contemporary world, including managerial practices, have promoted "moral blindness" by placing economic calculus above moral concern (Bauman & Donskis, 2013). In prisons, it has been observed that "virtual prisons" have been constructed based upon performance data and remote management, which is different from the experiences of those who live and work in a prison (Owers, 2007: 16). This is characteristic of managerialism, as was highlighted by the public inquiry into the failures in patient care at Mid-Staffordshire NHS Foundation Trust in 2013, where excessive concentration on financial and performance measures meant that insufficient attention was given to the quality of patient experiences (Francis, 2013). These examples expose that managerialism can encourage a process in which managers develop "moral indifference" in which the everyday requirements of their organisational role and cultural expectations dull their moral reflexes and critical perspectives (Cohen, 2001: 98). In prisons, this can mean an environment where managers are desensitised to intolerable conditions (Hardwick, 2014) such as those later seen at HMP Liverpool, where the Chief Inspector of Prisons described an abject failure to offer a safe, decent and purposeful environment, without alarm bells being sounded by managerial measures or internal scrutiny (Justice Select Committee of House of Commons, 2018). A further example of pervasive moral indifference occurred in 2010, when it was uncovered that prison managers in two prisons arranged for prisoners to be transferred for the duration of their respective inspections to manipulate the image presented to inspectors (Prison Reform Trust, 2010). The then Chief Inspector of Prisons, Anne Owers, described that this incident revealed an "underlying mind-set: that prisoners are merely pieces to be moved around the board to meet performance targets or burnish the reputation of the prison" (Prison Reform Trust, 2010). The rise and evolution of managerialism brought with it an alteration in how prison managers, as subjects, engaged with the emotional life of the institution. There was a movement towards a dispassionate approach to prisoners, or at least an approach where emotion is contained and diminished in favour of economic rationality and managerial compliance.

The increased economic rationality did not, however, go uncontested. Even during the austerity period, individual prison managers valued and wanted to conserve a focus on good staff–prisoner relationships (Bennett, 2015b). On a broader structural level, in some periods, there were attempts to reinvigorate the notion of a more relational and empathic approach to prison management. This was apparent in the reform prisons operated between 2016 and 2017 (Bennett, 2019), which sought to re-engineer the "mindset" of employees, so rather than being reliant upon a directive hierarchy, they would take greater self-responsibility, acting as "role models" and "enablers", taking "personal responsibility". With prisoners, there was an intention to create improved staff–prisoner interactions, participation by prisoners in the internal community, enhanced opportunities for rehabilitation and a social climate that supported rehabilitation (see also Roberts et al., 2020). The desire to create a stronger sense of internal community can be seen as a way of giving prisoners a stake in the institution in which they live, to produce legitimacy (Sparks et al., 1996). The reimagining of social relations in the reform prisons in part appeared to be a re-emergence of "managerialism-plus" with a stronger focus on the well-being of staff and prisoners. That, however, was not the whole picture. These reforms were also an attempt to deploy soft power (Crewe, 2009), such as incentives, relationships, persuasion and education, to co-opt staff and prisoners, reshaping their habitus to be active corporate citizens, self-managing in alignment with a strategic intent. As one manager observed: "…you're empowered but you still need to go in a certain direction".

During the pandemic, the managerial infrastructure was disrupted over a two-year period (Bennett, 2023). In the absence of managerial targets and scrutiny, managers turned their attention to the internal community. Many managers described that they had more time to be visible, interacting directly with colleagues and prisoners. Investing in relationships and communication had an instrumental value in enabling them to identify and resolve problems, reduce resistance and secure engagement. This was also considered by many managers as having an affective quality, as a way of building cohesiveness between colleagues, and between staff and prisoners. The altered relationships were described as less hierarchical, summarised by a custodial manager:

> It was a good team effort. If we're gonna give the lads, the men, what they need then we're all going to have to work together. Whether you're wearing a suit or whether you're a cleaner…we're all in it together.

For some of them, the pandemic brought a shift between staff and prisoners, encapsulated by a supervisory officer:

> [Covid] reps were prisoners who helped with communication. We knew we needed buy in from the men, so having communication from other prisoners was helpful. The discussions we had helped to humanise us, and we shared that we had our own anxieties, vulnerable family members at home. It was important that we showed that we weren't just black and white, that we were more than a uniform. We had to work together.

Breaking down social barriers enabled the nurturing of a sense of togetherness in the face of shared adversity. This description is not intended to ignore the very real material effects of the pandemic for people in prison. The independent inspectorate of prisons concluded that although the measures put in place reduced fatalities, this "has been achieved at significant cost to the welfare and progression of prisoners" (HM Chief Inspector of Prisons, 2021: 7). Many prisoners were left experiencing "helpless and hopeless, stuck in limbo", with "a crushing sense of boredom" and falling into "a deep malaise" (Taylor & Bennett, 2022: 72). There was, nevertheless, a period in which a shared and significant experience gave rise to a greater sense of community and emotional connectedness for those who live and work in prisons, including managers.

This section has sought to explore the role of emotions in prison governance. It has illustrated how prison managers have been the object of governance through emotions. Managerialism has not simply been a system imposed through hard power, including threat and force. Instead, there has been a gradual process in which the professional habitus of managers has altered so that they have come to accept and even embody the managerial approach. The accounts of prison managers have shown that the habitus is not solely about rationalisations, logical perceptions and reasoning, but also has an emotional dimension, encompassing how prison managers feel about their work and how emotions shape their behaviour. From this vantage point, prison managers have been governed through their emotions. This section has also explored how managers, as subjects, approach the governance of prisoners. It has been argued that managerialism has been a dehumanising process in which prisoners have come to be increasingly perceived through the lens of economic rationality. This has not, however, been an untrammelled process. Individuals have resisted this tendency in their own practice, but also there have been moments, in particular the reform prisons and during the pandemic, in which there has been a reinvigoration of attention to the emotional and relational aspects of prison governance. In both cases, this was for a combination of instrumental and normative reasons; emotions and social relations were seen as reflecting desirable values but also a way to get the business of the organisation done in the most effective way. Governing through emotions has become a tool in the repertoire of prison managers in the age of managerialism.

Emotional labour

As described previously, emotional labour has attracted significant attention in the sociology of work, including prison work. This section will describe the ways in which managerialism has created increasing demands for emotional labour and will argue that the burdens of emotional labour have been unequally distributed, exacerbating existing inequalities.

It is widely accepted that management and leadership involve high degrees of emotional labour in creating the right conditions for effective team performance (e.g. Smith & Grandey, 2022). The increasing demands of emotional labour on prison managers can be illustrated by considering their experiences implementing austerity policies. These changes were described earlier and included reducing staff and changing job roles. Managers had to lead these changes while experiencing significant anxiety, concerned that they would have a detrimental impact on staff, prisoners and service quality.

The demands were summed up in the words of one manager:

> If you are leading on something and you express your anxieties, you can transfer your anxieties onto others…if you are transferring your anxieties, what faith are they going to have in you in leading through that change? … sometimes you have to swallow hard and get on with it, take a deep breath and go for it.

As well as creating an appropriate presentation to colleagues, managers were attempting to corral the feelings and actions of those they led to encourage compliance and reduce resistance:

> I met with the team and had a series of "toolbox" talks…The content was largely taken from centrally produced narratives which we had to use. We…put a more positive spin on it saying it might not be all bad. Basically, we said you have to go with it.

Given the significance of the changes and the impact on those they managed, prison managers had to face protracted and intense emotional reactions and part of their role was to absorb and diffuse this. One manager described:

> On a daily basis for the first six months we had to soak up the negativity… I felt a bit stuck in the middle, holding a line between uniform staff and senior management. Sometimes the change seemed relentless and it was important to be a sounding board for staff…We had to bear the brunt of it from staff and prisoners and we did feel the impact. There were times when I thought "bloody hell, I don't know what I'm going to get today". I felt powerless, all I could do was appease people.

Managers themselves experienced significant uncertainty and anxiety. For some, there was a residual concern that prisons would be privatised in the future and that the current changes were a further step in this direction. There were some managers directly affected by or involved in changes such as the closing of smaller prisons, with staff transferred to work elsewhere, or the redeployment of staff from one place to another due to the impact of cost reductions. In addition, many managers felt that their role and the expectations placed upon them were changing, and they felt that their skills were no longer useful or valued. The cumulative impact of these changes left some managers feeling overwhelmed and powerless:

> There was a lot of uncertainty. It was the worst part of my career. I found myself some days in the car park, thinking "where are we going?". There was so much uncertainty…It was an unhappy time. As a manager it was

difficult to look forward and put it in a good light when you didn't know what was around the corner yourself. ...There was a big bulldozer coming through and you had to jump on board.

The period of implementing austerity intensified the emotional labour expected of prison managers. The more fluid, changing work environment reflected the features of "new capitalism" (Sennett, 2004; Doogan, 2009). Managers experienced anxiety and uncertainty and were not always convinced that the changes were positive. They offered "disaffected consent", that is compliance that is reserved and begrudging, even calculated, and without satisfaction, commitment or enthusiasm (Clarke & Newman, 2012: 315). Nevertheless, they managed their emotions and undertook their role as local agents of national change, producing a front-stage performance in which their emotions were masked or minimised and they attempted to generate support, or at least reduce resistance amongst their colleagues.

While the example of austerity shows how prison managers generally experienced intensification in emotional labour, there were some staff who experienced additional but often hidden burdens. In particular, women managers and those from minority ethnic communities described how they faced a hostile working environment. The number of women managers has been increasing, and they now comprise around 40% of managers, while minority ethnic managers make up around 6% of managers, compared to 18% of the general population (HM Prison & Probation Service, 2023).

Women managers often described that there was a predominantly masculine culture in which their suitability and capability were viewed sceptically. They were sometimes described as bringing unwelcome "emotional baggage" (cited in Bennett 2015a; see also Smith, 2021), such as showing empathy or displaying their feelings openly, for example by crying. Women described having to adapt to the expectations of the environment, often in ways that were inauthentic for them. In contrast, men displaying feelings such as fear, competitiveness and aggression did not have their behaviour described as "emotional" at all, and indeed these emotions were often perceived as culturally acceptable (Wajcman, 2000). Managers who were Black or members of minority ethnic communities also described experiencing suspicion and scepticism from colleagues, sometimes being perceived as the beneficiaries of positive discrimination rather than achieving their role on merit. They claimed that their authority was tested and that they could not count on the support of more senior colleagues. These managers had to engage in additional emotional labour, presenting a culturally acceptable façade, often while experiencing a profound sense of injustice and social isolation (see also Morgan, 2018). The persistent microaggressions created "hidden injuries" (Sennett & Cobb, 1972), including a diminished sense of belonging and professional esteem. Managerialism with its targets, audits and other measures was often presented by prison managers as having created an objective standard and having levelled the playing field for everyone. The appearance of objectivity, however, masked the lived experience of some managers, including the harmful, deleterious effects of microaggressions. Rather than creating a level playing field, managerialism enabled the obscuration and denial of the harms experienced by women and minority ethnic managers.

It has become more widely recognised that emotional labour is a core feature of the contemporary working world. As has been illustrated here, it is an integral, even increasing, aspect of the work of prison managers. The experiences of women and minority ethnic managers show that the burdens of emotional labour are not evenly distributed and are implicated in racial and sex-based disparity, generating a context of affective inequalities in the workplace.

Conclusion

This chapter has attempted to explore emotions in *prison* managerialism and the working lives of prison managers.

On a macro level, emotional rhetoric has been an instrument of managerialism. In the late 1990s and early 2000s, managerialism was presented as offering the prospect of a more ordered approach in which progressive ambitions could be translated into reality. This played upon both the fears and anxieties of the past and the hopes for the future. This rhetoric was intended to create the emotional context in which change was possible. As the practices of managerialism became accepted, the rhetoric shifted during the austerity period. The justifications no longer rested on a hope of a more positive future, but rather played upon the fear of privatisation and economic collapse. The intention was to ensure that managerialism was conserved. The rhetoric of managerialism illustrates how the emotions – the hopes and fears – of citizens and workers are consciously managed to create change or conserve the status quo.

At a meso level, the professional culture and habitus of prison managers have been altered by the coming of managerialism. The accounts of prison managers show how the habitus encompasses not only how they think about the world, but also how they feel. Emotions are an integral aspect of the habitus. The alteration of the habitus, including emotions, is a critical aspect of contemporary governance. This chapter also explored how managerialism altered the ways in which emotion is distributed and deployed. *Prison* managerialism, combining the traditional subordination of prisoners with the economic rationality of managerialism, can contribute to creating an environment that enables dehumanisation. Although this is not uncontested, prisoners have in some circumstances been treated as commodities to be utilised to managerial ends rather than thinking, feeling agents whose lived experience is valued.

At a micro level, the chapter considered experiences of emotional labour. In common with the working world more broadly, prison managers are increasingly having to engage in emotional labour. Yet, the burdens of emotional labour do not fall evenly, but instead replicate and reinforce patterns of power and inequality, particularly for women and managers from minority ethnic communities.

This chapter has applied ideas from the sociology of emotions, using long-term data collected from prison managers in England. It has illuminated how emotions have become part of the technology of governance. Emotions are used to mobilise and constrain prison managers; accessing their subjective capacities including their emotions is one way in which the organisation exercises increasing control; and managers have become more adept at regulating their own emotions and those of others to achieve corporate objectives. By examining the inter-relationship between individual emotions, institutional structures and the social context, this chapter is attempting to reveal an "affective economy" (Ahmed, 2014) in which emotions do not solely reside within any individual but are instead one point in a wider network of power and social order. In this case, the emotional lives of prison managers and the affective landscape of *prison* managerialism are entangled with the context of neo-liberalism.

References

Ahmed, S. (2014). *The cultural politics of emotion*. Second Edition. Edinburgh: Edinburgh University Press.
American Psychological Society (2024) www.apa.org/topics/emotions
Bauman, Z. & Donskis, L. (2013). *Moral blindness: The loss of sensitivity in liquid modernity*. Cambridge: Polity Press.
Bell, E. (2011). *Criminal justice and neoliberalism*. Basingstoke: Palgrave Macmillan.
Bennett, J. (2015a). *The working lives of prison managers: Global change, local cultures and individual agency in the late modern prison*. Basingstoke: Palgrave Macmillan.
Bennett, J. (2015b). Managing prisons in an age of austerity. *Prison Service Journal* 222: 15–24.
Bennett, J. (2019). Reform, resistance and managerial clawback: The evolution of 'Reform Prisons' in England. *The Howard Journal of Crime and Justice* 58(1): 45–64.
Bennett, J. (2020). Against prison management. *Prison Service Journal* 247: 4–13.
Bennett, J. (2023). Disrupting prison managerialism: Managing prisons in an age of pandemic. *Incarceration* 4. https://doi.org/10.1177/26326663231169716
Bennett, J. (2024). *Managing prisons: Managerialism, austerity and moral blindness*. Cham: Palgrave MacMillan.
Blyth, M. (2013). *Austerity: The history of a dangerous idea*. Oxford: Oxford University Press.

Bourdieu, P. (1977). *Outline of a theory of practice*. Cambridge: Cambridge University Press.
Brookes, S., Smith, K. & Bennett, J. (2008). The role of middle and first line managers. In Bennett, J., Crewe, B. & Wahidin, A. (eds) *Understanding prison staff*. Cullompton: Willan, p. 262–276.
Bryans, S. (2007). *Prison governors: Managing prisons in a time of change*. Cullompton: Willan.
Bryans, S. & Wilson, D. (2000). *The prison governor: Theory & practice*. Second Edition. Leyhill: Prison Service Journal.
Carvalho, H. & Chamberlen, A. (2016). Punishment, justice, and emotions. In *Oxford handbooks online (criminology and criminal justice, punishment theories)*. New York: Oxford University Press.
Cheliotis, L. (2006). How iron is the iron cage of new penology? The role of human agency in the implementation of criminal justice policy. *Punishment and Society* 8(3): 313–340.
Clarke, J. (2016). Fearful asymmetry: Circuits of paranoia in governing through school inspection. In Jupp, E., Pykett, J. & Smith, F. M. (eds) *Emotional states: Sites and spaces of affective governance*. Abingdon, OX: Routledge, p. 129–143.
Clarke, J. & Newman, J. (2012). The alchemy of austerity. *Critical Social Policy* 32(3): 299–319.
Cohen, S. (2001). *States of Denial: Knowing about atrocities and suffering*. Cambridge: Polity Press.
Coyle, A. (2008). Change management in prisons. In Bennett, J., Crewe, B. & Wahidin, A. (eds) *Understanding prison staff*. Cullompton: Willan, p. 231–246.
Crewe, B. (2009). *The prisoner society: Power, adaptation and social life in an English prison*. Oxford: Clarendon Press.
Crewe, B. & Liebling, A. (2015). Governing governors. *Prison Service Journal* 222: 3–10.
Doogan, K. (2009). *New capitalism? The transformation of work*. Cambridge: Polity Press.
Foucault, M. (1977). *Discipline and punish: The birth of the prison*. London: Allen Lane.
Francis, R. (2013). Report of the mid Staffordshire NHS foundation trust public inquiry: Executive summary. Available at https://assets.publishing.service.gov.uk/government/uploads/system/uploads/attachment_data/file/279124/0947.pdf. Accessed on 04 August 2023.
Garland, D. (2001). *The culture of control: Crime and social order in contemporary society*. Oxford: Oxford University Press.
Gooch, K. & Treadwell, J. (2020). Prisoner society in an era of psychoactive substances, organized crime, new drug markets and austerity. *The British Journal of Criminology* 60(5): 1260–1281.
Gove, M. (2015). The treasure in the heart of man – Making prisons work. Speech given at Prisoners Learning Alliance on 17 July 2015. Available at www.gov.uk/government/speeches/the-treasure-in-the-heart-of-man-making-prisons-work. Accessed on 02 May 2021.
Hardwick, N. (2014). Perrie Lecture: Lessons for the Prison Service from the Mid-Staffs inquiry. *Prison Service Journal* 211: 3–13.
Harrison, K., Mason, R., Nichols, H. & Smith, L. (2024). *Work, culture, and wellbeing among prison governors in England and Wales*. Basingstoke: Palgrave MacMillan.

HM Chief Inspector of Prisons (2013). *Annual report 2012–13*. London: The Stationary Office.
HM Chief Inspector of Prisons (2014). *Annual report 2013–14*. London: The Stationary Office.
HM Chief Inspector of Prisons (2015). *Annual report 2014–15*. London: The Stationary Office.
HM Chief Inspector of Prisons for England and Wales (2021). *Annual report 2020–21*. Available at www.justiceinspectorates.gov.uk/hmiprisons/wp-content/uploads/sites/4/2021/07/6.7391_HMI-Prisons_Annual-Report-and-Accounts-2020_21_v6.1_WEB.pdf. Accessed 18 December 2022.
HM Prison & Probation Service (2023). *Annual staff equalities report: 2022 to 2023*. Available at www.gov.uk/government/statistics/hm-prison-probation-service-staff-equalities-report-2022-2023/hm-prison-and-probation-service-annual-staff-equalities-report-2022-to-2023. Accessed 11 September 2024.
Hochschild, A. (1983). *The managed heart: The commercialisation of human feeling*. Berkeley: University of California Press.
Institute for Government (2012). *Competition in prisons*. Available at www.instituteforgovernment.org.uk/sites/default/files/publications/Prisons%20briefing%20final.pdf. Accessed on 24 October 2023.
Justice Select Committee of House of Commons (2018). *Oral evidence: HM Inspectorate of prisons report on HMP Liverpool*, HC 751. Available at http://data.parliament.uk/writtenevidence/committeeevidence.svc/evidencedocument/justice-committee/hm-inspectorate-of-prisons-report-on-hmp-liverpool/oral/77512.pdf. Accessed on 02 August 2019.
Kennedy, P. (2010). *Local lives and global transformations: Towards world society*. Basingstoke: Palgrave Macmillan.
Liebling, A. (2011). Perrie Lecture: The cost to prison legitimacy of cuts. *Prison Service Journal* 198: 3–11.
Liebling, A. assisted by Arnold, H. (2004). *Prisons & their moral performance: A study of values, quality and prison life*. Oxford: Oxford University Press.
Liebling, A. & Crewe, B. (2013). Prisons beyond the New Penology: The shifting moral foundations of prison management. In Simon, J. & Sparks, R. (eds) *The Sage handbook of punishment and society*. London: Sage, p. 283–307.
Morgan, M. (2018). *Black women prison employees: The intersectionality of gender and race*. Lewiston, NY: Edwin Mellen Press.
Mulholland, I. (2014). Perrie Lecture 2013: Contraction in an age of expansion: An operational perspective. *Prison Service Journal* 211: 14–18.
National Offender Management Service (2012). *Fair and sustainable: Revision to proposals for working structures in HM Prison Service following the consultation with trade unions*. London: Ministry of Justice.
National Offender Management Service (2014). *Business plan 2014–15*. London: National Offender Management Service.
Nylander, P. & Bruhn, A. (2020). The emotional labour of prison work. In Phillips, J., Westaby, C., Fower, A. & Waters, J. (eds) *Emotional labour in criminal justice and criminology*. London: Routledge, p. 69–84.
Owers, A. (2007). Imprisonment in the twenty-first century: A view from the inspectorate. In Jewkes, Y. (ed) *Handbook on Prisons*. Cullompton: Willan, p. 1–21.

Parker, M. (2002). *Against management: Organization in the age of managerialism.* Cambridge: Polity Press.

Prime Minister & Minister for the Cabinet Office (1999). *Modernising government.* London: HMSO.

Prison Reform Trust (2010). *'Unacceptable' prisoner swaps undermined duty of care.* Prison Reform Trust 06 October 2010. Available at https://prisonreformtrust.org.uk/unacceptable-prisoner-swaps-undermined-duty-of-care/. Accessed on 17 May 2024.

Prison Service Pay Review Body (2014). *Thirteenth report on England and Wales 2014.* London: The Stationary Office.

Pykett, J., Jupp, E. & Smith, F. (2017). Introduction: Governing with feeling. In Pykett, J., Jupp, E. & Smith, F. (eds) *Emotional states: Sites and spaces of affective governance.* London: Routledge, p. 1–17.

Roberts, E., Sharrock, S., Pullerits, M., Barnard, M. & Turley, C. (2020). *The reform prisons pilot: Research report on lessons learnt.* London: Ministry of Justice. Available at https://assets.publishing.service.gov.uk/media/5f0c578a3a6f40038682639b/reform-prisons-report.pdf. Accessed on 24 April 2024.

Rose, N. (1999). *Governing the soul: The shaping of the private self.* Second Edition. London: Free Association Books.

Rutherford, A. (1993). *Criminal justice and the pursuit of decency.* Oxford: Oxford University Press.

Sennett, R. (2004). *The culture of the new capitalism.* New Haven: Yale University Press.

Sennett, R. & Cobb, J. (1972). *The hidden injuries of class.* New York: Norton & Company.

Smith, V. (2021). The experiences of women prison governors. *Prison Service Journal* 257: 22–28.

Smith, D. & Grandey, A. (2022, November 2). The emotional labor of being a leader. *Harvard Business Review.* Available at https://hbr.org/2022/11/the-emotional-labor-of-being-a-leader. Accessed on 25 May 2024.

Sparks, R., Bottoms, A. & Hay, W. (1996). *Prisons and the problem of order.* Oxford: Clarendon Press.

Spurr, M. & Bennett, J. (2008). The interview: Michael Spurr. *Prison Service Journal* 177: 54–61.

Taylor, C. & Bennett, J. (2022). Inspecting prisons during a pandemic and recovery. *Prison Service Journal* 259: 69–75.

Turner J. & Stets J. (2005) *The Sociology of Emotions.* Cambridge: Cambridge University Press.

Wajcman, J. (2000). It's hard to be soft: Is management style gendered? Grint, K. (ed) *Work and society: A reader.* Cambridge: Polity Press, p. 254–273.

Wheatley, P. (2005). Managerialism in the prison service. *Prison Service Journal* 161: 33–34.

Wilson, D. (1995). Against the culture of management. *Prison Service Journal* (98): 7–9.

10
RELATIONAL ASPECTS OF PRISON WORK AND INSTITUTIONAL CHANGE

Reflections on Uruguay's Prison Reform

Ana Vigna

Introduction

Prison officers have been considered as the *'face of the state behind the walls'* (Shannon & Page, 2014: 631). Therefore, the ways in which they conceive and carry out their task have a strong impact on the quality of life in prisons, and on the possibilities for the incarcerated population to access and exercise their rights.

Prison staff in Latin America face particular challenges, given the extreme levels of violence inside facilities (Ariza & Tamayo Arboleda, 2020; Bergman & Fondevilla, 2021), widespread overcrowding and inhumane living conditions (Darke and Karam, 2016; Salla et al., 2015) and different expressions of self-governance and co-governance (Sozzo, 2022; Nunes Dias et al., 2022; Skarbek, 2020; Darke, 2013). Additionally, the region exhibits the highest incarceration rates in the world, which have increased steadily in recent years (Sozzo, 2022; Bergman, 2023). In this context, Latin American prisons not only show low inmate to correctional officers' ratio, but also high levels of corruption and institutional violence (Sanhueza & Brander, 2021; Zaffaroni, 2015). The strong military and police tradition that characterizes prison systems in the region explains the high concentration of custodial officers with a security background and their pervasive mistrust of the civilian world. Moreover, prison work is marked by appalling working conditions, which are related to high levels of turnover and absenteeism, intensifying the problem of staff shortages (Galvani, 2012).

Uruguay, far from being an exception, has faced international scrutiny due to high levels of overcrowding and the harsh conditions of imprisonment (United Nations (UN), 2022). In an effort to transform the authoritarian hegemony that has historically governed its prison system, an institutional change process was implemented between 2010 and 2020. This chapter examines the links between professional culture, emotions and prison reform in Uruguay. In particular, it explores the different ways in which civilian and police officers conceived and carried out their duties. The findings indicate that, despite the formal changes introduced during the reform—particularly regarding role definition and training—the relational dimension of prison work, often overlooked in contexts of institutional change, remains central to everyday work inside prison facilities, perpetuating routine practices embedded in the hegemonic occupational culture.

Conflicts and Dilemmas in Prison Officers' Occupational Culture

A recent systematic review of Latin American prison officers' literature (Vigna, forthcoming) shows that the majority of the studies in the region come from psychology and are focussed on the effects of work on officers' emotional and mental health (Abello et al., 2023). Most of these studies address topics such as suicidal thoughts, depression, burnout, problems related to alcohol and drug consumption, insomnia, fatigue etc. (Álvarez-Cabrera et al., 2018; Tapias Saldaña et al., 2007; Gomes, 2016; Lima et al., 2019; Bravo et al., 2022; Albuquerque & Araújo, 2018; Santos et al., 2010).

With a different lens, several social science studies have highlighted the tragic position occupied by prison staff, representing a double exclusion: they are neither part of the outside world (which undervalue them) nor part of the inside world (to which they must constantly distinguish themselves) (Mouzo, 2010; Bodê de Moraes, 2013). In this liminal position, officers need to understand the customs, language and dynamics of the incarcerated population in order to obtain information and prevent conflicts (Bodê de Moraes, 2013; Claus, 2015). However, this prolonged contact has detrimental effects on their identity, as they risk going through a prisonization process similar to that observed in inmates (Lourenço, 2010; Bodê de Moraes, 2013; Bogo Chies et al., 2005).

Other Latin American studies explore the production of the 'correctional subject' and focus on the dispute over the content and the process of acquisition of prison knowledge that takes place beyond formal training (Galvani, 2016). Among them, some authors have highlighted the relevance of critical moments—such as riots—in shaping the 'esprit de corps' among colleagues (Mouzo, 2010). These elements create an occupational culture based on tradition and camaraderie that is closed to outside scrutiny.

Despite its peculiarities, these conflicting elements observed in Latin America are in line with that observed in other parts of the world. While prison organizations are rigid settings, prison staff exercise considerable discretionary power (Gilbert, 1997; Liebling, 2011). Indeed, literature highlights the existence of a significant discrepancy between formal regulations and the informal rules that govern daily life in prisons (Sparks & Bottoms, 1995; Gilbert, 1997; Liebling, 2011). In this context, norms are necessarily limited in stipulating precisely how to proceed in each situation, given that the administration in question concerns the entire life of a group of human beings living together against their will. Even when those rules exist, officers frequently decide not to apply them, or to apply them selectively. Therefore, prison officers could be thought of as 'street-level bureaucrats' (Lipsky, 1980) referring to those employees who interact directly with the public, often in complex and ambiguous situations, and are responsible for interpreting and implementing the abstract policy on a daily basis. In this position, frontline officers possess significant discretionary power in the allocation of benefits and sanctions and control information and resources that their superiors cannot directly supervise.

To illustrate the heterogeneity in prison officers' attitudes and behaviours, two main orientations towards prison work can be distinguished (Kauffman, 1988). On the one hand, officers who adhere to a relational perspective tend to express a more positive view of inmates and interpret criminality as the result of social inequality and the context of vulnerability in which inmates were raised. On the other hand, officers who espouse a distant perspective are more likely to hold a conceptualization of crime as an individual matter of choice or failure. From this perspective, the very idea of developing a bond with inmates is strongly rejected. Therefore, in the context of conflicting orientations, the definition of the 'optimal' distance between officers and inmates is one of the most contentious aspects of their work (Liebling, 2011).

The attitudes prison officers have towards inmates are also related to the ways in which they interpret and deal with prison violence. Whether explicit or latent, and through its various manifestations, violence is a constitutive part of the carceral dynamics and affects those who inhabit it (Crawley, 2004). In order to explain the staff's ability to endure the pains of imprisonment suffered by inmates (whether derived from prison conditions or directly inflicted by other inmates or officers), Scott (2008) revisits Stanley Cohen's (2001) work on 'techniques of denial'. Denial is presented as opposed to acknowledgement, which is identified as taking place:

...when a person has knowledge of human suffering, recognises the full reality of the pain and harm this information imparts, and identifies the personal implications of possessing such knowledge, leading ultimately to some form of action that attempt to mitigate or end the injuries inflicted upon their fellow humans.

(Scott, 2008: 169)

On the contrary, denial occurs when officers are aware of prisoners' suffering yet reinterpret this information in a manner that legitimizes their inaction.

Among the denial techniques are the classic 'neutralization techniques' highlighted by Sykes and Matza (1957): (i) *denial of responsibility* (inmates themselves are responsible for their imprisonment, having chosen to commit the crime); (ii) *denial of injury* (the treatment given to inmates is even too good for what they deserve); (iii) *denial of victim* (inmates do not suffer the situation or do not fully understand it); (iv) *condemnation of the condemners* (discrediting those external critics who, without experiencing carceral dynamics, denounce it from the outside); and (v) *appeal to higher loyalties* (the need to protect the rights of other vulnerable collectives, such as the victims of crime or the workers themselves). Drawing on Herzfeld (1992), Cohen (2001) adds *moral indifference* as a new technique of denial, which directly implies that the officer believes in the rightness of prisoners' suffering. In the extreme case, moral indifference can lead to a self-perception by prison officers as 'respectable victims' of imprisonment, while the suffering of inmates is not only justified but even regarded as desirable (Scott, 2008).

Therefore, violence frames the development and reproduction of occupational culture and has strong moral effects on personnel. Emotional labour entails dealing with one's own emotions, whether stemming from forced coexistence with inmates, the reaction generated by knowing the crimes committed, officers' limited possibility of distancing themselves from 'morally questionable' actions (such as pat-downs and searches), or various conflictive situations that may arise in day-to-day interactions (Nylander et al., 2011). In line with the idea of 'moral indifference', Kauffman (1988) highlights that officers often end up considering the prison as a separate moral environment, where different standards prevail compared to that of the 'free world', in a sort of 'numbing effect'. Depersonalization, detachment or attempts to suppress 'weak feelings', such as fear or anxiety, are among the emotional strategies developed by workers to deal with the emotional costs of their job (Nylander et al., 2011).

Furthermore, the emotional costs of prison work frequently end up tainting staff's families and home lives (Garrihy, 2021). Therefore, many must make a real effort to 'behave' appropriately at home or directly distance themselves from their families as a strategy to keep them away from the suffering of the prison.

However, in contrast to the simplistic image of prison guards performing a purely custodial task, literature has highlighted that their work involves a delicate emotional management and a professional use of power (Liebling et al., 2011; Bennett et al., 2008). Indeed, numerous authors have asserted that the defining characteristic of prison work is the capacity to reconcile 'welfare and discipline' or 'care and power' (Crewe, 2011; Crewe et al., 2011; Liebling, 2011).

Furthermore, this tension arises within an institutional context that is strongly domestic in nature, characterized by mundane aspects of daily routine related to housekeeping and the reproduction of life (Crawley, 2004). Within this framework, debates introduced by feminist criminologists regarding the incorporation of women into organizational settings traditionally dominated by men (Britton, 2003) underscore the need to take into account the gender dimension in the analysis of hegemonic practices, values and emotions within the prison. Whereas some traits traditionally associated with hegemonic masculinity (such as aggressiveness, courage and physical strength) are highly valued within the prison occupational culture, the expression of certain emotions related to femininity (such as fear or empathy) are considered incompatible or even counterproductive within the prison setting (Crawley, 2004; Britton, 2003; Zimmer, 1987; Tait, 2011). Therefore, the feminization of the prison workforce challenges the traditional view of the attitudes and knowledge required to do the job properly (Malochet, 2005) and brings to the forefront the role of care and dialogue in prison work (Tait, 2011; Liebling, 2011).

Within this context, this chapter aims to explain how several key aspects of prison work—mainly related to human interactions—have been challenged during prison reform in Uruguay, particularly with the introduction of civilian officers. Following this section, the methodology and data used in this study are presented. The analysis then focusses on the relational dimension of prison work, highlighting the most salient differences between police and civilian personnel. The chapter concludes with reflections on the relevance of frontline officers' values and attitudes in either fostering or hindering institutional change.

Context and Methodological Approach

Uruguay has the South American highest incarceration rate, with 449 inmates per 100,000 inhabitants in 2024.[1] This enormous incarcerated population, which is three times the global average, is a key factor in explaining the profound crisis of the Uruguayan prison system, characterized by human rights violations and high levels of overcrowding (Parliamentary Commissioner for the Penitentiary System, 2023).

To address this situation, during the 'progressive era' that took place between 2005 and 2020, the government implemented a prison reform (2010–2020) that focussed on combating inhumane prison conditions, moving from a custodial model to one based on human rights. The administration sought to build a strong institutional framework for prison management and to *depoliciliaze* prisons, which were (and still are) under the responsibility of the Ministry of Interior. In 2010 the National Institute for Rehabilitation ('Instituto Nacional de Rehabilitación', INR) was created as the governing body of the prison system. The figure of 'operador penitenciario'—a civilian officer specially selected and trained to work in prisons—was created in the same year. 'Operadores penitenciarios' began to carry out their duties alongside police officers, who were exclusively in charge of prison work until 2011.

Therefore, prison reform sought to radically change not only the conformation of the 'penitentiary body' but also the role of prison staff, now intended to be centred on relational work and welfare rather than on custody and punishment. According to the First National Census of Prison Officers (2016), compared to police officers, civilian staff were mostly women, became prison officers at older ages and were over-represented in welfare and rehabilitation tasks (Vigna, 2021).

Regarding staff training, Dammert and Zúñiga (2008) note that in most Latin American countries, a secondary education is required to become a prison officer, although not necessarily completed. In some countries, having finished primary education is sufficient to enter the profession. In Uruguay, according to the First National Census of Prison Staff (2016), while over 14% of police officers had primary education as their highest level of schooling (whether completed or not), the proportion of civilian staff in this situation was 5%. At the other end of the spectrum, nearly one-third of civilian staff had attained tertiary or university education (whether completed or not), whereas this applied to fewer than one in ten police officers.

In relation to the specific training process to become a prison officer, Dammert and Zúñiga (2008) observe that, in most countries of the region, initial training lasts between two and four months. In Uruguay, according to the First National Census of Prison Staff (2016), almost one-third of the staff received no training for working in prisons. That was the situation of approximately 43% police officers and 7% of civilian staff.

This chapter examines a specific period in the history of the Uruguayan prison system when the concept and role of the prison officer were expected to undergo transformation. Evidence is derived from the research I conducted as part of my doctoral dissertation (Vigna, 2021). Here I draw on interviews conducted with 35 officers working in six facilities, covering different security levels: high (Units No. 3 Libertad and No. 4 COM.CAR), medium (Units No. 5 Femenino and No. 13 Maldonado) and low (Units No. 6 Punta de Rieles and No. 18 Durazno). Participants were diverse in terms of gender and rank (civilian and police staff), as well as in terms of their working area (welfare-rehabilitation and administrative, internal security and external security). The interviews were conducted inside facilities without the presence of third parties. The testimonies presented here have been anonymized.

Table 10.1 presents the distribution of the interviewees in terms of the dimensions considered for their selection. It illustrates the concentration of men and police officers in high-security prisons, as well as in surveillance activities.

The interviews aimed to delve into the ways in which prison officers made sense of their career trajectories, their conceptions of the job, the way

TABLE 10.1 Distribution and characteristics of interviewed officers

Security level	Working area			Total
	Internal security	Welfare-rehabilitation and administrative	External security	
Low	4 (3 civilian, 1 police officer; 3 men, 1 woman)	4 (4 civilian officers; 1 man, 3 women)	4 (4 men; 4 police officers)	12
Medium	3 (3 civilian officers; 1 man, 2 women)	6 (6 civilian officers; 2 men, 4 women)	3 (3 men; 3 police officers)	12
High	5 (5 police officers; 5 men)	4 (4 civilian officers; 2 men; 2 women)	2 (2 men; 2 police officers)	11
Total	12	14	9	35

in which they exercised their power and the relationships they developed with other actors with whom they shared the daily dynamics of prison life (inmates, colleagues and authorities).

Regime and Working Conditions: 'It's another world'

Correctional facilities in Uruguay expose great heterogeneity, resulting in significant disparity in the regime and working conditions. While most civilian officers work shifts of between 6 and 10 hours per day, a large portion of police officers work on a 'week on, week off' regime. This regime involves 12-hour shifts for seven consecutive days. Due to the distance of the correctional facilities from their homes, this regime often implies staying at the facility for the entire week. In the bigger and more complex units, in addition to the 12-hour daily shifts, officers have two weekly 'overtime' shifts of 6 extra hours each, resulting in 18-hour workdays. This working regime and the impossibility of leaving the prison for a whole week are key factors in explaining the processes of 'prisonization' observed in many police officers, strengthening the sense of isolation and the idea of the prison as a 'separate world' (Kauffman, 1988).

The low ratio of staff to prisoners reinforces the perception of 'constant threat' from the officers' point of view and is identified from their perspective as a reason to focus on surveillance activities to the detriment of relational work. Widespread turnover and absenteeism can be seen as individual acts of resistance to the harsh working environment (Galvani, 2012, 2016), yet they have a perverse effect on colleagues, further exacerbating the structural issue of staff shortages.

> We have to cover the work of many [colleagues], because they are certified or because they are absent. That generates stress. For example, when we

started working on the floor, there were, I don't know, 50 inmates, and we had 6 or 7 officers working. Eventually, we ended up with just one officer. And of course, when you are alone, you have to prevent from doing many things that you can't do. Because you can't manage, you can't leave, you can't do anything. You have to limit yourself to a phone or a walkie-talkie.
(Civil officer, male, medium-security facility, welfare-rehabilitation area)

Despite the implementation of a progressive prison reform intended to enhance the living conditions within correctional facilities, the persistent increase in the prison population and the shortage of staff impeded the enactment of a radical transformation. Overcrowding and staff shortage, compounded by material conditions that were frequently undignified, affected the physical and emotional well-being of staff members. The following quotation illustrates disgust (see Aliverti, 2025) as an element present in the working routine of these officers, who share the degrading living conditions endured by a large part of the prison population in Uruguay.

You have to work in places where you step in water all day, whether it's sewage water or not, but you step in water all day. You feel that nauseating smell of garbage, human sweat all day long. And there you have to eat and drink. It's impossible to keep that place clean.
(Police officer, male, high-security facility, internal security area)

Ultimately, the work regime, staff shortages and degrading working conditions reinforce the perception of prison as a 'world of its own', isolated from the rest of society. These structural conditions strongly influence staff attitudes, shaping the context in which occupational culture and everyday practices are formed and reproduced—beyond the knowledge acquired through formal training.

Attitudes towards Inmates

As literature has stated (Shannon & Page, 2014; Lerman & Page, 2012; Lambert et al., 2007; Kauffman, 1988), there is a great deal of diversity in staff attitudes towards inmates. To those officers who define inmates as individuals with values different—or directly opposed—to those of the rest of society, adherence to the relational dimension of work will be severely limited.

You can't rehabilitate a rapist, who has raped and killed. You release them onto the street, and they're like animals. I'm telling you because I talk to them, you won't rehabilitate them. (...) I see guys the same age as my son

killing each other over a cigarette. So people who don't value life, I don't know how to instil values in them, how to integrate them into society.
(Police officer, male, high-security facility, internal security area)

This attitude (more frequently observed among police staff) is associated with the development of the techniques of denial mentioned by Scott (2008). From this perspective, responsibility for the hardships experienced in prison is placed on inmates. In fact, these officers perceive inmates' rights as directly opposed to those of other actors (such as crime victims or officers themselves). While they point to the violence suffered by officers at the hands of inmates as a persistent issue (regardless of the frequency with which these incidents actually occur), they perceive their own violent behaviour towards inmates as 'deserved' (Kauffman, 1988). In this context, some officers perceived the human rights perspective and concerns about institutional violence—promoted as part of prison reform—as a 'constraint' on their work and a sign of insufficient support for staff.

Everything has changed, the laws have changed a lot (...) a prisoner has more support than a policeman. It's not like before. I joined in 2000 and in 2000 the prisoners respected the police. (...) Now, if you shoot a prisoner, you have to go to court afterwards, write a report about why you shot, why you didn't avoid the greater evil, a whole issue (...) Now you can't shoot anymore, because it gets complicated.
(Police officer, male, high-security facility, external security area)

However, this is not the only way to conceptualize prison work. On the contrary, many officers emphasize the need to develop an empathetic perspective towards inmates. Most of these officers understand inmates' involvement in crime as a consequence of the hardships they experienced in their lives.

There are people here who are in for theft, who steal because when they were children, they stole because they were hungry, because their parents abandoned them. (...) A child like that ends up stealing, and if you've already stolen when you're older, you'll keep stealing. It's a social problem.
(Police officer, male, medium-security facility, external security area)

Thus, while some officers interpret crime as a result of moral failure or individual choice, others adopt a more empathetic perspective. The way staff perceive inmates significantly influences their willingness to establish relationships with them (Wooldredge & Steiner, 2016). However, the meaning each officer assigns to the concept of 'relationship' is particularly noteworthy. This understanding shapes officers' perceptions of both the appropriateness and desirability of the type and frequency of interactions with inmates (Liebling, 2011; Klofas & Toch, 1982).

In the case of civilian officers, relational work is considered a constitutive part of their function. However, it is difficult for them to define exactly what constitutes a 'proper' relationship. While some believe that developing a close relationship is essential for performing their job effectively, others see such involvement as problematic, as it may hinder 'impartial' decision-making. The following quotations illustrate the diversity of opinions among 'operadores penitenciarios':

> I believe [officers] have to engage with the issues of the inmates because it's the only way to contribute to the rehabilitation process. Because if I'm not interested in what happens to others, it's like you're never going to help in anything
> *(Civil officer, woman, medium-security facility, welfare-rehabilitation area)*

> We can't have a bond [with the inmates]. The fact of getting involved already creates a problem. You're getting involved, you care, you're interested, so that already affects making a correct decision.
> *(Civil officer, man, high-security facility, welfare-rehabilitation area)*

Additionally, some emphasize the role problems derived from establishing a relationship of listening and trust when simultaneously performing custodial functions (Liebling, 2011). This contradiction has been highlighted as leading to frequent confusion and misunderstandings.

> When I'm the keeper, I'm the one who locks the keys and who doesn't allow them out into the yard. I'm the one who says 'no'. So, it's not the same as the work a person can do in the labour or education sector. You can't play both roles (...) You're handling a key in the sector, and everything that comes with handling a key.
> *(Civil officer, woman, medium-security facility, welfare-rehabilitation area)*

Conversely, prison officers who view inmates as manipulative individuals driven by self-interest perceive interpersonal relationships as a constant threat and risk. From this perspective, relationships between officers and inmates should be based on subordination to hierarchy and the demonstration of respect for authority.

> I try not to be tempted by what's easy. Here, they [inmates] always ask you for something: 'Can you bring me this?' I always try to think that I have a family outside and that I'm not going to let myself be dragged down by one of these. I have more to lose than to gain.
> *(Police officer, man, high-security facility, internal security area)*

If I respect you, I expect you to respect me. We spend 12 hours a day with the prisoners. We spend more time with them than with our families. So the bond has to be based on respect and on knowing who is in charge. Sometimes the prisoners get confused and disrespect us. Then people say that we are repressing them.
(Police officer, man, high-security facility, internal security area)

In this sense, beyond the formal definition of their role, it is clear that staff values and the emotions elicited by contact with inmates play a crucial role in shaping the daily implementation of prison policy. Staff perceptions of inmates' character and their explanations of the causes of crime influence their everyday practices, the ways they exercise power and the type of relationship they deem appropriate to establish with this population.

Correctional Preferences

Officers' attitudes do not automatically derive from their rank but are evidently shaped by the type of facility in which they work. Specifically, police officers are over-represented in larger, more densely populated prisons, where staff shortages are more acute and the prison population profile is more complex. In contrast, civilian staff are more commonly found in smaller prisons, where the provision of a human-centred service is more likely. It is evident that these structural factors significantly shape how officers conceptualize and fulfil their professional responsibilities.

In high- and medium-security facilities custodial aspects take a central place. In these contexts most police officers explicitly distance themselves from rehabilitation and emphasize that their role is to 'contain' and repress. In this classical view, the more confinement, the fewer problems.

We are the police; we are here to suppress. I'm not talking about using axes and machetes, no, it's not like that, but we're not here to bring prisoners to school; this isn't a park. The other day there was a meeting with I don't know how many people, and they told us: 'but they [the inmates] spend the whole day locked up,' and I told them, 'well, yes, they are prisoners'.
(Police officer, man, high-security facility, internal security area)

Despite this custodial attitude, many police officers show concern for relational tasks, generally because they consider them instrumental for maintaining prison order. However, these officers often feel a deficit in their training to address this aspect of their role. In these cases, the possibility to provide human service is generally associated with experience, and with the existence of structural conditions that enable a more personalized intervention.

> Inmates who have problems with his family, a sick mother... many times we talk, not to everyone, but we talk, because that prevents many things: that the prisoner self-harms, that he gets into fights with others, so that prevents a greater evil. So the police officer should have some preparation, I'm not saying he should be a psychologist, but he should have social skills.
> *(Police officer, man, low-security facility, external security area)*

On their part, the majority of civil officers adhere to a relational work perspective, understanding that the development of an active listening attitude and the pursuit of motivation for change constitute key elements of their role. However, many officers mention that the context in which they carry out their job prevents them from putting it into practice, leaving them limited to the development of merely custodial tasks. The limited availability of human and material resources imposes significant constraints on welfare initiatives. In this context, beyond the paradigmatic opposition, the contradictions between rehabilitation and custody also manifest in terms of their 'conditions of possibility'.

Meanwhile, the conceptualization of prison work is significantly shaped by gender norms. In the Uruguayan context, the substantial influx of civilian personnel led to a process of workforce feminization, which was first met with strong resistance from male colleagues. The prevailing hegemonic culture portrays female staff as more susceptible to manipulation by male prisoners and less competent in exerting authority. These prejudices, aimed at devaluing women's contributions, were reinforced by a paternalistic rhetoric that framed men as the protectors of female staff's well-being.

> There are tasks that women can't do. A woman's head is much lighter than a man's, the inmate has a lot of influence. (...) I've always said that the prison is for men, and only men should work here.
> *(Police officer, man, medium-security facility, external security area)*

However, some police officers acknowledge that, although they initially reacted negatively to the entry of women into the workforce, they now understand that they can introduce certain elements in their interactions with inmates that improve coexistence and reduce violence. From this standpoint, the value of female contribution is acknowledged as long as it aligns with traditional gender roles.

> It's perfect [the incorporation of women] because we've noticed a change in them [the inmates]. It's like, with a woman, I don't know if they see her as a mother, but they feel a different kind of support than with a man. It's different. It has helped a lot.
> *(Police officer, man, low-security facility, internal security area)*

In summary, the clear-cut opposition between custodial and human service attitudes becomes more nuanced when new dimensions of analysis are considered, extending beyond the distinction between civilian and police officers. The 'conditions of possibility' for exploring alternative approaches to prison work, along with the persistent concern for maintaining order (Sykes, 1958), bring together attitudes that may initially seem irreconcilable. This, in turn, makes it difficult to radically transform the everyday practices and values that underpin occupational culture.

Violence and the Emotional Impact of Prison Work

As stated before, the high levels of violence that permeate prison dynamics leave their mark on the well-being of the personnel. Police officers, in particular, mentioned having experienced situations of extreme violence at work. The stress and anxiety derived from this context do not end when the workday is over. On the contrary, they generate lasting effects on the physical and emotional health of staff, affecting their family and social lives (Garrihy, 2021).

> You see things that you don't see elsewhere. There are people who have never seen someone stabbed, never seen a dead body, never seen anything. And here you have everything, you see dead bodies, you see stabbings, stabbings all the time. Sometimes they try to attack you. The atmosphere here is not good, it's complicated, and there comes a point where it affects you.
> *(Police officer, man, medium-security facility, external security area)*

However, a symbolic barrier hinders the acknowledgement of fear and weakness, elements that are incongruent with the prevailing hegemonic masculinity that permeates the occupational culture.

> When I entered the force, I was afraid, trembling (...) They tried to hold a psychology workshop for police officers (...) but we police officers are reserved, mostly out of shame, because of machismo, including myself.
> *(Police officer, man, high-security facility, internal security area)*

In response to these circumstances, staff develop a variety of strategies for coping with their emotions that end up reinforcing the idea of prison as a 'separate moral environment' (Kauffman, 1988). On one hand, some officers engage in a process of emotional numbing, which enables them to continue with their daily activities. On the other hand, others seek to maintain a strict separation between their personal and professional lives, pretending that suffering does not exist at home.

At first, it impacts you, the first death, the first hanging you see. Then it becomes routine, that's why I tell you, it's a whole different world.
(Police officer, man, high-security facility, internal security area)

In my house I don't mention anything about my job, you understand? Sometimes they find out something from the television, but I can't talk about this.
(Police officer, man, high-security facility, internal security area)

Thus, working in prisons, particularly under the critical conditions in which most Uruguayan prisons operate, has long-lasting effects on the physical and mental health of staff, as well as on their family and community environments. Nevertheless, the prevailing mandates within the organizational culture, deeply rooted in the concept of hegemonic masculinity, hinder staff members' ability to openly express their emotions and seek assistance when needed.

Discussion

The analysis presented allows us to observe the different ways in which police and civilian staff conceived their roles and made sense of their interactions with inmates. On the one hand, civilian staff experienced role problems related to the difficulty of reconciling the care and control aspects of their job, as well as the lack of adequate resources to carry out their tasks properly. On the other hand, despite the greater specificity of police work (focussed on maintaining order and carrying out custodial tasks), these officers faced a process of questioning their hegemonic values and the traditional knowledge that has historically guided their practices.

Among police personnel, there is a marked emphasis on custody and a general reluctance towards relational work, whereas civilian officers tend to favour human service and rehabilitation. However, beyond the ethical and philosophical considerations underlying these attitudes, structural factors—such as the type of facility or the specific working area—play a crucial role in enabling or constraining the translation of initial predispositions into concrete behaviours. Within this framework, officers' perceptions of constant threat emerge as significant factors influencing everyday practices. Moreover, the emotional consequences of exposure to an inherently violent work environment, both for the workers, their social environment, as well as for the inmates themselves, must be taken into account by any policy that seeks to modify the scope and effects of imprisonment.

The recent prison reform in Uruguay involved the incorporation of civilians as prison officers, with the intention to transform the goals of imprisonment, as well as the skills and knowledge valued in prison work. While the programmatic guidelines were modified, the precarious material conditions of prisons persisted. Thus, the progressive ideals that inspired the reform were in practice aspirational and only partly effectively implemented. This situation created a context in which, in the presence of contradictory, changing and ambiguous institutional guidelines, the perceptions of the staff regarding the causes of crime and the type of person they believe offenders to be, as well as the emotions derived from prolonged contact with this population, end up strongly conditioning the way in which prison work was carried out on a daily basis.

Addressing these issues from Latin America, where incarceration rates have reached world's records, the presence of the state is weakened, and violence in prisons is a widespread phenomenon, represents a conceptual and empirical challenge that remains open.

Note

1   www.prisonstudies.org/country/uruguay

References

Abello, C., Pacheco, M., & Sanhueza, G. (2023). Funcionarios penitenciarios en América Latina: calidad de vida, condiciones laborales y principales problemáticas. *Revista Española de Sanidad Penitenciaria*, 25(1), 20–29. https://dx.doi.org/10.18176/resp.00063

Albuquerque, D., & Araújo, M. (2018). Precarização do trabalho e prevalência de transtornos mentais em agentes penitenciários do estado de Sergipe. *Revista Psicologia e Saúde*, 10(1), 19–30. https://dx.doi.org/10.20435/v10i1.456

Aliverti, A. (2025) Disgust at the border: Border work as dirty work. In Aliverti, A., Carvalho, H., Chamberlen, A. & Tawfic, S. (Eds.) *The Embodied State: Emotions, State Power and Social Marginalisation*. Abingdon: Routledge.

Álvarez-Cabrera, P., Chacón Fuertes, F., Sánchez-Moreno, E., & Araya Urquiola, Y. (2018). Síndrome de Burnout y variables psicosociales en funcionarios penitenciarios de Arica- Chile. *Fides et Ratio. Revista de Difusión cultural y científica de la Universidad La Salle en Bolivia*, 16(16), 49–79.

Ariza, L., & Tamayo Arboleda, F. L. (2020). El cuerpo de los condenados. Cárcel y violencia en América Latina. *Revista De Estudios Sociales*, 73, 83–95.

Bennett, J., Crewe, B., & Wahidin, A. (2008). *Understanding Prison Staff*. London: Willan Publishing.

Bergman, M. (2023). *El negocio del crimen. El crecimiento del delito, los mercados ilegales y la violencia en América Latina*. Ciudad Autónoma de Buenos Aires: Fondo de Cultura Económica.

Bergman, M., & Fondevilla, G. (2021). *Prisons and Crime in Latin America*. Cambridge University Press. https://doi.org/10.1017/9781108768238

Bodê de Moraes, P. (2013). A identidade e o papel de agentes penitenciários. *Tempo Social. Revista de sociologia da USP*, 25(1), 131–147.

Bogo Chies, L., Barros, A., Silva Lopes, C., & Oliveira, S. (2005). Prisionalização e sofrimento dos Agentes Penitenciários: fragmentos de uma pesquisa. *Revista Brasileira de Ciências Criminais*, 52, 309–335.

Bravo, D., Gonçalves, S., Girotto, E., González, A., Melanda, F., Rodrigues, R., & Mesas, A. (2022). Condições de trabalho e transtornos mentais comuns em agentes penitenciários do interior do estado de São Paulo, Brasil. *Ciência & Saúde Coletiva*, 27(12), 4559–4567. https://doi.org/10.1590/1413-812320222712.10042022

Britton, D. (2003). *At Work in the Iron Cage*. New York: New York University Press.

Claus, W. (2015). El trabajo penitenciario como "trabajo sucio". Justificaciones y normas ocupacionales. *Delito y Sociedad*, 40, 115–138.

Cohen, S. (2001). *States of Denial: Knowing about Atrocities and Suffering*. Cambridge: Polity.

Commissioner for the Penitentiary System (2023). Annual Report 2023. Available at: https://parlamento.gub.uy/sites/default/files/DocumentosCPP/Informe_2023_A delanto_web.pdf

Crawley, E. (2004). *Doing Prison Work. The Public and Private Lives or Prison Officers*. London: Routledge. Taylor & Francis Group.

Crewe, B. (2011). Soft power in prison: Implications for staff–prisoner relationships, liberty and legitimacy. *European Journal of Criminology*, 8(6), 455–468.

Crewe, B., Liebling, A., & Hulley, S. (2011). Staff culture, use of authority and prisoner quality of life in public and private sector prisons. *Australian & New Zealand Journal of Criminology*, 44(1), 94–115.

Dammert, L., & Zúñiga, L. (2008). *La cárcel: problemas y desafíos para las Américas*. Santiago de Chile: FLACSO.

Darke, S. (2013). Inmate Governance in Brazilian prisons. *The Howard Journal*, 52(3), 272–284.

Darke, S., & Karam, M. (2016). Latin American prisons. In Jewkes, Y., Bennett, J. & Crewe, B. (Eds.) *Handbook on Prisons* (pp. 460–474). Abington: Routledge.

Galvani, I. (2012). Cuestión de "cintura". Formas de obedecer y desobedecer en el personal subalterno del Servicio Penitenciario Bonaerense. In Frederic, S., Galvani, I., Garriga Zucal, J. & Renoldi, B. (Eds.) *De armas llevar: estudios socio antropológicos de los quehaceres de policías y de las fuerzas de seguridad* (pp. 115–145). La Plata: Ediciones de Periodismo y Comunicación. Facultad de Periodismo y Comunicación Social. Universidad Nacional de la Plata.

Galvani, I. (2016). *Entre la arbitrariedad y la inflexibilidad. El personal penitenciario bonaerense y su relación con las reglas*. Buenos Aires: Universidad Nacional de San Martín.

Garrihy J. (2021). 'That Doesn't Leave You': Psychological dirt and taint in prison officers' occupational cultures and identities. *The British Journal of Criminology*. https://doi.org/10.1093/bjc/azab074. Available at SSRN: https://ssrn.com/abstr act=3907870

Gilbert, M. (1997). The illusion of structure: A critique of the classical model of organization and the discretionary power of correctional officers. *Criminal Justice Review*, 22(1), 49–64.

Gomes, S. (2016). *Liderança em contextos instáveis: stresse e stressores dos gerentes prisionais e agentes penitenciários das unidades prisionais do Estado da Bahia*. Tese (Doutor em Psicologia). Universidade Autónoma de Lisboa.

Herzfeld, M. (1992). *The Social Production of Indifference Exploring the Symbolic Roots of Western Bureaucracy*. Chicago: University of Chicago Press.

Kauffman, K. (1988). *Prison Officers and Their World.* Cambridge: Harvard University Press.
Klofas, J., & Toch, H. (1982). The guard subculture myth. *Journal of Research in Crime and Delinquency,* 19(2), 238–254.
Lambert, E., Paoline, E., Hogan, N., & Baker, D. (2007). Gender similarities and differences in correctional staff work attitudes and perceptions of the work environment. *Western Criminology Review,* 8(1), 16–31.
Lerman, A., & Page, J. (2012). The state of the job: An embedded work role perspective on prison officer attitudes. *Punishment & Society,* 14(5), 503–529.
Liebling, A. (2011). Distinctions and distinctiveness in the work of prison officers: Legitimacy and authority revisited. *European Journal of Criminology,* 8(6), 484–499.
Liebling, A., Price, D., & Shefer, G. (2011). *The Prison Officer.* London: Willan Publishing. Prison Service Journal.
Lima, A., Dimenstein, M., Figueiró, R., Leite, J., & Dantas, C. (2019). Prevalência de Transtornos Mentais Comuns e Uso de Álcool e Drogas entre Agentes Penitenciários. *Psicologia: Teoria E Pesquisa,* 35. https://doi.org/10.1590/0102.3772e3555
Lipsky, M. (1980/2010). *Street-Level Bureaucracy: Dilemmas of the Individual in Public Services.* New York: Russell Sage Foundation.
Lourenço, L. (2010). Batendo a tranca: Impactos do encarceramento em agentes penitenciários da Região Metropolitana de Belo Horizonte. *Dilemas – Revista de Estudos de Conflito e Controle Social,* 3(10), 11–31. ISSN: 1983-5922.
Malochet, G. (2005). Dans l'ombre des hommes: La féminisation du personnel de surveillance des prisons pour hommes. *Sociétés Contemporaines,* 59, 199–220.
Mouzo, G. K. (2010). *Servicio Penitenciario Federal. Un estudio sobre los modos de objetivación y de subjetivación de los funcionarios penitenciarios en la Argentina actual.* Buenos Aires: Tesis para optar por el título de Doctora en Investigación en Ciencias Sociales. Facultad de Ciencias Sociales. Universidad de Buenos Aires.
Nunes Dias, C., Salla, F., & Alvarez, M. (2022). Governance and legitimacy in Brazilian prison: From solidarity committees to the Primeiro Comando Da Capital (PCC) in São Paulo. In Sozzo, M. (Ed.) *Prisons, Inmates and Governance in Latin America* (pp. 35–62). London: Palgrave Macmillan.
Nylander, P.-A., Lindberg, O., & Bruhn, A. (2011). Emotional labour and emotional strain among Swedish prison officers. *European Journal of Criminology,* 8(6), 469–483.
Salla, F., Ballesteros, P., Espinoza, O., Martínez, F., Litvachky, P., & Museri, A. (2015). *Democracy, Human Rights and Prison Conditions in South America.* São Paulo: Núcleo de Estudos da Violência Center for the Study of Violence, University of São Paulo NEV/USP. www. nevusp. org/downloads/down249. pdf
Sanhueza, G., & Brander, F. (2021). Centralidad de la relación interno-funcionario en cárceles chilenas: implicancias para la reinserción y el control de la corrupción. *URVIO, Revista Latinoamericana de Estudios de Seguridad* 29, 78–95. ISSN: 1390-3691.
Santos D., Dias J., Pereira M., Moreira T., Barros D., & Serafim A. (2010). Prevalence of common mental disorders among prison officers. *Revista Brasileira de Medicina do Trabalho,* 8(1), 33–38.
Scott, D. (2008). Creating ghosts in the penal machine: Prison officer occupational morality and the techniques of denial. In J. Bennett, B. Crewe, & A. Wahidin (Eds.) *Understanding Prison Staff* (pp. 168–186). London: Willan Publishing.

Shannon, S., & Page, J. (2014). Bureaucrats on the cell block: Prison officer' perceptions of work environment and attitudes toward prisoners. *Social Service Review*, 88(4), 630–657.

Skarbek, D. (2020). *The Puzzle of Prison Order. Why Life Behind Bars Varies around the World*. New York: Oxford University Press.

Sozzo, M. (Ed.) (2022). *Prisons, Inmates and Governance in Latin America*. London: Palgrave Macmillan.

Sparks, R., & Bottoms, A. (1995). Legitimacy and order in prisons. *The British Journal of Sociology*, 46(1), 45–62.

Sykes, G. (1958). *The Society of Captives: A Study of a Maximum Security Prison*. Princeton: Princeton University Press.

Sykes, G., & Matza, D. (1957). Techniques of neutralization: A theory of delinquency. *American Sociological Review*, 22(6), 664–670.

Tait, S. (2011). A typology of prison officers' approach to care. *European Journal of Criminology*, 8(6), 440–454.

Tapias Saldaña, Á., Salas-Menotti, I., & Solórzano, C. (2007). Descripción de las Estadísticas de Problemáticas Psicosociales en Guardianes Penitenciarios de Colombia. *Suma Psicológica*, 14(1), 7–22. ISSN: 0121-4381.

United Nations (UN) (2022). Human Rights Committee. Concluding observations on the sixth periodic report of Uruguay. Available at: https://tbinternet.ohchr.org/_layouts/15/treatybodyexternal/Download.aspx?symbolno=CCPR%2FC%2FURY%2FCO%2F6&Lang=en

Vigna, A. (2021). *Funcionarios penitenciarios y ejercicio del poder: rol ocupacional en un modelo en transición*. Tesis Doctorado en Sociología, UdelaR.

Vigna, A. (forthcoming). Prison officers in Latin America: A systematic review of the literature. In: Sozzo, M. & Iturralde, M. (Eds.) *Routledge Handbook on Crime and Punishment in Latin America*.

Wooldredge, J., & Steiner, B. (2016). The exercise of power in prison organizations and implications for legitimacy. *The Journal of Criminal Law and Criminology*, 106(1), 125–165.

Zaffaroni, E. (2015). La filosofía del sistema penitenciario en el mundo contemporáneo. In Bardazano, G., Corti, A., Duffau, N. & Trajtenberg, N. (Eds.) *Discutir la cárcel, pensar la sociedad. Contra el sentido común punitivo* (pp. 15–36). Montevideo: Trilce-CSIC.

Zimmer, L. (1987). How women reshape the prison guard role. *Gender and Society*, 1(4), 415–431.

11

THE AFFECTIVE TURN IN THE CRIMINAL PROCESS

Stakeholders' Emotional Labour in Child Sexual Abuse Cases in India

Shailesh Kumar

11.1 Introduction

Courtrooms are emotional spaces (Karstedt, 2002). Stakes in criminal cases are very high, as loss of personal liberty, love, limb, and life of the victims, the accused, and their family members are involved. Human beings, being a warehouse of emotions, experience and express different feelings throughout the criminal process, depending on their role in a case, their societal position and culture, as well as the complex group dynamics – emotional, social, and political – of their community, office, profession, and those inherent in the adversarial system (Bandes, 2006a; Bandes & Blumenthal, 2012; Blumenthal, 2005; Morrison, 1968). For example, jurors, judges, prosecutors, defence lawyers, police officers, and court staff members might have their decisions, behaviour, and engagements with victims, accused, and their families, informed by existing power asymmetry and the way it shapes their emotions (Bandes, 2006b; Cross & Whitcomb, 2017; Webster, 2020).

Emotions, therefore, as Ahmed (2014) argues, do not reside solely within individuals but circulate between people, objects, and communities; they arise through interactions, and are relational in nature, for they shape and are shaped by power, identity, and social relations. Such a relational and social account – alongside an individual-centric account – of emotion plays an important role in the criminal justice system. This is particularly the case in the lower-level criminal courts, which are adult-centric, and where the majority of criminal cases – involving people from mostly socio-economically marginalised communities – are tried and adjudicated. In common law jurisdictions like India, these courts perform adversarial trials that act as public fora and a communicative process, with procedures normatively tailored to not only hold defendants accountable for their criminal conduct, but also to challenge claims of wrongdoing made against them (Duff et al., 2007).

In rape cases, such procedures have enabled the defence to deploy all sorts of grilling techniques, such as character assassination, use of the survivor's sexual history, repeated questioning, lack of breaks during trial, and performing in a loud voice. These techniques, combined with sharing courtroom space with the accused, generate pain, fear, and nervousness in survivors, taking away their dignity during deposition, and act as a tool to exclude them in the courtroom. Such deliberate infliction of pain, as Cover (1986) argues, does not only resist survivors' language but also destroys it, thereby destroying their normative world. These emotional experiences of fear and nervousness are shaped by the context in which they occur, including cultural-legal norms and socio-economic hierarchies (Ahmed, 2014) between the survivor, the accused, and the court practitioners as state agents.

In child sexual abuse (CSA) cases, child survivors' limited vocabularies and cognitive and social skills compared to those of an adult, the language barrier when they speak a different language than the one used in court, and the inherent power imbalance between them and court authorities, i.e., police, lawyers, judges, and support persons, exacerbate their anxieties. Testifying by child survivors:

> may be accompanied by a range of triggers that resurrect the intensity of emotions surrounding the original trauma [...] Delays, adjournments, repeated continuances, and appeals can mean that children remain in a state of high anxiety for sustained periods of time.
> *(Cossins & Rowden, 2021: 145)*

Such anxieties and uncertainties become sources of children's secondary victimisation and trauma when interacting with legal actors or during deposition in courts, particularly in an adversarial trial system (Cossins & Rowden, 2021; Hoyano, 2015; Magnusson et al., 2017). In the Indian context, child survivors' vulnerability and experience with the criminal justice system worsen when they belong to subaltern castes and classes (Kumar, 2019, 2021, 2022). A lack of stakeholder training on how to interact with such vulnerable children can affect how stakeholders emotionally react to them and their responses and how they expect children to react emotionally (Kumar, 2022).

While academic literature and the Protection of Children from Sexual Offences (POCSO) law have often focused on CSA survivors' emotions, this chapter shifts the focus to court practitioners and aims to examine their perceptions and experiences of their own and other court users' emotional labour, and how they constitute, mobilise, and embody emotions vis-à-vis the power relationships they have as state agents with CSA survivors. The chapter shares findings from a larger project (Kumar, 2023), which explores and examines stakeholder perceptions of whether reforms under the POCSO Act 2012, a special law dealing exclusively with CSA cases – improved access to justice for CSA survivors. It is based on qualitative empirical methods – in-depth face-to-face individual semi-structured interviews with 49 adult stakeholders (judicial officers, lawyers, police officers, and support persons dealing with the POCSO cases), and observation of POCSO special courts and trials, conducted during six months' fieldwork (2019–2020) in Delhi and Bihar.[1]

The main argument of the chapter is that the procedural changes brought by the POCSO law can be seen to ground an "affective turn" in the Indian criminal process dealing with the CSA cases, and that the stakeholders highlight the relational and cultural features of emotions that are at play, while they exert state power on the ground facing a heavy demand to manage their emotions in a stressful work environment without any specific training. I discuss the nature of trial courts, the procedural reforms brought by the POCSO law, and the workload of POCSO special courts in the second section. In the third section, I report findings on how the court practitioners perform role enactment, engage emotional labour, and interact with court users, and the implications these procedural changes, gender, and the socio-legal culture of the locations under study have on these aspects. This section also offers insights on the contradictions, dilemmas, and challenges of morality, reason, and affect that the stakeholders embody, and how do they navigate these while carrying the burden of enacting state power at the ground level.

11.2 POCSO Reforms, Special Courts, and Their Workload

In India, trial courts are a set of lower courts that function as a socio-legal public arena at the district level. The spatial and physical disposition of people within these courts is also relevant for understanding the ways in which power relations both influence and structure face-to-face interactions throughout the trial, as during the examination, both the prosecutor and the defence attorneys may end up physically quite close to the witness (Berti, 2011). These courts, which have traditionally been adult-centric, applying the adult normative framework to CSA survivors and lacking in sensitivity towards them (Baxi, 2014), have been designated as POCSO special courts. Attempts have been made by the state in the last few decades to make these courts "child-friendly"[2] to improve survivors' access to justice (Kumar, 2023). Primarily, this has been done by bringing procedural changes in the criminal process of the CSA cases by the POCSO law.

The POCSO law prescribes special court personnel like judges, prosecutors, and support persons, and stakeholder training on several procedural changes in how they should interact with CSA survivors during the pre-trial and trial stages (Kumar, 2022). However, the law does not mention the ways in which these stakeholders should emotionally react or respond during such complex engagements. The objective behind having such special courts and personnel is also to ensure a speedy trial[3] and deliver quicker justice to CSA survivors, as lengthy delays and long waiting periods in trial and disposal of such cases might lead them to experience "anticipatory stress", meaning they will suffer varying degrees of anxiety (Cossins & Rowden, 2021). The POCSO law demands the trial court judge to use a screen or such arrangements where a CSA survivor does not see the accused, to have a *woman* judge hear CSA cases, to use translators when needed, to not ask questions on sexual history and character of CSA survivors, and the questions by lawyers to be given in writing to the judge, who would then put them to the child survivor. Furthermore, a CSA survivor's statement during the pre-trial stage is to be recorded by the police and a judicial officer in the presence of a friend, relative, or social worker whom the child trusts, and for its proper implementation, videotape or CCTV is to be utilised. Similarly, during trial, courts must preferably have a "neutral" adult and supportive *woman* as a support person to inspire the child's confidence.

These requirements are an invocation of criminal law to further therapeutic objectives of the criminal process by legally making both pre-trial and trial stages of CSA cases child-friendly and present several challenges before the court practitioners, as courtroom tours for CSA survivors have not been incorporated in the law. This is also a shift away from the traditional approach of applying a dogmatic method of interaction and cross-examination informed by age-neutrality and suggests a move towards a radical approach of healing[4] and child-friendliness in courtroom space and criminal process while dealing with child survivors (Kumar, 2023). This notion of healing appears to be an insertion of ideals and emotional objectives that come from a medicalised therapeutic context, and its premise raises questions about its viability in courts. As Perlin asks, "how can a system that prides itself on adversariness heal?" (2000: 407). This is where comes a synthesis of the two opposing approaches, bringing to the fore a kind of "therapeutic jurisprudence" (TJ) and opening up the opportunity to explore the role of the law as a potentially therapeutic agent (Wexler, 1993; Winick, 2002). This new model, Perlin argues,

> recognizes that substantive rules, legal procedures and lawyers' roles may have either therapeutic or anti-therapeutic consequences and questions whether such rules, procedures and roles can or should be reshaped so as to enhance their therapeutic potential, while preserving due process principles.
>
> *(2000: 408)*

If we focus on the workload of the POCSO special courts, the number of cases recorded by the police across India has approximately doubled in just five years – from 32,608 in 2017 to 63,414 in 2022. To deal with these cases, as on May 2023, a total of 412 exclusive POCSO special courts were functional across India, i.e., around 154 POCSO cases per special court in 2022.[5] Its impact is reflected in the National Crime Records Bureau (NCRB) data, which show that the rate of court disposal of POCSO cases, i.e., percentage of total cases in which trial has been completed, is around only 10%, resulting in an exponential growth in the number of POCSO cases pending trial at the end of each year – from 84,143 in 2017 to 268,038 in 2022. Meanwhile, the conviction rate in POCSO cases whose trial was completed was only 14% during the first decade, i.e., from 2012 until 2022.[6] Such data reveal that the large caseload, and thereby constant work pressure to dispose CSA cases quickly on POCSO court personnel, is very high, all while following the special procedures prescribed by the POCSO law. Moreover, despite these legislative efforts to alleviate the burden on, and traumatic experience of, the CSA survivors in the criminal justice system, the existing research shows that many challenges remain in implementing the POCSO law (Ali et al., 2017; Bhawnani, 2022; Centre for Child and the Law, 2016, 2018; Gupta, 2023; Kothari & Ravi, 2015; Patkar & Kandula, 2016).

11.3 Practitioners' Emotional Labour: Stakeholder Perceptions and Challenges on Managing Emotions

Law and criminal justice, as several social theorists have noted, including Durkheim, Elias, and Weber, are deeply embedded in the emotional culture of societies, and intricately linked to the structural and institutional patterns of society (Karstedt, 2002; Weber, 1978). Law recognises certain relational aspects of emotions between victims and accused as important factors, such as romance, trust, and hate, and offers leeway in the form of defences like "loss of control," "self-defence," "heat of passion," "diminished responsibility," and insanity. On the other hand, the conventional story of law, argues Bandes (1999), portrays a narrowly defined list and proper roles for emotions in the legal realm, so that emotions do not interfere into the true preserve of law – reason, and that they are assigned to the criminal courts, confined mostly to those without legal training – witnesses, the accused, the public. Yet, others argued that rather than "precluding rational action," as is the common belief, "emotions may facilitate a 'rational response' – for example, to the experience of injustice" (Karstedt, 2002: 301).

Scholars have shown that emotional labour is present in everyday work by the trial court practitioners – judges, lawyers, and the support staff members, who have the onus of enacting state power at the ground level (Phillips et al.,

2021; Roach Anleu & Mack, 2005, 2017). Such management and regulation of emotions acquire even more importance when these court practitioners are dealing with CSA cases, which not only have honour, social shame, and stigma attached to them but also involve the vulnerable children. While these factors make it challenging for a CSA survivor to speak about their experience of sexual violence, these same factors pose challenges for court practitioners to get the CSA survivor to recall and share that experience in a new environment with a new person. Despite there being a relation between these two sets of challenges, while the POCSO law appears to recognise the emotionality of child survivors, it does not speak about the issue of the emotional work and coping mechanisms of court practitioners engaged in CSA cases.

These practitioners not only need to build a trust relationship with the child for them to open up and speak but must listen to the horrifying stories of sexual abuse directly from children who suffered the abuse and belong to mostly marginalised communities, often quickly, as they also need to think of the case backlog. They are exposed to highly disturbing stories and evidence of a range of child sexual offences, including child rape, and must face the difficult task of not only acknowledging and managing their feelings of frustration, outrage, anger, and pity, but also those of others, all the while maintaining the appearance of impartiality (Maroney, 2011). Given the Indian socio-cultural context, they also need to engage with the child's parents and relatives. Considering these challenges and the legal vacuum on how to emotionally react in such difficult situations, these practitioners, performing the state's role on the ground, express themselves as they deem fit, without knowing whether and how they can indulge in affective engagement with children and their families.

This section examines the perceptions and experiences of these court practitioners of engaging their own and other court users' emotional labour, and how they constitute, mobilise, and embody emotions vis-à-vis the power asymmetries they have with CSA survivors. It explores the ways in which these practitioners negotiate the emotional norms for appropriate judicial and courtroom conduct.

11.3.1 Managing Emotion to Ensure Institutional Integrity and Legitimacy

One judicial magistrate (BJM1), explaining how she performed emotional labour to maintain judicial neutrality while recording a CSA survivor's statement in the pre-trial stage, said, "Whatever she [child] narrates, you must write it down in the first person only. 'I went to home like this,' or 'the accused approached me in this manner and did this to me'." She further argued that "it is her version, and you have to just write it down," and "it is just a way of, you know, that neither she can go back on that statement and then we can later on use it." However, she mentioned that it is difficult not to empathise when you record in writing a child's statement, "Yeah, the victims in POCSO are basically small girls, so it is very emotional kind of a thing to hear their stories and, you know, how such things can happen. It is sad." She, however, did not let it reflect on herself while recording the statement to achieve institutional impartiality.

When I asked a prosecutor whether dealing with such cases affects his emotions, he said, "Yes, yes, it does. [But] I would say I look at legality. I keep aside the emotive part (DPP1)." On enquiring if and how the emotion plays out in the courtroom, another prosecutor responded, "Yes, yes. It happens. I become more, you know, disturbed, with the whole thing (DPP3)." He then went on to share the account of his engagement with the father of a 16-year-old girl who went away with her lover "consensually" and got married but was dragged into a POCSO case as her consent was legally invalid:

> Once I was involved in recording the statement of a father. So, speaking off the record, I was trying to ask him: What happened? [Father said:] "She went with him without telling me." Then I said: okay, she went with him. Now has she got married or is she living [with her partner]? Is he not a proper person? Can you marry him? [Father said:] "No, how can you do it? In our *community*, it is not possible."
>
> *(DPP3)*

Although this was not part of the trial and would never get into the court record, it reflects the prosecutor's attempt to secure institutional integrity, as he could see the weaponisation of criminal law by the father against his daughter's lover. His action might seem against the law as he was asking a prosecution witness to take back the prosecution's case, being a prosecutor himself. He further added how he emotionally interacted to convince the father not to pursue this case and rather to understand the matter in a pragmatic manner:

> You are living in Delhi. Since when you are living in Delhi? [Father said:] "It has been ten-fifteen years." He came from Bihar [a poorer state]. I said: you had left Bihar now; you are living in Delhi. The boy is earning and eating well. You marry her to him.

Although the prosecutor acknowledged his patriarchal questioning, when he asked the father, "why did he not keep his daughter in control?", he said he tried to link progressivism on the gender front with progressivism in intimate sexual relationships:

> You are going for work. Your mother and your wife are also going for work. Girl…you know [is] vulnerable. She became friendly [with the accused].

The fellow [accused] is also not a robber...not a thief...not a cheater. He simply got infatuated with your daughter, and she also got infatuated, and they [consensually] went away before their marriageable age.

Highlighting that we have a stringent POCSO law, the prosecutor asked the father not to be adamant: "you still have the same [feudal-casteist] mindset. You should change. You are not living there in Bihar among the *Zamindars*." He then went on to express his dissatisfaction by saying that the POCSO Act is a sensitive law, but for a society where most people are educated, and not where there is so much illiteracy, unemployment, and where people do not even have access to the minimum requirements of life. With anger, he said that wrongs are normalised, as "We have a society where wrong is taking place ten times a day in a, you know, these slums, to a child or to a lady by a *Zamindar* or landlord."

While the POCSO law does not allow these informal interactions/ reprimands, such behaviour is something inherent in the Indian legal system. All the three stakeholders – one Magistrate and two prosecutors – above attempted to manage their emotions to ensure the integrity and legitimacy of the criminal justice system, even when it meant going beyond the law.

11.3.2 Eliciting Appropriate Emotion and Care in Oneself and Others and Humanisation of State Power

Despite the law's demand to ensure that the child does not see the accused during testimony, this was not so in all the POCSO courts I observed, particularly in Bihar. When I asked a lawyer (BNGO) from a charity organisation supporting public prosecutors (PPs) in CSA cases, whether he found a CSA survivor being scared or nervous or acting violently after seeing the accused either in the courtroom or during identification, he replied affirmatively, but said he is unable to intervene in such situations. He, however, noted that in one such encounter, the CSA survivor became very violent and emotional and after seeing the accused deposed very well in the court. On the same question, a court clerk in a Delhi POCSO court (DCS1) told me that there were several instances where he found children feeling uncomfortable by seeing the accused in courtroom: "It becomes a big problem for the victim when they see the accused during identification, as then they become emotionally and physically vulnerable, and get tensed and have anxieties too." So, in such situations, he intervened and gave the child drinking water and made them feel calm. Not only did he have to not get emotionally burdened by the situation, but he also had to provide emotional support to the child to make her feel comfortable during the testimony.

As support persons have become a new state institution in the wake of the POCSO Act and play an important part in its implementation,

I interviewed one in Delhi (DCS3) and asked her about the role she plays in the criminal process. She said that support persons bring the CSA survivor from her home for the purpose of Prosecution Evidence, i.e., to record their testimony during trial. Despite being aware of the sexual abuse the child might have gone through, she keeps herself relaxed and gives them snacks, toffee, and biscuits, to create a particular kind of environment, one that is child-friendly, which she calls is not court-like, "where someone is being punished, or someone is being sentenced to death." When I asked her why she is bringing the death sentence specifically, she narrated a story of a girl child victim who asked her: 'if I will testify then will he [the accused] be sentenced to death?' So, "these things, such child psychology," she argued, "weakens the Prosecution case somewhere. Because after all, emotionally, they are just children." Highlighting the role of the Rape Crisis Cell (RCC) of the Delhi Commission of Women (DCW), which she was a member of, and her own role, she said,

> Whatever we have talked about until now, you...remove the RCC from the picture, you won't be able to provide access to justice to children in such situations. To perform these processes in such an emotional manner, to answer such questions from children and to convince her to speak, is to help child victims access justice.
>
> *(DCS3)*

She then linked her own gender identity and that of the CSA survivors (mostly girls) to emotional labour and justice, highlighting a gendered approach to practitioners' recruitment as well as to being empathetic and sharing pain:

> In rape cases, one cannot compensate. But due to time and our efforts, pain can be lesser. And why [do you think] *ladies* have been made to sit [as POCSO judges], why the RCC [member] is a *lady*, there is a reason behind that. A male may not be able to feel that [pain]. We...*ladies* go through that pain. So, we can understand...how much pain she must have been in. When hymen of a [girl] child is broken, you just think how much pain she will have. A male cannot do the qualitative and quantitative analysis of that. He can think emotionally. But he cannot feel *that* thing.
>
> *(DCS3)*

At this juncture, she discussed the complex relation of emotion with justice,

> Now, I understand that justice is not based on emotion. But it is based on evidence, and many other things. And emotion does not even influence. But it is also wrong to say that emotion does not influence. Zero emotion can never deliver justice.

In her opinion, judging requires a judge to understand how much pain the other person (CSA survivor) has suffered, and how much truth or fabrication is involved in the child's statement about their suffering. Even to become a successful prosecutor, she said, one must understand what the small child wants to say, and without feeling the child's pain, one would not understand that pain. She further justified the move by the state to have females as judges in POCSO cases, and that emotion does not bring bias in justice delivery, "they [female judges] know how the small child suffered when such a brutal incident happened with her. There is no biasness here. It is a tool to do the analysis of the situation at hand."

Another important aspect that respondents highlighted where emotion management and labour was required, and where stakeholders faced one of their biggest challenges, was in incest cases, particularly involving poor families and children. One DCW member working as a support person (DCS5) narrated her experience of engaging with a poor 14-year-old CSA survivor who was raped by her stepfather. The child told her that she did not want to file the case, as she wanted to forgive her stepfather and to have him released from jail. This support person then had to convince her otherwise:

> You tell me, what he has done, is it forgivable? He has brought the relation of father-daughter to disrepute. How will a daughter believe her father? You had a baby afterwards. What was the fault of the baby? That baby is in orphanage now, father is in jail, and you are incapable to keep her.

The support person further commented, "When you [practitioners] come to the court, many times we have to become emotional, sometimes [it is] tricky to explain to the party." In this incest case, she had to invoke God to convince the child to testify truthfully and to prevent her from becoming hostile, "when you [CSA survivor] come to the Court, leave some things to the God. You just have to speak the truth." Afterwards, the girl child responded affirmatively when the lady asked if she was raped. But things were not so simple. The support person had to be cautious, as such victim interaction, she said, might push the child to say to the court that it was she who asked the child to say that the incident took place. Furthermore, the lady also did not speak about whether the conviction was guaranteed in this case, and that the accused would get life imprisonment, as she feared the victim might not have testified. She just asked the child to speak the truth, which she ultimately did.

While this conversation showcased the importance of the newly created state institution of support persons and how they exert state power in a humanised manner in securing child testimony that would strengthen the prosecution's case, it also reveals a gap that exists in the criminal process regarding the role of special PPs appointed to deal exclusively with POCSO cases. This gap was clear when she (DCS5) acknowledged,

> PP [Public Prosecutor] madam said [to me]: "because of your presence, we have a lot of benefits, as this bonding is not there between us (PP and CSA survivor), and it is me (PP) who feel most hurtful when the victim becomes hostile"[7]

"So, we have strengthened the bonding between the state agencies and child victims," she (DCS5) added.

She pointed out that it is the failure of the state when CSA survivors become hostile, which could be due to several socio-economic-familial reasons. Berti (2013) through her observation of a child rape case in India analyses the contrasting relationship between the written and the oral in the production of judicial proof related to the problem posed by hostile witnesses and how judicial procedures are influenced by extra-judicial power dynamics resulting from local relationships of dominance. This raises a crucial issue of how Indian trial courts and the justice system function, when rooted in colonialism and centred on a regime of proof and truth derived from elsewhere, in a society still largely governed by hierarchical relationships and local dominance based on religion, gender, caste status and economic dependence, and on feudal, family, or territorial allegiances (Berti, 2013).

Here, the NGO lawyer, court clerk, and support persons not only manage their emotions but elicit appropriate emotions and care for the CSA survivors, their family members, and other court practitioners, while dealing with the abovementioned social forces. They fill an important void in the criminal process by humanising state power for the Prosecutor, who, as she reported, felt bad for CSA survivors becoming hostile, but was unable to interact with them to build a trust relationship and convince them to depose.

11.3.3 Building Inter-institutional Support and Trust for Affective and Effective State Power

The previous sub-section discussed how respondents – a court clerk and support persons – elicit appropriate emotion and care in themselves and others and attempt to humanise state power on the ground on behalf of the prosecutors in POCSO cases. This section moves further and demonstrates why building inter-institutional support and trust is essential in enacting affective and effective state power in processing POCSO cases. My findings suggest that at the heart of such support also lies private emotional labour – a short-term interaction with fellow professionals such as lawyers and court clerks, considered as part of the "game" (Harris, 2002).

One female Delhi police officer (DCS7) shared her experiences of working on the ground, as an investigating officer (IO) in POCSO cases, and raised the issue of a lack of trust from the higher police officials. While reflecting on the lack of peer trust, she shared how it frustrates her to see the senior official's perception that she wants to rush or emotionally "detach" from the issues at stake in the case. She told me how, rather than being provided support, she is perceived as not doing her work properly, yet she never raised this issue before the police department, demonstrating that she suppresses her feelings and does not share them with her senior officials.

The issue of inter-institutional support was also raised by one Delhi judge (DPJ1), although in relation to child sex-trafficking. He talked about the problems in cases of recovery raids in Delhi's G.B. Road – a red-light area – to recover girl victims of sex-trafficking from Nepal and Indian states like Assam, Bihar, and West Bengal. So, he claimed, it becomes difficult to secure their presence, especially in cases where the victim is from Nepal, because of the lack of a treaty with Nepal. He explained that, as it is done through the MEA (Indian Ministry of External Affairs) and the Nepal Embassy, there are acquittals in these cases, and CSA survivors also return to their homes when the investigation takes longer.

Another judge (DPJ3) discussed how building a good relationship with defence lawyers was important to have them follow the new procedures. Public emotional labour has been stated as akin to "front stage" emotional labour, i.e., where the "actor" is playing to a critical audience and is the centre of attention to all present during public court work (Harris, 2002). The judge kept a check on defence lawyers, employing public emotional labour, when he perceived the CSA survivor speaking truth while deposing,

> then it is very important to guard him [the child] in the Cross [examination]. Or else there will be a big trouble. If there has been such grave crime against a young child, and only to wrap up the matters quickly if we wind up the matter, then it is very problematic. They [defence lawyers] run their own...whatever tricks and tips they have.

He reported that they also try to delay the proceedings by making everyone wait, "they would just pick up a fight on some issue in court, be it either with the prosecution, or even with him; anything stupid... [they will say] no, this cannot be asked in this way." These statements suggest the frustrations staff face in navigating the complexities of inter-institutional encounters.

This sub-section demonstrated how the police officer and the judges built or failed to build inter-institutional support and trust by employing different forms of emotional labour for affective and effective state power that could impact justice delivery in CSA cases.

11.3.4 Emotion Management and Judges' Relational Work

Moving away from institutional support and diving into technological support, one judge in Delhi (DPJ1) shared his experience of recording a child's testimony via videoconferencing. He highlighted how this aspect of reform has not only helped CSA survivors during deposition but has also eased their relational work as judges in managing the survivors' emotions during trial:

> The child witnesses can give their testimony without any fear in the Vulnerable Witness Deposition Room[8]. The victims do not become emotional. So, establishment of exclusive POCSO courts here has been a boon.

Another judge (DPJ3) also discussed testimony, but in the context of how in some cases despite a lack of documentary or medical evidence, and one where he thought that the accused was innocent, he convicted the accused solely on the victim's testimony as the law mandates it. He acknowledged that in such situations, his thought process as well as his emotions runs wild. When I enquired what he feels and how he deals with such cases, he responded, "I feel nothing. I just give my decision based on evidence. That is what I feel." He further consolidated his belief:

> Never ever something like that came that I did something wrong. If there is a wrong thing to do, then I will do acquittal. But if…there is no rebuttal, the statement is not being falsified by equally probable document or evidence, then I must work by taking only that into consideration. I believe in sticking to the law…And I also believe that justice for a Judge is only when he follows the law.

He argued that deviating from the law will make judges commit more grave errors and that "I am a different kind of Judge, who has always followed the law. I…am heartless. No sentiments." Though, he later acknowledged that courts involving matters of children like the POCSO court required a change in approach,

> it is…necessary for us to understand the child psychology. After coming to these Courts, I saw that things cannot work in that [traditional] manner. You will have to necessarily bring the emotional factor, and if we do not bring in that factor, then somewhere injustice can take place.

A female Delhi judge (DPJ4) explained to me how child rape is very different and unique offence in terms of its implications on the survivors,

> In the case of murder, a victim is dead, in case of dacoity, a victim is looted of his material property, but in rape, the loss to the victim is the

loss to a person which is not material in nature, but rather psychological, emotional, and physical loss.

She recalled an adolescent child rape survivor telling her, "Ma'am, that offence was for five minutes, but I see it everywhere. When I stand in front of a mirror, I see it in mirror." She said she gives a patient listening as she understands and empathises with the child because it is very difficult for CSA survivors during court testimony to express what they went through.

This sub-section focused on the tension between judges' understanding of their role as rational, dispassionate actors, and the new emphasis on the need to care for CSA survivors' emotions and how their emotional displays emotionalise the court actors.

11.4 Conclusion: Emotion Work, Performativity, and Social Change

It was during the eighteenth and early nineteenth centuries, in England and the United States, respectively, that both judge and jury came to conform closely to the ideals of neutrality and passivity (Landsman, 1983). This neutral and passive judging approach was transplanted in the Indian justice system during British colonialism. In a shift from this approach, in the last couple of decades, scholars have written extensively not only on judicial emotion management and labour, including judicial empathy, but also on how lawyers express themselves emotionally when interacting with victims in court settings. Such development, though, has been restricted mostly to the West, with rare presence in the South Asian context (Ahmed, 2013).

The findings in this chapter suggest that the procedural changes brought by the POCSO law can be seen to ground an "affective turn" in the Indian criminal process dealing with the CSA cases. It is not, however, a turn to affect or emotions *per se*, but a heavy demand on court actors to do emotion work – a demand which they often feel can conflict with what they understand their job is about, all while faced with an unrealistic caseload and work pressure.

Practitioners in POCSO special courts have been employing emotional labour to exert state power and showcase how healing in the criminal process is understood and translates on the ground. However, they are working by themselves on how they ought to emotionally react while interacting with CSA survivors and other court users dealing with POCSO cases. It is also evident that some of them have had their approach to judging and the role of emotional labour in it changed in the wake of the POCSO reforms. This is because while the POCSO law emphasises CSA survivors' emotionality and its impact on the criminal process through new procedures, personnel, and institutions, it is silent on how these stakeholders, embodying the state as its agents, should employ emotion. This also tells us that there is an interesting sense in which the state presents itself as the guardian of emotion.

There also appear to be negative effects of emotional labour on the respondents, as they reported their vulnerabilities and challenges. Yet, how their emotional labour benefited the CSA survivors or other court users and supported the state in creating an affective, humanised, and child-friendly criminal process was the positive side. There is also an implication emanating from gender-based division, albeit based on most CSA survivors being girls, in the recruitment of court practitioners handling POCSO cases, as the women might be disproportionally affected by emotional labour. The findings also offer relational and cultural accounts of emotion, particularly where female court actors linked their gender identity to empathise with CSA survivors' pain and suffering. Bandes (2006b: 340) argues, "the emotional costs of lawyering are rarely considered worthy of mainstream legal discussion," and I would add that this applies to all court actors in POCSO cases. Moreover, the nature of the interaction between these stakeholders working as state agents for CSA survivors is critical to the successful and meaningful implementation of the law.

Ultimately, there is an absence of coherence in approach by court actors when dealing with CSA cases, which is further worsened by a lack of formalised training – structured and need-based – and one that is informed by the socio-cultural contexts in which trial courts function. Training on the role and impact of caste, class, gender, disability, race, religion, and sexuality on emotional labour ought to be pursued to negate its subjective application by court actors that might lead to injustice to CSA survivors and accused. Such training is also important to make them aware of performing their role without adversely affecting themselves, to bring about any social change by delivering justice in POCSO cases. This would mean improving their job satisfaction and leading to better and positive survivor and accused experiences with the criminal process. Knowing that justice is a deeply emotive notion, the Indian legal and judicial profession needs to overcome its hostility to acknowledge and address the emotional aspects of lawyering and judging for the affective turn in criminal process to have any positive social impact.

Notes

1 Interviews were numbered and given an alphabetic code to specify the jurisdiction and category of the interviewee. For example, BJM 1, B = Bihar, JM = Judicial Magistrate, 1 = Interviewee number 01. Other codes include the following: D = Delhi, PP = Public Prosecutor, CS = Court Staff, PJ = POCSO Special Judge, and NGO = NGO representative. Some professional details of the respondents have also been concealed to further the objective of anonymity.

2 S. 33(4), POCSO Act says: "The Special Court shall create *a child-friendly atmosphere* by allowing a family member, a guardian, a friend or a relative, in whom the child has trust or confidence, to be present in the court." This is the only place where the term "child-friendly" appears in the entire special legislation. The POCSO (Protection of Children from Sexual Offences) Rules 2012 do not even mention this term.
3 S. 28, POCSO Act 2012.
4 While the POCSO Act does not use the word "healing," the 240th Report on the POCSO Bill, 2011, by the Department-Related Parliamentary Standing Committee on Human Resource Development, 2011, mentions that the National Commission for Protection of Child Rights (NCPCR) – the leading government of India institution working on child rights protection – strongly emphasized that "the judicial process of adjudication in the case of child victim (of sexual offences) should be the *process of healing* and not that of re-victimization." See para 2.7 of the Report.
5 09 August 2023, Press Information Bureau, Delhi, accessed on 5 April 2024, available at: https://pib.gov.in/PressReleaseIframePage.aspx?PRID=1947050
6 A Decade of POCSO Law, Vidhi Centre for Legal Policy, Delhi. See 14% conviction in POCSO; in a fourth of cases, accused known to victims, says study |India News – The Indian Express.
7 In the UK's context, this is different. The CPS guidelines state that as

> it is important that the need for support for child victims is identified early and kept under close review during the progress of the case, Prosecutors should proactively raise this matter in "case discussions" with the police and other relevant agencies so that victims are given the best possible support.

The guidelines further say that

> the prosecutor has an important part to play in ensuring that the requisite support is provided and should be asking questions about this from the outset of their involvement in the case. Prosecutors should be aware of the type of support available and, if necessary, should be able to signpost this support to the child or young person (or their parent/carer) via the police officer in the case or the Witness Care Unit, as appropriate.

See Child Sexual Abuse: Guidelines on Prosecuting Cases of Child Sexual Abuse issued in relation to section 15A of the Sexual Offences Act 2003, 11 January 2023, available at: www.cps.gov.uk/legal-guidance/child-sexual-abuse-guidelines-prosecuting-cases-child-sexual-abuse (accessed on 25 March 2024).
8 To know about the Vulnerable Witness Deposition Room, see Kumar (2025).

Bibliography

Ahmed, F. E. (2013). The Compassionate Courtroom: Feminist Governance, Discourse, and Islam in a Bangladeshi *Shalish*. *Feminist Formations*, 25(1), 157–183. https://doi.org/10.1353/ff.2013.0005

Ahmed, S. (2014). *The Cultural Politics of Emotion* (Second). Edinburgh University Press.

Ali, B., Adenwalla, M., & Punekar, S. (2017). *Implementation of the POCSO Act: Goals, Gaps and Challenges- Study of Cases of Special Courts in Delhi & Mumbai (2012–2015)*. http://haqcrc.org/wp-content/uploads/2018/02/implementation-of-the-pocso-act-delhi-mumbai-study-final.pdf

Bandes, S. A. (1999). Introduction. In *The Passions of Law*. New York University Press.
Bandes, S. A. (2006a). Loyalty to One's Convictions: The Prosecutor and Tunnel Vision. *Howard Law Journal, 49*, 475.
Bandes, S. A. (2006b). Repression and Denial in Criminal Lawyering. *Buffalo Criminal Law Review, 9*(2), 339–389. https://doi.org/10.2139/ssrn.223079
Bandes, S. A., & Blumenthal, J. A. (2012). Emotion and the Law. *Annual Review of Law and Social Science, 8*(1), 161–181. https://doi.org/10.1146/annurev-lawsocsci-102811-173825
Baxi, P. (2014). The Child Witness on Trial. In *Public Secrets of Law: Rape Trials in India* (pp. 117–173). https://doi.org/10.1093/acprof:oso/9780198089568.003.0003
Berti, D. (2011). Courts of Law and Legal Practice. In I. Clark-Decès (Ed.), *A Companion to the Anthropology of India* (pp. 353–370). Blackwell Publishing Ltd.
Berti, D. (2013). Local Powers and Judicial Constraints in a Case of Rape in India. *Diogenes, 60*(3–4), 97–115. https://doi.org/10.1177/0392192115589274
Bhawnani, G. (2022). The Mother's "character" on Trial in Child Sexual Abuse Cases. *Indian Law Review, 6*(2), 189–208.
Blumenthal, J. A. (2005). Law and the Emotions: The Problems of Affective Forecasting. *Indiana Law Journal, 80*(2), 155–238. https://doi.org/10.2139/ssrn.497842
Centre for Child and the Law. (2016). *Report of Study on the Working of Special Courts under the POCSO Act, 2012 in Delhi* (Issue January). www.nls.ac.in/ccl/jjdocuments/specialcourtPOSCOAct2012.pdf
Centre for Child and the Law. (2018). *Implementation of the POCSO Act, 2012 by Special Courts: Challenges and Issues*.
Cossins, A., & Rowden, E. (2021). The Child Sexual Assault Trial: Reconceptualising the Design of Court Spaces According to Trauma-Informed Principles. In *Courthouse Architecture, Design and Social Justice* (pp. 140–166). https://doi.org/10.4324/9780429059858-9
Cover, R. M. (1986). Violence and the Word. *Yale Law Journal, 95*, 1601–1629.
Cross, T. P., & Whitcomb, D. (2017). The Practice of Prosecuting Child Maltreatment: Results of an Online Survey of Prosecutors. *Child Abuse and Neglect, 69*(January 2016), 20–28. https://doi.org/10.1016/j.chiabu.2017.04.007
Duff, A., Farmer, L., Marshall, S., & Tadros, V. (Eds.). (2007). *The Trial on Trial (Volume 3): Towards a Normative Theory of the Criminal Trial*. Hart Publishing.
Gupta, A. (2023). Child Sexual Abuse by Fathers in India: Exploring the Layers of 'Honour' in Trials. *Australian Feminist Law Journal, 49*(2), 267–292. https://doi.org/10.1080/13200968.2023.2281463
Harris, L. C. (2002). The Emotional Labour of Barristers: An Exploration of Emotional Labour by Status Professionals. *Journal of Management Studies, 39*(June). https://doi.org/10.1111/1467-6486.t01-1-00303
Hoyano, L. C. (2015, February). Reforming the Adversarial Trial for Vulnerable Witnesses and defendants. *Criminal Law Review* 2, 107–129.
Karstedt, S. (2002). Emotions and Criminal Justice. *Theoretical Criminology, 6*(3), 299.
Kothari, J., & Ravi, A. (2015). *The Myth of Speedy and Substantive Justice: A Study of the Special Fast Track Courts for Sexual Assault and Child Sexual Abuse Cases in Karnataka*. Bangalore: Centre for Law & Policy Research.
Kumar, S. (2019). Shifting Epistemology of Juvenile Justice in India. *Contexto Internacional, 41*(1), 113–140. https://doi.org/10.1590/s0102-8529.2019410100006

Kumar, S. (2021). The Rebirth of Delinquent 'Adult – Children': Criminal Capacity, Socio-Economic Systems and the Malleability of Penality of Child Delinquency in India. In A. Cox & L. S. Abrams (Eds.), *The Palgrave International Handbook of Juvenile Imprisonment* (pp. 107–139). Palgrave Macmillan.

Kumar, S. (2022). Child Sexual Abuse Cases in India and Judicial Officers' Perceptions and Experiences of POCSO-Related Special Training. *Socio-Legal Review*, 18(2), 264–300.

Kumar, S. (2023). *Access to justice and sexual violence against children in India: an empirical study of the reforms under the POCSO (Protection of Children from Sexual Offences) Act 2012*. Birkbeck, University of London.

Kumar, S. (2025). Criminal Law, Court Architecture, and the Space of Justice: Stakeholder Perceptions of 'special' Courts Used in Child Sexual Abuse Trials in India. In M. Szczyrbak (Ed.), *More than (Just) Words: Legal and Non-Legal Narratives in the Courtroom and Beyond* (pp. 293–318). De Gruyter Mouton.

Landsman, S. (1983). A Brief Survey of the Development of the Adversary System. *Ohio State Law Journal*, 44(3), 713–739.

Magnusson, M., Ernberg, E., & Landström, S. (2017). Preschoolers' Disclosures of Child Sexual Abuse: Examining Corroborated Cases from Swedish Courts. *Child Abuse and Neglect*, 70(May), 199–209. https://doi.org/10.1016/j.chiabu.2017.05.018

Maroney, T. A. (2011). Emotional Regulation and Judicial Behavior. *California Law Review*, 99(6), 1485–1555.

Morrison, C. (1968). Social Organization at the District Courts: Colleague Relationships among Indian Lawyers. *Law & Society Review*, 3(2/3), 251–268.

Patkar, P., & Kandula, P. (2016). *Four Years since POCSO: Unfolding of the POCSO Act in the State of Maharashtra*.

Perlin, M. L. (2000). A Law of Healing. *University of Cincinnati Law Review*, 68(2), 407–432.

Phillips, J., Westaby, C., Fowler, A., & Waters, J. (2021). Emotional Labour in Criminal Justice and Criminology. In *Emotional Labour in Criminal Justice and Criminology*. Routledge. https://doi.org/10.4324/9780429055669

Roach Anleu, S., & Mack, K. (2005). Magistrates' Everyday Work and Emotional Labour. *Journal of Law and Society*, 32(4), 590–624. https://doi.org/10.3868/s050-004-015-0003-8

Roach Anleu, S., & Mack, K. (2017). *Performing Judicial Authority in the Lower Courts*. Palgrave Macmillan.

Weber, M. (1978). *Economy and Society: An Outline of Interpretive Sociology* (G. Roth & C. Wittich (Eds.)). University of California Press.

Webster, E. (2020). The Prosecutor as a Final Safeguard against False Convictions: How Prosecutors Assist with Exoneration. *Journal of Criminal Law and Criminology*, 110(2), 245–305.

Wexler, D. B. (1993). Therapeutic Jurisprudence and the Criminal Courts. *William and Mary Law Review*, 35(1), 279–299.

Winick, B. J. (2003). Therapeutic Jurisprudence and Problem Solving Courts. *Fordham Urban Law Journal*, 30(3), 1055–1090.

PART 4
Unsettling institutionalised emotions

PART 4
Unsettling institutionalised emotions

12
DISGUST AT THE BORDER

Border Work as Dirty Work[1]

Ana Aliverti

Introduction

Scholars of the state have traditionally theorised state bureaucracies as disembodied. Distinct from society, the state is on this familiar view hierarchical, rational, anonymous and incapable of ethical reasoning, hence prone to moral indifference (Bauman 1991, Herzfeld 1992). The supposedly disembodied nature of state bureaucracies is particularly marked and enduring in characterisations of legal bureaucracies which evoke the Weberian model of rational and impartial judgement, even so and particularly in highly emotional cases such as those involving hideous crimes (Vaisman and Barrera 2020). Yet, in recent decades, social scientists have unsettled this imagery to illuminate our understanding of statehood as embodied and profoundly underpinned by moral sentiments (Navaro-Yashin 2002, Fassin 2015, Zacka 2017, Cooper 2019). They call for greater attention to how political authority is constructed, maintained and unsettled through emotional and sensorial registers (Jupp *et al.* 2017, Laszczkowski and Reeves 2018). In studying the state from the bottom up – through the everyday lives of its agents – this scholarship has been critical for scrutinising the moral and emotional lives of 'the state' and for 'humanising' it.

In this chapter, I build on this work to reflect on the moral and emotional lives of British immigration officers. I pay particular attention to the place of disgust in their everyday work.

Disgust is uniquely connected to the body: it is intrinsically linked to 'tactile' senses (touch, smell, taste), and its primary objects (semen, blood, sweat, faeces, urine) signal a visceral revulsion to our embodied, animal self. It attempts to insulate us from these objects through magical thought of contagion and creates disgust-based social subordination by attributing polluting features to certain human beings considered emblematic of the animal (Douglas 2002 [1966]). Disgust is said to pervade certain occupations considered 'dirty' or 'tainted': morally, physically and socially. Border policing fits squarely within this category.

Morally, immigration officers embody one of the most delegitimised government departments in Britain – the Home Office – and their work is deeply felt by staff as morally contentious giving rise to strong reactions and controversy among the different publics. Physically, their work takes place in the 'backstage' of society where people at the margins work and leave. Due to the material precarity of these spaces, staff are exposed to various 'pollutants' – including diseases. Finally, their clientele features one of the most publicly despised populations in countries around the world, and more particularly in the Global North. As a former colonial power, the UK has a long history of demonising some immigrant groups as 'undesirable' and unwelcome (El-Enani 2020) (see also chapters by St Louis and McCurdy in this volume). Illustrating the constitutive function of racialised emotions in creating white spaces and 'ambient racism' (Bonilla-Silva 2019, Woody 2021), this emotional economy underpins the contemporary politics of migration contributing to restrict legal routes for migration and creating ever hostile conditions for people to leave and work. These conditions in turn shape 'animalized subjectivities'. Despite attempts to sanitise them through the corporate language of 'customers' or 'clients' to refer to this population, officers' perceptions and engagement with them constantly reproduce otherness and the racialised emotions that underpin them.

This chapter builds on the moral philosophy and psychology of emotions and the sociology of policing to illuminate our understanding of the significance of disgust in border policing. I draw on ethnographic material, including observations of enforcement operations and interviews, from various projects I conducted with British immigration officers since 2016 in English urban towns and at the Anglo-French border. Their everyday work involves identifying foreign national individuals without leave or with criminal records, and who are liable to removal or deportation from the UK. It also involves re-documenting people who arrive in the UK clandestinely, processing their asylum claim, making decisions on their immigration status and determining whether they should be detained or bailed. Much of the work of immigration officers is about making migrants legible to the British state. This labour of 'making legible' does not happen in a vacuum, but it is shaped by frames of recognition which in turn rely on affective and sensorial grids (Aliverti 2021b, 2023). These officers' daily work makes them familiar with sensorial norms, shot through by racial and gender stereotypes, about national groups (Parmar 2024). This is because officers' unique trained asset is their intuition, built on gut feelings about people and situations, as well as a heightened perception about risks. Their formal training involves various sessions on personal safety training (PST) which acquaint them with potential dangers they face from 'customers', and where they learn how to anticipate and avert them. Longstanding research with these officers made me privy to the embodied nature of their work which demands a delicate and careful management and training of the senses.

The chapter proceeds as follows. In the first section, I bring into conversation the philosophical and psychological scholarship on disgust with the sociological literature on dirty work to examine the everyday labour of British immigration officers. After situating immigration enforcement within this backdrop and conceptualising it as 'dirty work', the chapter seeks to excavate the functions of disgust in immigration enforcement and attend to the contradictions that its mobilisation evinces. In so doing, I trace the political potential of the focus on emotions in understanding state power and its effects. The chapter then queries: What is the vantage point of seeing the state through its embodied material self? How can the focus on disgust and its contradictory mobilisation offer an insight on the state and its effects?

The Anatomy of Disgust

In one of the most comprehensive and detailed examinations of disgust as a moral emotion, William Miller's *The Anatomy of Disgust* (1998) commences with a scene from Charles Darwin's *The Expression of the Emotions in Man and Animals*. In it, Darwin recounts the following encounter:

> In Tierra del Fuego a native touched with his finger some cold preserved meat which I was eating at our bivouac, and plainly showed disgust at its softness; whilst I felt utter disgust at my food being touched by a naked savage, though his hands did not appear dirty.
> *(Darwin 1872, 256 quoted in Miller 1998, 1)*

For Darwin, the feeling of the unpleasant, revolting and disgusting by the 'savage' and the 'civilized' signified the universality of the emotion and its persistence through human evolution. His work has shaped our understanding of disgust as a 'basic', visceral emotion, centred on taste, that develops during early childhood and is said to have a primal function of protecting us from oral contamination, through preventing the ingestion of dangerous, noxious substances. Yet, Miller argues that such conceptions of disgust as a 'primitive hard-wired reflex' (Miller 1998, 6) lose sight of its richly cognitive and social dimension and its role as a moral emotion.

Like Miller, other moral psychologists and philosophers characterised disgust as a moral emotion because it affects our moral judgements and is profoundly exclusionary, entrenching social inequalities, and inducing punitive treatment of minoritised social groups, like women, gays, migrants, the poor and the untouchable (Nussbaum 2004, Schnall *et al.* 2008, Strohminger and Kumar 2018, Inbar and Pizarro 2022). Such aversion, psychologist Paul Rozin and colleagues explain, follows a magical thinking that attributes contagion qualities to the person in contact with disgusting things (like semen, blood, vomit, sweat, faeces and urine) (Rozin *et al.* 1986). From being conceived as a primitive reaction to physical danger, they argue, disgust has expanded its functions to protect the soul (Rozin *et al.* 1999, 434). Building on Mary Douglas' *Purity and Danger* (Douglas 2002 [1966]), sociologists and anthropologists pointed to the symbolic meaning of dirt as a potential source of disgust in maintaining social ordering. As Sara Ahmed (2014) argues, the disgusting is quintessentially 'matter out of place', outside normal ordering, which serves to maintain bodily boundaries and social hierarchies. For Ahmed, disgust has a corporeal element, involving a relationship between bodies and objects, driving bodies to 'recoil' from proximity.

As a reminder of and a reaction to our common animal nature, disgust is known as 'the emotion of civilisation' (cf Elias 2000 [1939]). Historian Zachary Samalin (2021) traced the significance of this emotion in the affective re-organisation of social life during Victorian Britain. As a 'technology of sensorial legibility', disgust is central in the 'fantasy of the primal scene'. This is an imagined historical timeline when humans overcame their primitive humanity, a fantasy which serves 'to establish, for the modern person, the instinctivity that preceded rationality, the feeling anterior to the thought, the animal that came before the human, the natural before the social world' (Samalin 2021, 124). Modernity in this view cannot be understood without paying attention to its affective scaffolding, where disgust and the discursive struggles that permeate its formation are its constitutive parts. As he suggests, the history of disgust is constitutive of Europe's arrogation of modernity and dominance. In tracing this historical function, Samalin also points to the internal contradictions of its mobilisation. Disgust epitomises the physiological and visceral, the reflex, gut reaction, but it is also said to be a reasoned, deliberate, voluntary response to that what reminds us of our animal nature. It is a key mechanism of social stratification and exclusion, yet it is crucial for social cohesion, the baseline of affective sociality, and – *pace* Marx and Engels – a vehicle to denounce the malice of civilisation.

According to sociologists of work, emotions such as disgust are critical for understanding the embodied nature of labour and the way in which certain workers negotiate their gender, class and professional identity (Simpson *et al.* 2012). For Simpson and colleagues, disgust is a key resource in so-called dirty work which is 'given meaning in context and in specific interaction' (Simpson *et al.* 2016, 190). In documenting the performative role of emotions among butchers and waste collectors, they showcase the 'conflicting, ambiguous and intense affective experiences [of these workers], that complicate the clean/ dirty divide' and highlight the contradictions in the mobilisation of emotions and their effects (Simpson *et al.* 2016, 206).

Dirty work has been defined as tasks, occupations and/or roles that are likely to be perceived as disgusting or degrading (Hughes 1962). These are tainted both materially and symbolically, and socially perceived as dirty: physically, socially and/or morally. Policing has long been categorised as a 'tainted occupation' (Bittner 1970, 6) because it involves work regarded as physically, socially or morally dirty (Ashforth and Kreiner 1999, 414, Ashforth *et al.* 2017, De Camargo 2019). Historically, the police have been tasked to manage the social consequences of adverse economic and cultural restructuring of society (Loftus 2009, Frederic 2020), a task that is increasingly shared with border guards in a context of globalised capital and human mobility (Aliverti 2021a, b). Like other criminal justice workers (Mawby and Worrall 2013, Garrihy 2021), the daily work of police and immigration officers involve dealing with stigmatised, abject social groups. Crucially, their legal endowment to use physical violence (and their physical exposure to it) taints the policing profession in peculiar ways while also shaping their professional culture (Waddington 1999, Dick 2005). As police ethnographers documented, their relationship to coercion is morally ambiguous: although often referred to as a source of professional pride, it generates distinctive ethical dilemmas and legitimacy paradoxes (Fassin 2013, Jauregui 2016). For while the police are one of the most controversial institutions around the world (Fassin 2017), levels of public support remain high (Caldeira 2013, Hornberger 2013), even in countries like the UK where the forces routinely face accusations of racism, misogyny and xenophobia (Harkin 2015). Police violence then gives rise to ambivalent and oscillating moral sentiments of anxiety and disgust, and thrill and desire (see also chapters by Rodrigues and Spesny in this volume).

Even more complex is the relationship of immigration workers with violence in part due to the political polarisation that their labour produces, reflected in ongoing debates within political philosophy on the ethics of border controls (Abizadeh 2008, Wellman and Cole 2011, Song 2018). Despite efforts to moralise immigration law breaking and border protection, its 'moral core' remains at best elusive. In turn, this elusiveness impinges on immigration law enforcement's on its civic virtue and moral worth. Unsurprisingly, violence in this context is surrounded by institutional attempts at concealing and camouflaging it (through language and aesthetics) (Vega 2018, Aliverti 2021a). In the UK, immigration officers have limited coercive powers compared to the police: they have similar powers of arrest, and search and seizure of property, but cannot bear firearms and their powers are circumscribed spatially (to border areas) and restricted to immigration matters. Physical coercion is remarkably rare in this context (Aliverti 2021a), with most officers I talked to admitting to using their baton once or twice during their professional career; persuasion (in police jargon, 'tactical communication') is far more effective and less morally troubling, they insist. 'I have never in 23 years needed to use force', Chief Immigration Officer Jake tells me proudly as though a sign of emotional maturity and professionalism, 'I can communicate with people. I have seen force being used and that whole level of aggression…, you know, puffing up chests and going in their mob handed, it is not necessary'.

In recent years, the annexation of safeguarding and care agendas to immigration policing attempted at sanitising its nasty remit centred on the pursuit and ejection of people without papers (Bolt 2019). Yet, Immigration Enforcement, and its policing arm – the Immigration Compliance and Enforcement (ICE) Teams – remains a tainted agency and, to paraphrase Wacquant (2009), the embodiment of the right hand of the state. Like police work, ICE work is about order maintenance. As Katja Franko claims, under contemporary conditions, the kind of order that they seek to maintain is a 'bordered order'. Although modern civil order presupposes borders, Franko refers to the contemporary fixation with the enforcement of the external borders of the nation-state against unwanted foreigners. The production of such order also creates zones of disorder and lawless elsewhere (Comaroff and Comaroff 2006). Much of their work involves policing the economies of illegalities that proliferate in UK post-industrial metropolitan areas to serve rapidly changing consumption patterns, and that increasingly rely on migrant labour to satiate them. These are sites characterised by sheer material precarity and organised to evade the state's gaze (Aliverti 2022).

These sites and the emotional economies around them are reminiscent of the sordid and disenchanted Victorian critiques of industrial capitalism lamenting 'the rottenness and inhumanity of the modern way of life' (Samalin 2021, 180). In particular, they elicit Engels' invocation of disgust as a moral critique of capitalism and its resulting socioeconomic conditions, evoking well-rehearsed links between filth and moral ruin. As Simpson and colleagues urged, we need to understand the implications of the material dimensions of 'dirt' which includes the embodied experiences of dirty workers:

> Approaches to and experiences of the work are strongly affected by dirt's materiality, grounded in the pragmatics of dealing with/removing it; how it adheres to clothing and skin; and how it can be a source of contamination in a physical sense.
>
> *(Simpson et al. 2016, 238)*

It also involves paying attention to how dirt is productive of emotions, including disgust, that are corporeally experienced and shape moral judgements. I turn to exploring these social and moral dimensions of immigration enforcement work in the next sections.

Immigration Enforcement as Embodied Work

Disgust features prominently in the everyday work of immigration officers. During fieldwork I conducted on their work in metropolitan areas and at the Southern English maritime border, officers often expressed disgust at the material conditions they routinely encounter, characterised by overcrowding and filthiness, and plagued by pests and diseases. Their work makes them privy to the backstage of British society, where people without the right papers and their children are forced to work and sojourn: the poultry processing plant, the brothel, the cannabis 'farm', the construction site, the car handwash encampment and the veg-cutting warehouse. Despite wearing chunky boots and thick dark clothes, by the end of the shift many confessed to feeling dirty and smelly, and rushing to take their clothes off and have a shower; an urge I also shared after accompanying them in their daily shifts. Like their police counterparts, some of these officers devise cleansing routines (or rituals) to manage work-related 'dirt': they carry with them hand sanitisers, disposable gloves and face masks; they avoid sharing personal objects with their clientele; they swiftly clean surfaces and wash their uniforms at the end of every shift. Often though, these officers were at the receiving end of strong reactions – which we could frame as moral disgust – from sections of the public. To these officers, their work felt tainted: physically, socially and morally.

Inscribed in the moral and emotional economies of migration and its control, disgust connects to the broader context in which immigration enforcement work operates. The global (neo)liberal order shapes the labour market in particular ways that privilege certain clean, 'high-skilled' and sanitised activities (banking, tourism, shopping), while reproducing 'dirty' labour, that is the cleaning work behind the scenes that bears the brunt of maintaining and enabling such order. Its everyday upkeep systematically produces social stratifications along racial, gender, nationality and class lines, reproducing forms of labour characterised by highly precarious material and regulatory conditions. These occupations are increasingly filled by migrant labourers from the Global South (Wills *et al.* 2009, Simpson *et al.* 2016, 7, Bloch and Mckay 2017). In turn, other professional fields, such as care, become increasingly devalued and fulfilled by female migrant workers (Anderson 2007, Laugier 2016). Finally, neoliberal social order requires an expansion of violence work, like policing and enforcement labour, which is central for enforcing that order (occupied by mostly the vernacular working classes) (Neocleous 2000, Jauregui 2013, Aliverti 2020, 2022, Waseem 2022).

The political economy of migration and its control, I argue, forms a backdrop for understanding the moral and emotional economies that dominate immigration enforcement work where disgust features prominently. Much of my fieldwork involved accompanying teams of police and immigration officers doing 'harm reduction' visits to residences and workplaces, along with welfare workers (such as local council, housing and health and safety officers), where unauthorised migrants were allegedly harboured. I once visited a site enclosed by improvised and parched up wires, full of muddy puddles left behind by a string of rainy weather, where somehow paradoxically three people were hand-washing incoming cars. A small shed by the side provided shelter to workers during rests and parked further afield a lorry trailer, I was told, offered lodging for them. Officers were accompanied to these sites by local council officers who unsurprisingly found breaches of various health and safety and housing laws. Many of the workers there were paid less than the minimum wage and some of them had been refused asylum and hence were unable to work legally. Other than lecturing these men about their exploitative conditions, police and immigration officers found themselves impotent to tilt market forces within a world polarised by wealth inequality.

On another occasion, I attended a two-storey rundown townhouse situated in an impoverished suburban neighbourhood. The worn wooden gate led to a small paved front garden where a broken baby chair and an empty petrol container laid abandoned, and wires from the house hung loose. Officers were looking for a man from Hungary who was convicted of crimes back home, but as they approached the front door, they saw a little girl looking through the upstairs window. After some knocking with no response, they decided to force their way in. One of the officers inspected the kitchen downstairs, while the others went upstairs where they found the girl and a man lying sleeping in a soiled sheetless mattress. After their forceful entry and the shouting, the toddler started to cry. The man woke up and soothed her. She calmed down. By then I was allowed to come up through an uncarpeted, steep, narrow staircase leading to two small bedrooms. His torso bare and still clearly sleepy, the man told the officers he worked at night at a food processing company. His partner worked during daytime. After running some checks over the phone, they confirmed the veracity of his answers and that the man they were after had the same surname but was not the man in front of them. There was a bowl of half-eaten food on the mattress, rubbish on the floor and some £20 notes sprinkled around. The room had a large hole in the ceiling, letting the freezing wind squeeze in. The landlord had evaded repeated requests for repairing it, he told them resignedly. After taking pictures of the place, the officers left the man and his daughter alone as we moved on to check other similar sites. The visit was then an opportunity to intervene in the life of this family mistakenly entangled with immigration and led to a range of welfare interventions in the form of referrals to the local council to assess health and safety rules compliance and offer 'parenting training' from social services.

'This was not the worst we have been to', Police Constable (PC) Paul commented as we stopped at a nearby service station for a coffee, probably sensing my own perplexity. 'I can't believe someone could put a baby in those conditions', Immigration Officer (IO) Haley interjected. Such sentiments are frequently echoed by their colleagues who often rank the conditions of the places they visit in a hierarchy of the disgusting. With a mix of moral outrage and sympathy, they often express their aversion to these conditions that ultimately orientalise and moralise poverty, and muttered their aversion and bewilderment with a mix of moral outrage and sympathy that ultimately orientalise and moralise poverty. Reflecting the racialised and classed grammar of disgust, IO Serena recalled one of these visits and the emotions it provoked on her vividly:

> I can't bear to be in there for ten minutes without wanting, you know, [pause] feeling unwell. But that is where they live and they have no choice and they are being charged hundreds of pounds a week to stay there, and do they not know there is anything better? Or is that the best they can get? I think that is the thing that surprises me the most. People say they want a better life and they are willing to overstay their visas or come here illegally risking life and limb, for a better life and how bad must it be for that to be better?

Like his colleagues, IO Sam conveyed to me his astonishment at witnessing the conditions people live in and harshly judged them for putting their children at risk of constant hazards. He told me how he feels disgusted at the conditions in certain houses, overcrowded, dirty, with wires all over, kids running around. He must put his uniform to wash sometimes when he gets back home because he feels dirty, smelly. 'How can people live in those conditions?', he queried rhetorically. Because of the daily exposure to these conditions, Sam had decided to steer away from sunny and exotic holiday hotpots in the Global South and instead travel within Europe and North America. As our conversation trailed, he became less vociferous and assertive. He toned down his discourse and started to talk to me about the precariousness he had found in some places he visited.

> It doesn't matter now whether you are legal or illegal. Most probably, the Romanians who we saw today are worse off than this Albanian. Illegal work is narrowing down. The Romanians are now working in car wash for peanuts. We are doing a disservice by allowing people in, and left them to be subject to exploitation.

'Our job is very negative', he confessed. Hinting at the animalisation that his labour entails, he rounded off resignedly: 'There are no good results. Either they go back or are released into poverty'.

Lurking in the background of these officers' bewilderment is the perceived animalisation that advanced capitalism produces on people who, to paraphrase Marx, become alienated but in their animal, physiological functions (that is, eating, drinking, procreating). As their human, productive self is bereft of humanity, their physiological self remains the only dimension of life where they can exert some human agency. As it turns out, immigration enforcement workers realise that they are instrumental in this process.

Indeed, scholars have pointed to the creation of 'animalized subjectivities' through immigration enforcement discourses and practices which treat migrant people as animals (Hartley and Fleay 2017, Fernandez de la Reguera 2022, see also Fernandez de la Reguera this volume), by literally detaining them in an abandoned zoo in Tripoli or in cages in the USA–Mexico border. Nick Vaughan Williams (2015) argues that the animal imageries, language and spaces that structure contemporary bordering practices constitute a particular form of sovereign power, 'zoopolitical', which rests on the identification and exclusion of the animal from the realm of the 'human' and demonstrates the violent foundations of the 'human' sovereign political community. Animalised subjectivities further reinstate the intrinsic connections between nature and race that have long enabled civilisational missions and produced landscapes of purity and pollution. As Moore and colleagues put it, 'racial and spatial divides protect vulnerable bodies from the essentially dangerous. Crossing the borders of these exclusive spaces – national bodies, uninhabited wilds, racialized ghettos – unsettles natural orders' (Moore et al. 2003, 29–30). Emotions such as disgust and fear form part of the sensorial scaffold that maintains these natural orders and exclusionary geographies.

Historically, public health has been a central justification of border controls as immigrants were perceived as public health risks (Nasar 2021). Recently immigrants have been blamed for the increase in rates of infectious diseases – including COVID – in Europe and the USA (Collingwood 2015, Vignier et al. 2022) suggesting that this relationship is enduring. Evidencing the emotional underpinnings of public policy, such racialised sentiments of 'illegal migrants' as pollutants and carriers of diseases have buttressed anti-immigration policies across Europe and North America (Hennebry and KC 2020, Iliadou 2022). As a residual effect of COVID, epidemiological measures in the form of Perspex screens dividing interviewing desks, compulsory distance signs and bottles of hand sanitisers in their workplace continue to signal these occupational hazards to immigration officers, reinforcing the Otherness of their clientele. In the aftermath of the global pandemic, these practices could be understood as performative of disgust. Either because of institutional inertia or intention, their survival is telling of the deep institutional sensibilities that underscore border control work.

Indeed, dealing with 'dirt' and feelings of disgust feature prominently in immigration work. Tabitha, an immigration officer I shadowed for extensive periods, made that clear. She once explained that, unlike other colleagues, she does not share her pen with 'clients' and does not let them touch her office smart phone, if conducting an interview through a phone interpreter, fearing contagion and contamination. She suggests that they carry with them diseases and they have been in filthy places and have different hygienic standards. She once interviewed a man from Sudan who had entered the UK clandestinely in the back of a lorry through Northern France and, to claim asylum, he attended the police station where Tabitha was posted. Tabitha duly followed the scripts of questions. The pace of it was tedious in part because of the man's weariness, in part because of Tabitha's bureaucratic dryness. As her various attempts at eliciting information failed and the man started to pick his nose, she became progressively upset: her tone became louder and her body tense, and she resorted to threats of prosecution, despite her preference for casual conversations. The man clearly sensed this affective escalation and, as though defiant, he didn't budge. 'Stop that!', she suddenly wailed at his nose picking. 'That's why – she tells me – I don't let them touch my pen or phone'. While the man was still in the room, she turned to me and interjected: 'I can understand that they come here for a better life, that I can understand', but she bemoaned their ungratefulness and defiance.

Even without the moral overtones, immigration workers often related to these unwanted feelings. Many of her colleagues who have been repurposed to deal with the upsurge in the arrival of people through the southern coast of Dover mentioned cleaning after them as an aspect of their job with a mix of pride, disdain and revulsion. As a job that revolves around social hierarchies, immigration officers found themselves doing much of the looking after and upkeeping of the tents where migrants crossing the English Channel are ferried to. Asserting her class suitability for the job and distancing from her managers in Central London's elegant Home Office headquarters, Mary-Ann pointed out the harsh and undesirable but grounded character of their remit:

> Our London branch... Marshall Street... it is full of people that don't have the same background as me, they don't talk like me, don't dress like me and I think it is like two parallel worlds operating and behaving in different ways. So I am not sure someone from Marshall street could do the things that I do but I am sure that I could eventually learn to do the things they do. I am not sure somebody in Marshall Street could process a migrant or clean the toilets or do all of the crappy things we do or not get upset by what things we see. But then that is only because I have been doing it forever.

Ceasar, a colleague of hers, is adamant to show his endurance and adaptability to deal with whatever his job throws at him:

> if you want me to clean the bins, I will clean the bins, if you want me to run a team, I will run a team. I am perfectly capable, willing and able to do any of these things... I am always happy with what I am doing, you

know. As I say, if you want me to go and clean the toilets, I will go and clean the toilets.

Doing 'crappy things', like emptying bins and cleaning toilets, is the ultimate test of professional and committed workers. In Mary-Ann's and Ceasar's accounts, we see how disgust is mobilised to subvert hierarchies. Turning from migrants to Home Office elites as disgusting subjects, these accounts signify 'that the boundaries that separate vice from virtue, good from evil, pure from polluted are permeable, and worse, necessarily permeable' (Miller 1998, 185).

The maintenance of a bordered order requires immigration officers to get morally dirty. Their job makes them dirty also because of the moral stain attached to it. IO Farzan resents the negative reactions their work arouses among sectors of the public:

> We had people coming up to us saying 'oh thank you, you are doing a good job'. You have other people who are swearing, cursing and saying 'you are all just disgusting people, you are breaching human rights, you're doing this, you're doing that'. It is that aspect of the job which initially kind of caught me by surprise thinking I would have normally expected the illegal migrant population to be a bit more aggressive.

Being immersed in their worlds for a long period of time, I too felt morally troubled and dirty. As I recalled in my fieldnotes, the casual explanation of 'intelligence fielding' techniques, which rely on individuals in positions of trust and tasked with care functions such as firefighters, doctors and nurses, or drug rehabilitation advisors, to report families and vulnerable people (like heroin addicts) without papers, made me physically sick. The bodily signs of disgust – dry throat, blushing – often resisted my attempts to repress them while interacting with these professionals. Sensing perhaps this discomfort when I was leaving my final shift, one of the officers I shadowed for extended periods of time asked what I learnt from spending time with them and hoped I had changed my opinions about them: 'you probably thought we were horrible people, but we are humans'. The morally dirty nature of immigration policing engages us, as researchers, too (Jauregui 2013). It makes us query the purpose and limits of the task of bearing witness.

Embodying one of the most 'crisis-ridden' government departments, these officers are the receptacle of public disdain, mistrust and contempt. Known for its crisis-prone reputation, toxic working environment, bureaucratic insensitivity and heartless policies, the Home Office have been the target of mocking campaigns from critics (and even its own staff) expressing discomfort at policies such as the Rwanda scheme (iNews 2022, Gentleman 2022). A recent report by a Whitehall think-tank described the

Home Office as marred by persistent cultural and institutional problems, from longstanding low morale among employees, lack of compassion in decision making, aversion to external scrutiny and poor cross-department coordination (Clyne and Savur 2023). Although the Home Office brief is not limited to immigration, asylum and borders, this is by far the area depleting most of its resources and making up its most prominent (and infamous) face. Given the controversies that beset their remit, many officers prefer not to talk about work with friends and family and cover themselves up when they are wearing their uniform to avoid unexpected attacks from passers-by. Moreover, their working routines are designed to avoid this uncanny aspect of their work: there are immigration no-go areas to which police colleagues are sent instead; they carefully 'risk assess' places before raiding them and plan timings to avert trouble.

Conclusion

A focus on emotions in policing moves our analysis away from Weber's rational bureaucrat as the archetype of state's frontline worker: it allows a richer understanding of the state as embodied, whereby its power is enabled or unsettled through emotions. As scholars argued, state bureaucracies operate through the production and circulation of emotions (like fear, hope, disgust, love) as much as through practices of classification and inscriptions (Navaro-Yashin 2002, Laszczkowski and Reeves 2018). Under contemporary conditions where questions of crime, immigration and punishment are increasingly politicised, we need to attend to these 'emotionalised techniques of governance' (Jupp *et al.* 2017) and its social effects.

Attention to disgust offers insights on themes long researched by policing scholars (on the insularity and outsiderness of the police, on the notion of 'police property' and on suspicion, and gut feelings) as remarkable feature of police cultures. According to policing scholars, disgust can contribute to widespread patterns of burdensome and disparate policing against despised minorities (Goff and Rau 2020). It is a problematic emotion because it reinforces social thick boundaries creating unassimilable otherness and draws us into an unrealisable fantasy of purity. My analysis of the work of Britain's immigration police demonstrates that disgust is central for understanding a force tasked with enforcing status difference, by distinguishing who belongs and who does not, a distinction that largely hinges on racial cognitive maps and sensorial epistemologies (through smell, sight, touch, taste, sound) (Parmar 2024). Their work in turn takes place amidst a highly emotional backdrop of immigration politics in the Global North, where their work arouses strong emotions and often leaves them feeling tainted physically and morally.

Attending to the place of negative moral emotions such as disgust allows us to understand the deep-rooted nature of these structures of feelings that permeate policing culturally and institutionally. Such structures of feelings and the economy of emotions of policing that underscores police work have seldom featured in police reform agendas. All this begs the question of what form might policing without disgust take, if it is even possible? Rather than seeking to eliminate disgust from policing, my aim is to understand the potential of exploring its contradictions. The salience of the grammar of disgust in and around immigration enforcement provides a rich backdrop to pin down the tensions and contradictions in its mobilisation. Immigration officers perform disgust as a professional and moral resource to legitimise a controversial mandate and, in so doing, reproduce racialised hierarchies of belonging. Yet, as I also show, disgust is also seized as an affective resource to disrupt these hierarchies and criticise the social, political and economic conditions that make them possible. As I showed, disgust is often mobilised by enforcement officers to denounce the 'malice of civilization' and its effects on the animalisation of the global proletariat, sometimes conveying empathy for their predicament. Ultimately, this work shows the polyvalent nature of emotions and their potential for bringing to bear the embodied, fragmented and contradictory nature of state power.

Note

1 Drafts of this chapter were presented at the University of Oxford's Policing Discussion Group (January 2024), the University of Warwick's Embodied State workshop (May 2024), the Law and Society Association conference (Denver, June 2024) and Warwick's 'Fear Studies in an Age of Fears' conference (January 2025). I am grateful to participants and the editors of this volume for their questions and observations which help me develop this work. I am also grateful to the immigration officers from the Home Office that allowed me to shadow their work and discuss it in interviews. The research underpinning this chapter was made possible by the financial support of various grants from the Leverhulme Trust and the British Academy (PLP-2017-170; SG210082; RPG-2022-218).

References

Abizadeh, A. (2008). "Democratic Theory and Border Coercion: No Right to Unilaterally Control Your Own Borders." *Political Theory* 36(1): 37–65.

Ahmed, S. (2014). *The Cultural Politics of Emotion*. Edinburgh, Edinburgh University Press.

Aliverti, A. (2020). Doing the Dirty Job: Labour at the Intersections of Criminal Law and Immigration Controls. *Criminality at Work*. A. Bogg, M. Freedland, J. Collins and J. Herring. Oxford, Oxford University Press: 327–342.

Aliverti, A. (2021a). "Manufacturing Obedience: Coercion and Authority in Border Controls." *Punishment & Society* 25(2): 14624745211051320.

Aliverti, A. (2021b). *Policing the Borders Within*. Oxford, Oxford University Press.
Aliverti, A. (2022). "Law in the Margins: Economies of Illegality and Contested Sovereignties." *British Journal of Criminology* (https://doi.org/10.1093/bjc/azac078).
Aliverti, A. (2023). "Storytelling and Magic: Meaning Making in Immigration Policing." *International Journal for Crime, Justice and Social Democracy* 12(2): 25–35.
Anderson, B. (2007). "A Very Private Business." *European Journal of Women's Studies* 14(3): 247–264.
Ashforth, B. E. and G. E. Kreiner (1999). ""How Can You Do It?": Dirty Work and the Challenge of Constructing a Positive Identity." *The Academy of Management Review* 24(3): 413–434.
Ashforth, B. E., et al. (2017). "Congruence Work in Stigmatized Occupations: A Managerial Lens on Employee Fit with Dirty Work." *Journal of Organizational Behavior* 38(8): 1260–1279.
Bauman, Z. (1991). *Modernity and the Holocaust*. Cambridge, Polity.
Bittner, E. (1970). *The Functions of Police in Modern Society*. Washington DC: National Institute of Mental Health.
Bloch, A. and S. Mckay (2017). *Living on the Margins: Undocumented Migrants in a Global City*. Bristol, Policy Press.
Bolt, D. (2019). An inspection of the Home Office's approach to the identification and safeguarding of vulnerable adults February – May 2018. London, ICIBI.
Bonilla-Silva, E. (2019). "Feeling Race: Theorizing the Racial Economy of Emotions." *American Sociological Review* 84(1): 1–25.
Caldeira, T. P. R. (2013). The Paradox of Police Violence in Democratic Brazil. *Policing and Contemporary Governance: The Anthropology of Police in Practice*. W. Garriott. New York, Palgrave Macmillan US: 97–124.
Clyne, R. and S. Savur (2023). *Home truths: Cultural and institutional problems at the Home Office*. London: Institute for Government. Available at: https://www.instituteforgovernment.org.uk/sites/default/files/2023-05/cultural-and-institutional-problems-home-office_0.pdf.
Collingwood, J. (2015). Illegal immigration and the threat of infectious disease. SMA News: https://sma.org/illegal-immigration-and-the-threat-of-infectious-disease/
Comaroff, J. and J. Comaroff (2006). Law and Disorder in the Postcolony. An Introduction. *Law and Disorder in the Postcolony*. J. Comaroff and J. Comaroff. Chicago, University of Chicago Press: 1–56.
Cooper, D. (2019). *Feeling Like a State: Desire, Denial, and the Recasting of Authority*. Durham, Duke University Press.
Darwin, C. (1872). *The Expression of the Emotions in Man and Animals*. Chicago: Chicago University Press.
De Camargo, C. R. (2019). "'You feel dirty a lot of the time': Policing 'dirty work', Contamination and Purification Rituals." *International Journal of Police Science & Management* 21(3): 133–145.
Dick, P. (2005). "Dirty Work Designations: How Police Officers Account for Their Use of Coercive Force." *Human Relations* 58(11): 1363–1390.
Douglas, M. (2002 [1966]). *Purity and Danger: An Analysis of Concept of Pollution and Taboo*. Abingdon, Routledge.
El-Enani, N. (2020). *Bordering Britain: Law, Race and Empire*. Manchester: Manchester University Press.

Elias, N. (2000 [1939]). *The Civilizing Process*. Oxford, Blackwell.
Fassin, D. (2013). *Enforcing Order: An Ethnography of Urban Policing*. Cambridge, Polity.
Fassin, D., Ed. (2015). *At the Heart of the State: The Moral World of Institutions*. London, Pluto Press.
Fassin, D. (2017). Introduction: Ethnographying the Police. *Writing the World of Policing: The Difference Ethnography Makes*. D. Fassin. Chicago and London, University of Chicago Press: 1–20.
Fernandez de la Reguera, A. (2022). El asco como política y pedagogía de la detención migratoria en México. *Política y afectos. Poder, subjetividad y emociones*. H. Diaz Alvarez and R. Lince Campillo. Mexico DF, UNAM: 221-248.
Frederic, S. (2020). *La Gendarmeria desde Adentro. De Centinelas de la Patria al Trabajo en Barrios, Cuáles son sus Verdaderas Funciones en el Siglo XXI*. Buenos Aires, Siglo XXI.
Garrihy, J. (2021). "'That Doesn't Leave You': Psychological Dirt and Taint in Prison Officers' Occupational Cultures and Identities." *The British Journal of Criminology* 62(4): 982–999.
Gentleman, A. (2022). 'Paddington, go home: Home Office staff pin up faked deportation notices'. The Guardian. Available at: https://www.theguardian.com/uk-news/2022/jun/13/paddington-go-home-home-office-staff-pin-up-faked-deportation-notices.
Goff, P. and H. Rau (2020). "Predicting Bad Policing: Theorizing Burdensome and Racially Disparate Policing through the Lenses of Social Psychology and Routine Activities." *The ANNALS of the American Academy of Political and Social Science* 687(1): 67–88.
Harkin, D. (2015). "The Police and Punishment: Understanding the Pains of Policing." *Theoretical Criminology* 19(1): 43–58.
Hartley, L. and C. Fleay (2017). ""We are Like Animals": Negotiating Dehumanising Experiences of Asylum-Seeker Policies in the Australian Community." *Refugee Survey Quarterly* 36(4): 45–63.
Hennebry, J. and H. KC (2020). Quarantined! Xenophobia and migrant workers during the COVID-19 pandemic. International Organization for Migration (IOM). Geneva.
Herzfeld, M. (1992). *The Social Production of Indifference Exploring the Symbolic Roots of Western Bureaucracy*. Chicago, University of Chicago Press.
Hornberger, J. (2013). "From General to Commissioner to General—On the Popular State of Policing in South Africa." *Law & Social Inquiry* 38(3): 598–614.
Hughes, E. (1962). "Good People and Dirty Work." *Social Problems* 10(1): 3–11.
Iliadou, E. (2022). Quarantine Continuum: La medicalizzazione dei confini e la securitizzazione delle migrazioni e della salute in Grecia. *Corpi reclusi in attesa di espulsione. La detenzione amministrativa in Europa al tempo della sindemia*. F. Esposito, E. Caja and G. Mattiello, Turin: Edizioni SEB27: 167–196.
Inbar, Y. and D. A. Pizarro (2022). Chapter Three – How Disgust Affects Social Judgments. *Advances in Experimental Social Psychology*. B. Gawronski, Cambridge: Academic Press. 65: 109–166.
iNews (2022). *Tube adverts tell London Underground passengers stop people deported flights*. Available at: https://inews.co.uk/news/tube-adverts-tell-london-underground-passengers-stop-people-deported-flights-236918?srsltid=AfmBOorZ6RQWh-OuCQ6LPkYbnzVPy-MTZJgBs0qdw3IHhCNKfnZWJFuu and www.theguardian.com/uk-news/2022/jun/13/paddington-go-home-home-office-staff-pin-up-faked-deportation-notices.

Jauregui, B. (2013). Dirty Anthropology: Epistemologies of Violence and Ethical Entanglements in Police Ethnography. *Policing and Contemporary Governance: The Anthropology of Police in Practice.* W. Garriott. London, Palgrave: 125–153.

Jauregui, B. (2016). *Provisional Authority. Police, Order, and Security in India.* Chicago, Chicago University Press.

Jupp, E., et al., Eds. (2017). *Emotional States: Sites and Spaces of Affective Governance.* Oxford, Routledge.

Laszczkowski, M. and M. Reeves (2018). *Affective States: Entanglements, Suspensions, Suspicions.* New York and Oxford, Berghahn.

Laugier, S. (2016). "Politics of Vulnerability and Responsibility for Ordinary Others." *Critical Horizons* 17(2): 207–223.

Loftus, B. (2009). *Police Culture in a Changing World.* Oxford, Oxford University Press.

Mawby, R. and A. Worrall (2013). *Doing Probation Work Identity in a Criminal Justice Occupation.* Abingdon: Routledge.

Miller, W. (1998). *The Anatomy of Disgust.* Cambridge and London: Harvard University Press.

Moore, D., et al. (2003). *Race, Nature, and the Politics of Difference.* Durham: Duke University Press.

Nasar, S. (2021). "Patrolling Race and the UK's Medical Borders." *The Lancet* 397(10286): 1702–1703.

Navaro-Yashin, Y. (2002). *The Faces of the State: Secularism and Public Life in Turkey.* Princeton: Princeton University Press.

Neocleous, M. (2000). *The Fabrication of Social Order: A Critical Theory of Police Power.* London: Pluto Press.

Nussbaum, M. (2004). *Hiding from Humanity: Disgust, Shame and the Law.* Princeton:, Princeton University Press.

Parmar, A. (2024). "Feeling Race: Mapping Emotions in Policing Britain's Borders." *Identities* 31(1): 14–30.

Rozin, P., et al. (1999). Disgust: The Body and Soul Emotion. *Handbook of Cognition and Emotion.* T. Dalgleish and M. Power. London: John Wiley & Sons Ltd: 429–445.

Rozin, P., et al. (1986). "Operation of the Laws of Sympathetic Magic in Disgust and Other Domains." *Journal of Personality and Social Psychology* 50(4): 703-712.

Samalin, Z. (2021). *The Masses Are Revolting: Victorian Culture and the Political Aesthetics of Disgust.* Ithaca: Cornell University Press.

Schnall, S., et al. (2008). "Disgust as Embodied Moral Judgment." *Personality and Social Psychology Bulletin* 34(8): 1096–1109.

Simpson, R., et al. (2016). *Gender, Class and Occupation: Working Class Men Doing Dirty Work.* London, Palgrave Macmillan.

Simpson, S., et al. (2012). *Dirty Work: Concepts and Identities.* Basingstoke, Palgrave Macmillan.

Song, S. (2018). *Immigration and Democracy.* New York: Oxford University Press.

Strohminger, N. and V. Kumar, Eds. (2018). *The Moral Psychology of Disgust.* London and New York, Rowman & Littlefield.

Vaisman, N. and L. Barrera (2020). "On Judgment: Managing Emotions in Trials of Crimes against Humanity in Argentina." *Social & Legal Studies* 29(6): 812–834.

Vaughan-Williams, N. (2015). ""We are not animals!" Humanitarian Border Security and Zoopolitical Spaces in EUrope" *Political Geography* 45: 1–10.

Vega, I. I. (2018). "Empathy, Morality, and Criminality: The Legitimation Narratives of U.S. Border Patrol agents." *Journal of Ethnic and Migration Studies* 44(15): 2544–2561.

Vignier, N., et al. (2022). "Burden of Infectious Diseases among Undocumented Migrants in France: Results of the Premiers Pas Survey." *Frontiers in Public Health* 10.

Wacquant, L. (2009). *Punishing the Poor: The Neoliberal Government of Social Insecurity*. Durham and London: Duke University Press.

Waddington, P. (1999). *Policing Citizens*. London: UCL Press.

Waseem, Z. (2022). *Insecure Guardians: Enforcement, Encounters and Everyday Policing in Postcolonial Karachi*. London: Hurst & Co.

Wellman, C. H. and P. Cole (2011). *Debating the Ethics of Immigration: Is There a Right to Exclude?* Oxford: Oxford University Press.

Wills, J., et al. (2009). *Global Cities At Work: New Migrant Divisions of Labour*. London: Pluto Press.

Woody, A. (2021). "Emotions and Ambient Racism in America's Whitest Big City." *Social Problems* 70(4): 981–998.

Zacka, B. (2017). *When the State Meets the Street. Public Service and Moral Agency*. Cambridge, MA, Harvard University Press.

13
CREATIVE EMOTIONS

The governance of vulnerability and the caring ambivalence of arts therapeutic work in prisons

Sally Foreman and Anastasia Chamberlen

It is probably safe to assume that the image of prisoners participating in arts therapy sessions is unpopular among law-and-order politicians and punitive publics, tapping into enduring prejudices towards prisons, prisoners, and the arts alike (Cullen et al. 2000; Carvalho et al. 2020; Lynch 2004). It is an image that stands contrary to the largely coercive rationales of imprisonment – particularly within the recent revolving crises in safety, mental health, and wellbeing in England's overcrowded, understaffed prisons (Chamberlen and Carvalho 2019) – and which poses an affective provocation to post-austerity British society, with its devaluation of the arts more generally (Shaw and McGivern 2023). Today's political climate promotes a view of the arts as the preserve of a cultural elite, or as a recreational field without instrumental value. Consequently, the idea that convicted criminals are making art and receiving arts therapy while doing time provokes ambivalent emotions in many, belying moral unease: if punishment is right, then any activity that brings joy, pleasure, and colour into the prisoners' lives must be wrong.

For researchers of the prison, the emergence of arts therapies as a facet of contemporary imprisonment speaks to the contradictory objectives of incarceration, which oscillate between punitive and rehabilitative ideologies but in practice almost always lean towards the punitive (Norrie 2022; Carvalho and Chamberlen 2024). A key tension underpinning the research presented here, then, goes to the heart of the punishment–care nexus of the modern prison: how can an institution designed to produce incapacitation, repression, and pain also invest in and host therapeutic endeavours – particularly of those orientations which divert from the mainstream psycho-medical models and encourage creative expression that can take rather radical, broadly anti-institutional tones?

In this chapter, we look at prison-based arts therapists' experiences and perceptions as people who work in prisons but who are not employed by HM Prison and Probation Service (HMPPS). Arts therapists are accredited therapeutic professionals, contracted via the National Health Service (NHS), with a dual background in the arts and in psychotherapy. They specialise in a form of psychotherapy that relies on the creation of arts products during one-on-one or group therapy sessions; these creations form a central part of the therapeutic journey for patients. The chapter interrogates the very label of 'arts therapist' in the prison context. In so doing, in part, we unpack these arts therapists' complicity in the task of delivering rehabilitation and punishment agendas and explore their motivation to offer what appears to be an often-tricky form of therapeutic care in a coercive context that discourages free expression. We unpack the ambivalence that arts therapists express in connection with their work and suggest that the ways in which these practitioners feel and manage their emotions reveal enmeshed preoccupations with resistance and care. We contend that arts therapists – a marginalised group of prison workers assigned mainly to 'vulnerable' prisoners – occupy a shifting-liminal position inside the institution. This precarious position allows arts therapists to create a unique professional space in which they can hold conflicting affective states: they can express personal resistance and anti-carceral sentiments, while ultimately being in the service of the prison's oppressive and individualising-rehabilitative goals. The emancipatory potential of this space, we argue, is realised through the practice of a care aesthetics (Thompson 2022) that critiques and resists oppressive norms and seeks to transform the prisoners' sensory worlds.

This study draws on research with a group of arts therapists working in English prisons undertaken between November 2023 and April 2024 as part of the AHRC-funded project 'Captive Arts'. The broader project sought to interrogate the role of the arts in the lives of prisoners. The participants we draw upon in this chapter include women and men whose experience of working in prisons ranges from a couple of years to decades. The anonymised data presented here is based on 15 qualitative interviews analysed thematically. The participants specialise mostly in visual-arts psychotherapy, and a handful of them also practise a combination of visual, film-based, animation or drama-based psychotherapy. As all participants clarified from the outset, there is no 'typical' arts therapy session; the therapeutic process varies considerably from therapist to therapist and depends also on the specific needs of the patient (or patients, when the therapy is group-based). Nonetheless, most arts therapy relies on the patient/s creating some form of artwork during therapy sessions (e.g. a painting, drawing, collage, clay-work, or some combination of media and art forms to produce a visual or discursive output). Some patients create art from the first session, while others may not be able to create anything for several sessions. Some complete many arts outputs during the sessions, while others may work on a single piece of art through several sessions. The creations – which are retained by the therapists and form part of the patients' mental health files – are a catalyst for developing an expressive relationship with the therapist, who psychoanalytically analyses both the art product and the patient's conduct during the making of the art product. A unique feature of this type of therapy, then, is that it relies a lot less on what patients may say verbally, and a lot more on what they can express creatively.

The chapter begins by charting a brief history of the field of arts therapies in the UK and its evolving relationship with carceral institutions. We show how the role of the arts therapist is marginalised within the prison setting; their classification as health workers places them below prison management and forensic psychologists in the hierarchy, while therapeutic objectives are subordinate to the objectives of the justice system. Though demand for arts therapies in prisons is potentially increasing (albeit this is not yet fully established), there has been no systematic institutional transfer of authority to these professionals, who remain 'guests' of the prison. We suggest that this enables arts therapists to retain their sense of separation from punishment and control priorities, and to a lesser extent from rehabilitation goals. We discuss the influence that these therapists are in fact able to wield, despite expressing frustration at their lack of power.

The chapter continues with a critical examination of the allocation of arts therapies to 'vulnerable' prisoners – typically those groups deemed unsuitable for mainstream talking therapies due to non-verbal or non-responsive tendencies, or who are perceived as being unable to adapt to rehabilitation programmes or cope with daily prison life. There is a growing trend in prison policy and discourse to frame a complex range of conditions and experiences as 'vulnerabilities' (Vanliefde 2024), a vague category that many therapists employed to engage with said vulnerabilities are themselves unclear about. We analyse the complex effects of this discursive shift: on the one hand, labelling more prisoners as 'vulnerable' expands the domain of arts therapy and renders its provision more publicly acceptable by recasting criminals as (also) victims; on the other hand, this 'politics of pity' (Boltanski 1999) instrumentalises vulnerability by granting the institution moral legitimacy to deepen its control over a hard-to-reach population – a control in which the therapist is necessarily complicit.

Finally, we explore the emotional realities of delivering arts therapies in prison and unpack the ambivalence that defines the experience of this unique group of prison workers. We theorise that these practitioners bring an aesthetic quality to the therapeutic care they provide, which does not relate primarily to the art produced in therapy sessions but exists in the sensory experience of two bodies relating to one another across a shared moment and space (Thompson 2022; see also Thompson 2009). This caring, relational, embodied aesthetics works to counter the individualising experience of being singled out for punishment and disrupts the oppressive, desensitising regime of the prison. In this way, the embedding of arts therapies in the 'vulnerability' agenda of modern prisons presents a surprising yet opportune moment for a revival of the radical promise buried in the history of this profession.

Background: Arts therapies and their place in prisons

Arts therapies are forms of psychotherapy that use creative practices (primarily visual art-making, music, and drama) as methods for enabling patients to express, communicate, and understand complex feelings and traumas in a safe, therapeutic environment. Arts therapists usually have an artistic background and specialise via a postgraduate qualification in arts psychotherapy. Those practising through the NHS, including therapists contracted to work in prisons, are registered with the Health and Care Professions Council.

Before turning to the place of arts therapies today, it is worth starting with a brief history of the emergence of arts therapy as professional practice. Delving into this history will hopefully highlight the curious, if not ironic, rediscovery of arts therapies today, particularly in the context of our mostly punitive political stance on punishment. Between the 1930s and 1950s, arts therapies were mostly found in hospital-like institutional settings. Links with the anti-psychiatry movement and humanistic schools of thought meant that by the time the British Association of Arts Therapists (BAAT) was established in the 1960s, arts therapies positioned themselves as alternatives to the psychiatric and medical model of mental health and contributed to the wider informalisation of therapist–patient relations and to a more politically and socially attuned understanding of mental distress. Arts therapies were formally recognised as a profession in the UK in 1966 and at this point had been consistently informed by psychoanalytic, child arts education, and anti-psychiatry approaches (Walker 1991). In the 1980s, the profession established itself more fully in the public sector and began to move beyond hospital settings; during this period, the practice was informed by psychoanalytic and group systems theory. Since the 2000s, arts therapies have evolved in response to shifts in consumer demand, including from private individuals, and adopted a wide range of mixed approaches.

Arts therapies have a contentious history vis-à-vis prison. Arguably, their ideological and theoretical foundations complicate the standpoint of those working in forensic spaces with long legacies of imbrication of penal, disciplinary, and medical power (Sim 1990; Rock 1996). A pivotal moment in the British penal context was the creation in 1973 of the HM Barlinnie Special Unit (BSU) within Scotland's largest prison. The BSU pioneered a progressive therapeutic rehabilitative community, where arts training and arts therapy were blended and made available to a group of prisoners regarded as difficult and exceptionally dangerous. Many of these men (including the renowned sculptor Jimmy Boyle) thoroughly engaged with arts approaches, showcasing their rehabilitative value while simultaneously reframing the promise of the arts through the reputations the men developed beyond the prison as talented artists. The BSU experiment did much more than achieve indisputable success with rehabilitation goals; it was transformative, healing, and emancipatory. Perhaps unsurprisingly, the BSU could not survive at a time when punitive public sentiments were increasingly mobilised to call for a harsher, anti-progressive penal climate. The BSU closed in 1996 and now feels like a distant, almost mythical experiment (see Nellis 2010).

The availability of arts therapies today

The practice of arts therapies in contemporary prisons presents a compound set of objectives associated with broader rehabilitative rationales focused on desistance as well as more concretely therapeutic wellbeing and treatment aims. Arts therapies sometimes occupy a crossover space between healthcare and education provision, integrating mental health concerns with a wider curriculum in cultural and artistic training (Gussak 2019). However, this conflation is more likely to be observed in the US correctional context.

In a UK setting, arts therapies are deemed especially suitable for 'vulnerable' prisoners. This flexible designation is typically applied to certain groups of people, including individuals with trauma; women; children and young people; people with non-verbal and neurodivergent tendencies; people who fall outside the personality diagnostic disorder framework; and those for whom English is a second language (Bosworth and von Zinnenburg Carroll 2017; Maruna 2001). Current data on the availability of arts therapies in prisons is unclear, but we can estimate a gradual expansion. The Forensic Arts Therapy Group (FATAG) reports having around 500 members working in various establishments across the country, but it is not clear how many of these practitioners work exclusively in prisons. Participants in our study suggest that arts therapies are particularly available, and in high demand, in therapeutic prisons (e.g. HMP Grendon and Send), Young Offenders' Institutions, and secure forensic hospitals, and are increasingly available, though on a smaller scale, in mainstream prisons; nonetheless, they remain a marginalised provision targeting a marginalised population.

The recent rise in demand for arts therapies has led to increased efforts to 'prove' their efficacy. Studies measuring various mental health indicators, such as change in depression and locus of control, have found arts therapies to be effective in prison settings, including reporting that patients exhibited healthier emotional states after arts therapy than traditional psychotherapy

(Regev and Cohen-Yatsiv 2018; van den Broek et al. 2021). Nonetheless, as one research participant who is leading arts therapy provision across a series of prisons explained, these efficacy metrics rarely feature in decisions on whether arts therapies should be offered. Instead, these decisions appear to be made based on financial considerations when contracting with the NHS (arts therapists are usually on a higher salary band than junior psychological staff), and on different prisons' cultural dynamics and senior management's values and priorities. Most of our participants suggested that availability ultimately depends on facilitation by key individuals, such as prison governors and senior staff, rather than a systematic framework.

Defining the arts therapy 'space'

What we have called the 'marginalisation' of arts therapies in prisons is the consequence of a formal division between mental healthcare teams, who are contracted via the NHS, and in-house forensic psychological teams. The former are responsible for primary healthcare provision, while the latter are more aligned with HMPPS priorities involving, for instance, risk and parole assessments. One participant suggested that NHS staff are treated as 'guests of HMPPS', whose roles rank below the more 'serious' or urgent goals of the regime; another suggested that, from the prison's perspective, therapists are 'resources' and prisoners' needs are a demand for resources. Participants consistently mentioned a perceived hierarchy and dichotomy between forensic and mental health teams, in which the latter are treated as outsiders and feel powerless and vulnerable to changing institutional dynamics and values. The prison's cultural and moral practices are perceived to be constructed by lead forensic psychologists, some of whom appear to enjoy a considerable degree of authority (see Warr 2020). As one participant explains:

> So we are asked to write parole reports, but what we write doesn't hold as much importance as what they [forensic psychologists] write and, you know, I would have seen somebody for two years every week. And they would have met him for two hours, but because of their position, their report will be the one that is relied upon.

This perceived hierarchy and dichotomy is, of course, not only constructed via the prison's cultural and regime dynamics. Perceptions of differences in clinical expertise between those with a forensic clinical status and those, such as arts therapists, whose training may be deemed less 'scientific' are also at play.

However, participants also expressed a desire to make a difference in prisoners' lives by exercising their limited authority and felt that they had varying degrees of autonomy to do so. The influence that arts therapists can wield is partly derived from the fact that their concerns are somewhat siloed from the establishment's, and partly dependent on how well the therapist has been embedded within the institution, gaining recognition and credibility that better enables them to meet their patients' needs.

> I kind of have a particular reputation to be able to make my own decisions. All therapists, art therapists, have that, but I can really more or less see people for as long as I think it's necessary. And I discuss it with the woman [patient] rather than the team.

In principle, therefore, the role of arts therapists is to provide care rather than dispense justice, although as the participants in this study clarify, most – if not all – of the work that therapists do with patients is focused on addressing their offending histories rather than their overall mental health. In this way, we contend, the arts therapy space may be considered *distinct* from the prison's justice and punishment priorities, but it is not *independent* of the prison context.

Within this distinct therapeutic space, arts therapists acknowledge their power to define what they do and to make an impact on individual lives. One participant observed that the very idea of therapy is 'complicated': 'I don't really mention the word therapy because quite a lot of people [in prison] would run for the hills'. Arts therapists attempt to navigate this aversion, or stigma, creatively, by emphasising the artistic aspects of the work. Many participants suggested that the idea of 'getting better', in a conventional therapeutic sense, is secondary to providing containment and personal connection and facilitating artistic production, and that they enjoy considerable freedom in determining the pacing, content, and process that they follow in individual sessions: 'I'll try to talk to them about what they're making. But it's not usually that neat and tidy'. One participant working with young people explained that he rarely uses the terms 'therapy' or 'treatment' because he finds the creative aspects of arts therapy are perceived as more neutral and thus benevolent; medicalised notions of treatment raise questions of trust – as well as potentially false expectations of healing – among his young cohorts and can obstruct their focus on 'completing ... art projects'. This prioritisation of artistic outputs is not shared by all participants but demonstrates the flexibility of what occurs within the arts therapy space. We can see that, through this work, therapists and prisoners are actively co-constructing the arts therapy space, defining its priorities, characteristics, and outcomes, and liberating prisoners to express themselves – within this dynamic, marginal, temporally limited domain – on their own terms.

Arts therapies and 'vulnerable' prisoners

We have already mentioned that arts therapies are typically offered to prisoners who are deemed 'vulnerable' and are often withheld from the mainstream population. Participants in this study indicated that demand for arts therapies has increased in the past few years, and it is no surprise that this coincides with an observable rise in penal policy discourses concerned with the management of so-called vulnerable prisoners: an opaque category, the definitional boundaries of which are being drawn more and more broadly (Gilson 2016; Brown et al. 2017; Maguire 2021). This lack of clarity on what constitutes vulnerability is evident in the responses of our participants. As one senior arts therapist explains:

> Art therapists work with exceptionally vulnerable people … It's a kind of an ongoing joke that I am the sort of sponge [therapist]. And the women who can't engage in talking therapies, or who can't engage in skills-based therapies, kind of mop up.

Another participant notes that arts therapists tend to handle particularly intricate cases:

> I get some very complicated cases who can't articulate themselves very well or who are just self-harming a lot or causing trouble.

In broad strokes, in policy terms, vulnerability is assigned to specific cohorts, e.g., children in custodial settings; chronically and acutely ill prisoners; elderly prisoners; pregnant prisoners; and those at risk of self-harm, or of being exposed to bullying or grooming (HMPPS 2023). Participants indicated that the vulnerable prisoner category may include anyone with learning disabilities, a broad spectrum of mental health conditions and personality disorders, and those deemed to be 'poor copers' in the context of the prison regime (Liebling 1999). Vulnerable prisoners are likely to be found in prisons' segregation units but are also housed on mainstream landings, depending on various institutional factors and limitations.

The rise in demand for arts therapies coincides with the growing recognition of the overrepresentation of neurodivergence among prisoner populations. A recent Inspectorate of Prisons report (2021; see also Smith 2023) suggests that a considerable proportion of prisoners meet the criteria for autism and other neurodivergent conditions. This group of prisoners is understood to pose certain concrete vulnerabilities (e.g. around their ability to cope with the regime, or who are at risk of exposure to isolation, (self) harm, or bullying while in prison), which were particularly recognised and embraced by our participants. As one participant working in a young offenders' institution clarified, 'some of these boys don't want to, or can't really respond to any other education or therapy programme, especially the non-verbal or autistic ones really struggle with what prison's got to offer [aside from arts therapy]'.

A growing emphasis on 'vulnerability' in penal discourses makes the provision of arts therapies in prisons more politically palatable, since the label discursively transforms criminals (who deserve harsh punishment) into victims (who deserve pity, and some degree of help) (see Carvalho et al. 2025). This positions arts therapists as a distinct category of state-sponsored workers who are contracted to deal with particularly complex (read: problematic) prisoners, towards whom the harsh structures of the regime are not oriented, and who prove difficult to engage and manage in a regular way. In this vulnerability-infused climate, therefore, arts therapies serve a contradictory yet concrete penal function, since they can be deployed to serve therapeutic and rehabilitative (particularly concerning discipline and docility) objectives simultaneously (see Cheliotis 2014 on the arts' broader co-option in punishment). The imbrication of health and justice goals can be seen most clearly in US correctional settings, where research into the impact of the arts in corrections presents evidence of the arts' contribution to a wide range of institutional goals, including greater compliance; less impulsivity; elevation of mood; reduced depression; increased energy; and improvements in problem solving and following directions (Gussak 2019).

Despite arts therapists' inevitable implication in the regime that hires them, our participants expressed a strong sense of responsibility and care towards their patients and recognised that their position enables them to provide crucial support and empathy, and to advocate for prisoners within the system. This included therapists' direct or indirect interventions to obtain various institutional assistances (e.g. in signing up for courses, applying for appeals or parole, or advocating on prisoners' behalf to various other members of staff). This sense of care goes hand-in-hand with feelings of helplessness, given the institutional power dynamics and punitive priorities that constrain the therapists' professional agency. One participant who works in young offenders' institutions spoke about being unable to 'hold' her patients when they go to trial, expressing concern about not being able to provide supportive care at these most physically and mentally destabilising moments.

In the prison context, 'vulnerability' is both an institutional construction *and* a critical fact: prisoners are suffering, and they need care. Our findings suggest that arts therapists, through serving the 'vulnerability' agenda and accepting their inherent complicity in a cruel system, are reaching a growing number of prisoners who benefit from the supportive, emancipatory dynamics of the arts therapy space.

Managing and harnessing ambivalence: A compromised resistance

It is not unusual for prison workers, especially those tasked with rehabilitative and caring functions, to describe feeling torn by having to navigate the competing and contradictory objectives of the institution (Bennett et al. 2013; Crawley 2008, 2004). While the participants in our study were keen to differentiate and distance themselves from the carceral logics of prison by embracing their status as outsiders, many also embraced the prison as a unique professional setting that provides them with constructive, rewarding opportunities. We have identified two main sources of ambivalence across participants' accounts: towards the carceral system, its methods and ethics; and towards their profession, its compromises and limitations. The therapists' willingness to endure and confront these emotional conflicts demonstrates, we argue, a deeply humane, and necessary, commitment to providing care in a cruel environment. We further contend that these caring interactions provide more than temporary respite and that some participants perceive them to be acts of resistance; the embodied relations that are produced during arts therapy sessions are a protective factor against further traumatisation and injury and contain the potential to create joyful collaborations and a sense of community (Thompson 2022).

Ambivalence towards the carceral system

Most participants acknowledged the prison to be a deliberately harmful environment, describing the carceral setting as 'traumatic', 'hostile', and a place of 'dehumanisation'. The nature of this harmfulness is complicated by participants' reflections on the personal costs of working in this setting; reflections ranged from wondering whether the pain is perversely self-gratifying ('I wonder if there's something quite self-punitive about what I do. And I've certainly had supervisors that tell me I have a very harsh super ego') to acknowledging their privilege in the form of the protections built in to therapeutic work ('the other day I had a really, really awful dream [about a patient's crimes]... that was very disturbing. But I take it to supervision... I try to look after myself').

Nonetheless, participants seemed able to hold this picture of harm alongside a sense of acceptance. For one participant, the institutionalised nature of her work provides a sense of security:

> the boundaries of the prison make me feel quite contained. And I like working for a big organisation [NHS] that sorts out all my day and my pay and everything. I just feel kind of held by it all.

Aside from the institutional security, this participant also likely reflects a perception of professional security held in contrast to the more precarious, gig-economy jobs market that many arts-based and psychotherapy opportunities fall into.

Another participant expressed interest in the idea that prison might be a 'safe space' for women prisoners and considered what it means to accept this heavily conditioned safety. She also compared what she perceived as her 'bridging' role between authorities and inmates to the role that she played in her family as a child, relating her professional position to the position of navigating the competing expectations of her parents:

> I was really interested in the concept that prison was the safe space for them. And that although some of them really railed against it and hated it and didn't want to be labelled as a criminal, there was a sense that there was a kind of feeling of belonging and camaraderie with the other women. I was just really interested in the kind of splits and the dynamics and how quickly you could get sucked into colluding either with the women and the very anti authority kind of stuff. And I think again, going back to my own family dynamics that was, that's definitely the dynamic I had in my family of having to bridge the two 'enemies' [the prison authority and the anti-establishment]. Of finding a way to make that work. And you know clearly, unconsciously I get something from that too. You know, I benefit in some way from it. By connecting, connecting something in a conflict, kind of bridging the gap.

Comparing prison dynamics to family dynamics is a relatively common trope in the narratives of frontline workers in prisons and probation services (Crawley 2004, 2008), especially among the psychotherapeutically trained, suggesting a (possibly unconscious) view of the system as something natural and potentially nurturing, rather than something alien and inherently malevolent. It highlights a specifically affective, rather than moral, ambivalence towards the institution that provides work and determines its workers' conditions. When the aforementioned participant acknowledges that 'I get something from [the role I play] ... I benefit in some way from it', the implication is that the benefit isn't purely professional but also provides emotional gratification.

A recurring notion in participants' responses was that their work improves the system as a whole, as well as helping individuals. One participant saw herself as performing a supportive function for prisoners and prison officers by facilitating trauma-informed 'reflective practice' for both groups. She describes this split function in a positive, constructive light:

> there's an element of my work that is giving one-to-one art therapy or group therapy, but also [another part] is around supporting the [officer] teams around their thinking, supporting what the boys need.

It is her understanding that her support for the institution helps to ensure that prisoners will get the support they need in turn. This participant explicitly referred to herself as part of the institution: 'the only way we can make it happen as an establishment...'. Another participant accepts the duality of his role, but with more detectable ambivalence:

> Probably I am working for [in the service of punishment], but I don't feel that. But yeah, I see that I am doing that. I also kind of see that what I'm doing is resisting it because I think it's more rehabilitation than punishment.

A third participant evokes the entanglement between the prisoners and the institution:

> I always think about it [the system] as an enactment of the kind of lives these women live. I just sort of feel as if the whole institution is just a personification of the chaos and the kind of neglect in the women's lives. So, it's easy not to take it personally, but it's very frustrating.

Rather than focusing on the system's dehumanising aspects and impenetrability, this perspective presents the system as something the therapist knows how to work with: a giant, externalised, chaotic, and vulnerable psyche.

Across participants' responses, there was a sense that the emotional discomfort they feel in connection with the institution is justified by the chance to contribute something good. One participant talked about the 'magic' and 'miracles' that he witnessed through his work:

> Well, prisons are not easy places. I don't like going into prisons. They're difficult places. It's kind of nerve-wrecking, it's a very uncomfortable place and you're relieved to get out at the end of the day. But then the *magic* happens behind those walls. Really. And *that's what I'm after, that bit of magic*. And it's a miracle if anything happens. These are such difficult environments, but these miracles generally always happen, not every time but 90% of the time. Something magical will happen there.

Thus, participants tended to hold on to the promise of their practice, even as they acknowledged the wider violence of daily life in incarceration.

Professional ambivalence and blurred boundaries

Participants expressed frustration at the many challenges that arise when attempting to carry out creative and/or therapeutic work in a prison setting. A significant obstacle is the fact that the punitive–rehabilitative agenda of the prison, and the broader workings of the justice system, must take priority, so if a patient or a client (as participants interchangeably referred to the prisoners they work with) is relocated, or their case progresses, then their therapy will be interrupted (due to changes e.g. in one's prison location or release date). Inadequate prison staffing, cumbersome administrative procedures, and scheduling issues can all impede the delivery of therapy. One participant described doing the best she can to make up for institutional shortcomings:

> Just the procurement process is so long, and everything gets lost in the prison. So I generally do like to make one big order of arts stuff [supplies, including clay, paints, paper, etc.] that the NHS pays for, that's maybe £200 or something, and then everything else I'll just bring in myself.

Another participant expressed doubt that therapy can ever be effective in such conditions: 'it's a slightly false kind of expectation. People think they will get better. And that's not the way I see it, it's more complex than that, it's not like a medication'. Many participants' comments suggested that formal therapy, linked to the idea of healing, is a secondary aspect of their work, which is mostly focused on providing a sense of coping, personal connection, and, in some cases, on the production of art as an end in itself. One participant explained that prisoners are 'concerned about me getting inside [their] head', highlighting a long-standing scepticism among prisoners towards any form of treatment delivered by the perceived authorities. Fundamentally, therapy requires emotional openness in order to be effective, and the process intentionally provokes raw and vulnerable emotional states; participants recognised that prison is 'a very, very difficult place to show vulnerability... probably almost impossible' (see also Ricciardelli et al. 2015).

Although the goal of arts therapy is not primarily concerned with the aesthetic quality or skill level of what is produced in sessions, some participants recognised that, in a carceral setting, the artistic output may be more successful than the therapeutic one, particularly from a political standpoint. One participant who embeds art therapeutic techniques in animation workshops with young prisoners explained:

> I'm not saying you're going to get better from doing this ... I'm not saying 'how does that make you feel'... I'm trying to make it as safe as possible. But I'm not trying to get anywhere apart from getting them to finish and make a film. I think there are definitely therapeutic benefits, [and] social benefits, I almost think there are political benefits as well. People are given the voice. But it's not therapy in the traditional sense.

A number of participants became therapists after pursuing careers as artists; they continue to identify as artists and value their work helping prisoners to craft and 'complete' fully realised projects: 'thinking of it, I'm mostly commissioned as an artist, but I'm an art therapist'. Perhaps more than its aesthetic value, participants assigned moral and political value to prison art: the 'most important thing about the arts' is their 'humanising force'. One participant acknowledged that arts therapy is a political provocation: 'Imagine the *Daily Mail* reporting [that] prisoners get to do stock-frame animation'.

All of this means that participants often feel uncertain about their place and role and tend to take a rather fluid approach to the limits and boundaries of their job. Several participants described a sense of identification with the prisoners, which they narrated as self-gratifying. This may flow from the lack of a strictly maintained professional setting; instead of showing up as medical staff, the arts therapists show up as themselves. The style of the therapy also allows for considerable discretion and flexibility with regard to the relationships they develop with their patients. Indeed, some participants suggested that their own psychic histories and life experiences enabled them to understand the prison system and prisoners through what they perceived to be a uniquely sympathetic lens. These participants suggested that their biographies conferred on them political and social credibility and legitimacy as professionals tasked with the care of vulnerable people. This anti-establishment 'I understand prisoners' narrative belied a sense that the participants felt politically vulnerable and insecure in their roles and so sought to consolidate their niche 'capital' as a 'different' kind of therapist.

> in my misspent youth I've met quite a few people who have … had brushes with the criminal justice [system].
>
> I think [the prisoners] understand that I kind of look and sound a certain way. I think they can [sense]…that I've had some stuff.
>
> I went to boarding school when I was very young… There's been a lot of writing around boarding school and prisons… in both you're captive… I have a kind of empathy for the people inside the prisons … [I bring] my own narrative into these places and how I understand it.

Participants also expressed a broader political alignment with prisoners: 'I feel like I'm much more in the prison with the prisoners… I feel like I'm sort of doing time with the prisoner'. The idea that prisoners might recognise something 'like' themselves in the therapist seems to be a key belief that motivates arts therapists to enter prison settings.

This sense of identification, or bond, can foster strong positive feelings towards the prisoners. One participant recounted, 'there was one patient in particular…who I really loved'. Others expressed that they relate to, respect, and feel solidarity with their patients, particularly women therapists working in women's prisons: 'I kind of admired them, their survival'. One participant described how she decided to work in prisons when she felt the impact of providing vulnerable, isolated people with a sense of human connection: 'there was something very deep, quite profound, about a relationship that you can have when you're not really talking very much and you're very disturbed and you just need to kind of connect with someone'. The participant remains affected by this relationship – 'I still feel moved when I talk about [the patients] now' – and speaks about the need to guard against 'over-identify[ing] with them too much'.

One participant questioned whether the child prisoners he works with truly pose a danger to society, or whether they are unwell due to a lack of support; he expressed that 'there are very, very few people that need to be in prison', before pinpointing the crux of his confusion: 'holding in mind both the child's need and their offence is difficult'. Arguably, it is through this holding of ambivalence that arts therapists are able to make a change in prisoners' lives. It is precisely through resisting a conflict-resolving identification with one 'side' or the other, but instead navigating the difficult position of relating to both – choosing to engage constructively with institutional power *and* individual suffering – that arts therapists can act as mediators across this painful boundary. It is by fulfilling this inherently ambivalent role that the presence of arts therapies in prisons helps to ameliorate suffering and create space for a kind of activism that we, following Thompson (2022), call 'care aesthetics'.

Towards a carceral care aesthetics

The concept of care aesthetics is premised on the notion that social relations – or 'subject-to-subject attention, an orientation to the other' (Thompson 2022) – have an aesthetic, and that striving for aesthetic quality in our interpersonal interactions can be a powerful means of critiquing and resisting carelessness and cruelty. In a prison context, the relevance of this is clear: where the physical environment and daily regime are designed to produce deprivation and desensitisation, suffering and shame, then any interaction that does not produce these results is transformative, at least momentarily.

This is a theory of aesthetics that goes beyond the objective judgement of an object to encompass insight gained through immersion in embodied sensory experience. Thus, whether the prisoner-patient's work is artistically 'good' or 'not good' is not the sole determinant of aesthetic quality; what matters is the quality of the patient's attention to the object, and of the therapist's attention to the patient. This is a social, rather than an individualised, model of aesthetics. The responses of our participants speak to the truth of this idea: while they all express uncertainty about the aesthetic value of the art and the therapeutic value of the therapy, they have no doubt that their work brings something good into the prisoners' lives.

It is important to clarify that there is a difference between an aesthetic interaction and an everyday one, just as there is in 'traditional' aesthetics a difference between aesthetic appreciation and simply looking. Thompson (2022: 31) argues:

> For an experience to be aesthetic experience, it seems to need a certain structure, an enhanced sense of crafted intent, a particular stimulus of embodied response or affective involvement, and a certain stand out feature which engages with some or all our senses in a way that shifts them from their usual axis.

This resonates with the words of one participant, quoted above: 'there was something very deep, quite profound, about a relationship that you can have when you're not really talking very much and you're very disturbed and you just need to kind of connect with someone'. There is nothing ordinary or easy, for either prisoner or arts therapist, about the interaction that occurs between them; it is, undoubtedly, an interaction that 'must be searching for a quality that extends the diminished sensory register within which much of life, and so much care, is executed' (Thompson 2022: 32).

A social theory of aesthetics highlights that we do not live *in* a sensory world but are more *of* a sensory world, 'producing it through our actions, and produced by it as the sense acts of others interact with our affective lives' (Thompson 2022: 33). Drawing on our conceptualisation of the liminal-shifting arts therapy space, we contend that what takes place inside this space is the construction of new sensory realities that resist punitive agendas and institutionalised systems of control. Arts therapists may not enter prisons with abolitionist aims, but through the professionally crafted provision of care and empathy for suffering individuals, they refuse to maintain the oppressive sensory world created by carceral logics. Furthermore, arts therapists who do this work are exposed to a destabilising, often painful ambivalence, which they must hold and harness in order to be effective in a difficult professional setting.

Conclusion

This chapter has sought to examine the place of arts therapeutic work in UK prisons, drawing attention to the growing, yet institutionally marginalised and ambivalent, status of arts therapists. We have shown that these workers straddle a series of competing roles vis-à-vis the carceral establishments in which they work, their professional connection to therapeutic practice and the wider healthcare system that supports it, and towards the prisoners they see as patients (but whose offending histories they are there to primarily address). Moreover, some of them straddle additional complexities linked to holding a more compound status as therapists and independent artists, and, in some cases, even as activists. We have shown that their affectively complex labour and broader presence inside prisons enable them to craft a distinctive space for their patients and for those they work alongside (including prison staff and other forensic and mental healthcare teams).

This arts therapeutic space is often compromised by various institutional demands and restrictions, but when enabled, it is a space that allows expression (and potentially also healing). Importantly for these therapists, it is also a space that enables a sensorially inter-subjective connection, a kind of solidarity between therapist and prisoner which we analysed as a paradigmatic case of carceral 'care aesthetics' (Thompson 2022). The arts therapists who participated in this study perceive their roles as involving the provision of an *aesthetic space* – in the sensorial and social sense of the term, but also in the artistic sense – for their patients to creatively express themselves *together* in that shared space, despite the prison's wider repressive structures. The embodied connections enabled in arts therapy sessions, many of which involve very little talking but still manage to create a profound sense of connection between patient and therapist, are at the heart of this care aesthetic, which, we have argued, animates the complicated function of arts therapies in prisons.

The arts therapists in our study were motivated to enter carceral and forensic settings because they saw their own life trajectories, and the unique promise of arts therapy more generally, as especially well-suited for responding to the oppressive regimes of such spaces. In that sense, our participants expressed a sense of hesitant faith in their profession to bring about empathy and understanding inside settings that are otherwise hostile to prisoners. They see their jobs as separate from, but not independent from, other work taking place in prisons and acknowledge their distinctive position to respond to a growing cohort of 'vulnerable' prisoners, thus serving therapeutic as well as penal objectives. Though unclear and somewhat confused about the category of the 'vulnerable' prisoner, these participants seemed keen to grasp the professional opportunities arising from the expansion of the vulnerability agenda. Tasked with this growing population of patients, they expressed hope that their positionality in prison healthcare provision may slowly but steadily shift to offer them more professional recognition, legitimacy, and even authority to influence overall care practices in carceral settings.

This chapter has shown that these state-employed professionals see their roles as predominantly care-based, and that they acknowledge that, even though they are in higher demand now, they are still – at least for the time being – treated by prison personnel as 'guests' in these settings. For the most part, they are content with their liminal, part-outsider status. Though often compromising their ability to effect real change, as they tend to be cast in the lower ranks of the prison's professional power structure, this liminal, ambivalent status affords them a relative independence, which they see as indispensable for the work they do as therapists. This status also allows them a sense of political distancing from prison, and thus some ethical and political integrity against prisons' punitive and coercive structures. Herein lies, we have argued, these workers' affective struggle around their professional identities and work inside prisons, in addition to the radical promise they may hold in navigating the prison's punitive–rehabilitative complex.

Participants' accounts repeatedly drew on a desire to enact – through their arts and therapeutic practice, and through their unique, sensory engagements with prisoners – an anti-carceral, anti-authoritarian, cautiously humanitarian practice that sits in contrast with their place of work and the demands imposed upon them. Though not all participants identified as abolitionists, several did. Their narratives of profound connection with their patients remind us of what Norrie (2022) has termed, with regard to the work done at the BSU in the 1980s, the promise of enacting 'abolition from within'. Though that might be too optimistic a reading of the contemporary British prison and its professionals, we nonetheless wish to hold onto these arts therapists' desire to read their own work as an attempt to unsettle the prison's regimes of hostility, security, and repression.

Bibliography

Bennett, J., Crewe, B. and Wahidin, A. (eds.) (2013) *Understanding Prison Staff*, London: Willan.

Boltanski, L. (1999) 'The Politics of Pity'. In: *Distant Suffering: Morality, Media and Politics*. Cambridge Cultural Social Studies, Cambridge: Cambridge University Press, pp. 3–19.

Bosworth, M., and von Zinnenburg Carroll, K. (2017) 'Art and Criminology of the Border: The Making of the Immigration Detention Archive', *OAR: The Oxford Artistic and Practice Based Research Platform* (1), www.oarplatform.com/art-criminology-border-making-immigration-detention-archive/

Brown, K., Ecclestone, K. and Emmel, N. (2017) 'The Many Faces of Vulnerability', *Social Policy and Society*, Vol. 16 (3), pp. 497–510.

Carvalho, H. and Chamberlen, A. (2024) *Questioning Punishment*, London: Routledge.

Carvalho, H., Chamberlen, A. and Lewis, R. (2020) 'Punitiveness beyond Criminal Justice: Punishable and Punitive Subjects in an Era of Prevention, Anti-migration and Austerity', *British Journal of Criminology*, Vol. 60 (2), pp. 265–284.

Carvalho, H., Foreman, S., Tawfic, S., Aliverti, A., Chamberlen, A. and Rawson, B. (2025) 'Modern Slavery and the Punitive-Humanitarian Complex', *British Journal of Criminology*, Vol. 65 (1), pp. 93–109.

Chamberlen, A. and Carvalho, H. (2019) 'The Thrill of the Chase: Punishment, Hostility and the Prison Crisis', *Social & Legal Studies*, Vol. 28 (1), pp. 100–117.

Cheliotis, L. (2014) 'Decorative Justice: Deconstructing the Relationship between the Arts and Imprisonment', *International Journal of Crime, Justice & Social Democracy*, Vol. 3 (1), pp. 16–34.

Crawley, E. (2004) *Doing Prison Work*, London: Routledge.

Crawley, E. (2008) 'Prison Governors: Managing Prisons in a Time of Change', *The British Journal of Criminology*, Vol. 48 (1), pp. 105–108.

Cullen, F. T., Fisher, B. S. and Applegate, B. K. (2000) 'Public Opinion about Punishment and Corrections', *Crime and Justice*, Vol. 27, pp. 1–79.

Gilson, E. (2016) 'The Perils and Privileges of Vulnerability: Intersectionality, Relationality, and the Injustices of the U.S. Prison Nation', *PhiloSOPHIA*, Vol. 6 (1), pp. 43–59.

Gussak, D. (2019) *Art and Art Therapy with the Imprisoned: Re-creating Identity*, New York: Routledge.

HMPPS (2023) 'Prison Life: 4. Vulnerable prisoners'. [Accessed: 17 July 2024] available online: www.gov.uk/life-in-prison/print

Inspectorate of Prisons (CJJI) (2021) 'Neurodiversity in the Criminal Justice System: A review of evidence', London: Ministry of Justice. [Accessed: 17 July 2024] available online: www.justiceinspectorates.gov.uk/cjji/wp-content/uploads/sites/2/2021/07/Neurodiversity-evidence-review-web-2021.pdf

Liebling, A. (1999) 'Prisoner Suicide and Prisoner Coping', *Crime and Justice*, Vol. 26, pp. 283–359.

Lynch, M. (2004) 'Punishing Images: Jail Cam and the Changing Penal Enterprise', *Punishment & Society*, Vol. 6 (3), pp. 255–270.

Maguire, D. (2021) 'Vulnerable Prisoner Masculinities in an English Prison', *Men and Masculinities*, Vol. 24 (3), pp. 501–518.

Maruna, S. (2001) *Making Good: How Ex-convicts Reform and Rebuild Their Lives*, New York: American Psychological Association.

Nellis, M. (2010) 'Creative Arts and the Cultural Politics of Penal Reform: The Early Years of the Barlinnie Special Unit, 1973–1981', *Journal of Scottish Criminal Justice Studies*, Vol. 20, pp. 304–334.

Norrie, A. (2022) 'Restoration, Abolition and the Loving Prison: Jimmie Boyle and Barlinnie Special Unit', *Howard Journal of Crime and Justice*, Vol. 61 (1), pp. 103–116.

Regev, D. and Cohen-Yatziv, L. (2018) 'Effectiveness of Art Therapy with Adult Clients', *Frontiers in Psychology*, Vol. 29 (9), p. 1531.

Ricciardelli, R., Maier, K. and Hannah-Moffat, K. (2015). 'Strategic Masculinities: Vulnerabilities, Risk and the Production of Prison Masculinities', *Theoretical Criminology*, Vol. 19 (4), pp. 491–513.

Rock, P. (1996) *Reconstructing a Women's Prison: The Holloway Redevelopment Project 1968–88*, Oxford: Oxford University Press.

Shaw, A. and McGivern, H. (2023, July 11) 'Special Report: Funding Cuts and Weak Economy Send UK's Visual Arts into Crisis', *The Art Newspaper*, available online: www.theartnewspaper.com/2023/07/11/special-report-funding-cuts-and-weak-economy-send-uks-visual-arts-into-crisis

Sim, J. (1990) *Medical Power in Prisons: The Prison Medical Service in England 1774–1989*, Milton Keynes: Open University Press.

Smith, T. (ed.) (2023) *Autism and Criminal Justice: The Experience of Suspects, Defendants and Offenders in England and Wales*, London: Routledge.

Thompson, J. (2009) *Performance Affects: Applied Theatre and the End of Effect*, London: Palgrave Macmillan.

Thompson, J. (2022) *Care Aesthetics: For Artful Care and Careful Art*, London: Routledge.

van den Broek, E. P. A., Strijbos, N., Vromen, J., van Duursen, S., Cousijn, J., Bosschaert, L., Zeegers, L., van Zeeland, G., Pouwels, S., van den Berge, M.,

Vallentin, R., Korsten, D. and Keulen-de Vos, M. (2021) 'A Pilot Study of Arts Therapy Techniques to Evoke Emotional States in Forensic Patients', *The Arts in Psychotherapy*, Vol. 74, 101798.

Vanliefde, A. (2024) 'Vulnerability and Victimhood in Prison: Reflecting on the Concept of Vulnerability in Prisoner Victimisation Research'. In: Daems, T., Goossens, E. (eds) *Understanding Prisoner Victimisation*. Palgrave Studies in Victims and Victimology, London: Palgrave Macmillan, pp. 115–142.

Walker, D. (1991) *Becoming a Profession: The History of Art Therapy in Britain 1940–82*, London: Routledge.

Warr, J. (2020) *Forensic Psychologists: Prisons, Power, and Vulnerability* London: Emerald Publishing.

14
INSTITUTIONALISED HELPER INTERACTIONS AND STRUCTURALLY EMBEDDED EMOTIONS

Welfare assistance as a social form

Åsa Wettergren

Introduction

The aim of this chapter is to theorise state-organised social welfare to citizens and migrants as an institutionalised helper interaction enacting and reproducing structurally embedded emotions. Structurally embedded emotions are collective emotional dispositions which originate from institutionalised inequality (Barbalet 1998). Approaching the helper interaction as a social form, I will outline ideal-typical positions of the institutionalised helper interaction along with the emotion work and typical emotional outcomes for 'the helper' and 'the receiver'. Through this lens, I suggest, we can begin to see how structurally embedded emotions inform top-down engagement with poverty and how receivers of welfare become reified rather than empowered in their agency. While my focus will be on the Swedish welfare state, I suggest that the social form and its emotional components are theoretically generalisable to institutionalised helper interactions in similar modern welfare states, whether state-financed social welfare distribution is organised via the municipalities or via civil society organisations.

Inspired by Simmel, I here use the concept of social form as denoting a social event, building on common and recurrent interactions between at least two persons. The social form is arguably socio-culturally and historically contingent, but the type of interaction itself may be universal. The rich, or better off, giving to the poor, or people in need, is discussed by Mauss ([1925] 2025) as part of the magic or religious sets of beliefs of 'archaic' societies. In modern societies, the social form of redistribution from rich to poor takes on other, more secular emotiv-cognitive motives. Regarding this modern form of assistance to the poor, Simmel writes:

> The goal of assistance is (...) to mitigate certain extreme manifestations of social differentiation, so that the social structure may continue to be based on this differentiation. If assistance were to be based on the interests of the poor person, there would, in principle, be no limit whatsoever on the transmission of property in favor of the poor, a transmission that would lead to the equality of all. But since the focus is the social whole (...) there is no reason to aid the person more than is required by the maintenance of the social status quo.
>
> *(Simmel 1971 [1908]: 155)*

I will take this lucid statement of Simmel as a point of departure to discuss the emotions embedded in the structural and abstract relationships between the state as a giver and the receivers of welfare assistance. I will argue that despite the rational 'unemotional' and objective ('disembodied') appearance of state-organised welfare, the conditioned micro-relation between the social worker/frontliner and the welfare recipient communicates the emotive-cognitive ideology of ruling groups. While the idea that social relations of inequality and hierarchy are regulated and anchored by emotion is far from new (e.g. Neckel 1991) it may still be controversial to say that emotions are not simply the unintended outcomes of the way that societies are organised, but rather, societies are organised in specific ways *because* of certain *desired* emotional outcomes.

The overall purpose of my argument is to highlight welfare state assistance as a function of 'the emotional' state (Jefferson, this volume). I will argue that (i) the institutionalised helper interaction is a distinct social form oriented by structurally embedded emotions; (ii) this form moulds the emotive-cognitive roles of helpers (social/frontline workers) and receivers (vulnerable citizens and migrants) and constricts the action space of those roles. Both helpers and receivers are locked in their roles with detrimental consequences for both; (iii) If the goal of the welfare state is, at least, to forge collective emotions of solidarity, security, and belonging, among all categories of people living within its territorial boarders, the construction of the institutionalised helper interaction must be reconsidered, specifically acknowledging its fundamental significance for the long-term emotive-cognitive effects on the targeted vulnerable groups.

The reader should keep in mind that when the argumentation outlines the institutionalised helper interaction as a social form, this is a distilled theoretical approach akin to Weber's (1978) ideal-type and Durkheim's (1964) social fact. Previous studies of the intersection of humanitarian and disciplinary measures of the Swedish welfare state abound with sociological indignation at the misdirected and humiliating effects of what is set up to be an expression of the state's respect for human rights and a nation's good intentions (e.g. Barker 2012). In my own previous research, I studied the reception of forced migrants in Italy and Sweden and was shaken by discovering how the well-intended assistance to this group, albeit differently organised and with very different access to resources in the two countries, effectively eroded the self-feelings (self-confidence, pride, and recognition) of receivers and diminished their chances of successful integration. The concept of the institutionalised helper interaction developed in this paper, I propose, can be used as a theoretical sensitiser to enhance understanding of how such outcomes are conditioned by the locked positions of both the frontline worker and the receiver.

The institutionalised helper interaction consists of emotional exchange at two levels; on the one hand, the micro-setting of the one-to-one relation between giver and receiver, and on the other, of the institutionalised set-up, in which the helper role is ultimately determined by 'the emotional state' (Jefferson, this volume). In the following two sections, I will clarify what I mean by this, taking Simmel's discussion as a point of departure. Thereafter, I continue to expand on the social form of the institutionalised helper interaction, its roles, and its inherent emotional careers.

Emotional micro-exchanges

Simmel discusses two forms of assistance to the poor, the one-to-one relation (e.g. giving money to a beggar) and the state-organised welfare assistance. In this section I focus on the one-to-one relation on the micro-level and expand on the emotional exchange, which is underdeveloped in Simmel's essay. Helping the poor is governed by the giver's 'moral instinct' Simmel (1971: 164) argues. This can be understood in terms of Clark's (1997) theory of sympathy – 'feeling sorry for or with another person' (Clark 1987:291) – as a fundamental social emotion (see also Smith [1759] 2006). Sympathy is a 'role-taking emotion' and thus premised on empathy, which is not an emotion but the act of imagining oneself in the situation of the other (Morton 2013). Sympathy offered when asked for is an important sign of recognition, or put differently, sympathy signals recognition of the other's suffering. As an emotion of reciprocal recognition, sympathy is surrounded by social feeling rules that produce and are produced by hierarchies in social organisation, in turn confirming and reinforcing relations of power and intimacy between actors (Clark 1987).

Expanding on the structuring function of sympathy, Clark (1987) introduces the notion of sympathy as a resource exchanged under market-like conditions, the sympathy economy, relating to 'sympathy biography' and 'sympathy accounts'. Mutual exchange of sympathy establishes equality, trust, and intimacy in a relationship, but this reciprocity also depends on the change of positions of the actors over time. The sympathiser at one point in time opens a sympathy account with the sympathisee, to be retrieved when the former sympathiser instead is in need of sympathy. Accepting sympathy thus implicitly entails that a present sympathiser will accept the sympathisee's sympathy offered in return, in the future. If sympathy is not offered, or if it is rejected, trust and intimacy are at risk, and the equality of the relationship is disrupted. Offering or rejecting sympathy can be part of a negotiation of status through emotional exchange, that is 'emotional micro-politics' (Clark 1990).

Following the norms of the sympathy economy, in asymmetrical relationships, sympathy is usually offered downwards. Reversing this order represents a risky claim to intimacy and equality by the inferior actor. Instead, the expected recognition in return for downwards sympathy is *gratitude* (Clark 1987). In this light, the one-to-one offering of assistance to the poor is an exchange of sympathy for gratitude, making the giver feel good. But this emotional exchange also reproduces the superior-inferior positions: in exchange for recognition of their need and money, regardless of how much is given, the receiver must perform the emotion work of evoking feelings of goodness in the giver (cf Hochschild 1983).

The one-to-one assistance, Simmel further argues, may establish an emotional bond (in Simmelian terms 'moral induction') that requires continued giving (Simmel 1971: 163–4). However, following Clark (1987), a one-sided offering of sympathy over a long time wears on a relationship – the receiver will eventually be perceived as a carrier of a 'deviant' sympathy biography. Eventually, the giver will close the account and ignore the other's suffering.

This brings us to the other side of assistance to the poor, which is denied sympathy, evoking shame and humiliation in the micro-political exchange of emotions. Shame, according to Scheff (1990), is a 'master emotion' fundamental for social conformity with norms and feeling rules. Shame is a painful self-reflective feeling of low self-worth in the eyes of others, informing the actor of a potential 'threat to the social bond' (Scheff 1990), i.e. of pending social exclusion. The relationship between shame and humiliation is elucidated by Smith (2001), who defines humiliation as

> the forced ejection and/or exclusion of individuals or groups from social roles and/or social categories with which they subjectively identify in a way that conveys the message that they are fundamentally inadequate to fill those roles or belong to those categories.
>
> *(Smith 2001:542)*

If the function of shame is conformity with regulations and social norms (Scheff 1990), the function of humiliation is to shame and ultimately to exclude.

The emotional state

The second form of assistance to the poor discussed by Simmel (1971:165–6) is when this is taken over by the state and ceases to be a one-to-one relationship. The relation between giver and receiver then passes 'from the immediate sensate form to the abstract' and the 'immediate visibility' of misery turns into a 'general concept of poverty'. The welfare state also instates *assistance as a right*, removing it, Simmel claims, from the domain of morality to the domain of citizenship and legally confirmed rights. Claiming assistance as a right, it becomes easier for the poor to avoid 'the humiliation, shame, and *déclassement* that charity implies' (Simmel 1971:152 emphasis in original).

This argument echoes the modern conviction that rationality and emotion could be separated (Barbalet 1998), asserting that modern bureaucratic rationality has nothing to do with emotions (Weber 1998). Refuting this, it should be noted that political ideologies are saturated by emotions and explicit or implicit feeling rules (Stearns 1994, Stearns and Stearns 1985; Scheer 2021; Johnson et al. 2010, Johnson 2013). Political power comes with an emotional regime (Reddy 2001) embedded in ideological discourses informing social morality, distinctions between the deserving and the undeserving, the good and the bad, prioritising some groups on behalf of others (Jacobsson and Johansson 2025). Emotion communicates meaning and laws, regulations, distinctions, and categories, all of which become truly meaningful only when actors *feel* them, that is, care about them and therefore adapt their behaviour accordingly (cf. Helm 2009; Wettergren 2025). A government's political composition and its ideological discourses have direct consequences not just for the policy and practice of the welfare state, but also, via the implicit feeling rules, for how the policy feels (Holt 2025; Therborn 2018; Taylor-Gooby et al. 2018; Neckel 1996). Given the history of the labour movement and the ideological goal of more equal societies, the intention behind the Swedish social democratic welfare state until the 1980s may well have been to protect the citizen from poverty and unemployment (Broström 2015; Esping-Andersen 1990; Mau 2015). Through the right to social and unemployment benefits, and by depersonalising the asymmetrical sympathy exchange of the helper interaction, assistance would no longer involve either humiliation or shame, as it would be effectuated on objective grounds and by rational bureaucratic means (Weber 1998).

The 'objective' grounds in case of the social democratic welfare state were fuelled and oriented by structurally embedded collective emotions of *care* for the working class and *resentment* towards capitalism (Barbalet 1998; cf Broström 2015). Even so, as noted by Simmel (1971), the person receiving welfare benefits *is* in fact required to return it with gratitude and loyalty to the giving state and with different kinds of submissiveness to the abuses of personal integrity inherent to means tests[1] and other terms and conditions of assistance (Hansen-Löfstrand 2005; Broström 2015; Philipson Isaac 2024). This is even more accentuated in the present by the quid pro quo discourse of the political emotional regime after the breakthrough of neoliberalism in the 1980s (Holt 2025; Philipson Isaac 2024; Therborn 2018; Broström 2015). In Sweden, access to social assistance has become markedly more conditional, much less trusting, and certainly much less generous (Jacobsson and Johansson 2025). But it is also true that collective solidarity of the social democratic welfare state, at least until the 1980s, presumed a shared moral consciousness dictating *not* seeking social assistance, claiming fellow taxpayers' money, unless as a last resort. Hence, the reception of social assistance was always associated with potential shame of being seen as a 'sponger' (Neckel 1996; Monrad 2024; Broström 2015; Fraser and Gordon 1994). I suggest that the function of this risk of being shamed, in any welfare state, is to protect the welfare institution from abuse. If this function was implicit in the past, it is rather explicit in the present, which brings us back to the relation between shame and humiliation.

I will focus on two types of humiliation, advanced by Smith (2001: 543), which are especially pertinent to the situation of low status groups in society: *expulsion-humiliation* as the ejection of an individual or group from 'a society to which they previously [believed that they] belonged', for instance through banishment; and *reinforcement-humiliation* as the 'routine abuse of inferiors in order to maintain the perception that they are, indeed, inferior'. Successful reinforcement humiliation in effect removes the link between humiliation and shame since the 'standards of superior beings are not applicable to inferiors' (Smith 2001: 545, compare de la Reguera, this volume). This said, the structural conditions under which humiliated actors accept an inferior position without shame are challenged by modern norms and values of individualism, equal opportunities, and human rights. Scheff (1990) argues that in this context shame is socially distributed to keep the lower classes convinced of their inabilities while idealising the abilities of the elite classes. I suggest that the distribution is effective by means of different humiliation rituals that produce and reproduce shame among the lower classes. In the context of institutionalised helper interactions, means testing is a systemic humiliation ritual, signalling that a claimant of social assistance may not be *needing enough*.

Controlling, for instance, claimants' income and assets may lead to rejection of assistance because they own their apartment (this is true for about 60% of Swedish households since the selling out of social housing began in the 1990s). The claimant must sell their home and live off that money. The unemployed must provide proof of a certain number of job applications each week, within and below their qualifications, close to their home, or at the other end of the country, to receive unemployment benefits.

The long-term sick must prove they are all but dying to be deemed worthy of public health insurance, and the same goes for the elderly in need of public home care service. These examples illustrate expulsion humiliation. They are not just about the possible denial of the right to assistance, but foremost about the denial of rights taken for granted by taxpaying citizens – *to whom the claimants believed that they belonged*. Add to this the invention of quid pro quo activities like time-consuming courses and coaching, or unpaid community service, all of which are primarily set up to control their time (cf. Philipson Isaac 2024), and we have reinforcement humiliation. These humiliation rituals function to deter abuse of welfare assistance through shaming, in line with a dominant political discourse of distrust and contempt of the poor and dependent (cf Fraser and Gordon 1994). Already 25 years ago, Rantakeisu and Starrin (1999) showed that the meaning of these rituals is indeed *felt*, as reported shame and experience of being shamed turned out as one of the explanatory factors in the occurrence of the disproportionate amount of ill-health among the unemployed and recipients of welfare benefits, as compared to the general population.

The amount of shame induced by dependency on welfare services and the character and extent of the humiliation rituals are thus associated with dominant discourses about the character of welfare recipients, which are in turn shaped by the emotional regimes of political ideologies (Johnson 2010). Contingent on the dominant discourse, through laws and directives, the relations between citizen and frontline worker move on a continuum between top-down trust and distrust, with an impact on both the popular and the professional (social/frontline worker) imagery of the welfare recipients (cf Esping-Andersen 1990).

While the category of the receiver has so far been discussed in general terms, there is a marked difference between citizens and non-citizens. Citizens have the right to claim the state's protection and welfare services, but forced migrants' rights vis-à-vis the receiving state are conditioned by its discretion and willingness to offer help to non-citizens (cf Derrida 2001; Khosravi 2006). Indeed, the receiving state is the one responsible for realising forced migrants' human rights, since there are no supranational institutions to fulfil this function (e.g. Castles 2003). The reception of asylum seekers may thus ideally be seen as a benevolent and humanitarian act, an act of helping those in need by accepting them in the nation state and granting them access to (some restricted version of) welfare services (e.g. Ticktin 2014, 2016). When looking at the role of institutionalised helper interactions and how these are imbued by emotions in line with the current state emotional regime, reflecting its view of the poor, migrants can analytically be seen as an extreme case of receivers (Aliverti, de la Reguera, this volume).

The social form of the institutionalised helper interaction is thus the state's means to regulate both symbolic and material resources, managing different group's feelings of belonging to the nation. In the following two sections, I will elaborate on the roles and emotional careers involved.

The social form of the institutionalised helper interaction

That public shaming felt by the receiver of social assistance is linked to the loss of status in a socio-cultural context of individualism (Bauman 1997; Neckel 1996; Sennett 1998), where dependency is judged by a moral register as 'an individual character trait like lack of will power or excessive emotional neediness' (Fraser and Gordon 1994: 312). I argued in the previous sections that the degree of shame ties in with the dominant political discourses. In the practice of the institutionalised helper interaction, the intensity of felt shame relates to the humiliation rituals, where the experience of expulsion humiliation may generate more shame, while experiencing reinforcement humiliation may eventually lead to numbing, and thus repressed shame (Hochschild 1983; Smith 2001). As mentioned earlier, ultimately, shaming is a tool of the welfare state economy, regulating the number of people, at any given moment, who depend on welfare state services of any kind, from sickness and unemployment benefits to social welfare benefits. Consequently, if the state is short of money or if the people in need are 'too many', shaming mechanisms may encompass more humiliation rituals. In the context of migrants, these rituals can become forces of expulsion humiliation, literally removing migrant physically and morally from rights-entitled citizens (Philipson Isaac 2024).

Migrants experience expulsion humiliation when they realise that their claims to the right to protection (established by the 1951 Geneva Convention) are dependent on the host nation's will to guarantee it (Derrida 2001; Derrida and Dufourmentelle 2000; Rosello, 2001). The migrant is literally expelled through the widely endorsed practice of deportation, often involving both mental and physical violence of the kind that not only deny the migrant access to recognition as a potential member of a nation, but also deliberately ignores their universal human rights (Castles and Davidson 2000; Ellerman 2006; Hansen 2008; Guiraudon and Lahav 2000; Khosravi 2006). It is ultimately from the aspired belonging to a community of humans, having human rights, that the unwelcome forced migrant is expelled.

Reinforcement humiliation is experienced by migrants as they are deliberately kept on the margins of the welfare state, its standards of rights for citizens. Humiliation with the purpose of making it clear that the migrants are inferior to host country citizens is explicitly employed as a deterrence strategy (Fassin 2005; Brekke and Sörholt 2005; Gibson 2003; Wettergren and Wikström 2013). But also after the migrant has received their residence permit, the intertwined processes of reinforcement and expulsion humiliation continue, now within the perimeters of the nation state (Wettergren 2013; Flam and Beauzamy 2008). This is arguably exacerbated by the increasingly restrictive migration regimes, a path followed by Sweden in the wake of the 2015 'refugee crisis', entailing a shift from permanent to temporary resident permits for accepted forced migrants, and a multitude of new humiliation rituals (Philipson Isaac 2024).

The roles

The institutionalised helper interactions control the range of options available to the client, assessing their person and its symbolic and cultural capital with regard to the standards and requirements of the institution. Emotional rewards for a social benefit recipient, for instance, pertain to the recognition that may be received for behaving as a 'good' client (Hansen-Löfstrand 2005), but inhabiting and performing this role forecloses other potential roles of the recipient because these either complicate or are irrelevant for the institutionalised helper interaction. In other words, locking the recipient in the role of receiver of help by way of the power invested in the social worker reduces the agency of the recipient.

On the other end of the interaction, we find the helper, the social/frontline worker. They may be working for a private company, an NGO, or the state, but in each case, the helper is invested with the power to decide or at least influence decisions concerning whether, how much, and what assistance to offer to particular claimants. The help offered consists wholly or partly of state resources, and the helper's relation to distributing these resources is contingent on the political and organisational discourses about the value of the resources and the 'general character' of the potential receivers of help (Aliverti, Braddock et al., this volume). The helper may either consider their position primarily as a 'guardian of scarce resources' or as a 'humanitarian agent' (e.g. Nario-Lopez, this volume). In line with the neoliberal turn, the public sector of Swedish and European welfare states has been steadily shrinking, along with deregulation, privatisation, and the lowering of taxes, while state resources have been geared towards maintaining the living standards of the middle classes, through various subsidies and tax deductions (Therborn 2018; Mau 2015; Koch 2021). This gives some ground for the 'guardian' perspective, arguing that public social services operate with scarce resources. In addition, new public management, the preferred neoliberal form of management of public institutions, prioritises budget-goals over organisational core-activities, encouraging and conceiving those who assume the 'guardian' role as loyal to the organisation (Holt 2025). Along with the political emotional regime implicit in this governing of social welfare services, the person inhabiting the role of helper finds themselves in a situation that effectively paves the way for particular patterns of emotive-cognitive behaviour towards the receiver (Jacobsson and Johansson 2025).

The recognition and emotional energy retrieved by fulfilling one's role as helper derive from a continuum where power over the receiver is emphasised on the one end (the guardian), and disregarded or refuted on the other (the humanitarian agent) (Maynard-Moody and Musheno. 2003). If power is emphasised, the helper is likely to act as guardian of scarce resources where distrust is the emotive-cognitive starting point, and receivers must prove that they are not trying to swindle the state out of money. At this end of the continuum, the helper is unlikely to receive recognition (e.g. gratitude) from interacting with the receiver. The helper is instead likely to get 'feelings of goodness' from peers in the organisation; the harsher the decisions they take, overcoming 'personal feelings' of sympathy for the client while reproducing the norms and rules governing the allocation of help, the more they will be recognised as a good, loyal professional (Wettergren 2010).

If the humanitarian agent is instead enacted, power will be disregarded to emphasise trust in, and sympathy for, the receivers' 'authentic' need of assistance. The helper is then likely to gain feelings of goodness from the interaction with the receiver due to gratitude and recognition from the latter. The helper's power may be concealed, but it still defines the form of the interaction, which is an asymmetrical helper interaction premised on scarce resources. The helper may go beyond the rules and give more of their time and engagement than prescribed by the organisation (Nario-Lopez, this volume). The receiver may be allowed more space for expressing him or herself but must keep navigating between the authentic suffering (worthy) and the inauthentic suffering (unworthy) receiver. Any sign of too much self-confident agency or dissatisfaction with the help given may 'reveal' them as cheaters (but see Monrad 2024).

Based on the roles outlined here, in the following, I will discuss some possible emotional outcomes, in terms of emotional careers (Wettergren 2015b) of each role. This builds on patterns found in my previous research on the reception of asylum seekers in Italy and Sweden and is therefore derived from typical cases of long-term institutional helper interactions. The institutional helper's emotional career is, I argue, shaped by the duration of their professional occupation and the great number of people in need who, often, have very similar stories. This said, empathic engagement with long-term recipients can make the limitations of the help offered particularly apparent and push an emotive-cognitive reframing of the meaning of their work. On the receiving end, a long-term positioning as receiver of assistance is likely to affect their personal emotional careers, by exacerbating the elements of shame and humiliation with long-term consequences for the actor's self-feelings (Wettergren 2015b).

Emotional careers of helper interaction roles

The helper: From sympathy to professional 'empathy' or the cynic

Professional helpers often begin as humanitarian agents, believing that they will 'make a difference' but eventually finding themselves locked in a structurally superior position, their task being defined by rules and regulations and, perhaps most importantly, by budget and productivity goals (Wettergren 2010; Holt 2024, Jacobsson and Johansson 2025, see also Bennett, this volume). Insofar as they do feel sympathy for their clients, legal restrictions put on the help they can offer may invoke feelings of shame, if the client expects more from them than they can offer, and guilt as they must perform as agents of a system that demands humiliating submissiveness from the client (Kemper 2001). These emotions, signalling a degree of identification with the client, may, if nothing else, bolster sympathy for the client's situation.

We may recall that sympathy is not required for the institutionalised helper interaction to function, but it seems hard to avoid in the beginning. For instance, frontliners in refugee reception describe an emotional career from intensely felt sympathy (including pity, compassion, grief) when they first began to work with the migrants, through to a process of professionalisation where they distanced themselves from the migrants (Wettergren 2013). This is an emotional career in which professional distancing takes place primarily in response to the general emotional overload of the job. Professionalisation in this case proactively protects against, or is an effect of, sympathy burnout (Clark 1997). Through professionalisation, the frontliner shifts from loyalty to the goal of frontline social work (to really help), to loyalty to the organisation (keeping the budget) as a way to protect the self from painful emotions. A variant of this emotional career develops when a client is caught making what the social/frontline worker perceives as false claims to sympathy: for instance, when a migrant is caught lying about key events or about her or his identity. Such 'wake-up calls' can evoke shame for being a bad ('naive' or 'too kind') professional and tend to be seen as *a cue* to professionalisation (Wettergren 2013; Holt 2025).

Professionalisation may go in different emotional directions. In some institutionalised helper organisations, *empathy* is regarded as a management ideal that should be part of being professional. A restricted version of empathy is here employed, as a way to keep a distance *without acting disrespectfully* towards the client (Jacobsson and Johansson 2025; Larsson 2014; Holt 2025, see also Zacka 2017). Implying respect but not sympathy, it means that helpers try to stay attuned only to those dimensions of the clients that are meaningful to the type of help they can or may offer (cf Wettergren and Bergman Blix 2016). In other words, professional empathy accompanies *clientisation*, that is, '[t]he processing of people into clients, assigning them to categories for treatment by bureaucrats, and treating them in terms of those categories' (Lipsky 1980: 59; see also Hansen-Löfstrand 2005). Professionalisation means that frontliners begin to orient their emotions *away* from the clients *towards* the performance of the job and the emotional regime of the organisation. Rewards in terms of recognition and feelings of goodness of a job well done are retrieved from colleagues and superiors in the organisation for the successful performance of the professional emotive-cognitive script, not for successfully helping a client (Wettergren 2010; Jacobsson and Håkansson 2025).

If professionalisation instead occurs following a client's *false claim to sympathy* (understood by the social/frontline worker as revealing of inauthentic suffering), the distancing of the professional helper may be fuelled by feelings of broken trust (disappointment, self-doubt, and generalised distrust, see e.g. Barbalet 2009) and strong feelings of resentment. The trust breach is fundamentally humiliating for the professional helper, who is now instead shamed and exposed to colleagues as 'emotional', aka 'unprofessional' (Wettergren 2010). But it is not anger that appears to be the dominant emotion directed at receivers in response to such an experience; it is *disgust*, because the other has claimed undeserved status (Kemper 2001). Frontliners and social workers call this emotional career 'becoming cynical' (Wettergren 2010; Holt 2025, see also Aliverti, this volume). In my own study of the reception of asylum seekers (Wettergren 2010), some frontliners thought cynicism was an inevitable outcome of staying in the job for too long, indicating that professionalisation can eventually be a trajectory towards becoming a guardian of scarce resources.

The receiver: From dignity protection to the humiliated habitus

As mentioned previously, the receivers in focus here are the ones engaged in long-term relations with social assistance, such as long-term sick leave, long-term unemployment, or homelessness in combination with drug or alcohol addiction. These long-term receivers of assistance resemble the forced migrants participating in my study (Wettergren 2013).

The receivers' emotional careers begin with the hopes they nurture for a future improved situation by means of the assistance they can get (cf Wettergren 2025). For forced migrants, this hope contains the dream of 'a normal life' (Herz et al. 2022; Wettergren 2013). The kind of assistance typically sought by those who leave their country due to war, persecution, climate catastrophes, or poverty is a place to live and economic means to get by, while searching for a job, possibly via education first. In the long run, migrants who held, or aspired to, middle-class positions in the country of origin hope to be able to achieve something like the middle class in the host country. This means, forced migrants generally wish, and often expect, initial and quick help to self-help; to settle and get started, work and pay taxes, in the new country (Wettergren 2013). For people who are already included in the welfare state, like citizens, and who have come across serious trouble that requires long-term support, the needs and hopes may include other things. The long-term sick, for instance, may hope for a permanent disability pension. Perhaps the most noteworthy characteristic of the emotional career of the forced migrant is that their expectations to quickly get to support themselves are usually not met. Instead, they get locked in a long-term helper interaction that requires constant monitoring and disciplined emotion work to protect the self from shame and humiliation (Wettergren 2015a). This may also be true for citizens who are long-term receivers of welfare assistance (e.g. Hansen-Löfstrand 2005). In general, people 'in dependency' develop strategies to suppress feelings of shame, anger, resentment, and disappointment; they cannot allow themselves the freedom to express such emotions, and in some cases not even to 'feel' them, and thus avoid introspecting their emotional well-being (Wettergren 2015a). Firstly because they need to focus firmly on the future hope-object – e.g. the dream of a 'normal' life or a disability pension – in order to maintain feelings of hope, and secondly because the priority of definition of their situation is in the hands of the helpers; the receivers' emotional expressions are watched and interpreted by others with the power to give or to deny the help needed.

In terms of humiliation and shame, long-term receivers of help have no choice but to endure and cope with it. Migrants share this situation with the groups of citizens or denizens in the host country who are on the lowest level of the social status ladder. If they enter the institutionalised helper interaction with self-confidence and belief in their right to assistance, the longer they stay in the situation of dependency, the more they risk having their feelings of self-worth eroded. If the helper is a 'humanitarian agent', the receiver may start out with sincere expectations to really get the help needed to get going. When these expectations are disappointed, reacting with a sense of entitlement is risky. Acting with too much confidence and competence can raise the helper's irritation and dislike, and suspicion of false claims (Wettergren and Wikström 2013; Hansen-Löfstrand 2005). At this point, they realise that they are confined to the role of either a worthy or unworthy receiver. In other words, receivers will need to continuously display the emotive-cognitive script of a person in righteous need, bearing a reasonable amount of suffering and gratitude in recognition of the help they get, whether it promotes or hinders any substantial change in their life (Philipson Isaac 2024).

The helper-interaction is contingent on rules and regulations of the organisation or bureaucratic institution, which is usually running with tight budget-goals. This means that the austerity embedded in the regulations will become sensed by the receiver as structural distrust and contempt, despite the helping 'humanitarian agent' who cannot help but disappoint the hopes of the receiver. The 'good and worthy' receiver may then shift into the 'bad and unworthy', if nothing else, to maintain a sense of self-worth and dignity (Wettergren 2015b). This may be done in secret, for instance, a migrant taking on undeclared work to improve the insufficient cash flow, or an unemployed person pursuing education while on unemployment benefits. In relation to the helper, the actor continues to perform the good receiver by 'surface acting' the required humility and gratitude (Hochschild 1983).

Being forced to separate the displayed self from the 'real' self leads to such 'secondary arrangement' understood by Goffman (1961: 189) as: 'any habitual arrangement by which a member of an organisation employs unauthorised means, or obtains unauthorised ends, or both, thus getting around the organisation's assumptions as to what he should do and get and hence what he should be'. Secondary arrangement is a way to preserve dignity for oneself by actually refusing enforced humiliation rituals to govern one's life. Surface acting is the emotion work of secondary arrangements. If suspected, it will increase control measures, which will in turn increase humiliation and shame, going both ways in the interaction, as well as mutual dislike in the helper interaction. In other words, this strategy nurtures the popular imagery of the 'fake' needing – *demanding sympathy on false grounds* – and plays into the hands of the cynical guardian of resources on the helper side.

If the helper is a guardian of scarce resources, the receiver will be made aware of the significance of obedience to rules and regulations at the outset, and is likely to sense the helper's distrust and antipathy. In line with Smith's (2001) argument that humiliation does not evoke feelings of shame if it appears reasonable or just, an alternative for the receiver is to attempt to grasp the logic of the institution that offers help. This strategy allows the subject to protect dignity while accepting humiliation as 'the way it needs to be', primarily because they 'understand' that access to help must be controlled in order to protect the system against others who may abuse it. Thereby, individual actors distance themselves from the shamed fellows in misfortune, claiming to be *different*. This is a way to forge authentic suffering in interaction with the guardian helper. Accordingly, the receiver will submit to humiliating rituals of obedience, to make themselves worthy.

I suggest that what Hochschild (1983) instead terms 'deep acting' is the process at work here. Deep acting means cognitively reframing an event to evoke the desired emotion, and although it involves working on a multitude of (conflicting) potential emotional outcomes, it eventually enables the subject to 'truly' feel what is expressed. By reframing the interaction as one in which both helper and receiver are structurally locked in with limited options, migrants can, for example, avoid shame and still submit to humiliating procedures and feel gratitude (Wettergren 2015b). However, they may also engage in feeling and showing *sympathy*, thus positioning themselves as equal – or even superior – to the helper's situation. As argued earlier, such status challenges may trigger everything from slight irritation to disgust in the helper, leading to instances of reinforcement/expulsion-humiliation subtly disguised as 'rules' and 'procedures' (Graham 2002).

Contrary to the 'surface acting' clients, who neither believe in the procedures they are submitting to nor rely on successful interaction rituals with professional helpers for their self-feelings, deep-acting clients invest 'the whole person' in the helper interaction and depend on the professional helper's recognition. According to Hochschild (1983), long-term deep acting in situations that entail attacks to the self may lead to self-estrangement through emotional numbing. Ultimately, when faced with institutionalised help that is not meant to achieve any substantial difference, and which is fraught with empty rituals of obedience and control, the 'bad and unworthy' receiver, resorting to secondary arrangements, may be the only way to protect the self from deterioration.

Conclusions

In this chapter I have outlined institutionalised helper interactions aka welfare assistance as a social form and part of how the emotional state regulates structural inequality, recognition, and belonging, and the distribution of structurally embedded shame. I have argued that institutionalised helper interactions are intrinsically humiliating because most (if not all) help/ sympathy offered comes with the expectation of a gift in return. When the relationship between giver and receiver is unequal, sympathy offered requires acts of gratitude and loyalty/submissiveness in return. In the context of the welfare state, institutionalised helper interactions demand submission to integrity breaches and to various forms of humiliation rituals. Clients, whether migrants of citizens, are thereby deprived of the status as equal to non-dependent citizens they are treated as *less* than that. They are denied recognition as members of a community 'in good standing' as autonomous and capable individuals and thus – depending on their previous standing – experience expulsion-humiliation and/or reinforcement-humiliation. The institutionalised helper interaction is thereby organised in such a way as to generate shame as a deterrence strategy.

This said, the public discourse on welfare recipients can be more or less shaming due to contextual factors such as dominant political ideology. The dominant ideology, such as post-1980s neoliberalism or the care of the social democratic welfare state of the 1980s, influences the position of the helper in terms of resources and goal-orientation. Most people choosing to work as social workers or frontline bureaucrats often wish to make a difference and really help people in need, but these ambitions can be thwarted by various organisational restraints. I have highlighted the scarcity of resources and loyalty with keeping the budget-goals as examples that exhaust the 'humanitarian agent' while it promotes 'the guardian of scarce resources'. The different positions of the helper on the continuum between the humanitarian and the guardian extremes have not been discussed but deserve further scrutiny (see e.g. Maynard-Moody and

Musheno, 2003). My suggestion is that the institutionalised helper interaction, in line with the assumption that it is never truly in the interest of the ruling class to eliminate inequality, will always be restricted as compared to the ambition of the humanitarian helper. That said, the dominant political emotional regime of the state will likely push towards one of the ends.

On the side of the receivers of assistance, these can be differentiated in terms of time (how long they remain in the helper interaction) and degree of membership in society. I have discussed forced migrants as an extreme case of vulnerable receivers of assistance, due to their legal and social dependence on the willingness of the host state to protect their human rights. I showed how receivers of help seem destined to end up as 'unworthy' receivers if they try to insist on or protect their dignity and agency in the institutionalised helper interaction. It is hard to see the logic of that institutional outcome except as a way to deter people from seeking assistance. Still, the institutionalised helper interaction as a social form and analytical lens that I have begun to outline here needs to be developed in future theoretical and empirical work.

The discussion of the emotive-cognitive micro and structural dynamics involved in institutionalised helper interactions has also served to forge the point that emotional exchanges do not occur merely between persons in situated/micro interactions. Put simply, as the state consists of people in power, powerful people's emotions saturate the state and its institutions and shape the nation's emotional regime. While this takes place on the level of the collective, laws, regulations, norms, and values distribute and communicate the emotions and feeling rules of the state. Individuals interacting with state institutions as clients or employees will feel the emotional regime and react to it in different ways depending on their social position, resources, group, or class identity. Hence, if the goal of the state is to achieve collective emotions of solidarity, security, trust and belonging among its members, the emotional significance of purportedly rational arguments for the 'objective' organisation of specific tasks, like assistance to the poor, should be reconsidered. By this I mean that while 'assistance' to people in need may be based on a universal human logic that Simmel calls 'moral instinct', enacting feelings of goodness in the giver and gratitude in the receiver, this does not per se make all forms of welfare assistance destined to reproduce structural inequality. But when it is constituted within a social order that is perceived, and justified, by privileged groups as the righteous outcome of individual and group competition and achievement, assistance takes on the grim form and conflict-generating emotional careers highlighted in this chapter.

Note

1 This refers to, for instance, allowing checks on bank accounts, assets, and tax returns. Other terms and conditions include detailed checks on physical status (in

case of illness or disability) or, as in the case of unaccompanied refugee children in contemporary Sweden, submitting to physical examinations and wrist X-rays to determine their age ('skeletal maturity').

References

Barbalet, J. 1998. *Emotion, Social Theory, and Social Structure – A Macrosociological Approach*, Cambridge, Cambridge University Press.

Barbalet, J. 2009. A Characterization of Trust, and Its Consequences. *Theory and Society*, 38, 367–382.

Barker, V. 2012. Nordic Exceptionalism Revisited: Explaining the Paradox of a Janus-Faced Penal regime. *Theoretical Criminology*, 17, 5–25.

Bauman, Z. 1997. *Postmodernity and Its Discontents*, Cambridge, Polity Press.

Brekke, J.-P. & Söholt, S. 2005. *I velferdsstatens grenseland. En evaluering av ordningen med bortfall av botilbud i mottak for personer med endelig avslag på asylsöknaden*, Oslo, Institutt for samfunnsforskning.

Broström, L. 2015. *En industriell reservarmé i välfärdsstaten. Arbetslösa socialhjälpstagare 1913–2012*. Gothenburg University of Gothenburg. School of Business Economics and Law.

Castles, S. 2003. Towards a Sociology of Forced Migration and Social Transformation. *Sociology*, 37, 13–34.

Castles, S. & Davidson, A. 2000. *Citizenship and Migration: Globalization and the Politics of Belonging*, New York, Routledge.

Clark, C. 1987. Sympathy Biography and Sympathy Margin. *American Journal of Sociology*, 93, 290–321.

Clark, C. 1990. Emotions and Micropolitics in Everyday Life. Some Patterns and Paradoxes of "Place". *In*: Kemper, T. D. (ed.) *A Research Agenda in the Sociology of Emotions*, New York, State University of New York Press, 305–333.

Clark, C. 1997. *Misery and Company: Sympathy in Everyday Life*, Chicago, University of Chicago Press.

Derrida, J. 2001. *On Cosmopolitanism and Forgiveness*, London, Routledge.

Derrida, J. & Dufourmentelle, A. 2000. *Of Hospitality*, Stanford, Stanford University Press.

Durkheim, E. 1964. *The Rules of Sociological Methods*, New York, Free Press.

Ellerman, A. 2006. Street-Level Democracy: How Immigration Bureaucrats Manage Public Opposition. *West European Politics*, 29, 293–309.

Esping-Andersen, G. 1990. *The Three Worlds of Welfare Capitalism*, Cambridge, Cambridge Polity Press.

Fassin, D. 2005. Compassion and Repression: The Moral Economy of Immigration Policies in France. *Cultural Anthropology*, 20, 362–387.

Flam, H. & Beauzamy, B. 2008. Symbolic Violence: On Natives, Migrants and Their Emotions. *In*: Delanty, G., Wodak, R. & Jones, P. R. (eds.) *Identity, Belonging, and Migration*, Liverpool, University of Liverpool Press, 221–240.

Fraser, N. & Gordon, L. 1994. A Genealogy of Dependency: Tracing a Keyword of the U.S. Welfare State. *Signs: Journal of Women in Culture and Society*, 19(2), 309–336.

Gibson, S. 2003. Accommodating Strangers: British Hospitality and the Asylum Hotel Debate. *Journal for Cultural Research*, 7, 367–386.

Goffman, E. 1961. *Asylums: Essays on the Social Situation of Mental Patients and Other Inmates*, New York, Anchor Books.

Graham, M. 2002. Emotional Bureaucracies: Emotions Civil Servants, and Immigrants in the Swedish Welfare State. *Ethos*, 30, 199–226.

Guiraudon, V. & Lahav, G. 2000. The Reappraisal of the State Sovereignty Debate. *Comparative Political Studies*, 33, 163–195.

Hansen, P. 2008. *EU's migrationspolitik under 50 år. Ett integrerat perspektiv på en motsägelsefull utveckling*, Lund, Studentlitteratur.

Hansen-Löfstrand, C. 2005. *The Politics of Homelessness. Local Policy and Practice*, Gothenburg, Gothenburg University. Department of Sociology.

Helm, B. W. 2009. Emotions as Evaluative Feelings. *Emotion Review*, 1, 248–255.

Herz, M., Lalander, P. & Elsrud, T. 2022. Governing through Hope: An Exploration of Hope and Social Change in an Asylum Context. *Emotions and Society*, 4, 222–237.

Hochschild, A. R. 1983. *The Managed Heart – Commercialization of Human Feeling*, Los Angeles, University of California Press.

Holt, F. 2025. *Emotion and Social Work – Role Performances in a Contradictory Emotional Regime*, Gothenburg, Gothenburg University. Department of Social Work.

Jacobsson, K. and Johansson, H. 2025. *Governing Street-Level Bureaucracies. The Organizational Shaping of Caseworkers*, London: Routledge..

Johnson, C. 2010. The Politics of Affective Citizenship: From Blair to Obama, *Citizenship Studies*, 14(5), 495–509.

Johnson, C. 2013. From Obama to Abbott. *Australian Feminist Studies*, 28, 14–29.

Kemper, T. D. 2001. A Structural Approach to Social Movement Emotions. In: Goodwin, J., Jasper, J. M. & Pollitt, F. (eds.) *Passionate Politics -- Emotions and Social Movements*. Chicago: University of Chicago Press, 58–73

Khosravi, S. 2006. Territorialiserad mänsklighet: irreguljära immigranter och det nakna livet (Territorialized Humanity: Irregular Migrants and the Naked Life). *In*: Reyes, P. D. L. (ed.) *Om välfärdens gränser och det villkorade medborgarskapet (On the Limits of Welfare and the Conditional Citizenship)*. Stockholm: Statens offentliga utredningar SOU, 37.

Koch, I. 2021. The Guardians of the Welfare State: Universal Credit, Welfare Control and the Moral Economy of Frontline Work in Austerity Britain. *Sociology*, 55, 243–262.

Larsson, B (2014) Emotional Professionalism in a Bureaucratic Context: Emotion Management in Case Handling at the Swedish Enforcement Authority. *International Journal of Work Organisation and Emotion*, 6(3), 281–294.

Lipsky, M. 1980. *Street-Level Bureaucracy*, New York, Russell Sage Foundation.

Mau, S. 2015. *Inequality, Marketization and the Majority Class: Why Did the European Middle Classes Accept Neo-Liberalism?*, London, Palgrave Pivot.

Mauss, M. [1925] 2025. *The Gift*, Oxford, Taylor and Francis Ltd.

Maynard-Moody, S., & Musheno, M. (2003). *Cops, Teachers, Counselors. Stories from the Front Lines of Public Service*. The University of Michigan Press.

Monrad, M, 2024. Emotional Capital in Citizen Agency: Contesting Administrative Burden through Anger, *Journal of Public Administration Research and Theory* 34(4), 611–623.

Morton, A. 2013. *Emotion and Imagination*, Cambridge, Polity Press.

Neckel, S. 1991. *Status und Scham - Zur symbolischen Reproduktion Sozialer Ungleichheit*, Frankfurt: Campus.
Neckel, S. 1996. Inferiority: From Collective Status to Deficient Individuality. *The Sociological Review*, 44, 17–34.
Philipsson Isaac, S. 2024 *Temporal Dispossession: The Politics of Asylum and the Remaking of Racial Capitalism in and Beyond the Borders of the Swedish Welfare State*, Doctoral dissertation. Gothenburg: Gothenburg University
Rantakeisu, U., Starrin, B. & Hagquist, C. 1999. Financial Hardship and Shame: A Tentative Model to Understand the Social and Health Effects of Unemployment. *The British Journal of Social Work*, 29(6), 877–901.
Reddy, W. 2001. *The Navigation of Feeling — A Framework for the History of Emotions*. Cambridge: Cambridge University Press.
Rosello, M. 2001. *Postcolonial Hospitality: The Immigrant as Guest*. Stanford: Stanford University Press.
Scheer, M. 2021. *Enthusiasm. Emotional Practices of Conviction in Modern Germany*. Oxford: Oxford University Press.
Scheff, T. J. 1990. *Microsociology. Discourse, Emotion, and Social Structure*. Chicago: The University of Chicago Press.
Sennett, R. 1998. *The Corrosion of Character: The Personal Consequences of Work in the New Capitalism*. New York; London: Norton.
Simmel, G. 1971. The Poor. *In*: LEVINE, D. N. (ed.) *Georg Simmel. On Individuality and Social Forms*. Chicago: University of Chicago Press, 150–178.
Smith, A. [1759] 2006. *The Theory of Moral Sentiments*. New York: Dover Publications Inc.
Smith, D. 2001. Organizations and Humiliation: Looking beyond Elias. *Organization*, 8, 537–560.
Stearns, P. N. 1994. *American Cool — Constructing a Twentieth-Century Emotional Style*. New York: New York University Press.
Stearns, P. N. & Stearns, C. Z. 1985. Emotionology: Clarifying the History of Emotions and Emotional Standards. *The American Historical Review*, 90, 813–836.
Taylor-Gooby, P., Hvinden, B., Mau, S., Leruth, B., Schoyen, M. A. & Gyory, A. 2018. Moral Economies of the Welfare State: A Qualitative Comparative Study. *Acta Sociologica*, 62, 119–134.
Therborn, G. 2018. *Kapitalet, överheten och alla vi andra*. Lund: Arkiv.
Ticktin, M. (2014) Transnational Humanitarianism. *Annual Review of Anthropology*, 43, 273–289.
Ticktin, M. (2016) Thinking Beyond Humanitarian Borders. *Social Research: An International Quarterly*, 83, 2.
Weber, M. 1978. The Types of Legitimate Domination. *In*: Roth, G. & Wittich, C. (eds.) *Economy and Society — An Outline of Interpretive Sociology*. Berkeley: University of California, 212–299.
Weber, M. 1998. Bureaucracy. *In*: Gerth, H. H. & Mills, C. W. (eds.) *From Max Weber: Essays in Sociology*. New York: Routledge, 196–244.
Wettergren, Å. 2010. Managing Unlawful Feelings: The Emotional Regime of the Swedish Migration Board. *International Journal for Work, Organisation and Emotion*, 3, 400–419.
Wettergren, Å. 2013. *A Normal Life: Reception of Asylum Seekers in an Italian and a Swedish Region*, Gothenburg, Gothenburg University, https://gupea.ub.gu.se/handle/2077/33252

Wettergren, Å. 2015a. How Do We Know What They Feel? *In:* Flam, H. & Kleres, J. (eds.) *Methods of Exploring Emotions.* London: Routledge, 115–124.

Wettergren, Å. 2015b. Protecting the Self against Shame and Humiliation: Unwanted Migrants' Emotional Careers. *In:* Kleres, J. & Albrecht, Y. (eds.) *Die Ambivalenz der Gefühle: Über die verbindende und widersprüchliche Sozialität von Emotionen [The Ambivalence of Emotions: On the Connective and Contradictory Sociality of Emotions].* Wiesbaden: Springer, 221–245.

Wettergren, Å. 2025. Emotionalising Hope in Times of Climate Change. *Emotions and Society,* 7(1), 133–151.

Wettergren, Å. & Bergman Blix, S. 2016. Empathy and Objectivity in the Legal Process: The Case of Swedish Prosecutors. *Journal of Scandinavian Studies in Criminology and Crime Prevention,* 17, 19–35.

Wettergren, Å. & Wikström, H. 2013. Who Is a Refugee? Political Subjectivity and the Categorisation of Somali Asylum Seekers in Sweden. *Journal of Ethnic and Migration Studies,* 40, 566–583.

Zacka, B. (2017). *When the State Meets the Street.* Harvard: Belknap Press

15
BEYOND THE COURTROOM

Emotions, affects and embodied senses of justice in ground-level interventions in the judicialisation of an environmental disaster

Leticia Barrera

Introduction: Judicialisation of social inequalities, embodied senses of justice and contestation over the boundaries of law

The last decades of expansion of litigation in social and political conflicts in Argentina have shown the domestic courts adopting a novel and progressive approach to social, cultural, economic and environmental rights (Abramovich and Pautassi 2009; Arcidiácono and Gamallo 2023; Bercovich and Maurino, 2013; Smulovitz 2010). In this field, judicialisation has been promoted in different formats: through individual or collective claims resulting from elite case-lawyers' (Public Defenders, NGOs) rights advocacy strategies; legal mobilisation of social groups; or claims for rights enforcement before international courts. In many of those cases, lawsuits were filed before the courts to pursue structural transformations (Bergallo 2005) or judicial remedies for the breach of constitutional rights without having a broader impact other than on the individual case.

This move towards judicialisation of conflicts and the adoption of a Human Rights perspective by certain key figures in the juridical field have impacted upon agents' and groups' understandings of adjudication, or rather, of what can be achieved through litigation in contemporary Argentina. Consequently, with the courts' willingness to expand their powers to entertain and adjudicate public policy issues, a blanket idea of judicialisation as the pathway towards social change gained momentum in some circles (Bergallo 2005; Bergallo 2014; Gargarella and Bergallo 2014; Puga 2012). However, the imaginaries about justice that may circulate among the agents and groups involved in social rights litigation cannot be taken as mirroring the responses from state agencies to their claims. Moreover, since judicial intervention in the field of social rights in Argentina has been large and involved a multiplicity of agents (in many cases, subordinate groups), accounts of the social representations of law and justice by the actors included must be understood within a complex landscape and reflect the existence of different and even contradictory orientations among them.

In their study of lawsuits involving poor and marginalised populations around large urban areas in Argentina, anthropologist Cristina Cravino and sociologist Carla Fainstein note that the residents' perspectives on law and justice have not been explored sufficiently by socio-legal scholars (2023). As they interestingly remark, representations of justice and its workings are inherent to the agents' worldviews, specifically, about their place in society, the city and the territory that they inhabit, and their capacity to transform relations of force with the State and their previous experiences in community organisations (2023: 149). In other words, actors' social representations of justice cannot be separated from their practices; they involve moral and political conceptions and should be considered as *situated* (2023: 150).

A similar understanding of justice as an embodied practice is advanced by anthropologists Sandra Brunnegger and Karen Faulk (2016). Drawing on ethnographic explorations of the concept of "justice in practice" elaborated by various authors in diverse Latin American milieus, Brunnegger and Faulk come up with an understanding of justice as a "sense" that individual actors or movements experience, construct and frame in multiple ways. A sense of justice—not an abstract but a grounded one—is nurtured, Brunnegger and Faulk argue, by "the embodied expression of memory, mapped out spatially, and is continuously negotiated in dialogic practice" (Brunnegger and Faulk 2016: 17). Consequently, there is a variability of meanings, ideas and experience attached to justice that may coexist within spatial settings, scales and layers (Brunnegger and Faulk 2016: 4). In the same way, these authors stress the need to pay attention to the lived experience of justice and its role in the production of legal subjectivity (2006: 9).

With respect to the plurality of meanings of justice that may unfold from the actors' experiences, situations and environments, it is also worth noting here anthropologist Jonas Bens's assertion that differences in peoples' culturally socialised values do not suffice to explain the judgements that they make on justice (2022: 15). Based on his extensive ethnographic study conducted in the field of international criminal justice, Bens describes that people assess the justice or injustice of a given case always in relation to the normative orders that present them with the criteria to make their assessments, and that is *sentiment* what allows them to "navigate this normative pluralism" (2022: 15) (italics added). In the context of his research, this author explains that the term sentiment refers to "the role of affect and emotion in the formation of political opinions, normative assessments, and assertions of justice or injustice" (2022: 13).

Following these authors' insights, I propose to approach the study of judicialisation of social conflicts in Argentina by moving away from normative analysis that frames litigation and its results in terms of failure or success—whether, in a concrete case, judicialisation has been the effective remedy to overcome social inequality or not. Instead, I aim to elaborate a more nuanced understanding of this phenomenon by integrating into the analysis the actors' perspectives. In particular, I intend to explore ethnographically some ordinary interstices of the legal process that may account for their efforts to make sense of justice through practices that are culturally and spatially situated (Cravino and Fainstein 2023), senses forged by their trajectories and lived experiences of the conflict they are facing (Brunnegger and Faulk 2016), and the emotions and affects that judicialisation mobilises, enabling the circulation of sentiments of what is just or unjust (Bens 2022).

The chapter draws on a leading case in public interest litigation for the enforcement of diffuse and collective rights in Argentina: the so-called Mendoza case[1] or the Riachuelo case, a long-standing environmental pollution conflict that for 20 years has extended through multiple jurisdictions (national, provincial and municipal) and became the largest lawsuit filed before domestic courts. Particularly, I inquiry on ground-level bureaucratic encounters enacted by the ongoing enforcement proceedings of the Supreme Court decision delivered in the case in 2008. More concretely, I am interested in the interactions that unfold in town hall forums or meetings that are held periodically in local government facilities where residents[2] from areas affected by the environmental disaster and the agents from different bureaucracies involved in the Court sentence enforcement all assemble. As I will explain further, in these settings the agents navigate dimensions of the conflict other than the legal (moral, political, affective, emotional), seeking to reconfigure it in their own and sometimes conflicting terms.

In looking at the development of the *Mendoza* lawsuit at the ground level requires, I am trying to push the analysis beyond a normative and spatialised notion of judicial adjudication that takes the courts as the only authoritative source of knowledge-making. As I briefly suggested earlier, such a narrow understanding of the case neglects its multiple dimensions and places the actors' perspectives on the conflict and justice-making practices attached to it in realms outside the law. Likewise, a conceptualisation of the conflict involved in *Mendoza* through the lens of binary categories such as legal *versus* political (or social, moral, emotional); or formal-informal overlooks the material and symbolic effects that may emerge out of a tailor-made mode of exercising jurisdiction at different scales.

In the vein, by giving an ethnographic account of the ordinary interventions that the *Mendoza* lawsuit mobilises among the subjects on the ground, I also expect to show that analytical boundaries drawn between the law and the moral, emotional, political and affective dimensions of the conflicts are blurred.

This chapter proceeds as follows. The next section provides a short description of the *Mendoza* lawsuit for the environmental pollution of the basin of the *Riachuelo* and *Matanza* rivers filed before the Supreme Court of Argentina in 2004. It explains some features of the larger socio-environmental conflict involving the judicial case, the Court's approach to the subject-matter, the decision reached in the case and its enforcement. I will also stress the relevance of this case for socio-legal research of justice in action and propose to expand the scope of its analysis to integrate the political, moral and affective dimensions that the judgement implementation opens on the ground. The subsequent section turns to an ethnographic description and analysis of the dynamics displayed in a series of town hall meetings that I attended and observed over seven months of fieldwork (from August 2019 to February 2020). The meetings were convened by the authorities of one of the districts in the Province of Buenos Aires that form part of the contaminated region. In this district, a large number of residents live in shantytowns, slums and squatter settlements that line the highly contaminated banks of the basin. The encounters bring together local government bureaucrats, officers from other state agencies and residents from the district. The chapter concludes with reflections that summarise my analysis of the ground-level interactions in which this conflict unfolds, and ultimately with a claim for a more-nuanced understanding of a multi-layered environmental social rights conflict like that of the *Riachuelo*. I built my analysis on data collected from observations of the meetings and larger public events held in other locales of the same district, semi-structured interviews and informal conversations conducted with Public Defense agents and dwellers.

The *Mendoza* lawsuit: Enduring environmental problems, structural inequality and multi-scale governance.

I first encountered the *Mendoza* case during long-term ethnographic research that focused on the contemporary forms and practices of knowledge-making and circulation within Argentina's Supreme Court of Justice (Barrera 2012). Indeed, *Mendoza* burst onto the judicial scene, bringing to the forefront the spectacle of public oral advocacy before the Court—a then-unusual practice— in September 2006. The chance to observe the parties delivering their oral argument and watch expert witnesses reporting their opinions to the Court in an open and public fashion was a unique event. It allowed me to enquire into the instances of knowledge-making beyond those that unfolded through the documentary practices that I had encountered in the Court thus far and which had become the focus of my analysis of judicial decision-making. At the same time, *Mendoza* was gaining even more relevance among legal professionals, scholars, environmental activists, and grassroots organisations. The complexity of the issues at stake had made the Court broaden the scope of its jurisdiction, formally introduce new modes of operation (public oral hearings) to its adjudication process, adopt an innovative remedial plan and establish a network of mechanisms for its implementation. *Mendoza* was, in effect, a "paradigmatic case" (Puga 2008).

The main conflict that triggered the *Mendoza* litigation was the longstanding pollution of the basin of the *Matanza* and *Riachuelo* rivers that affects the health and well-being of almost 5 million people. This is an industrial metropolitan area that extends approximately 39 miles into 14 municipalities in the province of Buenos Aires and reaches the southeastern edge of the homonymous city, Argentina's federal capital. Lacking access to water and sewage services, a significant number of slums, shantytowns, and squatter settlements line the highly contaminated banks of the rivers. Different actors, such as the federal ombudsperson and non-profit environmental organisations, brought the problem of the deteriorated socio-environmental living conditions of the population to the political authorities on many occasions, but they failed to address it for decades. In the 1990s, Federal (national) government authorities announced an ambitious plan to clean and remove pollution from the river within a three-year period, but contamination, environmental degradation and health rights violations continued and even increased dramatically.

After many years of neglect, the conflict gained political momentum in 2004 through judicialisation. A group of workers and residents from *Villa Inflamable* (Flammable), a highly polluted shantytown in the petrochemical port Dock Sud, and medical professionals from *Hospital Interzonal de Agudos Pedro Fiorito* (Pedro Fiorito Acute Care Regional Hospital), both in the district of Avellaneda in the province of Buenos Aires, filed a lawsuit before the Argentine Supreme Court against the province, the City of Buenos Aires, the federal administration and 44 private corporations that operated in the area. The plaintiffs sought remedies for individual and collective damages and the rebuilding of the environment. In a series of preliminary decisions, the Court rejected the individual claims but accepted the collective case because it involved an inter-jurisdictional pollution problem. In addition, the Court ordered the defendants to submit an environmental management plan to clean the river and establish a river authority.

In response to the Court's mandate, the Argentine Congress passed Law 26.168 (B.O. November 15, 2006) which created an inter-jurisdictional river basin authority (*Autoridad Nacional para la Cuenca Matanza Riachuelo,* hereinafter ACUMAR) responsible for coordinating the plan.[3] At the same time, the judicial process continued before the Supreme Court, which, in turn, held a series of public hearings during its 2006 and 2007 terms for all the parties to the case and the interested parties to which the Court had granted standing, to express their views on the claims and on the authorities' plan to clean the basin.

On July 8, 2008, the Court delivered its ruling on the case. To this day, such a decision is considered a landmark in environmental litigation. The Supreme Court ordered the National Government, the Province of Buenos Aires and the City of Buenos Aires not only to clean the river basin, but also to prevent future environmental harm and remove the industrial pollution, clean up the landfills, clean the riverbanks, expand potable water networks, construct proper storm drainage and sewage sanitation systems, establish an emergency health plan and inform the public about the measures taken. The execution of the Court sentence quickly exposed the structural problems that extended beyond the environmental conflict (for instance, access to decent housing) and the inadequacies of pre-existing public policies to address the vast array of unsatisfied basic needs of the affected population (Auyero and Swistun 2009; Merlinsky 2013; Chelillo et al. 2014; Carman 2019).

To ensure compliance with its judgement, the Court established several oversight mechanisms in its 2008 decision. Particularly, it decided that the execution of the ruling would lie on a set of institutional arrangements that would expand across different jurisdictions—national, provincial and municipal. In addition, it created an interorganisational committee (a coalition of several NGOs and the Nation's ombudsperson) to monitor compliance with the judgement. Through this multi-level governance scheme, the Court assembled the workings of state agencies, private and state-owned utility companies, and first-instance federal courts vested with jurisdiction to oversee and make decisions with respect to the judgement application, among other. However, the Court reserved for itself the power to monitor and decide on the development of new public policies and institutions created through its judgement. To do so, the tribunal would convene public hearings at its facilities to follow up on the progress of the environmental management plan. Unexpectedly, the Supreme Court's decision refused to entitle the plaintiffs and other residents from the polluted area with legal standing, despite granting them the status of victims of environmental harm ("affected dwellers", as the Court named them).

As the enforcement mechanisms developed at the ground level, they gave room to entities, actors, roles and interactions that were not anticipated when the ruling was issued in the distant and removed setting of the courthouse. This can be seen in the case of the Office of Public Defense that assumed legal representation of the affected dwellers lacking legal standing in the lawsuit. Along the same lines, as it will be explained below, the kinds of interactions generated on the ground in the context of this evolving case contributed to destabilising previously established representations of actors' knowledges, practices and narratives associated with their roles and positions in the conflict. Agents from the Office of Public Defense, for instance, not only provided legal counsel to the dwellers but were also involved in social work in the affected territories and turned to political activism for their clients' rights in arenas beyond the judicial (Scharager 2019). Dwellers, for their part, learned through extended judicialisation of their social conflicts to resort to a rights discourse to frame and advance their legal and political claims (Delamata, Sethman and Ricciardi 2014; Bercovich, Garone, Tarbuch and Ureta 2014). And even sometimes bureaucrats resisted the roles associated with their workings and routines in the state structure. Likewise, for the actors, justice and adjudication practices may take the form and be enacted in the everyday through different relationships, either collaborative or conflictive. In this light, justice rendering in the *Mendoza* case is not limited to proceedings held in formally designated times and places.

Bureaucracy matters: Unfolding the *Mendoza* case through everyday administrative interactions

From August 2019 to the end of February 2020, I attended and observed 6 town hall meetings and 1 large public event in 1 of the 14 local districts in the Province of Buenos Aires. As previously noted, this is an area affected by the environmental pollution of the *Riachuelo-Matanza* basin and thus included in the integral sanitation and cleaning project (*Plan Integral de Saneamiento Ambiental*, or PISA) implemented following the Court's mandate in *Mendoza* lawsuit. The last meeting of that series was held only a couple of weeks before the lockdown ordered by the Argentine Government on April 20 in response to the COVID-19 pandemic. During the lockdown, meetings were held remotely, but in this piece, I focus only on the in-person encounters that I attended before then. The meetings were held monthly at the Municipality's main building (Town Hall) and gathered civil servants (municipal agents), ACUMAR personnel, agents from the Public Defense Office and a group of dwellers, many of whom lived in the largest settlement of the district and were the target of policies of regularisation of land ownership, urbanisation, and relocation. The main purpose of the meetings was to discuss and review the status of compliance with PISA and the agreement for urbanisation of the settlements, shantytowns and slums, and the relocation of families exposed to environmental harm.

At first glance, town hall meetings resembled informal gatherings rather than officially organised sessions. No spatial organisation seemed to be planned: participants sat in a big circle next to each other, and there was no spot reserved for local government officers. The environment was relaxed, and participants usually addressed each other in a casual and appropriate manner. Some civil servants, however, would tend to rely more on some formal attitudes and engage in elite ways of speaking to take distance from their interlocutors' critiques. Dwellers, for their part, would perform passionate, vigorous and wholehearted interventions in the course of the meetings. The absence of protocol did not obscure the fact that the attendees were positioned on two sides of a divide: on the one hand, there were the affected dwellers and the Public Defense agents who provided the former with legal counselling before the federal first instance court that oversees the progress of the plan, and assistance with their bureaucratic claims. "We co-create the judicial work with the residents and communities. We think together about the judicial strategy to pursue before the court, although most of the problems are solved in the administrative instance. Ours is community-based work", an agent from the Public Defense explained to me.[4] In addition to the Public Defense staff that participated in all the meetings that I attended, I saw local political figures (for instance, a councilperson) showing up in some of the town hall forums to back the dwellers' claims. Certainly, the group of dwellers that I encountered at those meetings was not homogeneous. Some of them lived in neighbourhoods with access to some basic public services and had experience in community organisations and activism. Other residents' living conditions were more precarious, and they had no organisational and advocacy skills. Nonetheless, a sense of community infused the dwellers' side.

At the meetings, the dwellers appeared as what Carman, following Butler's (2010: 54) and Laclau's (2009: 300, 307) insights, calls a "moral community" (2019). Such a community—and the subjects that make it up—she argues, is not constituted beforehand but

> emerges when in the diverse claims of a group that shares a class habitus and certain symbolic structure, operates an equivalent logic that creates unity amidst the heterogeneity of the different actors, who nonetheless are situated on the same side of the antagonistic frontier.
>
> *(Carman 2019: 128)*

This sense of moral community among the affected dwellers that participated in the meetings became palpable in the statement made by one of them in the second meeting that I attended: "Our fight is for the entire community", said vehemently María, one of the dwellers to the whole audience.[5] This notion of community that merged the dwellers' different positions in the space of the meetings was also made clear to me when, after one of the gatherings, a Public Defense lawyer and a community delegate mentioned to me that not all the dwellers that participated and brought their claims to the authorities were formally included in the *Mendoza* litigation. Those neighbours, they explained to me, were not settled in the contaminated area demarcated by the case and thus were not formally subject to the implementation of any plan within the legal framework provided by the judicial decision. Following my query about their attendance at the meetings and acting as if they had been legally recognised as "affected dwellers", they responded: "we did not say anything to the authorities about their situation. No one did". The fact that in the meetings there were dwellers who had not been officially recognised as "victims of environmental harm" and thus not included in public policies implemented through the *Mendoza* litigation did not mean for my interlocutors that those subjects were not suffering the same kind of problems. On the contrary, they saw the "non-affected" dwellers as their fellows and also entitled to petition the authorities in the same terms, as they actually did in the course of the town hall meetings.

On the other hand, the meetings gathered civil servants from different areas of the municipal government and agents from ACUMAR. They were chaired by an officer (usually a lawyer) from the Municipality's Legal and Technical Office who had also held the role of convening the encounters. Many of the government actors that attended the meetings in that district were responsible for the execution of the environmental management plan for the basin. Some of them, however, did not have a direct role in the implementation of the plan at the ground level but had to supervise the workings of other units involved and were bound by orders issued by the first-instance court. Except for the meeting chair and the ACUMAR's agents that attended almost all the encounters (of all the encounters that I attended, the ACUMAR staff did not show up in only one meeting due to a workers' strike), the attendance of government actors varied from one meeting to another. This would happen because no item related to their area of competence was included on that month's meeting agenda, or the meeting organiser did not have the power to compel them to attend. For instance, none of the meetings that I attended included staff from the public utility companies (gas and electricity), even though they had been requested to do so by the convening authority. Public utility companies are run by private corporations; thus, the meeting chair alleged that she could not oblige them to come. The fact that no personnel from those corporations joined the meetings showed the limits of the local bureaucracy's power to fully enforce participation of all the institutions responsible for the execution of the ongoing project of sanitation and cleaning of the polluted region. Also importantly, those absences spawned a sense of frustration and disappointment among the dwellers since nobody would take their claims on crucial issues for their daily lives.

Despite the apparently relaxed and informal atmosphere of the encounters, town hall meetings exhibited various features that afforded them a formal appearance and an official character. Indeed, the meetings were held in a discrete institutional venue, open to the public, had an agenda previously set and were convened and chaired by a local government authority. Also, they were transcribed in official minutes that had to be signed by all the participants. But most importantly, these gatherings were framed within the scope of the Supreme Court's decision. This legal framework not only afforded the encounters a legal character but also operated symbolically on the dwellers' strategies to advance their claims.

As part of the routine and dynamics that became established in the course of successive town hall meetings, the sessions usually started half an hour later than the scheduled time due to the late arrival of the chairperson and typically lasted 3 hours. It was difficult for all the participants to follow the order of the items listed on the agenda and keep the meeting on track. A collection of themes relating directly to the execution of the environmental plan were addressed and discussed recurrently in every encounter; for instance, the relocation of the families that inhabited the most contaminated areas, the existence of waste-fills in open air, problems in the system of garbage collection and toxic spills from the industries located in the district affecting a large urban area that included slums, shantytowns and squatter settlements. But also importantly, discussion pivoted to the issues that concerned the residents mostly: "urbanisation"[6]; that is, access to potable water networks, electricity distribution grids, gas supply services and sewage sanitation systems. Housing needs, besides relocation, were also emphasised in the meetings. Dwellers requested from the government a timeline for granting title deeds to the families that had been living for decades in slums settled on publicly owned lands. In addition, other issues also important to residents' everyday lives were raised, even if they had been previously included or not on the agenda. And also, in some cases, discussions on particular issues were handled informally among the dwellers, public defenders and local bureaucrats, and thus, no record of them was noted in the meeting minutes.[7] These particularities of the meetings often made it difficult to keep the discussion on point.

"Disobedient" subjects:[8] Emotions, lives at the margins and experiences of resistance

"We are patient! We have been patient for 30 years!" claimed Juan, one of the residents affected by the environmental pollution. "We are accused of being irrational or crazy because we go and knock on the doors of the Ministries. But what do they want??!! We know how it is. We go and hand out our little piece of paper, but nothing happens afterwards".[9]

As noted above, the sentence enforcement proceedings have made even more palpable the structural inequality that affects the inhabitants of the *Matanza* and *Riachuelo* basin and the inefficient public policies aimed at improving their living conditions. Recurrent discussions on these issues in the town meetings that I observed reminded me the sense of extended "waiting" that Auyero and Swistun (2009) describe as inherent to the population of *Villa Inflamable*, one of the polluted shantytowns also located in the Riachuelo river basin. Residents, they argue, wait for the government to take action to improve their living conditions and thus make their right to a healthy environment effective. Consequently, in contexts where vulnerable populations lack access to basic needs, "waiting" functions, according to these authors, as a tool of control and subordination. Similarly, drawing on a larger ethnographic research that includes a study of people waiting for social benefits and administrative services in state agencies facilities in Buenos Aires, Auyero (2012) reflects on welfare bureaucracies' capacities to turn the poor into "patients of the State" rather than citizens with rights. The act of waiting—waiting indefinitely—for others to decide is a temporal process that reproduces political domination, he argues (2012). The everyday experience of endless waiting to which the poor are subject is an exercise of state power that secures submission and obedience (2012). However, a different appreciation of waiting emerges from the sites of bureaucratic interventions that I observed. Indeed, the sense of waiting that I encountered among my research subjects contests somehow the idea of passivity and obedience once associated with their roles and positions in this conflict.

The quotation that opens this section illustrates the dwellers' stance in face-to-face encounters with sentence enforcement bureaucracies. Those words recount a resident's reaction to a local government agent's demand for more patience to await a response from other bureaucratic units. That resident, Juan, was the most vocal figure on the victims' side in the town hall meetings that I attended. He had been living with his family for decades in the largest slum of the district and had been active in advocating for his community's rights before local authorities, even before the conflict was turned into a legal case. He was part of a social organisation that brought together his fellow neighbours, and at the time of my arrival in the field, he was serving as their delegate. The execution of the environmental and relocation plan demanded Juan's participation in multiple activities, like the town hall meetings, larger public hearings convened by the authority of the basin and frequent trips to La Plata, the capital city of the Province of Buenos Aires. He was tasked with making claims to higher-level administrative authorities, particularly against their non-compliance with the integral sanitation plan. At the meetings that I attended, he used to serve as the spokesperson for his neighbours as well as for the residents from other settlements that also came to these encounters, even though they were not considered formally included as affected subjects in this legal case. Juan had a clear idea about his fellow neighbours' needs and demands and was very tenacious and persistent in the pursuit of an official response. When the discussion on one topic became sidetracked, he urged all the participants to stay on topic. He was very critical of the little progress made by the local government in the implementation of the plan, and he had a strong conviction regarding who was accountable for that lack of progress. "We still have a State [the Government]" I heard Juan complain very energetically before the authorities during the first town hall meeting I attended. He was reacting to the meeting chair's statement about her inability to compel public supply companies to sit at the table. "The State must take responsibility and comply with its obligations" he insisted and concluded: "When we do not have the State, then we will go and face the private actor".

In addition to the data collected from those ground-level encounters, other empirical studies on the *Matanza-Riachuelo* litigation process have documented similar reactions by organisations or groups of residents from the affected area (Carman 2019; Cravino and Fainstein 2017, 2023; Fainstein 2020; Merlinksy 2013, 2020; Scharager 2019). These works also question the idea of passiveness associated with this populace. Fainstein in particular argues that the history of the social movements settled in this territory and the public policies directed at this segment of the population indicates that "the way to get things done" by the oppressed sectors is through confrontation and action (in its multiple forms) and not by becoming passive and obedient subjects (2020: 174; Ferraudi Curto 2014: 4). This insight on vulnerable groups' practices of collective action, in addition to the rich literature on social movements, allows a more complex understanding of the effects of waiting upon certain social actors.

Between policy and practice

The kinds of meetings that I describe in this chapter are unique venues to appreciate dwellers' actual positions in this case regardless of their judicial statuses. Such positions are infused by their experiences, trajectories (Cravino and Fainstein 2023) and long-term struggles with the enduring conflict of the *Riachuelo*, and also mobilise imaginaries of justice and adjudication practices that may emerge in concrete spatial-temporal interactions beyond the courtroom. Indeed, as Brunnegger and Faulk recall, notions of justice can be layered and even vary within the same community, influencing the way in which formal systems of law are used and experienced by participants (2016: 11). Undoubtedly, for the dwellers involved in the *Mendoza* litigation, their experiences of "environmental suffering" (Auyero and Swistun 2009) and the material and symbolic structures of their communities shaped their views and engagements with judicialisation (Fainstein 2020). In other words, motivations, desires, perceptions and struggles have made social actors into particular kinds of subjects (Ong 1999: 5–6). However, within the community of dwellers that actively participated in the monthly town hall meetings that I observed, a representation of justice and judicial decision-making arose in very concrete and material terms: as a problem that must be solved, or a need to be satisfied through direct bureaucratic action. Both in the dwellers' discourses and actions displayed in the meetings, adjudication took the form of the actual interventions that they demanded from government officers. Accordingly, justice is not a prospective and indeterminate concept, or the promise of accessing rights (i.e. the right to a clean habitat, to decent housing, to a healthy environment, and to be part of a city on equal terms). Rather, justice can be rendered through tangible and specific actions such as the building of sewage and sanitation systems, access to ordinary electricity networks and gas provision, drinking water supply systems, all of which have been at the core of the residents' enduring request for urbanisation, pursued even before the legal case started.

If the dwellers advanced an idea of justice embodied in bureaucrats' concrete steps conducive to urbanisation, these latter subjects also seemed to convey a different understanding of adjudication, according to the roles they found themselves playing within the intricate web of relations and institutional arrangements that constitute the judicial case. Accordingly, bureaucrats' practices and discourses displayed in the context of the town meetings enacted a conception of adjudication as a multi-layered and procedural phenomenon performed within a formal system of law. For them, the pathway to justice follows a large chain of sequential and simultaneous interventions to be performed by multiple entities at different scales. From this point of view, adjudication rests on a division of labour among administrative agencies and public institutions. At the meetings, this scheme was palpable in bureaucrats' reactions to dwellers' claims about the non-compliance with the environmental and sanitation plan. At different times, I observed local agents making statements about their (bureaucrats') lack of power to perform certain activities, like the meeting's chair's constant failure to bring third parties to the debate, or deferring to other units and agents the handling of concrete problems brought by the residents to the discussion table.

But also interestingly, the officers of the local government who convened the town hall meetings and participated in them did not see themselves as bound to perform the direct actions that dwellers demanded from them. Indeed, bureaucrats refused to play the role of front-line, street-level agents responsible for the direct fulfilment of dwellers' needs according to the Court's mandate. On the contrary, they saw themselves as facilitators, intermediate-level bureaucrats who operated in the interstice between policy and practice. For instance, in one of the encounters that I attended, after protesting the non-attendance of any staff member of the public services companies, one of the participant dwellers stood up and approached the representative of the environmental unit of the Municipal government. She showed the officer a letter that she had sent directly to that government area informing them of recurrent flooding issues they had in the slum where she lived. The agent glanced over the dweller's copy and asked that woman to file her claim before the Municipality's General Reception Desk so that her request could be registered properly and she [the resident] would get a file number to follow up on the status of her petition. On another occasion, in response to the failure and frustration of the meeting chair to make public service companies participate in town hall forums to address the dwellers' requests, she turned to the one of members of the Public Defense that was assisting the dwellers and indicated "you should notify the court about their [privately-run public service companies] reluctance to come. The judge can summon them to appear".[10]

Concluding remarks

In this work, I have drawn on the wider phenomenon of judicialisation of social conflicts in Argentina by engaging ethnographically with the interactions developed at the ground level in the context of a public interest litigation of an environmental disaster. More concretely, I have focused on discrete bureaucratic settings such as the periodical town hall forums organised by local authorities to discuss the progress of a very complex remedial plan with the victims of the environmental harm.

The ongoing enforcement proceedings of the Court's 2008 innovative decision brought attention to the material conditions of social inequality that most of the affected residents endured for decades. In the meetings that I described in this chapter, the dwellers incessantly presented the other attendees with concrete effects of social injustices on their everyday lives. Also, as I explained before, these meetings were formally embedded in a larger legal process and held in local government facilities. Nonetheless, the aesthetics and dynamics of those encounters created a somewhat informal or casual atmosphere that enabled the dwellers to visibilise their everyday struggles while requesting the authorities for better living conditions under the Court's framework. Indeed, at this ground level, the dwellers' opinions on the future orientations of the public policies to implement the Court's remedies intermingled with their embodied experiences of living at the margins, community attachments, moral and political obligations, affective states, and emotions. In this sense, following other authors' insights, I have advanced the idea that the modes in which actors make sense of justice in particular cases are mediated by their lived experiences. These embodied experiences, in turn, may enable a plurality of meanings of justice and forms of legal subjectivity.

In addition to this, I have argued that the town hall forums that I studied were unique venues to see the different engagements with justice among the subjects involved and that their understanding and handling of this case were permeated by their experiences and trajectories in dealing with the larger environmental conflict. Moreover, I suggested that certain forms of legal subjectivity displayed in this case might be understood as some actors' or groups' means of resistance and contestation on the conditions imposed by "subalternisation" (Bleger and Stella 2020).

Along the same lines, I have explained that in such discrete settings, the actors' senses and representations of justice and the meanings of judicial adjudication could be approached by paying attention to their discourses, actions and displays of agency. I have argued that for the affected dwellers, justice could be materially enacted through concrete interventions of local bureaucracies. Meanwhile, government agents advanced a notion of adjudication and justice-making practices as a multi-sited and non-linear process that assembled a network of agents and entities within a formal system of law. In this configuration, those bureaucrats saw themselves as mediators who operate in the liminal space between policy and practice.

In bringing to the attention the unfolding of the *Mendoza* case in bureaucratic milieus such as town hall meetings, I have tried to shed light on the mode in which the case operates on the ground by looking closely at the actors' interventions and the moral, emotional and political components that litigation mobilises. In this light, through my ethnographic description of these micro-level interactions, I also sought to demonstrate that normative assessments of the effects and workings of judicialisation of social injustices do not capture the complexities that it engenders, and leave apart, for instance, its affective and emotional dynamics. As I have shown in my ground-level development of the *Mendoza* lawsuit, the multiple lives of the wider conflict at issue are integrated into the embodied practices by which the subjects pursue justice and advance their legal claims. In this sense, analytical boundaries between the law and other realms (moral, political, emotional and so on) are contested on the ground. Ultimately, in this chapter, I have advocated for a more comprehensive approach to this conflict that allows moving socio-legal inquiry beyond the kind of dichotomies such as legal-political, formal-informal that usually break up its development—as well as its analysis—in different and fragmented domains.

Acknowledgements

I want to thank Ana Aliverti, Henrique Carvalho and Simon Tawfic for their helpful comments on this chapter. An earlier version also benefited from the careful reading and feedback from Karina Ansolabehere, Noa Vaisman, and Mariana Valverde. Specially, I would like to express my gratitude to all my interlocutors from the field who generously shared their time, knowledge and experiences of this very complex and enduring conflict. Some of them are referred in this piece by pseudonyms while others have been anonymised. Due to my research ethics, I decided to not mention them by their actual names.

Notes

1 CSJN M 1569, XL —*originario*— "*Mendoza, Beatriz Silvia y otros c/ Estado Nacional y otros s/ daños y perjuicios (Daños derivados de la contaminación*

ambiental del Río Matanza Riachuelo)", Supreme Court ruling, July 8, 2008.
2 I use the words "residents" and "dwellers" indistinctively to refer the people affected by the environmental pollution.
3 The plan's main objectives were the regularisation of land titles, the urbanisation of shantytowns, slums and settlements through the provision of public service infrastructure; and the relocation of the families settled in surrounding urban areas that were at risk of imminent environmental harm.
4 Interview, October 28, 2020.
5 Fieldnotes, September 20, 2019.
6 Interview, October 28, 2020.
7 Interview, October 28, 2020.
8 This expression borrows from Bleger and Stella's (2020).
9 Fieldnotes, August 23, 2019.
10 Fieldnotes November 29, 2019.

Works Cited

Abramovich, Víctor and Pautassi, Laura (2009). "El enfoque de derechos y la institucionalidad de las políticas sociales", in Victor Abramovich and Laura Pautassi (comps.), *La revisión judicial de las políticas. Estudio de casos*. Buenos Aires: Del Puerto, pp. 147–169.

Arcidiácono, Pilar and Gamallo, Gustavo (2023) *La otra ventanilla. Judicialización de los conflictos sociales en Argentina*. Buenos Aires: Eudeba.

Auyero, Javier (2012). *Patients of the State: The Politics of Waiting in Argentina*. Durham, NC: Duke University Press.

Auyero, Javier and Swistun, Débora (2009): *Flammable: Environmental Suffering in an Argentine Shantytown*. New York: Oxford University Press.

Barrera, Leticia (2012). *La Corte Suprema en Escena. Una Etnografía del mundo judicial*. Buenos Aires: Siglo XXI.

Bens, Jonas (2022). *The Sentimental Court: The Affective Life of International Criminal Justice*. Cambridge: Cambridge University Press.

Bercovich, Luciana and Maurino, Gustavo (comps.). (2013). *Los derechos sociales en la Gran Buenos Aires. Algunas aproximaciones desde la teoría, las instituciones y la acción*. Buenos Aires: EUDEBA.

Bercovich, Luciana, Garone, Noelia, Tarbuch, Laura, and Ureta, Fernando (2014). "La participación de los afectados en el 'Caso Mendoza': Un derecho en construcción", *Revista Institucional de la Defensa Pública de la Ciudad de Buenos Aires*, 2014, año IV, N°6, Buenos Aires, 123–138.

Bergallo, Paola (2005). "Justice and Experimentalism: The Judiciary's Remedial Function in Public Interest Litigation in Argentina", SELA working papers.

Bergallo, Paola (2014). "La causa "Mendoza": una experiencia de judicialización cooperativa sobre el derecho a la salud", in Gargarella, Roberto (coord.), *Por una justicia dialógica: el Poder Judicial como promotor de la deliberación democrática*. Buenos Aires: Siglo XXI, pp. 245–291.

Bleger, Mariel and Stella, Valentina (2020). "La espera desobediente. Análisis de un caso etnográfico sobre una comunidad Mapuche en Bariloche (Rio Negro)", *AVÁ* 36, June 2020, 43–64.

Brunnegger, Sandra and Faulk, Karen (2016). "Introduction: Making Sense of Justice", in Sandra Brunnegger and Karen Faulk (eds.), *A Sense of Justice: Legal Knowledge and Lived Experience in Latin America*. Stanford: Stanford University Press, pp. 1–21.

Butler, Judith (2010). *Marcos de guerra. Las vidas lloradas*. Buenos Aires: Paidós (cited in Carman, Maria (2019) "La fabricación de una comunidad moral. El caso de los afectados de la causa Matanza-Riachuelo", *EURE*, 2019, XLV, N°135, Santiago de Chile, 111–130).

Carman, María (2019). "La fabricación de una comunidad moral. El caso de los afectados de la causa Matanza-Riachuelo", en *EURE*, XLV, N°135, Santiago de Chile, 111–130.

Chelillo, Mauro, López, María Julia, Royo, Laura, Sagasti, Ignacio, and Territoriale, Agustín (2014). "El 'qué'. Las relocalizaciones en el marco de la causa Riachuelo y el derecho a la ciudad", *Revista Institucional de la Defensa Pública de la Ciudad Autónoma de Buenos Aires*, año IV, N°6: "La causa 'Mendoza': la relocalización de las familias y el derecho a una vida digna. Las personas no son cosas" Buenos Aires, 23–40.

Cravino, María Cristina and Fainstein, Carla (2017). "Disputas por el acceso al ambiente sano y a la vivienda en la ribera del Riachuelo: derechos de los vecinos, acción de la justicia y políticas públicas", in María Cristina Cravino (comp.), *Detrás de los conflictos. Estudios sobre desigualdad urbana en la Región Metropolitana de Buenos Aires*. Los Polvorines: Ediciones Universidad Nacional General Sarmiento, pp. 53–113.

Cravino, María Cristina and Fainstein, Carla (2023). "Asentamientos populares y judicialización de los conflictos: representaciones sociales sobre la justicia", in Pilar Arcidiácono and Gustavo Gamallo (coord.), *La otra ventanilla. Judicialización de conflictos sociales en Argentina*. Buenos Aires: Eudeba, pp. 147–188.

Das, Veena (2014). "Políticas de la vida cotidiana: memoria y presente". Public lecture given at EIDAES, Universidad Nacional de San Martín Buenos Aires, Argentina, August 14, 2014, available at www.youtube.com/watch?v=SS6C0SQNqi0

Delamata, Gabriela, Sethman, Alejandro, y Ricciardi, María Victoria (2014). "Más allá de los estrados. Activismo judicial y repertorios de acción villera en la ciudad de Buenos Aires", in Laura Pautassi (dir.), *Marginaciones sociales en el Área Metropolitana de Buenos Aires, Acceso a la justicia, capacidades estatales y movilización legal*. Buenos Aires: Editorial Biblos, pp. 397–444.

Fainstein, Carla (2020). "Problemas del mientras tanto. Espera y justicia en la causa Mendoza", *AVÁ* 36, June 2020, 165–193.

Ferraudi Curto, María Cecilia (2014). *Ni punteros ni piqueteros: urbanización y política en una villa del conurbano*. Buenos Aires: Editorial Gorla.

Gargarella, Roberto and Bergallo, Paola (2014). "Presentación", in Roberto Gargarella (comp.), *Por una justicia dialógica. El Poder Judicial como promotor de la deliberación democrática*. Buenos Aires: Siglo XXI, pp. 9–13.

Laclau, Ernesto (2009). *La razón populista*. Buenos Aires: Fondo de Cultura Económica (cited in Carman, Maria (2019) "La fabricación de una comunidad moral. El caso de los afectados de la causa Matanza-Riachuelo", *EURE*, 2019, XLV, N°135, Santiago de Chile, 111–130).

Merlinsky, Gabriela (2013). *Política, derechos y justicia ambiental: el conflicto del Riachuelo*. Buenos Aires: Fondo de Cultura Económica.

Merlinsky, Gabriela (2020). "Introducción. Cosmopolíticas de lo común", en *Cartografías del conflicto ambiental III*. Buenos Aires: Ediciones Centro de Integración, Comunicación, Cultura y Sociedad.

Ong, Aihwa (1999). *Flexible Citizenship. The Cultural Logics of Transnationalty*, Durham, NC: Duke University Press.

Puga, Mariela (2008). ¿A dónde va la Corte en las causas Verbitsky y Riachuelo? Ni uñas ni dientes, intervenciones experimentalistas", en *Revista del Colegio de Abogados de La Plata*, 2008, año L, N°69, La Plata, 151-165.

Puga, Mariela (2012). *Litigio y cambio social en Argentina y en Colombia*. Buenos Aires: CLACSO.

Scharager, Andrés (2019). "Judicialización y política en un proceso de relocalización: estrategias y discurso de la Defensa Pública de Buenos Aires", en *Revista Direito e Práxis*, 2019, vol. X, N°2, Rio de Janeiro, abril-junio de 2019, 846-870.

Smulovitz, Catalina (2010). "Judicialization in Argentina: Legal Culture or Opportunities and Support Structures?", In *Cultures of Legality: Judicialization and Political Activism in Latin America*, edited by Javier Couso, Alexandra Huneeus, and Rachel Seider, 234-253. Cambridge: Cambridge University Press.

16
IN SEARCH OF INSTITUTIONAL AFFECT IN SIERRA LEONE'S PRISONS

Andrew M. Jefferson

Introduction

This chapter examines the institutional affect of prisons in Sierra Leone as this envelops frontline officials, incarcerated persons and the researcher. It demonstrates how state power is embodied and affectively enforced not only through frontline state officials but also through often effaced and naturalised structures and institutions. While taking seriously the first-person perspectives of state officials and their affective histories, I focus on the agentic force and expression of the penal institution itself. I tentatively refer to this agentic force and expression as 'structural intentionality'. I focus on the ways in which affect is *embedded* in materials, structures, and routines and *embodied* in relations of power. By so doing I allow for analysis of linkages between moral and affective dimensions of state power and structural intentionality, the latter understood not in terms of volition or intention but in terms of momentum, drive and weight. My aim is to try to discern the structural drive behind institutional harm that is evidenced by affective forces and dynamics that are embedded in brickwork and bodies, and revealed in everyday practice. To put it colloquially, institutions are not simply containers – they do stuff, and they do stuff purposefully and with feeling.[1]

Conceptually, I am inspired by work by Sara Ahmed (2004, 2014) and Annika Lindberg (2022), and by Millicent Churcher and colleagues (2022) who lay out an influential concept of affect that draws on Spinoza via Deleuze. They identify the 'critical role played by institutions in shaping, enabling, and preserving entire ecologies of affect and habituated behaviours that reflect and reproduce inequalities of power and privilege' (2022: 1). My core assumption is that prisons, as hyper-emotive, amplifying, affective crucibles, do this in highly charged ways. Constrictive, limiting, and controlling, prisons call forth strong reactions; they have also been shown to deaden, to numb, and to dull the senses (Carrabine 2005; Crewe 2011). But the emotivity of prisons is not limited to the effects on their inhabitants. Affect resides in infrastructures, relations, and imaginaries. It is differentially distributed in events, paperwork, family life, and contestations (Stoler 2004: 5, 9). Often it is a mess of conflicting forces, a 'sensorium' (Laszczkowski and Reeves, 2017: 5–6) which makes studying it like 'chasing tiny fireflies' (Laszczkowski and Reeves, 2018: 5–6). Researcher immersion is necessary, Churcher et al (2022) argue, to get at these dynamics. This chapter is based on material that was gathered through such immersion.

In 2006 I spent seven months in Sierra Leone – a small West African country of around 6 million inhabitants (at that time) – ethnographically exploring dynamics and experiences of confinement. This involved hanging out in prisons and poor urban neighbourhoods in different parts of the country and getting to know their occupants or former occupants. I was specifically interested in the experiences of ex-combatants, that is people involved in the civil war (1990–2001). In 2006 the total prison population was less than 2,000, distributed across 13 prisons, with around half held in the central prison in the capital, Freetown. (Further details on the country context are presented later.)

The situated affectivity of institutions

'Institutional affect', argue Churcher et al., should be understood as 'inherently relational and as a key conduit for power to operate and exert its effects' (2022: 2–3). In fact, I am less interested, in this chapter, in how 'actors and their situated affectivity give life to an institution' (Churcher et al. 2022: 13) (though this is considered in section three) and more in how the situated affectivity of institutions gives life, or makes particular forms of life available, to actors. My primary concern is to trace the institutional affect of the penal apparatus and illustrate the way it adheres to places (e.g. the gate lodge), people (prisoners and staff), and times (affective histories of war).

My interest is affective phenomena and the ways they are bound to penal practice. I pay particular attention to 'affective arrangements' (Slaby 2019 in Slaby and von Scheve, 2019), 'affective affordances' (Fuchs and Koch 2014), 'dynamic web[s] of affectivity' (Churcher et al. 2022: 4), affect's 'embodied agency' (Linke 2006: 207 cited by Laszczkowski and Reeves, 2018: 3), and the way affect is embedded in infrastructures (cf Street 2012; Draper 2012; Christie 1978). The role of infrastructure is arguably 'underappreciated... in shaping and inflecting institutional affect' and conditioning actors (Churcher et al. 2022: 4), though Nils Christie astutely suspected as long ago as 1978 that 'in the last resort, *buildings* and personnel will prove more resistant to change than the public and the politicians' (1978: 187, my emphasis).

The intersection between actors and institutional landscapes is the subject of Alice Street's insightful analysis of a postcolonial hospital landscape in Papua New Guinea that draws on ideas from critical geography and postcolonial theory (Thrift 2007; Stoler 2008 etc.). Street is particularly concerned with spaces of affect that are generated by the layering of spatial infrastructural practices through time (new buildings tagged onto old, for example). She considers the hospital as an 'institution of improvement' (an ascription that believers in prisons might also use), as an 'affective technology'. Her empirical focus is the ambivalent affective states invoked by the hospital environment and atmosphere in frontline staff, and in local residents offered tours of the premises and grounds in an effort to rekindle faith in state provision and development.[2] Following Gieryn (2002: 41), Street characterises the hospital as a 'walk-through machine(s)' (46) emphasising the agentic qualities and effects of institutions on people passing through and working in them. Conceiving of affect as 'an emergent property of relationships and encounters (between persons and between persons and things)' (46), Street foregrounds actors, but nevertheless registers that 'space is a particular vehicle for and transmitter of affect' and even, as I will, that emotions 'reside in the landscape itself' (54).

Embodying the state?

My approach to state power is informed by Hansen and Stepputat's (2001; 2005) ethnographic approach to understanding the state. In their groundbreaking work on sovereignty and state formation, they put forward the view that the state is always in a process of construction, best understood not by attending to an assumed central source of power but to the margins, that is to everyday practices of state-making (see also Das and Poole 2004). From this perspective the conditioning conditions and affective practices I pursue in this chapter are instantiations of a state-in-the-making, not a 'fragile state' or a 'post-conflict state' as Sierra Leone was commonly described in policy and political science circles.[3] Such a theorisation avoids a deficit-oriented approach that assesses the character of peripheralised states up against an assumed Western norm and enables a relational view that takes seriously the provisional character of state forms.

This approach has implications for the way we think about the embodiment of the state, whether institutionally or personally. What might it mean to embody a state in flux? If sovereignty is dispersed and resides in multiple sites and diverse actors, how do we know it when we find it? Do state employees (prison staff, for example) naturally embody the state or might they too best be understood as polyvalent, conflicted reflections of statehood-in-the-making? When is institutional affect 'of the state' as it were? Might prison staff be 'performing' the state and be targets of the state simultaneously? To what extent is state power internalised as well as externalised?[4]

I turn now from contextual framing and sources of inspiration to the empirical material and analysis.

The affective force of prisons

My approach has been to revisit detailed field notes made during initial and follow-up visits to selected prisons in Sierra Leone in search of examples of the operation of affective forces. I begin by looking at some of the punitive conditions which 'condition' and qualify the affective force of prisons in Sierra Leone. And then proceed to explore the ways structural intentionality and institutional affect are embedded and embodied in them.[5] This section is divided into four parts: first, observations in the gate lodge and other areas of the prison; second, reflections on prison-like and unprison-like prisons; third, the affective histories of staff; and fourth, history's affect.

Conditioning conditions[6]

Like many postcolonial prisons in sub-Saharan Africa, many of the prisons in Sierra Leone are unfit for purpose (Morelle, Le Marcis and Hornberger 2021; Martin and Jefferson 2019; Jefferson and Martin 2016). They are over-populated and feature high levels of physical and ontological insecurity. Prisoners are held in cramped, claustrophobic dormitory cells. Staff are disillusioned and demoralised; casual cruelty is common, health care is below par, and, as in many jurisdictions, there are discrepancies between rules on the page and rules as practised. Apart from the occasional VIP prisoner or politician, most prisoners are from materially and socially marginalised communities, where everyday survival is a struggle,[7] poverty is essentially criminalised, and policing is predatory. Imprisonment is still often the only punitive response available to judges and magistrates at sentencing, and while release on bail prior to sentencing has become somewhat easier, there are still high numbers of prisoners awaiting trial, often for very long periods. The wheels of justice turn slowly and are associated with much uncertainty. The idea of the separation of powers is not well-embedded in Sierra Leone's political culture, and imprisonment remains a means through which politicians can dispel the threat of rivals through temporary or sometimes lengthy incapacitation. Such conditions persist despite – or because of – efforts by internationally supported reform projects in the legal, justice, and security sectors.[8]

Out in the field(s)

I did not spend weeks or months inside prisons, but I did make multiple visits to multiple institutions. I spent most of my time in the Central Prison in

Freetown, known colloquially as Pademba.⁹ Seldom did it feel the same. And it never became so familiar that I got used to it. The place where I spent most time was unsurprisingly the entrance. There was only one, another one having been bricked up, I was told, after a riot in 1967, and so each visit featured at least two encounters – one in one out – with this quite particular space.

1. Sites of passage

Gate areas are key observation sites (Jefferson and Schmidt 2019) where the researcher can witness repetitive behaviour and experience surprise when rhythms are interrupted. At the gate the porous and securitised quality of the prison is on clear display. And the gate area has a peculiar affective quality as a point of entry and exit, carrying at one and the same time projected onto it elements of foreboding (on entry) and liberation (on release).

In some prisons the entrance is endowed with architectural grandeur and symbolism. In others it is a simple doorway. Quite often – though not everywhere – there are two gates situated one after the other, and only after the first gate is secured does the second gate open. In between the two gates, the arriving person (i.e. detainee, lawyer, monitor, NGO rep, service provider, staff member, or whoever), at a minimum, registers their arrival and may well be shuffled off into a side office to be processed.

For the researcher, as for others, the gate area is an iterative rite of passage, a space passed through repeatedly, a threshold marking beginnings and endings but also a space that is redolent of material through which to learn the language of the prison. The gate area is unavoidable and cannot be hidden from the researcher, even by a system intent on 'defensive concealment' (Jefferson and Schmidt 2019). Just about everybody and everything passes through the gate, making the gate area a potent and affective space to examine the 'emotivity' of prisons (Jefferson et al. 2025).

Affective infusions

My first entry involved passing through a metal gate that opened onto a quite extensive gate area that I registered as 'twice as long' as a prison gate area I was familiar with in Nigeria. A registration book rested on a waist-high podium to the left, where an officer recorded my details and took my phone and my cash. The gate area was wide and tall enough for a vehicle to pass through. A couple of desks stood on the left side of the space between the external and internal gates. I noted how the internal gate consisted only of bars, whereas the external gate was sheet metal with a grate for communication. The atmosphere, I recorded, was 'light-hearted'.

On the right-hand side before the internal barred gate was a stairway leading to an area used for visits and to the records office and the office of the Officer-in-Charge (OiC)[10]; there were rooms off to the right and left and, on the right, a short corridor leading to the 'female quarters' and the section designated for remand prisoners. On the left another short corridor led towards an adjacent reception area. I registered this the following day:

> You pass through a short corridor opposite the stairs leading to the OiC's office and the records office, and then into the open air turning left heading for the external wall past a separate building that once was the reception but got burned during an electrically caused fire (burning many records). It is currently not in use. Turn right again and a much smaller office comes into view with a fence leading from the left side of the building to the external wall against which several prisoners lean and converse. 4 staff were present. The OiC, 2iC, 4iC and a tall man dressed in civilian clothes. The 2iC and 4iC are women. In the open space onto which the office opens are congregated prisoners waiting to be summoned for prison transport to court. They looked surly. I imagined they were newly arrested rather than going to court.
>
> *(10/05/06)*

Infusing the descriptions of the spaces (and dividing lines) through which I moved and passed are articulations of past events (a destructive fire) and expressions of the ways in which contemporary spaces are populated. Present are relatively senior male and female staff – some uniformed, some not – as well as prisoners whom I characterised as 'surly'. Populated and historical structures together carry affect and evoke questions: what caused the fire, who is the figure in civilian clothes, and what are the prisoners waiting for? What kind of a place is this? Remember this is only my second day in prison .... But it was not long before the logic of the place began to draw me into its web. A police officer arrived. I recorded events as follows:

> He is in charge of conveying remand prisoners to court. He makes fun with the female 4iC touching her shoulders and face. She tells him to desist and he leaves but not before pausing to ask whether I saw anything, as if to say 'nothing happened here, eh?' The female officer explained to me that he had only been making fun. They have no quarrel between them. She tells me it's the same 3 or 4 cops who pick up the prisoners for court each day.
>
> *(10/05/06)*

Here, I am witness to and implicated in an incident of sexual harassment that is made light of and dismissed by the female prison officer. It's banter, she implies, and probably a regular occurrence given the way she shares that it is the same police officers who come by each day. Thus, the embodied tone of interaction between differently positioned members of the security sector is publicly revealed, and I am invited to be complicit in the everyday microaggressions that characterise interactions in the prison.

Affective, embodied, sensorial order

I regularly observed such aggressions in the gate lodge as prisoners were made ready for court but also other relational dynamics. On court days the gate lodge became an ordering space. On one occasion (11/05/06) I sat outside the gate watching as prisoners mounted the prison truck, having been cross-checked and cuffed inside the gate. There is space for 40, but sometimes 85 are crammed in. I watched as 53 were loaded on board. I could see through the open door of the truck. There were metal bench seats. Yet, as more and more men were crowded in, these could not be sat upon but only stood upon with prisoners clutching at the ventilation grate high above them both for balance and to peer out. As we sat, all the junior officers suddenly sprang to attention as the chief superintendent entered the prison. I was slow to react but later as a white Land Rover passed carrying the Director of Prisons, I was more alert and managed to reach my feet before he had passed by, much to the amusement of the surrounding officers. 'You want to be one of us!?' they exclaimed half questioning, half stating. Not quite but my embodied echo of their movement was teaching me about the way affective submission to authority was instantiated in everyday prison practice.

In fact – I was to note a month later – compared to what I knew of Nigerian prisons at least, there was much less 'hierarchical paraphernalia… less marching and saluting' on display in Sierra Leone (07/06/06). Relations between junior and senior staff were not quite as accentuated (though certainly not inconsequential). The OiC would, for example, pass through the gate lodge almost without noticing the hurried salutes of his subordinates, creating, I noted on one occasion, 'a distinguished look of efficiency' (29/06/06). This was partly a reflection of his particular mode of quietly and efficiently exuding authority, but it does seem to reflect a less militarised affective climate than the one I had experienced in Nigeria (Jefferson 2007).

The atmosphere at the gate varied, sometimes simply dull and other times quite tense. Already after a couple of weeks of going in and out, I noted 'The tension of the gate deserves more reflection' (22/05/06). Six weeks later (11/07/06), I watched a drama unfold as a notorious VIP prisoner (a former rebel spokesperson charged, at the time, with treason) was prepared for court. I noted how 'a stilled hush descended, though only briefly'. It followed a speech by the prisoner, vaguely directed towards me, and following a minor verbal altercation at the far end of the gate lodge. He cried out, 'This is the third time we have not been to court, the third bloody time… so called treason trial…'. He had not seemed to notice me at first, even though he had walked right past me. The commotion featured the treason trialist and the elderly chief prison officer who supervised him and his co-accused in the separate 'old female section', reserved for special prisoners. The grievance was a spill-over from there, where they had been protesting the delay in being produced for court. The treason trialist remonstrated in Krio with the guards but switched to English, moving out of the throng at the other end and taking the centre of the gate lodge as his launch pad. There had been a small delay whilst the gate pass was being signed on the desk at which I sat. It was this delay that gave him the chance to apparently gather himself and implement his tactic of making me aware of the difficulties they faced and implicating me in their struggles. He addressed me without addressing me, and I adopted a blank stare. He compromised neither himself nor me, and my acting as though I was not paying attention was a similar gesture. He spoke as if on a parade ground issuing orders, reminiscent, I noted, of the way on another occasion I had witnessed him 'thundering' in the high court (see Jefferson 2013). It was after this speech that a still hush fell. Was it awe, shock, or fear, I wondered? The silence dissolved almost as quickly as it descended as the front gate closed and the prisoners disappeared, finally on their way to court.[11]

This experience serves as a powerful example of affect rising and fading against a backdrop of enduring dynamics of control and conflict. It is obvious that my presence – as a privileged outsider – partially enabled the performance, but there was much about it that had nothing to do with me. The grievance was carried over from the three VIP prisoners' special quarters. Its expression was informed by frustration at the slow process of the trial and no doubt more deeply by the allegations they faced and the circumstances of being incarcerated. But also by the physical environment that served as an echo chamber for his voice, his message, and his affective disposition.

My notes also contain observations of sensory and affective aspects of prison life beyond the gate. For example, I noted the high level of activity yet studious and calm atmosphere in workshops, one 'lit up by the sizzling light of welding equipment' (09/05/06); the 'smell of flour drifting out of the door' of the bakery; the way staff in the women's section protected bathing prisoners from my intrusive presence. Once the sound of raised voices and a quarrel caught my attention. Two prisoners began to exchange blows just outside Blyden cell block. The officer I had been talking to became increasingly attentive to his chalkboard task as the quarrel gained momentum. No other officers were in sight. The two men were separated by their fellow prisoners. But as they were, one of them picked up a rock and looked to return to the melee. The second also grabbed a large stone, and they looked set to resume the fight, before one of them thought better of it and retreated, rubbing at his sore head. Words continued to be exchanged, but from a safer distance, whereby blows were ruled out.

In this section I have explored the affect-laden atmospheres that generate emotive carceral landscapes with particular focus on the '*conditions and surfaces* out of which or around which certain patterns of expressed emotion seem to form or coagulate' (Jefferson et al. 2025, p. 92, my emphasis). I have shown how affect is borne, reflected, produced, and reproduced in the gate lodge and in other spaces, revealing the affective agency of the institution. Institutional affect is generated in the moment at the intersection between structural conditions and modes of inhabiting them. The brickwork that formed the echo chamber of the gate lodge and the stones and rocks that lay in the dust by the cell blocks are integral aspects of the affective violent spaces that comprise the prison experience.[12] Presence or co-presence also seems significant. In the gate lodge, my presence contributed to the performance even while I was ostensibly ignored. It is impossible to assess the extent to which the presence of the officer updating the chalkboard while ostensibly ignoring the fight contributed to the quarrel between the prisoners. Yet seeing while pretending not to see (what we would colloquially term 'turning a blind eye') and even talking while pretending not to talk (as we shall see below) are common features of carceral spaces.

2. Contrasting senses of institutional affect

Central Prison captures many of the affective dynamics of other prisons in Sierra Leone, but due to its size and location in the capital, it is also unique. It is therefore worthwhile taking a short glimpse at some of the smaller prisons to consider the way affect plays out there. One particular trope invoked in my notes is a contrast between prison-like and unprison-like prisons. Clearly, this is a distinction highly dependent on stereotypical imaginaries of what a prison looks like. I reproduce it nevertheless as it serves to emphasise the variety of structural forms generating affect. Two excerpts are illustrative:

> I ask where the prison entrance is and I am directed to a standard size door in the side of a building. I had tried to find the prison once before without luck at first because it resembles just a standard [residential] compound. There is nothing very prison like about it, though once one gets closer to the door the standard prison grill is evident. What is missing I later found out is a perimeter wall.
>
> *(Makeni, 25/05/06)*

On the other hand,

> I was shocked by the prison-like state of Kenema prison. It seemed like something out of a bygone age. It felt malign in a way that the new

UNDP sponsored prisons do not. It felt brutal.... The [new, modern] court building in contrast is spectacular and magnificent, a site of splendour, actually looking down on the prison, a stark contrast.

(Kenema, 13/06/06)

In Makeni, I had perhaps been looking for the big imposing gate, and all I discovered was a 'standard'-sized door, albeit with a viewing grill. And I'd been expecting a perimeter wall, one of the most ubiquitous security features of prisons globally, but actually a feature missing in both the ostensibly unprison-like prison in Makeni and – to my mind – the distinctly unmodern, almost prototypical (post)colonial prison in Kenema.

My notes feature the use of contrasts and distinctions: between expected and unexpected, standards and actuality, contemporary and bygone, old and new, dilapidation and splendour. It was through such contrasts that I sought to capture the dynamic affect of the institutions as I initially perceived them.

My more detailed description of Makeni prison as I first encountered it is illustrative of the everyday vibe of some of the smaller prisons I visited:

> The OiC's office, the 2iC's office (also reception) the wireless room, and the store (containing soap, flour and strangely toilet paper) all opened out onto the prison yard which really is only a yard, containing hens and a goat as well as prisoners. Confinement in Makeni is confined. The lack of an outer perimeter gives the impact of the yard an immediacy lacking in other prisons I have visited. It is as if a layer is missing. There are fewer rites of passage before the final entry. I was thrust into the atmosphere which was not exactly teeming with activity but felt close and energetic. In the compact yard prisoners were moving around. Given the lack of an outer perimeter the back walls of the male cells are the outside of the prison. [13]
>
> *(25/05/06)*

During a walk around the outside of the prison, the OiC was vocal about the cracking walls and foundations, the non-functioning pump for the well, and the absence of a perimeter wall. He pointed to the patched-up back of cell three, the rendering indicating a place where prisoners had escaped, breaking straight through their cell wall to freedom. The goat is his. He brings it to work each morning for safekeeping, feeds it, and takes it home again in the evening. Safe custody for the goat. He was not keen for me to note this. He showed me his cassava plantation and told me how he has no help to harvest except prisoners, whom he rewards with tobacco.

The following extract conveys my first impressions of Kenema prison:

> Not much movement inside really. A busy early morning claustrophobic atmosphere seemed to constrain our movement, the two-storey building

having a kind of overbearing, foreboding character to it... Kenema prison may be the oldest in Sierra Leone. As stark and ugly and prison-like on the inside as it looks on the out. Just a yard surrounded on four sides by a two-storey structure. An example of confining, claustrophobic confinement... Prisoners had just been opened and there was a just-woken-up-getting-going atmosphere with a harsh subtext. Voices could be heard even from outside the walls. There is no perimeter so the only thing separating outsiders from insiders in their cells is the cell wall... The kitchen is a small jutting annex off the right side of the complex. A narrow corridor between the cells runs to it. Already three paces into the corridor my eyes begin to sting from the smoke from the wood fire beneath the large iron cauldron. Closer in where the corridor opens into a room the stinging was barely bearable. A prisoner stoked the flames and tended to the contents of the cauldron. Others pointed to the roof indicating the holes in the zinc. One big hole above the cauldron was clearly designed to let out smoke. But the problem is the rain. Not only does the room fill with smoke; it also floods.
(13/06/06)

Women comprise a small proportion of the prison population in Sierra Leone. Today there are two designated prisons for women, one in Freetown and one in Kenema. Back in 2006, there were none, and women were held in separate sections or sometimes simply in staff offices used as cells in the men's prisons. In Makeni there were six women prisoners whom I observed 'looked isolated as well as confined'. Their section was rectangular, with two cells at the far end and a washroom taking up much of the space, adding to the sense of closeness and claustrophobia that was created by the fact that the space was no wider than the height of the surrounding walls. It felt like 'being in a shoe box'.

This section further demonstrates the way affect is material as well as relational. Affects are felt even when not delivered by individual agents and sometimes in spite of their best or worst intentions. Walls, smoke, the organisation, and inhabitation of space (e.g. by a goat) act as do the lack of such features and commodities (e.g. perimeter walls, medical supplies, clean water, livelihood opportunities). Institutional affect is of course mediated via personal trajectories and experiences as I consider below.

3. Affective histories – dreary loops, belligerent frustration, and resignation

Staff felt trapped, too. The OiC encouraged the female officer supervising the women's compound to make some positive remarks about her situation; when she mumbled small complaints about the lack of an office, he did not deny it but dismissively moved on, emphasising that 'we thank God anyway'. The woman officer's job involved supervising the female prisoners as they cleaned the compound and made food. The OiC remarked they mostly just sat around: 'One gets a salary the other does not', a vivid illustration of staff confinement (Makeni, 25/05/06).

In another prison (in Bo, 13/06/06), I witnessed a woman prisoner cooking her own food over a wood fire. Her cell was once the office of the OiC. An officer says he can see she is eating too well and getting fat. She ignores his abuse, gazing flatly in his direction, her apparently deliberate lack of affect conveying its own message. Once again, not hearing, or pretending not to hear, presents as a feature of the carceral space in a manner akin to not seeing (and not 'talking'), as referred to above. Institutional affect comprises absences as well as presences.

Churcher et al write of the 'sedimentation' of 'institutional arrangements' in 'material surroundings, to which stereotypical institutional agents and their affective demeanor contribute in a dreary feedback loop...' (2022: 10). In this section I cast some light on the morale and demeanour of prison staff (and the 'dreary feedback loops' in which they partake) in the light of their trajectories and personal histories. In one sense this can be read as an attempt to contextualise staff's state of mind and body in the light of enduring penal norms and recent developments in Sierra Leone's penal history. The affective force of the institution reveals itself in staff's adaptive responses to it, whether these take the form of belligerent frustration or resignation.[14]

Staff complained to me regularly about a lack of materials and tools, pointing to machines left over from colonial times as well as about poor salaries, long commutes to work, unpaid rice allowances, and the general difficulty of making ends meet. Resignation and frustration, as well as demoralisation and disillusionment, were common features of their narratives (see Jefferson, Feika and Jalloh 2014). They often compared themselves unfavourably to the police, resenting perceived better conditions of service and more prestige. 'We are tired', they would say, and my field notes testify at least four times to staff sleeping while on duty: one officer at headquarters was just dressing after waking from a Chloroquine-induced nap when I met him. An elderly instructor in the tailoring workshop was also sleeping when I arrived to see the premises, as was an officer in the records office on one occasion. In fact, the scene was set for the discovery of somnolent staff on my very first day in Central Prison in the office of the OiC. I was led through the gate lodge and up the stairs and instructed by the 2iC – dressed in bleached jeans and a colourful top – to sit. He alluded to a man sleeping barefoot on the couch, whose feet I could smell, as his boss. He was 'taking his rest', he said (09/05/06).

New recruits as well as old hands complained equally, though not always about the same things. Young new recruits are typically better educated than old-timers and complain about their seniors' lack of literacy and the fact that merit is rarely rewarded. Promotions, for example, were reportedly based on time in the job rather than aptitude. One young recruit recounted how senior staff tried to discourage the new recruits both from trying to achieve any form of success and from speaking up about conditions or 'how things really are'. His final remark to me during this conversation was to say that one recruit died because of the pressure. In fact, it wasn't really a conversation, more a monologue. All the while he spoke in relatively hushed tones, deliberately not looking at me but speaking warily into the air, conscious that, as he put it, 'focus was on us'. He appeared tense, cautious, and wary of the risks of being seen speaking with me.

It is possible, of course, that satisfied, contented staff did not choose to speak with me, but for the most part, it was I who sought out people to talk to rather than the other way around. One long-serving officer (23+ years) who had recently been – in his view, unjustly – demoted was keen to share his story with me. The case was three years old, and the result had just been announced. It related to a prisoner who had been permitted – against the rules but at the behest of a police officer to avoid a fracas at the court – to bring some goods with him in the truck from the court to the prison. The prison officer was charged with trafficking even though he had the prisoner declare the goods at the gate. A demotion was the thanks he got for 20 years of service: 'For 20 years I suffer for nothing', he said regretfully, capturing his sense that even before his current misery, his work life was characterised by suffering rather than satisfaction.

Another long-serving officer recounted a tale of promotions and demotions, making clear that any fear he experienced in the job did not relate to prisoners but to the machinations of the prison administration and to ethnically inflected rivalries. Similarly to the recruit, he shared a belief that education was not highly prized and that those who were educated were stigmatised and even subject to punishment postings. In May 1997, following a regime change, he felt as though he was targeted by his superiors. At the same time, he felt the prison service did not want him. 'Well trained but not well-placed', as he put it. He referred to enemies within the service blocking his progress, standing in the way of acknowledging merit and the merit of education. He alleged the authorities wanted to discourage him because he was an educated manager. He was withdrawn from a post that matched his skills and 'dumped' in an administrative position where, as he put it, 'If I went to work or not, no-one cared'. He explicitly used the words 'marginalised' and 'victimised' to refer to this period.

Another officer I met in the eastern part of the country described his lack of faith in the prison administration and the government. 'The government don't appreciate', he said. 'How can I wear the uniform and walk in the rain or the dust of Kailahun town? So mostly I don't wear uniform'. He lamented the lack of provision of a vehicle and compared the appearance of staff unfavourably with prisoners. 'Prisoners look better off than prison officers. Officers look haggard'. This certainly chimed with my impression of the somewhat bedraggled staff I found it hard to distinguish from prisoners during early visits to Central prison.

If the affective force of the institution is partially revealed by the state of frontline officials, might we also see a reflection of the state in their bedraggled, exhausted, frustrated, and resigned condition? Or, recalling discussion of Hansen and Stepputat's work earlier, might it be more productive not to project statehood onto persons but rather to see state officials as part of the performance of provisional state-making? In this version, state officials do not embody the state, but they do perform and thereby constitute it – though always only partially and provisionally. There is a tension in the narratives above between prison officers' self-perceptions and the idea that officials somehow embody or personify state power.[15] Statehood or state representativity may be projected onto prison staff (not least by international actors, intent on promoting professionalism and neutrality within an assumed rational-legal framework), but being a state official is clearly experienced quite differently. At the same time, whatever sufferings or histories may inform their actions and affective states, these officers are paramount players in constituting the state-in-the-making, however frustrated and fatigued they may feel. Another significant factor affecting prison staff was their historical experience of working during the civil war. I consider this briefly now.

4. History's affect

My fieldwork took place only five years after Sierra Leone's brutal civil war had ended (1990–2001). During that period prisons were targeted and ransacked by rebels, prisoners freed, and prison staff taken hostage. Given the often-long careers of prison staff, some of those I spoke with carried with them the memories and wounds of such experiences. The conflict played out mostly in areas outside of the capital, Freetown. But the infamous 'invasion' of 6 January 1999, also featured an attack on the Central prison and the liberation of prisoners.

An officer from Kabala shared his version of an attack he thought probably took place in 1994. There were only two officers on duty when the attack came sometime between 11 and midnight. The rebels broke through the gate, broke open the cells, and freed over 20 prisoners. At that time the prison was only fenced; there was no wall. He was not on duty himself but at his home on the other side of town. But his colleagues told him that when they heard the rebels approaching and the sound of shots, they locked the prison and fled into the bush. No officers were killed in Kabala, he told, in contrast to when prisons at Mafanta and Masanki were attacked. On a separate occasion, another officer shared how the prison plantation for the production of palm oil at Masanki was 'destroyed, devastated, vandalised, burned down to pieces by the rebel war'.

The well-trained but not well-placed officer mentioned above was not well placed during the attack on Freetown either, though he was not present when his place of work was burned to the ground. Neither was he well placed when a serious incident occurred at the courts, where prisoners went on the rampage and broke out of the holding cells. Just under half (9) of the prison services' 21 prisoners escaped. He described how he and others fought with the escapees and tried in vain to prevent the gate from breaking. Armed police came, but only after it was too late. He took sick leave, suffering from hypertension.

Another officer with over 40 years' experience described how in Bo on 13 February 1997 all the prisoners were illegally released. He walked the streets in plain clothes, afraid for his life and afraid of prisoners identifying him as a prison officer. Some rebels, he said, hunted prison officers to slaughter them. They fled to the countryside, 'fighting for our lives'. It was a 'strong problem… We were targets for them'. One colleague was captured, but serious resistance and an attack by civil defence forces led to his release (10/05/06).

Given these kinds of histories and the tensions between staff, and between staff and prisoners that seem endemic, the fact that staff were in a sorry state and largely invisible might not be so surprising.

Conclusion

Prisons in Sierra Leone – like prisons elsewhere – are historical, political, and populated. They are not merely sites of confinement but sites of everyday practices and relations, places where people engage in relations and transactions with one another, where quarrels take place and alliances develop, where 'people suffer, talk, eat, fight, work, laugh, tease, quarrel…' (Field Note 10/05/06), where affect is embedded, embodied and projected.[16]

State officials and the institutions in which they work – in this case prisons – are constituted and reconstituted in everyday social practices that are constrained and compelled as people interact with infrastructures, materials, buildings, rules, procedures, as well as each other. I have described some of these affect-laden constraints and compulsions. I have portrayed the gate lodge at Pademba as an example of an environment infused with affect, sedimented in physical structures and their arrangements, as well as in hierarchical norms and punitive, ordering procedures. Furthermore, I have contrasted the variety of carceral forms that frame and produce affect in post-war Sierra Leone. And finally, I have presented examples of the affective histories that inform prison staff's modes of surviving in the prison and performing the state.[17] All in pursuit of examples of the ways in which the prison itself demonstrates forms of embodied, emotive institutional agency. I am proposing that institutions *think* (Douglas 1986) and *act* (i.e. have effects) and demonstrate, deliver, and distribute affect through the enabling capacities embedded in arrangements of space and mobility, through the stonework, and through the norms governing modes of relating in punitive spaces 'containing' marginalised populations.

In Street's analysis of the hospital in Papua New Guinea, it is the 'spatial layering of inequalities' that produces the affective force of the hospital, not its ostensible function as site of improvement and healing. Perhaps it is necessary, she suggests, to consider the way such spaces 'might always already be ruined insofar as differentiations, exclusions, and inequalities are built into them and create spaces of relative wreckage from the start' (54). Prisons, I believe, invite the same indictment. In this chapter, I have considered the harm-filled structural intentionality – the force and expression of history-filled structures – that is embedded in prisons in Sierra Leone and the dynamics of affective force that sustain punitive conditions. I am left with a puzzle: if affect is resident and emanating from the brickwork and the structures, then who is accountable for harm? One implication of my analysis is that in punitive institutional contexts, harm is often done despite the absence of an easily identifiable, intentional, individual agent. Cause–effect relations are complex and rarely simply linear, and culpable agents of harm are ephemeral (cf Young 1990, 2011; McKeown 2021). Often referred to as collateral damage (but better understood following Condry and Minson (2021) as 'symbiotic harms'), institutional harm is commonly viewed as merely incidental to the operation of state power. This 'incidentality' renders observers oblivious to intent and too easily seduced by statements of benign purpose (or excuses in the form of 'we didn't mean to').

However, the notion of structural intentionality or institutional agency does not necessarily get decision makers or frontline actors off the hook, nor does it mean that people rendered vulnerable through the workings of institutional affect cannot be better protected. Situating decisions and actions, and dynamics and logics through deeper understandings of settings and circumstances compromised by affect-laden punitive structures and arrangements, helps us contextualise and explain their consequences. Recognising the way historical affect and affective histories inform prison staff's perspectives on the task at hand and acknowledging the affective force of the brickwork should allow us to better mitigate endemic and sedimented harms that marginalised populations are subject to in prisons – maybe not immediately, but once we (together with others perhaps) – have processed the implications. Thinking about prisons and their harmful effects in terms of institutional affect and structural intentionality may help us in that quest.

Notes

1 For previous attempts to grapple with this idea, please see our work on 'perpetrative institutions' (Jefferson and Gaborit 2015).

2 Street's data and methodology resemble mine, given their anchoring in observation and presence in the institution.
3 Elsewhere, I have characterized the Sierra Leonean state as 'trifurcated' reflecting the converging impact of the traditional, the colonial, and the contemporary global interventionist (the latter represented in 2006 by demobilization and disarmament initiatives; security and justice sector reform; humanitarian assistance to amputees as well as a truth commission, special court, and a massive UN military presence) (Jefferson 2013).
4 Thanks to Ana Aliverti, Henrique Carvalho, and Simon Tawfic for provoking these questions.
5 There is some resonance here with Åsa Wettergren's invocation of the notion of 'structural embeddedness'(this volume), though where Wettergren emphasises the way affect is embedded in 'social forms', I will additionally stress the way affect is *materially* embedded.
6 This is an alternative form of what I have elsewhere termed 'compromised circumstances' (Jefferson 2022).
7 In 2006 Sierra Leone was ranked 176/177 on the UN's Human Development Index, which compares countries along dimensions related to life expectancy, education, and per capita income: https://hdr.undp.org/system/files/documents/human-development-report-2006-english.human-development-report-2006-english
8 Some critical abolitionist scholars have argued that the persistence of prisons unfit for purpose is perpetuated by interventions that fail to take seriously deeply embedded ecologies of structural violence (e.g. Armstrong and Jefferson 2017; Drake 2018). See also Mathiesen (2000) on the 'fiasco' of the prison.
9 Named so because of its location on Pademba Road, which runs south from the roundabout in the city centre where the iconic cotton tree once stood.
10 Equivalent to a Prison Governor or Director in other countries.
11 This could be conceived of as an example of what Churcher et al conceive of as affect put into the service of 'instigating change', for example 'showing disaffection where affection is expected; expressing anger when polite deference is the norm' (2022: 19).
12 Philosopher Charles Taylor registers a similar idea when he discusses the way the *effect* of a Rodin sculpture is a product not only of the sculptor's hands or ideas but of 'the material itself' (2024: 197). An object – Taylor names an oak tree – can have an impact, an affect; it 'works on us' (2024: 174).
13 The capacity of the prison was 75. The population that day was 114. There were 28 officers attached: 7 women and 21 men.
14 Prisoners, of course, have their own affective histories that they bring with them, but this was not an area my prison fieldwork explored.
15 I have appreciated conversations with Henrique Carvalho around these matters and for reminding me of the connection between my thinking on institutional harm and Iris Marion Young's work on structural injustice. See later, and also Jefferson (2009).
16 By projection here I mean to reference the way affect is presented and distributed *across and between* people and things, actors, and objects and not simply 'contained' in or by them. Thanks to Amanda Wilson for pushing for clarity on this matter.

17 I have argued elsewhere that in the Sierra Leonean context, prisoners and staff share experiences of carcerality to a surprisingly high degree, such that it does make sense to think of prison staff surviving. One officer I spoke with, for example, described his regret about joining the service, comparing himself with former fellow students: 'Today' he said 'I have regretted it. Other graduates drive Jeeps and Mercedes Benz. I walk to work, not sure of a meal per day'.

References

Ahmed, S. (2004) *The Cultural Politics of Emotion*. New York: Routledge.
Ahmed, S. (2014) *The Cultural Politics of Emotion*. Edinburgh: Edinburgh University Press.
Armstrong, S. and Jefferson, A.M. (2017) Disavowing 'the' prison, pp. 237–267. In Moran, D. and Schliehe, A. (eds.) *Carceral Spatiality: Dialogues between Geography and Criminology*. Basingstoke: Palgrave.
Carrabine, E. (2005) Prison Riots, Social Order and the Problem of Legitimacy. *British Journal of Criminology* 45(6): 896-913.
Christie, N. (1978) Prisons in society, or society as a prison – a conceptual analysis, pp. 179–187. In Freeman, J.C. (eds.) *Prisons Past and Future*. London: Heinemann.
Churcher, M., Calkins, S., Böttger, J., and Slaby, J. (2022) The many lives of institutions, pp. 1–32. In Churcher, M. Calkins, S. Böttger, J. and Slaby, J. (eds.) *Affect, Power, and Institutions*. Abingdon: Routledge.
Condry, R. and Minson, S. (2021) Conceptualizing the effects of imprisonment on families: Collateral consequences, secondary punishment, or symbiotic harms? *Theoretical Criminology*, 25(4), 540–558.
Crewe B. (2011) Depth, weight, tightness: Revisiting the pains of imprisonment. *Punishment & Society* 13: 509-529.
Das, V. and Poole, D. (2004) *Anthropology in the Margins of the State*. Santa Fe, NM: School of American Research Press.
Douglas, M. (1986) *How Institutions Think*. New York: Syracuse University Press.
Drake, D. (2018) Prisons and state building: Promoting 'the fiasco of the prison' in a global context. *International Journal for Crime, Justice and Social Democracy*, 7(4), 1–15.
Draper, S. (2012) *Afterlives of Confinement, Spatial Transitions in Postdictatorship Latin America*. Pittsburgh, PA: University of Pittsburgh Press.
Fuchs, T. and Kock, S. (2014) Embodied affectivity: On moving and being moved. *Frontiers in Psychology*. Sec. Psychology for Clinical Settings, 5–2014.
Gieryn, T.F. (2002) What buildings do. *Theory and Society*, 31, 35–74.
Hansen, T.B. and Stepputat, F. (Eds.) (2001) *States of Imagination: Ethnographic Explorations of the Postcolonial State*. Durham, NC: Duke University Press.
Hansen, T.B. and Stepputat, F. (2005) *Sovereign Bodies: Citizens, Migrants, and States in the Postcolonial World*. Princeton, NJ: Princeton University Press.
Jefferson, A.M. (2007) Prison officer training and practice in Nigeria: Contention, contradiction and re-imagining reform strategies. *Punishment and Society*, 9(3), 253–269.
Jefferson, A.M. (2009) On hangings and the dubious embodiment of statehood in Nigerian prisons, pp. 122–138. In Jensen, S. and Jefferson, A.M. (eds.) *State Violence and Human Rights. State Officials in the South*. Abingdon: Routledge.

Jefferson, A.M. (2013) The situated production of legitimacy: Perspectives from the Global South, pp. 248–266. In Tankebe, J. and Liebling, A. (eds.) *Legitimacy and Criminal Justice: An International Exploration*. Oxford: Oxford University Press.

Jefferson, A.M. (2022). Prison reform and torture prevention under 'compromised circumstances'. *Criminology & Criminal Justice*, 24(2), 413-429.

Jefferson, A.M., Feika, M.C., and Jalloh, A.S. (2014) Prison officers in Sierra Leone: paradoxical puzzles. *Prison Service Journal*, 212, 39–44.

Jefferson, A.M. and Gaborit, L.S. (2015) *Human Rights in Prisons: Comparing Institutional Encounters in Kosovo, Sierra Leone and the Philippines*. Basingstoke: Palgrave Macmillan.

Jefferson, A.M. and Martin, T.M. (2016) Prisons in Africa, pp. 423–440. In Jewkes, Y., Crewe, B. and Bennett, J. (eds.) *Handbook on Prisons*, 2nd edition.. London: Routledge.

Jefferson, A.M. and Schmidt, B.E. (2019) Concealment and revelation as bureaucratic and ethnographic practice: Lessons from Tunisian prisons. *Critique of Anthropology*, 39, 155–171.

Jefferson, A.M., Nai Hla Yin, Lynn Thar Yar, Nwe Thar Gi, Bihlo Boilu and San Tayza (2025) *Everyday Prison Governance in Myanmar: Understanding Imprisonment Beyond the West*. Leeds: Emerald Publishing.

Laszczkowski, M. and Reeves, M. (Eds.) (2017) *Affective States: Entanglements, Suspensions, Suspicions*, 1st edition (Vol. 5). Oxford: Berghahn Books.

Lindberg, A. (2022) Feeling difference: race, migration, and the affective infrastructure of a Danish detention camp *Incarceration*, 3(1), 1–18.

Linke, U. (2006) Contact zones: rethinking the sensual life of the state. *Anthropological Theory*, 6(2), 205–225.

Martin, T.M. and Jefferson, A.M. (2019) Prison ethnography in Africa: reflections on a maturing field. *Politique Africaine*, 155(3), 131–152.

Mathiesen, T. (2000) *Prison on Trial*, 2nd edition. Winchester: Waterside Press.

McKeown, M. (2021) Structural injustice. *Philosophy Compass*, 16(7), e12757.

Morelle, M., Le Marcis, F., and Hornberger, J. (2021) *Confinement, Punishment and Prisons in Africa*. Abingdon: Routledge.

Slaby, J. (2019) Affective Arrangement Pp. 109-118. In Slaby, J. and von Scheve, C. (2019) *Affective Societies*: Key Concepts. Abingdon: Routledge.

Slaby, J. and von Scheve, C. (2019) *Affective Societies: Key Concepts*. Abingdon: Routledge.

Stoler, A.L. (2004) "Affective States." Pp. 4–29. In Nugent, D. and Vincent, J. (eds.) *A Companion to the Anthropology of Politics*. Oxford: Blackwell.

Stoler, A.L. (2008) Imperial debris: Reflections on ruins and ruination. *Cultural Anthropology*, 23, 191–219.

Street, A. (2012) Affective infrastructure: Hospital landscapes of hope and failure. *Space and Culture*, 15(1), 44–56.

Taylor, C. (2024) *Cosmic Connections. Poetry in the Age of Disenchantment*. Cambridge: Harvard University Press.

Thrift, N. (2007) *Non-Representational Theory: Space, Politics, Affect*. London: Routledge.

Young, I. M. (1990) *Justice and the Politics of Difference*. Princeton: Princeton University Press.

Young, I. M. (2011) *Responsibility for Justice*. Oxford: Oxford University Press.

PART 5
Navigating dilemmas of care and control

17
GOVERNING THROUGH FEAR

Affective ambivalences and violence in police work

Sara León Spesny

Introduction

It was a hot afternoon. Riveiro and Diego, the two soldiers I was accompanying on foot patrol, were focused on the intricate maze of alleyways of the favela. They held their .40 Glock handguns pointing forward at each corner.

Riveiro and Diego were soldiers of the military police in Rio de Janeiro, Brazil. They were part of a specialised branch called the 'Pacifying Police Unit' (*Unidade de Polícia Pacificadora or UPP*) created in 2008. The initiative was guided by proximity policing strategies and the values of human rights, democracy, and citizenship. It was also a highly militarised initiative, following the institutional history and police structure in Brazil. The UPP's aim was to bring state control into some favelas, reconquer the territory from traffic gangs (*o tráfico*), and gain the hearts and minds of favela residents. At the heart of the UPP were a series of contradictory tasks that confronted security and human rights, violence and legitimation, compassion and repression, and integration and inequality. These contradictions generated ambivalent goals for police soldiers. They demonstrated impulses of both compassion and repression and often opted for violence as a way to impose police order.

Riveiro and Diego arrived at a crossing path where three young black men were gathered. I felt Riveiro and Diego tense up and approach them determinately. I could see both soldiers scrutinising the young men as if trying to determine the level of danger they posed. Without any explanation or greeting, they positioned two of the young men against the wall. The rough stop-and-frisk began. The search was thorough. The young men seemed almost unresponsive to their handling. They remained silent, their faces looking at the wall. The soldiers still held their handguns as they checked the young men's bodies. Quickly enough they found a handful of marijuana and a lighter in one of the young men's pockets. What else? Cigarettes. Keys. Dark glasses. Nothing incriminating. The little amount of the drug helps the soldier quickly classify the men as drug users (*consumidores*). But even if effectively harmless, they must somehow be punished.

As the young men were being searched, their expressions were tense, their bodies rigid with fear. Soon enough the search was over. The young men kept looking down. I could only discern the young men's emotions through the thickness of silence and their avoidant eyes. They made sure they did not respond to the menacing gaze of the soldiers. You could almost smell the fear in the air. For soldiers, imposing fear seems to be a way to deter them from similar behaviour in the future and 'putting them in their place'. This feeling of fear, which I quickly became aware of during fieldwork, was also a shared intuition that violence was always just waiting to be woken.

One of the three young men broke the silence by greeting the soldiers (*bom dia oficiais, tudo bem com os senhores?*). His tone seemed ironic, implying that the police contact should have started with a greeting and introduction before the rough search. I could tell from previous patrols that this could be interpreted as a crime of treating a public agent with disrespect (*desacato*). Soon after the young man pronounced 'Hey, you don't even have respect! Huh?'. I saw the penetrable gaze of his big brown eyes. Immediately, Riveiro put his hand on the young man's chest, pushing him towards the wall with violence and insulting him briefly (*vagabundo! Bom dia um caralho, vocês estão portando droga!*), suggesting that they didn't need to greet because they were caught doing something illegal. He screamed at them, telling them that they should go to the police station (*delegacia*) for drug possession. Riveiro combined a repressive tone with an apparent benevolent action, as if they were being generous for not arresting them. But evidently, one small marijuana joint wasn't worth the inconvenience of taking them to the *delegacia*. Indeed, the civil police officer (*delegado*) would probably dismiss the whole case given the insignificant matter and release the young men after filing – or even without registering- the event (*ocorrência*).

Riveiro's screaming imparted a dose of public shaming and revealed – albeit fleetingly – the power of the police. He scolded the young men with a strong moral lecture about values, how they were wasting their lives with drugs, and how they would end up dead either by consumption or by getting involved with *o tráfico*. Implicitly, Riveiro's speech alluded to the risk of further police violence: Once the drug user became a trafficker (considered a natural escalation) the police would act differently. After the encounter, Riveiro professed that the rough handling and the moral scolding were, in fact, in the young men's best interest.

This ordinary interaction, like many others I witnessed, demonstrates how central emotions are in police encounters. Here, I am particularly interested in understanding how emotions shape policing practices and how institutional contexts shape the emotional responses of state agents. My approach seeks to understand emotions not merely as individual responses but as framed by historical and institutional frameworks and expectations.

Diego and Riveiro's interaction with the three young men highlights how emotions, especially fear, were expressed and produced through gestures and language. An ethnographic perspective allows us to see how the police's institutional history and context shape soldiers' perspectives. In this sense, soldiers made constant efforts to distinguish the level of threat favela residents pose: the good citizen (mostly women, children and workers), the annoying but harmless drug user or consumer (such as the three young men we encountered), and the traffickers (the *bandidos*, these did not deserve respect or dignity, and, on the contrary, deserved the full force of violence). The effort to distinguish who is who posed practical and moral challenges to soldiers and significantly shaped their emotions and attitudes towards residents.

Just as Riveiro and Diego, soldiers strived to distinguish and decide what treatment residents deserved. This constant classification became the central task of the Pacifying Police. Indeed, I observed soldiers constantly grappling with what I name affective ambivalences towards favela residents. Soldiers constantly displayed mixed feelings about their targets and the community more broadly. For example, Diego and Riveiro simultaneously expressed impulses to repress the young men (punish them in some way) and protect them (deterring them from further drug use and affiliation with a traffic gang).

The affective ambivalences of soldiers were related to the contradictory and equally ambivalent goals of the UPP. These reflected a tension between policies and institutional efforts that confronted security and human rights, violence and legitimation, compassion and repression, and integration and inequality. Thus, the institutional ambivalences were mirrored in soldiers' behaviours and perspectives. For instance, soldiers engaged in social projects (music and sports lessons for children, workshops for mothers, organising charity events and other services, etc.) and they often expressed sympathy towards children, women, and 'good' citizens who respected their authority. In this sense, soldiers often displayed strong feelings of protection and compassion for certain segments of the favela residents. At the same time, they considered enemies those who did not respect police authority, and violence was a key component of everyday policing.

Soldiers expressed a spectrum of sentiments and affects towards the residents. As other chapters in the book discuss, the embodiment of police work and policing as an activity is often related to a range of emotions, namely disgust (see Aliverti, this volume, and Fernández de la Reguera, this volume). However, there was a central emotion that underlies what I saw in the field: fear. Indeed, what structured soldiers' impulses of protection and repression was fear. For agents, fear was a productive emotion that grounded police order in the favela, and eliciting fear in residents was a core aspect to sustain pacification. Indeed, in a broad sense, fear is a crucial affective component of becoming a police soldier, as Eduardo de Oliveira Rodrigues illustrates in their chapter (this volume).

During pacification it was through the imposition of fear that soldiers managed the population in the favela. For Riveiro, as for many soldiers I patrolled with, fear was the only means necessary to impart respect and authority in the favela. Fear, in a way, is the basis of police work. Either by public humiliation or shaming, in minor cases such as the one described above, or by aggressive handling and arrests, or by much greater forms of violence, such as shootings and police killings. Fear is even useful to persuade 'good' citizens to adhere to police orders by expressing loyalty to them.

While I did not witness the greater forms of violence, I heard much about them: From the bragging sergeant with big tales of bravery, to the injured officer who perpetrated fear and hatred towards favela residents due to his own experience, or soldiers who were under administrative penalty for 'excessive force'. Stories of death and violence also circulated daily: News of killed or injured colleagues travelled fast and circulated in soldiers' communication channels, and videos. But the hardest were the personal stories of past experiences, notably injured or killed colleagues; these memories were shared very often in moments of vulnerability and sadness.

I ground my analysis in a 13-month-long ethnography of one station of the Pacifying Police (2014–2015). This station is in a favela in the Southern region of Rio de Janeiro, a wealthy part of the city. During my research I followed the daily life of soldiers, mostly their foot patrols and vehicle patrols, but also other tasks, such as workshops they organised for the community, errands they ran, testimonies they were called to provide to the judiciary, preparation of meals, visiting relatives, etc. While I spoke and interacted with higher and middle hierarchies of the police, I spent most of my time with the troops composed of the lower echelons of the police, the soldiers. Most of the troops were made up of young men, mostly black or brown, many of whom were favela residents themselves. The personal background of soldiers also contributed to their affective ambivalences, as they patrolled a population that oftentimes reflected their own circumstances and stories.

In this chapter, I first introduce the Pacifying Police as a novel and ambitious project that preached human rights, citizenship, and democracy, while retaining the militaristic style of the police. I then trace the moral economy of police violence, retracing some major shifts in the recent history of Brazil, placing the emergence of human rights as a keystone in contemporary police action, but being also one that ultimately perpetuates violent police practices. Thirdly, I focus on some of the affective relations between the police and favela residents, discussing the centrality of fear as a police tactic, but also highlighting some of the affective ambivalences expressed by soldiers. I conclude with a reflection on the 'duty of violence' that shapes the affects of soldiers.

Renewing state power: The pacification police

In 2007 Brazil was confirmed as the host country of the 2014 FIFA World Cup. And with the upcoming mega-event set, the city faced international pressure to contain violence. A couple of years later, the city would be confirmed as the host of the 2016 Olympic Games, which only added fuel to the initiative to integrate and secure the city. International anxieties around public security certainly prompted the local government to act (Saborio, 2014).

The Secretary of Public Security opted for a novel approach: The Pacifying Police Unit (UPP). At the end of 2008, the massive community policing programme was launched. Indeed, the entrance of the state into traffic-controlled communities established a benchmark for public security in Rio de Janeiro. It broke from the history of cyclical and distant relationships between the police and favela residents. The idea that the UPP had come to stay seemed a hopeful message. This recovery of lost territories now dominated by traffic gangs represented a renaissance of the military police. This renaissance was based on the modernisation of the force, known for its cruel and violent methods, corruption, and inefficiency (Caldeira, 2002; Human Rights Watch, 2009; Wacquant, 2008). It was translated into investment, training, infrastructure, weaponry, and human resources (police trained in a new perspective, including an emphasis on human rights). As a 2009 newspaper article entitled 'The military police seek requalification' explained, 'to recognise our flaws is the first step towards the process of purification and modernisation'.[1] There was a new wave of positive information about the police, both through an effective marketing strategy and thanks to coverage from national and international media outlets.[2] Also, the military police diversified their communication strategies and outlets to announce their positive actions and successes.[3] The feeling of fear and distrust was being replaced by hope and a sense of reparation.

Pacification was a dual initiative: securitarian and social. The Pacifying Police would bring public security and social integration. However, the social branch remained subjugated to the securitarian branch, and soon the social initiative faded completely (Misse, 2014; Henriques, 2012.). The result was that police agents became the only representatives of the state in the pacified favelas. Soldiers quite literally embodied the state, as favela residents would have to seek other services outside the contours of the favela.

The UPP became a political tool of the local government to promote a renewed integrated version of a city with a tumultuous history of socio-spatial segregation (Perlman, 2010). However, the pacification created a wave of uncertainty for residents, who experienced suspicion by and fear of the police and retaliation from traffic gangs, so this new occupation seemed unstable as well as threatening (Valle Menezes, 2014).

While the pacification also involved a high dose of violence and risk, the narrative of reconciliation between the police and favela residents began to dominate the national climate. While working to establish a new image of the military police, violence transitioned from troubling to intolerable, raising the idea of reconciliation between the police and residents: residents did not have to fear the police as they were used to. Police authorities explicitly clarified that they are not on a 'crusade against drugs, but the aim is to take away the power of traffickers over domination and death'.[4][5] Images of the police with *bandidos*, drugs, and weapons flourished in the news. Integration through social sanitation began.

The combination of these modernisation processes repositioned the police as a rational force. This rationality also applied to their use of violence, now used with measure, restraint, and proportionality. The military police recovered a sense of meaning and were able to fulfil some of the social demands to reduce police violence. But, pacification formalised the idea that there is space for legitimate violence as a means for peace, a mandatory phase, the instauration of 'order' through 'shock'. In this sense, pacification was framed within a continuum of violence.

Media outlets, NGOs, and society at large perpetuated sympathy for the residents as well as a sense of victory at integrating them into the formal city. Pacified favelas were portrayed as experiencing economic growth and social peace.[6]

According to media outlets, pacification has finally liberated favela residents. Thus, the time for reconciliation between the police and residents had come. But despite expectations of forgiveness and trust between the residents and the police, the reconciliatory process did not shatter the deeply seated fear that shaped the relationship between the police and residents.

Indeed, the Pacifying Police condensed the tensions between the traditional and the new, and in this sense, it continued to reproduce the same logic and rationalities of its past, where police violence is the norm and not the exception. This explains why fear continued to be central to the work of soldiers, such as Riveiro and Diego's patrol.

In the next section, I will retrace how the circulation and reproduction of collective values and moral emotions shape police violence as the force behind Pacifying Police work.

Fear and police work: A brief genealogy of police violence in Brazil

Violence was ubiquitous in police work, and violence was a significant contributor to soldiers' emotions, notably fear. Soldiers feared residents: they were constantly scrutinising and classifying them. They feared the sense that violence was always lurking in their daily lives (inside and outside work). But perhaps they feared the most not fulfilling institutional expectations and directives. As the previous section described, while the UPP was portrayed as a novel approach, it contained all the militaristic features of the institution.[7] This is why police violence, in this context, was developed amid a persistent tension between justification and control, management and regulation, incitement and condemnation.

A way to understand police violence is through the notion of moral economy (Fassin, 2009). A moral economy represents the production, circulation, and appropriation of values and affects within a particular social context. Moral economies unveil – for a specific historical moment and social space – how a social issue is constituted, through the display of judgments and moral sentiments that define a common sense and collective perspective of a problem (Fassin et al., 2013, p. 23). A moral economy refers to a social fact and is not limited to a specific professional group or social segment. Moral economies frame the construction of a social issue through the emotions this issue produces and reproduces. In this case, I trace a moral economy of police violence in Brazil.

The transformations and circulations of the values and affects around police violence represent not so much an objective reality as a subjective understanding of the social problem. Indeed, to discuss the moral economy of police violence is to understand it as a social fact, to identify the shared affects that shape it. This allows us to understand the nuances in Riveiro and Diego's police work, beyond their individual and moral subjectivities, but relating them to collective understandings about violence and institutional expectations of their work.

Police violence and the use of fear by the police can be traced back to the inception of the institution in Brazil. Initially created to control and punish enslaved people, the police were built to be at the service of the economic elites (Holloway, 1993).

Retracing the values and affects in Brazilian society regarding police violence reveals one key continuity: police violence has historically been directed towards certain 'suspicious classes'. At first, enslaved people, the fugitive slave, or those inciting revolts were the most severely punished. After the abolition of slavery, vagrants and vagabonds were criminalised and repressed by police forces. With the rise of military rule during the twentieth century, police gained expanded powers to repress anyone who seemed to represent a national threat. Poor and black people, especially favela residents, continued to represent these 'suspicious classes' in the eyes of the police throughout the past decades and until today (León Spesny, 2024).

Human rights emerged as a fundamental keystone in a rising democracy since the late 1980s. However, the democratisation also saw a sharp rise in crime, and public insecurity became a major issue in Brazilian society. The calls from activists to protect human rights for all often did not elicit public sympathy. Soon enough, human rights became equated with the protection of criminals (Alves, 2014; Caldeira & Holston, 1999). What did change was that police violence started to become troubling and intolerable to many, including top-level authorities of the military police and the Secretary of Public Security, if not directed appropriately.

Favelas have had a central place in discussions of police violence and human rights. Historically represented as a locus for the 'suspicious classes', favelas have been portrayed as urban enclaves of the immoral, unsanitary, and dangerous people (Zaluar & Alvito, 1998). In this sense, the emergence of *favela* residents as subjects worthy of non-violence and human rights – their progressive recognition as part of the human community – has redefined the boundaries of police work. In moral terms, the tension between the intolerable character of systematic violence and violence as a justified means to ensure social control has constituted the moral economy of police violence in Rio de Janeiro. Police violence in this sense has evolved in a constant tension between being justified and controlled, enhanced and regulated, incited and condemned.

Finally, it must be said that the military police are also represented not just as perpetrators of violence, but as victims of it (Minayo et al., 2007, 2008). Police agents have started being portrayed as heroes who offer their lives to secure the city. This recent shift has portrayed the police as fragile and vulnerable, but it simultaneously ensures a justification for repressive and lethal policing strategies. As the Secretary of Public Security stated, the stressful conditions under which police work in Rio de Janeiro make them potentially lethal. But agents must be understood and exculpated for their lethality, as the violence they receive justifies their retaliation. Because agents are victimised, police violence has become justified.

Conservative sectors have also passionately defended police violence, presenting it as the only means of fighting crime, reducing traffic gangs, regaining territorial control, and avoiding the spreading of violence throughout the city. For them, to restrain police violence is to take the side of the criminals and *bandidos*. Many deep polarisations remain around the issue of condemning or justifying violence. In this sense, human rights continue to be represented as the defence of *bandidos*. And the dominant logic remains that police violence is legitimate and appropriate if it is directed at those who deserve it (the *bandidos*) (Miranda, 2014; Silva, 2014; da Silva Leandro and Figueira, 2014). This is why Riveiro and Diego's work is highly focused on classifying appropriately and recognising if the suspects are indeed deserving of violence or not. It is an institutional expectation to punish appropriately those who deserve it. In this next section, I will focus on the mobilisation of fear and violence as part of the soldier's experience of work.

Soldiers' views towards favela residents: Distinguishing deserving citizens from the *bandidos*

Pacification established that the police were no longer capable of exercising violence in favela indiscriminately. Violence continues to be central to police work; however, it must be administered correctly. This makes distinctions crucial in police work; if violence is directed towards good people or honest workers, the police lose legitimacy. As the police were seldom held accountable, the growing number of claims and public outrages implanted a sense of restriction and limitation on police work.[8]

For Riveiro, nobody should witness the young men wasting their lives on drugs, and while the young men were not *bandidos*, they were dangerously close to them. The humiliation Riveiro imparted came hand in hand with outright aggressive behaviour – conveying a dose of fear – and was deemed as simply part of police work. I once asked Riveiro about the aggressiveness of patrols, and he confessed that he made great efforts to control it and only impart the necessary dose; however, he also acknowledged that violence is part of the profession and fear is just part of the job (Leon Spesny, 2020).

For the soldiers, when dealing with a public that cannot be taken to the *delegacia*, harsh or violent treatment was the means of maintaining control. Riveiro always justified it as his duty to impart 'lessons' and 'warnings' to young men so they wouldn't engage with the trafficking gangs. In this sense, fear is productive as a means to deter youth from joining traffic gangs. In a broader sense, it is also a way to ritually impart a dose of respect to young men and reassert police order in the favela.

Riveiro constantly threatened and scolded the youth, but he never engaged (at least never in front of me) in an actual arrest for possession, preferring verbal warnings about the devastating effects of drugs and the dangers of traffic gangs. Riveiro was otherwise respectful with residents and young men who were not involved with drugs or at least seemed not to be guilty of consuming or dealing. But despite his aggressive behaviour, unlike other police agents, Riveiro usually talked about residents with respect and cordiality, making clear that 'the real enemies were the drugs and the weapons', not the residents themselves, even if he chased his suspects almost obsessively. His duty as a police agent was to fight *o tráfico*, so correctly identifying the traffickers, as was the legal and moral objective of the pacification enterprise. Police goals should then be imparted in formal or informal matters. For the rest of the residents, Riveiro expressed a mix of indifference and sympathy.

As mentioned before, the central goal of pacification became to classify residents by filtering the traffickers and suspects from other social groups. This tended to place or classify people into three broad categories. The first, the worker or good person (*trabalhador ou pessoa de bem*). They represented the resident (*morador*), those who work for a living through dignified means.

They were morally associated with the good. If they adhered to the 'good' order of the police, they elicited sentiments of protection and respect. The second, the trafficker (*traficante ou bandido*), those belonging to the *o tráfico*. They were usually assigned a place outside the human community and generated strong feelings of fear and hatred among the police. The third, the drug user (*consumidor*), those who the police recognised as not belonging directly to *o tráfico*, but who sustained the drug economy through their consumption. While they were not respected, they were not despised with such intensity as the *traficante*. But since they were so dangerously close to *o tráfico*, they were also monitored and tormented. The young men that Riveiro and Diego interacted with were included in this last group because they had only a small quantity of marijuana and were not recognised by the agents as part of *o tráfico*.

Indeed, soldiers constructed social and moral classifications of residents. Profiling the *bandido* and distinguishing him from a good person was a common task of the police. The criminal was distinguished from the non-criminal with an array of adjectives expressing different degrees of suspicion.[9] While the first social category – the worker – was well defined, the figure of the *traficante* and the *consumidor* could be confused or blurred (depending on the circumstance of the patrol or exchange). Sometimes a *morador* might have been perceived as favourable or supporting the traffickers (*fávoravel ao tráfico*); other times they could have been unable to give the soldiers relevant information, or they simply 'did not want to collaborate'. This constant struggle to classify and obtain information often generated frustration, exasperation, and resentment from soldiers. In return, imparting fear became a common trading coin.

At the root, these social classifications relied on constructions of good and evil. For instance, one afternoon, Sargent Inácio was notified by an anonymous call that the police should patrol near a particular area because a motorcycle had been stolen. The stolen motorcycle was supposedly hidden in a house, and as they were organising a team to pay a visit, the sergeant said, 'I know where it is, there have been previous occurrences there, they are evil people' (*gente do mal*). This sense of evil also elicited strong affects from police agents. Under this register, most agents had a moral impulse to restore the good order and punish evil deeds.

I must clarify that these distinctions are not exclusive to the military police. On the contrary, the figures of *pessoa de bem* and *bandido*, among others, are widely used and define the limits of the human community in Brazilian society at large (Lembruger et al., 2017). But these categorisations are especially relevant in police work. Contrasting figures emerge within this classification of suspiciousness. While women and children are more likely to be perceived as *pessoas do bem*, men must show that they are workers – *trabalhador* – and not *bandidos*, associated or not with o *tráfico*.

The scene with Riveiro additionally exemplifies how the moralisation of repression can be used as a legitimate tool in the quest for pacification.

Instead of legal arguments, and technical rationalisations, police work is mostly based on the moral compass of agents. This is why social categories come with the moral duty of agents to act accordingly.

While it is true that ingrained violence is common in Brazilian military police, there were also many forms of genuine kindness and care from police soldiers. Soldiers would assist respected residents and even establish cordial relationships. Many of them had lunch at local restaurants and enjoyed their time chatting with residents. Soldiers also engaged with children and stepped out to play football or the like. In this sense, proximity policing created paradoxical effects. While it invited the legitimisation of the police through a certain familiarity during patrols, the police were simultaneously delegitimised when soldiers engaged in discriminatory and aggressive behaviour. The use of fear is rooted in this dichotomy. Police officers build acquaintanceships with certain groups and people: small entrepreneurs and merchants, restaurant owners, and participants in police activities such as a Christmas party or lessons and workshops offered at the station. The bricklayers who carry cement bags and materials near the station and up into the *morro* are recognised by soldiers and are thus labelled as workers. Someone who has asked for help from the police will be recognised afterwards, or someone who greets the police will often be recognised and labelled as good. Inversely, suspiciousness is also generated through implicit moral rules, such as going out at night; as one soldier pointed out, 'At night, anyone who's outside is suspicious, because they are up to no good'.

But proximity also prompted other forms of distinctions involving categories that may generate disorder, but are nonetheless considered non-threatening, as some individuals labelled as crazy or drunk who engaged in public disorder, but whom the police might treat more softly. For instance, on a lunch break, Sargent Valério received a call from a team of soldiers on patrol. They were concerned, and emotions were running high, as I could hear through the phone. A man was screaming that after the Olympics, the police would be in trouble. The soldiers were concerned about him scaring tourists and about their safety. They thought about the man as a threat, given what he was saying. However, the Sergeant asked for identifying traits, only to conclude,

> Use the military psychology, remember? Ignore. Just ignore. We know him, we know that he is just crazy and that he gets worse when he is drunk. Just stay calm, I need to finish my lunch and then I will personally go down there.

The permanent presence of the police inside the favela familiarised the police with residents, and shaped their responses towards them according to the level of threat they posed.

The force of punishment and repression runs deep within the veins of the military police in Brazil. While the pacification enterprise was created to moralise the police itself and establish the integration of some favelas through reconciliation and compassion, the proximity created paradoxical effects, as the new position of the police inside the favela also gave an extraordinary, renewed force and allowed the radicalisation of police repression as a moral duty. The soldiers' emotional responses were shaped by a process of moral classification of citizens to determine the appropriate route to take. This process of clarification was rooted in collective understandings of police violence, but also individual subjectivities of soldiers, on which I will focus in the final section.

Between individual trajectories and institutional expectations: Soldiers' ambivalences and the duty of violence

Riveiro was in his mid-20s, and he did a very long commute, having to sleep on the bus on his way to work; this seemed a better arrangement than living in another favela (where he lived previously). He was imposing and muscular and had many tattoos on his arms. Riveiro considered himself brown, and his parents had migrated from a northern region when he was a child. For Riveiro, as for many soldiers, those who got involved with *o tráfico* represented a lost cause. Interestingly, Riveiro constantly compared himself with those young men, stating that it was easy for them to take that road. This sense of the same origin, same difficulties, but different outcomes, created a reinforced sense of resentment and hatred. Riveiro once casually stated that he had never used drugs; he had had plenty of chances when he was young, but he always knew it was 'the wrong thing to do'. He then treated it as a personal duty to impart that fear into young men, as he justified, to protect them. He had worked in other favelas previously, in a very complicated environment. He was happy to have been assigned to this UPP, even if he expressed disillusionment with the institution. Many soldiers I spoke to had similar life pathways as Riveiro: they lived under economic strains, they experienced high control from the institution, they navigated racialisation in a generally racist institution, and they were convinced that it was up to them to sustain the good order of the police, despite not being recognised by society. This personal enmeshment with their work further shaped all sorts of ambivalence. From sympathy, familiarity, and complicity with favela residents to outright distrust, anger, and resentment.

The historical accumulation of violence is a haunting figure for police agents, who fear it while being ironically drawn to it. They avoid it but taunt it. They hold on to it while hoping it never gets them. In other words, violence is ubiquitous for police agents, both in its manifestation (through forms of violence that are acted, exerted, imparted, as well as received) or in hypothetical forms (the imagined, restrained, projected). Violence can materialise at any turn, expressing itself or remaining in the shadows. And violence is wrapped up in fear.

While actual violence occurs daily, its effects are so powerful that they go beyond the material and become metaphysical, or transcendental (Scheper-Hughes, 2015). In this sense, the magic or metaphysical power of the police in postcolonial settings emerges from their actual and imagined force to exert their power ritually over their subjects, especially favela residents. It seems that the military police manage favela residents via the accumulation of fear and distrust.

Whether the police are perpetrators or recipients of violence, police violence is usually naturalised and justified. Justifications of violence are rooted in the idea of what is morally just, precisely because targets (*bandidos* whom police soldiers must identify among favela residents) are considered immoral, with little or no value. They embody evil and are thus disposable: disposable in the double sense that their lives hold no value and that they will quickly be replaced. Ironically, the same logic applies to soldiers themselves.

Conclusion

During patrols, soldiers grappled with contradictory sentiments and affects as they categorised the residents they encountered. This moral categorisation was key to preserving police order: it aimed to win the hearts and minds of honest residents, divert consumers from joining traffic gangs, and expunge traffickers from the favela. Soldiers relied on swift and accurate categorisations to fulfil their mandate. These distinctions had one common and centralising emotion: fear.

Fear was considered a productive emotion by soldiers. On one hand, most soldiers patrolled in fear, and fear was considered an integral part of the job. On the other hand, soldiers sought to impose fear in the community. For soldiers, respect from residents meant a fearful acceptance of police order.

Contemporary moral economies of police violence consolidate a collective understanding that police violence is justified as long as it is directed towards certain categories of favela residents who deserve punishment. This shared morality legitimises the use of fear as a central feature of police work. Soldiers' trajectories and moral subjectivities further entrench resentment and ambivalent sentiments towards favela residents.

Ultimately, there is a sense of a lurking moral paradox in every task of police work. Protection and punishment are tied together. Most notably, policing is the site where contradictions and ambiguities regarding protection and repression take place.

The centrality of fear within the pacification programme can explain how the initiative fell short for residents and police soldiers alike. The Pacifying Police Unit sought to break from previous approaches to policing the favela. The UPP was grounded simultaneously in the values of human rights, democracy, citizenship, and the military logic of the institution. But the Pacifying soldiers grappled with competing tasks, such as gaining community support and cleansing the favela from armed traffic gangs. Even with the vision to win hearts and minds of favela residents, the UPP and its proximity policing principles ended up reinforcing violence, repression, and inequality.

Notes

1. *Jornal do Brasil* (RJ) 23/7/2009: *Polícia militar mira na requalificação*. The article explains that: *assumir as falhas é o primero passo no processo de depuração e modernização*.
2. Stories presenting an amicable and positive version of the police appeared on the news. For instance, *Jornal do Brasil* (RJ) 25/4/2010: *PM: corporação sem preconceito* Subtitle: *Estudo revela que Polícia Militar é a instituição que mais contrata e promove negros no Rio*.
3. Like other police forces around the world, the military police of Rio de Janeiro activated a series of communication channels, such as a Facebook page, Twitter, etc. These media present daily news, events, and actions of the police, often illustrated with scenes of action, photos of the apprehension of drugs or weapons, etc.
4. *Jornal do Brasil* (RJ) 3/1/2010: *Rocinha e Alemão já estão na mira*. Subtitle: *Comandante-geral diz que não quer uma cruzada contra as drogas, mas, sim, retirar dos traficantes o poder de morte e de dominação*.
5. *Jornal do Brasil* (RJ) 14/5/2009: *Polícia ocupará mais 7 comunidades* Subtitle: Beltrame afirma que ação no Leme é de pacificação e ordem, e não para 'caçar bandidos' arguing 'haverá ordem no morro e no asfalto'.
6. *Jornal do Brasil* (RJ) 2/4/2009: *Rio contra a pedra* Subtitle: *Santa Marta respira sem o crack* The article described that '*Ocupado pela PM, morro perde rotina de mau cheiro e dramas infantis na Praça do Cantão*' it mentions the '*viciados recuperados*', '*crianças-zumbies*' and '*cracolândia*' or *Jornal do Brasil* 22/3/2010: *Segurança que gera lucros* subtitle: *Chegada da UPPs em morros da Tijuca faz comércio do bairro prever aumento de 10% nas vendas*.
7. It is important to note that the Pacifying Police retained all the military codes and structures of the military police. And the police institution has a long history of punishment towards soldiers and repression of any inner calls for internal reform (Filho & Lima, 1944; Holloway, 1993).
8. Particularly notorious is the case of the killing in April 2017 of Maria Eduarda, a student who was shot by a police agent inside a school in Acari, or the many other cases of stray bullets that have taken the lives of residents (including infamous cases of child victims of stray bullets and even unborn babies). Often these stray bullets are from high-calibre weapons such as imported rifles that both traffickers and the police use.
9. Michel Misse, one of the leading sociologists in Brazil, established distinctions between *malandro, marginal* e *vagabundo*. These three designations are not mere stereotypes but are historically imbued with social meaning in the criminal world (Misse, 1999).

Bibliography

Alves, J. A. (2014). Neither humans nor rights: Some notes on the double negation of Black life in Brazil. *Journal of Black Studies*, 45(2), 143–162. https://doi.org/10.1177/0021934714524777

Beattie, P. M.. (2015).. *Punishment in Paradise. Race, Slavery, Human Rights, and a Nineteenth-Century Brazilian Penal Colony*. Duke University Press.
Caldeira, T. P. R. (2002). The paradox of police violence in democratic Brazil. *Ethnography*, 3(3), 235–263.
Caldeira, T. P. R., and Holston, J. (1999). Democracy and violence in Brazil. *Comparative Studies in Society and History*, 41(4), 691–729.
da Silva Leandro, Sylvia Amanda, & Figueira, L. E.. (2014). 'Não me venha com direitos humanos': Por uma compreensão do sujeito no 'homicídio por auto de resistência.' *DILEMAS: Revista de Estudos de Conflito e Controle Social*, 7(2), 261–291.
de Miranda, A. P. M. (2014). Militarização e direitos humanos: Gramáticas em disputa nas políticas de segurança pública no Rio de Janeiro/Brasil. *Forum Sociológico. Série II*, 25, 11–22. https://doi.org/10.4000/sociologico.886
de S. Minayo, M. C., de Souza, E. R., & Constantino, P. (2007). Perceived risks and victimization of military and civil police in the public (in)security domain. *Cadernos de Saúde Pública*, 23(11), 2767–2779. https://doi.org/10.1590/S0102-311X2007001100024
de S. Minayo, M. C., de Souza, E. R., & Constantino, P. (2008). *Missão prevenir e proteger: Condições de vida, trabalho e saúde dos policiais militares do Rio de Janeiro*. Editora FIOCRUZ. http://books.scielo.org/id/y28rt
Fassin, D. (2009). Les économies morales revisitées. *Annales. Histoire, sciences sociales* (Vol. 64, No. 6, pp. 1237–1266). Éditions de l'EHESS.
Fassin, D., Coutant, I., Fernandez, F., Fischer, N., Roux, S., & collectif. (2013). *Juger, réprimer, accompagner: Essai sur la morale de l'Etat*. Seuil.
Filho, M. B., & Lima, H. (1944). *Historia Da Policia Do Rio De Janeiro; Aspectos Da Cidade E Da Vida Carioca: 1870-1889*. A. Noite.
Henriques, R. (2012). Integrated Social and Urban Policies in the Favelas of Rio de Janeiro: The Experience of the UPP Social Program 1. In P. A. Ashley & D. Crowther (Eds.), Territories of Social Responsibility (1st ed., pp. 149–159). Routledge.
Holloway, T. H. (1993). *Policing Rio De Janeiro: Repression and Resistance in a 19th-Century City*. Stanford University Press.
Human Rights Watch. (2009). *Lethal Force: Police Violence and Public Security in Rio de Janeiro and São Paulo*. Human Rights Watch
Lembruger, J., Cano, I., & Musumeci, L. (2017). *Olho por olho? O que pensam os cariocas sobre "Bandido bom é bandido morto."* CENTRO DE ESTUDOS DE SEGURANÇA E CIDADANIA (CESEC).
Leon Spesny, S. (2020). The ethical soldier?: How the military police in Rio de Janeiro practice human rights morality. *Etnográfica*, 24, 133–154.
León Spesny, S. (2024). The law as a necropolitical tool: A genealogy of police violence in Brazil. *Critical Criminology*, 32, 587–607.
Misse, D. G. (2014). Cinco anos de UPP: Um breve balanço. *DILEMAS: Revista de Estudos de Conflito e Controle Social*, 7(3), 675–700.
Misse, M. (1999). *MALANDROS, MARGINAIS E VAGABUNDOS & a acumulação social da violência no Rio de Janeiro*. IUPERJ.
Perlman, J. (2010). *Favela: Four Decades of Living on the Edge in Rio de Janeiro*. Oxford University Press.
Saborio, S. (2014). From community police to proximity practices. New forms of control in the pacified favelas of Rio de Janeiro. *Autonomie Locali e Servizi Sociali*, 37(2), 271–286.

Scheper-Hughes, N. (2015). Death Squads and Vigilate Politics in Democratic Northeast Brazil. In J. Auyero, P. Bourgois, & N. Scheper-Hughes (Eds.), *Violence at the Urban Margins* (pp. 266–304). Oxford University Press.

Silva, K. (2014). Da resistência à violência de Estado a um novo projeto de formação nacional: Genealogias das políticas de Direitos Humanos no Brasil. *Anuário Antropológico, 39*(1) (2013), 39–71.

Valle Menezes, P. (2014). Os rumores da 'pacificação': A chegada da UPP e as mudanças nos problemas públicos no Santa Marta e na Cidade de Deus. *DILEMAS: Revista de Estudos de Conflito e Controle Social, 7*(4), 665–684.

Ventura, Z. (1994). *Cidade partida* (1era Edição). Companhia das Letras.

Wacquant, L. (2008). The militarization of urban marginality: Lessons from the Brazilian metropolis. *International Political Sociology, 2*(1), 56–74. https://doi.org/10.1111/j.1749-5687.2008.00037.x

Zaluar, A., & Alvito, M. (1998). *Um século de favela*. FGV Editora.

18
EMBODYING THE STATE IN PROBATION PRACTICE

Emotional labour and self-alienation

Jake Phillips, Sam Ainslie, Andrew Fowler and Chalen Westaby

Introduction

Probation work demands high levels of emotional labour from probation practitioners (Westaby et al., 2020). In this chapter we explore the concept of emotional labour in the field of probation in England and Wales by returning to Hochschild's (1983) original work, *The Managed Heart* in some depth. We start by exploring key concepts and definitions from her work and argue that probation work requires practitioners to embody the state by negotiating the emotional labour demands placed on them which are rooted in peoples' motivations for doing their jobs, organisational expectations and the society in which they are working. In this way we shed light on how probation workers embody the state as part of their practice and we explore this through Hochschild's concept of 'the pinch' (1983: 57) to argue that probation work leads to a significant conflict between what practitioners do feel, and what they think they should feel.

The chapter examines probation practice in England and Wales and probation practitioners' displays of emotion to bring to the fore the ways in which practitioners' emotions are appropriated by and for the ends of criminal justice. We do this through three thematic areas that cast light on how probation workers must perform emotional labour: (1) the disjunction between values underpinning their daily work and their role expectations; (2) the demand that practitioners use their emotions in increasingly efficient ways because of workload pressures; and (3) the ways emotional labour can be understood as a gendered practice. We situate this analysis in the context of the Marxist underpinnings of Hochschild's (1983) emotional labour theory and conclude by arguing that much of the emotional labour we see in probation increases the risk of practitioners suffering from some form of self-alienation. That said, whilst embodying the state through affective displays can result in adverse effects on probation staff, practitioners do not always experience emotional labour as external, alien and hostile to themselves but rather as an endeavour that allows them to express and actualise their professional selves. In this way, embodiment in this chapter concerns the emotional or affective displays that probation practitioners perform.

Emotional labour in probation

Central to Hochschild's work is the Marxist concept of transmutation. Whilst for Marx this relates to the circulation of money and the transmutation of money into commodities, Brook (2009) posits that we need to understand Hochschild's concept of transmutation as one which illustrates the way personal emotions are turned into commodities:

> Workers' feelings are commercialized as service through a 'transmutation' of 'private sphere' feelings into a package of emotions consumed by customers as a commodified interaction.
>
> *(Brook, 2009: 11)*

Hochschild's (1983) original formulation pertained to the commodification of emotions for the purposes of driving a profit. This, coupled with the requirement that 'the employer, through training and supervision, control the emotional activities of employees' (1983: 147), means her analysis focused on service workers rather than occupations which lacked direct supervision and as such an emotional labour script. However, these workers – although self-regulating – do perform emotional labour (Guy et al., 2008; Harris, 2002; Mastracci et al., 2011), and in the criminal justice context, workers' emotions are used by the criminal justice system to achieve goals such as rehabilitation, punishment and public protection. Thus, emotional labour involves the exploitation or appropriation of workers' feelings that – in turn – increase the organisation's ability to achieve its goals. For probation, this relates to the delivery of sentences imposed by the court, rehabilitation of people with convictions and protecting the wider public and victims.

Feeling rules

Emotional labour theory posits that emotional displays must be packaged in ways deemed appropriate by 'feeling rules': written and unwritten rules dictating how people should feel when carrying out their work (Hochschild, 1983: 59). There is an important distinction here between display rules which dictate the display of emotions (Ashforth & Humphrey, 1993) and feeling rules as described by Hochschild. Specifically, Hochschild considers how we recognise a feeling rule, which is achieved 'by assessing our feelings, how other people assess our emotional displays and by sanctions issuing from ourselves and from them' (1983: 58).

In the context of probation, the feeling rules which dictate how practitioners should feel have a particular quality. Societal feeling rules are rooted in what society thinks workers should feel while working and engaging with their customers or – for our purposes – people on probation. Thus, we can identify societal feeling rules by turning to public discourse on both probation and people on probation (Mann et al., 2014; Westaby et al., 2020). Whilst research on public opinion and knowledge of probation is limited, there are certain ways probation is portrayed and understood. In their study, Mawby and Worrall (2013: 105) suggest that probation had become tainted or dirty quoting probation workers who felt society reluctantly accepted the need for probation (Tidmarsh, 2024). In addition to regular proclamations in the media that when someone is sentenced to a community sanction they 'walk free from court' (Sentencing Council, 2024), probation is referenced in the media when a serious further offence is committed with blame often being placed on the doorstep of probation and – more recently – individual practices (see Das, 2024 for an example). Together, this implies that what the media and the public want from probation is the protection of the public through rigorous assessment, enforcement and punitive methods.

Probation work requires the balance of punitive working methods with more welfarist or rehabilitative endeavours such as working relationally with people on probation to support them in overcoming individual and structural factors which may result in offending. This means probation workers have to both support and condemn the people they work with, meaning they have to navigate the line between institutional, occupational and societal expectations. Engaging in such welfarist approaches to working with people on probation gives rise to a risk that this 'dirty work' stigmatises probation workers, resulting in conflict between societal display rules, and organisation and occupational display rules (Westaby et al., 2020). This approach to probation work as punitive and risk-focused implies a need for feelings that are hard and impersonal, standing in conflict with a form of probation work that is grounded in an 'ethics of care' (Dominey & Canton, 2022) and consistent with findings that individuals' motivations for entering probation are to help other people (Annison et al., 2008; Deering, 2010; Tidmarsh, 2024).

When we look to occupational feeling rules, we see the importance of emotions such as empathy and compassion for ensuring effective practice (Fowler et al., 2017). As such, these emotions are seen as central to developing what is often understood as the key tool of probation: the professional relationship (Durnescu, 2012; Fowler et al., 2017; Westaby et al., 2020).

Through this relationship probation workers can enable supervisees to build 'social capital and relationships likely to support the process of desistance' (Dominey, 2019). In this way we start to see some of the competing affective and moral tensions inherent to probation practice: practitioners must show empathy with people they work with whilst also expressing condemnation of their actions. Whilst not always thought of as a tension, the idiom 'condemn the sin and not the sinner' captures the difficulties for probation practitioners here. Practitioners know that judging people who have offended is likely to make it harder for those people to engage and comply with a sentence whilst also knowing that condemning the sinner is exactly what society wants them to do.

Occupational feeling rules are developed via processes of occupational acculturation. Occupational cultures, and relatedly occupational feeling rules, are grounded in shared values that are taught to new members, shaping their thoughts and feelings (Schein, 2004), by the development of a belief system (Kaushik, 2017), emotional logic and social consensus (Ingram, 2015). In relation to probation, practitioners may be particularly predisposed to wanting to adhere to occupational feeling rules because of their motivations to join the service (Grant, 2016). We can also understand the development and communication of occupational feeling rules as occurring through training (such as the Professional Qualification in Probation (PQIP), the academic aspect of which emphasises the importance of relationship building a key tenet of good quality probation practice) and professional socialisation (learning from peers). It is also interesting that despite being challenged by external forces (such as moves towards ever more punitive probation systems and organisational feeling rules that align with this), the probation 'habitus' has remained surprisingly durable (Grant, 2016).

A third and final set of feeling rules – organisational feeling rules – also shape the way probation workers embody the state. Here, we point to the importance of moves towards efficiency that have dominated organisational reforms in criminal justice over the last 30 years (see also Bennett this volume). This process started with the introduction of the principles of new public management in the early 1990s (Grant, 2016) and has continued with many examples of probation being governed and legitimated 'by numbers' (Carr & Robinson, 2021; Robinson, 2019). In a recent, pertinent example, the probation inspectorate found a 'culture of meeting performance measures as the absolute priority' (HMI Probation, 2024: 7) which 'diverted attention away from what was being delivered with people on probation' (HMI Probation, 2024: 3).

We start to see here how emotions and emotion work become focused – because of organisational feeling rules – on doing work as quickly as possible rather than as 'well' as possible. In an example of what Robinson (2019) calls 'McJustice', probation workers end up resorting to scripts and highly routinised forms of practice deployed to avoid 'opening a can of worms' (Robinson,

2019: 77) because of a lack of time. In addition to formal reforms which sought to 'speed up justice' (Robinson, 2018) and increase efficiency, workload pressures have meant probation practitioners spend less time with supervisees.

Hochschild (1983) argued there are gendered and social patterns to this transmutation of feeling, suggesting women are more often involved in the trade of emotion management for pay and that middle- and upper-class women are more likely to work with people as opposed to things (Hochschild, 1983: 28). The feminisation of probation over the last 50 years (Annison, 2007; Petrillo, 2007; Tidmarsh, 2023) highlights the link between the degradation of pay, working conditions and value of the work with the influx of women into this 'caring profession'. Further to these structural considerations, Petrillo (2007) brings to the fore the way female practitioners experience gendered relations in society in their work and the emotional impact of working mainly with men on probation. Elsewhere, Mawby and Worrall (2011) have identified how female practitioners consider being symbolic mothers inappropriate, although holding people on probation to account by being 'symbolic victims' is one of the ways in which gender feeds into probation practice. Men and women experience the importance of emotion work in different ways, something which Hochschild (1983: 163) attributed to women having less independent access to 'money, power, authority and status in society'. Thus, the feminisation of probation represents a useful lens through which to explore the way in which probation practitioners embody the state.

From this brief discussion of feeling rules, we can begin to see how there is potential for tension or conflict between different feeling rules in the context of probation. This tension can be seen to manifest within documentation that aims to guide practitioner behaviours. For example, in the Probation Institute Code of Ethics (2020) – which could represent occupational feeling rules – the requirement for practitioners to believe in the ability of people to change for the better is foregrounded, closely followed by an expectation to believe in 'the inherent worth and dignity' of those they supervise and to commit to promoting social justice and inclusion. By way of contrast, the Probation Professional Standards (MoJ, 2024) could be considered representative of the organisational feeling rules. Here, the beliefs and commitments expected by the occupation are notably absent. Instead, practitioners are not asked to *believe* (in other words, feel) but are expected to *behave* (display) in 'a professional and respectful manner at all times' and demonstrate they can 'balance protection of the public with the needs of the individual' (HMPPS 2024: 13). We might make links here to the way in which Goffman (1969) asserts that in work situations people present themselves in ways that convey a definition of the purpose of a given institution or workplace. As such, an analysis of the feelings that probation practitioners feel and display (which may differ or coincide) can provide us with deep insight into what probation seeks to do and how practitioners must embody the state as a result.

The 'pinch'

Whilst much work on emotional labour seeks to identify what workers do, it is more difficult to identify its proximate causes. In this chapter we endeavour to identify the drivers of feeling rules imposed upon probation workers and consider the expectations placed on them in terms of how they perform emotional labour through analysing Hochschild's concept of the 'pinch'. Hochschild (1983: 57) defines the pinch as the difference 'between what I do feel and what I should feel'. Doing this requires us to draw attention to the rule reminders which exist in the field of probation. Rule reminders tell workers what they are supposed to be feeling through what is described as a 'call for account'. Such calls for account can take the form of a self-assessment of one's feelings but can also be inferred from identifying how other people (such as colleagues, managers or people on probation) assess and react to an emotional or affective display. When one experiences a call for account, it implies that emotional conventions are not in order and need to be 'brought up to consciousness for repair' (Hochschild, 1983: 58).

Emotional labour can be performed through 'surface acting', which is where a person does not feel the emotions they display (Hochschild, 1983: 37). It can also be performed through 'deep acting', which is where a worker attempts to align their feelings with the emotional display they present (Rafaeli & Sutton, 1989: 12). The appropriation of emotions and the adherence to feeling rules (through surface and deep acting) can affect the well-being of workers. In this regard Hochschild argues (1983: 28) there is a 'cost to emotion work': the loss of hearing our feelings and what they tell us about ourselves (conceptualised as self-alienation) because of the successful transmutation of feeling. With this in mind, self-alienation is the final central concept for this chapter. Burkitt's (2024) research with people working in a job centre shows that self-alienation can result from practitioners feeling estranged from their own core values and feelings for others within a system that demands workers act in ways in opposition to those values because alienation is rooted in the ownership 'of domination in key social institutions' whereby the

> values that are central to that person's self-identity – such as care, empathy and solidarity – [are substituted] with the aims of a government acting in the interests of capital accumulation: the imposition of a punitive and disciplinary system of rules designed to further disadvantage.
> (Burkitt, 2024: 44–45)

In this way, we can start to identify the roots of self-alienation in the context of probation in the idea that practitioners' emotions are regulated – by societal and organisational feeling rules – in a way that is not in accordance with occupational feeling rules.

We now turn to our own analysis of three ways in which probation practitioners perform emotional labour focusing on three themes: being paid not to care, the efficient use of emotions and the gendered nature of embodying the state in probation.

Methods

The remainder of this chapter presents data collected via semi-structured interviews with probation practitioners in England and Wales to shed light on how people working in probation embody the state through their emotional labour. The data are drawn from two separate but linked studies. Study 1 was carried out in 2016, comprised interviews with practitioners and sought to generate data on the nature of emotional labour in the National Probation Service. Study 2, undertaken from 2020 to 2021, was a larger project which aimed to understand the implementation of reflective supervision and its impact on staff well-being. Within this study, we used a survey and interviews with staff in the National Probation Service to explore the concept of emotional labour in further depth and with a wider set of practitioners.

Across the two pieces of work, we have sought to understand how people perform emotional labour by asking them about the use of emotions in their work and probed participants around how emotions they were feeling might differ from those they displayed. In total we have carried out interviews with a total of 79 (18 from 2015 to 2016 and 61 from 2021) pseudonymised participants representing a range of grades in the Service including probation officer (PO), probation service officer (PSO) and senior probation officer (SPO). Overall, we interviewed 55 women and 23 men roughly representing the gender make-up of the wider service where nearly 75% of probation workers are female (HMPPS, 2024). For the purposes of this chapter, we have revisited this data with a view to identify examples of what it means to embody the state, focusing on POs and PSOs who supervise lower risk clients.

Findings

Being paid not to care

We know that probation workers often choose to enter the profession because of a desire to help people through relational work:

> Sitting in front of another human being and talking with them. Having a conversation. That's what probation practice is. Probation practice from my view isn't about doing a referral, about filling a form, that becomes a part of it but it's actually about human interaction and sitting in front of another human being and asking questions about their life.
>
> *(Kian, PO, Study 1[1])*

Therefore, it is expected that practitioners adhere to both organisational and occupational feeling rules when doing this type of work. Organisationally – in the Probation Institute's code of ethics, for example – we see emphasis on professionalism, neutrality and impartiality whilst occupational rules prioritise empathy, compassion and care towards service users (Canton, 2024; Fowler et al., 2017; Westaby et al., 2020). 'Integrative emotions' (Wharton & Erickson, 1993) (such as compassion and care) allow practitioners to display emotions that bind the service user to them as the probation practitioner. Thus, emotions such as empathy or happiness displayed towards service users, with accompanying requisite feelings, are recognised as being instrumental in the development of rapport and the building of effective working relationships (Fowler et al., 2017; Westaby et al., 2020).

However, the expectation that probation practitioners display these emotions stands in direct conflict with societal feelings rules which requires probation practitioners to perform emotional labour in a way that ensures the continued punishment of service users (Harper & Harris, 2017; Maruna & King, 2004). This tension is experienced as antithetical to the simultaneous need to be empathic, compassionate and caring:

> It is. I think it's difficult because you have to overcome everybody else's view of, 'Well, why are you even bothering? They're not worth it.' There's still the view that a lot of the people on my caseload should be shot and that it's a waste of money and when resources are tight why should we give it to offenders. So, you're constantly working against that.
> *(Sally, PO, Study 2)*

In other words, embodying the state here means being both caring and condemnatory although it appears that display rules practitioners conform to more readily are occupational (i.e. values-based) rather than societal. We see a similar tension when it comes to affective displays of care and risk management. In acknowledging organisational feeling rules relating to public protection and risk management, probation practitioners have described this aspect of their work as going into 'risk management mode' when a person is recalled in the knowledge that 'it's a last resort and it's not like I've not spelled it out to them that if this happens, then this will happen' (Wayne PO Study 1, quoted in Fowler et al., 2017: 254). Others comment on how they perform emotional labour to ensure their feelings and emotional displays are aligned with organisational feeling rules to create appropriate professional boundaries and the effective use of their authority as probation workers (Fowler et al., 2017):

> So yeah, even in these meetings everyone is sort of saying, 'Isn't it dreadful?', and I'm thinking, 'It's her choice, sort of thing, and we can do

what we can do to support her', but that's ultimately her choice of how she will lead her life in the next couple of weeks and months.

(Ryan PO Study 1, quoted in Fowler et al., 2017: 254)

Such affective displays can also be used to demonstrate an effective use of authority or convey frustration at a service users' behaviour. As Dillon (PO, Study 1) quoted in Westaby et al., 2020: 8) maintains:

> It is a bit frustrating ... you've just spent numerous hours, days or whatever trying to organise getting somebody accommodation ... that's kind of quite important and they just don't turn up for that ... I might tell them, occasionally I might [sigh] do you know it might come out like in a sigh or [frustrated sound] 'Why have you done that?... I suppose because we're pro social modelling; if I'm losing it, that's not very good for him is it? That just says, 'Oh well if people are frustrated it's alright to lose it' ... So I suppose you've kind of got to demonstrate that I'm normal and I have feelings and I do have thoughts.

Frustration is an example of a 'differentiating emotion' (Wharton & Erickson, 1993), which is used to instil hostility and contempt in others (Rafaeli & Sutton, 1989). Here we see probation practitioners are paid to be empathetic, compassionate and caring – to align with occupational feeling rules – and display differentiating emotions to ensure requisite boundaries are maintained, deploy effective use of authority and comply with societal and organisational feeling rules. As Hochschild (2012: 84) maintains, 'Even when people are paid to be nice, it is hard for them to be nice at all times'. We argue it is equally – if not more – challenging for probation staff to be paid *not* to be nice. This expectation about how practitioners embody the state results in situations where the 'pinch' is recognised and described by participants:

> I think it depends on how that [client] presents because I think also you have to be really careful because some people, it can be very easy to feel bad for somebody, but that's part of their grooming and manipulation. So, I think you always have to check in with yourself to do that and you do have to maintain some level of professional barrier. Not necessarily a barrier, but a bit of, you always have to wear a bit of a mask as well.
>
> *(Sally, PO, Study 2)*

Another way 'the pinch' manifests is through what we (Westaby et al., 2016: 119) have termed elsewhere 'altruistic imaginings'. These stem from the understanding of probation workers that they are expected *not* to be nice to people on probation by not physically connecting with them in certain ways. However, through altruistic imaginings our participants describe how they might help service users if they were able to:

> [A person on probation] said to me last week 'what am I going to do at Christmas? I'm on my own. I don't want to be on my own' ... but it is his problem ... many people are alone at Christmas and it's very sad but when you're driving home from that home visit and then you start thinking, '[sigh] could I have him for Christmas?' [Laughs] ... and then that's obviously gone in a second.
> *(Rose PO, Study 1, quoted in Westaby et al., 2016: 19–20)*

Altruistic imaginings serve to connect probation practitioners with the caring side of their profession. However, we also see evidence of the 'pinch' when participants want to *feel like they care*, but that feeling stands in tension with the requirement that they maintain both emotional and physical boundaries with their clients. Here we see feelings of 'guilt' acting as rule reminders signalling to practitioners that emotional conventions *not to be nice* are in place (Hochschild, 1983) and thus their feelings of care in that moment are misaligned.

This analysis suggests practitioners want to feel like they care but also feel they should not care and is an example of how organisational feeling rules and occupational feeling rules misalign because of the process of transmutation of emotion. Through analysis of this misalignment between feeling rules, we start to see how organisations serve to dehumanise people through expectations they suppress feelings of compassion. We would suggest that this is – to an extent – unique to probation because of its work with people who have been criminalised leading to probation work being understood as a form of dirty work (McMurray & Ward, 2014; Worrall & Mawby, 2013).

The temporal strains of probation work

Despite a history of organisational tumult, probation as an occupation has retained a commitment to relational practice (Robinson, 2023) whereby practitioners' emotions are expected to be used in the context of building a therapeutic alliance that can facilitate rehabilitation. Research pertaining to probation practice in England and Wales highlights not only breadth in *what* constitutes probation work but also the diversity in *how* it is to be delivered by practitioners within a context characterised by high workloads and a compromised workforce (CJJI, 2024).

Effective probation practice (conceptualised in the What Works era as practice empirically proven to result in reduced offending) is said to be underpinned by a set of Core Correctional Practices that can be characterised as either 'relationship skills' or 'structuring skills' (Bonta et al., 2017: 177).

In the context of emotional labour, these relationship skills require the practitioner to use their emotions to create caring, collaborative, respectful and motivating relationships with the individuals they supervise. In turn, the relationship provides the context for practitioners to bring to bear the structuring skills which can facilitate changes in behaviour and attitudes supportive of offending behaviour. Practitioners in England and Wales are trained from the outset to conceptualise relational practice as 'effective' in the context of reducing re-offending through interventions (delivered in groups or individually) that target 'criminogenic needs' in highly efficient ways.

However, given the growth in research that has sought to better understand how and why people move away from offending, probation practitioners are now also expected to build relationships that can initiate and sustain processes of desistance (Ainslie, 2021; McNeill & Weaver, 2010). Here, the focus of practice has shifted away from prescriptive delivery of groupwork programmes (Porporino, 2010) with greater recognition given to the critical role practitioners play in demonstrating a belief that change is possible (Maruna, 2001), holding hope in the face of barriers to change (McNeill, 2009), bearing witness to progress (Anderson, 2016) and supporting individuals as they navigate the emotional trajectories of desistance (Farrall et al., 2014) which takes both time and a great deal of emotional effort.

It is within this complex and emotionally laden context that practitioners are tasked with enforcing legal requirements by responding to acts of non-compliance through emotional displays that align to organisational and societal display rules that demand punitive action delivered in an efficient and highly managerialised manner. In this way neo-liberal technologies of managerialism and performativity mean that there is a need for practitioners to use their emotions effectively *and* efficiently.

In an example of how transmutation can fail, Hochschild (1983: 121) argues that when 'the time available for contact between flight attendants and passengers [reduces] it can become virtually impossible to deliver emotional labor'. Working practices which dictate how long and how often people on probation should be seen, along with models of delivery that emphasise the instrumental (i.e. effective) nature of relational work make emotional labour similarly difficult. Thus, participants talk about the 'relentless' nature of probation in the contemporary era where practitioners must balance writing reports, holding full caseloads and responding to people on probations' needs:

> We used to have to write one Pre-Sentence Report (PSR) a week, we've got to do two now and that's two days' work really. And then still have to manage a full caseload of high-risk cases which are more intensive. So the pressure of work's immense. It was always hard but it's doubly hard now... the quality of work I churn out now, is not... If you compare my

work now to fifteen years ago it's two totally different things. Everything's just cut corners now.

(Arlene, PO Study 1)

Similarly, the emphasis on administration that comes from the organisation's demands for staff to meet targets over and above building relationships places pressure on practitioners' abilities to do what they consider the important relational, emotional work fundamental to probation practice:

Stephen, PO:	Yeah too much, too many forms a lot of time spent at computers, all the usual sort of things and the thing that has to give on that is your contact time and with the people you're supposed to be working with basically.
Interviewer:	Right. And so that must be a bit of a challenge to you?
Stephen:	yeah. … I'm big on forming relationships at first rather than just getting into the work so you're just chit-chatting away basically, the first couple of weeks but you officially don't have time for that to build that relationships it's always get in, get the worksheets out or however you're going to do the work and away so I find it difficult I think if you're I find it rude to cut someone short if you know that they're in the thrust of a conversation, or if you go in and sort of say 'oh right we've only got fifteen minutes this week, or this fortnight to get done what we need to get done' that's just not going to be conducive to an open and positive working relationship really.

(Study 1)

More generally, workload pressures result in people having insufficient time to do their work putting pressure on the extent to which they can perform emotional labour. Importantly, participants told us that relational work is intense and this should be reflected somehow in workload management tools:

As much as the service says it values [relational work] and goes on about it, how important it is … where does that show on your workload management tool because that session that you've done and the aftermath, that will count as .1 on the algorithm as opposed to 1 for having done a report, done a written piece of work. That relationship work is real work and it's hard work, you know, but you don't always see how that's recognised in the systems I guess.

(Paul, PO, Study 2)

Practitioners seem to enjoy the emotional labour they do because it underpins the all-important relational side of their work. Crucially, it seems that in this context practitioners appear to try and avoid embodying what the state wants (through societal and organisational rules), instead seeking to align with occupational feeling rules even when they are eschewed in policy terms. In this way, we can start to see emotional labour as a not altogether negative element of probation work. Indeed, some scholars such as Bolton (2009) criticise Hochschild's Marxist analysis that emotional labour leads to self-alienation. Rather, emotional labour can allow practitioners to have a sense of professional and personal agency that exists because it is a form of resistance against organisational expectations. In the quote above, we see evidence of Paul's preference for deep acting which – despite having to be carried out outside formal guidelines and targets – creates satisfaction and a sense of fulfilment. As such, practitioners may not experience emotional labour as external, alien and hostile to themselves but rather as an endeavour that allows them to express and actualise their professional selves and so become willing to perform emotional labour because it tends to be intrinsically rewarding (Tsang & Wu, 2022).

The gendered nature of emotional labour

Whilst care and control in opposition may be an unhelpful dichotomy (Canton & Dominey, 2020), it is a useful heuristic device for showing how the legacy of the caring, 'advise, assist, befriend' approach in probation work comes into tension with the shift to a more punitive rhetoric (Garland, 2001). The Probation Service in England and Wales' current strapline is 'assess, protect and change' (HMPPS, 2021) and practitioners are expected to both care for and control service users. This dual role has resulted in a longstanding debate in the field (Harris, 1980; HMPPS, 2021; Willis, 1983). One example of how gender feeds into affective displays illustrates the ways structural inequalities around violence against women give meaning to how women practitioners experience their work and perform emotional labour:

> another reason I wouldn't show it [feeling scared] is because – this goes back to working with somebody years and years and years ago – I worked with somebody who was a knife point robber and he said he would always target women and he would always target women that looked vulnerable and I said 'but what do you mean by that?' and he said 'well I wouldn't target you because you're really confident.' ... if you sort of work along that theory, if I'm sat there in a room with somebody who I perceive could potentially become very aggressive and I'm sat there looking scared. I suppose there's more potential for them to, to attack me really than if I'm sort of confident and sort of on the ball, I think it's less likely to happen.
> *(Arlene, PO, Study 1)*

In this example, Arlene is expected to feel and display confidence to avoid looking 'unprofessional'. In this way she aligns with organisational display rules about what professionalism is whilst performing a form of gendered self-protection women must undertake in many areas of their personal and professional lives. We can further see how understandings of what professionalism is seen to be in probation create additional opportunities for tensions between what people feel, and what people show in the following highly gendered example:

> She discussed a lot about her children and how she's not going to get her kids back and she was very upset about that and it was a very emotional room ... I found it hard at first to separate myself from what was going on because I'd welcomed an emotional conversation, but there's still a way to hold that conversation not as if it's your best mate who you're sitting having a chat with and keeping it professional. So, as much as I felt for her and I wanted to be able to assist in every way that I could, I had my work brain on in the background as well. ... It had taken a lot to get through with her and not give yourself away ... So, it was a lot to keep up a nice professional image to her and then get back up to the office and crash when I got to the top with everything that had gone on.
> *(Esther, PQIP, Study 2)*

Female practitioners suppress their feelings in service to what Esther calls her 'work brain' which, in this scenario, was about being focused on finding solutions to keep up a 'professional image'. Esther highlights a call to account when she says she is not there to be a 'best mate', and she self-assesses her feelings to identify what is an appropriate emotional display. Again, we can hear how much effort this takes and the emotional cost when Esther 'crashes' when she returns to the office.

In Hochschild's (1983: 92) concept of the 'redefined self', workers must be able to 'distinguish between situations that call on her to identify herself and situations that call on her to identify her role and its relation to the company' and we heard examples that illustrate the potential for work to have an impact on peoples' private lives:

> the question that I get asked a lot and that I don't fully know how I do it is about how you do not let this damage you. So, how I detach myself. I don't really know how that happens, or if it does fully happen and it's something I think about a lot really because, I think does this job affect how I parent my kids? Yeah, it does. Absolutely. Does it affect how I view society? Yeah.
> *(Hazel, PO, Study 1)*

Probation work departs from Hochschild's stereotypical idea of women doing work which makes 'defensive use of sexual beauty, charm and relational skills' while men are more likely to do work where they 'wield anger and make threats' (1983: 112). Whilst unlikely to be wielding anger and making threats, Hazel accepts that the work affects her parenting and how she sees society. She experiences some uncertainty and difficulty explaining how she manages her feelings yet recognises the importance of minimising the emotional impact of the work as a skill. In Hochschild's reckoning the emotions that are used in work are the ones employees are likely to become 'estranged from' and it is here where we hear Hazel's attempts to avoid self-alienation.

We can also identify an impact on practitioners' relationships outside of work which stems from their inability to have control over emotions when at work. The control aspect of probation work requires practitioners to recognise and manage their emotions in response to the potential risk posed by service users. However, this can lead to what might be described as a 'skewed view on society' (Margaret PO, Study 1 and Hazel PO, Study 1, quoted in Westaby et al., 2016: 122), resulting in them becoming 'hypervigilant':

> That can be very unsettling [having physical threats made to you by a people on probation] and then it leaves you shaken and a bit rattled by it and then, again, when you know you're going to see them the next day or run into them or walking round the prison and you know that someone's made threats to have you potted or whatever, you're a bit hypervigilant.
>
> *(Nikki PO Prison, Study 2)*

Hypervigilance can lead to probation staff having what we have described as 'darker imaginings' which can spill over from their work role into their home life (Westaby et al., 2016: 121). This results in changes to how people see society and also manifests as changes to in the way probation practitioners manage their home life:

> I hate going to [the] fair, I will always say to my husband: 'you go stand round there and then if the ride stops around there you get him off and I'll–' so, I'd like to think it doesn't stop them doing what they should be doing, they play out, they go places, but it affects my anxiety levels … I do sometimes feel, think people have ulterior motives that probably don't, probably just really nice people and I immediately am on red alert … once it's in your head I can't get rid of the fact that I know that that happened. So that's the way it affects me.
>
> *(Hazel, PO, Study 1 quoted in Westaby et al., 2016: 122–123)*

These potentially deleterious effects of the embodiment of the state could be considered an example of how probation practitioners internalise emotional cues to such an extent that they are unable to feel 'normal' human emotions. If we return to the idea that emotional labour is about the difference between what I do feel and what I should feel, we can see that one product of embodying the state is that practitioners become unclear about how they should be feeling outside of work. Whilst practitioners conform to societal, organisational and occupational feeling rules at work, knowing how and whether to adhere to these rules outside of work is much less clear. This, then, is another example of how the need to embody the state as probation practitioners – especially as a woman – leads to potential self-alienation.

Conclusion

Based on this analysis, probation practitioners embody the state by feeling and displaying feeling in particular ways. The state asks practitioners to feel in ways that are often at odds with the emotions practitioners want to be transmutated into their work. Thus, probation is a prime site for self-alienation because societal, organisational and occupational feeling rules may conflict. That said, we should remember that affective displays and relational work also provide a great deal of job satisfaction for people who choose to work in probation. Through our analysis we can see how the tension that exists between care and control (not that they are mutually exclusive); the need to be highly efficient with the use of emotion; and the gendered nature of probation all give rise to certain affective displays.

Moreover, this analysis points to a deeper understanding of both what probation is – a penal institution which sits at the intersection of society's desire to be safe, condemn and rehabilitate – and its impact on staff. The consequences of embodying the state – whilst not all bad – (and particularly for women who make up most of the probation workforce) marshalling this boundary between society and people who commit offences, are potentially significant. Finally, we would conclude by emphasising the fact that the affective displays probation workers must perform require skill, resilience and experience and probation services would do well to remember this if they are to deal with low recruitment and high retention issues which are implicated in poor-quality probation work.

Note

1 Participant names are pseudonyms. PO denotes probation officer, PSO denotes probation services officer and SPO is a senior probation officer.

References

Ainslie, S. (2021). Seeing and believing: Observing desistance-focused practice and enduring values in the National Probation Service. *Probation Journal*, 68(2), 146–165. https://doi.org/10.1177/02645505211005031

Anderson, S. E. (2016). The value of 'bearing witness' to desistance. *Probation Journal*, 63(4), 408–424. https://doi.org/10.1177/0264550516664146

Annison, J. (2007). A gendered review of change within the probation service. *The Howard Journal of Criminal Justice*, 46(2), 145–161. https://doi.org/10.1111/j.1468-2311.2007.00462.x

Annison, J., Eadie, T., & Knight, C. (2008). People first: Probation officer perspectives on probation work. *Probation Journal*, 55(3), 259–271.

Ashforth, B. E., & Humphrey, R. H. (1993). Emotional labor in service roles: The influence of identity. *Academy of Management Review*, 18(1), 88–115.

Bonta, J., Bourgon, G., & Rugge, T. (2017). From evidence-informed to evidence-based: The Strategic Training Initiative in Community Supervision. In *Evidence-Based Skills in Criminal Justice International Research on Supporting Rehabilitation and Desistance* (pp. 169–192). Bristol University Press. https://bristoluniversitypressdigital.com/edcollchap/book/9781447332978/ch009.xml

Brook, P. (2009). The Alienated Heart: Hochschild's 'emotional labour' thesis and the anticapitalist politics of alienation. *Capital & Class*, 33(2), 7–31. https://doi.org/10.1177/030981680909800101

Burkitt, I. (2024). Emotional self-alienation and institutions: A Marxian approach to emotion and alienation in employment agencies and society. In H. Flam (Ed.), *Research Handbook on the Sociology of Emotion*. www.elgaronline.com/edcollchap/book/9781803925653/book-part-9781803925653-7.xml

Canton, R. (2024). Probation as social work. *Probation Journal*, 02645505241241588. https://doi.org/10.1177/02645505241241588

Canton, R., & Dominey, J. (2020). *Punishment and Care Reappraised*. Hart Publications. https://dora.dmu.ac.uk/handle/2086/19197

Carr, N., & Robinson, G. (2021). A legitimate business? Representations of privatised probation in England and Wales. *Crime, Media, Culture*, 17(2), 235–254. https://doi.org/10.1177/1741659020903771

CJJI. (2024). *Efficiency spotlight report: The impact of recruitment and retention on the criminal justice system*. CJJI. www.justiceinspectorates.gov.uk/cjji/inspections/joint-efficiency-spotlight-report-on-recruitment-and-retention/

Das, S. (2024, March 24). 'They signed her death warrant': How probation service failings left a violent man free to kill. *The Observer*. www.theguardian.com/society/2024/mar/24/father-michaela-hall-murder-victim-probation-service

Deering, J. (2010). Attitudes and beliefs of trainee probation officers: A 'new breed'? *Probation Journal*, 57(1), 9–26.

Dominey, J. (2019). Probation supervision as a network of relationships: Aiming to be thick, not thin. *Probation Journal*, 66(3), 283–302. https://doi.org/10.1177/0264550519863481

Dominey, J., & Canton, R. (2022). Probation and the ethics of care. *Probation Journal*, 69(4), 417–433. https://doi.org/10.1177/02645505221105401

Durnescu I (2012) What matters most in probation supervision: Staff characteristics, staff skills or programme? *Criminology and Criminal Justice* 12(2): 193–216.

Farrall, S., Hunter, B., Sharpe, G., & Calverley, A. (2014). *Criminal Careers in Transition: The Social Context of Desistance from Crime*. OUP.

Fowler, A., Phillips, J., & Westaby, C. (2017). Understanding emotions as effective practice. The performance of emotional labour in building relationships. In P. Ugwudike, P. Raynor, & J. Annison (Eds.), *Evidence-Based Skills in Community Justice: International Research on Supporting Rehabilitation and Desistance* (pp. 243–262). Policy Press.

Garland, D. (2001). *The Culture of Control: Crime and Social Order in Contemporary Society*. Clarendon.

Goffman, E. (1969). *The Presentation of Self in Everyday Life*. Allen Lane, The Penguin Press.

Grant, S. (2016). Constructing the durable penal agent: Tracing the development of habitus within English probation officers and Scottish criminal justice social workers. *The British Journal of Criminology*, 56(4), 750–768. https://doi.org/10.1093/bjc/azv075

Guy, M. E., Newman, M. A., & Mastracci, S. H. (2008). *Emotional Labor: Putting the Service in Public Service* (1 edition). Routledge.

Harper, C. A., & Harris, A. J. (2017). Applying moral foundations theory to understanding public views of sexual offending. *Journal of Sexual Aggression*, 23(2), 111–123. https://doi.org/10.1080/13552600.2016.1217086

Harris, L. C. (2002). The emotional labour of barristers: An exploration of emotional labour by status professionals. *Journal of Management Studies*, 39(4), 553–584. https://doi.org/10.1111/1467-6486.t01-1-00303

Harris, R. (1980). A changing service: The case for separating 'Care' and 'Control' in probation practice. *British Journal of Social Work*, 10(2), 163–184.

HMI Probation. (2024). *An inspection of probation services in Norfolk*. HMI Probation. www.justiceinspectorates.gov.uk/hmiprobation/wp-content/uploads/sites/5/2024/05/An-inspection-of-probation-services-in-Norfolk-1.pdf

HMPPS. (2021). *The Target Operating Model for probation services in England and Wales*. HMPPS.

Hochschild, A. R. (1983). *The Managed Heart: Commercialization of Human Feeling*. University of California Press.

Hochschild, A. R. (2012). *The Managed Heart: Commercialization of Human Feeling* (1st ed.) University of California Press. Available at: www.jstor.org/stable/10.1525/j.ctt1pn9bk

Ingram, R. (2015). *Understanding Emotions in Social Work: Theory, Practice and Reflection*. McGraw-Hill Education (UK).

Kaushik, A. (2017). Use of self in social work: Rhetoric or reality. *Journal of Social Work Values & Ethics*, 14(1), 21–29.

Mann, M., Menih, H., & Smith, C. (2014). There is 'hope for you yet': The female drug offender in sentencing discourse. *Australian & New Zealand Journal of Criminology*, 47(3), 355–373. https://doi.org/10.1177/0004865814523436

Maruna, S. (2001). *Making Good: How Ex-Convicts Reform and Rebuild Their Lives*. American Psychological Association.

Maruna, S., & King, A. (2004). Public opinion and community penalties. In A. E. Bottoms, S. Rex, & G. Robinson (Eds.), *Alternatives to Prison: Options for an Insecure Society* (pp. 83–112). Willan.

Mastracci, S. H., Guy, M. E., & Newman, M. A. (2011). *Emotional Labor and Crisis Response: Working on the Razor's Edge* (1st edition). Routledge.

Mawby, R., & Worrall, A. (2011). *Probation Workers and Their Occupational Cultures*. University of Leicester. www2.le.ac.uk/departments/criminology/research/current-projects/rim3_culture_probation

Mawby, R., & Worrall, A. (2013). *Doing Probation Work: Identity in a Criminal Justice Occupation* (Vol. 9). Routledge.

McMurray, R., & Ward, J. (2014). 'Why would you want to do that?': Defining emotional dirty work. *Human Relations*, 67(9), 1123–1143. https://doi.org/10.1177/0018726714525975

McNeill, F. (2009, September 8). Helping, holding, hurting: Recalling and reforming punishment. *The 6th Annual Apex Lecture*. The 6th Annual Apex Lecture, Edinburgh. www.sccjr.ac.uk/documents/Apex%20lecture%20-%20Fergus%20McNeill.pdf

McNeill, F., & Weaver, B. (2010). *Changing Lives? Desistance Research and Offender Management*. Scottish Centre for Crime and Justice Research.

Ministry of Justice (MoJ). (2024). *Probation Professional Register Policy Framework*. Ministry of Justice. Available at: www.gov.uk/government/publications/probation-professional-register-interim-policy-framework (accessed 24 April 2025).

Petrillo, M. (2007). Power struggle: Gender issues for female probation officers in the supervision of high risk offenders. *Probation Journal*, 54(4), 394–406. https://doi.org/10.1177/0264550507083538

Porporino, F. J. (2010). Bringing sense and sensitivity to corrections: From programmes to 'Fix' offenders to services to support desistance. In J. Brayford, F. Cowe, & J. Deering (Eds.), *What Else Works? Creative Work with Offenders* (pp. 61–85). Willan.

Probation Institute. (2020). *Code of Ethics*. Probation Institute. http://probation-institute.org/code-of-ethics/

Rafaeli, A., & Sutton, R. I. (1989). The expression of emotion in organizational life. *Research in Organizational Behavior*, 11, 1–42.

Robinson, G. (2018). Transforming probation services in Magistrates' courts. *Probation Journal*, 65(3), 316–334. https://doi.org/10.1177/0264550518776778

Robinson, G. (2019). Delivering McJustice? The probation factory at the Magistrates' court. *Criminology & Criminal Justice*, 19(5), 605–621. https://doi.org/10.1177/1748895818786997

Robinson, G. (2023). Can probation be rehabilitated? *The Howard Journal of Crime and Justice*, 62(2), 264–276. https://doi.org/10.1111/hojo.12504

Schein, E. H. (2004). *Organizational Culture and Leadership*. Jossey-Bass.

Sentencing Council. (2024). Non-custodial sentences – walking free from court? – Sentencing. www.sentencingcouncil.org.uk/blog/post/non-custodial-sentences-walking-free-from-court/

Tidmarsh, M. (2023). Gender in a 'caring' profession: The demographic and cultural dynamics of the feminisation of the probation service in England and Wales. *Probation Journal*, 02645505231221240. https://doi.org/10.1177/02645505231221240

Tidmarsh, M. (2024). Making, unmaking, remaking: Mapping the boundaries of professional legitimacy, identity and practice in probation in England and Wales. *Criminology & Criminal Justice*, 24(3), 568–584. https://doi.org/10.1177/17488958221135108

Tsang, K. K., & Wu, H. (2022). Emotional labour as alienated labour versus self-actualized labour in teaching: Implications of the outbreak of the COVID-19 pandemic for the debate. *Educational Philosophy and Theory*, 1–5. https://doi.org/10.1080/00131857.2022.2108399

Westaby, C., Fowler, A., & Phillips, J. (2020, June). Managing emotion in probation practice: Display rules, values and the performance of emotional labour. *International Journal of Law, Crime and Justice*, *61*, 100362. https://doi.org/10.1016/j.ijlcj.2019.100362

Westaby, C., Phillips, J., & Fowler, A. (2016). Spillover and work–family conflict in probation practice: Managing the boundary between work and home life. *European Journal of Probation*, *8*(3), 113–127. https://doi.org/10.1177/2066220316680370

Wharton, A. S., & Erickson, R. J. (1993). Managing emotions on the job and at home: Understanding the consequences of multiple emotional roles. *The Academy of Management Review*, *18*(3), 457–486. https://doi.org/10.2307/258905

Willis, A. (1983). The balance between care and control in probation: A research note. *British Journal of Social Work*, *13*(1), 339.

Worrall, A., & Mawby, R. C. (2013). Probation worker responses to turbulent conditions: Constructing identity in a tainted occupation. *Australian & New Zealand Journal of Criminology*, *46*(1), 101–118.

19
CIRCUITS OF OUTRAGE AGAINST AND WITHIN THE ENGLISH STATE OF HOMELESSNESS

Simon Tawfic

> It is an affront to this country that last winter, one of the coldest on record, there were people still sleeping rough on our streets ... In a civilised society, this is totally unacceptable ... Together I am confident that we can make a real impact, with the ambition to end the uncertainty, indignity and suffering of rough sleeping.
>
> *(Cameron 2011: 4)*

In metropolitan England, cycles of moral outrage at the endurance of homelessness keep staging returns. At the dawn of austerity, however, Westminster's claims to care took on an increasingly strident tone, voiced in Prime Minister Cameron's foreword to the *Vision to end rough sleeping* white paper. In contrast to the Thatcher-era insistence that 'there is no such thing as society' (Thatcher 1987), Conservative-led governments of the 2010s sought to evoke a sense of collective moral duty, culminating in the 2018 Rough Sleeping Initiative: a £1.2 billion grandstand package to fund NGOs in the business of ending homelessness. The Initiative was designed to enact the Conservative Party's manifesto pledge to 'halve rough sleeping over the course of the parliament and eliminate it altogether by 2027' (Conservative Party 2017: 58). This language – of urgency, rescue and moral responsibility – echoes broader humanitarian discourses, where suffering is framed as a moral scandal and intervention as a civilizational imperative.

While much scholarship has framed humanitarian regimes as a politics of compassion, this chapter highlights the place of outrage as a central affect in everyday pursuits to govern suffering. Scholars of humanitarianism suggest such interventions often rely on entrenched hierarchies of deservingness that guide the distribution of aid – drawing on idealized images of bodily suffering – and, in doing so, reproduce the very exclusions they claim to redress (Ticktin 2011; Fassin 2012). Meanwhile, Andrea Muehlebach's study of welfare restructuring in 2000s Northern Italy traces how the state's retreat from service provision was accompanied by efforts to instill a collectivist ethic of care among disenfranchised citizens, who were recast as heartfelt volunteers to fill the space left behind. Her work suggests that austerity governance depends on projects of moralization that aim to produce emotionally bonded publics – in a manner not dissimilar to Cameron's familiar calls for a 'Big Society' – unified by compassion, sacrifice and co-suffering. Taken together, these analyses tend to foreground the affective power of humanitarianism to bind publics around a moral consensus.

The analysis in this chapter departs from this prevailing framing, examining how moral outrage – rather than merely compassion – animates frontline workers' everyday pursuits to end homelessness in an English metropolitan town I call Castlebury.[1] Firmly situated in the post-austerity setting, I conducted participant observation as a volunteer and caseworker between September 2018 and March 2020 in Castlebury's homelessness industry across its series of homeless NGOs that offered a set of services – 'a pathway out of single homelessness' – and experienced exponential growth under the Rough Sleeping Initiative.

This chapter focuses on the everyday relations between two NGOs central to Castlebury's homelessness industry – Churches of Castlebury Housing Project (CCHP) and the Noah Community night shelter – as well as Castlebury local authority. It traces the circulation of outrage between workers in these settings and the manner in which they contested each other's legitimacy. In their role as multiagency partners, frontline workers' everyday pursuits to care across these organizations featured regular, pointed moral critiques of each other who they blamed for why their work is impossible; and they claimed often that their purpose was precisely to 'fight' the other. My analysis suggests that their moral outrage is a hardwired characteristic of their will to care – to enact care is to feel outrage – that tells a story about the wider emotional politics of post-austerity England.

If compassion tends to eschew attributing causes or assigning responsibility (Barnett 2013) – favoring urgent action over critical reflection – moral outrage inspires action precisely through the assignment of blame. In Castlebury, moral outrage is how my former colleagues related to 'the system' – the fragmented field of agencies who share in the business of ending homelessness, including their government funders – by using vivid imagery to attribute responsibility for suffering homeless bodies. In doing so, they use idioms that translate the everyday effects of austerity into a moral and somatic register, enabling them to contest the state of homelessness. This blame-work enables frontline workers to cast themselves as the 'righteous and rightful' guardians of their clients (Bornstein & Sharma 2016), securing moral authority by contrasting their care with rival agencies. In stabilizing a fractured moral field, this self-positioning locks workers into circuits of emotional excess (see also Christinaki & Burman, this volume). Outrage inhibits identification across the industry, foreclosing recognition of shared ambivalences or complicities. Instead, it sustains feedback loops of hostility, serving as an affective outlet for the injustices frontline workers sense but struggle to redress.

This chapter proceeds in four sections. First, it traces a history in which Westminster promises to end rough sleeping collide with austerity policies that deepen it, demonstrating how these contradictions set up frontline actors for moral indignation in pursuit of an impossible goal. Second, it moves ethnographically into CCHP's advice office, analyzing the bodily idioms and psychodynamics through which its caseworkers understand the local authority as a hostile other. The third section turns to the neighboring Noah Community night shelter to illustrate a mirror image of outrage – one directed at CCHP, organized around purity, contagion and the defense of a bounded home. The chapter returns ethnographically to CCHP to analyze the limits of righteous anger and the feelings of futility it can leave behind. The conclusion suggests that, while central to the affective economy of England's homelessness industry, moral outrage sharpens boundaries, amplifies moral distress and participates in the same feedback loop of state failure and virtuous firefighting it decries. Across these settings, I show how frontline workers' moral outrage actively 'makes up' the state: constructing and contesting its moral character through everyday practices of blame and care.

An outrageous system?

Moral outrage is a distinct, relational and embodied political affect that merits close examination (Johansen et al. 2018). As mentioned, scholars of humanitarianism tend to emphasize the importance of sympathy, pity and compassion as crucial moral sentiments that mobilize political interventions in the lives of suffering others (Ticktin 2011; Fassin 2012). However, this chapter draws inspiration from emerging historical scholarship on the abolition of slavery in the British Empire – a key archetype of humanitarian action – which rediscovers how abolitionist rhetoric relied as much (if not more) on the putative villainy of slave traders as on compassion for their victims (Woods 2015). Such a recognition of the place of outrage in inspiring humanitarian projects is critical. It reveals the character of moral outrage as a profoundly civilizational emotion: expressions of moral outrage tend to accompany claims to moral superiority, recur in (post-)colonial historical moments and crises and often emerge from actors in positions of relative privilege to their beneficiaries (see also Aliverti, this volume). While moral outrage resembles anger, anthropologists and social psychologists have differentiated the two terms by pointing to outrage's tendency to index the wrongdoings of others – it is 'an emotional response to what other people do, not what we do ourselves' (Goodenough 1997: 5) – which tends to have the effect of (re)asserting the boundaries between outraged and outrageous actors, limiting actors' recognition of the commonalities and shared complicities across the outrage divide (Batson et al. 2007; Täuber & van Zomeren 2013).

When performed by electoral figures in Westminster, such forms of moral outrage tend to enact a form of symbolic distancing from its causes – an aesthetic of regret without attribution that staves off critique by offering catharsis. The paradox that confronted my interlocutors lies in the 2010s revival of moral sentiments in an era of fiscal austerity (Clarke & Newman 2012). On the one hand, the then Conservative–Liberal Democrats Coalition pledged that it would ensure 'nobody has to spend a second night out on the streets', a 'commitment' it placed 'at the centre' of its wider promise to 'protect the most vulnerable and promote social justice' (Department for Communities and Local Government 2011: 5, 12).

At the same time, the inequitable effects of the 2010–2019 austerity program frequently made headlines. In 2019, the Local Government Association criticized central government funding reductions to local council budgets of up to 60%, claiming it created a financial 'black hole' and hindered councils' ability to provide dignified care. Newspaper columnists and anti-poverty groups opposed rental subsidy cuts, highlighting research showing less than 5% of inner-city tenancies were viable for single claimants in 2019 (Booth 2019; Chartered Institute of Housing 2019). The Bureau of Investigative Journalism's *Dying Homeless* project estimated the rising death toll from these policies (McClenaghan 2020). And the UN Special Rapporteur on extreme poverty (2019: 1) linked rising homelessness to austerity, describing the policy as replacing the post-WWII welfare state with 'a harsh and uncaring ethos'.

The contradictory nature of this narrative – pledging to end rough sleeping while the effects of austerity hinder such pursuits – is a hallmark of UK governmental responses to homelessness since the 'shocking' (re)discovery of homelessness in the wake of the 1966 BBC play *Cathy Come Home* (Tawfic 2022). *Cathy*'s capacity to inspire outrage owes largely to its unflinching depiction of a fictional white working-class nuclear family's descent into destitution and decrepit single-sex Poor Law dormitories. Eventually, Westminster passed the Housing (Homeless Persons) Act 1977 as an explicit tribute to the suffering of the titular character, Cathy. Enduring in modified form in the 1996 Housing Act, it enshrines a legal duty on local authorities to secure accommodation for a restrictive and ambiguously defined subset of claimants, relying on the discretion of local authority street-level bureaucrats – what CCHP advice workers sought to 'fight' decades later when contesting eligibility decisions on their clients' behalf.

Despite its promise of being the first modern legislative provision to address homelessness, the Act was already 'out of time' from the outset (Cowan 2019). Judicial precedent emerged shortly after that signaled the senior judiciary's disapproval of having to hear appeals of local authority decisions in the first place; and a leading precedent held that it is 'an Act to assist persons who are homeless, *not* an Act to provide them with homes' (*R. v Hillingdon LBC Ex p. Puhlhofer* [1986] A.C. 517). The state-initiated disposal of public housing in 1980 under Right to Buy – according to 2021 estimates (Department for Levelling Up, Housing and Communities 2022), there has been a 70% reduction in local authority housing stock in England since 1980 – broke the link between homelessness and public housing, if one even reliably existed.

The need for a growing state-sponsored industry of homelessness charities, night shelters and advice services stems precisely from the apparent failures of the Act to rise to the challenge. By the time I started fieldwork in Castlebury's homelessness industry, seeking council housing did not just seem like a pipedream to my casework colleagues: it was not even remotely on their radars. Between September 2018 and April 2020, none of the clients, guests or service users that I knew ultimately obtained council housing, even though a few were on the waiting list for it. Indeed, a former senior colleague of over five years' service in CCHP sharply observed to me, 'the wait I've been told [by the local authority] is 15 years', referring to an eligible client whose epilepsy, brain injury and severe hearing impairment plausibly imply high priority on the waiting list. Moreover, the introduction of cuts to publicly funded legal representation in 2012 has heightened barriers to access solicitors to legally challenge decisions under the Act, often leaving CCHP workers to fill this niche despite their lack of legal professional accreditation.

Similarly to the predicament of aid workers in the arena of international development (Fechter 2016), the business of ending homelessness in England systemically enrolls the moral labor of its workforce as a buffer against moral and civilizational decline. '[I]nhabiting the situation and accommodating this knowledge while expending one's effort on making strides' was the very premise of my interlocutors' roles: to perform their labor in 'awareness of at least partial futility of their professional endeavors' (Fechter 2016: 232). In CCHP, for example, such feelings of futility stem not least from their own structural disadvantage in relation to their governmental sponsors: as beneficiaries whose reliance on unpredictable, discretionary fixed-term funding reached 51% of total revenue in 2019/2020. This chimes with the austerity-era scholarship on UK state–charity relations which echoes the contradictory *re*-centralization of power that increased funding to charities has entailed (Dagdeviren et al. 2019). Acclimatizing to the constraints of such roles – in the words of its workers, to 'firefight' while feeling 'set up to fail' – demands regular confrontation with the impossibility of the promise to end homelessness.

For CCHP, its workers regularly encountered the contradictions of the work of holding the local authority to account while lacking the effective capacity to do so, a predicament which commonly led to the projection of antagonism back toward its funders as well as Noah, CCHP's closest neighbor. For Noah's founding figures, meanwhile, the night shelter disciplinary regime they constructed enshrined an ethic of care that sought to function as a moral corrective to the shortcomings of CCHP and 'the British state' writ large. The profoundly differentiated ethoses of these projects corresponded to the distinct personalities of its leading figures – a contested landscape with fragmented notions of humanitarian action – who were inspired by profound forms of indignation that assumed a life of their own in a circuit of outrage. The chapter moves now to focus on the CCHP-local authority flow within this circuit.

Enemies, absent limbs and moral pains

When a person first seeks housing advice from CCHP, its caseworkers need to quickly prejudge whether the prospective client fulfills the following Housing Act criteria, which serve as a sorting mechanism:

> *Housing Act 1996*
> <u>188 Interim duty to accommodate in case of apparent priority need.</u>
>
> (1) If the local housing authority have reason to believe that an applicant may be **homeless, eligible for assistance** and have a **priority need**, they must secure that accommodation is available for the applicant's occupation.

This is due to several reasons. First, CCHP defines itself – and receives funding in its capacity – as a 'single homeless charity', purposely setting its stall to serve those to whom the Act affords limited coverage on paper. If a person presents to the office with children, this implies that they 'are priority need', that is, presumably unquestionably eligible for state support. Accordingly, they are given advice to this effect at the CCHP reception, redirecting them to 'approach the council'. Second, if a prospective single client is on the face of it 'priority need' – typically by virtue of its complex subsidiary test, 'vulnerability' – the anticipated task becomes 'fighting the council' as CCHP advice workers regularly called it. This refers to the challenge of activating a client's entitlement by persuading local authority decision makers that the person satisfies the criteria.

'All of the stuff about the Housing Act, all of the benefits [rules]: I had no knowledge of any of this when I started working there', Lily observed, even joking off-handedly that the CCHP training budget had been slashed when she was in post but at least there was still 'Google'. In this regard, Lily is representative of my former paid colleagues in the Castlebury homelessness industry. None of them reported having a legal qualification or prior legal experience, even though their role requires them to interpret legal documents regularly (such as tenancies, eviction letters and appeals about benefit and statutory legislation). Further, only 15% of them reported that they had any previous employment in another homeless service before commencing their current post. For most of them, their then employers represented their first in the industry. This deprofessionalization of advice is commonplace in the UK homelessness industry (Tawfic 2022: 85–86); it relies on visceral, heartfelt forms of moral persuasion rather than a legalistic conception of justice. In this role, their brief is to be outraged mediators.

Despite her status as one of CCHP's most decorated caseworkers, Lily's own assessment of her achievements was arrestingly sober. Movingly, she described to me how, following her departure from CCHP, she 'was going through some sort of purge' in which she was 'crying all the time'. Lily used the words 'trauma' and 'disillusionment' – a term to characterize her experience of working in CCHP – as an explanation for the source of her prolonged feelings of distress. What was traumatic, Lily indicated, was not merely the 'vicarious' experiences of another's suffering that her role demands; she observed that the lack of aftercare and institutional support contributed more to the 'burnout' than the routinized witness of suffering itself.[2] What made her 'disillusioned' was the gradual realization that the intrinsic effect of her labor was to 'institutionalize' her clients in a 'capitalistic system' with which she profoundly disagrees. I asked her to elaborate on what she meant by 'the system':

> Well, I say council is probably enemy number one because they make it impossible [...] You might as well just have four limbs missing and you're still going to have to make a case for yourself. So that was all horrible at the council business.

Lily was not the first to offer to me the unprompted suggestion that local authorities are inclined to obstruct claims from applicants who lack limbs. I had first encountered this claim almost four years earlier in East Axlow, another local authority area 7 miles away from Castlebury, among caseworkers in a similar service to CCHP's advice service:

> Ingrid: I wonder what training they get [local authority officials]. Alfred [Ingrid's colleague] told me that they lose all emotion, have to become a

completely different person. It's so tough. You [would] literally need to bring all the evidence [of disability] to a presentation, even their prosthetic legs – I'm not actually joking!

Shortly after, Ingrid observed exasperatedly that local authority officials often imported additional extralegal requirements in order to decline eligibility, such as 'local connection' and 'significant' priority need.[3] She also noted that local authorities commonly suggested to applicants that they approach Ingrid's organization for assistance instead of them, even when it was precisely her advice organization advocating to the local authority on the applicant's behalf. It is often a 'deadlock', Ingrid reiterated, claiming that local authority officials were 'dead inside'.

Meanwhile, when I challenged Lily on her perception of housing officers as 'not well-meaning', she interjected, 'No no no, [they are] absolutely not [well-meaning]', continuing:

> Why the hostility? It's beyond me. Like why they are just so horrible and frankly vicious to people who are having the shittiest time of their lives is beyond me. You can say no to somebody without shouting at them. I don't know. I don't know how you get into being a housing officer.

Lily and Ingrid's critique of their respective counterparts rehearses a common form of moral outrage at English local authorities that forecloses any discernible identification with the fiscal constraints they face.[4] *Guardian* columnists, legal advocates and a few scholars in social policy echo such criticisms of local councils' 'gatekeeping practices' (e.g., Cowan 1997; Butler 2011; Fearn 2015; Alden 2015; Marsh 2020).

The character of these contentions compares usefully with John Clarke's study (2016) of pervasive cultures of antagonism that are hardwired in the contemporary English schooling inspection regime. For Clarke, excess emotional intensities – of anger, fear, anxiety – and perverse forms of mutual hostility characterize the field of relationships between Ofsted (the Inspectorate) and English schooling personnel. He argues the Ofsted inspection system is both a product and producer of a 'shared paranoid sensibility' among actors (2016: 139), culminating in an institutional field where 'circuits of paranoia' predominate, the psychodynamics of which feature ' "splitting" (the binary and absolutist distinction of Good and Bad) and "projection" (the phantastic imagery of good and bad people)' (2016: 135).

The psychodynamics of moral outrage comprise splitting and projection too – these reveal and set in motion moralized economies of hostility and emotional excess. Lily suggested that her local authority counterparts lacked any positive qualities – they were necessarily not well-meaning, horrible and vicious – and so she drew on readily circulating binary images of council homelessness officials as reflections of the Bad. Alongside Ingrid's reflections that such workers have to become a 'different person', this reflects a commonsensical view among homelessness NGO workers that council officials embody the Bad and so are necessarily a distinct class of person. This distinction positions both the NGO workers here and the people on whose behalf they advocate, as emplaced on the side of the Good – a shared position which is premised on the worker's outrage and their client's suffering.

Notably, the moral outrage expressed by Lily and Ingrid relies on distinctively bodily imagery: an appeal to morality with recourse to the body as its rhetorical focal point. The coincidental example of a claimant without limbs serves as a rhetorical device to depict local authorities' supposed depravity; the claim that such officials were 'dead inside' demonstrates these workers' belief that inhabiting the local authority role figuratively removes a certain life force from its personnel. This draws on a contrasting expression of NGO workers' outrage and compassion: as both evidence of their continued embodied capacity to feel and their belief that their moral imperative is to save life when it is most disfigured. From this aspect, it is a quintessentially humanitarian mode of action with the image of the suffering body at its heart as the morally legitimate object for compassion (Ticktin 2011), entailing an inevitable objectification of the suffering other in those terms. Lily and Ingrid's belief that eligibility appeals on the grounds of medical vulnerability are morally persuasive is tragic, however: local authorities most effectively contest claims not on the grounds of vulnerability, but by disputing the sincerity of the claimant's very status as homeless (Tawfic 2022: ch. 6).

On the part of my NGO interlocutors, the absence of any discernible capacity to identify with local authority workers was striking and pervasive: the ability to feel ambivalent, or to identify with the shared experience of austerity, seemed to be written out of their job description. Sebastian, one of Lily's former colleagues in CCHP, described the process through which he tried to activate local authority entitlement for a claimant with profound hearing loss:

> I fought with the council so much. [Lucien Pendleton], I despise you and I need that on record. Named and shamed, man. [They] just refused. This council worker refused. Like, [they] just wouldn't. [They] were so obstinate, everything. And I just fought so much. I fought really hard for this guy, and I stand by it.

When I asked a managerial CCHP colleague if he could empathize with local authority constraints, he responded with some bewilderment:

> Do I have sympathy for the local authority? No, I don't. I can't. Because to me at CCHP, we're seeing the people who are suffering. And just my

principles, my morals, my values, my beliefs, means that I believe that everybody deserves a home.

This relational and personal attunement to suffering, informed by a professedly embodied ethic of witnessing, is what makes CCHP, as Jonas put it, 'distinct from the local authority'. He hinted that the local authority lacks the capacity to 'see' suffering, does not similarly perceive the need to alleviate it and is perhaps even responsible for it in the first place. The visceral and repeated claim that their job is to 'fight' the council reveals the extent to which antagonism is written into their charter. Scaling up beyond Lily, Jonas and even CCHP, this represents a positive feedback loop in which homeless charities and government institutions 'make up' each other (cf. Hacking 1986) and the wider industry.

A bioethics of consumption: Noah against the state, against CCHP

CCHP's charter to feel outrage against the council has an uncanny mirror image: how neighboring organization the Noah Community night shelter instilled and communicated a sense of outrage toward CCHP along parallel lines. Even though CCHP and Noah were neighbors during my fieldwork – sharing respective halves of St Mark's Church Hall separated by a fabricated party wall – personnel within these organizations rarely communicated with each other and shared a distrust of those in the other organization; there was no common area in the building for Noah and CCHP personnel to mingle and the entrances were segregated – each organization stuck firmly to its own side of the wall.

Noah's mercurial and muscularly masculine founding and final manager, Kev, framed CCHP's relationship with the local authority as categorically profane, viewing the CCHP-local authority dynamic as improperly close and uncritical, describing CCHP's proximity to central and local government as 'getting in bed with the devil'. For him, that relationship characterized the very antithesis of his home-making project.

Kev's desire to distance and boundary himself from CCHP, the local authority and other homeless NGOs in Castlebury was palpable, observing to me that he purposefully declined invitations to local multiagency forums. Moreover, CCHP's proximity to the state engendered an awareness in Noah beyond Kev that the nature of Noah's pursuits morally differed from its neighbors. I once asked deputy manager Sara what distinguished the two organizations. She observed that CCHP were 'caseworkers', whereas Noah was 'lifeworkers', perceiving that CCHP resembled their local authority counterparts and funders, whereas Noah was in the business of 'changing lives', as she put it. This was not entirely dissimilar to how Kate, a CCHP support worker, once put it – 'CCHP are the brains, Noah is the brawn' – spinning her organization's more conventionally professional approach as a virtue. In each case, the casework/lifework and brains/brawn dichotomy expressed subtle praise for one's respective organizational style and veiled denunciation in relation to the other. This reflected Noah's unpopularity with its neighbors – a status that often garnered pride within Noah.

Noah's legitimacy – for its primary architects, Kev and Andrew[5] – was precisely the fact that it was an anti-state endeavor. Charting the state's history back to the 'dissolution of the monasteries' in Reformation England, they both described it as an institution that engendered 'greed' and the 'growth of individualism' to the extent that it led to the systematic exclusion of 'homeless people'; and they termed their project as 'a center of hospitality' at the forefront of reversing this history. 'These days, society is trying to put you into boxes – "gay", "straight" – and women eventually go off with daddies: they've never felt like they've belonged', Kev put it, reserving his right as the manager to adapt Noah's rules on a case-by-case basis, even though – or perhaps precisely because – he wrote them. He maintained the right to enroll guests onto the shelter's closed guest list – and evict them – at his discretion, estimating to me that he had evicted one in two guests since Noah's establishment. Similarly, Kev asserted his personal right to admit and exclude volunteers. Crucially, he cast himself as an authority about homelessness, derived his identification with his clientele, often recounting a former time sleeping rough and engaging in criminality.

The Noah night shelter presented reformative discipline as the antidote to moral decline, with bodily practice at its heart. Diet was critical. Kev reminded me at my volunteer induction – and guests at the weekly Community meetings that only he convened – that Noah's approach to the 'recovery' from homelessness was key. 'We insist that everyone eats together on the table', he emphasized regularly, referring to the home-cooked meal served up nightly by the volunteers, according to a daily dinner rota conceived by paid staff; he digressed by complaining about volunteers he reprimanded for serving special meals for 'picky guests' upon request, such as the occasional baked beans on toast. This was the basis for the shelter's 'foods for moods' policy. 'You can't recover if you eat like shit', Kev noted. 'We keep the food the same for everyone because it's good food! Not pre-packaged, pre-made shit; no white bread'. 'Coca-Cola is only good for cleaning drains and the bottles for planters in the garden', he declared sagely. Neither white nor brown sugar was supplied for hot drinks: only honey, due to its status as a 'natural' (i.e., putatively unprocessed) ingredient.

Drug abstinence was the second component of Noah's disciplinary mind–body regime: it had a zero-tolerance policy against its guests 'using', as Kev described it, and operated on the presumption that its guests were necessarily recovering addicts; this was enforced through (the possibility of) on-demand urine tests. Describing himself as an 'addict', Kev observed that 'if you have never *been* addicted – if you don't *understand* addiction – you just wouldn't know', continuing that the meaning of the term comes from the Latin 'addictus': 'I surrender [...] to surrender your will'. He called this will a 'demonic force that wants to keep you in bondage' and that he was in 'the warzone' of addiction. A further key component to his 'recovery' from homelessness, he told me, was 'the gym'. Kev's devotion to fitness was palpable: his office doubled up as an exercise studio, and an optional part of Kev's mentorship toward recovery involved offering his guests a program of personal fitness.

A grammar of purity and contagion underlies Kev's reformative bioethics and his perspective on multiagency politics. Kev recounted how he arrived unannounced one night in a 'black Land Rover' to the car park that CCHP and Noah shared, accompanied by several of his 'big guys', stood resolutely cross-armed in front of the 4x4 in a bid to 'non-violently' evict several trespassers who had set up camp and whom Kev suspected were 'using'. Kev viewed the proximity of drug consumption to Noah as imperiling his guests who try to 'keep with the project' of abstinence, once describing them as 'the casualties of a spiritual war [and] our warriors on the battlefield'. Meanwhile, he critiqued CCHP for failing to contribute to these efforts and for attracting what Kev termed 'rubbish' to the church grounds: the bodies of CCHP clients were categorically morally contagious for him. This chimed with his resolute insistence to exclude CCHP staff from the Noah night shelter kitchen. He justified this on the basis that Noah had a five-star food hygiene rating and so the admission of other workers and volunteers might precipitate a breach of 'food safety'.

The psychodynamics of this grammar of purity and contagion feature the same processes of splitting and projection, featuring a moral rhetoric of the body at its heart. The difference here, however, from the CCHP-local authority case is the way in which Kev moralized homeless bodies. Whereas for CCHP, the homeless body is coded as putatively vulnerable and so morally deserving of (state) compassion, Kev's outrage at the 'users' reveals a conception of (some) homeless bodies as contagious, an unwanted outside presence that threatens the bodies and souls of his guests on the inside.

A form of boundary work, Kev's outrage has a spatial component through which *all* bodies from the 'outside' may imperil Noah's integrity – it features a hostile orientation that demands defending 'the home'. Although this entwinement of pure bodies and pure home-making is a product of Noah's eclectic ethos, it also reflects the division of labor between CCHP and Noah that is commonplace across the homelessness industry and welfare: the former as an advice agency and the latter as an accommodation provider. In other words, Kev's highly moralized attempts at gatekeeping are unexceptional insofar as he sought to *repel* from 'his' home-making project what he views as the evil in a largely uncaring world. In contrast to repulsion, CCHP's ethical orientation to the local authority was *confrontational*. In this, CCHP, Noah and the local authority mobilized and prompted each other's outrage in a circuit of emotional excess characterized by hostility.

One afterlife of outrage: Adrift in futility

This final ethnographic section returns to Sebastian in CCHP, analyzing an interaction he had with a client shortly before he resigned from his post.

A Friday late afternoon, the CCHP office was gearing down for the bank holiday weekend. The majority of its staff were wrapped up in various plenary meetings; its drop-in was now closed until Tuesday morning. Meanwhile, Sebastian attended to a cascade of financial spreadsheets. He sat alone in the main office; for a pleasant change, he was not tied up in the meetings that occupied his other colleagues.

The doorbell rang; it was now 4:30 p.m. Sebastian welcomed into the empty waiting room a woman, who he would later describe as Arabic and 'four foot ten, almost child-like'. Communication was not easy. Sebastian quickly discerned that the woman, Clarissa, is profoundly hard-of hearing and relies on lip reading while nonetheless articulating English well; Sebastian wondered if the woman has an intellectual disability. She presented him what looked like a ream of official paperwork: documents from the Department for Work and Pensions that show her maximum entitlement to disability benefits and NHS-headed letters showing that she needs a cochlear implant. Sebastian began to learn that the woman was being evicted on Tuesday by her live-in landlord. As a lodger, she has no ready means of contesting or delaying the eviction. She visited the council housing offices for assistance that afternoon, Sebastian discovered, before being told that she should instead visit CCHP as the council cannot help her.

Despite being one of CCHP's most experienced staff members, Sebastian did not know how to respond. The only housing advisor on site was in an uninterruptible meeting, and so was Sebastian's manager, Jonas. Sebastian interrupted anyway to be told that the woman would have to return on Tuesday for the drop-in between 10 a.m. and 1 p.m. Sebastian did not think this was a reasonable solution: the woman would have a critical medical appointment at 10:30 a.m. in a hospital 1 hour away that day; and drop-in is unpredictably busy, sometimes closing early if there is a shortage of advisors – as would be the case on Tuesday.

Sebastian feared that this was a non-solution that would place her in grave peril. So Sebastian returned to the woman with a list of housing solicitors' contact details in his hand, and they attempted to telephone each one without any positive response. This was the product of local authority 'cruelty', surmised Sebastian; and he felt profoundly unsupported by his employers, being left to his own devices to assist the woman without any debrief, aftercare or even the means to do so. 'She cried to me and I cried with her', Sebastian would later recall to me, continuing, 'I felt so helpless'.

The impossibility of mobilizing a response, for Sebastian, prompted an encounter with what anthropologist Jarrett Zigon (2007) terms a 'moral breakdown'. Zigon's concept refers to a conscious moment out of the flow of the everyday in which an actor is presented with a 'dilemma, difficulty or trouble' and becomes enfolded 'uncomfortably and uncannily in the situation-at-hand'; a type of experience in which 'the very process of stepping-out and responding to the breakdown in various ways alters, even if ever so slightly, the aspect of being-in-the-world' upon return (Zigon 2007: 138). Sebastian's meeting with Clarissa prompted a situation outside of the usual flow of the everyday for him: no colleagues or lawyers available for him to refer Clarissa, nor with whom to vent or blame the local authority, a feeling that there is no time left for a person profoundly in peril.

The usual 'outlets' for outrage were absent, and yet Sebastian felt an excess of emotion. The lack of colleagues to whom to vent was unusual and precipitated a disruption in the typical splitting-projection dynamics that tend to idealize CCHP as morally positive in a zero-sum game at the expense of local authority. The awareness that he was alone at the nexus of outrage and suffering, dependent on absent others to enact compassion, was viscerally distressing: the difference between CCHP and the local authority now seemed to feel less real. For Lynn Froggett (2002: 37, cited by Clarke 2016), such dynamics of splitting-projection typically feature in disaffected welfare clients who idealize one welfare worker at the expense of another with whom the client may have had a negative experience, in a manner akin to preferring and identifying with one parent over the other. Froggett's insights are also useful for understanding outrage among welfare workers themselves, as she points to the psychodynamics of hope – and hopelessness in fact – in such fraught settings where there may be no-one to idealize nor with whom to identify as a vehicle of hope. In these cases, the focus of the emotional excess expresses itself 'inwards', leading Sebastian to identify only and perhaps perversely with Clarissa.

What aspect of being-in-the-world is experienced upon return for disaffected workers such as Sebastian? These forms of moral distress – occupational helplessness – are a professional hazard in such settings in austerity England. Even though it appears to be an essential component of these workers' job specifications, it tends to drive worker attrition due to the emotional toll (James & Killick 2012). This applied for Sebastian, as it did similarly for Lily earlier in this chapter, when she framed her experiences as 'trauma' and her state upon resigning as 'disillusioned'. Yet these forms of helplessness and disillusionment do not seem to yield an awareness for ambivalence that scholars such as Froggett anticipate, which is an eventual capacity to see the 'bigger picture' in its wholeness and complexity. Instead, frontline workers' disillusionment often reinforced an unsustainable sense that they came to resemble the object of their critique.

Although feelings of futility might well prompt an awareness of the ambivalent nature of their roles, such an awareness appears by design to be incompatible with the job. Instead, prominent expressions of resentment toward the system – and their former employers – feature in the narratives of Lily and Sebastian, both of whose interviews were conducted after departure. The excess of emotion settled into a form of deeply felt betrayal at being neglected in the role; if Lily had the chance to address her former employers, she described a desire to say 'thanks for making me mentally ill'.

Conclusion: Circuits of outrage

The English homelessness industry demands and institutionalizes outrage. In doing so, its workers paradoxically make up 'the state' in the process of critiquing 'the system' by attributing straightforward forms of moral responsibility in a fragmented field. Their critiques seek to salvage some sense of separation from what they view as morally dubious, and it presupposes an in-group of similarly outraged spectators. The paradox here is that it conceals the inevitability of contagion and ambivalence which is written into their roles but must be denied to cultivate legitimacy. This places demands on the intimate self that are apt to generate moral distress when the impossibilities of the charter are experienced alone, amplifying the atomization of an already fragmented political field.

This chapter has depicted the affective feedback loop between outrageous state failure and outraged virtuous firefighting that characterizes the politics of homelessness in the UK, offering an analysis that extends to the governance of vulnerability writ large. As scholars of the emotional life of states remind us, the institutions in this chapter – and 'the state' itself – are 'affective formations', with emotion as its 'connective tissue' giving meaning and substance to these unstable social fields (Hunter 2016: 162). The role of moral outrage as such a connective force is critical in a contemporary political conjuncture where normalized forms of division and scapegoating processes seem to hold such currency (Newman 2016; Carvalho et al. 2024; Koch 2018: ch. 7). Scaling up, the moral outrage that circulates is at once a call to action and an invitation to perform individualized renditions of virtue: it divides as much as it mobilizes, producing new attachments and disaffections with 'the state' in the process.

Notes

1 Similarly to the town where I conducted fieldwork, my interlocutors and host organizations are also pseudonymized to preserve their anonymity.
2 Lily described a common grievance that caseworkers feel toward their employers: a shortage of peer- or practitioner-led psychological support. One outreach worker observed to me that he felt figuratively like he was 'going to have a brain hemorrhage' due to the unfulfilled promise of clinical supervision.
3 Local connection is a legal criterion in the Housing Act but its use to determine eligibility is a misapplication. It is instead designed, upon a positive decision, to determine which local authority is responsible for securing accommodation.
4 Due to the UK's complex system of devolved government, the regime governing access to housing support varies significantly; as a result, the system discussed in this chapter exists only in England.
5 The vicar of the Church Hall where Noah resided since its founding, and so *ex officio* chair of its Board of Trustees.

Bibliography

Alden, S. (2015). Discretion on the frontline: The street level bureaucrat in English statutory homelessness services. *Social Policy and Society*, 14(1), 63–77.

Barnett, M. N. (2013). Humanitarian governance. *Annual Review of Political Science*, 16, 379–398.

Batson, C. D., Kennedy, C. L., Nord, L.-A., Stocks, E. L., Fleming, D. A., Marzette, C. M., Lishner, D. A., Hayes, R. E., Kolchinsky, L. M., & Zerger, T. (2007). Anger at unfairness: Is it moral outrage?. *European Journal of Social Psychology*, 37(6), 1272–1285

Booth, R. (2019, July 7). UK housing crisis deepens as benefit claimants priced out by high rents. *The Guardian*. Retrieved from: www.theguardian.com/society/2019/jul/07/ukhousing-crisis-deepens-as-benefit-claimants-priced-out-by-high-rents

Bornstein, E., & Sharma, A. (2016). The righteous and the rightful: The technomoral politics of NGOs, social movements, and the state in India. *American Ethnologist*, 43(1), 76–90.

Butler, P. (2011). Cuts warning to councils: Don't ignore homelessness. *The Guardian*. Retrieved from: www.theguardian.com/society/patrick-butler-cutsblog/2011/jul/06/ombudsman-warning-to-council-on-homelessness

Cameron, D. (2011). Prime Minister's foreword. In *Vision to end rough sleeping: No Second Night Out nationwide*, 4. Retrieved from: https://assets.publishing.service.gov.uk/government/uploads/system/uploads/attachment_data/file/6261/1939099.pdf

Carvalho, H., Foreman, S., Tawfic, S., Aliverti, A., Chamberlen, A., & Rawson, B. (2024). Modern slavery and the punitive-humanitarian complex. *British Journal of Criminology*, 65(1), 93–109.

Chartered Institute of Housing. (2019). *Frozen Out: The real value of the local housing allowance in the final year of the benefit freeze*. Retrieved from: www.cih.org/media/nypi2ki0/frozen-out-nov-2019.pdf

Clarke, J. (2016). Fearful asymmetry: Circuits of paranoia in governing through school inspection. In E. Jupp, J. Pykett, & F. Smith (Eds.), *Emotional states: sites and spaces of affective governance*, 129–143. Routledge.

Clarke, J., & Newman, J. (2012). The alchemy of austerity. *Critical Social Policy*, 32(3), 299–319.
Conservative Party. (2017). *Forward, Together: Our plan for a stronger Britain and a prosperous future*. London: Conservative Party. Retrieved from: https://ucrel.lancs.ac.uk/wmatrix/ukmanifestos2017/localpdf/Conservatives.pdf
Cowan, D. (1997). *Homelessness: The (in-) appropriate applicant*. Ashgate.
Cowan, D. (2019). Reducing homelessness or re-ordering the deckchairs? *Modern Law Review*, 82(1), 105–128.
Dagdeviren, H., Donoghue, M., & Wearmouth, A. (2019). When rhetoric does not translate to reality: Hardship, empowerment and the third sector in austerity localism. *The Sociological Review*, 67(1), 143–160.
Department for Communities and Local Government. (2011). *Vision to end rough sleeping: No Second Night Out nationwide*. Retrieved from: https://assets.publishing.service.gov.uk/government/uploads/system/uploads/attachment_data/file/6261/1939099.pdf
Department for Levelling Up, Housing and Communities. (2022, May 12). *Table 104 Dwelling stock: by tenure, England (historical series)*. Retrieved from: https://assets.publishing.service.gov.uk/government/uploads/system/uploads/attachment_data/file/1075242/LT_104.ods
Fassin, D. (2012). *Humanitarian reason: A moral history of the present*. University of California Press.
Fearn, H. (2015). The scandal of councils turning away the homeless is finally being exposed. *The Guardian*. Retrieved from: www.theguardian.com/housing-network/2015/feb/27/council-gatekeeping-scandal-homeless-exposed
Fechter, A. M. (2016). Aid work as moral labour. *Critique of Anthropology*, 36(3), 228–243.
Froggett, L. (2002). *Love, hate and welfare: Psychosocial approaches to policy and practice*. Policy Press.
Goodenough, W. H. (1997). Moral outrage: Territoriality in human guise. *Zygon*, 32(1), 5–27.
Hacking, I. (1986), Making up people. In T. C. Heller, M. Sosna, & D. Wellbery (Eds.), *Reconstructing individualism: Autonomy, individuality, and the self in Western thought*, 161–172. Stanford University Press.
Hunter, S. (2016). The role of multicultural fantasies in the enactment of the state: The English National Health Service (NHS) as an affective formation. In E. Jupp, J. Pykett, & F. M. Smith (Eds.), *Emotional states: Sites and spaces of affective governance*, 161–176. Routledge.
James, D., & Killick, E. (2012). Empathy and expertise: Case workers and immigration/asylum applicants in London. *Law & Social Inquiry*, 37(2), 430–455.
Johansen, M. L., Sandrup, T., & Weiss, N. (2018). Introduction: The generative power of political emotions. *Conflict and Society*, 4(1), 1–8.
Koch, I. (2018). *Personalizing the state: An anthropology of law, politics, and welfare in austerity Britain*. Oxford University Press.
Local Government Association. (2019). *Opinion: it's time to put the funding crisis facing our local services on centre stage*. Retrieved from: www.local.gov.uk/opinion-its-time-putfunding-crisis-facing-our-local-services-centre-stage
Marsh, S. (2020). English councils breaking law in 'secretly' relocating homeless people. *The Guardian*. Retrieved from: www.theguardian.com/society/2020/jul/01/english-councils-breaking-law-in-secretly-relocating-homeless-people

McClenaghan, M. (2020). *No fixed abode: Life and death among the UK's forgotten homeless.* Picador.

Muehlebach, A. (2012). *The moral neoliberal: Welfare and citizenship in Italy.* University of Chicago Press.

Newman, J. (2016). Rationality, responsibility and rage: The contested politics of emotion governance. In E. Jupp, J. Pykett, & F. M. Smith (Eds.), *Emotional states: Sites and spaces of affective governance*, 21–35. Routledge.

Tauber, S., & van Zomeren, M. (2013). Outrage towards whom? Threats to moral group status impede striving to improve via out-group-directed outrage. *European Journal of Social Psychology, 43*(2), 149–159..

Tawfic, S. (2022). *The state of homelessness: Fragmentation and the will to care in metropolitan England.* Doctoral dissertation, London School of Economics and Political Science.

Thatcher, M. (1987). *Interview with Woman's Own.* Retrieved from: www.margarett hatcher.org/document/106689

Ticktin, M. (2011). *Casualties of care: Immigration and the politics of humanitarianism in France.* University of California Press.

United Nations General Assembly. (2019). Special Rapporteur for extreme poverty and human rights to the United Nations Human Rights Council. *Visit to the United Kingdom of Great Britain and Northern Ireland.* United Nations General Assembly. Retrieved from https://digitallibrary.un.org/record/3806308/files/A_HRC_41_39_Add-1-EN.pdf?ln=en

Woods, M. E. (2015). A theory of moral outrage: Indignation and eighteenth-century British abolitionism. *Slavery & Abolition, 36*(4), 662–683.

Zigon, J. (2007). Moral breakdown and the ethical demand: A theoretical framework for an anthropology of moralities. *Anthropological Theory, 7*(2), 131–150.

20
PLATO AND THE PENAL REFORMER'S DILEMMA

Ambivalence, blocked trinity and the failure of integration

Amanda Wilson and Alan Norrie

> punishment is better viewed in terms of tragedy than comedy.
> (Garland 1990, 292)

> Socrates was making them agree that...he who is a tragic poet by art is a comic poet too.
> (Plato trans. 1991: 223d)

Identifying the problem

The prison as tragic

Any serious consideration of the modern prison is likely to be drawn to the view of punishment as tragedy expressed by David Garland over 30 years ago. If things have changed since he wrote, they have probably got worse. The recent decade of austerity has brought the British prison system to a situation of crisis in terms of overcrowding, resources and control, but we should remember Michel Foucault's observation that the western prison has always been in crisis and that efforts radically to rethink its character are almost as old as the institution itself (Foucault 1977). In the United Kingdom today, there is insufficient space to deal with a serious outbreak of civil lawlessness, to which the seemingly inevitable 'solution' is to let some prisoners out now and build 'super-prisons' for the longer term. The logic is for more of the same and a persistent ratcheting up of prison numbers.

The problem is not however one simply of numbers. It is rather a question of how the prison is used as a kind of warehouse, but human beings are not goods. They live and love, breathe, have emotions and organise themselves. They are capable under favourable circumstances of doing better than they do, of doing well. The problem is that prison does not offer favourable circumstances. Returning to Foucault, the old model of the disciplined subject as the outcome of punishment remains to the fore, regardless of whether it succeeds. The present problem is indeed that prisons do not even effectively produce discipline, as opposed to a containment prone to breakdown. Even where discipline succeeds, human change seems miles away. A better approach would be to find ways of harnessing people's humanity, supporting them to reflect on their lives, and encouraging them to be better versions of themselves. But this seems a distant prospect, rendering Garland's observation valid. Or is it?

Prison reform

What we have said above is accurate but not entirely so. Prisons are indeed tragic places, but are they places entirely without hope, in the sense at least of commitment to change?[1] Against the tragic view, one argument worth canvassing is that of the 'prison reformer', by which deliberately capacious term we include all those committed to changing prison life, be it at the level of the system, or at that of the individual prisoner. Whether articulated or not, such a person may argue that the parlous nature of the prison is due to its bad use rather than its necessary character. There are too many prisoners, but many should not be there. The answer is not to build more prisons but to modernise the prison estate and limit the numbers sent there. The aim of prison is neither containment nor discipline but reform or rehabilitation. The prison estate includes both mainstream and high security provision *and* therapeutic establishments. Less of the former and more of the latter would make things better. Similarly, women's and young offenders' imprisonment can open a door to different ways of proceeding even if they often fail for poor resources or because they get subsumed in control strategies. Punishment may remain central to prisons, but only as the deprivation of liberty; restorative projects should be promoted. Prison staff are not all callous and cynical, even if some are. Many staff believe in their work and seek to help prisoners, though they may be ground down by the system. Many institutional practitioners in and beyond the prison look for routes to reform for both prisons and prisoners. This includes academics who articulate a discourse of change or who find a higher reformative purpose in the reformed prison (Liebling 2012, 2020; Maruna 2001). If Garland's overall view might classify the penal system as tragic, there is a lot of effort to try to make something good within it.

To this it might be replied that the tragedy is in part that so many good intentions are spent trying to reform the unreformable. All reform is superficial, serving only to legitimate an otherwise morally unacceptable and necessarily failing system. Without wishing to adopt a reformative agenda, we doubt that this is an adequate response. It is relevant, we think, to note an underlying reconciliative dimension in the prison from its earliest days. Just as prisons have always failed (Foucault's point), so have they also always contained ideas and commitments to change. This is noted even by so staunch a critic as Didier Fassin who observes the historical, religious and democratic impulses behind a humanising strategy in western penal systems and suggests that these 'perhaps even [offer] potentialities for the future' (Fassin 2018, 55–58; see Norrie 2019). What this might mean, or how it might work, Fassin does not say, but consider also the radical prison abolitionist Angela Davis who has observed the role of prison writing and educational programmes in the 1960s and 1970s in delivering change for prisoners. She notes that these programmes were subsequently closed down, just as they became successful for prisoners such as Malcolm X (Davis 2003, ch.3). Malcolm X was no tragic figure and there is a whiff here of radical change from within. Similarly, one of us has written of the experience of Glasgow's Barlinnie Special Unit in the 1970s as a 'loving prison' (Norrie 2022, 2025, ch.11). We acknowledge a degree of paradox in the term, and that such a prison may be seen as exceptional. We think however that exceptions should also be studied for they both prove rules and show their limits.

A deeper level: The blocked trinity

In what follows, we argue for the deeper truth of the prison reformer's dilemma. We wish to hold onto the fundamental criticisms of the prison, as contained in the tragic view. However, we think it is important to acknowledge the role of penal reform in not just legitimating a bad system, but in bringing a commitment to bear that plays a significant part in the modern prison. This is a commitment to loving integration, even if this is thwarted and even turned against itself within the modern prison. In adopting this position, we move beyond simplistic understandings of the prison as either wholly tragic ("there is nothing good about the prison") *or* inherently promising ("we just need to harness human love in the prison"). Ours is a middle ground that holds something of both together while accepting neither by itself.

Are we then simply saying two contradictory things: that the prison is both tragically unreformable and the place where redemption is possible? To answer this question, we want to take seriously the claim about penal tragedy by thinking more seriously about what tragedy is, how it works, and how this is relevant to the modern prison. Taking tragedy seriously takes us, first, back in time, to Plato's *Symposium*, where the question of the relationship between tragedy and comedy is first raised in an oblique but penetrating way. Thereafter, we will argue that this relationship, properly understood, is relevant to thinking through the nature of the prison as an unreformable place where reform may occur. Our account is not one of conceptual transplantation: we do not transplant tragedy and comedy qua the *Symposium* and read them into the modern prison. Rather, we see the issue as being one of how tragedy is intertwined with something else. In Plato, it is with comedy, though there is a failure to integrate the two. In the modern prison, there is a similar failure of integration of a kind we will consider below. In brief, we say that the prison reformer's dilemma involves a failure of integration between three elements within a structure that works against it. The integration we argue for is neither simple nor straightforward in a structural holding pattern we will call a 'blocked trinity'. The three elements at stake are punishment, reform and loving care. The key point here is how a structure fails to integrate these, as we first see in turning to Plato and Socrates.

The contribution this essay makes to the present volume is to provide a moral psychological account of what underlies dilemmas faced by institutional actors—in our case, the penal reformer's dilemma—in criminal justice settings. It connects to other contributions through deepening our understanding of why best intentions for meaningful change become thwarted (Bennett) and theorising the underlying tension that gives effect to shifting liminal positions on the front line (Foreman and Chamberlen). Its account of penality in the modern state acknowledges the grip of punitive power through identifying it as the 'structure in dominance', yet recognises the role of those acting in reform-oriented ways.

Plato's *Symposium*: A tragi-comic understanding

Beginning at the end

Just before the breaking of dawn, a sleepy Aristodemus awakes to find some guests from his party departed and others asleep. The only people still awake are Aristophanes, Agathon, and Socrates who are drinking from a large bowl, passing it anticlockwise. In his sleepy state, Aristodemus recalls 'that Socrates was making them agree that the same man knows how to compose comedy and tragedy, and he who is a tragic poet by art is a comic poet too' (223d). As Jonathan Lear (1998) notes, these parting words of Socrates have been puzzled over by western philosophy for centuries. Plato clearly thought that there was something important in Socrates's comment, but what? These are the last lines of the *Symposium* and Socrates himself does not explain. All we know from Aristodemus is that '[c]ompelled to these admissions, and not quite following' (223d), Aristophanes and Agathon fall asleep. The matter remains drunkenly enigmatic: after 'putting them to sleep, Socrates got up and left...' (223d). What should we take from Socrates's claim that comedy and tragedy are connected?

According to Lear (1998, 150), Socrates's point is that 'a tragic poet ought to be able to write a single drama which can be read both as a tragedy and a comedy' and, further, that the *Symposium* might be such a drama. As we shall go on to elaborate in the next section, we suggest that this tragi-comic insight can usefully be extended in a different setting to the modern prison, enabling a more adequate understanding of how the penal system operates and the dilemmas it gives rise to. In reading the tragedy *and* comedy of the *Symposium*, what we find is that it reveals something of the complexity of what it means to be human, what it would mean to flourish as a human, and how this pertains to our human connectedness. The underlying issue becomes one of ethical integration, and this is also relevant, we shall argue, to the modern prison.

The scene of which Plato writes is a dinner party, a symposium, where various speeches in honour of the god of love (Eros) are performed. It presents a rich dialogue that traverses ethical and metaphysical issues that remain alive today concerning the vicissitudes of love, the soul, beauty, wisdom, reason, and transcendence. This is a serious discussion, though one well-oiled by wine. The Greeks took divinity seriously and believed the gods were powerful puppeteers that intervened in the human realm. Honouring the god of love is a way of keeping Eros onside and, so doing, reaffirming the difficult relation between the human and the divine. Yet in the general bonhomie of the occasion, familiar seeds of the comic poet's craft are sown. There is much talk about the human body and its functions—sex, drunkenness, hangovers and so on. There are two main elements we consider: Aristophanes account of what the gods did to the humans, and the love games played by Alcibiades, Socrates (yes, him) and Agathon.

Tragedy and comedy: Aristophanes's story

At one point, Eryximachus gives advice to Aristophanes on how to stop some pesky hiccups preventing him from giving a speech on love. Thanks to these tips (the last of which is to sneeze), the hiccups cease and he proceeds to offer a speech that, on one reading, is comical. He conjures an image of humans as once being whole and round with 'four arms and an equal number of legs, and two faces...and four ears and two sets of pudenda', somersaulting and rolling around the Earth as omniscient beings (190a). These spherical, rolling beings were 'terrible in strength and force' and hatched a plan to conspire against the gods to displace them. To stop them getting above themselves, Zeus cuts them in two making them weaker and forcing them to contemplate their difference from the gods and to be forever destined to search for their other halves. The image of these humans is ridiculous, but the punishment meted out by Zeus and its attendant suffering is also tragic: humans are unable to be whole again.[2]

Through Aristophanes's story, we begin to grasp a deeper understanding of what comedy and tragedy might be taken to mean by Plato. Human beings are made out to be ridiculous for trying to "play god" and the gods, in turn, play a joke on them which blocks their (human) ascent to a fully flourishing state. This also creates a decisive split between the human realm and the divine realm. No matter how hard they try, these ridiculous creatures cannot reunite with their other halves, a situation that is both tragic from a human context and comic from a divine one.

This blocking of the path from the human to the divine is also seen in a different way in Socrates's recounting of his conversation with Diotima (which constitutes his speech to the symposium). This indicates how the human and divine realms are kept apart as Diotima wonders what it would be like 'if it were possible for someone to see the Beautiful itself, pure, unalloyed, unmixed, not full of human flesh and colours, and the many kinds of other nonsense that attach to mortality' (211e). This would be the truly beautiful but it is not available to humans and the inability to achieve it counterposes what humans are and may aspire to. From one point of view this is tragic, but from another it consigns humans to a life of comedy (the 'nonsense' of mortal life). This then sets the scene for the foolish love rivalry among the humans that is to follow, in which none other than Socrates himself plays a leading role.

Tragedy and comedy: Naughty Socrates

A licentious farce is played out between Alcibiades, Socrates and Agathon. The back story is that Socrates had previously seduced then abandoned Alcibiades, and now both are in pursuit of Agathon. The scene starts when a very drunk Alcibiades, crowned in 'a bushy wreath of ivy and violets and a multitude of fillets [ribbons]', stumbles into the symposium, looking for his lover, Agathon (212e). He has come to crown the 'beautiful' Agathon with his ridiculous fascinator, but the ribbons dangling in his eyes get in the way. He accordingly does not see Socrates, his former lover, and now his competitor in seduction, lying next to Agathon. Alcibiades is, we might say, freaked out by this:

> What's this! Socrates here! Lying in ambush for me again...And why do you come now? And again, why lie here, and not beside Aristophanes or somebody else who is funny and wishes to be? Instead you've contrived to lie next to the most beautiful person in the room.
>
> *(213c)*

Socrates response is comical, like that of a 'camp queen' (Lear 1998, 161), complaining of Alcibiades's jealousy: 'Ever since I fell in love with him, it's no longer possible for me to look or even talk to a single beautiful person'. He turns to Agathon, his new object of desire, to protect him from Alcibiades: 'I very much tremble at his madness and his love for hating lovers' (213e). Socrates is known for his games of seduction, as Alcibiades later warns Agathon, '[i]t isn't just me he has treated this way, but...many others as well whom he seduces as a lover and ends up himself as beloved instead of lover' (222a).

The descent of the dinner party from praise of divine love and beauty to games of jealousy and seduction has both a tragic and a comic side. Human beings know that true love exists but when they try to pursue it, they get hijacked into a much baser form. That is funny but it is also sad. The point is also revealed in the specific reactions of Alcibiades and Socrates. Alcibiades is still completely in thrall to Socrates and deeply wounded that Socrates should have discarded him. His speech is not on Eros at all but rather on the beauty that is Socrates. This is full of both admiration and a degree of animus. Socrates possesses qualities of the divine on the one hand (holding the images of the gods within him) and the goat-like (like the satyr Marsyas) on the other. The latter is a dig at his old age and animalistic features, but also what Marsyas was known for: 'his music alone causes possession and reveals, because it is divine, those who need the gods and rites of initiation'. Socrates differs from him only in that he accomplishes 'the same thing by bare words without instruments...when someone hears you...we are amazed and possessed' (215c–215d).

Then there is a small twist. Alcibiades reveals that Socrates never in fact sought to take advantage of him sexually. Even when he threw himself at Socrates, the latter always declined his advances. We might be tempted to think that Socrates's virtuous retreat reflects his nobility of soul, but we know that Socrates is a very capable seducer. An alternative view might be that he simply did not fancy Alcibiades, though Alcibiades would find that hard to entertain. Instead he experiences his rejection by the great man as a continuing enslavement to him. Socrates makes him feel a failure in allure and ethics, one who always feels he must fall short of an ideal standard. Alcibiades knows this, but instead of doing something about it, we might say 'growing up', he wallows in a cycle of unrequited flirtation. In the remainder of his speech, Alcibiades depicts Socrates as an 'erotically disposed', dishonest old seducer of young men. He seeks our pity as 'like a man who's been bitten by a snake' (218a). Yet he continues to project the divine in Socrates and would be like him. At one point he says that he once saw the images of the gods within Socrates and 'thought they were so divine and golden, so marvellously beautiful, that whatever Socrates might bid, in short, must be done' (217a). If only he could be more like this ideal love object, but he can't and continues himself to play the games of seduction, to seduce Agathon and still to be seduced by Socrates (though not, it seems, at the same time).

But if this is Alcibiades, how different is Socrates? Lear suggests that Socrates has made the journey that Alcibiades cannot. He 'has become as divine as humanly possible, and although he remains in the human realm, he is no longer part of it. He looks on the humanity of the human world with the indifference of the gods' (Lear 1998, 164). Yet, his response to Alcibiades's praise is to fuss about seating arrangements and to seek to charm Agathon. For all his approach to the divine (the speech on Diotima, the 'selfless' behaviour with Alcibiades), Socrates is eager to play the game of seduction, and to use Alcibiades's coarseness to draw Agathon in. For all his wisdom and beauty of soul, Socrates is also a messy human being. What he says is undermined by what he does; he points to divine wisdom but behaves all too humanly. So if Alcibiades lacks the moral and emotional maturity to reach beyond the sexual games, we have to say this is his responsibility and not Socrates's. But we *also* have to say that the grand old goat stays with his corrupting desires long after he should have known better. Where Alcibiades idolises Socrates in an example of what Lear (1998, 158) calls 'transference as resistance', Socrates is himself caught in a form of psychological resistance, this time as the repetition of seduction. He really should know better.

Wisdom won from integration: Loving Socrates

Now we can see how Aristophanes's story of the primal splitting of human being frames the later shenanigans. Yet, behind the games of seduction and farcical antics lurk the higher terms of love, truth and beauty. The tragedy that the *Symposium* brings to the fore is that human beings cannot access these. They remain stuck in shallow, conflicting, comic appearances, either as half-humans or as unreflective desiring bodies. Comedy and tragedy are both here, indeed they are necessary bedfellows. There is a blockage such that the human can never get beyond its earthly follies to participate in the divine. Zeus made the first (literal) cut, and both Alcibiades and Socrates must live with it. From the gods' perspective, the outcome is comic; from the human perspective, it is perhaps comic along the way but this masks an underlying tragedy.[3] Not even Socrates can become what he should have the power to be.

Two questions come to mind now as we prepare to leave the *Symposium* and to think about the modern prison. The first is that there may be a blockage between the human and the divine, and this must perhaps always be endured in the Platonic mindset,[4] but is there a way out? The second is to wonder what this blockage, the split between the human and the divine, could possibly tell us about the nature of the modern prison and the place of the prison reformer? The second question is pursued in the next section, but here is an initial response to the first which indicates the way forward in the second. An answer to both concerns the nature of a structural blockage and how it might be resolved by an integration.

To consider the nature of the blockage at play in the *Symposium*, we can return to its very end, when Socrates has sought to convince his friends that tragedy and comedy go together, and what happens thereafter. In making this claim, could he perhaps be recognising his own flaws and that his behaviour itself reflects the split between the divine and the human, the tragic and the comic? Across two and a half millennia, the flavour of a drunken party ending with heartfelt, fundamental, truths (*in vino veritas*) and their weary acceptance by those who have given up the will to argue is clear:

> Compelled to these admissions, and not quite following, they drowsed, and Aristophanes fell asleep first, and then, just as it was becoming light, Agathon. So after putting them to sleep, Socrates got up and left...He went to the Lyceum and bathed, passed the rest of the day as if he would any other, and after that he went home in the evening and rested.
> (223d)[5]

We find these closing lines of the *Symposium* in a way the most moving. Socrates has not slept so the prospect of going home to rest must seem very attractive. He goes about his usual business and, most importantly, he tucks his friends in before departing the scene. Agathon remains safe, no dramatic sexual triumphs are announced; rather a new day without melodrama starts, and Socrates goes about his business. He is a normal person with normal friends whom he treats with a degree of care and attention. In the end, there is a quiet wisdom which points us in the direction of a third position beyond comedy and tragedy. In this, love and care are present as real human experiences rather than as *either* over-elevated divine ideals *or* as personally diminishing sexual games. The human condition, it turns out, is one where real human care and affection are possible, even if these appear right at the edge of the tragic and the comic in the *Symposium*.

Note, however, that this does not *cancel* the problems encountered therein. Rather, the problem becomes different from what Plato's account suggests. The broken and split discourse of the divine and ideal, on the one hand, and the 'human all too human' sexual games, on the other, becomes a deeper question of how it might have been possible in Plato's Athens to connect and integrate the blocked relationship between three things: real, caring human love, divine ideal love and narcissistic sexual love, all of which are present in the *Symposium*. It is the *disconnected* nature of these three that is key to what is going on. The way forward that is yet to be achieved is to integrate human love and care with both the aspiration towards the divine and noble and embodied sexual self-expression. The key underlying motivation is human affection, love and care for self and other, such as Socrates exhibits in the end, but this should be intrinsically connected or integrated with both the desire to live one's embodied life and the ambition to live beyond it. To do so would be to establish a situation in which humans are genuinely enabled to flourish as unified beings. The question underlying Plato's *Symposium* is then how human beings may flourish, while its problematic is how this is blocked by an inability to *integrate* love's three facets, as care for self and other, desire and transcendence. Without integration, divine idealism sets up the human as comic while 'all too human' game-playing appears ultimately as tragic, and so we get to Socrates's argument. What, as it were, he has failed to see is the importance of the story's final scene as coda, his affectionate human farewell.

This however is no simple failure on Socrates's (and Plato's) part to bring these three elements together. With Lear, we suggest that what is being represented is the failure of an historical culture to integrate the different elements in a blocked structure. Greek philosophy is based upon a split between the ideal and the actual which is most clear in Plato's thought and this affects the ability to synthesise the three terms. As Lear (1998, 164) has argued, the difficulty of the *Symposium* has significance for Greek society as a whole:

> From the vantage of Athenian culture, this encounter between Alcibiades and Socrates must be judged a failure of inestimable cost. Nothing less is at stake than the future of one of the world's great civilizations.

In short, and establishing the argument we will develop below with regard to the prison, we suggest that the Greek trichotomy represents a structural blockage, or a 'blocked trinity', that is a structural setting in which three things that should be integrated cannot be. We turn to this now.

The dilemma of prison reform

The modern prison is no philosophical dinner party but we think that Socrates's claim that the tragic and the comic are intellectual bedfellows is relevant in the way we have considered it here. We now argue first that the source of what is the modern penal tragi-comedy is the consistent promise of a reform purpose that is systematically undermined by a political and institutional process that blocks it. Second, the analysis we have developed above of an unintegrated and split conception of human being, where the ultimate promise of human flourishing is a present absence, can be related to modern prison life, and the nature of the desire for prison reform. Here unintegrated lies the modern trinity of the potential for human flourishing, the systemic will to punish and the desire for penal reform. These function as a blocked trinity in the modern penal system. We begin by making the case for the comparison.

Parallel bars: From Plato to the prison

In the *Symposium*, even the best of humans, Socrates, is blocked by bodily desire and ego from attaining divine being on earth, condemned to repeat worn-out tropes of seduction into old age. Taking an overall, god-like, view of his behaviour, this looks quite comic but his conduct at the dinner party is both tragic (he ought to do so much better) and comic (how ridiculous he looks in contrast with his ethical ambition). Tragically, we might say, Socrates is condemned to be a comic figure; and then, we might add, if only he could integrate his underlying affection for his friends with a sense of how to behave nobly and in a manner sexually befitting his years and nurturing those around him.

That modern prison life is also tragic hardly needs elaboration, but there is also something comic here. Punishment (with prison as its apex) pronounces itself a place where people may reform (this is its higher purpose, its as it were 'divine' mission),[6] but it condemns many if not most prisoners to a life of containment. Here personal moral development is not just extremely difficult but is contra-indicated, and a more likely outcome is the repetition of offending behaviour. We would say that the conjunction of Socrates's ambition to achieve the divine and his sexual recidivism parallels the prison's aspiration to rehabilitate the prisoner alongside the ensuing repetition of crime and punishment. The resulting gap between penal aspiration and outcome is systemically predetermined, so that from the human point of view, the experience is tragic. It is the contrast between the promise and the outcome that generates the tragedy.

What of prison comedy? Prison life can also be represented in comedic terms. Think of the popular UK sitcom *Porridge*, though it may be said that comedy is achieved by misrepresenting the prison reality. Prisons don't actually look like that. Yet, the idea of prisoners finding ways and means to turn an intolerable reality into something they can survive, while turning prison officers into figures of fun has a reality to it. Certainly, prison humour is likely to be of the gallows form, but there is a bitter comedy to be gleaned from the contrast between the pretensions of a system, maintained with ever-noble sentiments, and the truth of what it achieves. It is hard not to view, for example, the recent official calculation of how best to manage unmanageable prison numbers by trimming prisoners here and adding to them there without a sense that human comedy is at work. The way to get more prisoners into the system is to release more prisoners! Certainly from the point of view of 'the gods', if we had any, the overall contrast between professed ambition and ensuing outcome suggests there is something strange and humorous going on in the politics of the system. Similarly, of the prisoners themselves, as in Aristophanes's story, the metaphor of people who are damaged and not 'fully formed' fits many prison inmates perfectly.[7] As in his story, there is no way of achieving greater wholeness on offer. Condemned to inhabit its halls, inmates wander the system with the aspiration that they should become whole in a setting that makes this impossible. At some point the reality and the contrast with the aspiration maintained for 200 years becomes bitterly comical. Plato's divine comedy is replaced here by one that is only too human.

Common ground: The blocked trinity

What then of the question of integration, of a potential to flourish, held at bay by practices of punishment and reform in a blocked, three-part arrangement? The deeper question raised by the comparison above concerns the overall structure of the penal system as involving a split and unintegrated quality, such that our overall analysis of the *Symposium* is relevant here too. Our starting point is the potential in human beings to live in loving and caring relationship with others as the basis for flourishing. That is the telling point at the end of Plato's story, when drink, sex and noble argument have been laid aside and Socrates makes his friends comfortable before heading about his business. This starting point, at the very end point of the *Symposium*, is supplied gratis by Socrates's basic humanity, and, setting aside any claim that the penal system endorses or actions such an underlying quality, we think that what is true of Socrates in the end is also true of many who work in the prison, and indeed of many of its inmates. Underneath any system constraints, and often suppressed by them, there is the possibility that human beings can show care and concern for each other and that this, in another environment, would be the starting point for human flourishing. We see such an aspiration and conviction among many who work in prisons, that they should be places where care and concern for others is possible. While we accept that the prison environment may wear it down, warp and constrict it, we do not think this kind of commitment lacks an underlying authenticity that could be expressed more fully in another setting. The question then becomes how to understand its place in the prison setting, and this leads us, as with Plato, to the question of integration and its blockage.

If we call the potential for care and concern with the possibility for this to develop into a flourishing situation a basic starting point for integration, we have to understand how this potential sits in the penal setting. Remember that in the *Symposium*, we observe a failure to integrate so that basic love and care fail to become the core of a flourishing human life in which care and concern, noble aspiration and embodied desire are synthesised. In the time and place of the Greeks, desire falls back into self-centred, physical satisfaction that mocks nobility and is out of kilter with a flourishing life. Beauty of soul becomes an abstract and unattainable ideal.

As suggested above, we see this as a structural failing in the life of the Greek polis, which could not transcend the human/divine split.[8] In the modern prison, a basic commitment to love, care and human flourishing encounters a structure of being that denies it. Here there are also two elements. On the one hand, there is, in the 'major' key, an essentially punitive and security-based mindset that sees the prison as lesser eligibility payback for offenders that deserve to be there, who may be dangerous and must be disciplined. On the other, in the 'minor' key, we recognise a lesser role for commitments to reform of prisoner and improvement of the prison regime to make this possible. The problem then becomes one of thinking about how the major punitive key and the minor reformative key work together, and how they *both* relate to the basic human dimension of flourishing through care for the other. As with the *Symposium*, we see here a basic tripartite arrangement, a blocked trinity, in which an underlying human quality fails to be integrated with two competing aspects, neither of which can be synthesised with it.

The modern prison, the structure of punishment and the failure to integrate

In the major key within modern punishment, there is a punitive mindset, and we trace it back in human being not to love and care but to instinctual self-protection, reactive anger and hostility. We see this as a primitive, early or reactive component of human moral psychology, one that constitutes an initial reaction to a threat or violation, and one that can be overtaken in time by a different, more considered reaction. The initial desire to punish, to hurt someone who has hurt us can lead to a later, more mature reflection (Norrie 2022, 2025, ch.8; Wilson 2020, 2021, 2022). The initial angry reaction is experienced by many, if not us all, as when someone bangs into us out of the blue, triggering a fight or flight response. The immediate effect is to stand in the way of a reaction based on love and care that is essentially restorative and reconciliative in its form. Over time this deeper reaction becomes possible (Norrie 2025, 262–5), but it needs space to develop. The problem for the institutionalised form of crime and punishment, and therefore for the prison, is that this initial reaction is given a significant role in the ideology and practice of the penal system. Acting punitively towards a prisoner in the court sentence or the mainstream prison contains a good measure of this kind of reaction and this is the primary block on the development of flourishing, care and love in the system. Its outcome in the penal system is to hold but not progress the inmate, so that it fails to address problems of violation and their repetition which led to the prison in the first place.

In the minor key and alongside this, the prison is also a place which permits reform strategies designed to make prisons more liveable, give prisoners' lives some meaning, enable a degree of therapeutic engagement, and to harness the commitment of staff who seek to do well by prisoners. This is the restorative dimension which exists in the penal system, but it is significant that the major punitive key is structural in its effects and therefore dominates and shapes it. There is a *structure in dominance* at play, in which the punitive is the overall space in which the restorative is channelled, shaped, moulded, distorted and even turned against itself. The two elements in the prison are the punitive and the reformative, with the former as the dominant element structuring its minor co-partner. In this regard, the process of containing and blocking reflects the similar structure of ethical life found in Plato. In both, two elements cannot collaborate and require an integration that is missing. Crucially, as concerns the underlying human possibility for care and flourishing, this remains at a remove from the reformative element in penal life. There is not an unmediated connection between the two so that the practical workings of one directly reflect the underlying potential of the other, as we shall explain below.

In sum, the structurally dominant punitive form of the penal with its control of the lesser reformative dimension, and an underlying human capacity for care and concern, represent a parallel modern problematic to the splitting of the Greek world into flourishing, the sacred and the profane. There, the unreachability of the divine casts a dark shadow over possibilities for the human, which are rendered either comic (from the point of view of the gods) or tragic (from the human point of view). In the modern prison, human striving to better itself is real, for both prisoners and staff, yet is blocked by the overall punitive structure, while efforts at reform are limited by it. From the point of view of participants in the system, this looks like tragedy as the will to reform repeatedly runs up against (what turns out to be) a brick wall, despite the system's ongoing assertion that it wants people and prisons to change. From the bird's eye point of view of the disinterested onlooker, the modern equivalent of the divine, so much good energy dissipated in struggles to achieve the unachievable looks as comical as tragic. Today, we are not permitted the vantage point of divine comedy, but we can still appreciate the black humour of human failure even as we understand its tragic aspect. Penal reform is present but shaped and distorted by the punitive structure in dominance. This is the reason for the gap between earnest aspiration and disappointed outcome. What is generally lacking is a way to integrate a desire for human flourishing within the system, rather than observe its disconnection from and thwarting by the penal structure in its combined punitive and reformative elements. The ensuing blocked trinity explains why the reformers' role appears both possible and impossible at the same time.

The blocked trinity: A concrete example

We cannot make a developed case for the blocked trinity here, but the final episode of the recent BBC documentary series *Inside Barlinnie* (2025) offers a modest indication of how it operates in practice. The episode sets out to show how Barlinnie prison in Scotland has changed positively over the years, but what it ends up showing is how the failure of integration marches on, repeating itself in the present.

A cornerstone of modern Barlinnie is said to be its empathetic approach to prisoners and its focus on their welfare. A prison officer contends that nine times out of ten, you can get around issues 'just by talking to people'. We observe a Governor doing daily rounds of the Segregation and Reintegration Unit, checking in on prisoners, most of whom are there for mental health reasons. The documentary contrasts this present day reality to the horrible history of the prison. A 19 year old sentenced to death by hanging writes letters to his parents telling them he loved them before walking from his condemned cell to the gallows. The forms of extreme segregation that were to control non-compliant prisoners were abolished. Interviewed in the documentary, Jimmy Boyle was one such prisoner. Sentenced to life imprisonment at age 22, he describes feeling like his was a 'death sentence': 'I knew my life was finished…so I acted as if my life was finished'. He broke the jaw of the prison Governor, had violent confrontations with prison officers, broke up and tore down every cell he was placed in, fighting the system 'with every fibre of my being'. Barlinnie (and the other prisons to which he was sent) responded with brutal containment, first in the Silent Cells—where a war of attrition raged on between being beaten 'to fuck' and protesting by smearing himself in excrement or biting officers before being knocked unconscious—and later in specially built cages in Inverness. Boyle recounts: 'They just couldn't cope. And they put me naked in a cage. One blanket. The rule list on the wall says nobody should be there more than six months. I was there four and a half years'. But even this extreme brutality did not snuff the fight in Boyle and others. Brutality begot brutality and neither the prison nor people like Boyle were prepared to back down. This stalemate resulted in a 21 year-long experiment: the Barlinnie Special Unit. The brutal war of attrition was abolished by a very different kind of prison within a prison: a loving prison.[9]

The nub of the Special Unit (Norrie 2022) was that it offered a radically different way of thinking about the relationship between staff and prisoners and, by extension, what a prison officer and prisoner are inside and beyond prison walls. As Boyle puts it: '…at a point we just all became human'. This paved the way for the bringing out of love *in* the prison. But after 21 years of providing a space for seeing how care and concern for others could be integrated with penal reform and against punishment, the prison service turned its back on the Unit. Following its closure, Barlinnie once again resorted to segregation qua the Separation and Reintegration Unit where we had earlier seen the Governor doing his "welfare" rounds for dealing with difficult prisoners. Dirty protests (prisoners covering themselves in their own excrement) are common. The episode ends with a tour of the Wellbeing Centre at Barlinnie and an overview of the various activities available to prisoners designed to encourage practical skills, self-reflection and collaboration where the aim is to create a relaxed environment, to build empathetic and respectful relationships. As one officer put it, 'we're trying to humanise more, we're trying to move towards a more individualised approach' but this occurs in the shadow of the Separation and Reintegration Unit as a real alternative.

Tracking Barlinnie's past and present history reveals three elements: empathy and welfare; segregation and control; and the promise of the Special Unit. These three elements reflect the unintegrated trinity: the potential for human flourishing; the systemic will to punish; and the desire for reform. How are we to make sense of a reality that holds these three elements together yet keeps them apart?

The ambivalence of penal reform

As we see it, the penal reformer starts from the desire for change and to promote human flourishing, but this is a desire that remains unintegrated with the reality of the prison environment. That reality blocks the potential for reform and reshapes it in potentially damaging ways. Filtering the reformative desire through the will to punish and control disrupts the link between human flourishing and penal reform. This initial desire, we would say, is a modern representation of Socrates's wish to see his friends tucked up before he goes about his daily business. Just as his basic love and care for his friends was unintegrated with his vision of the divine and his failure to get beyond a degraded sexuality, so the penal reformer's position is one of reaching out for human flourishing and finding it blocked and distorted by the punitive reality of the prison. The reformer is stuck with a commitment to flourishing that is unintegrated with the reform process available in the penal system, as this is structured by the punitive. Yet the penal reformer remains committed to a reformative role, so it is a question of how to characterise this. We suggest that the way to do so is to distinguish the idea of a general commitment to flourishing and reconciliation from one that is reformative or restorative *in the shadow of the punitive*. The latter expresses the former, but in a stunted or misshaped form by virtue of its location in a structure in dominance organised around the punitive. It does not integrate it. This is the ambivalence of penal reform. The failure to integrate is often expressed but not always understood, as the following words from Barlinnie's current Governor, Mick Stoney (*Inside Barlinnie*, Ep.3), demonstrate:

> Everybody wants a pound of flesh. There's a retributive kind of approach to punishment...everything else should be focused on positive rehabilitation and positive supports...prison can make a difference to people, a real difference, and designed to allow people to thrive in it.

The problem is that those bent on making a 'real difference' to inmates' 'thriving' must do so in an environment designed to take the 'pound of flesh'. This is the blocked trinity in action.

Conclusion

We can conceive of a world better set up than ours in which all forms of punishment and captivity would indeed be abolished and human flourishing would be possible. In that world, we would agree with the retributivist Immanuel Kant (and before him Plato) that no punishment would be required. In this present world, however, we are stuck with the practical reality of prisons and the punitive and no clear sight of a path forward that could take us to something different. We think what we would call a deep or tendential abolitionist approach is defensible (Norrie 2025), but in the present we want to affirm the possibility of reform as something both intrinsic to and ambivalent in the modern prison. This essay affirms its possibility while thinking through its structural limits in a system based overall on punishment. A punitive culture, which dominates the modern prison, drives a wedge between reformative commitments and the underlying possibility of care and flourishing so that these remain unintegrated.

Suppose, however, that a commitment to flourishing and reform were central to the work of dealing with violation, and that the punitive dimension had been restricted or abandoned. We suggest that the present coupling of punishment and reform reflects the complexity of our moral psychology. Behind the angry reaction that blocks flourishing lies the real possibility of mature development that tends towards it. Penal reform and reformers gesture (to varying degrees) towards flourishing and, with it, the hope of integration, even if that hope is controlled and often disfigured by the structural dominance of the major (punitive) over the minor (restorative) key. The problem lies in how the punitive structure blocks the connection to love, care and flourishing on the one hand and limits, shapes and distorts the commitment to reforming, restorative and reconciliatory practices on the other.

That the Special Unit was able to bring out the love within people like Boyle indicates the possibility for loving integration. This is not to say that the answer to the prison reformer's dilemma is to turn all prisons into Barlinnie Special Units. For fully fledged integration is only possible beyond the prison. But it is to say that the Special Unit reveals how love might be integrated in the prison. Indeed, love in the prison at its best is not the best execution of love *just because* it is in the prison, but it can reflect something of a genuine move towards integration. This helps us to make sense of the deeper ambivalence in Boyle's remark that 'Barlinnie prison destroyed me. But it also built me up and made me into a better person'. The structural forces behind this paradox remain in place.

Notes

1 Our conception of hope here is not to be confused with the kind of hope frequently discussed in prison literature (see, for example, Liebling et al. 2019).

In our account, hope is more radical; concerned with (concrete) emancipatory possibilities.
2   The story continues that initially when the halves did find one and another, they tried to be one again which led to their perishing from 'hunger and inactivity… because they were unwilling to do anything apart from one another' (191b). Zeus took mercy on the humans and rotated their pudenda so that the human race could continue, but this merely provides for erotic human love (sex). Wholeness belongs to the realm of the divine: '…the soul of each [human] clearly wishes for something else it can't put into words; it divines what it wishes, and obscurely hints at it…Eros then is a name for the desire and pursuit of wholeness' (192d–193a).
3   As Lear argues, the author

> needs to be able to portray an event like the meeting of Socrates and Alcibiades from both a human and divine perspective. Tragedy purports to give an account of the intersection of divine and human realms, but it does so from a purely human perspective. Comedy represents the best human attempt to give an account of that same intersection from a divine perspective.
>
> *(Lear 1998, 165)*

4   C.f. Lear (1998).
5   A warmer translation is that 'Socrates made them both comfortable, and got up to leave himself…' (see Plato *Symposium and Phaedrus (Everyman's Library Classics Series)*, trans. T. Griffith, Random House, New York (2001)).
6   'People are sent to prison as punishment, not for it'. Really?
7   As Stan Cohen wrote many years ago, it is obvious 'to anyone who has spent five minutes in a court or prison' that 'the damage has already been done' (Cohen 1979, 35, 41).
8   While Lear portrays the split between the two players as expressing the division between the human and the divine, we see it as expressed in the standpoint of both of them: Socrates is also a seducer.
9   To clarify, by 'loving prison' we do not mean a loving institution (prison). Instead, we use the term as a placeholder for human capacities to love *in* the prison.

References

Cohen, S. (1979), 'Guilt, Justice and Tolerance: Some Old Concepts for a New Criminology' in D. Downes and P Rock (eds), *Deviant Interpretations*. Martin Robertson: Oxford, 35–41.
Davis, A. Y. (2003), *Are Prisons Obsolete?*, Seven Stories Press: New York.
Fassin, D. (2018), *The Will to Punish*, Oxford University Press: New York.
Foucault, M. (1977), *Discipline and Punish: The Birth of the Prison*, Allen Lane: London.
Garland, D. (1990), *Punishment and Modern Society: A Study in Social Theory*, Clarendon Press: Oxford.
Lear, J. (1998), *Open Minded: Working Out the Logic of the Soul*, Harvard University Press: Cambridge.
Liebling, A. (2012), 'Can Human Beings Flourish in Prison?' Paper presented at the Prison Phoenix Trust, London.
Liebling, A. (2020), 'Prisons, Personal Development, and Austerity', in P. Ugwudike, H. Graham, F. McNeill, P. Raynor, F. S. Taxman & C. Trotter (eds.) *The Routledge*

Companion to Rehabilitative Work in Criminal Justice, Routledge: London, 193–206

Liebling, A., Laws, B., Lieber, E., Auty, K., Schmidt, B. E., Crewe, B., Gardom, J., Kant, D. & Morey, M. (2019), 'Are Hope and Possibility Achievable in Prison?', *The Howard Journal of Crime and Justice*, 58: 104–126.

Maruna, S. (2001), *Making good: How Ex-convicts Reform and Rebuild Their Lives*, American Psychological Association: Washington, DC.

Norrie, A. (2019), 'Beyond Persecutory Impulse and Humanising Trace: On Didier Fassin's *The Will to Punish*', *Criminal Law and Philosophy*, 13: 681–688.

Norrie, A. (2022), 'Restoration, Abolition and the Loving Prison: Jimmy Boyle and Barlinnie Special Unit', *The Howard Journal of Crime and Justice*, 61: 103–116.

Norrie, A. (2025), *Rethinking Criminal Justice: Punishment, Abolition and Moral Psychology*, Cambridge University Press: Cambridge.

Plato. (1991), *The Dialogues of Plato Volume II: The Symposium*, trans. R. E. Allen, Yale University Press: New Haven.

Wilson, A. (2020), 'Shame, Guilt and Martha Nussbaum's Immaturing Process: Alethic Truth and Human Flourishing', *Journal of Critical Realism*, 19(4): 380–397.

Wilson, A. (2021), 'Guilt Beyond Guilt: From Political Theory to Metaphysics with Herbert Morris', *The Modern Law Review*, 84: 89-117.

Wilson, A. (2022), 'What a Shame! Restorative Justice's Guilty Secret', *The Howard Journal of Crime and Justice*, 61: 39–52.

21

EMOTIONAL LABOUR AND FEMINISATION OF WORK

The case of a 'spontaneous arrival' at a refugee camp in Greece

Artemis Christinaki and Erica Burman

Introduction

How do emotions inform, or else interfere with, psychosocial labour within migration and humanitarian terrain? To put it more sharply, have you ever asked a humanitarian aid worker how many hours they work in the field and how this 'excess of work', in terms of actual working overtime as well as emotional toll, is understood within institutionalised psychosocial humanitarian work in migration? This chapter discusses emotional labour in humanitarian work in relation to wider political and gendered economies of emotions in the field of migration. By emotional labour (Phillips et al., 2020; Hochschild, 1983), we refer to the way frontline humanitarian aid workers are required to manage their emotions as well as the emotions of their 'service recipients' – in this case, migrants[1] – while following the protocols of the organisation they work for. We also bring to the fore the alignment of traditionally gendered notions of care that are mobilised and capitalised upon by humanitarian work. By discussing humanitarian gendered and political economies of emotions, we engage the gendered and racialised complexities on which humanitarianism and psychology both converge and the mutually contested modes of practices, work, and power around migration, as they arise in encounters within the space of camps.

The chapter draws attention to an example occurring during the first author, Artemis Christinaki's doctoral research on the politics of psychosocial support (PSS) in the refugee camps of Greece (Christinaki, 2022a). Taking the documented example of the 'spontaneous arrival' of a family in a refugee camp in mainland Greece, who were asked to leave the camp as they were not registered there, we focus on two important aspects of what we name as

DOI: 10.4324/9781032617060-27

the 'emotional excess' of work in the field of humanitarianism and migration. The first aspect refers to humanitarian and political economies of emotions in relation to the discourse of psychology (itself already a feminised arena, Burman, 2007). We specifically address how the political economy of both space and emotions unfolds within the camp. Inspired by feminist geographers' discussion of the 'feminisation' of asylum (Hyndman and Giles, 2011), which we extend here also to the humanitarian care workers, the second aspect interrogates what the concept of 'feminisation' could bring to the field of humanitarianism and especially humanitarian work within migration (see also Burman, 2014 and Palmary et al., 2010). As such, we discuss what the concept of 'feminisation of work' may signify in the programme of PSS in the refugee camps of Greece.

Before we introduce our case study from the first author's doctoral research in the refugee camps of Greece, it is worth recalling how, since 2014, the situation in the Mediterranean Sea has been named and tackled as a 'refugee crisis'. In the name of this 'crisis', migrants have been accommodated in 'hotspots'[2] and camps where there has been a constant call for and attention to humanitarian aid and support, clustered by the notion of 'emergency'. As discussed elsewhere (Christinaki, 2022b), scholars from critical migration studies (New Keywords Collective, 2016) have questioned the concept of a 'humanitarian refugee crisis', arguing that there are, instead, a plurality of crises. De Genova et al. (2018) point out that this allows for the situating and conceptualising of migration within a nexus of crises. This nexus includes the economic crisis (i.e. the fiscal crisis in Greece since 2008 which has since extended across Europe), the political crisis of Europe (i.e. the rise of far-right movements, tightening of migration and restriction of movement, border control) with its internal re-bordering (e.g., Brexit), and the epistemic crisis 'at stake in the governmental labelling and administration of migrants' and refugees' heterogeneous mobilities' (De Genova et al., 2018, 255).

To support thinking at and across the borders of these economic, political, and epistemic crises in Greece and Europe (Tazzioli & De Genova, 2023; Mezzadra, 2021), it is important to situate the intricacies of both emotions and work in the field of migration and humanitarian aid. In the context of Greece from 2008 onwards, graduates of social sciences (including the first author) were struggling to find jobs (in psychology, sociology, social work, and education, among others in the social sciences). In that sense, the 'refugee crisis' opened up job opportunities for the jobless national youth in Greece. This point is important not only to highlight how the political economy of the refugee crisis started unfolding in the context of the economic crisis in Greece, but also to show how work in this humanitarian terrain was already 'emotionally' invested. For many of the jobless national youth getting a job in the Greek humanitarian and refugee terrain meant, in simple terms, that there was a chance to stay at 'home' and not become migrants themselves.

In this context, there are several reasons why we link 'emotional labour' in institutionalised humanitarian work with the role of psychology in the field of migration. In her doctoral thesis, Christinaki (2022a) argued that psychology infuses the humanitarian terrain as a discourse that, besides individualising, pathologising, gendering, and racialising migrants and refugees, also subjectifies aid workers. By 'subjectify', we refer to Foucauldian-informed approaches that attend to the doubled character of subjectivity, where to be a subject (or locus of thinking and action) is also to be subject to particular regimes of institutionalisation and accountability. The reflexive work involved in providing PSS constitutes a prime site for the constitution and exercise of professional and disciplinary identities and practices (Burman, 2011, 2004), which also includes the cultural alignment of reflexivity with femininity. It also organises ideas around how refugees are seen as passive, vulnerable, and traumatised, as well as how workers should work, organise, and deal with emotions arising from their encounters with refugees.

In that sense, and in line with Pykett et al. (2017), we are concerned with what happens when emotions are entangled with governmental and institutional forms of power, including humanitarian governance (Fassin, 2012); that is, with how emotions are put to work, circulated, performed, and guarded as a form of governing, while also constituting a way to disrupt and create forms of solidarity. In the next section, we discuss an extract from an interview with an aid worker on the programme of PSS in one of the refugee camps in mainland Greece to consider how emotions are spatialised within a political economy of humanitarian labour. To clarify, across the chapter, we are not concerned with defining what emotions are, or when and where they manifest. Rather, our focus is on what they do and what they provoke within the humanitarian-migration matrix and apparatus. Specifically, we address emotions as part of an institutional response and praxis, a strategy for control and management (Christinaki, 2023, 2022a, b), rather than as psychic expressions or claims about the experiences of certain individuals.

Case study: A 'spontaneous arrival'

The following lengthy extract invites analysis of how the study of 'emotions' has to be placed within wider historical, political, institutional, and economic contexts, that is, contexts that address both the state and the humanitarian forms of governance during the so-called refugee crisis in Greece. The extract comes from an interview the first author conducted in 2018 with a humanitarian aid worker in a refugee camp in mainland Greece. The interview was conducted in Greek and was translated by Artemis. The aid worker was employed by a national humanitarian organisation, working in a medium-to-small-sized camp in mainland Greece that had around 500 refugees and about 70 containers (used as shelters/homes). The camp primarily offered health and education services, with the organisation providing a PSS programme that included social workers, psychologists, lawyers, and language teachers. The broader study involved interviews with workers, ethnographic observation, map and photograph analysis, and political reflexivity. Gender, professional role, and camp location are not disclosed either here or in the doctoral study, to protect the anonymity of workers, as some roles had only one worker per profession and camp. Withholding this information (for appropriate ethical reasons) may frustrate and appear to muddy our claims somewhat, yet we also invite readers to consider what work seemingly secured attributions of gender and work role do in anchoring certain assumptions about the relevance of particular models or concepts.

This response came after Artemis asked the aid worker if they would like to share some of the experiences they had at the refugee camp.

> Aid worker: ...once, there was a family, here, that was a spontaneous arrival, so they had not been moved here via the ministry and there was not any container [housing allocated to accommodate them]. They learned on their own that there was a camp here and they came, expecting that they would be given a space to stay; these people were homeless for one month in [the capital city], and, somehow, they managed to come here [to the camp]. However, because they had not been transferred via the ministry [which is the official route and procedure], the manager of the camp left them outside the camp, without accommodating them anywhere. For about a month they stayed, there, in front of the camp in the covered kiosk.
>
> The first day that they came here, the woman was not at all well, she crashed, and she was crying all the time. We approached them, we offered them something to eat and drink, because they seemed to us [pause] I don't know, in an awful condition. The woman was not well at all, and she was trying to commit suicide. She had taken a scarf, the scarf that she had on her neck and she was trying to hang herself from a tree [pause] and this continued happening, so if we did not watch her for 10 minutes, she was trying to go and do that thing.
>
> In the end, I decided to accompany her to the psychiatrist to do an assessment and see whether she needed to be hospitalised or something like that, based on the degree of suicide intention. I was guessing that it was very possible to keep her at the hospital, which in the end did not happen. They did not Section [compulsorily detain] her, because [the psychiatrist] considered [pause] that her reactions were an outcome of external stress factors and not of an endogenous condition let's say. [...]. The direction that [pause] the camp manager had given to our organisation, not myself personally, to my supervisors, was that [pause] we should not bring them back, to avoid giving the impression that they would stay here. What

I did, following the direction of my supervisors, was to leave them in a nearby town.

These people, coincidentally, managed to come back because [pause] after we abandoned them there, err because [pause] I was told anyway, to buy them some stuff from the supermarket to have food, but because they did not cooperate, I just gave them the money, which is something that is typically forbidden to give directly money to a beneficiary, but at that moment I considered that [pause] ok let me give them the money to take something to eat [pause] and it seemed that they used the money to take a taxi and come from the nearby city, here, in the camp. It was 15 euros.

We will continue with this extract shortly. But let us pause for a moment to start unpacking how emotions unfold in the narrative between the bodies of individual subjects within a body of state and humanitarian policy. To begin, 'spontaneous arrivals' refer to those arriving in refugee camps without official recognition from the state. In this sense, they were (only) 'spontaneous' because they did not have approval from the Ministry of Migration. Without official approval and registration, usually, the individuals or families arriving in camps would not have the authorisation to stay there. As the extract suggests, despite being homeless in Athens, the capital city of Greece, and managing to arrive in another city in mainland Greece, the camp manager could not 'accommodate' them in the camp. This specific camp, in mainland Greece, comprised only containers, and usually families would stay together or share a container with another family.

It is clear from this account that the camp manager was positioned as allied with or representative of the State and Ministry. Hence, affective economies (Ahmed, 2004) already started unfolding between the state and the humanitarian landscape by providing and safeguarding different forms of access and services within the camp. However, 'emotions' and their gendered and other political economies at play here touch upon three different intersections and complex politics within the field of migration. First is how the state imposes limits on who can access the space of the camp, as well as how humanitarian aid is constrained by state policies. This opens up 'emotional responses' from both the migrants and the humanitarian aid workers. As noted, the woman responds to the state's attempt to 'gatekeep' or regulate who receives the right to access accommodation by pushing herself to the limit, attempting repeatedly, as the extract suggests, to commit suicide. The second intersection concerns how the woman's attempt to commit suicide is approached by both humanitarian and psychological discourse (i.e. the referral to the psychiatrist). A third intersection, which we will take up by continuing with the extract below, is how the aid worker's emotional 'excess' (in terms of what they have been asked to do and their subsequent emotional response to this) is managed (or rather not managed) by institutionalised humanitarianism. This opens up questions more broadly about the gendered and reflexive politics of work in the migration field, as what we will discuss as 'feminisation of work'. The aid worker continued:

> This is the biggest mistake I have made in my life because we abandoned some people, we harmed them simply to serve the micropolitics of the camp.
>
> *Artemis:* When they came back to the camp, what happened?
> *Aid worker:* They continued living outside and after a long time, one day there was a heavy storm, a very heavy storm, it had 10 cm of water, you were coming out and your whole feet were wet, and of course, the people became wet, they had 4 or 5 children, I can't remember how many, but they were many, and they were wet as well. The children were risking getting sick, so after that, they put the family temporarily in the common men's area. Also, another very big family, approximately 10 members [who] had been given 2 containers, offered on their own to merge in one container and give the other container to this family.
> *Artemis:* How many days did the family stay in front of the camp?
> *Aid worker:* They stayed for a long time, about a month. I just think that what we did to them, we harmed them, we did not help them. This is the most important mistake I have made here; I would say it was from negligence of the broader context.

A clear matter for reflection is the intricacies of accessing 'accommodation' in this example and how the 'stubborn' (Mezzadra, 2021) strategies used provoked a nexus of responses – from the state (i.e. the camp manager's decision to leave the family for a month outside the camp), the humanitarian organisation (which followed the camp manager's directions), the aid worker (who both followed and then resisted the supervisors' suggestions and camp management policies), the migrant woman (with her repeated attempts to commit suicide), and the refugees (who showed active solidarity). This prompts our discussion in the next section of how emotions become both spatialised and gendered to create different 'affective economies' (Ahmed, 2004) within the field of migration and the humanitarian terrain.

Spatialised emotions: Affective economies

Sara Ahmed (2004) coined the provocative phrase 'affective economies' to indicate how

> emotions *do things*, and how they align individuals with communities – or bodily space with social space – through the very intensity of their

attachments. Rather than conceiving of emotions as psychological dispositions, emotions work, in concrete and particular ways, to mediate relationships between the psychic and the social, and between the individual and the collective.

(p. 4)

In that sense, 'affective economies' combine the psychic, social, and material. We add to this notion how emotions are (always already, through gendered ideologies) feminised and as such are subject to discourses of privatisation and minimisation (Burman, 2007, 2009a, b).

Returning to our example, when the family arrived at the space of the camp, there was already a material, social, and political nexus in place. It was not only that, as a 'spontaneous arrival', they could not be 'accommodated' in the camp. It was also that what was considered 'spontaneous' and 'not welcomed' within the space of the camp was kept institutionally 'outside' of, but nonetheless physically within, the camp.[3] This paradox of being inside the camp but outside official and institutionalised support from the state (as indicated by the camp manager's response who refused to provide a container) led, on the one hand, to the 'humanitarian aid' providing only 'the basics' – literally food, water, and medical assistance – and, on the other hand, to closely monitor the woman and the family to ensure their safety (in a limited sense) while enacting the wider camp management policy to remove the family from the space of the camp.

From a psychoanalytic point of view, the term 'spontaneous' carries a certain meaning and significance. In psychoanalytic theory, what comes suddenly or 'spontaneously' is the return of the repressed, which in Freud's interpretation (1900, but also Freud, 1915, 1939) is situated in the unconscious field. The family's arrival within the camp can be read as a form of a repressed affective economy because it signifies what happens to those who fall into the cracks between or contest the power of state borders and institutional policies. This 'spontaneous' return, manifested in the arrival of the family, which was not registered on the state and camp management's lists, set in train a certain humanitarian and political economy of emotions within the space of the camp. More broadly, it could also be argued that migrants are 'the return of the repressed' as they signify Europe's colonial and imperial history, which, in the second half of the chapter, we approach as 'coloniality of power' (Quijano, 2000, but also Gutiérrez-Rodríguez, 2013).

Again, inspired by psychodynamic theory and group analysis in the field of institutions (Dajani, 2022; Layton & Leavy-Sperounis, 2020; Wilke, 2018; Fotaki et al., 2012; Obholzer & Roberts, 1994), it is worth noting how the state, in the form of the camp management, remained unmoved at the beginning by the arrival of the family and the woman's desperate emotional state. While the humanitarian organisation, as the main provider for the PSS in the camp, responded by providing 'the basics', the aid worker mobilised an additional institutional mechanism in their attempt to help the woman (and by extension also the family). By deciding to refer the woman to the psychiatrist, the institutional authority of professional mental health, i.e. psychiatry, was mobilised to intervene in and 'name' the woman's psychic response as well as (being anticipated) to offer a temporary solution for both the aid worker and the refugee woman. As the aid worker said,

> *I was guessing that it was very possible to keep her at the hospital, which in the end did not happen. They did not Section her, because [the psychiatrist] considered...that her reactions were an outcome of external stress factors and not of an endogenous condition.*

The institutional power of psychiatry offered an interpretation of the attempt to commit suicide as 'an outcome of external factors', and in that sense confirmed that what affected the woman's response was the camp management's decision to exclude the family from the camp (but stay just about within the camp). Yet what is striking is the commitment on the part of the state (in the form of camp management) to maintain its 'procedures and rules' at all costs. While the possibility of the woman being Sectioned and so admitted to the hospital could have offered temporary relief for the camp manager and the humanitarian organisation (in the sense that she would not return to the camp), the decision of the psychiatrist to allow the woman to return to the camp enforced yet another return of 'the repressed': not only the return of the woman and family but also a wilful mobilisation of a much-contested binary within psychiatry between 'endogeneous' and 'reactive' depression or distress. In this case, this binary appears to be being opportunistically deployed by both parties, with psychiatric authority 'trumping' that of the camp management by refusing to name 'suicidal ideation' and/or disorder. In highlighting this, we do not align with the psychiatrisation of care, but rather to show the limitations of both the state and psychiatry and to expose the intentional harm enacted by the migration regime and matrix (in which both the state and psychiatry are implicated).

As De Genova et al. (2018) elaborate, alongside their victimisation, migrants can be seen within radical positions, gaining autonomy, challenging and diluting borders and orders, nations and states. Alongside this, the psychiatrist's decision to approach the woman's emotional response as 'an outcome of external factors', rather than frame it as a disorder (i.e. to 'psychiatrise it'), fragmented both the state, in the form of camp management and mainstream humanitarian assistance, and the psychiatric power and ideology that often goes hand in hand with the state. Naming her emotional response as an outcome of external factors shows how the psychiatric discourse can paradoxically work against the psychiatrisation of the woman, so both underestimating the impact the state's decision had on the woman's response (by refusing to acknowledge how she was psychologically at risk of suicide), precisely by withholding this institutional, in this case, psychiatric, 'care'. These are the same mechanisms that force or decide to legitimise which migrants will survive in disgraceful conditions, like those refugee camps that shouldn't exist in the first place.

As argued elsewhere (see Christinaki, 2022a, b, Burman et al., 2004), the psychologisation and the psychiatrisation of migrants (De Vos, 2011; Summerfield, 2001) has become a powerful tool and form of alienation that disregards the psychosocial politics of space and avoids acknowledging and considering in practice how space and time within camps and 'hotspots' become what Kapsali and Mentinis (2018) name as the 'traumatic present'. As Kapsali and Mentinis highlight, the 'traumatic present' portrays how

> thousands of migrants are piled up under terrible conditions, exposed to danger and the fear of natural, psychological and sexual violence and are trapped for a long period in a vicious bureaucratic circle and continuous dead ends in terms of asylum procedures but also their everyday needs (medical care, clothes, legal services, etc.).
>
> *(p. 79–80)*

Freud's (1919) notion of 'the uncanny' (*unheimlich*), with its analysis of how the 'unhomely' is always present alongside and as the underside of the 'homely', highlights the politico-affective dynamics enacted, institutionally and materially, in refusing to 'accommodate' the woman and her family. The 'spontaneous' (that is, unexpected, unplanned) 'arrival' of the family is met with a protracted, elaborate, and deliberate repudiation by those whose job is to receive and 'host' them. That is, this inhuman practice of supposed humanitarianism confronts Europe with the limits of its 'hospitality' and even more with how its very existence belies its 'civilised' constructed identity and exposes its exclusionary practices. As with the return of the repressed, migrants are 'here' because 'we' were – and still are – 'there' (Centre for Contemporary Cultural Studies (CCCS), 1982; Bhattacharyya, 2014), and so their embodied presence in 'our' (European) spaces speaks uncomfortably of colonialisms that are all too current in the very creation of camps as a key nexus of the migration regime.

Returning to this case example, while the referral at the hospital was unsuccessful, the return of the family to the camp opened up new and contradictory dimensions in the affective economies of the state in its policies and procedures on migration and more specifically in the camp management, the non-governmental aid, and the different forms of emotional labour within the camp. The dead end of the state's bureaucracy, which was already apparent in the way migrants are made to live within 'hotspots' and camps, was further clarified. Indeed, this example concerns migrants who were not even allowed to be recognised within the premises of the camp.

Notably, the unsuccessful referral provoked a certain form of emotional labour on the part of the aid worker who was obliged to lead the family away from the camp and accompany them from the hospital to the closest city, to leave them there and not give them the impression, as the camp manager suggested, that they could come back to the camp.

The institutional pressure exercised by the camp manager led both the humanitarian organisation and the aid worker to proceed with this request, irrespective of the family's circumstances and the woman's psychological state. Yet, in another 'return', confronted with the desperate circumstances of the woman and her family, the worker's effort to mitigate the exclusionary practice that they were obliged to enact, haunts them as *'the biggest mistake I have made in my life... I just think that what we did to them, we harmed them, we did not help them. This is the most important mistake I have made here'*. That is, whereas the camp manager and the psychiatrist wilfully deploy arbitrary bureaucratic institutional rules to maintain the overall policy of exclusion, the frontline worker takes their own compliance as a personal failing: *'we abandoned some people, we harmed them simply to serve the micropolitics of the camp'*. Significantly, the worker not only portrays themself as at fault, internalising the injustice as a matter of personal responsibility but also accuses the whole migration management apparatus.

Naming it as 'a mistake' that does not initially identify or specify *whose* mistake it is in one way demonstrates their speaking position as a responsible worker who does not want to (or perhaps cannot) publicly criticise their managers/seniors. Yet it rapidly becomes specified and owned as the worker's own mistake. They take responsibility for their part in this larger process and then speak of it as situated within the 'micropolitics' or the 'institution'; that is, identifying or accusing the wider decision-making authorities only in broader terms. Just as Menzies Lyth (1990) highlighted so long ago as a core dynamic at play in nurses dropping out of their hospital training, what this leaves the worker with is all the responsibility and none of the agency. They must manage their conflicting feelings of anger and desperation, which must surely be directed to those more senior to them, along with the frustration and perhaps even disgust (as Menzies Lyth also highlighted) that likely mixes with compassion towards the woman and her family. This 'excess' emotional labour is what leads to what organisations name as 'burnout' – another psychologised interpretation that hides the exploitation and excess of this work and apparatus.

Pykett et al. (2017, p. 3) argue that emotional forms of governance include the way state agencies, civil servants, and public services involve emotional negation, excess dilemmas, rhetorical fantasy, emotional celebration, and commitment. From the professional experience of the first author, all these reflect the everyday reality within the migration apparatus of work and aid in the refugee camps in Greece, and the way emotions work as 'affective economies' in the extract above. It requires emotional *negation* (or denial of reality) on the part of the camp management to decide to eject a family from the camp to follow the state's policies and protocols. There is both an excess and a dilemma on the part of the humanitarian organisation (located also within the worker) regarding what to do and how (much) to help the woman and family. There is a 'rhetorical' fantasy in the humanitarian labour that suggests 'there is only so much you can do' so that protocols are required to help workers keep an 'emotional distance' from those humanitarian governance names and subjectifies as 'beneficiaries'. Although this distance is celebrated institutionally as a professional and necessary emotional commitment to the 'rules' of work, it ends up creating harm, negation, and excess emotional charge.

However, emotions in the form of 'affective economies' were also performed and manifested in another way in the extract above. This was through the affective solidarity another family in the camp showed, which led to the 'spontaneous arrival' family finding (or being offered) a place to stay. This highlights not only the ways that emotions are entangled with governmental and institutional forms of power, but also how emotions can become a way to create forms of solidarity (see also Pykett et al., 2017). Judith Butler (2004) offers an understanding of vulnerability and precariousness as entangled with human existence, which is also central to co-existence with others in the world. Aliverti (2020), commenting on Butler, indicates how 'vulnerability emerges from sociability and indicates conditions of physical dependency on one another. We are, therefore, required to take moral stock of such [social] bonds and interdependence; we are ethically implicated and responsible for others' lives' (p. 1121). It appears this is precisely what the other refugee family did by offering and sharing their second container with the 'spontaneous arrival' family. Deciding to literally 'contain' all their ten family members in a very small, and almost uninhabitable space, they recognised the existence of the other family and intervened in the dominant exclusionary (micro)politics of the refugee camp and space.

Drawing upon our case study and having addressed how emotions are spatialised in the form of 'affective economies' in the camp, we move now to suggest that what links feminisation, asylum, and work together is the constant and intentional precarity and conditions of work, along with how emotions, reflexivity, and labour are tied together within managerial practices of subordination and control.

Feminisation, asylum, and work

From the professional work and doctoral research of the first author in migration, and the feminist research and critical mental health practice experience of the second author, it has been evident that work in the field of forced migration, and especially within 'hotspots' and camps, arouses strong and conflicting feelings.[4] In the extract above, the removal of the family from the camp was not only an unwelcome task for the aid worker, but also involved continuous emotional labour of the aid worker in trying to assist the family, which then brought them into greater conflict with the camp management's decision to remove the family. As the aid worker reflected, *'this is the biggest mistake I have made in my life because we abandoned some people, we harmed them simply to serve the micropolitics of the camp'*.

Despite the worker's resistance and the undoubted personal effort to help the woman, questions remain. How can a worker, any worker, tolerate so much 'emotional labour' in this job? To reiterate, by 'emotional labour' (Phillips et al., 2020; Hochschild, 1983), we refer to the way frontline humanitarian aid workers are required to manage their emotions. Beyond this, we also refer to how their role demands of them to manage the emotions of their service recipients. Group psychoanalytic theory of institutions (see Menzies Lyth, 1990; Wilke, 2018; Fotaki et al., 2012; Obholzer & Roberts, 1994) has addressed how the care professions are split both by interprofessional hierarchies and by distinguishing professionals from service recipients. Indeed, depersonalising service users is an immediate effect of institutions' failures to sustain the emotional labour of the work because the exploitation and alienation of both workers and service users exceeds any form of 'well-being'. In the case of migration, we argue that this is even more complicated. As the extract discussed indicates, what connected the psychic, social, and material economies of the state's and humanitarian's position was the bureaucracy, and, of course, the ideology concerning who is permitted to enter a certain territory, who is excluded from it, and how the overall existence of camps came to sustain the migration regime.

Even if the aid worker reflects on the removal of the family from the camp as *'the biggest mistake'* that caused harm, going against the professional principle to 'do no harm', the migration regime and state-bureaucracy nexus forced both the humanitarian organisation and the aid worker to proceed with the family's removal. At the same time, the decision of the organisation and the aid worker to refer the woman to the hospital and psychiatrist was a way of attempting to manage the refugee woman's emotions alongside the worker's concerns.

Although we addressed the complexities and contradictions of this hospital referral above, it is worth noting how the language of psychology in forced migration can also be used to extract a story of confession (see Christinaki, 2023). Narrating refugees' stories within what we would characterise as a White Western psychological discourse (i.e. one focused on vulnerability, pain, inactivity, and trauma, among other things, see Christinaki, 2022a) offers a canonical linear, sometimes obligatory, story to access, and gain asylum (and often access to services). In that way, it disregards intricate, interwoven histories of racial capitalism and colonialism, gender, and class. This is, of course, not new, but this example highlights the miniaturisation and intensification of the bordering of states in the name of who (and how someone) is allowed to enter 'another's home' as well as how aid and support are sometimes offered and facilitated. It is worth noting that there has been growing critical literature about the forms of vulnerability and threat that the language of humanitarianism and psychology foregrounds, drawing from work conducted in 'hotspots' and camps in Greece (see Mantzari and Mentinis, 2024; Christinaki, 2022a; Christinaki and Mylonas, 2020; Kapsali and Mentinis, 2018).

From the extract above, we note how the state, and to some extent the humanitarian organisation, presumed that the family would be passive, and that, with the removal of the woman from the hospital and the rest of the family from the camp, the whole family would not return from the nearby city to the refugee camp. Scholars from feminist geography and migration studies have discussed how the portrayal of refugees in such protracted situations as immobile and passive contributes to a feminisation of asylum (see Hyndman and Giles, 2011). By 'feminisation' here, we draw on Nancy Fraser's work (1989 as cited in Hyndman and Giles, 2011, p. 363) to discuss

> *how systems of entitlement and charity are valued differently, how the [so-called] beneficiaries of such assistance are gendered subjects and how this gendering feminizes some programmes more than others. Feminization can lead to the attribution of certain practices and identities as passive, helpless, or static, but it can also signal the gendering of labour market segmentation and the production of inequalities.*

A glimpse of this is how the worker assumed responsibility, with the mistake constructed as their own. This is a particularly noxious institutional identification that internalises blame, even as it retrospectively attempts to envisage a different set of outcomes.

However, while this example demonstrates how the migrant family were far from 'passive', it also highlights how aid work embraces emotions and labour involved in the removal of the family. To put it differently, what links the feminisation of asylum or migration with the forms of labour unravelled in this context?

In the Greek setting, which was under severe economic recession from 2007 to 2008, the constitutive context concerns not only that the 'refugee crisis' opened the state and humanitarian market for the jobless 'youth' to find a job in the Greek territory and avoid being migrants themselves. Beyond this, the programme of PSS – offered mainly by psychologists, social workers, educators, and lawyers – comprises professions that are already gendered.

Psychology, social work, and education are often seen as 'female professions'. Moreover, during the professional work and experience of the first author, work in the humanitarian landscape was also precarious, meaning that an aid worker in a national or local humanitarian organisation would have a job only as long as there was funding. Despite being lucky to 'continue having a job', they were becoming internal migrants to 'save their job'. Thus, precarity and feminisation of labour are linked.[5]

As the first author noted in her doctoral research (Christinaki, 2022a, p. 158):

> Moving from one area to another, from camp-to-camp, aid workers became internal migrants in the Greek terrain, depending on where assistance was needed. The latter signified not only a chance to work, but that they were also becoming another object of humanitarian assistance; an 'object' which was yet another cheap labour force since their contracts within humanitarian organisations were adjusted to fit but exceed national financial (pay)scales. Hence, this work was more tempting than the contracts of the [state] public sector, but they were cheaper than Geneva's international financial agreements.

Gutiérrez-Rodríguez (2013, p. 197) argues 'feminisation not only refers to women's work and the increasing participation of women in paid work, but to a general mode of production'. Feminisation now describes a general process, transcending embodied gender identifications, of devaluing labour that entails deteriorating terms and conditions of employment, so that a large proportion of the labour force has come to experience 'feminised' (that is, poor and insecure) conditions of work. This occurs often through deregulation at the national level in favour of international capital. In our example, the concept of feminisation is not used to justify humanitarian governance and labour but to expose further its contradictions. Despite the 'job opportunities' the (international) humanitarian sector brought to crisis-stricken Greece, the politics of humanitarian labour became embedded in the financial politics of Greece and its transnational status, both within the EU and beyond. Although national NGOs usually offered a salary somewhat higher than the minimum wage, precarious work characterised humanitarian labour in Greece. Many had no other option but to work on three-month contracts or contracts advertised as 'permanent' but which were closely dependent on the international renewal of funding and thus effectively fixed-term.

While discussions of the 'feminisation' and precarity of labour within Greece and the field of humanitarianism shed some light on the politics of aid work, they remain limited without connecting such precarity to that of migrants within this context. Migrants have always been visible as a vulnerable but potentially well-exploited and cheap labour force in formal and informal sectors of imperial economies. Chakrabarty (2000) makes this clear in his work *Provincializing Europe*, and Gunaratnam and Lewis (2001) call for critical attention to how emotional labour is very often racialised. De Genova (2016) points out that, across the colonial history of Europe, the majority of Europe's labouring classes did not live in Europe but in Africa, Asia, and the Americas. He continues:

> Today, in the extended aftermath of decolonization for the hundreds of millions of people who formerly were largely confined to the mass prison labour camps that were Europe's colonies, Europe is now confronted with migrants and refugees from those same countries
>
> (p. 351)

It is therefore necessary to situate the feminisation of labour and precarity (of Southern European societies and beyond) within the context of the 'coloniality of power' (see also Quijano, 2000; Asher, 2017) in Europe.

Analyses of the coloniality of power offer additional lenses to understand precarity in Europe (and for domestic work, which is most obviously feminised, see Gutiérrez Rodríguez, 2010). Today, in Greece and Europe, this has an in-depth resonance with the European Union's (EU's) migration/refugee regime that reiterates certain forms of inclusion and exclusion to status and citizenship. Although, as Gutiérrez-Rodríguez (2013) argues, the EU does not use racial categories per se, its social classification system creates forms of exteriority, especially for labour migrants (see also Mezzara & Neilson, 2013). Similarly, forms of exteriority are apparent in the very way the EU deals with refugees within its territory. EU migration policy prioritises accessing a cheap, disposable (thereby precarious and racialised) labour force, alongside seeking to reduce the number of refugees. Indicatively, during the professional work and doctoral fieldwork of the first author, examples were encountered of refugees working for 1 euro per hour!

This is where feminisation, asylum, and work come together. They are tied at the crossroads of the interconnected crises within Europe and the EU. These are crises that create and mark deep forms of precarity and exploitation for those who are racialised and gendered due to Europe's colonial histories, reflected and perpetuated in the current migration regime and apparatus. In the same vein, workers from the 'South' of Europe are also implicated. They are called upon 'to manage' what Europe named a 'refugee crisis', dealing with precarity and a constant 'excess' of work intertwined with specific and intensified 'affective economies'.

Conclusion

Within the refugee terrain, 'emotional labour' addresses both the management of migrants in the form of feelings, existence, and recognition and the management of workers, specifically around an 'excess of work', within what we have discussed as 'affective economies'. As shown in the chapter, this 'excess' of work cannot be shrunk into a psychologised understanding of 'managing' feelings, 'managing' migrants overall, and 'managing' work. On the contrary, 'excess' is infiltrated with and attests to interconnected crises that intensify forms of precarity and exploitation (what we named 'feminisation') for both workers and migrants, embedded in Europe's colonial history and the world's aggressive racial capitalist annihilation. While 'emotional labour' became indicative of discussing what Pykett et al. (2017) so eloquently named 'governing with feeling', it also attests to how emotions and labour within migration are deployed within a 'coloniality of power' and management of control and extraction.

Despite the call for clinical supervision and individual therapy in humanitarian work, which we think sustains the humanitarian industry of governing with feeling, further questions remain about the status of workers' emotions within the state-humanitarian nexus and apparatus. We are aware that, in the case example we offered, emotions may be left unaddressed. Yet just as the family appeared at the camp as a 'spontaneous arrival', like an uncanny return of the repressed of Fortress Europe, the emotions discussed seem to express the excess of the migration injustices and control at play.

It is often the case that organisations draw on the discourse of psychology to privilege emotions that reflect detachment ('being professional'). This coexists with an emotional commitment to the 'rules of work'. In the context of the humanitarian work discussed here, this includes working in a constant mode of emergency, having precarious contracts, not getting paid on time, being ready to move but also shielding yourself to keep a distance and thus not becoming 'too emotional' while you are doing your 'job' – a job that, as shown, may ask from you to act 'spontaneously' to maintain the state's and humanitarianism's harming demands and migratory rules. This affective job nexus works alongside a migration apparatus to further sustain Europe's coloniality, national borders, and bordering regimes, as well as a humanitarian industry of profits, regimes, and governance. Ironically, if workers find it unbearable to work under these exploitation regimes for both themselves and migrants, then emotional excess is transformed into the organisational and psychologised category of 'burnout'.

Standing with an abolitionist political practice, we are against all forms of imperial power and borders, including humanitarian services. Europe's migration and border regime reflect both the exploitation of its workers and how it sets out 'rules' to justify migrants surviving (or as we showed in the chapter, attempting to survive) in horrible and disgraceful conditions within 'hotspots' and camps, spaces that shouldn't exist in the first place, waiting for years to receive their asylum decision. The same stands for building fences in the name of safety, pushing back, and letting people die and getting drawn into the Mediterranean's blood-stained Sea in an attempt to guard their fortress, Europe.

Notes

1. Across the chapter, the reader will notice that we mostly refer to 'migrants' and occasionally to 'refugees'. This is intentional. Following Wendy Brown's (1995) analysis of the exclusionary work that identity categories (especially for us in the field of forced migration) perform and her suggestion to refuse the use of 'refugee', we use the word 'migrant' as an attempt to intervene whenever possible in those divisive identity categories.
2. The term 'hotspot' signifies, here, the space and name of the registration centres which are used to identify, register, and fingerprint refugees during the so-called refugee crisis in Greece. It was officially adopted in May 2015, and refugees who are based in a 'hotspot' are allowed to move inside and outside of this space, but they are not allowed to leave the region where the 'hotspot' is based. For a critical discussion on this, see Neocleous and Kastrinou (2016).
3. The space where the family camped for a month was just inside the security perimeter gate of the camp. This area was away from any container used by either the humanitarian organisations or refugees within the camp.
4. As another indication, we offer the example of 'evictions'. Social workers, especially in mainland Greece, had to facilitate the eviction of families (single or not) that had been recognised under refugee status but who could no longer stay under the international protection and the urban accommodation programme of UNHCR. This created much frustration, especially for those workers who shared a leftist and activist background.
5. Indicatively, during the one-year professional work of the first author as an aid worker-psychologist in Greece, she was twice reallocated to different projects/ funding and region because the funding of the organisation for that specific project and programme had come to an end.

References

Ahmed, S. (2004). Affective Economies. *Social Text*, 22(2(79)), 117–139.
Aliverti, A. (2020). Benevolent Policing? Vulnerability and the Moral Pains of Border Controls. *British Journal of Criminology*, 60, 1117–1135.
Asher, K. (2017). Spivak and Rivera Cusicanqui on the Dilemmas of Representation in Postcolonial and Decolonial Feminisms. *Feminist Studies*, 43(3), 512–524.
Bhattacharyya, G. (2014). Rereading the Empire Strikes Back. *Ethnic and Racial Studies*, 37(10), 1802–1807.
Brown, W. (1995). *States of Injury*. Princeton University Press.
Burman, E. (2004). Emotions in the Classroom: And the Institutional Politics of Knowledge. *Academy for the Study of the Psychoanalytic Arts*. Available at: www.academyanalyticarts.org/library.html
Burman, E. (2007). Feminismo(s) o Feminización? Entre el Triumfalismo Autónomo y la Victimización. In J. Donzelot, J. Walkowitz, I. Parker, J. Varela, E. Burman & J. Pastor (Eds.), *La Fragilización de las Relaciones Sociales* (pp. 111–130). Conorcio del Circulo de Bellas Artes.
Burman, E. (2009a). Resisting the De-radicalization of Psychosocial Analyses', *Psychoanalysis, Culture and Society*, 13, 374–378.
Burman, E. (2009b). Beyond Emotional Literacy in Feminist and Educational Research. *British Education Research Journal*, 35(1), 137–156.

Burman, E. (2011). Emotions and Reflexivity in Feminised Education Research. In I. Parker (Ed.), *Critical Psychology: Critical Concepts in Psychology* (pp. 234–253). Routledge.

Burman, E. (2014). Taking Women's Voices: The Psychological Politics of Feminisation. In N. Bozatzis & T. Dragona (Eds.), *The Discursive Turn in Social Psychology* (pp. 171–189). Taos Institute: Wordshare Books.

Burman, E., Smailes, S., & Chantler, K. (2004). "Culture" as a Barrier to Domestic Violence Services for Minoritised Women. *Critical Social Policy*, 24(3), 358–384.

Butler, J. (2004). *Precarious Life: The Power of Mourning and Violence*. Verso.

Centre for Contemporary Cultural Studies (CCCS) (1982). *Empire Strikes Back: Race and Racism in 70's Britain*. Routledge.

Chakrabarty, D. (2000). *Provincializing Europe: Postcolonial Thought and Historical Difference*. Princeton University Press.

Christinaki, A. (2022a). The Politics of Psychosocial Support in the Refugee Camps of Greece: Site—Psychology—Subject. The University of Manchester. Available at: https://research.manchester.ac.uk/en/studentTheses/the-politics-of-psychosocial-support-in-the-refugee-camps-of-gree

Christinaki, A. (2022b). Crisis, Ψ-Trauma, Refugees: Psycho-Political Questions at the Edge of Fortress Europe. *Psychotherapy and Politics International*, 20(4), 1–15.

Christinaki, A. (2023). Deconstructing Humanitarian Compassion: Ψ as Method. *European Journal for Counselling and Psychotherapy*, 25(1–2), 127–144.

Christinaki, A., & Mylonas, N. (2020). Refugees, Camps & NGOs, *Misfit 1* (in Greek).

Dajani, K. G. (2022). The Social Unconscious: Then and Now. *International Journal of Applied Psychoanalytic Studies*, 19(2), 179–186.

De Genova, N. (2016). The 'European' Question: Migration, Race, and Post-Coloniality in 'Europe'. In A. Amelina, K. Horvath & B. Meeus (Eds.), *An Anthology of Migration and Social Transformation European Perspectives* (pp. 343–356). Springer.

De Genova, N., Garelli, G., & Tazzioli, M. (2018). Autonomy of Asylum? The Autonomy of Migration Undoing the Refugee Crisis Script. *The South Atlantic Quarterly*, 117(2), 239–265.

De Vos, J. (2011). The Psychologization of Humanitarian Aid: Skimming the Battlefield and the Disaster Zone. *History of the Human Sciences*, 24(3), 103–122.

Fassin, D. (2012). *Humanitarian Reason: A Moral History of the Present*. University of California Press.

Fotaki, M., Long, S., & Schwartz, H. S. (2012). What Can Psychoanalysis Offer Organization Studies Today? Taking Stock of Current Developments and Thinking about Future Directions. *Organization Studies*, 33(9), 1105–1120.

Fraser, N. (1989). *Unruly Practices: Power, Discourse, and Gender in Contemporary Social Theory*. University of Minnesota Press.

Freud, S. (1900). *The Interpretation of Dreams*. The Standard Edition of the Complete Psychological Works of Sigmund Freud.

Freud, S. (1915). *Repression*. The Standard Edition of the Complete Psychological Works of Sigmund Freud.

Freud, S. (1919). The Uncanny. In J. Strachey (Ed.), *The Standard Edition of the Complete Psychological Works of Sigmund Freud* (Vol. 17, pp. 219–232). Hogarth Press.

Freud, S. (1939). *Moses and Monotheism: Three Essays*. The Standard Edition of the Complete Psychological Works of Sigmund Freud.

Gunaratnam, Y., & Lewis, G. (2001). Racialising Emotional Labour and Emotionalising Racialised Labour: Anger, Fear and Shame in Social Welfare. *Journal of Social Work Practice, 15*(2), 131–148.

Gutiérrez Rodríguez, E. (2010). *Migration, Domestic Work and Affect*. Routledge.

Gutiérrez-Rodríguez, E. (2013). The Precarity of Feminisation. On Domestic Work, Heteronormativty and the Coloniality of Labour. *International Journal of Politics, Culture, and Society, 27*, 191–202.

Hochschild, A. R. (1983). *The Managed Heart: The Commercialization of Human Feeling*. University of California Press.

Hyndman, J., & Giles, W. (2011). Waiting for What? The Feminization of Asylum in Protracted Situations. *Gender, Place & Culture, 18*(3), 361–379.

Kapsali, A., & Mentinis, M. (2018). *Psychologies of Compliance: Notes on the Psychopolitical Control of Migration*. Oposito (in Greek).

Layton, L., & Leavy-Sperounis, M. (2020). *Toward a Social Psychoanalysis: Culture, Character, and Normative Unconscious Processes*. Routledge.

Mantzari, D., & Mentinis, M. (Eds.) (2024). *Frontier Psychologies: Mapping Mental Health Care in the Refugee Field*. Oposito (in Greek).

Menzies Lyth, I. M. (1990). Social Systems as a Defense against Anxiety: An Empirical Study of the Nursing Service of a General Hospital. In E. Trist, H. Murray & B. Trist (Eds.), *The Social Engagement of Social Science, a Tavistock Anthology, Volume 1: A Tavistock Anthology: The Socio-Psychological Perspective* (pp. 439–462). University of Pennsylvania Press.

Mezzadra, S. (2021). Abolitionist Vistas of the Human. Border Struggles, Migration and Freedom of Movement. In H. Schwiertz and H. Schwenken (Eds.), *Inclusive Solidarity and Citizenship along Migratory Routes in Europe and the Americas* (pp. 20–36). Routledge.

Mezzadra, S., & Neilson, B. (2013). *Border as Method*. Duke University Press.

Neocleous, M., & Kastrinou, M. (2016). Commentary: The EU Hotspot. Police War against the Migrant. *Radical Philosophy, 200*, 3–9.

New Keywords Collective (2016). Europe/Crisis: New Keywords of 'the Crisis' in and of 'Europe'. *Near Futures Online, 1*. Available at: https://nearfuturesonline.org/europecrisis-new-keywords-of-crisis-in-and-of-europe/

Obholzer, A., & Roberts, V. Z. (1994). *The Unconscious at Work*. Taylor & Francis.

Palmary, I., Burman, E., Chantler, K., & Kiguwe, P. (2010). Gender and Migration: Feminist Interventions. In I. Palmary, E. Burman, K. Chantler & P. Kiguwe (Eds.), *Gender and Migration* (pp. 1–12). Zed Press.

Phillips, J., Westaby, C., & Fowler, A. (2020). Emotional Labour in Probation. Her Majesty's Inspectorate of Probation. Academic Insights. Available at: www.justiceinspectorates.gov.uk/hmiprobation/wp-content/uploads/sites/5/2020/04/Emotional-Labour-in-Probation.pdf

Pykett, J., Jupp, E., & Smith, F. M. (2017). Introduction: Governing with Feeling. In E. Jupp, J. Pykett & F. M. Smith (Eds.), *Emotional States: Sites and Spaces of Affective Governance* (pp. 1–18). Routledge.

Quijano, A. (2000). Coloniality of Power and Eurocentrism in Latin America. *International Sociology, 15*(2), 215–232.

Summerfield, D. (2001). The Invention of Post-Traumatic Stress Disorder and the Social Usefulness of a Psychiatric Category. *British Medical Journal, 322,* 95–98.

Tazzioli, M., & De Genova, N. (2023). Border Abolitionism: Analytics/Politics. *Social Text, 41*(3), 1–34.

Wilke, G. (2018). *The Art of Group Analysis in Organisations: The Use of Intuitive and Experiential Knowledge.* Routledge.

INDEX

Note: Figures are shown in *italics* and tables in **bold** type. Endnotes consist of the page number followed by "n" and the note number e.g. 55n2 refers to note 2 on page 55.

abandonment 104, 114, 155
abolitionism 13, 268, 270, 327n8, 339, 371, 389, 403, 421
access denial 113
accidental death verdict, of inquest 130–131
acquiescence 75, 145, 183
acting: deep 286, 287, 354, 361; surface 286, 287, 354
actual-existing postracial society 8, 59, 61, 62, 69
ACUMAR (*Autoridad Nacional para la Cuenca Matanza Riachuelo*) 297–298, 299, 301
aesthetics 109, 239; carceral care 11, 254, 256, 267–268, 269
affect: collective 54; and embodied mind 45–48; of history 324–325; institutional 311, 312–313, 314, 319–321, 321, 322, 326; mobilising 7–8; political 8, 22, 44, 45, 48–51; theory of 8, 45, 46
affective ambivalences 12, 335, 336, 337
affective capacity, of an inquest 9, 123, 125–126, 131, 132–133, 133
affective component, of governmentality 84; *see also* emotionalities of rule
affective economies 2, 7, 22; refugee camps as 410, 411–416, 420, 421; of state power 2, 7, 22; theory of 106

affective, embodied, sensorial order 317–319
affective experience 46, 47, 49, 51, 55, 239
affective force, of prisons 314–325
affective governance 9, 125
affective histories 311, 312, 314, 321–324, 325, 326, 327n14
affective infusions 315–317
affective life 43, 44, 50, 51, 55, 268
affective potential: of inquests 125, 130; of Prevent Duty 86–87
affective registers 9, 64, 123, 129, 130, 131, 133, 135; and state violence 124–126
affective relations 45, 46, 47, 48, 50, 52, 53, 336–337
affective turn 2, 84–85; in criminal process 217, 228, 229
affectivity 8, 44, 45, 52; situated (of institutions) 312–313
aggression 44, 45, 55n2, 125, 163, 164, 240; micro- 191–192, 317
Ahmed, Sara: on affective economies 106, 411–412; on disgust 107, 109–110, 238; on emotions 215
allegories 49, 50, 51
Althusser, Louis 49–50
altruistic imagining 357–358

ambivalence: of arts therapists 262–267; of emotion, and rationality 8, 59, 61, 62–64; of penal reform 402; of soldiers 344–345
anger 55n2, 222, 284, 285, 363; reactive 399; righteous 371–372
animalisation 243–244, 248
animalised subjectivities 236, 244
anthropology 39, 44, 52, 53, 55, 294, 371–372
anthropophagy 162–166
anticipatory stress 218
anxiety 45, 46, 48, 50, 52, 53, 54, 55, 239
appropriate emotion and care in oneself and others 222–225
Arendt, Hannah 64
Argentina, judicialisation of environmental disaster in 293–308
arts therapies: emergence as professional practice of 256; in prisons 253–270; therapeutic space of 258–259; and vulnerable prisoners 257, 260–261
assembling emotions 147–151
asylum 116, 117, 119n6, 125, 130; feminisation of 14, 407, 416–420; seekers of 73, 118, 134, 279, 282, 284
Asylums 141
attachments 12, 44, 45, 46, 55n2, 106, 179, 306, 383, 412
attitudes, of prison officers towards inmates 204–207
austerity 13, 50, 285, 387; and homelessness 369, 370, 371, 372, 377, 382; and prison managerialism 181, 183, 184, 186, 191, 192
authoritarian turn 60
Autoridad Nacional para la Cuenca Matanza Riachuelo (ACUMAR) 297-298, 299, 301
Awareness Course, in Prevent Duty online training 88

bad migrants *see* undeserving migrants
Badenoch, Kemi 62, 67, 68, 69, 70–71, 72
Baldwin, James 8, 59, 61–62, 66–67, 72, 75–76
bandidos, and deserving citizens 341–344
Bastille 7–8, 21, 23, 28–30, 40; demolition 33, 34–35, 36, 36, 37; iconography 7, 22; memory work 35–39, 36, 38; myth making 30–35, 31, 32, 33, 34; symbolic resurrection 37–38
Bauman, Zygmunt 186
being paid not to care 355–358
being paramilitary 145, 147, 150–151, 153, 155, 169n8
belligerent frustration 321–324
belonging 3, 11, 12, 49, 51, 280, 342; institutional 105, 107; to the nation 75, 280; racialised hierarchies of 248
Benjamin, Walter 166
Bens, Jonas 295
bereaved families 122, 123, 124, 125, 126, 128, 129, 130, 132, 133, 134, 135, 135n4
bioethics of consumption 378–381
BJMP *see* Bureau of Jail Management and Penology (BJMP)
Blair Peach inquest 123, 131–134, 135
blame 95, 132–133, 351, 370–371, 382, 418
blocked trinity 389–390, 396, 398–399, 400–402
bodilessness 5
body, the 4, 5, 46, 179, 377, 380; and disgust 235–236; ipseity of 23; optic of 27
border controls 3, 11, 59, 72, 76, 113, 239, 244, 407
border fatalities 9, 125, 127
border policing, disgust in 235–248
border regime 127, 129, 421
border work, as dirty work 235–248
bordered order 240, 246
bordering 244, 418, 421; re- 407
boundaries of law, contestation over 293–296
Bourdieu, Pierre 181, 186; *see also* habitus
bourgeoisie 24, 31, *31*
Braverman, Suella 60, 62, 66, 71, 72, 73, 74, 75, 76
Brazil, feud law among prospective police recruits in 157–169
Brexit 8, 50, 59–60, 63–64
British Bill of Rights 66
British Cabinet 60, 62, 67, 68, 71; ethnically-diverse 60, 71–72
British citizenship 66, 68–69
British identity politics 66–69
British openness 68, 71

Britishness 61, 68–69, 74, 75, 76
Brunnegger, Sandra 294, 304
BSU (HM Barlinnie Special Unit) 256–257, 270
bucket of urine 107, 111, 112
Bureau of Jail Management and Penology (BJMP) 142, 144, 145, 147, 150; Operations Manual 145, 147, 152, 153
bureaucracy 145, 153, 414–415, 417; and Mendoza case 299–302
bureaucratic rationality 277

Cabinet 60, 62, 67, 68, 71; ethnically-diverse 60, 71–72
Calais Migrant Solidarity (CMS) project 127
cannibalism 162–166
Captive Arts 254–255
carceral care aesthetics 267–268
care and control 12–14, 210, 361, 364
care sector 1, 86, 91
Carville, James 62
Cass Report 132, 133
Cathy Come Home 372
CCHP *see* Churches of Castlebury Housing Project (CCHP)
Centro de Derechos Humanos Fray Matías de Córdova A.C. 111, 112
Channel Course, in Prevent Duty online training 88, 90–91
charged affective register 125
charity 277, 335, 373, 374, 418; *see also* INQUEST charity
child rape 220, 223, 224, 225, 227–228
child sexual abuse (CSA), in India 215–230; survivors of (CSA survivors) 216–217, 218, 219, 220, 222, 223, 224, 225, 226, 227, 228–229
Churches of Castlebury Housing Project (CCHP) 370, 371, 372, 373, 374, 375–376, 377–379, 380, 381, 382
circuits of outrage 383
Ciudad Juarez immigration detention centre fire 118
civilian staff, of prisons 202, 207, 210
civilizational emotion 372; *see also* moral outrage
class struggle 24, 25
CMS (Calais Migrant Solidarity) project 127
CNDH (*Comisión Nacional de Derechos Humanos*) 104, 111

collaboration 44, 152, 262, 299, 342, 359, 400, 401–402
collective affects 54
colonialism 64, 74, 225, 228, 414, 418
coloniality 421; of power 412, 420, 421
Colonizer and the Colonized, The 74
Colonne de Juillet 38, 40
Comisión Nacional de Derechos Humanos (CNDH) 104, 111
Commission on Race and Ethnic Disparities (CRED) 67, 69, 70, 71, 72
compassion 2, 3, 9, 86; and death investigations 125; and homelessness 370, 371, 377, 380, 382; in police work 333, 335, 344; politics of 369; in probation 351, 356, 358; for radicalisation suspects 89, 91–93, 94, 95, 96–97, 98
competition 24, 44, 49, 50, 65, 144, 183–184, 185, 288
completeness, myth of 2
condemnation of the condemners 200
conditioning conditions 313, 314, 327n6
consciousness: of objects 55n4; political 48–49, 54; practical 51–52, 55; shared moral 278; subjective 55n4
Conservative party 8, 60, 61, 62, 65, 66, 67, 68, 69, 70, 73, 76, 369; *see also* minority-ethnic Conservative politicians
consumption, bioethics of 378–381
contamination 108, 237, 240, 245, 296, 297, 300, 302
CONTEST 89
contestation over boundaries of law 293–296
contextualisation 3–6
control *see* care and control
cooperation 49, 50, 153, 154
Core Correctional Practices 358–359
coroner's court 122, 123–124, 128, 131
correctional preferences 207–209
counter-radicalisation 83, 84, 87, 91, 93, 96; *see also* Prevent Duty; Prevent Duty training
counter-terrorism 85, 86, 87, 90–91, 92; and emotions 84–85; *see also* CONTEST; PREVENT; Prevent Duty
Counter-Terrorism and Security Act 83
COVID-19 pandemic 182, 184, 188, 189, 244, 299
creative emotions 253–270

CRED (Commission on Race and Ethnic Disparities) 67, 69, 70, 71, 72
criminal justice officers 52, 53, 54, 55
criminal process, affective turn in 217, 228, 229
criminology of emotions 3
critical theory 2, 47, 49
cruel sentimentality 76; *see also* Baldwin, James
CSA *see* child sexual abuse (CSA), in India
cultural scripts 144
custody: police 134, 135n3; prison 202, 208, 210

daily punishment 9, 106, 118
danger formations 50
dangerousness 50, 86, 95
darker imagining 363–364
Darwin, Charles 237
DCW (Delhi Commission of Women) 223, 224
death by misadventure verdict, of inquest 130, 131, 132, 133
Declaration of the Rights of Man and Citizen 21, 28
deep acting 286, 287, 354, 361
defense of honor 164
dehumanisation 9, 75, 76, 128, 189, 192–193, 262, 264, 358; in immigration detention 103, 104, 105, 106, 117, 118
Delhi Commission of Women (DCW) 223, 224
democracy 62–63, 339–340, 389; and French Revolution 23, 25
democratic welfare state 277, 278, 287
demolition, of Bastille 33, 34–35, 36, 36, 37
denial: access 113; of identity 163; of injury 200; and inquests 132, 133; and managerialism 192; overcompensation 90; of racism 72; of responsibility 200; of rights 163; of sympathy 276; techniques of 199–200; of victim 200
dependency, on welfare services 279, 280, 285
depersonalisation 5, 167, 274, 277, 417
depolicialization, of prisons 201–202
deportation 75, 106, 116, 119n6, 135n1, 236, 280

deservingness 6, 60, 71, 277, 341–344, 369–370
despotism 24, 30, 37; ministerial 28
DesPres, Terrence 103
detention centres: Ciudad Juarez fire 118; subjectivities in 106–107
differentiating emotions 357; *see also* frustration
differentiation 5, 109, 110, 151, 262, 274, 288, 326, 357, 372, 374
dignity 111, 117, 183, 216, 335, 353; protection of 284–287, 288
dirty work: border work as 235–248; definition of 239
discrimination 10, 61, 66, 75, 86, 115; positive 191; racial 136n9; White 71
disembodiment 5, 235
disgust: anatomy of 235–236, 237–240; in border policing 235–248; in immigration detention 105–118; and immigration law (exceptionality of) 115–117; learning to feel 109–111; as moral critique of capitalism 240; as pedagogy 109; as punishment 113–115; social cohesion through 110; and stigma 110–111, 114–115, 118
disobedient subjects 302–304
display rules 144, 149, 155, 350–351, 356, 359, 362
dispositions 2, 10, 150, 181, 186, 273, 412
dissatisfaction 54, 222, 282; *see also* satisfaction
distant perspective, on prison work 199
diversity 60, 61, 68, 72
dominance 50, 144, 225, 238; punitive 10, 13; structure in 390, 399–400, 402, 403
dominant phantasy-formations 50
domination 5, 24, 25, 94, 186, 303, 338, 354; male 178, 201
double exclusion, of prison staff 198
Douglas, Mary 238
dramaturgy 144
dreary loops 321–324
drug gangs 160, 161
duty of violence 344–345
dynamic security 9–10, 143, 144, 155; recalibrating 147–151

economic migrants 66, 73, 76
economic rationality 186, 187, 189, 192–193

embodied mind, and affect 45–48
embodied senses of justice 293–296
embodied work, immigration enforcement as 241–247
embodiment: dis- 5, 235; institutional 142–143, 152–154
embodying the state 51–54
emotion management 9, 200, 224, 228, 353; and judges' relational work 227–228; in Philippine city jail 143, 151, 152, 153, 154
emotion work: in child sexual abuse special courts 228–229; of Prevent Duty training 87–95
emotional baggage 191
emotional careers: of helpers 282–284; of receivers 284–287
emotional catharsis 163
emotional climate, of prison population 152, 153, 154
emotional economies, of state power 3, 6, 10–11, 14, 22–23, 240, 241–242
emotional energy 281–282, 283–284
emotional excess 371, 376, 381, 382; of humanitarian labour 14, 407, 421
emotional impact, of prison work 209–210
emotional labour: and feminisation of work 406–422; gendered nature of 361–364; and managerialism 189–192; in probation 349–355, 356, 359, 360–364; scripts 350; of trial court practitioners 219–228
emotional landscape, of prison managerialism 177–193
emotional management *see* emotion management
emotional manipulation 85
emotional micro-exchanges 275–276
emotional registers 66, 124, 130, 131
emotional state 12, 274, 275, 277–280, 287
emotional support 95, 163, 222
emotionalised governance 8–10
emotionalities of rule 84, 85, 98, 99
emotionally driven political action 63
emotions: assembling 147–151; civilizational 372; creative 253–270; criminology of 3; definitions of 179; differentiating 357; and governance 185–189; institutionalised 11–12; moral 11, 106, 237–238, 248, 338; political 64, 106, 107, 278, 281, 288;
and prison governance 179–181; and privilege 421; punitive 106; racialised 236; spatialised 411–416; structurally embedded 12, 273, 274; and terrorism 84–85
emotive-cognitive behaviour 11–12, 274, 281, 282, 284, 285, 288
empathy 2; judicial 228; professional 282–283
EMSXXI (*Estación Migratoria Siglo XXI*) 103–104, 105, 106, 111, 112, 114, 115
Engels, Friedrich 240
England: homelessness *see* homelessness, English state of; nationalism of 64
Enlightenment 28–29, 37, 65
environmental pollution 295, 296, 297, 298, 299, 302, 308n2
environmental problems 296–299
epistemology 4–5, 109, 247, 407
Estación Migratoria Siglo XXI (EMSXXI) 103–104, 105, 106, 111, 112, 114, 115
Estates-General 29
ethical integration 391
ethical rationality 63
ethnic inequality 68
ethnically-diverse Cabinet 60, 71–72
ethnography: of affective ambivalences in police work 333–346; of affective forces in prisons 314–325; of Churches of Castlebury Housing Project (CCHP) 374–383; of disgust in border policing 235–248; and illicit police activities 169n7; of Mahammat Abdullah Moussa inquest 126–131, 134–135; of Mendoza lawsuit 295–302, 307; in a Philippine city jail 141–155, 146; of prison managerialism 177–193; of a professional driver and aspiring police recruit 158–162; of state bureaucracies 1–2, 12; of violence in police work 333–346; of waiting for social benefits and administrative services 302–306
European Convention on Human Rights 66, 124
everyday state 5, 6
exceptionality of immigration law, and disgust 115–117
exclusion 5, 125, 129–130, 136n8, 238, 276, 379, 415, 420; double 198

expedient managerialism credo 180
experience: meaning of 70–71; personal 68, 71, 76
experiential positionalities 70
Expression of the Emotions in Man and Animals, The 237
expressive controls, institutional embodiments through 152–154
expulsion dreams 73–75
expulsion humiliation 278, 279, 280–281, 286, 287
extreme punishment 118
extremism 62, 75, 93, 95–96, 98, 99, 131–132

failure of integration 390, 400
fairness 70, 75, 76
Fassin, Didier 6, 158, 167, 389
FATAG (Forensic Arts Therapy Group) 257
Faulk, Karen 294, 304
favelas 333, 335–337, 338, 339, 340, 344–346; soldiers' views of residents of 341–344
fear: of consequences of not reporting radicalisation suspects 89, 93–95; of consequences of reporting radicalisation suspects 89–91; and police work 338–340
feeling rules: occupational 351, 352, 353, 354, 356, 357, 358, 361, 364; Prevent Duty 87, 88, 91, 98; probation 350–353, 354, 356, 357, 358, 361, 364; welfare assistance 275, 276, 277, 288
feminisation 14, 353, 407, 416–420
feminism 2, 5, 14, 63, 201, 407, 416–417, 418; humanist 63
feud law 157, 164–165, 166
Forensic Arts Therapy Group (FATAG) 257
Foucault, Michel 387, 388
framing rules 88–89
Fraser, Nancy 418
French Revolution 7, 21, 23–26, 27, 28, 39; visual representation of 25–28
Freud, Sigmund 45, 55n5, 412, 414
frontline staff 1–2, 6, 7, 8, 45, 313
frontline workers 8–9, 12, 84, 247, 263, 274, 370–371, 383
frustration 45, 95, 134, 255, 264–265, 301, 306, 318; belligerent 321–324; as differentiating emotion 357

full determination 49–50, 51
Fundación para la Justicia y el Estado Democrático de Derecho A.C. 105, 114
futility 13, 371, 373, 381–383

gangs 147–148; drug 160, 161; traffic 73, 333, 337, 338, 340, 341, 345, 346
gender: and emotional labour 361–364; identity 150, 223, 229, 419
Goffman, Erving 141, 143, 144, 149, 150, 151, 153, 155
good migrants *see* deserving migrants
governance: and emotions 8–10, 185–189; multi-scale 296–299; prison 9, 10, 178, 183, 189, 179–181
governmentality 84; *see also* emotionalities of rule; Prevent Duty
gratitude 276, 277–278, 282, 285, 286, 287, 288
Greece, spontaneous arrival at refugee camp in 14, 406–407, 408–411, 412, 416, 421
guilt 47, 110, 133, 141, 283, 341, 358

habitus 181, 186; class 300; humiliated 284–287; managerial 186, 188, 189, 192; probation 352
happiness 179, 185, 356
hate 45, 46, 55n2, 67, 167, 219, 263, 363; racist 64, 73
hegemonic masculinity 163, 201, 209, 210
helper interactions *see* institutionalised helper interactions
hierarchies: racial 11, 65, 248; social 108, 238, 245
history, affect of 324–325
HM Barlinnie Special Unit (BSU) 256–257, 270
HM Prison and Probation Service (HMPPS) 254, 258
Hochschild, Arlie Russell 357, 359; deep acting 286, 287, 354; display rules 144; emotion work 87; emotional labour 179; feeling rules 350–351, 353; pinch 354; surface acting 354
Holocaust 103
Home Office 90, 130, 236, 245, 246–247
homelessness, English state of 369–384; and compassion 370, 371, 377, 380, 382

honour 163, 164, 220
hostility 44, 50, 108, 110, 181, 229, 270, 357, 399; and homelessness 371, 376, 381
Housing Act 372, 374, 375, 384n3
Housing (Homeless Persons) Act 372–373
human agency 5, 244
human flourishing 8, 59, 396, 398–399, 400, 402, 403
human life, value of 9, 123, 143
human rights 150, 201, 205, 246, 293; and immigration detention 104, 105, 111, 116, 117, 118–119n1, 119n5; and police work 333, 335, 336, 339–340; and welfare assistance 275, 278, 279, 280, 288; *see also* European Convention on Human Rights
humanisation, of state power 222–225
humanist feminism 63
humanitarian aid 406, 407, 408, 410, 412, 417
humanitarian labour 14, 408, 416, 419; emotional excess of 14, 407, 421
humanitarianism 369–370, 371, 406, 407, 411, 414, 418, 419
humiliated habitus 284–287
humiliation: definition of 276; expulsion 278, 279, 280–281, 286, 287; reinforcement 278, 279, 280, 287; rituals of 278, 279, 280, 281, 286, 287; and shame 276, 277, 278, 279, 280, 282, 283, 285, 286, 287
hypervigilance 363

ICE (Immigration Compliance and Enforcement) 240
iceberg metaphor, in Prevent Duty online training 94
icon, definition of 47
iconic representation, of state power 22, 43, 48, 51, 52, 53, 54, 55
iconicity 47
iconography: of Bastille 7, 22; revolutionary 37
identity: denial of 163; gender 150, 223, 229, 419; politics of 66–69; self- 70, 354
illicit police activities 169n7
imagining 5, 46, 275; altruistic 357–358; darker 363–364; unconscious 45; *see also* phantasy
immigration: attacks on 72; mass 61, 66, 71, 76
immigration agents, subjectivities of 105

Immigration Compliance and Enforcement (ICE) 240
immigration control 8, 59, 61, 62
immigration detention: centres *see* immigration detention centres; culture of disgust in 106–108; culture of punishment in 106–108; disgust in 105–118
immigration detention centres 104, 105–106, 107, 108, 117, 118, 119n2; Ciudad Juarez fire 118; degrading conditions in 113–114
immigration enforcement 237, 240, 248; as embodied work 241–247
immigration law 115–117, 239
immigration officers 11, 105, 106, 110; and disgust 235, 236, 237, 239, 241–242, 244, 245, 246, 248; and violence 239–240
immigration policing 11, 240, 246
inclusion 5, 61, 72, 75, 125, 353, 420
Independent Review of Prevent 97
India, child sexual abuse in 215–230
individual subjectivities 4, 339, 344
individual trajectories, and institutional expectations 344–345
individualisation 135, 164, 254, 256, 267, 402, 408
individualism 4, 178, 278, 280, 379
inequality 6, 10, 11, 193; and emotional labour 181; ethnic 68; institutionalised 273; social 12, 199, 237–238, 293–296, 306; social relations of 274; structural 287, 288, 296–299, 302; wealth 242
informants 83, 89
INM *see Instituto Nacional de Migración* (INM)
inmates of prisons, attitudes of officers to 204–207
INQUEST charity 132, 133, 134, 135n1, 135n4, 136n9
inquests 122–124, 134–135; accidental death verdict 130–131; affective potential 125, 130; bereaved families *see* bereaved families; Blair Peach 123, 131–134, 135; death by misadventure verdict 130, 131, 132, 133; Mahammad Abdullah Moussa 9, 123, 126–131, 133, 134–135; therapeutic function 125, 126; unlawful killing verdict 124, 132
insecurity 45, 51, 53, 184, 185, 186, 266, 314, 339, 419; ontological 50

institutional affect, in Sierra Leone prisons 311, 312–313, 314, 319–321, 321, 322, 326
institutional belonging 105, 107
institutional change 198, 201
institutional embodiments 142–143; through expressive controls 152–154
institutional expectations, and individual trajectories 344–345
institutional integrity 220–222
institutional legitimacy 220–222
institutional punishment 106
institutionalised emotions, unsettling of 11–12
institutionalised helper interactions 273, 278, 279, 281, 287, 288; as social form 275, 279–281, 287, 288
institutionalised helper roles 281–282
institutionalised inequality 273
Instituto Nacional de Migración (INM) 103, 104, 105–106, 108, 110, 111, 112, 113–114, 114–115, 116, 117
integration 390, 394–396, 398, 400, 403; into Britishness 68; ethical 391; failure of 390, 400; loving 389, 403; racial 68; social 337, 338
inter-institutional support and trust, for affective and effective state power 225–226
internalization 151
international protection 9, 105, 106, 116, 117, 422n4
interpersonal relations 54, 206
isolation 88, 128, 191, 203, 260

job satisfaction 229, 364
Joensuu, Eleonora 109, 118
judges' relational work, and emotion management 227–228
judicial empathy 228
judicialisation, of social inequalities 293–296, 297, 299, 304, 306, 307
just following orders 145
justice: embodied senses of 293–296; in practice 294

Kant, Immanuel 403
Kristeva, Julia 107

languages of stateness 22, 28
Latin American prisons 197, 198–199, 202, 211
leadership 180, 189–190

Lear, Jonathan 390–391, 393–394, 396, 404n3, 404n8
'left behind' 63, 66
lettres de cachet 21, 22, 35
liberal humanitarian credo 180
liberty 27, 28, 32, 34, 118, 215, 388
living conditions 9, 106, 197, 204, 297, 300, 302, 303, 306
love 45, 46, 55n2, 92, 391, 392–393, 394, 395, 398, 399, 402, 403, 404n9
loving integration 389, 403
loving prison 389, 401, 404n9

Mahammat Abdullah Moussa inquest 9, 123, 126–131, 133, 134–135
male domination 178, 201
Managed Heart, The 349
managerial clawback 182, 183
managerial habitus 186, 188, 189, 192
managerial infrastructure 182, 183, 184, 188
managerialism 177–179; expedient 180; -plus 183, 186, 188; prison *see* prison managerialism
marginalised populations 1, 3, 6, 54, 257, 294, 326
Marx, Karl 24, 49–50, 238, 243–244, 350
Marxism 24, 25, 349–350, 361
masculinity 178; hegemonic 163, 201, 209, 210
mass immigration 61, 66, 71, 76
mayores 148–149, 152, 153
Memmi, Albert 74
memory work, of Bastille storming 35–39, 36, 38
Mendoza case 295–302
mental health 133, 135n2, 198, 210, 401, 413, 416–417; and arts therapy in prisons 253, 255, 256, 257–258, 259, 260; and immigration detention 104, 113, 117
methodology 1, 5, 7, 14, 23, 62, 142, 201–203, 203
microaggressions 191–192, 317
migrant crisis 62, 67, 75, 76
migrant welfare 60, 66
migrants: bad 60, 66, 71, 277; deserving 60, 71, 277; economic 66, 73, 76; good 60, 71, 277; undeserving 60, 66, 71, 277
Migration Law 104, 118–119n1
military police of Rio de Janeiro (PMERJ): feud law 10, 158, 159, 160, 165, 168n3, 168n6; governing

through fear 12–13, 333, 337, 338, 340, 342, 343–344, 345, 346n3, 346n7
Mills, Charles W. 64
ministerial despotism 28
minority ethnic communities 71, 191, 193
minority ethnic Conservative politicians 59, 61, 62, 69, 71, 72, 74, 75, 76
minority ethnic politicians 60, 71–72, 74, 76
misadventure verdict, of inquest 130, 131, 132, 133
mobilising affect 7–8
modern prison 13, 253–254, 256; and penal reformer's dilemma 387, 389, 390, 391, 394, 396, 397, 398–399, 399–400, 403
moral blindness 186
moral breakdown 382
moral communities 110, 166, 300
moral economies 339; of migration 241; of police violence 13, 336, 345; of resistance 22–23; of state power 2, 3, 7, 22–23, 61
moral emotions 11, 106, 237–238, 248, 338
moral indifference 187, 200, 235
moral instinct 275, 288
moral outrage 369, 370, 371–374, 376–377, 378, 380; afterlife of 381–383; circuits of 383
moral pains 3, 374–378
moral psychology 13, 399, 403
moral subjectivities 339, 345
Moussa inquest 9, 123, 126–131, 133, 134–135
multi-scale governance 296–299
Muslims 85, 86, 87, 89
myth: of Bastille storming 30–35, *31, 32, 33, 34*; of completeness 2; of the state 28; 39

National Assembly 29, 30, 37
National Health Service) 254, 256, 258, 262, 265
National Offender Management Service 181–182
National Probation Service 355
nationalism 60, 64, 69; English 64; populist 63, 64
negligence 104, 155, 411
neurodivergence 257, 260–261

NHS (National Health Service) 254, 256, 258, 262, 265
No More Deaths 133
Noah Community 370, 371, 374, 378–381, 384n5
nobility 24, 28, 29, 33, 37, 398
normalisation 65, 66–67, 72, 86, 179, 222
normative subjectivities 5
Nussbaum, Martha 107, 109, 110, 115

object relations theory 45, 46–47, 48, 55n4
occupational culture, of prison officers 198–201
occupational feeling rules 351, 352, 353, 354, 356, 357, 358, 361, 364
offensiveness 107
one-to-one assistance 276
ontology 23, 50, 70, 314
open borders 67, 68, 73
Operations Manual, of Bureau of Jail Management and Penology 145, 147, 152, 153
ordering 3, 5, 30, 238, 317, 325
orders 110, 145, 147, 150, 301, 318, 336; just following 145
outrage, moral 369, 370, 371–374, 376–377, 378, 380; afterlife of 381–383; circuits of 383
overcompensation denial 90
overcrowding 9, 114, 118–119n1, 142, 183, 197, 201, 204, 241, 387
over-determination 49–50, 51, 53–54, 54–55

Pacifying Police Unit (UPP) 333, 335, 337–338, 339, 344, 345–346
pain 216, 223, 224, 229
Palloy, Pierre-François 33, *33*, 34–36
pandemic, COVID-19 182, 184, 188, 189, 244, 299
paramilitary 145, 147, 150–151, 153, 155, 169n8
Patel, Priti 62, 66, 67, 71, 72, 73, 74
patriarchy 50, 63, 221
Peach inquest 123, 131–134, 135
pedagogy 95, 109, 165
penal reformer's dilemma 387–404
penal system 13, 388, 389, 391, 396, 398, 399, 402
performativity 61, 67, 142, 143, 228–229, 359

perpetrative institutions 12, 326n1
persecution 45, 46, 47, 50, 52, 53, 55, 66, 72, 284
persecutory phantasy-formation 52
PFD (Prevention of Future Death) reports 124, 133
phantasy: action causation by 47; formation of *see* phantasy-formation; political 8, 45, 49, 50, 51, 53–54, 55; socially situated 45, 48, 49
phantasy-formation 48, 49, 51, 52, 54–55; dominant 50; 49, persecutory 52; political 50, 53–54, 55
Philippine city jail 141–155, *146*
philosophes 28–29
pinch, the 349, 354, 357–358
Place de la Bastille 37, *38*, 39
Plato 387, 390, 396–398, 400, 403; *see also Symposium*
PMERJ *see* Military Police of Rio de Janeiro (PMERJ)
POCSO *see* Protection of Children from Sexual Offences (POCSO) Act
police brutality 10; *see also* police violence
police feuds 10, 166, 167, 169n9
police property 247
police recruits 10, 158, 161, 163, 166, 167
police violence 160, 239, 334, 344, 345; genealogy of (in Brazil) 338–340; moral economy of 13, 336, 345; *see also* police brutality
police work: compassion in 333, 335, 344; fear in 338–340; violence in 333–346
policing: border (disgust in) 235–248; immigration 11, 240, 246; military *see* military police of Rio de Janeiro (PMERJ)
political action 62, 63
political affect 8, 22, 44, 45, 48–51
political consciousness 48–49, 54
political domination 5, 303
political emotionality 64, 106, 107, 278, 281, 288, 307
political persecutory phantasy-formation 52
political phantasy 8, 45, 49, 50, 51, 53–54, 55; formation of 50, 53–54, 55
political repression 40
political violence 85, 157

politics of sentiment 64–66
pollution 107, 108, 244; environmental 295, 296, 297, 298, 299, 302, 308n2
poor, the 2, 11–12, 273, 274, 275, 276, 277, 279, 288, 303
populism 50, 63, 64
positive discrimination 191
post-Brexit Britain 59–60
postcolonialism 5, 313, 314, 345
postracial de-toxification, of racism 69–72
postracial gatekeeping 69, 73–74
postracial racism denial 72
postracial sentimentality 8, 59; and British identity politics 66–69; and 'price of the ticket' 75–76; and relativity of privilege 73–75
postracial society 69; actual-existing 8, 59, 61, 62, 69
Powell, Enoch 61, 65, 66, 68, 69
power relations 7, 39, 50, 54, 74, 142, 179, 216–217; and immigration detention 105, 106–107, 113
practical consciousness 51–52, 55
precarity 6, 50, 236, 240, 416, 419–420, 421
prejudice 47, 75, 85, 86, 208, 253
premature revenge 157–169
presentation 8, 47, 48, 179, 190
PREVENT 8–9
Prevent Duty 83–84, 85, 98–99; affective potential of 86–87; compassion 89, 91–93; contradictions of 95–98; manufacturing informants 83, 89; online training *see* Prevent Duty online training; prevention 89, 93–95; and public sector workers 84, 85, 86, 87, 88, 89, 90, 91–92, 93, 94–95, 95–96, 96–97, 98; safeguarding 89–91
Prevent Duty online training: emotion work of 87–95; iceberg metaphor in 94; material 90, 93, 95, 96
Prevention of Future Death (PFD) reports 124, 133
preventive punishment 104
'price of the ticket', and postracial sentimentality 75–76
prison governance 9, 10, 178, 183, 189; and emotions 179–181
prison inmates, attitudes of officers to 204–207

prison life 13, 184, 203, 255, 318, 388, 396, 397
prison management 9–10, 177–178, 181, 187, 201, 255; of Philippine city jail 143, 148, 149; *see also* dynamic security
prison managerialism 178, 185, 186, 192–193; emotional landscape of 177–193; rhetoric of 182–184
prison officers, occupational culture of 198–201
prison order 9–10, 148, 149, 207
prison population, emotional climate of 152, 153, 154
prison reform 13, 388–389; ambivalence of 402; dilemma of 396–402; in Uruguay 10, 197–211, 203
prison security, in Philippines 143, 144–147, *146*
prison staff, double exclusion of 198
prison work: distant perspective on 199; emotional impact of 209–210; relational aspects of 197–211, 203; relational perspective on 199
prisons: affective force of 314–325; arts therapeutic work in 253–270; civilian staff of 202, 207, 210; depolicialization of 201–202; Latin American 197, 198–199, 202, 211; reform 182, 184, 187, 189; Sierra Leone 311–328; as tragic 387–388
privilege 72, 241, 262, 311–312, 371; and emotions 421 relativity of 73–75
probation: compassion in 351, 356, 358; emotional labour in 349–355, 356, 359, 360–364; habitus of 352; practice of 349–364
producing the state 8–10
professional empathy 282–283
professional relationship 351–352
professionalisation 152, 283–284
property 4, 27, 37, 110, 227–228, 239, 274; police 247
protection 6, 74, 239, 262, 335–336, 340, 342; dignity 284–287, 288; international 9, 105, 106, 116, 117, 422n4; of migrants 279, 280; and Prevent Duty 90, 93; public 350, 351, 353, 356; and public order 126; and punishment 345; self- 362, 399; of vulnerable people 3, 86, 91, 97
Protection of Children from Sexual Offences (POCSO) Act 216–217, 220, 221, 222–223, 224, 225, 226, 227, 228–229, 230n2, 230n4, 230n6; reforms of 217–219; special courts 11, 217–219, 228
psychoanalysis 22, 45, 46–47, 48
psychoanalytic theory 8, 45, 46, 412, 417
psychotherapy 254, 256, 257–258, 263
public health 104, 109, 124, 184, 244, 279
public interest litigation 295, 306
public protection 350, 351, 353, 356
public racism 72
public sector workers, and Prevent Duty 84, 85, 86, 87, 88, 89, 90, 91–92, 93, 94–95, 95–96, 96–97, 98
public security 86, 98, 99, 119n3, 337
punishment: daily 9, 106, 118; definition of 108; disgust as 113–115; extreme 118; in immigration detention 106–108; institutional 106; preventive 104; retributive 108
punitive credo 180
punitive dominance 10, 13
punitive emotion 106
punitive turn, in criminal law and criminal justice 3
punitive-humanitarian complex 6
punitiveness 3, 179
Purity and Danger 238

race equality 8, 59, 60, 61, 62, 65–66, 67, 71–72, 75, 76; attacks on 72
race relations 61, 65
Race Relations Act 66
racial authenticity 70, 71
racial contract 64
racial discrimination 136n9
racial eliminativism 62
racial hierarchies 11, 65, 248
racial integration 68
racial thinking 64, 65
racial trace 72
racialisation 61, 62, 64–66, 134, 344; lived experience of 70
racialised emotions 236
racialised experience 70–71
racism: denial of 72; postracial detoxification of 69–72; public 72
racist hatred 64, 73
radicalisation 9, 83, 85, 87, 89, 90, 93, 95–96, 96–97; susceptibility to 84,

97–98; suspects *see* radicalisation suspects; vulnerability to 84, 86, 88, 91, 92, 94, 96, 97–98
radicalisation suspects 9, 83, 84, 87, 98; compassion 89, 91–93, 94, 95, 96–97, 98; prevention 89, 93–95; safeguarding 89–91
rape 216, 220, 223, 224, 225, 227–228
Rape Crisis Cell (RCC) 223
rationality: and ambivalence of emotion 8, 59, 61, 62–64, 277; bureaucratic 277; economic 186, 187, 189, 192–193; ethical 63; instinctivity preceding 238; of police 338
RCC (Rape Crisis Cell) 223
reactive anger 399
re-bordering 407
redefined self 362
Referral Course, in Prevent Duty online training 88
reform of prisons *see* prison reform
reform prisons 182, 184, 187, 189
refugee camps, spontaneous arrival at 14, 406–407, 408–411, 412, 416, 421
Regulation 28 reports *see* Prevention of Future Death (PFD) reports
rehabilitation 142, 246, 350, 358, 388, 402; and arts therapeutic work 254, 255, 257, 264; and prison managerialism 179, 180, 187; in Uruguay prisons 203, 204, 206, 207, 208, 210
reinforcement humiliation 278, 279, 280, 287
relational aspects: of emotions between victims and accused 219; of leadership 180; of prison governance 183, 189; of prison work 197–211, **203**
relational work: judges 227–228; prisons 199, 202, 203, 206, 208, 210; probation 355–356, 359, 360, 364
relationality 5–6, 46, 48
relationship skills 358, 359
relativity of privilege, and postracial sentimentality 73–75
representation: iconic (of state power) 22, 43, 48, 51, 52, 53, 54, 55; of the state 7–8, 52; visual (of French Revolution) 25–28
repression 28, 40, 253–254, 270; and police work 333, 336, 342, 343–344, 345, 346, 346n7
resident leaders *see mayores*

residents groups 148
resignation 321–324
restorative justice 124–125
retaliation 67, 163, 338, 340
retributive punishment 108
revenge: anthropophagic 162–166; premature 157–169
revolutionary iconography 37
rhetoric, of prison managerialism 182–184
Riachuelo case *see* Mendoza case
Right to Buy 373
righteous anger 371–372
Rio de Janeiro city and its Metropolitan Region (RMRJ) 158, 165, 168n2
rituals 7, 8, 22; anthropophagic 164; of French Revolution 25, 37, 38–39; humiliation 278, 279, 280, 281, 286, 287
'Rivers of Blood' speech 61, 65–66, 68, 69, 73
RMRJ (Rio de Janeiro city and its Metropolitan Region) 158, 165, 168n2
Robert, Hubert 36–37, *36*
role performance 9–10, 144, 149, 150, 152, 154–155
Rough Sleeping Initiative 369, 370
Rutherford, Andrew 180

safe driving, dangerous policing 159–162
safeguarding, and Prevent Duty 83–84, 85, 86, 89, 90, 91, 92, 93, 95, 96, 97, 98
Sartre, Jean-Paul 64–65, 67, 73
satisfaction 65, 108, 185, 186, 191, 323, 361, 398; job 229, 364; *see also* dissatisfaction
Schama, Simon 23
Schumpeter, Joseph 62–63
Scott, Joan 70–71
scripts 88, 128–129, 145, 151, 245, 352–353; cultural 144; emotional labour 350; emotive-cognitive 284, 285
security: dynamic 9–10, 143, 144, 147–151, 155; prison 143, 144–147, *146*; public 86, 98, 99, 119n3, 337; *see also* insecurity
self, the 2, 87, 107, 275, 284, 285, 287
self-alienation 354, 361, 363, 364
self-debasement 76

self-identity 70, 354
self-interest 4, 63, 206
self-protection 362, 399
self-sufficiency 2
semiotics 8, 22, 27, 37
senior Conservative minority ethnic politicians 59, 61, 62, 69, 71, 72, 74, 75, 76
sensibilities 4, 21, 36, 54–55, 244, 376
sensory world, of prisoners 3, 254, 255–256, 267, 268, 270, 318
sentimentality: Baldwin's definition of 8, 59, 67; cruel *see* cruel sentimentality; postracial *see* postracial sentimentality
sexual abuse of children, in India 215–230
shame 2, 110; and humiliation 276, 277, 278, 279, 280, 282, 283, 285, 286, 287
shared moral consciousness 278
Shawcross, William 97
Sierra Leone, institutional affect in prisons of 311, 312–313, 314, 319–321, 321, 322, 326
Simmel, Georg 273, 274, 275, 276, 277–278, 288
sites of passage 315
situated affectivity, of institutions 312–313
situatedness 6, 44, 48, 51
Smith, Ashley 118
social barriers 188–189
social change, and child sexual abuse special courts 228–229
social cohesion 110, 148, 238
social conflicts 25, 299; judicialisation of 295, 306
social control 61, 340
social experience 43, 47, 48, 54, 55
social fantasy 28, 39
social form 273–274; of institutionalised helper interaction 275, 279–281, 287, 288
social hierarchies 108, 238, 245
social inequalities 12, 199, 237–238, 306; judicialisation of 293–296
social integration 337, 338
social marginalisation 2, 3–6, 71
social relations 2, 9, 44, 187–188, 189, 215, 267, 274; in Philippine city jail 141, 148, 149, 152–153
social services 61, 242, 281
social welfare 273, 280, 281
social world 4, 55, 179, 238

socially situated phantasies 45, 48, 49
Socrates 387, 390, 391, 396–397, 398, 404n3, 404n5, 404n8; loving 394–396; naughty 392–394
soldiers: ambivalences of 344–345; views of favela residents 341–344
solidarity 11, 50, 127, 163, 178, 266, 269, 354; and refugee camp arrival 408, 411, 416; and welfare assistance 274, 278, 288
sovereign power 5, 244
sovereignty 30, 38, 64, 313
spatialised emotions 411–416
special courts, Protection of Children from Sexual Offences 11, 217–219, 228
spontaneous arrival, at refugee camp in Greece 14, 406–407, 408–411, 412, 416, 421
state, the: embodying 51–54; myth of 28, 39; producing 8–10; representing 7–8, 52
state centralisation 24
state failure 24, 371, 383
state modernisation 24
state officials 54, 55, 143, 311, 324, 325; as iconic representation of state power 22, 43, 48, 52, 53, 54, 55
state power: affective economies of 2, 22; emotional economies of 3, 6, 10–11, 14, 22–23, 240, 241–242; humanisation of 222–225; iconic representation of 22, 43, 48, 51, 52, 53, 54, 55; inter-institutional support and trust for affective and effective 225–226; moral economies of 2, 3, 7, 22–23, 61; renewal of 337–338; state officials as iconic representation of 22, 43, 48, 52, 53, 54, 55; symbols of 51–52
state racism 59–76
state representative 8, 52
state violence, and inquests 122, 123, 131, 135; and affective registers 124–126
statecraft 6
statehood 1–2, 235, 313, 324
stateness, languages of 22, 28
stereotyping 86, 87, 89, 141, 236, 319, 322, 346n9, 363
stigma 49, 160, 220, 239, 259, 323, 351; and disgust 110–111, 114–115, 118

street-level bureaucracy 199, 305
street-level practices 61
stress 3, 180, 203–204, 209, 409, 413; anticipatory 218
structural inequality 287, 288, 296–299, 302
structural intentionality 12, 311, 314, 326
structurally embedded emotions 12, 273, 274
structure in dominance 390, 399–400, 402, 403
structuring skills 358, 359
subjective consciousness 55n4
subjectivities 2, 10, 12, 70, 167, 294, 306, 408; animalised 236, 244; in detention centres 106–107; of immigration agents 105; individual 4, 339, 344; moral 339, 345; normative 5
suicide 134, 409, 410, 411, 413, 414
Sunak, Rishi 60, 62, 68–69, 70–71
Supreme Court of Justice (Argentina) 295, 296, 297–298, 301, 307–308n1
surface acting 286, 287, 354
surveillance 83, 85, 93, 119n2, 149, 178, 185, 202, 203
survivors, of child sexual abuse (CSA survivors) 216–217, 218, 219, 220, 222, 223, 224, 225, 226, 227, 228–229
susceptibility, to radicalisation 84, 97–98
Swedish welfare state 273, 274–275
symbolic action 166
symbolic resurrection, of Bastille 37–38
symbols, of state power 51–52
symmetry of interaction 152
sympathy: denied 276; economy of 275, 276; theory of 275–276
Symposium 389, 390–396, 396–397, 398, 399

tainted occupations 11, 236, 239, 240, 241, 247, 351
Tapachula 104, 105, 111, 115
temporal strains, of probation work 358–361
terrorism 83; and emotions 84–85; *see also* Prevent; Prevent Duty
theory: of affect 8, 45, 46; of affective economies 106; critical 2, 47, 49; of object relations 45, 46, 47; psychoanalytic 8, 45, 46, 412, 417; of sympathy 275–276

therapeutic function, of inquests 125, 126
therapeutic jurisprudence 218
Tocqueville, Alexis de 24, 64
torture 34–35, 105, 113, 114, 117, 164, 165
totalitarianism 25
town hall meetings 295, 296, 299–302, 303, 304–306, 307
traffic gangs 73, 333, 337, 338, 340, 341, 345, 346
transmutation 350, 353, 354, 358, 359
trauma 3, 133, 216, 257, 263, 375, 382–383
trial court practitioners, emotional labour of 219–228
Trump, Donald 63, 64
Tupinambás 164, 166–167

Uber 158, 159, 161, 163
UK coroner's court 122, 123–124, 128, 131
uncanny, the 414, 421
uncertainty 5, 117, 154, 190–191, 267, 314, 338, 363, 369
Uncle Tom's Cabin 66, 67, 72
unconscious imagining 45
undeserving migrants 60, 66, 71, 277
UNHCR (United Nations High Commissioner for Refugees) 111, 422n4
Unidade de Polícia Pacificadora (UPP) 333, 335, 337–338, 339, 344, 345–346
United Nations High Commissioner for Refugees (UNHCR) 111, 422n4
unlawful killing verdict, of inquest 124, 132
unsettling institutionalised emotions 11–12
UPP (*Unidade de Polícia Pacificadora*) 333, 335, 337–338, 339, 344, 345–346
uprisings 29, 30–31, 32, 36, 38
Uruguay, prison reform in 10, 197–211, 203

values 1, 6, 10, 14, 53
violence: duty of 344–345; and emotional impact of prison work 209–210; and immigration workers 239–240; in police work 333–346

visual representation, of French Revolution 25–28
vital needs 44, 46, 55n1
vulnerability, to radicalisation 84, 86, 88, 91, 92, 94, 96, 97–98
Vulnerability Assessment Framework 92
vulnerable prisoners 254, 255, 257, 269; and arts therapies 260–261
Vulnerable State, The 3, 6–7

waiting for social benefits and administrative services 302–306
wealth inequality 242
welfare services, dependency on 279, 280, 285
welfare state 179–180, 372; assistance 11–12, 273, 274, 275, 279, 285, 287, 288

wellbeing 13, 86, 114, 253, 257
White discrimination 71
white supremacy 64
whiteness 70, 75–76
'woke' 62, 66, 67, 72, 75
Wollheim, Richard 45, 47, 55n5
women prison managers 191
work, feminisation of 407, 411
working conditions, in Uruguayan prisons 197, 203–204
working environment 191, 203, 246
Workshops to Raise Awareness of Prevent (WRAP) 88

xenophobia 60, 239

Zigon, Jarrett 382

For Product Safety Concerns and Information please contact our
EU representative GPSR@taylorandfrancis.com Taylor & Francis
Verlag GmbH, Kaufingerstraße 24, 80331 München, Germany